A HISTORY OF THE

ENGLISH LANGUAGE

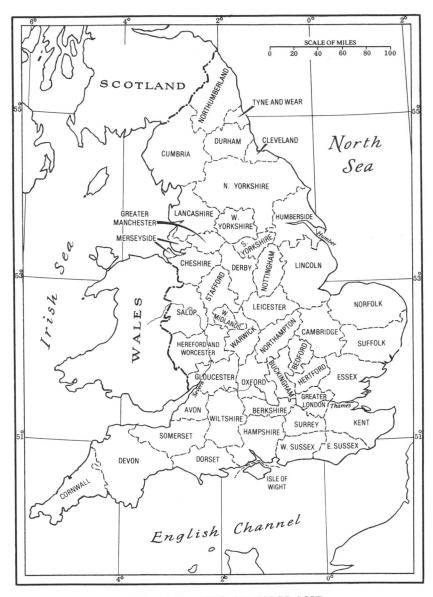

THE COUNTIES OF ENGLAND

A HISTORY OF THE
ENGLISH LANGUAGE

⌈ THIRD EDITION ⌉

Albert C. Baugh

University of Pennsylvania

Thomas Cable

University of Texas

PRENTICE-HALL, INC., Englewood Cliffs, New Jersey 07632

Library of Congress Cataloging in Publication Data

BAUGH, ALBERT CROLL, 1891–
 A history of the English language.

 Includes bibliographical references and index.
 1. English language—History.   I. Cable, Thomas,
1942–   joint author.   II. Title.
PE1075.B3 1978   420′.9   77–26324
ISBN 0-13-389239-5

Printed in the United States of America

10   9

PRENTICE-HALL INTERNATIONAL, INC., *London*
PRENTICE-HALL OF AUSTRALIA PTY. LIMITED, *Sydney*
PRENTICE-HALL OF CANADA, LTD., *Toronto*
PRENTICE-HALL OF INDIA PRIVATE LIMITED, *New Delhi*
PRENTICE-HALL OF JAPAN, INC., *Tokyo*
PRENTICE-HALL OF SOUTHEAST ASIA PTE. LTD., *Singapore*
WHITEHALL BOOKS LIMITED, *Wellington, New Zealand*

CONTENTS

MAPS

ILLUSTRATIONS

PREFACE

In the first edition of this book the aim of the writer was explained as follows:

The present book, intended primarily for college students, aims to present the historical development of English in such a way as to preserve a proper balance between what may be called internal history—sounds and inflections—and external history—the political, social, and intellectual forces that have determined the course of that development at different periods. The writer is convinced that the soundest basis for an understanding of present-day English and for an enlightened attitude towards questions affecting the language today is a knowledge of the path which it has pursued in becoming what it is. For this reason equal attention has been paid to its earlier and its later stages.

The relation between the French and English languages in England in the period following the Norman Conquest has been treated in some detail and with rather full documentation, not only because the subject is one of great interest in itself but because it has so often been dealt with only in broad outline and unsupported generalization. The footnotes will be useful to him who wants them; to him who does not, they will be sufficiently harmless. The chapter bibliographies are intended as a guide to the scholarship on the subjects treated. The discriminating teacher can readily indicate those items which will prove of value to the more elementary student.

In this third edition, as in the second, the original plan and purpose have not been altered. However, in the two decades that have elapsed since the book was last revised linguistic scholarship has been exceptionally active. Its achievements are reflected in the treatment of certain topics, in many small changes and additions throughout the book, and in the bibliographies to the various chapters. The two authors whose names now appear on the title page have worked in close cooperation throughout and are jointly responsible for the views expressed. But the senior member of the team wishes to pay warm tribute to his junior partner. The expansion of the chapter on the Indo-European family and the updating of the treatment of the modern dialects of English are mostly his, and without his younger legs and younger point of view this book would have been the poorer in many other places. We trust that we have represented fairly the views of the many linguists whose work we summarize or discuss. Our indebtedness, we hope, has always been specifically acknowledged.

Two maps have been revised and updated: the counties of England and the dialects of American English.

At the request of the publisher the manuscript was read by Morton W. Bloomfield (Harvard University), Julian Boyd (University of California at Berkeley), and Joseph L. Subbiondo (University of Santa Clara). We have been happy to profit by their comments and suggestions. The debt to our wives cannot be measured—their forbearance, their help with the proofs, and the many small chores which they have uncomplainingly taken on.

A workbook to accompany the text is in preparation by Diane Bornstein and Thomas Cable.

A. C. B.

T. C.

A HISTORY OF THE
ENGLISH LANGUAGE

PHONETIC SYMBOLS

[ɑ] in father
[a] in *French* la
[ɒ] in not in England (a sound
    between [ɑ] and [ɔ])
[æ] in mat
[ɛ] in met
[e] in mate
[ɪ] ·in sit
[i] in meat
[ɔ] in law
[o] in note
[ʊ] in book
[u] in boot
[ʌ] in but

[ə] in about
[y] in *German* für
[eɪ] in play
[oʊ] in so
[ɑɪ] in line
[ɑʊ] in house
[ɔɪ] in boy

[ŋ] in sing
[θ] in thin
[ð] in then
[ʃ] in shoe
[ʒ] in azure
[j] in you

[ ] enclose phonetic symbols and transcriptions.
ː after a symbol indicates that the sound is long.
ˈ before a syllable indicates primary stress: [əˈbʌv] *above*.
In other than phonetic transcriptions ẹ and ọ indicate open vowels, ẹ and ọ
    indicate close vowels.
* denotes a hypothetical form.
> denotes 'develops into'; < 'is derived from'.

[1]

English Present and Future

1. *The History of the English Language a Cultural Subject.* It was observed by that remarkable twelfth-century chronicler, Henry of Huntington, that an interest in his past was one of the distinguishing characteristics of man as compared with the other animals. And in these days when the cultivated man or woman is conscious of deficiencies in his education without some knowledge of economics, medieval history, recent advances in the basic natural sciences, so also he may discover a desire to know something of the nature and development of his mother tongue. The medium by which he communicates his thought and feelings to his fellow men, the tool with which he conducts his business or the government of millions of people, the vehicle by which have been transmitted to him the science, the philosophy, the poetry of the race is surely worthy of study. It is not to be expected that everyone should be a philologist or should master the technicalities of linguistic science. But it is reasonable to assume that the liberally educated man should know something of the structure of his language, its position in the world and its relation to other tongues, the wealth of its vocabulary together with the sources from which that vocabulary has been and is being enriched, and in general the great political, social, and cultural influences which have combined to make his language what it is. The purpose of the present book, then, is to treat the history of the English language not only as being of interest to the special student but as a cultural subject within the view of all educated people, while including enough references to technical matters to make clear the scientific principles involved in linguistic evolution.

2. *Influences at Work on Language.* The English language of today reflects many centuries of development. The political and social events that

1

have in the course of English history so profoundly affected the English people in their national life have generally had a recognizable effect on their language. The Christianizing of Britain in 597 brought England into contact with Latin civilization and made significant additions to our vocabulary. The Scandinavian invasions resulted in a considerable mixture of the two peoples and their languages. The Norman Conquest made English for two centuries the language mainly of the lower classes while the nobles and those associated with them used French on almost all occasions. And when English once more regained supremacy as the language of all elements of the population, it was an English greatly changed in both form and vocabulary from what it had been in 1066. In a similar way the Hundred Years' War, the rise of an important middle class, the Renaissance, the development of England as a maritime power, the expansion of the British Empire, and the growth of commerce and industry, of science and literature, have, each in its way, contributed to make the English language what it is today. In short, the English language reflects in its entire development the political, social, and cultural history of the English people.

3. Growth and Decay.   Moreover, English, like all other languages, is subject to that constant growth and decay which characterize all forms of life. It is a convenient figure of speech to speak of languages as living and as dead. While we cannot think of language as something that possesses life apart from the people who speak it, as we can think of plants or of animals, we can observe in speech something like the process of change that characterizes the life of living things. When a language ceases to change, we call it a dead language. Classical Latin is a dead language because it has not changed for nearly two thousand years. The change that is constantly going on in a living language can be most easily seen in the vocabulary. Old words die out, new words are added, and existing words change their meaning. Much of the vocabulary of Old English has been lost, and the development of new words to meet new conditions is one of the most familiar phenomena of our language. Change of meaning can be illustrated from any page of Shakespeare. *Nice* in Shakespeare's day meant *foolish; rheumatism* signified a cold in the head. Less familiar but no less real is the change of pronunciation. A slow but steady alteration, especially in the vowel sounds, has characterized English throughout its history. Old English *stān* has become our *stone; cū* has become *cow.* Most of these changes are so regular as to be capable of classification under what are called "sound laws." Changes likewise occur in the grammatical forms of a language. These may be the result of gradual phonetic modification, or they may result from the desire for uniformity commonly felt where similarity of function or use is involved. The man who says *I knowed* is only trying to form the past tense of this verb in the same way that he forms the past tense of so many verbs in English. This process is known as the operation of *analogy*, and it may affect the sound and meaning as well as the form of words. Thus it will be part of our task to trace the influences that are constantly at work tending to alter a language from age to age as spoken and written, and that have brought about such an extensive alteration in English as to make the language of 900 quite unintelligible to the people of 1900.

4. *The Importance of a Language.* So intimate is the relation between a language and the people who speak it that the two can scarcely be thought of apart. A language lives only so long as there are people who speak it and use it as their native tongue, and its greatness is only that given to it by these people. A language is important because the people who speak it are important—politically, economically, commercially, socially, culturally. English, French, and German are important languages because they are the languages of important peoples; for this reason they are widely studied outside the country of their use. But Romanian and Serbian and Malay are seldom learned by any save the native populations. Sometimes the cultural importance of an ethnic group or nation has at some former time been so great that their language remains important among cultivated people long after it has ceased to represent political, commercial, or other greatness. Greek, for example, is studied in its classical form because of the great civilization which its literature preserves the most complete record of; but in its modern form as spoken in Greece today the Greek language is largely neglected by the outside world.

5. *The Importance of English.* The importance of the English language is naturally very great. Spoken by more than 340 million people as a first language in the United Kingdom, the United States, and the former British Empire, it is the largest of the occidental languages. English, however, is not the largest language in the world. Western estimates of the population of China would indicate that Chinese is spoken by more than 880 million people in China alone.[1] But the numerical ascendancy of English among

---

[1] This figure is rather misleading. According to the general view, there are six regional varieties of Chinese, of which Mandarin is the largest (600 million). Each is divided into subdialects. Spoken Mandarin and Cantonese, for example, are no more mutually intelligible than English and Dutch. See John De Francis, *Nationalism and Language Reform in China* (Princeton, 1950), chap. 11: "Dialects or Languages"; Yuen Ren Chao, "Languages and Dialects in China," *Geographical Journal*, 102 (1943), 63–66, with a valuable map.

European languages can be seen by a few comparative figures. Spanish, next in size to English, is spoken by about 210 million people, Russian by 200 million,[1] Portuguese by 115 million, German by 105 million, French by 80 million native speakers (and a large number of second-language speakers), Italian by 62 million. Thus at the present time English has the advantage in numbers over all other western languages.

But the importance of a language is not just a matter of numbers or territory; as we have said, it depends also on the importance of the people who speak it. The importance of a language is inevitably associated in the mind of the world with the political role played by the nations using it and with their influence in international affairs; with the extent of their business enterprise and the international scope of their commerce; with the conditions of life under which the great mass of their people live; and with the part played by them in art and literature and music, in science and invention, in exploration and discovery—in short, with their contribution to the material and spiritual progress of the world. English is the mother tongue of nations whose combined political influence, economic soundness, commercial activity, social well-being, and scientific and cultural contributions to civilization give impressive support to its numerical precedence.

Finally there is the practical fact that a language may be important as a *lingua franca* in a country or region whose diverse populations would otherwise be unable to communicate. This is especially true in the former colonies of England and France where the colonial languages have remained indispensable even after independence and often in spite of outright hostility to the political and cultural values which the European languages represent.

6. *The Future of the English Language.* The extent and importance of the English language today make it reasonable to ask whether we cannot speculate as to the probable position it will occupy in the future. It is admittedly hazardous to predict the future of nations; the changes during the present century in the politics and populations of the developing countries have confounded predictions of fifty years ago. Since growth in a language is primarily a matter of population, the most important question to ask is which populations of the world will increase most rapidly. Growth

[1] The population of the Union of Soviet Socialist Republics was 241.7 million in the census of 1970, and it has been increasing at a rate of .9 percent. Fifty-nine percent of the 1970 population named Russian as their mother tongue, and another 17 percent indicated fluency in Russian. These figures and the figure in the text do not include Ukrainian or White Russian. It is said that there are 149 languages and significantly different dialects within the total population. On the languages in Russia, see W. K. Matthews, *Languages of the U.S.S.R.* (Cambridge, 1951), and E. Glyn Lewis, "Migration and Language in the U.S.S.R.," *International Migration Rev.*, 5 (1971), 147–79.

of population is determined mainly by the difference between the birth rate and the death rate. Although international migration has been an important factor in the past, demographic projections based on trends of recent years indicate that migration will make only a minor difference in the distribution of populations during the next century.[1] The single most important fact about current trends is that the less-developed countries of the world—in Africa, Asia, and Latin America—have experienced a precipitous drop in mortality during the twentieth century without a corresponding drop in the birth rate. As a result, the population of these areas is younger and growing faster than the population of the developed countries in Europe and North America. The effect of economic development upon the growth of population is especially clear in Asia, where the Soviet Union and Japan are growing at rates only slightly higher than that of Europe, while South Asia is growing at a rate more than twice as high. By one authoritative projection, India, Pakistan, and the other countries of South Asia will account for 43 percent of the increase in world population between the mid-1970's and the end of the century.[2] China is growing at a moderate rate, between that of Europe and South Asia, but with a population presently in excess of 880 million, the absolute increase will be very high. The one demographic fact which can be stated with certainty is that the proportion of the world's population in the economically developed countries will shrink during the next century in comparison with the proportion in the presently developing countries. From a majority of slightly more than two to one, the populations of the developing countries will increase their majority to perhaps three and a half to one by the year 2000. Since most of the native speakers of English live in the developed countries, it can be expected that this group will account for a progressively smaller proportion of the world's population.

If the future of a language were merely a matter of the number who use it as a first language, English would appear to be entering a period of decline after four centuries of unprecedented expansion. What makes this prospect unlikely is the fact that English is widely used as a second language throughout the world; estimates of the number of speakers with varying degrees of proficiency range between 50 million and 300 million. In some of the developing countries which are experiencing the greatest growth, English is one of the official languages, as it is in India, Nigeria,

[1] *World Population Prospects as Assessed in 1968*, United Nations Population Studies, no. 53 (New York, 1973), pp. 7–8 *et passim*.
[2] *The Determinants and Consequences of Population Trends*, United Nations Population Studies, no. 50 (New York, 1973), I, 564.

and the Philippines. The situation is complex because of widely varying government policies which are subject to change and which often do not reflect the actual facts (see § 229). Although there are concerted efforts to establish the vernaculars in a number of countries—Hindi in India, Swahili in Tanzania, Tagalog in the Philippines—considerable forces run counter to these efforts and impede the establishment of national languages. In some countries English is a neutral language among competing indigenous languages, the establishment of any one of which would arouse ethnic jealousies. In most developing countries communications in English are superior to those in the vernacular languages. The unavailability of textbooks in Swahili has slowed the effort to establish that language as the language of education in Tanzania. Yet textbooks and other publications are readily available in English, and they are produced by countries with the economic means to sustain their vast systems of communications.

The complex interaction of these forces defies general statements of the present situation or specific projections into the distant future. Among European languages it seems likely that English, Spanish, and Russian will benefit from various developments. The Soviet government's continuing effort to make Russian a language of communication throughout the Soviet Union and Eastern Europe will reinforce with additional numbers the status which that language has from a large and important native-speaking population. The growth of Spanish, as of Portuguese, will come mainly from the rapidly increasing populations of Latin America, while the growth in English will be most notable in its use throughout the world as a second language. It is also likely that pidgin and creole varieties of English will become increasingly widespread in those areas where English is not a first language.

7. *Will English Become a World Language?* The probable extension of English in the future leads many people to wonder whether English will some day become the language of all the world. In many cases the wish is father to the thought, and the wish springs partly from considerations of national pride, partly from a consciousness of the many disadvantages that result from a multiplicity of tongues. How much pleasanter travel would be if we did not have to contend with the inconveniences of a foreign language. How much more readily we could conduct our business abroad if there were but a single language of trade. How greatly would the problem of the scientist and the scholar be simplified if there were one universal language of learning. And how many of the misunderstandings and prejudices that divide nations would be avoided, how much the peace of the world would be promoted if there were free interchange of national thought and feeling—if only we could make effective the French proverb, *Tout comprendre, c'est tout pardonner*. That the world is fully alive to the need for an international language is evident from the number of attempts that have been made to supply that need artificially. Between 1880 and 1907 fifty-three universal languages were proposed. Some of these enjoyed an amazing, if temporary, vogue. In 1889 Volapük claimed nearly a million adherents. Today it is all but forgotten. A few years later Esperanto experienced a similar vogue, but interest in it now is kept alive largely by local groups and organizations. Apparently the need has not been filled by any of the laboratory products so far created to fill it. And it is doubtful if it ever can be filled in this way. An artificial language might serve sufficiently the needs of business and travel, but no one has proved willing to make it the medium of political, historical, or scientific thought, to say nothing of the impossibility of making it serve the purposes of pure literature, involving sustained emotion and creative imagination. Even if an artificial language were shown to be adequate for art and learning, the history of language policy in the twentieth century makes it unlikely that any government will turn its resources to an international linguistic solution which benefits the particular country only indirectly. Without the support of governments and the educational institutions which they control, the establishment of an artificial language for the world will be impossible. Recent history has shown language policy to be a highly emotional issue, the language of a country often symbolizing its independence and nationalism.

The emotions which militate against the establishment of an artificial language work even more strongly against the establishment of a single foreign language for international communication. The official languages of the United Nations are English, French, Russian, Spanish, Chinese, and Arabic. Since it is not to be expected that the speakers of any of these six languages will be willing to subordinate their own language to any of the other five, the question is rather which languages will likely gain ascendancy in the natural course of events. Just over a century ago French would have appeared to have attained an undisputed claim to such ascendancy. It was then widely cultivated throughout Europe as the language of polite society, it was the diplomatic language of the world, and it enjoyed considerable popularity in literary and scientific circles. During the nineteenth century its prestige, though still great, gradually declined. The prominence of Germany in all fields of scientific and scholarly activity made German a serious competitor. Now more scientific research is probably published in English than in any other language, and the preeminence of English in commercial use is undoubted. The revolution in communications during this century has contributed to the spread of several European languages, but especially of English because of major broadcasting and motion picture industries in the United States and Great Britain. It will be the combined effect of economic and cultural forces such as these rather than explicit legislation by national or international bodies that will determine the world languages of the future.

Since World War II, English as an official language has claimed progressively less territory among the former colonies of the British Empire while its actual importance and number of speakers have increased rapidly. At the time of the first edition of this history (1935), English was the official language of one-fourth of the earth's surface, even if only a small fraction of the population in parts of that area actually knew English. As the colonies gained independence, English continued to be used alongside the vernaculars. In many of the new countries English is either the primary language or a necessary second language in the schools, the courts, and business. The extent of its use varies with regional history and current government policy, although stated policy often masks the actual complexities. In Uganda, for example, where no language is spoken as a first language by more than 16 percent of the population, English is the one official language; yet less than one percent of the population speak it as a first language.[1] In India, English was to serve transitional purposes only until 1965, but it continues to be used officially with Hindi and fourteen other national languages. In Tanzania, Swahili is the one official language, but English is still indispensable in the schools and the high courts. It is nowhere a question of substituting English for the native speech. Nothing is a matter of greater patriotic feeling than the mother tongue. The question simply concerns the use of English, or some other widely known idiom, for international communication. And as John Galsworthy remarked, "any impartial scrutiny made at this moment of time must place English at the head of all languages as the most likely to become, in a natural, unforced way, the single intercommunicating tongue."

8. *Assets and Liabilities.* Since English seems likely to occupy an increasingly prominent place in international communication, it is worth pausing to inquire into its qualifications for so important a mission. We may assume without argument that it shares with the other highly developed languages of Europe the ability to express the multiplicity of ideas and the refinements of thought that demand expression in our modern civilization.

---

[1] Peter Ladefoged *et al.*, *Language in Uganda* (London, 1972), pp. 18–20.

The question is rather one of simplicity. How readily can it be learned by the foreigner? Does it possess characteristics of vocabulary and grammar that render it easy or difficult of acquirement? To attain a completely objective view of one's own language is no simple matter. It is so easy to assume that what we have in infancy acquired without sensible difficulty will seem equally simple to those attempting to learn it in maturity. What virtues can we honestly attribute to English and what shortcomings must we recognize as handicaps to be acknowledged and, where possible, overcome?[1]

9. Cosmopolitan Vocabulary. Prominent among the assets of the English language must be considered the mixed character of its vocabulary. English is classified as a Germanic language. That is to say, it belongs to the group of languages to which German, Dutch, Flemish, Danish, Swedish, and Norwegian also belong. It shares with these languages similar grammatical structure and many common words. On the other hand, more than half of its vocabulary is derived from Latin. Some of these borrowings have been direct, a great many through French, some through the other Romance languages. As a result, English also shares a great number of words with those languages of Europe which are derived from Latin, notably French, Italian, Spanish, and Portuguese. All of this means that English presents a somewhat familiar appearance to anyone who speaks either a Germanic or a Romance language. There are parts of the language which he feels he does not have to learn, or learns with little effort. To a lesser extent the English vocabulary contains borrowings from many other languages. Instead of making new words chiefly by the combination of existing elements, as German does, English has shown a marked tendency to go outside her own linguistic resources and borrow from other languages. In the course of centuries of this practice English has built up an unusual capacity for assimilating outside elements. We do not feel that there is anything "foreign" about the words *chipmunk, hominy, moose, raccoon, skunk*, all of which we have borrowed from the American Indian. We are not conscious that the words *brandy, cruller, golf, duck* (light canvas), *isinglass, measles, selvage, wagon, uproar* are from Dutch. And so with

[1] These kinds of questions have concerned linguists and language planners increasingly during the past two decades, after several decades during which descriptive linguistics generally considered evaluative judgments inappropriate for linguistic science. For various views of the question of linguistic efficiency, see Punya S. Ray, *Language Standardization* (The Hague, 1963); Einar Haugen, "Linguistics and Language Planning," in *Sociolinguistics*, ed. William Bright (The Hague, 1966), pp. 50–71; Valter Tauli, *Introduction to a Theory of Language Planning* (Uppsala, 1968); and the collection of studies edited by Joan Rubin and Björn H. Jernudd, *Can Language Be Planned?* (Honolulu, 1971).

many other words in daily use. From Italian come *balcony, canto, duet, granite, opera, piano, umbrella, volcano;* from Spanish, *alligator, cargo, contraband, cork, hammock, mosquito, sherry, stampede, tornado, vanilla;* from Greek, directly or indirectly, *acme, acrobat, anthology, barometer, catarrh, catastrophe, chronology, elastic, magic, tactics, tantalize,* and a host of others; from Russian, *steppe, drosky, vodka, ruble;* from Persian, *caravan, dervish, divan, khaki, mogul, shawl, sherbet,* and ultimately from Persian *jasmine, paradise, check, chess, lemon, lilac, turban, borax,* and possibly *spinach.* A few minutes spent in the examination of any good etymological dictionary will show that English has borrowed from Hebrew and Arabic, Hungarian, Hindi-Urdu, Bengali, Malay, Chinese, the languages of Java, Australia, Tahiti, Polynesia, West Africa, and from one of the aboriginal languages of Brazil. And it has assimilated these heterogeneous elements so successfully that only the professional student of language is aware of their origin. So cosmopolitan a vocabulary is an undoubted asset to any language that seeks to attain international use.

10. *Inflectional Simplicity.* A second asset which English possesses to a preeminent degree is inflectional simplicity. The evolution of language, at least within the historical period, is a story of progressive simplification. The farther back we go in the study of the languages to which English is most closely allied, the more complex we find them. Sanskrit, Greek, and Latin, for example, as classical languages of early date, have inflections of the noun, the adjective, the verb, and to some extent the pronoun that are no longer found in Russian or French or German. In this process of simplication English has gone further than any other language in Europe. Inflections in the noun as spoken have been reduced to a sign of the plural and a form for the possessive case. The elaborate Germanic inflection of the adjective has been completely eliminated except for the simple indication of the comparative and the superlative degrees. The verb has been simplified by the loss of practically all the personal endings, the almost complete abandonment of any distinction between the singular and the plural, and the gradual discard of the subjunctive mood. The complicated agreements that make German difficult for the foreigner are absent from English. However compensated for, such a reduction of inflections can hardly be considered anything but an advantage.

11. *Natural Gender.* In the third place, English enjoys an exceptional advantage over all other major European languages in having adopted natural in place of grammatical gender. In studying other European languages the student labors under the heavy burden of memorizing, along with the meaning of every noun, its gender. In the Romance languages, for example, there are only two genders, and all nouns which would be neuter in English are there either masculine or feminine. Some help in these languages is afforded by distinctive endings which at times characterize the two classes. But even this aid is lacking in the Germanic languages, where the distribution of the three genders appears to the English student to be quite arbitrary. Thus in German *sonne* (sun) is feminine, *mond* (moon) is masculine, but *kind* (child), *mädchen* (maiden), and *weib* (wife) are neuter. The distinction must be constantly kept in mind, since it not only affects the reference of pronouns but determines the form of inflection and the agreement of adjectives. In the English language all this was stripped away during the Middle English period, and today the gender of every noun in the dictionary is known instantly. Gender in English is determined by meaning. All nouns naming living creatures are masculine or feminine according to the sex of the individual, and all other nouns are neuter. Attributive gender, as when we speak of a ship as feminine, sun and moon as masculine or feminine, is personification and a matter of rhetoric, not grammar.

12. *Liabilities.* The three features just described are undoubtedly of great advantage in facilitating the acquisition of English by foreigners. On the other hand, it is equally important to recognize the difficulties which the foreign student encounters in learning our language. One of these difficulties is the result of that very simplification of inflections which we have considered among the assets of English. It is the difficulty, of which foreigners often complain, of expressing themselves not only logically but idiomatically. An idiom is a form of expression peculiar to one language, and English is not alone in possessing such individual forms of expression. All languages have their special ways of saying things. Thus a German says *was für ein Mann* (what for a man) where in English we say *what kind of man;* the French say *il fait froid* (it makes cold) where we say *it is cold.* The French visitor who had learned the English idiom *to press a person to do something* was making a natural mistake when he said *Can we not squeeze the young lady to sing?* His substitution was in a way logical but not idiomatic. Languages with a minimum of inflection are very likely to depend more than others on stereotyped expressions or idioms. Their mastery depends largely on memory. The distinction between *My husband isn't up yet* and *My husband isn't down yet*, or the quite contradictory use of the word *fast* in *go fast* and *stand fast* seems to the foreigner to be without reasonable justification. It is doubtful whether such idiomatic expressions are so much commoner in English than in other languages—for example, French—as those learning our language believe, but they undoubtedly bulk large in the mind of foreigners.

A more serious criticism of English by those attempting to master it is the chaotic character of our spelling and the frequent lack of correlation between spelling and pronunciation. Writing is merely a mechanical means of recording speech. And theoretically the most adequate system of spelling is that which best combines simplicity with consistency. In alphabetic writing an ideal system would be one in which the same sound was regularly represented by the same character and a given character always represented the same sound. None of the European languages fully attains this high ideal, although many of them, such as Italian or German, come far nearer to it than English. In English the vowel sound in be*lieve*, re*ceive*, *leave*, ma*chine*, *be*, *see* is in each case represented by a different spelling. Conversely the symbol *a* in *father, hate, hat*, and many other words has nearly a score of values. The situation is even more confusing in our treatment of the consonants. We have fourteen spellings for the sound of *sh: shoe, sugar, issue, mansion, mission, nation, suspicion, ocean, nauseous, conscious, chaperon, schist, fuchsia, pshaw*. And although the *s* and *ss* of *mansion* and *mission* are really the same as in *sugar* and *issue*, there remain a full dozen completely different spellings to testify to our lack of uniformity. This is an extreme case, but there are many others only less disturbing, and it serves to show how far we are at times from approaching the ideal of simplicity and consistency.

We shall consider in another place the causes that have brought about this diversity. We are concerned here only with the fact that one cannot tell how to spell an English word by its pronunciation or how to pronounce it by its spelling. The English-speaking child undoubtedly wastes much valuable time during the early years of his education in learning to spell his own language, and to the foreigner our spelling is appallingly difficult. To be sure, it is not without its defenders. There are those who lay stress on the useful way in which the spelling of an English word often indicates its etymology. Again, a distinguished French scholar has urged that since we have preserved in thousands of borrowed words the spelling which those words have in their original language, the foreigner is thereby enabled more easily to recognize the word. It has been further suggested that the very looseness of our orthography makes less noticeable in the written language the dialectal differences that would be revealed if the various parts of the English-speaking world attempted a more phonetic notation on the basis of their local pronunciation. And recently some phonologists have argued that this looseness permits an economy in representing words that contain predictable phonetic alternants of the same morphemes (e.g., *divine* ∼ *divinity, crime* ∼ *criminal*). But in spite of these considerations, each of which is open to serious criticism, it seems as though some improvement might be effected without sacrificing completely the advantages claimed. That such improvement has often been felt to be desirable is evident from the number of occasions on which attempts at reform have been made. In the early part of the present century a movement was launched, later supported by Theodore Roosevelt and other influential men, to bring about a moderate degree of simplification (see § 230). It was suggested that since we wrote *has* and *had* we could just as well write *hav* instead of *have*, and in the same way *ar* and *wer* since we wrote *is* and *was*. But though logically sound, these spellings seemed strange to the eye, and the advantage to be gained from the proposed simplifications was not sufficient to overcome human conservatism or indifference or force of habit. It remains to be seen whether the extension of English in the future will some day compel us to consider the reform of our spelling from an impersonal and, indeed, international point of view. For the present, at least, we do not seem to be ready for simplified spelling.

BIBLIOGRAPHY

An influential introduction to the study of language, and still indispensable, is Leonard Bloomfield, *Language* (New York, 1933). Among older treatments an honored place should be reserved for W. D. Whitney, *Language and the Study of Language* (New York, 1867). Excellent books of more limited scope or briefer treatment are E. H. Sturtevant, *Linguistic Change: An Introduction to the Historical Study of Language* (Chicago, 1917), and *An Introduction to Linguistic Science* (New Haven, 1947); Edward Sapir, *Language: An Introduction to the Study of Speech* (New York, 1921); Otto Jespersen, *Language, Its Nature, Development and Origin* (New York, 1922); J. Vendryes, *Language: A Linguistic Introduction to History*, trans. P. Radin (London, 1925); Willem L. Graff, *Language and Languages: An Introduction to Linguistics* (New York, 1932); Louis H. Gray, *Foundations of Language* (New York, 1939); and Ferdinand de Saussure, *Cours de linguistique générale* (*Course in General Linguistics*), ed. C. Bally *et al.*, trans. Wade Baskin (New York, 1959). Among the many general works which incorporate recent linguistic advances, see especially Ronald W. Langacker, *Language and Its Structure* (2nd ed., New York, 1973); Victoria Fromkin and Robert Rodman, *An Introduction to Language* (New York, 1974); Winfred P. Lehmann, *Descriptive Linguistics: An Introduction* (2nd ed., New York, 1976); and Ronald Wardhaugh, *Introduction to Linguistics* (2nd ed., New York, 1977). Of great historical importance and permanent value is Hermann Paul's *Principien der Sprachgeschichte*, trans. H. A. Strong under the title *Principles of the History of Language* (rev. ed., London, 1891). Recent introductions to historical linguistics are Winfred P. Lehmann, *Historical Linguistics: An Introduction* (2nd ed., New York, 1973); Robert D. King, *Historical Linguistics and Generative Grammar* (Englewood Cliffs, N.J., 1969); Raimo Anttila, *An Introduction to Historical and Comparative Linguistics* (New York, 1972); and Anthony Arlotto, *Introduction to Historical Linguistics* (Boston, 1972). The advanced student may consult Henry

M. Hoenigswald, *Language Change and Linguistic Reconstruction* (Chicago, 1960).
H. Pedersen's *Linguistic Science in the Nineteenth Century*, trans. John W. Spargo
(Cambridge, Mass., 1931; reprinted as *The Discovery of Language*, 1962), gives
a very illuminating account of the growth of comparative philology, while a
briefer record will be found in Book I of Jespersen's *Language*. A concise history
of linguistic study is R. H. Robins, *A Short History of Linguistics* (Bloomington,
Ind., 1968), and a generally excellent series which surveys both the study and the
substance of linguistics is Thomas A. Sebeok, ed., *Current Trends in Linguistics*
(14 vols., The Hague, 1963–1976).

Statistics on the number of people speaking the languages of the world may
be found in Siegfried H. Muller, *The World's Living Languages* (New York,
1964); Kenneth Katzner, *The Languages of the World* (New York, 1975); and
C. F. Voegelin and F. M. Voegelin, *Classification and Index of the World's
Languages* (New York, 1977). The figures in A. Meillet and Marcel Cohen, *Les
Langues du monde* (nouv. ed., Paris, 1952), are not now up to date, but the book
is full of information that is still useful. For current statistics and bibliography,
see the quarterly journal *Population Index* (Office of Population Research,
Princeton). Leon Dominian's *The Frontiers of Language and Nationality in
Europe* (New York, 1917) is a fascinating account of the situation then, illustrated
with many maps. Of similar scope is A. Dauzat, *L'Europe linguistique* (Paris,
1953). Since the spread of English is largely a matter of population, the question
of population growth is of importance. Authoritative statistics and projections
are discussed in *The Determinants and Consequences of Population Trends* (New
York, 1973) and *World Population Prospects as Assessed in 1968* (New York,
1973), which may be supplemented by up-to-date statistics in the *Statistical
Yearbook* and *Demographic Yearbook*, all published by the United Nations.
Readable accounts of recent demographic trends appear in Ronald Freedman,
ed., *Population: The Vital Revolution* (Chicago, 1964); Glenn T. Trewartha, *The
Less Developed Realm* (New York, 1972); Tomas Frejka, *The Future of Population
Growth* (New York, 1973); and a special number of *Scientific American*, vol. 231,
no. 3 (1974). On the cosmopolitan character of the English vocabulary, see Mary
S. Serjeantson, *A History of Foreign Words in English* (London, 1935).

The future of English in international communication is related to the movement for a universal language. An account of this movement is given by A. L.
Guérard, *Short History of the International Language Movement* (New York,
1921), and L. Couturat and L. Leau, *Histoire de la langue universelle* (2nd ed.,
Paris, 1907). An exhaustive bibliography is P. E. Stojan, *Bibliografio de internacia
lingvo* (Geneva, 1929). See also Mario Pei, *One Language for the World* (New
York, 1958). More recent studies in bilingualism have recognized the formidable
complexities of language planning. See especially William F. Mackey, *Bilingualism
as a World Problem* (Montreal, 1967); Joshua A. Fishman *et al.*, eds., *Language
Problems of Developing Nations* (New York, 1968); Joan Rubin and Björn H.
Jernudd, *Can Language Be Planned?* (Honolulu, 1971); Einar Haugen, *The
Ecology of Language* (Stanford, 1972); and Joshua A. Fishman, *Advances in
Language Planning* (The Hague, 1974).

Among the better known older histories of English the following may be listed:
G. P. Marsh, *Lectures on the English Language* (1860; rev. ed., New York, 1885),
and *The Origin and History of the English Language* (1862; rev. ed., New York,
1885); T. R. Lounsbury, *A History of the English Language* (2nd ed., New York,
1894); O. F. Emerson, *The History of the English Language* (New York, 1894);
Henry Bradley, *The Making of English* (1904; rev. Bergen Evans and Simeon
Potter, New York, 1967); Otto Jespersen, *Growth and Structure of the English*

Language (1905; 9th ed., London, 1938); H. C. Wyld, *The Historical Study of the Mother Tongue* (New York, 1906), and *A Short History of English* (1914; 3rd ed., London, 1927); G. P. Krapp, *Modern English, Its Growth and Present Use* (1909; rev. A. H. Marckwardt, New York, 1969); René Huchon, *Histoire de la langue anglaise* (2 vols., Paris, 1923–1930); and G. H. McKnight, *Modern English in the Making* (New York, 1928; reprinted as *The Evolution of the English Language*, 1968). Later titles have become too numerous to list. They may readily be found in bibliographies and publishers' catalogues. The history of English syntax receives its most impressive documentation in F. T. Visser, *An Historical Syntax of the English Language* (3 vols., Leiden, 1963–1973), and the development of selected patterns is given a transformational analysis by Elizabeth C. Traugott, *A History of English Syntax* (New York, 1972). For all references prior to 1923, the student should consult the invaluable *Bibliography of Writings on the English Language* by Arthur G. Kennedy (Cambridge and New Haven, 1927). R. C. Alston, *A Bibliography of the English Language . . . to the Year 1800* (Leeds, 1965–), is in progress. The most complete record of current publications is the *Bibliographie linguistique des années 1939–1947* (2 vols., Utrecht-Brussels, 1949–1950) and its annual supplements, published with the support of UNESCO. See also the annual bibliography of the Modern Language Association (vol. 3, *Linguistics*) and Harold B. Allen's selective and convenient *Linguistics and English Linguistics* (New York, 1966). Helmut Gipper and Hans Schwarz, *Bibliographisches Handbuch zur Sprachinhaltsforschung* (2 vols., Köln and Opladen, 1962–), is being published by the Rheinisch-Westfälische Akad.

[2]

The Indo-European Family of Languages

13. *Language Constantly Changing.* In the mind of the average person language is associated with writing and calls up a picture of the printed page. From Latin or French as he meets it in literature he gets an impression of something uniform and relatively fixed. He is likely to forget that writing is only a conventional device for recording sounds and that language is primarily speech. Even more important, he does not realize that the Latin of Cicero or the French of Voltaire is the product of centuries of development and that language as long as it lives and is in actual use is in a constant state of change.

Speech is the product of certain muscular movements. The sounds of language are produced by the passage of a current of air through cavities of the throat and face controlled by the muscles of these regions. Any voluntary muscular movement when constantly repeated is subject to gradual alteration. This is as true of the movements of the organs of speech as of any other parts of the body, and the fact that this alteration takes place largely without our being conscious of it does not change the fact or lessen its effects. Now any alteration in the position or action of the organs of speech results in a difference in the sound produced. Thus each individual is constantly and quite unconsciously introducing slight changes in his speech. There is no such thing as uniformity in language. Not only does the speech of one community differ from that of another, but the speech of different individuals of a single community, even different members of the same family, is marked by individual peculiarities. Members of a group, however, are influenced by one another, and there is a general similarity in the speech of a given community at any particular time. The language of any district or even country is only the sum total of the individual speech habits of those composing it and is subject to such changes as occur in the speech of its members, so far as the changes become general or at least common to a large part of it.

Although the alteration that is constantly going on in language is for the most part gradual and of such a nature as often to escape the notice of those in whose speech it is taking place, after a period of time the differences that grow up become appreciable. If we go back only six generations we find Alexander Pope writing

> Good-nature and good-sense must ever join;
> To err is human, to forgive, divine. . . .

where it is apparent that he pronounced *join* as *jine*. Again he says

> Here thou, great Anna! whom three realms obey,
> Dost sometimes counsel take—and sometimes Tea.

It is demonstrable that he pronounced *tea* as *tay*. Elsewhere he rimes *full—rule; give—believe; glass—place; ear—repair; lost—boast; thought— fault; obliged—besieged; reserve—starve*. Since Pope's time the pronunciation of at least one in each of these pairs has changed so that they would no longer be considered good rimes. If we go back to Chaucer, or still further, to King Alfred (871–899), we find still greater differences. King Alfred said *bān* (bone), *hū* (how), *hēah* (high); in fact all the long vowels of his pronunciation have undergone such change as to make the words in which they occur scarcely recognizable to the ordinary English-speaking person today.

14. Dialectal Differentiation. As previously remarked, where constant communication takes place among the people speaking a language, individual differences become merged in the general speech of the community, and a certain conformity prevails. But if any separation of one community from another takes place and lasts for a considerable length of time, differences grow up between them. The differences may be slight if the separation is slight, and we have merely local dialects. On the other hand, they may become so considerable as to render the language of one district unintelligible to the speakers of another. In this case we generally have the development of separate languages. Even where the differentiation has gone so far, however, it is usually possible to recognize a sufficient number of features which the resulting languages still retain in common to indicate that at one time they were one. It is easy to perceive a close kinship between English and German. *Milch* and *milk*, *brot* and *bread*, *fleisch* and *flesh*, *wasser* and *water* are obviously only words which have diverged from a common form. In the same way a connection between Latin and English is indicated by such correspondences as *pater* with English *father*, or *frāter* with *brother*, although the difference in the initial consonants tends somewhat to obscure the relationship. When we notice that *father* corresponds to Dutch *vader*, Gothic *fadar*, Old Norse *faðir*, German *vater*, Greek *patēr*, Sanskrit *pitar-*, and Old Irish *athir* (with loss of the initial consonant), or that English *brother* corresponds to Dutch *broeder*, German *bruder*, Greek *phrātēr*, Sanskrit *bhrātar-*, Old Slavic *bratŭ*, Irish *brathair*, we are led to the hypothesis that the languages of a large part of Europe and part of Asia were at one time identical.

15. The Discovery of Sanskrit. The most important discovery leading to this hypothesis was the recognition that Sanskrit, a language of ancient India, was one of the languages of the group. This was first suggested in the latter part of the eighteenth century and fully established by the beginning of the nineteenth. The extensive literature of India, reaching back further than that of any of the European languages, preserves features of the common language much older than most of those of Greek or Latin or German. It is easier, for example, to see the resemblance between the English word *brother* and the Sanskrit *bhrātar-* than between *brother* and *frāter*. But what is even more important, Sanskrit preserves an unusually full system of declensions and conjugations by which it became clear that the inflections of these languages could likewise be traced to a common origin. Compare the following forms of the verb *to be:*

Old English	Gothic	Latin	Greek	Sanskrit
eom (*am*)	im	sum	eimi	asmi
eart (*art*)	is	es	ei	asi
is (*is*)	ist	est	esti	asti
sindon (*are*)	sijum	sumus	esmen	smas
sindon (*are*)	sijuþ	estis	este	stha
sindon (*are*)	sind	sunt	eisi	santi

The Sanskrit forms particularly permit us to see that at one time this verb had the same endings (*mi, si, ti, mas, tha, nti*) as were employed in the present tense of other verbs, e.g.:

Sanskrit	Greek	
dádāmi	dídōmi	(*I give*)
dádāsi	dídōs	
dádāti	dídōsi	
dadmás	dídomen	(*dial.* dídomes)
datthá	dídote	
dáda(n)ti	didóāsi	(*dial.* dídonti)

The material offered by Sanskrit for comparison with the other languages of the group, both in matters of vocabulary and inflection, was thus of the greatest importance. When we add that Hindu grammarians had already gone far in the analysis of the language, had recognized the roots, classified the formative elements, and worked out the rules according to which certain sound-changes occurred, we shall appreciate the extent to which the discovery of Sanskrit contributed to the recognition and determination of the relation that exists among the languages to which it was allied.

16. Grimm's Law. A further important step was taken when in 1822 a German philologist, Jacob Grimm, following up a suggestion of a Danish contemporary, Rask, formulated an explanation which systematically accounted for the correspondences between certain consonants in the Germanic languages and those found for example in Sanskrit, Greek, and Latin. His explanation, although subsequently modified and in some of the details of its operation still a subject of dispute, is easily illustrated. According to Grimm, a *p* in Indo-European, preserved as such in Latin and Greek, was changed to an *f* in the Germanic languages. Thus we should look for the English equivalent of Latin *piscis* or *pēs* to begin with an *f*, and this is what we actually find, in *fish* and *foot* respectively. What is true of *p* is true also of *t* and *k:* in other words, the original voiceless stops (*p, t, k*) were changed to spirants (*f, þ, h*). So Latin *trēs* = English *three*, Latin *centum* = English *hundred.* A similar correspondence can be shown for certain other groups of consonants,[1] and the formulation of these correspondences is known as Grimm's Law. The cause of the change is not known. It must have taken place sometime after the segregation of the Germanic from neighboring dialects of the parent language. There are words in Finnish borrowed from Germanic which do not show the change, and which therefore must have resulted from a contact between Germanic and Finnish before the change occurred. There is also evidence that the shifting was still occurring as late as about the fifth century B.C. It is often assumed that the change was due to contact with a non-Germanic population. The contact could have resulted from the migration of the Germanic tribes or from the penetration of a foreign population into

[1] The aspirates (*bh, dh, gh*, which some hold to have been really spirants) became voiced spirants (*v, ð, ʒ*) or voiced stops (*b, d, g*). Consequently Sanskrit *bhárāmi* (Greek φέρω) = English *bear*, Sanskrit *dhā* = English *do*, Latin *hostis* (from **ghostis*) = English *guest*, Latin *hortus* = English *yard*, etc. And the original voiced stops (*b, d, g*) changed to voiceless ones in the Germanic languages, so that Latin *cannabis* = English *hemp*, Latin *decem* = English *ten*, Latin *genu* = English *knee*. In High German some of these consonants underwent a further change, known as the Second or High German Sound-Shift. It accounts for such differences as we see in English *open* and German *offen*, English *eat* and German *essen*.

Germanic territory. Whatever its cause, the Germanic sound-shift is the most distinctive feature marking off the Germanic languages from the languages to which they are related.

Certain apparent exceptions to Grimm's Law were subsequently explained by Karl Verner and others. It was noted that between such a pair of words as Latin *centum* and English *hundred* the correspondence between the *c* and *h* was according to rule, but that between the *t* and *d* was not. The *d* in the English word should have been a voiceless spirant, that is, a *þ*. In 1875 Verner showed that when the Indo-European accent was not on the vowel immediately preceding, such voiceless spirants became voiced in Germanic. In West Germanic the resulting *ð* became a *d*, and the word *hundred* is therefore quite regular in its correspondence with *centum*. The explanation was of importance in accounting for the forms of the preterite tense in many strong verbs. Thus in Old English the preterite singular of *cweþan* (to say) is *ic cwæþ* but the plural is *we cwǣdon*. In the latter word the accent was originally on the ending, as it was in the past participle (*cweden*), where we also have a *d*.[1] The formulation of this explanation is known as Verner's Law, and it was of great significance in vindicating the claim of regularity for the sound changes which Grimm's Law had attempted to define.

17. *The Indo-European Family.* The languages thus brought into relationship by descent or progressive differentiation from a parent speech are conveniently called a family of languages. Various names have been used to designate this family. In books written a century ago the term Aryan was commonly employed. It has now been generally abandoned and when found today is used in a more restricted sense to designate the languages of the family located in India and the plateau of Iran. A more common term is Indo-Teutonic or Indo-Germanic, the latter being the most usual designation among German philologists, but it is open to the objection of giving undue emphasis to the Germanic languages. The term now most widely employed is Indo-European, suggesting more clearly the geographical extent of the family. The parent tongue from which the Indo-European languages have sprung had already become divided and scattered before the dawn of history. When we meet with the various peoples by whom these languages are spoken they have lost all knowledge of their former association. Consequently we have no written record of the common Indo-European language. By a comparison of its descendants,

---

[1] Cf. the change of *s* to *z* (which became *r* medially in West Germanic) in the form of *cēosan—cēas—curon—corèn* noted in § 46.

however, it is possible to form a fair idea of it and to reconstruct with approximate accuracy its vocabulary and inflections.

The surviving languages show various degrees of similarity to one another, the similarity bearing a more or less direct relationship to their geographical distribution. They accordingly fall into eleven principal groups: Indian, Iranian, Armenian, Hellenic, Albanian, Italic, Balto-Slavic, Germanic, Celtic, Hittite, and Tocharian. These are the branches of the Indo-European family tree, and we shall look briefly at each.

18. *Indian.* The oldest literary texts preserved in any Indo-European language are the Vedas or sacred books of India. These fall into four groups, the earliest of which, the *Rig-veda*, is a collection of about a thousand hymns, the latest, the *Atharva-veda*, a body of incantations and magical formulas connected with many kinds of current religious practice. These books form the basis of Brahman philosophy and for a long time were preserved by oral transmission by the priests before being committed to writing. It is therefore difficult to assign definite dates to them, but the oldest apparently go back to nearly 1500 B.C. The language in which they are written is known as Sanskrit, or to distinguish it from a later form of the language, Vedic Sanskrit. This language is also found in certain prose writings containing directions for the ritual, dogmatic commentary, and the like (the *Brahmanas*), meditations for the use of recluses (the *Aranya-kas*), philosophical speculations (the *Upanishads*), and rules concerning various aspects of religious and private life (the *Sutras*).

The use of Sanskrit was later extended to various writings outside the sphere of religion, and under the influence of native grammarians, the most important of whom was Panini in the fourth century B.C., it was given a fixed, literary form. In this form it is known as Classical Sanskrit. Classical Sanskrit is the medium of an extensive Indian literature including the two great national epics, the *Mahabharata* and the *Ramayana*, a large body of drama, much lyric and didactic poetry, and numerous works of a scientific and philosophical character. It is still cultivated as a learned language and formerly held a place in India similar to that occupied by Latin in medieval Europe. At an early date it ceased to be a spoken language.

Alongside of Sanskrit there existed a large number of local dialects in colloquial use, known as Prakrits. A number of these eventually attained literary form; one in particular, Pāli, about the middle of the sixth century B.C. became the language of Buddhism. From these various colloquial dialects have descended the present languages of India, Pakistan, and Bangladesh, spoken by some 600 million people. The most important of these are Hindi, Urdu (the official language of Pakistan), Bengali (the official language of Bangladesh), Punjabi, and Marathi. Urdu is by origin and present structure closely related to Hindi, both languages deriving from Hindustani, the colloquial form of speech which for four centuries was widely used for intercommunication throughout northern India. Urdu differs from Hindi mainly in its considerable mixture of Persian and Arabic and in being written in the Perso-Arabic script instead of Sanskrit characters. The language of the Gypsies, sometimes called Romany, represents a dialect of northwestern India which from about the fifth century of our era was carried through Persia and into Armenia, and from there has spread through Europe and even into America, wherever, indeed, these nomads in the course of their long history have wandered.

19. *Iranian.* Northwest of India and covering the great plateau of Iran is the important group of languages called Iranian. The Indo-European population which settled this region had lived and probably traveled for a considerable time in company with the members of the Indian branch. Such an association accounts for a number of linguistic features which the two groups have in common. Of the people engaged in this joint migration a part seem to have decided to settle down on this great tableland while the rest continued on into India. Subsequent movements have carried Iranian languages into territories as remote as southern Russia and central China. From early times the region has been subjected to Semitic influence, and many of the early texts are preserved in Semitic scripts which make accurate interpretation difficult. Fortunately the last few decades have seen the recovery of a number of early documents, some containing hitherto unknown varieties of Iranian speech, which have contributed greatly to the elucidation of this important group of languages.

The earliest remains of the Iranian branch fall into two divisions, an eastern and a western, represented respectively by Avestan and Old Persian. Avestan is the language of the Avesta, the sacred book of the Zoroastrians. It is sometimes called Zend, although the designation is not wholly accurate. Strictly speaking, Zend is the language only of certain late commentaries on the sacred text. The Avesta consists of two parts, the Gathas or metrical sermons of Zoroaster, which in their original form possibly go back as far as 1000 B.C., and the Avesta proper, an extensive collection of hymns, legends, prayers, and legal prescriptions which seem to spring from a period several hundred years later. There is considerable difference in the language of the two parts. The other division of Iranian, Old Persian, is preserved only in certain cuneiform inscriptions which record chiefly the conquests and achievements of Darius (522–486) and Xerxes (486–466). The most extensive is a trilingual record (in Persian,

Assyrian, and Elamite) carved in the side of a mountain at Behistan, in Media, near the city of Kirmanshah. Besides a representation of Darius with nine shackled prisoners, the rebel chieftains subjugated by him, there are many columns of text in cuneiform characters. A later form of this language, found in the early centuries of our era, is known as Middle *Pehlevi* Iranian or Pahlavi, the official language of church and state during the dynasty of the Sassanids (226–652). This is the ancestor of modern Persian. Persian has been the language of an important culture and an extensive literature since the ninth century. Chief among the literary works in this language is the great Persian epic, the *Shahnamah*. Persian contains a large Arabic admixture so that today its vocabulary seems almost as much Arabic as Iranian. In addition to Persian, several other languages differing more or less from it are today in use in various provinces of the old empire —Afghan or Pushtu and Beluchi in the eastern territories of Afghanistan and Beluchistan, and Kurdish in the west, in Kurdistan. Besides these larger groups there are numerous languages and dialects in the highlands of the Pamir, on the shores of the Caspian, and in the valleys of the Caucasus, of which we have still but an imperfect knowledge.

20. *Armenian.* Armenian is found in a small area south of the Caucasus Mountains and the eastern end of the Black Sea. The penetration of Armenians into this region is generally put between the eighth and sixth centuries B.C. They evidently came into their present location by way of the Balkans and across the Hellespont. The newcomers conquered a population of which remnants are still perhaps to be found in the Caucasus, and whose language may have influenced Armenian in matters of accent and phonology. Armenian shows a shifting of certain consonants which recalls the shift in Germanic described above and which, like that, may be due to contact with other languages. Moreover, like the south Caucasus languages, Armenian lacks grammatical gender. Armenian is not linked to any other special group of the Indo-European family by common features such as connect Indian with Iranian. It occupies a somewhat isolated position. But in ancient times Thrace and Macedonia were occupied by two peoples, the Thraco-Phrygians, whom Herodotus mentions as very numerous, and the Macedonians, whose kings for a time adopted Greek and enjoyed a short but brilliant career in Greek history. The Phrygians, like the Armenians, passed into Asia Minor, and are familiar to us as the Trojans of Homer. Their language shows certain affinities with Armenian, and, if we knew more about it, we should probably find in it additional evidence for the early association of the two peoples. Unfortunately we have only scanty remains of Phrygian and Macedonian—chiefly place-names, glosses, and inscriptions—enough merely to prove their Indo-European character and give a clue to the linguistic affiliation.

Armenian is known to us from about the fifth century of our era through a translation of the Bible in the language. There is a considerable Armenian literature, chiefly historical and theological, extensive rather than important. The Armenians for several centuries were under Persian domination and the vocabulary shows such strong Iranian influence that Armenian was at one time classed as an Iranian language. Numerous contacts with Semitic languages, with Greek, and with Turkish have contributed further to give the vocabulary a rather mixed character.

21. *Hellenic.* At the dawn of history the Aegean was occupied by a number of populations which differed in race and in language from the Greeks who entered these regions later. In Lemnos, in Cyprus, and Crete especially, and also on the Greek mainland and in Asia Minor, inscriptions have been found written in languages which may in some cases be Indo-European, in others are certainly not. In the Balkans and in Asia Minor were languages such as Phrygian and Armenian, already mentioned, and certainly Indo-European, as well as others (Lydian, Carian, and Lycian) which show some resemblance to the Indo-European type but whose relations are not yet determined. In Asia Minor the Hittites, who spoke an Indo-European language (see § 27), possessed a kingdom which lasted from about 2000 to 1200 B.C.; and in the second millennium B.C. the eastern Mediterranean was dominated, at least commercially, by a Semitic people, the Phoenicians, who exerted a considerable influence upon the Hellenic world.

Into this mixture of often little-known populations and languages the Greeks penetrated from the north shortly after a date about 2000 B.C. The entrance of the Hellenes into the Aegean was a gradual one and proceeded in a series of movements by groups speaking different dialects of the common language. They spread not only through the mainland of Greece, absorbing the previous populations, but into the islands of the Aegean and the coast of Asia Minor. The earliest great literary monuments of Greek are the Homeric poems, the *Iliad* and the *Odyssey*, believed to date from the eighth century B.C. Of the Greek language we recognize five principal dialectal groups: the Ionic, of which Attic is a subdialect, found (except for Attic) in Asia Minor and the islands of the Aegean Sea; Aeolic in the north and northeast; Arcadian-Cyprian in the Peloponnesus and Cyprus; Doric, which later replaced Arcadian in the Peloponnesus; and Northwest Greek in the north central and western part of the Greek mainland. Of these, Attic, the dialect of the city of Athens, is by far the most important. It owes its supremacy partly to the dominant political and commercial position attained by Athens in the fifth century, partly to the great civilization which grew up there. The achievements of the Athenians in architecture and sculpture, in science, philosophy, and literature in the great age of Pericles (495–429 B.C.) and in the century following were such that it is difficult to overestimate their importance for subsequent civilization. In Athens were assembled the great writers of Greece—the dramatists Æschylus, Euripides, and Sophocles in tragedy, Aristophanes in comedy, the historians Herodotus and Thucydides, the orator Demosthenes, the philosophers Plato and Aristotle. Largely because of the political and cultural prestige of Athens, the Attic dialect became the basis of a *koiné* or common Greek which from the fourth century superseded the other dialects; the conquests of Alexander (336–323 B.C.) established this language in Asia Minor and Syria, in Mesopotamia and Egypt, as the general language of the eastern Mediterranean for purposes of international communication. It is chiefly familiar to modern times as the language of the New Testament and, through its employment in Constantinople and the Eastern Empire, as the medium of an extensive Byzantine literature. The various dialects into which the language of modern Greece is divided represent the local differentiation of this *koiné* through the course of centuries. At the present time two varieties of Greek (commonly called Romaic, from its being the language of the eastern Roman Empire) are observable in Greece. One, the popular or demotic, is the natural language of the people; the other, the "pure," represents a conscious effort to restore the vocabulary and even some of the inflections of ancient Greek. Both are used in various schools and universities, but the demotic seems to be gaining favor among the younger intellectuals.

22. Albanian. Northwest of Greece on the eastern coast of the Adriatic is the small branch named Albanian. It is possibly the modern remnant of Illyrian, a language spoken in ancient times in the northwestern Balkans, but we have too little knowledge of this early tongue to be sure. Moreover our knowledge of Albanian, except for a few words, extends back only as far as the fifteenth century of our era, and, when we first meet with it, the vocabulary is so mixed with Latin, Greek, Turkish, and Slavonic elements owing to conquests and other causes, that it is somewhat difficult to isolate the original Albanian. For this reason its position among the languages of the Indo-European family was slow to be recognized. It was formerly classed with the Hellenic group, but since the beginning of the present century it has been recognized as an independent member of the family.

23. Italic. The Italic branch has its center in Italy, and to most people

Italy in ancient times suggests Rome and the language of Rome, Latin. But the predominant position occupied by Latin in the historical period should not make us forget that Latin was only one of a number of languages once found in this area. The geographical situation and agreeable climate of the peninsula seem frequently and at an early date to have invited settlement, and the later population represents a remarkably diverse culture. We do not know much about the early neolithic inhabitants; they had been largely replaced or absorbed before the middle of the first millennium B.C. But we have knowledge of a number of languages spoken in different districts by the sixth century before our era. In the west, especially from the Tiber north, Etruscan was spoken by a powerful and aggressive people who did not speak an Indo-European tongue. In northwestern Italy was situated the little known Ligurian. Venetic in the northeast and Messapian in the extreme southeast were apparently offshoots of Illyrian, already mentioned. And in southern Italy and Sicily, Greek was the language of numerous Greek colonies. All these languages except Etruscan were apparently Indo-European. More important were the languages of the Italic branch itself. Chief of these in the light of subsequent history was Latin, the language of Latium and its principal city, Rome. Closely related to Latin was Umbrian, spoken in a limited area northeast of Latium, and Oscan, the language of the Samnites and of most of the southern peninsula except the extreme projections. All of these languages were in time driven out by Latin as the political influence of Rome became dominant throughout Italy. Nor was the extension of Latin limited to the Italian peninsula. As Rome colonized Spain and Gaul, the district west of the Black Sea, northern Africa, the islands of the Mediterranean, and even Britain, Latin spread into all these regions until its limits became practically co-terminous with those of the Roman Empire. And in the greater part of this area it has remained the language, though in altered form, down to the present day.

The various languages which represent the survival of Latin in the different parts of the Roman Empire are known as the Romance or Romanic languages. Some of them have since spread into other territory, particularly in the New World. The most extensive of the Romance languages are French, Spanish, Portuguese, and Italian. French is primarily the language of northern France although it is the language of literature and education throughout the country. In the Middle Ages it was divided into a number of dialects, especially Norman, Picard, Burgundian, and that of the Ile-de-France. But with the establishment of the Capetians as kings of France and the rise of Paris as the national capital, the dialect of Paris or the Ile-de-France gradually won recognition as the official and literary language. Since the thirteenth century the Paris dialect has been standard French. In the southern half of France the language differed markedly from that of the north. From the word for 'yes' the language of the north was called the *langue d'oïl*, that of the south the *langue d'oc*. Nowadays the latter is more commonly known as Provençal. In the twelfth and thirteenth centuries it was the language of an important literature, the lyrics of the troubadours, but it has since yielded to the superior political and social prestige of French. A patriotic effort at the close of the nineteenth century, corresponding to similar movements in behalf of Irish, Norwegian, and other submerged languages, failed to revive the language as a medium of literature, and Provençal is today merely the peasant speech of southern France. In the Iberian peninsula Spanish and Portuguese, because of their proximity and the similar conditions under which they have developed, have remained fairly close to each other. In spite of certain differences of vocabulary and inflection and considerable differences in the sounds of the spoken language, a Spaniard can easily read Portuguese. The use of Spanish and Portuguese in Central and South America and in Mexico has already been referred to. Italian has had the longest continuous history in its original location of any of the Romance languages, since it is nothing more than the Latin language as this language has continued to be spoken in the streets of Rome from the founding of the city. It is particularly important as the language of Dante, Petrarch, and Boccaccio, and the vernacular language in which the cultural achievements of the Renaissance first found expression. Romanian is the easternmost of the Romance languages, the least important of the six principal tongues forming the group. In addition to these six languages a few minor members may be mentioned: Catalan in northeastern and Galician in northwestern Spain, the former showing a certain affinity to Provençal, the latter to Portuguese; Rhaeto-Romanic, a group of nonliterary dialects in southeastern Switzerland and adjacent parts of the Tyrol; and Walloon, a dialect of French spoken in southern Belgium.

The Romance languages, while representing a continuous evolution from Latin, are not derived from the Classical Latin of Cicero and Virgil. Classical Latin was a literary language with an elaborate and somewhat artificial grammar. The spoken language of the masses, Vulgar Latin (from Latin *vulgus*, the common people), differed from it not only in being simpler in inflection and syntax but to a certain extent divergent in vocabulary. In Classical Latin the word for horse was *equus*, but the colloquial word was *caballus*. It is from the colloquial word that French *cheval*, Provençal *caval*, Spanish *caballo*, Italian *cavallo*, etc., are derived. In like manner where one wrote *pugna* (fight), *urbs* (city), *os* (mouth), the man in the street said *battualia* (Fr. *bataille*), *villa* (Fr. *ville*), *bucca* (Fr. *bouche*). So *verberare* = *battuere* (Fr. *battre*), *osculari* = *basiare* (Fr. *baiser*), *ignis* = *focus* (Fr. *feu*), *ludus* = *jocus* (Fr. *jeu*). It was naturally the Vulgar Latin of the marketplace and camp that was carried into the different Roman provinces. That this Vulgar Latin developed differently in the different parts of Europe in which it was introduced is explained by a number of factors. In the first place, as Gustav Gröber observed, Vulgar Latin like all language was constantly changing, and since the Roman provinces were established at different times and the language carried into them would be more or less the language then spoken in the streets of Rome, there would be initial differences in the Vulgar Latin of the different colonies.[1] These differences would be increased by separation and the influence of the native populations who adopted the new language. The Belgae and the Celts in Gaul, described by Caesar, differed from the Iberians in Spain. Each of these people undoubtedly modified Latin in accordance with their own speech habits.[2] It is not difficult to understand the divergence of the Romance languages, and it is not the least interesting feature of the Romance group that we can observe here in historical time the formation of a number of distinct languages from a single parent speech by a process of progressive differentiation such as has brought about, over a greater area and a longer period of time, the differences among the languages of the whole Indo-European family.

24. Balto-Slavic. The Balto-Slavic branch covers a vast area in the eastern part of Europe. It falls into two groups, the Baltic and the Slavic, which, in spite of differences, have sufficient features in common to justify their being classed together.

The Baltic languages are three in number: Prussian, Lettish, and Lithuanian. Prussian is now extinct, having been displaced by German since the seventeenth century. Lettish is the language of about two million people in Latvia. Lithuanian is spoken by about three million people in the

---

[1] The Roman colonies were established in Corsica and Sardinia in 231 B.C., Spain became a province in 197 B.C., Provence in 121 B.C., Dacia in A.D. 107.

[2] The principle can be illustrated by a modern instance. The Portuguese spoken in Brazil has no sound like the English *th*. The Brazilian who learns English consequently has difficulty in acquiring this sound and tends to substitute some other sound of his own language for it. He says *dis* for *this* and *I sink so* for *I think so*. If we could imagine English introduced into Brazil as Latin was introduced into Gaul or Spain, we could only suppose that the 100 million people of Brazil, almost 50 percent of whom can neither read nor write, would universally make such a substitution, and the *th* would disappear in Brazilian English.

Baltic state of Lithuania. It is important among the Indo-European languages because of its conservatism. It is sometimes said that a Lithuanian peasant can understand certain simple phrases in Sanskrit. While the statement implies too much, Lithuanian preserves some very old features which have disappeared from practically all the other languages of the family.

The similarities among the various languages of the Slavic group indicate that as late as the seventh or eighth century of the Christian era they were practically identical or at least were united by frequent intercourse. At the present time they fall into three divisions: East Slavic, West Slavic, and South Slavic. The first two still cover contiguous areas, but the South Slavs, in the Balkan peninsula, are now separated from the rest by a belt of non-Slavic people, the Hungarians and the Romanians.

The earliest form in which we possess a Slavic language is a part of the Bible and certain liturgical texts translated by the missionaries Cyril and Methodius in the ninth century. The language of these texts is South Slavic, but it probably approximates with considerable closeness the common Slavic from which all the Slavic languages have come. It is known as Old Church Slavonic or Old Bulgarian and it continued to be used throughout the Middle Ages and indeed well into modern times as the ecclesiastical language of the Orthodox Church.

The East Slavic includes the three varieties of Russian. Chief of these is Great Russian, the language of about 200 million people. It is found throughout the north, east, and central parts of the Soviet Union, was formerly the court language, and is still the official and literary language of the country. It is what is understood when in ordinary use we speak of "Russian." White Russian is the language of about 9 million people in the Belorussian S.S.R. and adjacent parts of Poland. Little Russian or Ukrainian is spoken by about 40 million people in the south. Nationalist ambitions in the past have led the Ukrainians to stress the difference between their language and Russian, a difference which, from the point of view of mutual intelligibility, causes some difficulty with the spoken language. Great, White, and Little Russian constitute the largest and most important group of the Slavic languages.

West Slavic includes four languages. Of these Polish is the largest, spoken by about 36 million people within Poland, by about three million in the United States, and by smaller numbers in the Soviet Union and other countries. Next in size are the two official, mutually intelligible languages of Czechoslovakia: Czech, spoken by about 10 million people, and Slovak, spoken by 5 million. The fourth language, Sorbian or Wendish, is spoken by only a little over 100,000 people in Germany, in a district a little northeast of Dresden.

South Slavic includes Bulgarian, Serbo-Croatian, and Slovenian. Bulgarian was spoken in the eastern part of the Balkan peninsula when the region was overrun by a non-Slavic race. But the conqueror was absorbed by the conquered and adopted his language. Modern Bulgarian has borrowed extensively from Turkish for the language of everyday use, while the literary language is even more heavily indebted to Russian. Serbo-Croatian represents the union of Serbian, formerly the language of Serbia, and Croatian, spoken before World War I by the Croats of Bosnia and Croatia. The two languages are practically identical. Slovenian is spoken by about a million and a half people at the head of the Adriatic. Serbo-Croatian and most of Slovenian are within the territory of Yugoslavia.

The Slavic languages constitute a more homogeneous group than the languages of some of the other branches. They have diverged less from the common type than those, for example, of the Germanic branch, and in a number of respects preserve a rather archaic aspect. Moreover the people speaking the Baltic languages must have lived for many centuries in fairly close contact with the Slavs after the two had separated from the parent Indo-European community.

25. Germanic.   The common form which the languages of the Germanic branch had before they became differentiated is known as Germanic or Proto-Germanic. It antedates the earliest written records of the family and is reconstructed by philologists in the same way as is the parent Indo-European. The languages descended from it fall into three groups: East Germanic, North Germanic, and West Germanic.[1]

The principal language of East Germanic is Gothic. By the third century the Goths had spread from the Vistula to the shore of the Black Sea and in the following century they were Christianized by a missionary named Ulfilas (311–383), whose father seems to have been a Goth and his mother a Greek (Cappadocian). Our knowledge of Gothic (sometimes called

---

[1] It has seemed best to retain the grouping here given, although in recent years it has been challenged. A division into North Germanic, Anglo-Frisian (or North-Sea Germanic), and South Germanic has been proposed, without as yet having gained general acceptance. In this classification Gothic is a part of North Germanic, with which its affinity has long been recognized. For a convenient summary of the newer views, see Ernst Schwarz, *Deutsche und Germanische Philologie* (Heidelberg, 1951). For fuller discussion, the student may consult the same author's *Goten, Nordgermanen, und Angelsachsen* (Bern, 1951; *Bibliotheca Germanica*, no. 2) and F. Maurer, *Nordgermanen und Alemannen* (3rd ed., Bern, 1952; *Bibliotheca Germanica*, no. 3). Further references will be found in the Schwarz book mentioned above.

Mœso-Gothic) is almost wholly due to a translation of the Gospels and other parts of the New Testament made by Ulfilas. Except for some runic inscriptions in Scandinavia it is the earliest record of a Germanic language we possess. For a time the Goths played a prominent part in European history, including in their extensive conquests both Italy, by the Ostrogoths, and Spain, by the Visigoths. In these districts, however, their language soon gave place to Latin, and even elsewhere it seems not to have maintained a very tenacious existence. Gothic survived longest in the Crimea, where vestiges of it were noted down in the sixteenth century. To the East Germanic branch belonged also Burgundian and Vandalic, but our knowledge of these languages is confined to a small number of proper names.

North Germanic is found in Scandinavia and Denmark. Runic inscriptions from the third century preserve our earliest traces of the language. In its earlier form the common Scandinavian language is conveniently spoken of as Old Norse. From about the eleventh century on, dialectal differences become noticeable. The Scandinavian languages fall into two groups: an eastern group including Swedish and Danish, and a western group including Norwegian and Icelandic. Norwegian ceased to be a literary language in the fourteenth century, and Danish (with Norwegian elements) is the written language of Norway.[1] Of the early Scandinavian languages Old Icelandic is much the most important. Iceland was colonized by settlers from Norway about A.D. 874 and early preserved a body of heroic literature unsurpassed among the Germanic peoples. Among the more important monuments are the Elder or Poetic Edda, a collection of poems that probably date from the tenth or eleventh century, the Younger or Prose Edda compiled by Snorri Sturluson (1178–1241), and about forty sagas, or prose epics, in which the lives and exploits of various traditional figures are related.

West Germanic is of chief interest to us as the group to which English belongs. It is divided into two branches, High and Low German, by the operation of a Second (or High German) Sound-Shift analogous to that described above as Grimm's Law. This change, by which West Germanic

---

[1] The union of Norway and Denmark for four hundred years made Danish the language of culture. The latter half of the nineteenth century witnessed the beginning of a movement to make the Norwegian dialects into a national language (*Landsmaal*), but this regeneration of the national speech has not succeeded in displacing Dano-Norwegian (*Rigsmaal*) as the dominant language. An amalgam of rural speech in normalized form (*Nynorsk*) is trying to compete in literature, the theatre, etc. and is further complicating the linguistic problem. The whole conflict is treated historically in Einar Haugen, *Language Conflict and Language Planning: The Case of Modern Norwegian* (Cambridge, Mass., 1966).

p, t, k, d, etc. were changed into other sounds, occurred about A.D. 600 in the southern or mountainous part of the Germanic area, but did not take place in the lowlands to the north. Accordingly in early times we distinguish as Low German tongues Old Saxon, Old Low Franconian, Old Frisian, and Old English. The last two are closely related and constitute a special or Anglo-Frisian subgroup.[1] Old Saxon has become the essential constituent of modern Low German or Plattdeutsch; Old Low Franconian, with some mixture of Frisian and Saxon elements, is the basis of modern Dutch in Holland and Flemish in northern Belgium; and Frisian survives in the Dutch province of Friesland, in a small part of Schleswig, in the islands along the coast, etc. High German comprises a number of dialects (Middle, Rhenish, and East Franconian, Bavarian, Alemannic, etc.). It is divided chronologically into Old High German (before 1100), Middle High German (1100–1500), and Modern High German (since 1500). High German, especially as spoken in the midlands and used in the imperial chancery, was popularized by Luther's translation of the Bible into it (1522–1532), and since the sixteenth century has gradually established itself as the literary language of Germany.

26. Celtic. The Celtic languages formed at one time one of the most extensive groups in the Indo-European family. At the beginning of the Christian era the Celts were found in Gaul and Spain, in Great Britain, in western Germany, and northern Italy—indeed, they covered the greater part of western Europe. A few centuries earlier their triumphal progress had extended even into Greece and Asia Minor. The steady retreat of Celtic before advancing Italic and Germanic tongues is one of the surprising phenomena of history. Today Celtic tongues are found only in the remoter corners of France and the British Isles; in the areas in which they were once dominant they have left but the scantiest trace of their presence.

The language of the Celts in Gaul who were conquered by Caesar is known as Gallic. Since it was early replaced by Latin we know next to nothing about it. A few inscriptions, some proper names (cf. *Orgetorix*), one fragmentary text, and a small number of words preserved in modern French are all that survive. With respect to the Celtic languages in Britain we are better off, although the many contradictory theories of Celticists[2]

---

[1] The West Germanic languages may be classified in different ways according to the features selected as the basis of division. Thus it is very common to divide them into an Anglo-Frisian group and a German group which includes Old Saxon. The division given in the text is none the less basic and is here retained for the sake of simplicity.

[2] For a summary of these theories, see T. Rice Holmes, *Ancient Britain and the Invasions of Julius Caesar* (2nd ed., Oxford, 1936), pp. 444–58. See also Myles Dillon and Nora K. Chadwick, *The Celtic Realms* (2nd ed., London, 1972), chaps. 1, 2, and 9.

make it impossible to say with any confidence how the Celts came to England. The older view, which is now questioned, holds that the first to come were Goidelic or Gaelic Celts. Some of these may have been driven to Ireland by the later invaders, and from there may have spread into Scotland and the Isle of Man. Their language is represented in modern times by Irish, Scottish Gaelic, and Manx. The later Cymric or Britannic Celts, after occupying for some centuries what is now England, were in turn driven westward by the Teutons in the fifth century after Christ. Some of the fugitives crossed over into Britanny. The modern representatives of the Britannic division are Welsh, Cornish, and Breton.

The remnants of this one-time extensive group of languages are everywhere losing ground at the present day. Spoken by minority elements in the population of France and the British Isles, they are faced with the competition of two great languages of the world and some seem destined not to survive this competition. Cornish became extinct in the eighteenth century, and Manx, once spoken by all the native inhabitants of the Isle of Man, has died out since the second world war. In Scotland Gaelic is found only in the Highlands. It is spoken by 75,000 people, of whom fewer than 5,000 do not know English as well. Welsh is still spoken by about one quarter of the people, but the spread of English among them is indicated by the fact that the number of those who speak only Welsh had dropped from 30 percent in 1891 to 2 percent in 1950 and is still slowly decreasing. Irish is spoken by about 500,000 people, most of whom are bilingual. Whether nationalist sentiment will succeed in arresting the declining trend which has been observable here as in the other Celtic territory remains to be seen. If not, it seems inevitable that eventually one important branch of the Indo-European family of languages will disappear from use.

27. *Recent Discoveries*. Besides the nine branches described above, recent discoveries have added two new groups to the family: Hittite and Tocharian. Until recently the Hittites have been known to us chiefly from references in the Old Testament. Abraham bought the burial place for Sarah from a Hittite (Gen. 23), and Bathsheba, whom David coveted, was the wife of Uriah the Hittite (2 Sam. 11). Their language was preserved only in a few uninterpreted documents. In 1907, however, an archaeological expedition uncovered the site of the Hittite capital in Asia Minor, at Boghazköi, about ninety miles east of Ankara, containing the royal archives of nearly 10,000 clay tablets. The texts were written in Babylonian cuneiform characters and some were in Babylonian (Akkadian), the diplomatic language of the day. Most of the tablets, however, were in an unknown language. Although a number of different languages seem to have been spoken in the Hittite area, nine tenths of the tablets are in the principal language of the kingdom. It is apparently not the original language of the district, but it has been given the name Hittite. The sudden opening up of so extensive a collection of texts has permitted considerable progress to be made in the study of this language. The most remarkable effect upon Indo-European studies has been the confirmation of a hypothesis made by Ferdinand de Saussure in 1879. On the basis of internal evidence Saussure had proposed certain sound patterns for Indo-European which did not occur in any of the languages then known. Twenty years after the discovery of the Hittite tablets it could be demonstrated that Saussure's phonological units, which had become known as "laryngeals," occurred in Hittite much as he had proposed for Indo-European. The number and phonetic features of laryngeals in Indo-European are still a matter of debate, but there is general agreement that at least one laryngeal must be posited for the parent language.[1] In the reconstruction of Indo-European syntax, a subject which until recently has suffered general neglect, Hittite has provided invaluable evidence. A strong argument can now be made that Hittite and the oldest hymns of the *Rig-veda* represent the Object-Verb structure of Indo-European, which by the time of Classical Greek and Latin had been largely modified to a Verb-Object pattern.[2] A large proportion of the Hittite vocabulary comes from an unidentified non-Indo-European source. The contamination with foreign elements appears to be as great as in Albanian. By some scholars Hittite is treated as co-ordinate with Indo-European, and the period of joint existence is designated Indo-Hittite. It is sufficient, however, to think of Hittite as having separated from the Indo-European community some centuries (perhaps five hundred years or more) before any of the other groups began to detach themselves. Tocharian is the name given to the language in which some fragmentary texts were discovered in the early part of the present century in central Asia (Chinese Turkestan). Some of them contain the name of a king who according to Chinese evidence reigned in the early part of the seventh century of our era. To the philologist the discovery is of some importance since the language belongs with the Hellenic, Italic,

---

[1] See Winfred P. Lehmann, *Proto-Indo-European Phonology* (Austin, 1952), pp. 22–35, 85–114, *et passim*, and the essays in *Evidence for Laryngeals*, ed. Werner Winter (The Hague, 1965).

[2] See Winfred P. Lehmann, "Contemporary Linguistics and Indo-European Studies," *PMLA*, 87 (1972), 976–93, and *Proto-Indo-European Syntax* (Austin, 1974), pp. 34–35, 238–51, *et passim*. See also Calvert Watkins, "Preliminaries to the Reconstruction of Indo-European Sentence Structure," in *Proceedings of the Ninth International Congress of Linguists*, ed. Horace G. Lunt (The Hague, 1964).

Germanic, and Celtic groups as a *centum* language rather than with the eastern or *satem* groups (see p. 38), with which we should expect it to be most closely related.[1]

28. *The Home of the Indo-European Family.* It is obvious that if the languages just described represent the progressive differentiation of an original speech, this speech, which we may for convenience call the Indo-European mother tongue, must have been spoken by a population somewhere at some time. What can be learned of these people and their early location?

Concerning their physical character, apart from the obvious fact that they belonged to the white race, practically nothing can be told. Continuity in language and culture does not imply biological descent. It is a not uncommon phenomenon in history for a people to give up their own language and adopt another. Sometimes they adopt the language of their conquerors, or of those whom they have conquered, or that of a people with whom they have simply become merged in a common territory. The Indo-European languages are spoken today in many cultures which until recently have had completely unrelated heritages. And to judge by the large variety of people who have spoken these languages from early times, it is quite possible that the people of the original Indo-European community already represented a wide ethnic diversity. Neither can we form any very definite idea of the date at which this people lived as a single, more or less coherent community. The period of their common life must have extended over a considerable stretch of time. It is customary to place the end of their common existence somewhere between 3500 and 2500 B.C.

With respect to the location of this community at a time shortly before their dispersal we are in a somewhat better position to form an opinion. We have at least a basis for inference. To begin with, we may assume that the original home was in that part of the world in which the languages of the family are chiefly to be found today, and we may omit from consideration Africa, Australia, and the American continents since we know that the extension of Indo-European languages in these areas has occurred in historical times. History, and its sister sciences, anthropology and archaeology, enable us also to eliminate certain other regions such as the British

---

[1] It has been suggested that the Tocharians, perhaps originally from the Balkans, formed part of the extensive migration from Europe into eastern Asia in the eighth and ninth centuries B.C., a migration which resulted in the overthrow of the Chou dynasty in China in 771 B.C. On the basis of archaeological and other evidence it is believed that Illyrians, Thracians, Phrygians, and Teutons (especially Scandinavians) were among those that took part in the movement. See Robert Heine-Geldern, "Das Tocharerproblem und die Pontische Wanderung," *Saeculum*, 2 (1951), 225–55.

Isles and the peninsulas of southern Europe. Early literary tradition occasionally preserves traces of a people at a former stage in their history. The earliest books of the Hindus, for example, the Vedas, show an acquaintance with the Indus but know nothing of the Ganges, indicating that the Indo-Europeans entered India from the northwest. In general, we may be fairly sure that the only regions in which it is reasonable to seek the original home of the Indo-European family are the mainland of Europe and the western part of Asia.

Prior to the middle of the nineteenth century it was customary to assume an Asiatic home for the family. Such an opinion was the natural result of biblical tradition which placed the Garden of Eden in the neighborhood of Mesopotamia. This notion seemed to find confirmation in the discovery that Sanskrit, situated in Asia, not only was an Indo-European language but was in many ways closest in form to the parent speech. Finally, Europe had seen the invasion of the Hun and the Turk and other Asiatic hordes, and it seemed natural to think of the movements of population as generally westward. But it was eventually recognized that such considerations formed a very slender basis for valid conclusions. It was observed that by far the larger part of the languages of this family have been in Europe from the earliest times to which our knowledge extends. Was it not more natural to suppose that the few representatives of the family in Asia should have made their way eastward than that nearly all the languages of Europe should have been the result of Asiatic incursions? In the course of the nineteenth century the comparative study of the Indo-European languages brought to light a number of facts that seemed to support such a supposition.

The evidence of language itself furnishes the most satisfactory criterion yet discovered on which to base a solution of the problem. It is obvious that those elements of the vocabulary which all or a considerable number of the branches of the family have in common must have formed a part of the original word-stock. In fact, a word common to two or three branches of the family, if the branches have not been in such proximity to each other as to suggest mutual influence, is likely to have been in the original language. Now the Indo-European languages generally have a common word for 'winter' and for 'snow'. It is likely that the original home of the family was in a climate which at certain seasons at least was fairly cold. On the other hand it is not certain that there was a common word for the sea. Instead, some branches of the family, when in the course of their wanderings they came into contact with the sea, had to develop their own words for the new conception. The original community was apparently an inland one, although not necessarily situated at a great distance from the coast. Still more instructive is the evidence of the fauna and flora known to the Indo-European community. As Harold H. Bender, whose *Home of the Indo-Europeans* is an admirable survey of the problem, puts it, "There are no anciently common Indo-European words for elephant, rhinoceros, camel, lion, tiger, monkey, crocodile, parrot, rice, banyan, bamboo, palm, but there are common words, more or less widely spread over Indo-European territory, for snow and freezing cold, for oak, beech, pine, birch, willow, bear, wolf, otter, beaver, polecat, marten, weasel, deer, rabbit, mouse, horse, ox, sheep, goat, pig, dog, eagle, hawk, owl, jay, wild goose, wild duck, partridge or pheasant, snake, tortoise, crab, ant, bee, etc." The force of this list is not in the individual items but in the cumulative effect of the two groups. Two words in it, however, have been the object of special consideration, *beech* and *bee*. A word corresponding to English *beech* is found in a number of Indo-European languages and was undoubtedly part of the parent vocabulary. The common beech (*Fagus silvatica* Linnaeus) is of relatively limited range: it is practically confined to central Europe and is not native east of Poland and the Ukraine.[1] The testimony of this word as to the original home of the Indo-European family would be persuasive if we could be sure that in the parent speech the word always designated what we know as the beech tree. But while this is its meaning in Latin and the Germanic languages, the word means 'oak' in Greek, 'elder' and 'elm' in other languages.[2] In like manner the familiarity of the Indo-European community with the bee is evident from a common word

[1] This is the area of the "beech line," which earlier arguments drew while ignoring that the eastern beech (*Fagus orientalis*) differs very little from the common beech and constitutes about one quarter of the tree population of the Caucasus east to the Caspian Sea. See Paul Friedrich, *Proto-Indo-European Trees* (Chicago, 1970), pp. 112–13.

[2] The validity of the evidence drawn from the beech tree receives strong support from Wilhelm Wissmann, *Der Name der Buche* (Berlin, 1952; *Deutsche Akad. der Wissenschaften zu Berlin, Vorträge und Schriften*, Heft 50). Problems in the etymologies of the various forms are treated by George S. Lane, "The Beech Argument: A Re-evaluation of the Linguistic Evidence," *Zeitschrift für vergleichende Sprachforschung*, 81 (1967), 197–212. Mention may be made of an interesting bit of evidence more recently brought forward. The word for salmon in some of the Germanic languages (German *Lachs*, Swedish *lax*, etc.), which occurs also in Balto-Slavic, is not found in Greek or Latin. It was formerly thought to be a word later acquired by those branches located around salmon-bearing waters, i.e., rivers emptying into the North Sea and the Baltic. But the discovery that the word occurs in one of the dialects of Tocharian shows that it was Indo-European. The salmon is naturally not found in Turkestan, and *laksi* in Tocharian has the generalized meaning 'fish'. Such a change of meaning would be natural among a people who had once lived in a region where the salmon was the fish *par excellence*. The word is another indication pointing to a fairly northern location of the original home. See Paul Thieme, *Die Heimat der indogermanischen Gemeinsprache* (Wiesbaden, 1953; *Akad. der Wissenschaften und der Literatur in Mainz, Abhandlungen der Geistes- und Sozialwissenschaftlichen Klasse*).

for honey (Latin *mel*, Greek μέλι, English *mil*dew, etc.) and a common word for an intoxicating drink made from honey, called *mead* in Old English. The honeybee is indigenous over almost all Europe but is not found in those parts of Asia which have ever been considered as possible locations of the Indo-European community. From evidence such as this a European home for the Indo-European family has come to be considered more probable.

One other linguistic consideration which figured prominently in past discussions is worth citing because of its intrinsic interest. The branches of the Indo-European family fall into two well-defined groups according to the modification which certain consonants of the parent speech underwent in each. They are known as the *centum* and *satem* groups from the word for hundred in ⟨Latin and Avestan respectively⟩ The *centum* group includes the Hellenic, Italic, Germanic, and Celtic branches. To the *satem* group belong Indian, Iranian, Armenian, Balto-Slavic, and Albanian. A line running roughly from Scandinavia to Greece separates the two, and suggests a line of cleavage from which disperson eastward and westward might have taken place. Although this division has been cited as supporting a homeland in central Europe—in the general area of the present Baltic states—linguists have been unable to find additional characteristics that would have been associated with such a fundamental split. With increasing knowledge about the classification of dialects and the spread of linguistic change, it has become more plausible to view the *centum-satem* division as the result of a sound change in the eastern section of the Indo-European speech community which spread through Indo-Iranian, Armenian, Slavic, and into Baltic.[1] It is still useful to speak of *centum* and *satem* languages, but the classification itself does not permit deductions about early migrations.[2]

From the nature of the case, the original home of the Indo-European languages is still a matter of much uncertainty, and many divergent views are held by scholars. During the past twenty years the most impressive new discoveries have come from archaeological excavations in the Soviet Union. Graves in the steppe area between the River Don and the Urals have yielded evidence of an Indo-European "Kurgan" culture that existed north of the Caspian Sea from the fifth through the third millennia B.C. It is especially interesting to note the characteristic flora and fauna of the area during that period, as described by Marija Gimbutas: "The Kurgan people

---

[1] See Winfred P. Lehmann, *Historical Linguistics* (2nd ed., New York, 1973), pp. 27–28.

[2] Accordingly Tocharian, as a *centum* language in *satem* territory, is no longer regarded as the anomalous problem that it was in earlier studies. See George S. Lane, "Tocharian: Indo-European and Non-Indo-European Relationships," in *Indo-European and Indo-Europeans*, p. 79.

lived in the steppe and forest-steppe zone, but in the fifth and fourth millennia the climate was warmer and damper than at present and what is now the steppe zone was more forested. Mixed forests, including oak, birch, fir, beech, elder, elm, ash, aspen, apple, cherry and willow, extended along rivers and rivulets in which such forest animals as aurochs, elk, boar, wild horse, wolf, fox, beaver, squirrel, badger, hare, and roe deer were present."[1] Gimbutas, who first proposed the name of the culture, believes that the Kurgan people were the original Indo-Europeans, an opinion shared by many archaeologists and linguists. Some scholars accept the descriptions by American and Soviet archaeologists of the early periods of Kurgan culture but propose different directions of migration.[2] Although the Indo-European homeland may prove impossible to locate precisely, one can expect new evidence and new interpretations of old evidence from both linguistics and archaeology. At present it is sufficient to observe that most of the proposed locations can be accommodated in the district east of the Germanic area stretching from central Europe to the steppes of southern Russia.

The civilization which had been attained by the people of this community at the time of their dispersal was approximately that known as neolithic. Copper was, however, already in use to a limited extent. The Indo-Europeans were no longer purely nomadic but had settled homes with houses and some agriculture. Here the evidence drawn from the vocabulary must be used with caution. We must be careful not to attribute to words their modern significance. The existence of a word for plow does not necessarily indicate anything more than the most primitive kind of implement. The Indo-Europeans raised grain and wool and had learned to spin and weave. They kept cattle and had for food not only the products of their own labor but such fruit and game as have always served the needs of primitive communities. Their system of society was patriarchal and they had some sort of king. They recognized the existence of a soul, believed in gods, and had developed certain ethical ideas. Without assuming complete uniformity of achievement throughout the area covered by this linguistic group, we may believe that the cultural development attained by the Indo-European was already considerable.

[1] "Proto-Indo-European Culture: The Kurgan Culture during the Fifth, Fourth, and Third Millennia B.C.," in *Indo-European and Indo-Europeans*, pp. 159–60.

[2] It has been argued that the traditional linguistic evidence in favor of the north European plain is sufficient to assume that the Kurgans migrated east at an early date. See Ward H. Goodenough, "The Evolution of Pastoralism and Indo-European Origins," in *Indo-European and Indo-Europeans*, pp. 253–65.

BIBLIOGRAPHY

The standard work on the Indo-European languages is K. Brugmann and B. Delbrück's *Grundriss der vergleichenden Grammatik der indogermanischen Sprachen* (2nd ed., Strassburg, 1897–1911). See also H. Hirt's *Indogermanische Grammatik* (7 vols., Heidelberg, 1921–1937). Good brief handbooks are A. Meillet, *Introduction à l'étude comparative des langues indo-européennes* (8th ed., Paris, 1937); J. Schrijnen, *Einführung in das Studium der indogermanischen Sprachwissenschaft*, trans. W. Fischer (Heidelberg, 1921); and Oswald Szemerényi, *Einführung in die vergleichende Sprachwissenschaft* (Darmstadt, 1970). A recent book that is useful to the student who wishes a summary of what is known about the many languages in this important family is W. B. Lockwood, *A Panorama of Indo-European Languages* (London, 1972). The Indo-European vocabulary is discussed in illuminating detail by Emile Benveniste, *Indo-European Language and Society*, trans. Elizabeth Palmer (London, 1973). The standard etymological dictionary is Julius Pokorny, *Indogermanisches etymologisches Wörterbuch* (2 vols., Bern, 1959–1969), which may be used with Calvert Watkins' helpful appendix to *The American Heritage Dictionary of the English Language* (New York, 1969) for examining Indo-European roots with reflexes in Modern English. Important studies of Indo-European morphology are by Jerzy Kuryłowicz, *The Inflectional Categories of Indo-European* (Heidelberg, 1964), and Calvert Watkins, *Geschichte der indogermanischen Verbalflexion*, vol. 3, part 1, of *Indogermanische Grammatik*, ed. J. Kuryłowicz (Heidelberg, 1969). Recent studies in Indo-European phonology and syntax are cited in the notes on p. 34, above. For the Germanic languages H. Paul's *Grundriss der germanischen Philologie* (2nd ed., Strassburg, 1900–1909, with some parts published separately in a third edition, extensively revised) is indispensable to the advanced student. T. E. Karsten's *Die Germanen: Eine Einführung in die Geschichte ihrer Sprache und Kultur* (Berlin, 1928) is a part of the third edition and is available in a French translation which incorporates some revisions: *Les Anciens Germains* (Paris, 1931). Basic works in their field are W. Streitberg, *Urgermanische Grammatik* (Heidelberg, 1896), and E. Prokosch, *A Comparative Germanic Grammar* (Philadelphia, 1939). A good brief treatment of the Germanic languages is A. Meillet, *Caractères généraux des langues germaniques* (4th ed., Paris, 1930), trans. W. P. Dismukes, *General Characteristics of the Germanic Languages* (Coral Gables, Fla., 1970). For essays on incorporating twentieth-century linguistic advances into Germanic grammars, see *Toward a Grammar of Proto-Germanic*, ed. F. van Coetsem and H. L. Kufner (Tübingen, 1972). Hermann Collitz's "A Century of Grimm's Law," *Language*, 2 (1926), 174–83, gives an interesting account of the development of this important earmark of the Germanic languages.

Of the more recently discovered branches, Hittite and Tocharian, the literature is scattered. An admirable statement of the Hittite question will be found in J. Friedrich, "Die bisherigen Ergebnisse der Hethitischen Sprachforschung," in *Stand und Aufgaben der Sprachwissenschaft: Festschrift für Wilhelm Streitberg* (Heidelberg, 1924), and the same author's *Hethitisch und 'Kleinasiatische' Sprachen* (Berlin, 1931). Advanced students may supplement this with E. H. Sturtevant's *A Comparative Grammar of the Hittite Language* (Philadelphia, 1933) and the same author's papers in *Language* and the *Trans. Amer. Philol. Assoc.* They may also consult Ferdinand Sommer, *Hethiter und Hethitisch* (Stuttgart, 1947), and J. Friedrich, *Hethitisches Elementarbuch*, I (2nd ed., Heidelberg, 1960). The principal facts in regard to Tocharian are contained in A. Meillet's article,

"Le Tokharien," *Indogermanisches Jahrbuch*, 1 (1913), 1–19; see also the introduction to A. J. Van Windekens, *Morphologie comparée du Tokharien* (Louvain, 1944; *Bibliothèque du Muséon*, vol. 17), and Holger Pedersen, *Tocharisch vom Gesichtspunkt der indoeuropäischen Sprachvergleichung* (Copenhagen, 1941; *Det Kgl. Danske Videnskabernes Selskab., Hist.-filol. Meddelser*, vol. 28, no. 1).

The most convenient account of the question of the original home of the Indo-European family is Harold H. Bender, *The Home of the Indo-Europeans* (Princeton, 1922). Other views may be found in M. Much, *Die Heimat der Indogermanen im Lichte der urgeschichtlichen Forschung* (Berlin, 1902); H. Hirt, *Die Indogermanen, ihre Verbreitung, ihre Urheimat und ihre Kultur* (2 vols., Strassburg, 1905–1907); S. Feist, *Kultur, Ausbreitung und Herkunft der Indogermanen* (Berlin, 1913), chap. 20, and *Indogermanen und Germanen* (Halle, 1914); and the popular but scholarly little book *Die Indogermanen*, by O. Schrader (2nd ed., Leipzig, 1916). Hirt has summed up his own views and given an excellent account of the question in the first volume of his *Indogermanische Grammatik* (1927), chap. 6. In addition to the important monograph of Thieme mentioned on p. 37, the following may be consulted: a group of interesting, though sometimes highly speculative papers assembled from various contributors by Wilhelm Koppers under the title *Die Indogermanen- und Germanen-Frage*, in vol. 4 of the *Wiener Beiträge zur Kulturgeschichte und Linguistik* (1936); Ernst Meyer, *Die Indogermanenfrage* (Marburg, 1948), with a useful bibliography; Hans Krahe, *Sprache und Vorzeit: Europäische Vorgeschichte nach dem Zeugnis der Sprache* (Heidelberg, 1954); and Walter Porzig, *Die Gliederung des indogermanischen Sprachgebiets* (Heidelberg, 1954). Impressive developments in archaeology during the past two decades have not settled the question. Marija Gimbutas argues for the lower Volga steppe and W. H. Goodenough for central Europe in their contributions to *Indo-European and Indo-Europeans*, ed. G. Cardona *et al.* (Philadelphia, 1970). This valuable collection of essays consolidates much recent Indo-European scholarship in both archaeology and linguistics.

$\begin{bmatrix} 3 \end{bmatrix}$

Old English

29. *The Languages in England before English.* We are so accustomed
to think of English as an inseparable adjunct to the English people that we
are likely to forget that it has been the language of England for a comparatively short period in the world's history. Since its introduction into the
island about the middle of the fifth century it has had a career extending
through only fifteen hundred years. Yet this part of the world had been
inhabited by man for thousands of years, 50,000 according to more
moderate estimates, 250,000 in the opinion of some. During this long
stretch of time, most of it dimly visible through prehistoric mists, the
presence of a number of races can be detected; and each of these races had
a language. Nowhere does our knowledge of the history of mankind carry
us back to a time when man did not have a language. What can be said
about the early languages of England? Unfortunately, little enough.

What we know of the earliest inhabitants of England is derived wholly
from the material remains that have been uncovered by archaeological
research. The classification of these inhabitants is consequently based upon
the types of material culture that characterized them in their successive
stages. Before the discovery of metals man was dependent upon stone for
the fabrication of such implements and weapons as he possessed. Generally
speaking, the Stone Age is thought to have lasted in England until about
2000 B.C., although the English were still using some stone weapons in the
battle of Hastings in 1066. Stone, however, gradually gave way to bronze,
as bronze was eventually displaced by iron about 500 or 600 B.C.[1] Since the

---

[1] The Iron Age begins in southern Europe rather earlier. The metal was apparently
just coming into use in the eastern Mediterranean in Homeric times. One of the prizes
in the funeral games in the *Iliad*, by which Achilles commemorated the death of his
friend Patroclus, was an ingot of iron.

Stone Age was of long duration, it is customary to distinguish between an earlier and a later period, known as the Paleolithic (Old Stone) Age and the Neolithic (New Stone) Age.

Paleolithic Man, the earliest inhabitant of England, entered at a time when this part of the world formed a part of the continent of Europe, when there was no English Channel and when the North Sea was not much more than an enlarged river basin. He was short of stature, averaging about five feet, long-armed and short-legged, with a low forehead and poorly developed chin. He lived in the open, under rock shelters or later in caves. He was dependent for food upon the vegetation that grew wild and such animals as he could capture and kill. Fortunately, an abundance of fish and game materially lessened the problem of existence. His weapons scarcely extended beyond a primitive sledge or ax, to which he eventually learned to fix a handle. More than one race is likely to be represented in this early stage of culture. The men whose remains are found in the latest paleolithic strata are distinguished by a high degree of artistic skill. But representations of boar and mastodon on pieces of bone or the walls of caves tell us nothing about the language of their designers. Their language disappeared with the disappearance of the race, or their absorption in the later population. We know nothing about the language, or languages, of Paleolithic Man.

Neolithic Man is likewise a convenient rather than scientific term to designate the races which, from about 5000 B.C., are possessed of a superior kind of stone implement, often polished, and a higher culture generally. The predominant type in this new population appears to have come from the south and, from its widespread distribution in the lands bordering on the Mediterranean, is known as the Mediterranean race. It was a dark race of slightly larger stature than Paleolithic Man. The people of this higher culture had domesticated the common domestic animals and developed elementary agriculture. They made crude pottery, did a little weaving, and some lived in crannogs, structures built on pilings driven into swamps and lakes. They buried their dead, covering the more important members of society with large mounds or barrows, oval in shape. But they did not have the artistic gifts of late Paleolithic Man. Traces of these people are still found in the population of the British Isles, especially in the dark-haired inhabitants of Scotland, Ireland, and Wales. But their language has not survived among these people, and since our hope of learning anything about the language which they spoke rests upon our finding somewhere a remnant of the race still speaking that language, that hope, so far as England is concerned, is dead. In a corner of the Pyrenees mountains of Spain, however, there survives a small community that is believed by some to represent the last remnant of the race. These people are the Basques, and their language shows no affiliation with any other language now known. Allowing for the changes which it has doubtless undergone in the centuries which have brought us to modern times, the Basque language may furnish us with a clue to the language of at least one group among Neolithic Man in England.

The first people in England about whose language we have definite knowledge are the Celts. It used to be assumed that the coming of the Celts to England coincided with the introduction of bronze into the island. But the use of bronze probably preceded the Celts by several centuries. We have already described the Celtic languages in England and called attention to the two divisions of them, the Gaelic or Goidelic branch and the Cymric or Britannic branch. Celtic was the first Indo-European tongue to be spoken in England and it is still spoken by a considerable number of people. One other language, Latin, was spoken rather extensively for a period of about four centuries before the coming of English. Latin was introduced when Britain became a province of the Roman Empire. Since this was an event that has left a certain mark upon later history, it will be well to consider it separately.

30. *The Romans in Britain.* In the summer of 55 B.C. Julius Caesar, having completed the conquest of Gaul, decided upon an invasion of England. What the object of his enterprise was is not known for certain. It is unlikely that he contemplated the conquest of the island; probably his chief purpose was to discourage the Celts of Britain from coming to the assistance of their kinsmen in Gaul, should the latter attempt to throw off the Roman yoke.[1] The expedition that year almost ended disastrously, and his return the following year was not a great success. In crossing the Channel some of his transports encountered a storm which deprived him of the support of his cavalry. The resistance of the natives was unexpectedly spirited. It was with difficulty that he effected a landing, and he made little headway. Since the season was far advanced, he soon returned to Gaul. The expedition had resulted in no material gain and some loss of prestige. Accordingly the following summer he again invaded the island, after much more elaborate preparations. This time he succeeded in establishing himself in the southeast. But after a few encounters with the natives, in which he was moderately successful, he exacted tribute from them (which was never paid) and again returned to Gaul. He had perhaps succeeded in his purpose,

---

[1] In the opinion of R. G. Collingwood, Caesar's intention was to conquer the whole island. See R. G. Collingwood and J. N. L. Myres, *Roman Britain and the English Settlements* (2nd ed., Oxford, 1937), p. 34.

but he had by no means struck terror into the hearts of the Celts, and Britain was not again troubled by the Roman arms for nearly a hundred years.

31. *The Roman Conquest.*   It was in A.D. 43 that the Emperor Claudius decided to undertake the actual conquest of the island. With the knowledge of Caesar's experience behind him, he did not underestimate the difficulty of the task. Accordingly an army of 40,000 men was sent to Britain and within three years had subjugated the tribes of the central and southeastern regions. Subsequent campaigns soon brought almost all of what is now England under Roman rule. The progress of Roman control was not uninterrupted. A serious uprising of the natives occurred in A.D. 61 under Boudicca (Boadicea), the widow of one of the native chiefs, and 70,000 Romans and Romanized Britons are said to have been massacred. Under the Roman Governor Agricola (78–85) the northern frontier was advanced to the Solway and the Tyne and the conquest may be said to have been completed. The Romans never penetrated far into the mountains of Wales and Scotland. Eventually they protected the northern boundary by a stone wall stretching across England at approximately the limits of Agricola's permanent conquest. The district south of this line was under Roman rule for more than three hundred years.

32. *Romanization of the Island.*   It was inevitable that the military conquest of Britain should have been followed by the Romanization of the province. Where the Romans lived and ruled, there Roman ways were found. Four great highways soon spread fanlike from London to the north, the northwest, the west, and the southwest, while a fifth cut across the island from Lincoln to the Severn. Numerous lesser roads connected important military or civil centers or branched off as spurs from the main highways. A score of small cities and more than a hundred towns, with their Roman houses and baths, temples and occasional theaters, testify to the introduction of Roman habits of life. The houses were equipped with heating apparatus and water supply, their floors were paved in mosaic, and their walls were of painted stucco—all as in their Italian counterparts. Roman dress, Roman ornaments and utensils, and Roman pottery and glassware seem to have been in general use. By the third century Christianity had made some progress in the island, and in 314, bishops from London and York attended a church council in Gaul. Under the relatively peaceful conditions that existed everywhere except along the frontiers, where the hostile penetration of the unconquered natives was always to be feared, there is every reason to think that Romanization had proceeded very much as it had done in the other provinces of the empire. The difference is that in Britain the process was cut short in the fifth century.

33. *The Latin Language in Britain.* Among the other evidences of Romanization must be included the use of the Latin language. A great number of inscriptions have been found, all of them in Latin. The majority of these proceed no doubt from the military and official class and, being in the nature of public records, were therefore in the official language. They do not in themselves indicate a widespread use of Latin by the native population. Latin did not replace the Celtic language in Britain as it did in Gaul. Its use by native Britons was probably confined to members of the upper classes and the inhabitants of the cities and towns. Occasional *graffiti* scratched on a tile or a piece of pottery, apparently by the workman who made it, suggest that in some localities Latin was familiar to the artisan class. Outside the cities there were many fine country houses, some of which were probably occupied by well-to-do natives. The occupants of these also probably spoke Latin. Tacitus tells us that in the time of Agricola the Britons, who had hitherto shown only hostility to the language of their conquerors, now became eager to speak it. At about the same time a Greek teacher from Asia Minor was teaching in Britain and by A.D. 96 the poet Martial was able to boast, possibly with some exaggeration, that his works were read even in this far-off island. On the whole, there were certainly many people in Roman Britain who habitually spoke Latin or upon occasion could use it. But its use was not sufficiently widespread to cause it to survive, as the Celtic language survived, the upheaval of the Germanic invasions. Its use probably began to decline after 410,[1] the approximate date at which the last of the Roman troops were officially withdrawn from the island. The few traces that it has left in the language of the Germanic invaders and that can still be seen in the English language today will occupy us later.

34. *The Germanic Conquest.* About the year 449 an event occurred which profoundly affected the course of history. In that year, as commonly stated, began the invasion of Britain by certain Germanic tribes, the founders of the English nation. For more than a hundred years bands of conquerors and settlers migrated from their continental homes in the region of Denmark and the Low Countries and established themselves in the south and east of the island, gradually extending the area which they occupied until it included all but the highlands in the west and north. The events of these years are wrapped in much obscurity. While we can form a general idea of their course, we are still in doubt about some of the tribes that took part in the movement, their exact location on the continent, and the dates of their respective migrations.

---

[1] Cf. J. Loth, *Les Mots latins dans les langues brittoniques* (Paris, 1892).

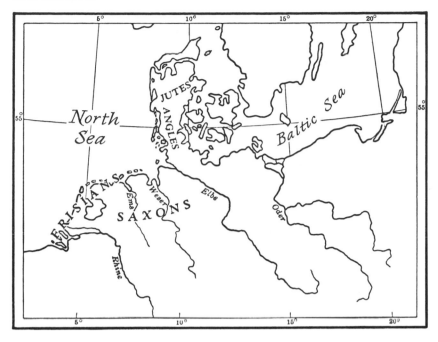

THE HOME OF THE ENGLISH

Note. The location of the Germanic tribes that invaded England is still a matter of dispute. The above map presents the traditional view, based upon the rather late testimony (eighth century) of Bede. An alternative opinion places the Angles on the middle Elbe and the Jutes near the Frisians.

The traditional account of the Germanic invasions goes back to Bede and the Anglo-Saxon Chronicle. Bede in his *Ecclesiastical History of the English People*, completed in 731, tells us that the Germanic tribes which conquered England were the Jutes, Saxons, and Angles. From what he says and from other indications, it seems altogether most likely that the Jutes and the Angles had their home in the Danish peninsula, the Jutes in the northern half (hence the name Jutland) and the Angles in the south, in Schleswig-Holstein, and perhaps a small area at the base. The Saxons were settled to the south and west of the Angles, roughly between the Elbe and the Ems, possibly as far as the Rhine. A fourth tribe, the Frisians, some of whom almost certainly came to England, occupied a narrow strip along the coast from the Weser to the Rhine together with the islands opposite. But by the time of the invasions the Jutes had apparently moved down to the coastal area near the mouth of the Weser, and possibly also around the Zuyder Zee and the lower Rhine, thus being in contact with both the Frisians and Saxons.

Britain had been exposed to attacks by the Saxons from as early as the fourth century. Even while the island was under Roman rule these attacks had become sufficiently serious to necessitate the appointment of an officer known as the Count of the Saxon Shore, whose duty it was to police the southeastern coast. At the same time the unconquered Picts and Scots in the north were kept out only at the price of constant vigilance. Against both of these sources of attack the Roman organization seems to have proved adequate. But the Celts had come to depend on Roman arms for this protection. They had, moreover, under Roman influence settled down to a more peaceful mode of life and had lost some of the barbaric power in war. Consequently when the Romans withdrew in 410 the Celts found themselves at a disadvantage. They were no longer able to keep out the warlike Picts and Scots. Several times they called upon Rome for aid, but finally the Romans, fully occupied in defending their own territory at home, were forced to refuse assistance. It was on this occasion that Vortigern, one of the Celtic leaders, is reported to have entered into an agreement with the Jutes whereby they were to assist the Celts in driving out the Picts and Scots and to receive as their reward the isle of Thanet.

The Jutes, who had not been softened by contact with Roman civilization, were fully a match for the Picts and Scots. But Vortigern and the Celts soon found that they had in these temporary allies something more serious to reckon with than their northern enemies. The Jutes, having recognized the superiority of England over their continental home, decided to stay in the island and began making a forcible settlement in the southeast, in Kent.[1] The settlement of the Jutes was a very different thing from the conquest of the island by the Romans. The Romans had come to rule the native population, not to dispossess it. The Jutes came in numbers and settled on the lands of the Celts. They met the resistance of the Celts by driving them out. Moreover the example of the Jutes was soon followed by the migration of other continental tribes. According to the Anglo-Saxon Chronicle some of the Saxons came in 477, landed on the south coast, and established themselves in Sussex. In 495 further bands of Saxons settled a little to the west, in Wessex.[2] Finally in the middle of the next century the Angles

---

[1] On the basis of archaeological evidence it has been maintained that the bulk of those who settled in Kent were Franks from the lower Rhine area, and it is suggested that with the Frisians they joined leaders who were Jutes, possibly from Jutland. See C. F. C. Hawkes, "The Jutes of Kent," in *Dark-Age Britain: Studies Presented to E. T. Leeds* (London, 1956), pp. 91–111. We must remember, however, that the possession of an ornament docs not establish its maker or place of manufacture. See the remarks of T. C. Lethbridge in the same volume, p. 114.

[2] It will be recalled that the King Arthur of romance is thought by some to represent a military leader of the Celts, possibly a Roman or Romanized Celt, who led this people, at the beginning of the sixth century, in their resistance to the Germanic invaders, and who enjoyed an unusual, if temporary, success.

occupied the east coast and in 547 established an Anglian kingdom north of the Humber. Too much credence, of course, cannot be put in these statements or dates. There were Saxons north of the Thames, as the names Essex and Middlesex (the districts of the East Saxons and Middle Saxons) indicate, and the Angles had already begun to settle in East Anglia by the end of the fifth century. But the entries in the Chronicle may be taken as indicating in a general way a succession of settlements extending over more than a century which completely changed the character of England.

35. *Anglo-Saxon Civilization.* It is difficult to speak with surety about the relations of the newcomers and the native population. In some districts where the inhabitants were few, the Anglo-Saxons probably settled down beside the Celts in more or less peaceful contact. In others, as in the West Saxon territory, the invaders met with stubborn resistance and succeeded in establishing themselves only after much fighting. Many of the Celts undoubtedly were driven into the west and sought refuge in Wales and Cornwall. In any case such civilization as had been attained under Roman influence was largely destroyed. The Roman towns were burnt and abandoned. Town life did not attract a population used to life in the open and finding its occupation in hunting and agriculture. The organization of society was by families and clans with a sharp distinction between *eorls,* a kind of hereditary aristocracy, and the *ceorls* or simple freemen. The business of the community was transacted in local assemblies or moots, and justice was administered through a series of fines—the *wergild*—which varied according to the nature of the crime and the rank of the injured party. Guilt was generally determined by ordeal or by compurgation. In time various tribes combined either for greater strength or, under the influence of a powerful leader, to produce small kingdoms. Seven of these are eventually recognized, Northumbria, Mercia, East Anglia, Kent, Essex, Sussex, and Wessex, and are spoken of as the Anglo-Saxon Heptarchy. But the grouping was not very permanent, sometimes two or more being united under one king, at other times kingdoms being divided under separate rulers. In the early part of the seventh century Northumbria gained political supremacy over a number of the other kingdoms and held an undoubted leadership in literature and learning as well. In the eighth century this leadership passed to Mercia. Finally, in the ninth century, Wessex under the guidance of Egbert (802–839) began to extend its influence until in 830 all England, including the chieftains of Wales, acknowledged Egbert's overlordship. The result can hardly be called a united nation, but West Saxon kings were able to maintain their claim to be kings of all the English, and under Alfred (871–889) Wessex attained a high degree of prosperity and considerable enlightenment.

36. The Names "England" and "English."   The Celts called their Germanic conquerors *Saxons* indiscriminately, probably because they had had their first contact with the Teutons through the Saxon raids on the coast.[1] Early Latin writers, following Celtic usage, generally call the Teutons in England *Saxones* and the land *Saxonia*. But soon the terms *Angli* and *Anglia* occur beside *Saxones* and refer not to the Angles individually but to the Teutons generally. Æthelbert, king of Kent, is styled *rex Anglorum* by Pope Gregory in 601, and a century later Bede called his history the *Historia Ecclesiastica Gentis Anglorum*. In time *Angli* and *Anglia* become the usual terms in Latin texts. From the beginning, however, writers in the vernacular never call their language anything but *Englisc* (*English*). The word is derived from the name of the Angles (O.E. *Engle*) but is used without distinction for the language of all the invading tribes. In like manner the land and its people are early called *Angelcynn* (Angle-kin or race of the Angles), and this is the common name until after the Danish period. From about the year 1000 *Englaland* (land of the Angles) begins to take its place. The name *English* is thus older than the name *England*.[2] It is not easy to say why England should have taken its name from the Angles. Possibly a desire to avoid confusion with the Saxons who remained on the continent and the early supremacy of the Anglian kingdoms were the predominant factors in determining usage.[3]

37. The Origin and Position of English.   The English language of today is the language which has resulted from the fusion of the dialects spoken by the Germanic tribes who came to England in the manner described. It is impossible to say how much the speech of the Angles differed from that of the Saxons or that of the Jutes. The differences were certainly slight. Even after these dialects had been subjected to several centuries of geographical and political separation in England, the differences were not great. As we

---

[1] The Teutons, on the other hand, called the Celts *Wealas* (foreigners), from which the word *Welsh* is derived.

[2] The spelling *England* no longer represents the pronunciation of the word. Under the influence of the nasal –*ng* the *e* has undergone the regular change to *i* (cf. O.E. *streng* > *string*; M.E. *weng* > *wing*). The spelling *Ingland* occurs in Middle English, and the vowel is accurately represented in the Spanish *Inglaterra* and Italian *Inghilterra*.

[3] The term *Anglo-Saxon* is occasionally found in Old English times and is often employed today to designate the earliest period of English. It went out of use after the Norman Conquest until revived in the sixteenth century by the antiquarian William Camden. While amply justified by usage, it is logically less defensible than the term *Old English*, which has the advantage of suggesting the unbroken continuity of English throughout its existence, but it is too convenient a synonym to be wholly discarded.

have seen above (§ 25) English belongs to the Low West Germanic branch
of the Indo-European family. This means in the first place that it shares
certain characteristics common to all the Germanic languages. For example,
it shows the shifting of certain consonants described above (§ 16) under the
head of Grimm's Law. It possesses a "weak" as well as a "strong"
declension of the adjective and a distinctive type of conjugation of the
verb—the so-called weak or regular verbs such as *fill, filled, filled*, which
form their past tense and past participle by adding *–ed* or some analogous
sound to the stem of the present. And it shows the adoption of a strong
stress accent on the first or the root syllable of most words,[1] a feature of
great importance in all the Germanic languages, since it is chiefly responsible for the progressive decay of inflections in these languages. In the
second place it means that English belongs with German and certain other
languages because of features which it has in common with them and which
enable us to distinguish a West Germanic group as contrasted with the
Scandinavian languages (North Germanic) and Gothic (East Germanic).
These features have to do mostly with certain phonetic changes, especially
the gemination or doubling of consonants under special conditions, matters
which we do not need to enter upon here. And it means, finally, that
English, along with the other languages of northern Germany and the Low
Countries, did not participate in the further modification of certain
consonants, known as the Second or High German Sound-Shift.[2] In other
words it belongs with the dialects of the lowlands in the West Germanic
area.

38. *The Periods in the History of English.* The evolution of English in
the fifteen hundred years of its existence in England has been an unbroken
one. Within this development, however, it is possible to recognize three
main periods. Like all divisions in history, the periods of the English
language are matters of convenience and the dividing lines between them
purely arbitrary. There is no break in the process of continuous transition.
But within each of the periods it is possible to recognize certain broad
characteristics and certain special developments that take place. The period
from 450 to 1150 is known as Old English. It is sometimes described as the
period of full inflections, since during most of this period the endings of the
noun, the adjective, and the verb are preserved more or less unimpaired.

---

[1] This is obscured somewhat in Modern English by the large number of words
borrowed from Latin.

[2] The effect of this shifting may be seen by comparing the English and the German
words in the following pairs: English *open*—German *offen*; English *water*—German
wasser; English *pound*—German *pfund*; English *tongue*—German *zunge*.

From 1150 to 1500 the language is known as Middle English.[1] During this period the inflections, which had begun to break down towards the end of the Old English period, become greatly reduced, and it is consequently known as the period of leveled inflections. The language since 1500 is called Modern English. By the time we reach this stage in the development a large part of the original inflectional system has disappeared entirely and we therefore speak of it as the period of lost inflections. The progressive decay of inflections is only one of the developments which mark the evolution of English in its various stages. We shall discuss the other features which are characteristic of Old English, Middle English, and Modern English in their proper place.

39. *The Dialects of Old English.* Old English was not an entirely uniform language. Not only are there differences between the language of the earliest written records (about A.D. 700) and that of the later literary texts, but the language differed somewhat from one locality to another. We can distinguish four dialects in Old English times: Northumbrian, Mercian, West Saxon, and Kentish. Of these Northumbrian and Mercian are found in the region north of the Thames settled by the Angles. They possess certain features in common and are sometimes known collectively as Anglian. But Northumbrian, spoken north of the Humber River, and Mercian, between the Humber and the Thames, each possess certain distinctive features as well. Unfortunately we know less about them than we should like since they are preserved mainly in charters, runic inscriptions, a few brief fragments of verse, and some interlinear translations of portions of the Bible. Kentish is known from still scantier remains, as is the dialect of the Jutes and their probable associates in the southeast. The only dialect in which there is an extensive collection of texts is West Saxon, which was the dialect of the West Saxon kingdom in the southwest. Nearly all of Old English literature is preserved in manuscripts transcribed in this region. The dialects probably reflect differences already present in the continental homes of the invaders. There is evidence, however, that some features developed in England after the settlement.[2] With the ascendancy of the West Saxon kingdom, the West Saxon dialect attained something of the position of a literary standard, and both for this reason and because of the abundance of the materials it is made the basis of the study of Old

---

[1] Some of the developments which distinguish Middle English begin as early as the tenth century, but a consideration of the matter as a whole justifies the date 1150 as the general line of demarcation.

[2] See David DeCamp, "The Genesis of the Old English Dialects," *Language*, 34 (1958), 232–44.

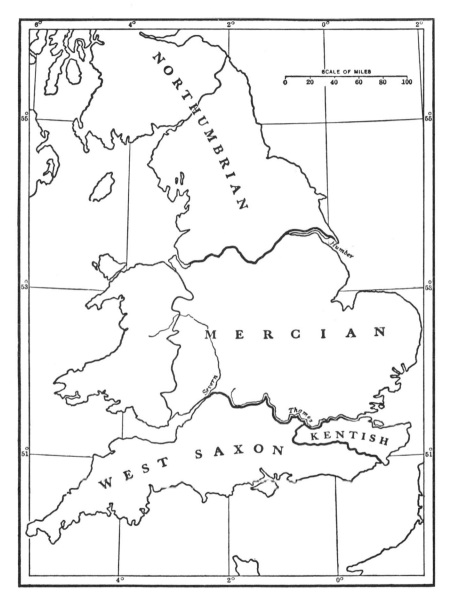

THE DIALECTS OF OLD ENGLISH

Note. Only the major dialect areas are indicated. That the Saxon settlements north of the Thames (see § 34) had their own dialect features is apparent in Middle English.

English. Such a start as it had made toward becoming the standard speech of England was cut short by the Norman Conquest which, as we shall see, reduced all dialects to a common level of unimportance. And when in the Middle English period a standard English once more began to arise, it was on the basis of a different dialect.

40. *Some Characteristics of Old English.* The English language has undergone such change in the course of time that one cannot read Old English without special study. In fact a page of Old English is likely at first to present a look of greater strangeness than a page of French or Italian because of the employment of certain characters that no longer form a part of our alphabet. In general the differences which one notices between Old and Modern English concern spelling and pronunciation, the vocabulary, and the grammar.

The pronunciation of Old English words commonly differs somewhat from that of their modern equivalents. The long vowels in particular have undergone considerable modification. Thus the Old English word *stān* is the same word as Modern English *stone*, but the vowel is different. A similar correspondence is apparent in *hālig—holy*, *gān—go*, *bān—bone*, *rāp—rope*, *hlāf—loaf*, *bāt—boat*. Other vowels have likewise undergone changes in *fōt* (foot), *cēne* (keen), *metan* (mete), *fȳr* (fire), *riht* (right), *hū* (how), *hlūd* (loud), but the identity of these words with their modern descendants is still readily apparent. Words like *hēafod* (head), *fæger* (fair), or *sāwol* (soul) show forms which have been contracted in later English. All of these cases represent genuine differences of pronunciation. However, some of the first look of strangeness which Old English has to the modern reader is due simply to differences of spelling. Old English made use of two characters to represent the sound of *th: þ* and *ð*, as in the word *wiþ* (with) or *ðā* (then), which we no longer employ. It also expressed the sound of *a* in *hat* by a digraph *æ*, and since the sound is of very frequent occurrence, the character contributes not a little to the unfamiliar appearance of the page. Likewise Old English represented the sound of *sh* by *sc*, as in *scēap* (sheep) or *scēotan* (shoot), and the sound of *k* by *c*, as in *cynn* (kin) or *nacod* (naked). Consequently a number of words which were in all probability pronounced by King Alfred almost as they are by us present a strange appearance in the written or printed text. Such words as *folc* (folk), *scip* (ship), *bæc* (back), *þorn* (thorn), *bæð* (bath), *þæt* (that) are examples in point. It should be noted that the differences of spelling and pronunciation that figure so prominently in one's first impression of Old English are really not very fundamental. Those of spelling are often apparent rather than real, since they represent no difference in the spoken language, and those of pronunciation obey certain laws as a result of which we soon learn to recognize the Old and Modern English equivalents.

A second feature of Old English which would become quickly apparent to a modern reader is the absence of those words derived from Latin and French which form so large a part of our present vocabulary. Such words make up more than half of the words now in common use. They are so essential to the expression of our ideas, seem so familiar and natural to us, that we miss them in the earlier stage of the language. The vocabulary of Old English is almost purely Germanic. A large part of this vocabulary, moreover, has disappeared from the language. When the Norman Conquest brought French into England as the language of the higher classes, much of the Old English vocabulary appropriate to literature and learning died out and was replaced later by words borrowed from French and Latin. An examination of the words in an Old English dictionary shows that about 85 percent of them are no longer in use. Those that survive, to be sure, are basic elements of our vocabulary, and by the frequency with which they recur make up a large part of any English sentence. Apart from pronouns, prepositions, conjunctions, auxiliary verbs, and the like, they express fundamental concepts like *mann* (man), *wīf* (wife), *cild* (child), *hūs* (house), *benc* (bench), *mete* (meat, food), *gærs* (grass), *lēaf* (leaf), *fugol* (fowl, bird), *gōd* (good), *hēah* (high), *strang* (strong), *etan* (eat), *drincan* (drink), *slǣpan* (sleep), *libban* (live), *feohtan* (fight). But the fact remains that a considerable part of the vocabulary of Old English is unfamiliar to the modern reader.

The third and most fundamental feature that distinguishes Old English from the language of today is its grammar.[1] Inflectional languages fall into two classes: synthetic and analytic. A *synthetic language* is one which indicates the relation of words in a sentence largely by means of inflections. In the case of the Indo-European languages these most commonly take the form of endings on the noun and pronoun, the adjective and the verb. Thus in Latin the nominative *murus* (wall) is distinguished from the genitive *muri* (of the wall), dative *muro* (to the wall), accusative *murum*, etc. A single verb form like *laudaverunt* (they have praised) conveys the idea of person,

synthetic lang.

---

[1] The principal Old English grammars, in the order of their publication, are F. A. March, *A Comparative Grammar of the Anglo-Saxon Language* (New York, 1870), now only of historical interest; P. J. Cosijn, *Altwestsächsische Grammatik* (Haag, 1883–1886); E. Sievers, *An Old English Grammar*, trans. A. S. Cook (3rd ed., Boston, 1903); K. D. Bülbring, *Altenglisches Elementarbuch* (Heidelberg, 1902); Joseph and Elizabeth M. Wright, *Old English Grammar* (2nd ed., Oxford, 1914), and the same authors' *An Elementary Old English Grammar* (Oxford, 1923); Karl Brunner, *Altenglische Grammatik* (3rd ed., Halle, 1965), based on Sievers; Randolph Quirk and C. L. Wrenn, *An Old English Grammar* (2nd ed., London, 1973); and Alistair Campbell, *Old English Grammar* (Oxford, 1959).

number, and tense along with the meaning of the root, a conception which we require three words for in English. The Latin sentence *Nero interfecit Agrippinam* means " Nero killed Agrippina." It would mean the same thing if the words were arranged in any other order, such as *Agrippinam interfecit Nero*, because *Nero* is the form of the nominative case and the ending *–am* of *Agrippinam* marks the noun as accusative no matter where it stands. In Modern English, however, the subject and the object do not have distinctive forms, nor do we have, except in the possessive case, inflectional endings to indicate the other relations marked by case endings in Latin. Instead, we make use of a fixed order of words. It makes a great deal of difference in English whether we say *Nero killed Agrippina* or *Agrippina killed Nero*. Languages which make extensive use of prepositions and auxiliary verbs and depend upon word order to show other relationships are known as *analytic* languages. Modern English is an analytic, Old English a synthetic language. In its grammar Old English resembles modern German. Theoretically the noun and adjective are inflected for four cases in the singular and four in the plural, although the forms are not always distinctive, and in addition the adjective has separate forms for each of the three genders. The inflection of the verb is less elaborate than that of the Latin verb, but there are distinctive endings for the different persons, numbers, tenses, and moods. We shall illustrate the nature of the Old English inflections in the following paragraphs.

41. *The Noun*.   The inflection of the Old English noun indicates distinctions of number (singular and plural) and case. The case system is somewhat simpler than that of Latin and some of the other Indo-European languages. There is no ablative, and generally no locative or instrumental case, these having been merged with the dative. In the same way the vocative of direct address is generally identical with the nominative form. Thus the Old English noun has only four cases. The endings of these cases vary with different nouns, but they fall into certain broad categories or declensions. There is a vowel declension and a consonant declension, also called the strong and weak declensions, according to whether the stem ended in Germanic in a vowel or a consonant, and within each of these types there are certain subdivisions. The stems of nouns belonging to the vowel declension ended in one of four vowels: *a*, *ō*, *i*, or *u*, and the inflection varies accordingly. It is impossible here to present the inflections of the Old English noun in detail. Their nature may be gathered from two examples of the strong declension and one of the weak: *stān* (stone), a masculine *a–* stem; *giefu* (gift), a feminine *ō–* stem; and *hunta* (hunter), a masculine consonant-stem:

Singular N.	stān	gief–u	hunt–a
G.	stān–es	gief–e	hunt–an
D.	stān–e	gief–e	hunt–an
A.	stān	gief–e	hunt–an
Plural N.	stān–as	gief–a	hunt–an
G.	stān–a	gief–a	hunt–ena
D.	stān–um	gief–um	hunt–um
A.	stān–as	gief–a	hunt–an

It is apparent from these examples that the inflection of the noun was much more elaborate in Old English than it is today. Even these few paradigms illustrate clearly the marked synthetic character of English in its earliest stage.

42. *Grammatical Gender*. As in Indo-European languages generally the gender of Old English nouns is not dependent upon considerations of sex. While nouns designating males are generally masculine and females feminine, those indicating neuter objects are not necessarily neuter. *Stān* (stone) is masculine, *mōna* (moon) is masculine, but *sunne* (sun) is feminine, as in German. In French the corresponding words have just the opposite genders: *pierre* (stone) and *lune* (moon) are feminine while *soleil* (sun) is masculine. Often the gender of Old English nouns is quite illogical. Words like *mægden* (girl), *wīf* (wife), *bearn* and *cild* (child), which we should expect to be feminine or masculine, are in fact neuter, while *wīfmann* (woman) is masculine because the second element of the compound is masculine. The simplicity of Modern English gender has already been pointed out (§ 11) as one of the chief assets of the language. How so desirable a change was brought about will be shown later.

43. *The Adjective*. An important feature of the Germanic languages is the development of a twofold declension of the adjective: one, the strong declension, used with nouns when not accompanied by a definite article or similar word (such as a demonstrative or possessive pronoun), the other, the weak declension, used when the noun is preceded by such a word. Thus we have in Old English *gōd mann* (good man) but *sē gōda mann* (the good man). The forms are those of the nominative singular masculine in the strong and weak declensions respectively, as illustrated on page 58.

This elaboration of inflection in the Old English adjective contrasts in the most striking way with the complete absence of inflection from the adjective in Modern English. Such complexity is quite unnecessary, as the English language demonstrates every day by getting along without it. Its elimination has resulted in a second great advantage which English possesses over most other languages.

	STRONG DECLENSION			WEAK DECLENSION		
	Masc.	*Fem.*	*Neut.*	*Masc.*	*Fem.*	*Neut.*
Singular N.	gōd	gōd[1]	gōd	gōd–a	gōd–e	gōd–e
G.	gōd–es	gōd–re	gōd–es	gōd–an	gōd–an	gōd–an
D.	gōd–um	gōd–re	gōd–um	gōd–an	gōd–an	gōd–an
A.	gōd–ne	gōd–e	gōd	gōd–an	gōd–an	gōd–e
I.	gōd–e		gōd–e			
Plural N.	gōd–e	gōd–a	gōd		gōd–an	
G.	gōd–ra	gōd–ra	gōd–ra		gōd–ena *or* gōd–ra	
D.	gōd–um	gōd–um	gōd–um		gōd–um	
A.	gōd–e	gōd–a	gōd		gōd–an	

44. The Definite Article. Like German, its sister language of today, Old English possessed a fully inflected definite article. How complete the declension of this word was can be seen from the following forms:

	SINGULAR			PLURAL
	Masc.	*Fem.*	*Neut.*	*All Genders*
N.	sē	sēo	ðæt	ðā
G.	ðæs	ðǣre	ðæs	ðāra
D.	ðǣm	ðǣre	ðǣm	ðǣm
A.	ðone	ðā	ðæt	ðā
I.	ðȳ, ðon		ðȳ, ðon	

While the ordinary meaning of *sē*, *sēo*, *ðæt* is 'the', the word is really a demonstrative pronoun and survives in the Modern English demonstrative *that*. Its pronominal character appears also in its not infrequent use as a relative pronoun (= who, which, that) and as a personal pronoun (= he, she, it). The regular personal pronoun, however, is shown in the next paragraph.

45. The Personal Pronoun. From the frequency of its use and the necessity for specific reference when used, the personal pronoun in all languages is likely to preserve a fairly complete system of inflections. Old English shows this tendency not only in having distinctive forms for practically all genders, persons, and cases, but also in preserving in addition to the ordinary two numbers, singular and plural, a set of forms for two people or two things—the dual number. Indo-European had separate forms for the dual number in the verb as well, and these appear in Greek and to a certain extent in Gothic. They are not found, however, in Old English. The distinction between the dual and the plural is an unnecessary complica-

---

[1] When the stem is short the adjective ends in *–u* in the nominative singular of the feminine and the nominative and accusative plural of the neuter.

tion in language and was disappearing from the pronoun in Old English. The dual forms are shown, however, in the following table of the Old English personal pronoun:

Singular	N.	ic	ðū	hē (*he*)	hēo (*she*)	hit (*it*)
	G.	mīn	ðīn	his	hiere	his
	D.	mē	ðē	him	hiere	him
	A.	mē (mec)	ðē (ðec)	hine	hīe	hit
Dual	N.	wit (*we two*)	git (*ye two*)			
	G.	uncer	incer			
	D.	unc	inc			
	A.	unc	inc			
Plural	N.	wē	gē		hīe	
	G.	ūser (ūre)	ēower		hiera	
	D.	ūs	ēow		him	
	A.	ūs (ūsic)	ēow (ēowic)		hīe	

46. The Verb. The inflection of the verb in the Germanic languages is much simpler than it was in Indo-European times. A comparison of the Old English verb with the verbal inflection of Greek or Latin will show how much has been lost. Old English distinguished only two simple tenses by inflection, a present and a past, and, except for one word, it had no inflectional forms for the passive as in Latin or Greek. It recognized the indicative, subjunctive, and imperative moods, and had the usual two numbers and three persons.

A peculiar feature of the Germanic languages was the division of the verb into two great classes, the weak and the strong, often known in Modern English as regular and irregular verbs. These terms, which are so commonly employed in modern grammars, are rather unfortunate since they suggest an irregularity in the strong verbs which is more apparent than real. The strong verbs, like *sing*, *sang*, *sung*, which represent the basic Indo-European type, are so called because they have the power of indicating change of tense by a modification of their root vowel. In the weak verbs, such as *walk*, *walked*, *walked*, this change is effected by the addition of a "dental," sometimes of an extra syllable.

The apparent irregularity of the strong verbs is due to the fact that verbs of this type are much less numerous than weak verbs. In Old English, if we exclude compounds, there were only a few over three hundred of them, and even this small number falls into several classes. Within these classes, however, a perfectly regular sequence can be observed in the vowel changes of the root. Nowadays these verbs, generally speaking, have different vowels in the present tense, the past tense, and the past participle. In some verbs the vowels of the past tense and past participle are identical, as in *break, broke, broken,* and in some all three forms have become alike in modern times (*bid, bid, bid*). In Old English the vowel of the past tense often differs in the singular and the plural; or, to be more accurate, the first and third person singular have one vowel while the second person singular and all persons of the plural have another. In the principal parts of Old English strong verbs, therefore, we have four forms, the infinitive, the preterite singular (first and third person), the preterite plural, and the past participle. In Old English the strong verbs can be grouped in six general classes, to which may be added a seventh, the reduplicating verbs. While there are variations within each class, they may be illustrated by the following seven verbs:

I.	drīfan	(*drive*)	drāf	drifon[1]	(ge) drifen
II.	cēosan	(*choose*)	cēas	curon[1]	coren
III.	helpan	(*help*)	healp	hulpon	holpen
IV.	beran	(*bear*)	bær	bǣron	boren
V.	sprecan	(*speak*)	spræc	sprǣcon	sprecen
VI.	faran	(*fare, go*)	fōr	fōron	faren
VII.	feallan	(*fall*)	fēoll	fēollon	feallen[2]

[1] The change of *s* to *r* is due to the fact that the accent was originally on the final syllable in the preterite plural and the past participle. It is known as Grammatical Change or Verner's Law for the scholar who first explained it (cf. § 16). In Modern English the *s* has been restored in the past participle (*chosen*) by analogy with the other forms. The initial sound has been leveled in the same way.

[2] The personal endings may be illustrated by the conjugation of the first verb in the above list, *drīfan*:

	INDICATIVE		SUBJUNCTIVE
	Present		*Present*
ic	drīf–e	ic	drīf–e
ðū	drīf–st (–est)	ðū	drīf–e
hē	drīf–ð (–eð)	hē	drīf–e
wē	drīf–að	wē	drīf–en
gē	drīf–að	gē	drīf–en
hīe	drīf–að	hīe	drīf–en
	Past		*Past*
ic	drāf	ic	drif–e
ðū	drif–e	ðū	drif–e
hē	drāf	hē	drif–e
wē	drif–on	wē	drif–en
gē	drif–on	gē	drif–en
hīe	drif–on	hīe	drif–en

In addition to these forms the imperative was *drīf* (sing.) and *drīfað* (plur.), the present participle *drīfende*, and the gerund (i.e., the infinitive used as a verbal noun) *tō drīfenne*.

The origin of the dental suffixes by which weak verbs form their past tense and past participle is not known. It was formerly customary to explain these as part of the verb *do*, as though *I worked* was originally *I work—did* (i.e., *I did work*). More recently an attempt has been made to trace these forms to a type of verb which formed its stem by adding *–to–* to the root. The origin of so important a feature of the Germanic languages as the weak conjugation is naturally a question to which we should like very much to find the answer. Fortunately it is not of prime importance to our present purpose of describing the structure of Old English. Here it is sufficient to note that a large and important group of verbs in Old English form their past tense by adding *–ede*, *–ode*, or *–de* to the present stem, and their past participles by adding *–ed*, *–od*, or *–d*. Thus *fremman* (to perform) has a preterite *fremede* and a past participle *gefremed; lufian* (to love) has *lufode* and *gelufod; libban* (to live) has *lifde* and *gelifd*. The personal endings except in the preterite singular are similar to those of the strong verbs and need not be repeated. It is to be noted, however, that the weak conjugation has come to be the dominant one in our language. Many strong verbs have passed over to this conjugation, and practically all new verbs added to our language are inflected in accordance with it.

47. *The Language Illustrated.* We have spoken of the inflections of Old English in some detail primarily with the object of making more concrete what is meant when we call the language in this stage synthetic. In the later chapters of this book we shall have occasion to trace the process by which English lost a great part of this inflectional system and became an analytic language, so that the paradigms which we have given here will also prove useful as a point of departure for that discussion. The use of these inflections as well as the other characteristics of the language so far pointed out may be seen in the following specimens. The first is the Lord's Prayer, the clauses of which can easily be followed through the modern form which is familiar to us from the King James version of the Bible.

> Fæder ūre,
> þū þe eart on heofonum,
> sī þīn nama gehālgod.
> Tōbecume þīn rīce.
> Gewurþe ðīn willa on eorðan swā swā on heofonum.
> Ūrne gedæghwāmlīcan hlāf syle ūs tō dæg.
> And forgyf ūs ūre gyltas, swā swā wē forgyfað ūrum gyltendum.
> And ne gelǣd þū ūs on costnunge,
> ac ālȳs ūs of yfele. Sōþlīce.

The second specimen is from the Old English translation of Bede's *Ecclesiastical History* and tells the story of the coming of the missionaries to England under St. Augustine in 597:

Ða wæs on þā tīd Æþelbeorht cyning hāten on Centrīce, and
Then (there)   was in   that time   a king named Æthelberht in Kent,   and (a)

mihtig: hē hæfde rīce oð gemæru Humbre strēames, sē tōscādeþ
mighty (one): he had dominion up to (the) confines of the Humber river,   which separates

sūðfolc Angelþēode and norðfolc. Þonne is on ēasteweardre Cent
the south folk of the English and the north folk.   Now   there is   in eastward   Kent

micel ēaland, Tenet, þæt is siex hund hīda micel æfter Angelcynnes
a large   island,   Thanet,   that is   six   hundred hides   large after the   reckoning of the

eahte. . . . On þyssum ēalande cōm ūp sē Godes þēow Augustinus
English. . . .   On   this   island   came   up   the   servant of God,   Augustine,

and his gefēran; wæs hē fēowertiga sum. Nāmon hīe ēac swelce him
and   his companions;   he was   one of forty.   Took   they likewise with them

wealhstodas of Franclande mid, swā him Sanctus Gregorius bebēad.
interpreters from Frank-land,   as   them Saint   Gregory   bade.

And þā sende to Æþelbeorhte ærendwrecan and onbēad þæt hē
And   then (Augustine) sent to Æthelberht a messenger   and   announced that he

of Rōme cōme and þæt betste ærende lædde; and sē þe him hīersum
from Rome had come and the   best   message brought (led); and he who   (if any) would

bēon wolde, būton twēon hē gehēt ēcne gefēan on heofonum and
be obedient to him, without doubt   he promised eternal happiness   in   heaven   and

tōweard rīce būton ende mit þone sōþan God and þone lifigendan.
a future kingdom without end   with the   true   God   and   the   living (God).

Ðā hē þā sē cyning þās word gehīerde, þā hēt hē hīe bīdan on þæm
When   the king   heard these   words,   then bade he them to bide   on   the

ēalande þe hīe ūp cōmon; and him þider hiera þearfe forgēaf, oð þæt
island   that they had come upon; and   them thither their   need   provided,   until that

hē gesāwe hwæt hē him dōn wolde. Swelce ēac ær þæm becōm hlīsa
he saw   what   he would do with them.   Likewise   ere that   had come to him

tō him þære crīstenan æfæstnesse, forþon hē crīsten wīf hæfde,
the fame   of the   Christian   religion,   since   he   had a   Christian wife,

him gegiefen of Francena cyningcynne, Beorhte wæs hāten. Þæt wīf
given him from   the royal family   of the Franks,   (who) was named Bertha. That wife

hē onfēng fram hiere ieldrum þære ārædnesse þæt hēo his lēafnesse
he received   from her parents (elders)   on   the   condition   that she should have his

hæfde þæt hēo þone þēaw þæs crīstenan gelēafan and hiere æfæstnesse
permission that she the   practice of the Christian   faith   and   her   religion

ungewemmedne healdan mōste mid þȳ biscope, þone þe hīe hiere
unimpaired   might   hold   with   the bishop   whom   they to her

tō fultume þæs gelēafan sealdon, þæs nama wæs Lēodheard.
for the help of   the (her)   faith   had given,   whose name   was   Leodheard.

Ðā wæs æfter manigum dagum þæt sē cyning cōm tō þǣm ēalande,
Then it was after many days that the king came to the island

and hēt him ūte setl gewyrcean; and hēt Augustinum mid his
and commanded (them) in the open air a seat to make him; and he bade Augustine with his

gefērum þider tō his sprǣce cuman. Warnode hē him þȳ lǣs hīe
companions to come thither to a (his) consultation. He guarded himself lest they

on hwelc hūs tō him inēoden; brēac ealdre hēalsunga, gif hīe hwelcne
in the same house with him should enter: he employed an old precaution in case they any

drȳcræft hæfden þæt hīe hine oferswīðan and beswīcan sceolden. . . .
sorcery had with which they should overcome and get the better of him. . . .

Þā hēt sē cyning hīe sittan, and hīe swā dydon; and hīe sōna him
Then the king bade them to sit, and they did so; and they soon to him

līfes word ætgædere mid eallum his gefērum þe þǣr æt wǣron,
the word of life together with all his companions that thereat were,

bodedon and lǣrdon. Þā andswarode sē cyning and þus cwæð:
preached and taught. Then answered the king and thus quoth:

"Fæger word þis sindon and gehāt þe gē brōhton and ūs secgað.
"Fair words these are and promises that ye have brought and say to us.

Ac forðon hīe nīwe sindon and uncūðe, ne magon wē nū gēn þæt
But since they new are and unknown, we may not yet consent to this

þafian þæt wē forlǣten þā wīsan þe wē langre tīde mid ealle
that we give up the ways that we longtime with all

Angelþēode hēoldon. Ac forðon þe gē hider feorran elþēodige
the English have held. But since ye hither from afar as strangers

cōmon and, þæs þe mē geþūht is and gesewen, þā þing, ðā ðe [gē]
have come and, as it seems to me and appears, the things that ye

sōð and betst gelīefdon, þæt ēac swelce wilnodon ūs þā gemǣnsumian,
believed true and best that likewise (ye) wished to impart them to us,

nellað wē forðon ēow hefige bēon. Ac wē willað ēow ēac fremsumlīce
we will not therefore on you be heavy. But we will you also kindly

on giestliðnesse onfon and ēow andleofne sellan and ēowre þearfe
in hospitality receive and give you food and your needs

forgiefan. Ne wē ēow beweriað þæt gē ealle, ðā þe gē mægen, þurh
provide for. Nor do we you forbid that ye all those that ye may through

ēowre lāre tō ēowres gelēafan ǣfæstnesse geðīeden and gecierren."[1]
your teaching to of your faith (the) religion may join and convert."

48. The Resourcefulness of the Old English Vocabulary. To one
unfamiliar with Old English it might seem that a language which lacked the
large number of words borrowed from Latin and French which now form

---

[1] The original is here somewhat normalized.

so important a part of our vocabulary would be somewhat limited in resources, and that while possessing adequate means of expression for the affairs of simple everyday life, it would find itself embarrassed when it came to making the nice distinctions which a literary language is called upon to express. In other words, an Anglo-Saxon would be like a man today who is learning to speak a foreign language and who can manage in a limited way to convey his meaning without having a sufficient command of the vocabulary to express those subtler shades of thought and feeling, the nuances of meaning, which he is able to suggest in his mother tongue. This, however, is not so. In language, as in other things, necessity is the mother of invention, and when our means are limited we often develop unusual resourcefulness in utilizing those means to the full. Such resource-fulness is characteristic of Old English. The language in this stage shows great flexibility, a capacity for bending old words to new uses. By means of prefixes and suffixes a single root is made to yield a variety of derivatives, and the range of these is greatly extended by the ease with which compounds are formed. The method can be made clear by an illustration. The word *mōd*, which is our word *mood* (a mental state), meant in Old English 'heart', 'mind', 'spirit', and hence 'boldness' or 'courage', sometimes 'pride' or 'haughtiness'. From it, by the addition of a common adjective ending, was formed the adjective *mōdig* with a similar range of meanings (spirited, bold, high-minded, arrogant, stiff-necked), and by means of further endings the adjective *mōdiglic* 'magnanimous', the adverb *mōdig-līce* 'boldly', 'proudly', and the noun *mōdignes* 'magnanimity', 'pride'. Another ending converted *mōdig* into a verb *mōdigian*, meaning 'to bear oneself proudly or exultantly', or sometimes, 'to be indignant', 'to rage'. Other forms conveyed meanings whose relation to the root is easily perceived: *gemōdod* 'disposed', 'minded', *mōdfull* 'haughty', *mōdlēas* 'spiritless'. By combining the root with other words meaning 'mind' or 'thought' the idea of the word is intensified, and we get *mōdsefa*, *mōd-geþanc*, *mōdgeþoht*, *mōdgehygd*, *mōdgemynd*, *mōdhord* (*hord* = treasure), all meaning 'mind', 'thought', 'understanding'. Some sharpening of the concept is obtained in *mōdcræft* 'intelligence', and *mōdcræftig* 'intelligent'. But the root lent itself naturally to combination with other words to indicate various mental states, such as *glædmōdnes* 'kindness', *mōdlufu* 'affection' (*lufu* = love), *unmōd* 'despondency', *mōdcaru* 'sorrow' (*caru* = care), *mōdlēast* 'want of courage', *mādmōd* 'folly', *ofermōd* and *ofermōd-igung* 'pride', *ofermōdig* 'proud', *hēahmōd* 'proud', 'noble', *mōdhete* 'hate' (*hete* = hate). It will be seen that Old English did not lack synonyms for some of the ideas in this list. By a similar process of combination a number of adjectives were formed: *micelmōd* 'magnanimous', *swīþmōd* 'great of soul' (*swīþ* = strong), *stīþmōd* 'resolute', 'obstinate' (*stīþ* = stiff, strong), *gūþmōd* 'warlike' (*guþ* = war, battle), *torhtmōd* 'glorious' (*torht* = bright), *mōdlēof* 'beloved' (*lēof* = dear). The examples given are sufficient to illustrate the point, but they are far from telling the whole story. From the same root more than a hundred words were formed. If we had space to list them, they would clearly show the remarkable capacity of Old English for derivation and word-formation, and what variety and flexibility of expression it possessed. It was more resourceful in utilizing its native material than Modern English, which has come to rely to a large extent on its facility in borrowing and assimilating elements from other languages

49. Self-explaining Compounds.   In the list of words given in the preceding paragraph there are a considerable number which we call self-explaining compounds. These are compounds of two or more native words whose meaning in combination is either self-evident or has been rendered clear by association and usage. In Modern English *steamboat, railroad, warning light, sewing machine, one-way street* are examples of such words. Words of this character are found in most languages, but the type is particularly prevalent in Old English, as it is in modern German. Where in English today we often have a borrowed word or a word made up of elements derived from Latin and Greek, German still prefers self-explaining compounds. Thus, for hydrogen German says *Wasserstoff* (water-stuff); for telephone *Fernsprecher* (far-speaker); and for fire insurance company *Feuer|versicherungs|gesellschaft*. So in Old English many words are formed on this pattern. Thus we have *lēohtfæt* 'lamp' (*lēoht* light + *fæt* vessel), *medu-heall* 'mead-hall', *dægred* 'dawn' (day-red), *ealohūs* 'alehouse', *ealoscop* 'minstrel', *ēarhring* 'earring', *eorþcræft* 'geometry', *fiscdēag* 'purple' (*lit.* fish-dye), *fōtādl* 'gout' (foot-disease), *gimmwyrhta* 'jeweler' (gem-worker), *fielleséocnes* 'epilepsy' (falling-sickness; cf. Shakespeare's use of this expression in *Julius Caesar*), *frumweorc* 'creation' (*fruma* beginning + work), and many more. The capacity of English nowadays to make similar words, though a little less frequently employed than formerly, is an inheritance of the Old English tradition, when the method was well-nigh universal. As a result of this capacity Old English seems never to have been at a loss for a word to express even the abstractions of science, theology, and metaphysics, which it came to know through contact with the church and Latin culture.

50. Prefixes and Suffixes.   As previously mentioned, a part of the flexibility of the Old English vocabulary comes from the generous use made of prefixes and suffixes to form new words from old words or to modify or extend the root idea. In this respect it also resembles modern German. Among the words mentioned in the preceding paragraphs there are several which are formed with the suffixes *–ig, –full, –lēas, –līce, –nes,* and *–ung.* Others frequently employed include the adjective suffixes *–sum* (*wynsum*) and *–wīs* (*rihtwīs*), the noun suffixes *–dōm* (*cyningdōm, eorldōm*), *–end,* and *–ere* denoting the agent, *–hād* (*cildhād*), *–ing* in patronymics, *–ung* (*dagung* dawn), *–scipe* (*frēondscipe*), and many more. In like manner the use of prefixes was a fertile resource in word-building. It is particularly a feature in the formation of verbs. There are about a dozen prefixes that occur with great frequency, such as *ā–, be–, for–, fore–, ge–, mis–, of–, ofer–, on–, tō–, un–, under–,* and *wiþ–.* Thus, with the help of these, Old English could make out of a simple verb like *settan* (to set) new verbs like *āsettan* 'place', *besettan* 'appoint', *forsettan* 'obstruct', *foresettan* 'place before', *gesettan* 'people', 'garrison', *ofsettan* 'afflict', *onsettan* 'oppress', *tōsettan* 'dispose', *unsettan* 'put down', and *wiþsettan* 'resist'. The prefix *wiþ–* enters into more than fifty Old English verbs, where it has the force of *against* or *away.* Such, for example, are *wiþcēosan* 'reject' (*cēosan =* choose), *wiþcweþan* 'deny' (*cweþan =* say), *wiþdrīfan* 'repel', *wiþsprecan* 'contradict', and *wiþstandan.* Of these fifty verbs *withstand* is the only one still in use, although in Middle English two new verbs, *withdraw* and *withhold,* were formed on the same model. The prefix *ofer–* occurs in over a hundred Old English verbs. By such means the resources of the English verb were increased almost tenfold, and enough such verbs survive to give us a realization of their employment in the Old English vocabulary.

In general one is surprised at the apparent ease with which Old English expressed difficult ideas adequately and often with variety. 'Companion-ship' is literally rendered by *gefērascipe*; 'hospitality' by *giestlīþnes* (*giest* stranger, *līþe* gracious); *gītsung* 'covetousness' (*gītsian =* to be greedy). *Godcundlic* 'divine', *indryhten* 'aristocratic' (*dryhten =* prince), *giefolnes* 'liberality' (*giefu =* gift), *gaderscipe* 'matrimony' (*gadrian =* to gather), *lǣcecræft* 'medicine' (*lǣce =* physician) illustrate, so to speak, the method of approach. Often several words to express the same idea result. An astronomer or astrologer may be a *tunglere* (*tungol =* star), *tungolcræftiga, tungolwītega,* a *tīdymbwlātend* (*tīd =* time, *ymb =* about, *wlātian =* to gaze), or a *tīdscēawere* (*scēawian =* see, scrutinize). In poetry the vocabu-lary attains a remarkable flexibility through the wealth of synonyms for words like *war, warrior, shield, sword, battle, sea, ship*—sometimes as many as thirty for one of these ideas—and through the bold use of metaphors. The king is the leader of hosts, the giver of rings, the protector of eorls, the victory-lord, the heroes' treasure-keeper. A sword is the product of files, the play of swords a battle, the battle-seat a saddle, the shield-bearer a warrior. Warriors in their woven war-shirts, carrying battle-brand or war-shaft, form the iron-clad throng. A boat is the sea-wood, the wave-courser, the broad-bosomed, the curved-stem, or the foamy-necked ship, and it travels over the whale-road, the sea-surge, the rolling of waves, or simply the water's back. Synonyms never fail the Beowulf poet. Grendel is the grim spirit, the prowler on the wasteland, the lonely wanderer, the loathed one, the creature of evil, the fiend in Hell, the grim monster, the dark death-shadow, the worker of hate, the mad ravisher, the fell spoiler, and the incarnation of a dozen other attributes characteristic of his enmity toward mankind. No one can long remain in doubt about the rich and colorful character of the Old English vocabulary.

51. *Old English Literature.* The language of a past time is known by the quality of its literature. Charters and records yield their secrets to the philologist and contribute their quota of words and inflections to our dictionaries and grammars. But it is in literature that a language displays its full power, its ability to convey in vivid and memorable form the thoughts and emotions of a people. The literature of the Anglo-Saxons is fortunately one of the richest and most significant of any preserved among the early Germanic peoples. Since it is the language mobilized, the language in action, we must say a word about it.

Generally speaking, this literature is of two sorts. Some of it was undoubtedly brought to England by the Germanic conquerors from their continental homes and preserved for a time in oral tradition. All of it owes its preservation, however, and not a little its inspiration to the introduction of Christianity into the island at the end of the sixth century, an event whose significance for the English language will be discussed in the next chapter. Two streams thus mingle in Old English literature, the pagan and the Christian, and they are never quite distinct. The poetry of pagan origin is constantly overlaid with Christian sentiment, while even those poems which treat of purely Christian themes contain every now and again traces of an earlier philosophy not wholly forgotten. We can indicate only in the briefest way the scope and content of this literature, and we shall begin with that which embodies the native traditions of the race.

The greatest single work of Old English literature is the *Beowulf*. It is a poem of some 3,000 lines belonging to the type known as the folk epic, that is to say, a poem which, whatever it may owe to the individual poet who gave it final form, embodies material long current among the people. It is a narrative of heroic adventure relating how a young warrior, Beowulf, fought the monster Grendel, which was ravaging the land of King Hrothgar,

slew it and its dam, and years later met his death while ridding his own
country of an equally destructive foe, a fire-breathing dragon. The theme
seems somewhat fanciful to a modern reader, but the character of the hero,
the social conditions pictured, and the portrayal of the motives and ideals
which animated men in early Germanic times make the poem one of the
most vivid records we have of life in the heroic age. It is not an easy life.
It is a life that calls for physical endurance, unflinching courage, and a fine
sense of duty, loyalty, and honor. No better expression of the heroic ideal
exists than the words which Beowulf addresses to Hrothgar before going
to his dangerous encounter with Grendel's dam: "Sorrow not. . . . Better
is it for every man that he avenge his friend than that he mourn greatly.
Each of us must abide the end of this world's life; let him who may, work
mighty deeds ere he die, for afterwards, when he lies lifeless, that is best
for the warrior."

Outside of the *Beowulf* Old English poetry of native tradition is represented by a number of shorter pieces. Anglo-Saxon poets sang of the things
that entered most deeply into their experience—of war and of exile, of the
sea with its hardships and its fascination, of ruined cities, and of minstrel
life. One of the earliest products of Germanic tradition is a short poem
called *Widsith* in which a scop or minstrel pretends to give an account of
his wanderings and of the many famous kings and princes before whom he
has exercised his craft. *Deor*, another poem about a minstrel, is the lament
of a scop who for years has been in the service of his lord, and now finds
himself thrust out by a younger man. But he is no whiner. Life is like that.
Age will be displaced by youth. *He* has his day. Peace, my heart! *Deor* is
one of the most human of Old English poems. The *Wanderer* is a tragedy
in the medieval sense, the story of a man who once enjoyed a high place
and has fallen upon evil times. His lord is dead and he has become a
wanderer in strange courts, without friends. Where are the snows of yester-
year? The *Seafarer* is a monologue in which the speaker alternately
describes the perils and hardships of the sea and the eager desire to dare
again its dangers. In *The Ruin* the poet reflects on a ruined city, once
prosperous and imposing with its towers and halls, its stone courts and
baths, now but the tragic shadow of what it once was. Two great war
poems, the *Battle of Brunanburh* and the *Battle of Maldon*, celebrate with
patriotic fervor stirring encounters of the English, equally heroic in victory
and defeat. In its shorter poems, no less than in *Beowulf*, Old English
literature reveals at wide intervals of time the outlook and temper of the
Germanic mind.

More than half of Anglo-Saxon poetry is concerned with Christian subjects. Translations and paraphrases of books of the Old and New Testament, legends of saints, and devotional and didactic pieces constitute the bulk of this verse. The most important of this poetry had its origin in Northumbria and Mercia in the seventh and eighth centuries. The earliest English poet whose name we know was Cædmon, a lay brother in the monastery at Whitby. The story of how the gift of song came to him in a dream and how he subsequently turned various parts of the Scriptures into beautiful English verse comes to us in the pages of Bede. Although we do not have his poems on Genesis, Exodus, Daniel, and the like, the poems on these subjects which we do have were most likely inspired by his example. About 800 an Anglian poet named Cynewulf wrote at least four poems on religious subjects, into which he ingeniously wove his name by means of runes. Two of these, *Juliana* and *Elene*, tell well-known legends of saints. A third, *Christ*, deals with Advent, the Ascension, and the Last Judgment. The fourth, *The Fates of the Apostles*, touches briefly on where and how the various apostles died. There are other religious poems besides those mentioned, such as the *Andreas* and *Guthlac*, a portion of a fine poem on the story of *Judith* in the Apocrypha; *The Phoenix*, in which the bird is taken as a symbol of the Christian life; and *Christ and Satan*, which treats the expulsion of Satan from Paradise together with the Harrowing of Hell and Satan's tempting of Christ. All of these poems have their counterparts in other literatures of the Middle Ages. They show England in its cultural contact with Rome and being drawn into the general current of ideas on the continent, no longer simply Germanic, but cosmopolitan.

In the development of literature, prose generally comes late. Verse is more effective for oral delivery and more easily retained in the memory. It is therefore a rather remarkable fact, and one well worthy of note, that English possessed a considerable body of prose literature in the ninth century, at a time when most other modern languages in Europe had scarcely developed a literature in verse. This unusual accomplishment was due to the inspiration of one man, the Anglo-Saxon king who is justly called Alfred the Great (871–899). Alfred's greatness rests not only on his capacity as a military leader and statesman but on his realization that greatness in a nation is no merely physical thing. When he came to the throne he found that the learning which in the eighth century, in the days of Bede and Alcuin, had placed England in the forefront of Europe, had greatly decayed. In an effort to restore England to something like its former state he undertook to provide for his people certain books in English, books which he deemed most essential to their welfare. With this object in view he undertook in mature life to learn Latin and either translated these books himself or caused others to translate them for him. First as a guide for the clergy he translated the *Pastoral Care* of Pope Gregory, and then, in order that his people might know something of their own past, inspired and may well have arranged for a translation of Bede's *Ecclesiastical History of the English People*. A history of the rest of the world also seemed desirable and was not so easily to be had. But in the fifth century when so many calamities were befalling the Roman Empire and those misfortunes were being attributed to the abandonment of the pagan deities in favor of Christianity, a Spanish priest named Orosius had undertaken to refute this idea. His method was to trace the rise of other empires to positions of great power and their subsequent collapse, a collapse in which obviously Christianity had had no part. The result was a book which, when its polemical aim had ceased to have any significance, was still widely read as a compendium of historical knowledge. This Alfred translated with omissions and some additions of his own. A fourth book which he turned into English was *The Consolation of Philosophy* by Boethius, one of the most famous books of the Middle Ages. Alfred also caused a record to be compiled of the important events of English history, past and present, and this, as continued for more than two centuries after his death, is the well-known Anglo-Saxon Chronicle. King Alfred was the founder of English prose, but there were others who carried on the tradition. Among these is Ælfric, the author of two books of homilies and numerous other works, and Wulfstan, whose *Sermon to the English* is an impassioned plea for moral and political reform.

So large and varied a body of literature, in verse and prose, gives ample testimony to the universal competence, at times to the power and beauty, of the Old English language.

BIBLIOGRAPHY

For the early peoples of Europe there is an abundant literature. In spite of its unconventional classification R. B. Dixon's *The Racial History of Man* (New York, 1923) is on the whole a satisfactory statement of the subject. H. F. Osborn's *Men of the Old Stone Age* (2nd ed., New York, 1916) is a fuller treatment of the oldest period. More recent discoveries and speculations are embodied in the early chapters of Carleton S. Coon's *The Story of Man* (2nd ed., New York, 1962) and the same author's *The Origin of Races* (New York, 1962). Robert Munro, *Prehistoric Britain* (London, 1913), and Norman Ault, *Life in Ancient Britain* (London, 1920), are excellent accounts of conditions in England, while T. Rice Holmes' *Ancient Britain and the Invasions of Julius Caesar* (Oxford, 1936) is invaluable for the advanced student. For the Roman occupation of England the work of F. Haverfield is authoritative, especially *The Romanization of Roman Britain*, rev. G. Macdonald (4th ed., Oxford, 1923), and *The Roman Occupation* of Britain (Oxford, 1924). R. G. Collingwood's Roman Britain (rev. ed., New York, 1934) is an admirable brief survey, and B. C. A. Windle's The Romans in Britain (London, 1923) is a readable account. Recent discoveries in archaeology and aerial photography are included in the complete revision of a standard handbook, R. G. Collingwood and Ian Richmond, The Archaeology of Roman Britain (rev. ed., London, 1969). For detailed studies of both the Roman occupation and the Germanic invasions, the best treatments are R. G. Collingwood and J. N. L. Myres, Roman Britain and the English Settlements (2nd ed., Oxford, 1937), and F. M. Stenton, Anglo-Saxon England (3rd ed., Oxford, 1971), both of them in the Oxford History of England, to which may be added R. H. Hodgkin, A History of the Anglo-Saxons (3rd ed., Oxford, 1953); Kenneth Jackson, Language and History in Early Britain (Edinburgh, 1953); P. Hunter Blair, An Introduction to Anglo-Saxon England (Cambridge, 1956); and Dorothy Whitelock, The Beginnings of English Society, Pelican History of England, Vol. 2 (1952; rev. ed., Baltimore, 1974). For divergent views the advanced student may consult A. Erdmann, Über die Heimat und den Namen der Angeln (Uppsala, 1890); H. M. Chadwick, The Origin of the English Nation (Cambridge, 1907); E. Thurlow Leeds, The Archaeology of the Anglo-Saxon Settlements (Oxford, 1913); Elis Wadstein, On the Origin of the English (Uppsala, 1927); and An Historical Geography of England before A.D. 1800: Fourteen Studies, ed. H. C. Darby (Cambridge, 1936). On early Germanic civilization F. B. Gummere's Germanic Origins (New York, 1892) is classic. It is now available with supplementary notes by F. P. Magoun, Jr., under the title Founders of England (New York, 1930). The importance for Anglo-Saxon studies of the Sutton Hoo excavation in 1939 is clearly documented in the text and illustrations of R. Bruce-Mitford, The Sutton Hoo Ship-Burial (2nd ed., London, 1972). Definitive volumes on the excavation are forthcoming from the British Museum. For the character of Old English the best source is the grammars mentioned on p. 55. A concise introduction to Old English syntax is Bruce Mitchell, A Guide to Old English (2nd ed., Oxford, 1968), chap. 5, which the advanced student may supplement with Paul Bacquet, La Structure de la phrase verbale à l'époque alfrédienne (Paris, 1962). The standard dictionary is J. Bosworth, An Anglo-Saxon Dictionary, ed. T. N. Toller (Oxford, 1898), with Toller's Supplement (Oxford, 1921). For a project designed to replace Bosworth–Toller, see Roberta Frank and Angus Cameron, eds., A Plan for the Dictionary of Old English (Toronto, 1973). Current bibliographies of Anglo-Saxon studies appear annually in the Old English Newsletter and Anglo-Saxon England.

[4]

Foreign Influences on Old English

52. *The Contact of English with Other Languages.* The language which has been described in the preceding chapter was not merely the product of the dialects brought to England by the Jutes, Saxons, and Angles. These formed its basis, the sole basis of its grammar and the source of by far the largest part of its vocabulary. But there were other elements which entered into it. In the course of the first seven hundred years of its existence in England it was brought into contact with three other languages, the languages of the Celts, the Romans, and the Scandinavians. From each of these contacts it shows certain effects, especially additions to its vocabulary. The nature of these contacts and the changes that were effected by them will form the subject of this chapter.

53. *The Celtic Influence.* Nothing would seem more reasonable than to expect that the conquest of the Celtic population of Britain by the Anglo-Saxons and the subsequent mixture of the two peoples should have resulted in a corresponding mixture of their languages; that consequently we should find in the Old English vocabulary numerous instances of words which the Anglo-Saxons heard in the speech of the native population and adopted. For it is apparent that the Celts were by no means exterminated except in certain areas, and that in most of England large numbers of them were gradually absorbed by the new inhabitants. The Anglo-Saxon Chronicle reports that at Andredesceaster or Pevensey a deadly struggle occurred between the native population and the newcomers and that not a single Briton was left alive. The evidence of the place-names in this region lends support to the statement. But this was probably an exceptional case. In the east and southeast, where the Germanic conquest was fully accomplished at a fairly early date, it is probable that there were fewer survivals of a Celtic population than elsewhere. Large numbers of the defeated fled to the west. Here it is apparent that a considerable Celtic-speaking population survived until fairly late times. Some such situation is suggested by a whole cluster of Celtic place-names in the northeastern corner of Dorsetshire.[1] It is altogether likely that many Celts were held as slaves by the conquerors and that many of the Anglo-Saxons married Celtic women. In parts at least of the island, contact between the two peoples must have been constant and in some districts intimate for several generations.

54. Celtic Place-names. When we come, however, to seek the evidence for this contact in the English language, investigation yields very meager results. Such evidence as there is survives chiefly in place-names.[2] The kingdom of *Kent*, for example, owes its name to the Celtic word *Canti* or *Cantion*, the meaning of which is unknown, while the two ancient Northumbrian kingdoms of *Deira* and *Bernicia* derive their designations from Celtic tribal names. Other districts, especially in the west and southwest, preserve in their present-day names traces of their earlier Celtic designations. *Devonshire* contains in the first element the tribal name *Dumnonii*, *Cornwall* means the 'Cornubian Welsh', and *Cumberland* is the 'land of the Cymry or Britons'. Moreover, a number of important centers in the Roman period have names in which Celtic elements are embodied. The name *London* itself, although the origin of the word is somewhat uncertain, most likely goes back to a Celtic designation. The first syllable of *Winchester, Salisbury, Exeter, Gloucester, Worcester, Lichfield*, and a score of other names of cities is traceable to a Celtic source, while the earlier name of Canterbury (*Durovernum*) and the name *York* are originally Celtic. But it is in the names of rivers and hills and places in proximity to these natural features that the greatest number of Celtic names survive. Thus the *Thames* is a Celtic river name, and various Celtic words for river or water are preserved in the names *Avon, Exe, Esk, Usk, Dover,* and *Wye*. Celtic words meaning 'hill' are found in place-names like *Barr* (cf. Welsh *bar* 'top', 'summit'), *Bredon* (cf. Welsh *bre* 'hill'), *Bryn Mawr* (cf. Welsh *bryn* 'hill' and *mawr* 'great'), *Creech, Pendle* (cf. Welsh *pen* 'top'), and others. Certain other Celtic elements occur more or less frequently such as *cumb* (a deep valley) in names like *Duncombe, Holcombe, Winchcombe; torr* (high rock, peak) in *Torr, Torcross, Torhill; pill* (a tidal creek) in *Pylle, Huntspill;* and *brocc* (badger) in *Brockholes, Brockhall,* etc. Besides these purely

---

[1] R. E. Zachrisson, *Romans, Kelts, and Saxons in Ancient Britain* (Uppsala, 1927), p. 55.

[2] An admirable survey of the Celtic element in English place-names is given by E. Ekwall in the *Introduction to the Survey of English Place-Names*, ed. A. Mawer and F. M. Stenton for the English Place-Name Society, 1, part 1 (Cambridge, 1924), 15–35.

Celtic elements a few Latin words such as *castra, fontana, fossa, portus*, and *vicus* were used in naming places during the Roman occupation of the island and were passed on by the Celts to the English. These will be discussed later. It is natural that Celtic place-names should be commoner in the west than in the east and southeast, but the evidence of these names shows that the Celts impressed themselves upon the Germanic consciousness at least to the extent of causing the newcomers to adopt many of the local names current in Celtic speech and to make them a permanent part of their vocabulary.

55. Other Celtic Loan-words. Outside of place-names, however, the influence of Celtic upon the English language is almost negligible. Not over a score of words in Old English can be traced with reasonable probability to a Celtic source. Within this small number it is possible to distinguish two groups: (1) those which the Anglo-Saxons learned through everyday contact with the natives, and (2) those which were introduced by the Irish missionaries in the north. The former were transmitted orally and were of popular character; the latter were connected with religious activities and were more or less learned. The popular words include *binn* (basket, crib), *bratt* (cloak), and *brocc* (brock or badger); a group of words for geographical features which had not played much part in the experience of the Anglo-Saxons in their continental home—*crag, luh* (lake), *cumb* (valley), and *torr*[1] (outcropping or projecting rock, peak), the two latter chiefly as elements in place-names; possibly the words *dun* (dark colored), and *ass* (ultimately from Latin *asinus*). Words of the second group, those that came into English through Celtic Christianity, are likewise few in number. In 563 St. Columba had come with twelve monks from Ireland to preach to his kinsmen in Britain. On the little island of Iona off the west coast of Scotland he established a monastery and made it his headquarters for the remaining thirty-four years of his life. From this center many missionaries went out, founded other religious houses, and did much to spread Christian doctrine and learning. As a result of their activity the words *ancor* (hermit), *drȳ* (magician), *cine* (a gathering of parchment leaves), *cross*, *clugge* (bell), *gabolrind* (compass), *mind* (diadem), and perhaps *stǣr* (history) and *cursian* (to curse), came into at least partial use in Old English.

It does not appear that many of these Celtic words attained a very permanent place in the English language. Some soon died out and others acquired only local currency. The relation of the two peoples was not such as to bring about any considerable influence on English life or on English

---

[1] Cf. E. Ekwall, "Zu zwei keltischen Lehnwörtern in Altenglischen," *Englische Studien*, 54 (1920), 102–10.

speech. The surviving Celts were a submerged race. Had they, like the Romans, possessed a superior culture, something valuable to give the Anglo-Saxons, their influence might have been greater. But the Anglo-Saxon found little occasion to adopt Celtic modes of expression and the Celtic influence remains the least of the early influences which affected the English language.

56. *Three Latin Influences on Old English.* If the influence of Celtic upon Old English was slight, it was doubtless so because the relation of the Celt to the Anglo-Saxon was that of a submerged race and, as suggested above, because the Celt was not in a position to make any notable contribution to Anglo-Saxon civilization. It was quite otherwise with the second great influence exerted upon English—that of Latin—and the circumstances under which they met. Latin was not the language of a conquered people. It was the language of a higher civilization, a civilization from which the Anglo-Saxons had much to learn. Contact with that civilization, at first commercial and military, later religious and intellectual, extended over many centuries and was constantly renewed. It began long before the Anglo-Saxons came to England and continued throughout the Old English period. For several hundred years, while the Germanic tribes who later became the English were still occupying their continental homes, they had various relations with the Romans through which they acquired a considerable number of Latin words. Later when they came to England they saw the evidences of the long Roman rule in the island and learned from the Celts a few additional Latin words which had been acquired by them. And a century and a half later still, when Roman missionaries reintroduced Christianity into the island, this new cultural influence resulted in a really extensive adoption of Latin elements into the language. There were thus three distinct occasions on which borrowing from Latin occurred before the end of the Old English period, and it will be of interest to consider more in detail the character and extent of these borrowings.

57. *Chronological Criteria.* In order to form an accurate idea of the share which each of these three periods had in extending the resources of the English vocabulary it is first necessary to determine as closely as possible the date at which each of the borrowed words entered the language. This is naturally somewhat difficult to do, and in the case of some words impossible. But in a large number of cases it is possible to assign a word to a given period with a high degree of probability and often with certainty. It will be instructive to pause for a moment to inquire how this is done.

The evidence which can be employed is of various kinds and naturally of varying value. Most obvious is the appearance of the word in literature. If a given word occurs with fair frequency in texts such as *Beowulf*, or the poems of Cynewulf, such occurrence indicates that the word has had time to pass into current use and that it came into English not later than the early part of the period of Christian influence. But it does not tell us how much earlier it was known in the language, since the earliest written records in English do not go back beyond the year 700. Moreover the late appearance of a word in literature is no proof of late adoption. The word may not be the kind of word that would naturally occur very often in literary texts, and so much of Old English literature has been lost that it would be very unsafe to argue about the existence of a word on the basis of existing remains. Some words which are not found recorded before the tenth century (e.g., *pīpe* 'pipe', *cīese* 'cheese') can be assigned confidently on other grounds to the period of continental borrowing.

The character of the word sometimes gives some clue to its date. Some words are obviously learned and point to a time when the church had become well established in the island. On the other hand, the early occurrence of a word in several of the Germanic dialects points to the general circulation of the word in the Germanic territory and its probable adoption by the ancestors of the English on the continent. Testimony of this kind must of course be used with discrimination. A number of words found in Old English and in Old High German, for example, can hardly have been borrowed by either language before the Anglo-Saxons migrated to England, but are due to later independent adoption under conditions more or less parallel, brought about by the introduction of Christianity into the two areas. But it can hardly be doubted that a word like *copper*, which is rare in Old English, was nevertheless borrowed on the continent when we find it in no less than six Germanic languages.

Much the most conclusive evidence of the date at which a word was borrowed, however, is to be found in the phonetic form of the word. The changes which take place in the sounds of a language can often be dated with some definiteness, and the presence or absence of these changes in a borrowed word constitutes an important test of age. A full account of these changes would carry us far beyond the scope of this book, but one or two examples may serve to illustrate the principle. Thus there occurred in Old English, as in most of the Germanic languages, a change known as *i–umlaut*.[1] This change affected certain accented vowels and diphthongs ($æ$, $ă$, $ŏ$, $ŭ$, $ĕa$, $ĕo$, and $ĭo$) when they were followed in the next syllable by an $ĭ$ or *j*. Under such circumstances $æ$ and $ă$ became $ĕ$, and $ŏ$ became $ĕ$, $ā$

---

[1] *Umlaut* is a German word meaning 'alteration of sound'. In English this is sometimes called *mutation*.

became $æ$, and $ŭ$ became $ȳ$. The diphthongs $ĕa$, $ĕo$, $ĭo$ became $ĭe$, later $ĭ$, $ȳ$. Thus *$baŋkiz$ > $benc$ (bench), *$mūsiz$ > $mȳs$, plural of $mūs$ (mouse), etc. The change occurred in English in the course of the seventh century, and when we find it taking place in a word borrowed from Latin it indicates that the Latin word had been taken into English by that time. Thus Latin $monēta$ (which became *$munit$ in Prim. O.E.) > $mynet$ (a coin, Mod. E. mint) and is an early borrowing. Another change (even earlier) that helps us to date a borrowed word is that known as *palatal diphthongization*. By this sound-change an $æ̆$ or $ĕ$ in early Old English was changed to a diphthong ($ĕa$ and $ĭe$ respectively) when preceded by certain palatal consonants (c, g,[1] sc). O.E. $cīese$ (L. $cāseus$, cheese), mentioned above, shows both *i–umlaut* and palatal diphthongization ($cāseus$ > *$cǣsi$ > *$cēasi$ > $cīese$). In many words evidence for date is furnished by the sound-changes of Vulgar Latin. Thus, for example, an intervocalic p (and p in the combination pr) in the late Latin of northern Gaul (seventh century) was modified to a sound approximating a v, and the fact that L. $cuprum$, $coprum$ (copper) appears in O.E. as $copor$ with the p unchanged indicates a period of borrowing prior to this change (cf. F. $cuivre$). Again Latin i changed to e before A.D. 400 so that words like O.E. $biscop$ (L. $episcopus$), $disc$ (L. $discus$), $sigel$, 'brooch' (L. $sigillum$), etc., which do not show this change, were borrowed by the English on the continent. But enough has been said to indicate the method and to show that the distribution of the Latin words in Old English among the various periods at which borrowing took place rests not upon guesses, however shrewd, but upon definite facts and upon fairly reliable phonetic inferences.

58. Continental Borrowing (*Latin Influence of the Zero Period*). The first Latin words to find their way into the English language owe their adoption to the early contact between the Romans and the Germanic tribes on the continent. Several hundred Latin words found in the various Germanic dialects at an early date—some in one dialect only, others in several—testify to the extensive intercourse between the two peoples. The number of Germans living within the empire by the fourth century is estimated at several million. They are found in all ranks and classes of society, from slaves in the fields to commanders of important divisions of the Roman army. While they were scattered all over the empire, they were naturally most numerous along the northern frontier. This stretched along the Rhine and the Danube and bordered on German territory. Close to the border was Treves, in the third and fourth centuries the most flourishing

---

[1] Representing the Germanic palatal spirant ȝ or Germanic initial *j*.

city in Gaul, already boasting Christian churches, a focus of eight military roads, where all the luxury and splendor of Roman civilization were united almost under the gaze of the Teutons on the Moselle and the Rhine. Traders, German as well as Roman, came and went, while German youth returning from within the empire must have carried back glowing accounts of Roman cities and Roman life. Such intercourse between the two peoples was certain to carry words from one language to the other.

The frequency of the intercourse may naturally be expected to diminish somewhat as one recedes from the borders of the empire. Roman military operations, for example, seldom extended as far as the district occupied by the Angles or the Jutes. But after the conquest of Gaul by Caesar, Roman merchants quickly found their way into all parts of the Germanic territory, even into Scandinavia, so that the Teutons living in these remoter sections were by no means cut off from Roman influence. Moreover, intercommunication between the different Germanic tribes was frequent and made possible the transference of Latin words from one tribe to another. In any case some fifty words from the Latin can be credited with a considerable degree of probability to the ancestors of the English in their continental homes.

The adopted words naturally indicate the new conceptions which the Teutons acquired from this contact with a higher civilization. Next to agriculture the chief occupation of the Germans in the empire was war, and this experience is reflected in words like *camp* (battle), *segn* (banner), *pīl* (pointed stick, javelin), *weall* (wall), *pytt* (pit), *strǣt* (road, street), *mīl* (mile), and *miltestre* (courtesan). More numerous are the words connected with trade. The Teutons traded amber, furs, slaves, and probably certain raw materials for the products of Roman handicrafts, articles of utility, luxury, and adornment. The words *cēap* (bargain; cf. Eng., *cheap*, *chapman*) and *mangian* (to trade) with its derivatives *mangere* (monger), *mangung* (trade, commerce), and *mangung-hūs* (shop) are fundamental, while *pund* (pound), *mydd* (bushel), *sēam* (burden, loan), and *mynet* (coin) are terms likely to be employed. From the last word Old English formed the words *mynetian* (to mint or coin) and *mynetere* (money-changer). One of the most important branches of Roman commerce with the Teutons was the wine trade: hence such words in English as *wīn* (wine), *must* (new wine), *eced* (vinegar), and *flasce*[1] (flask, bottle). To this period are probably to be attributed the words *cylle* (L. *culleus*, leather bottle), *cyrfette*

---

[1] The O.E. *flasce* should have become *flash* in Modern English, so that the word was probably reintroduced later and may have been influenced (as the *OED* suggests) by the Italian *fiasco*.

(L. *curcurbita*, gourd), and *sester* (jar, pitcher). A number of the new words relate to domestic life and designate household articles, clothing, etc.: *cytel* (kettle; L. *catillus, catīnus*), *mēse* (table), *scamol* (L. *scamellum*, bench, stool; cf. modern *shambles*), *teped* (carpet, curtain; L. *tapētum*), *pyle* (L. *pulvīnus*, pillow), *pilece* (L. *pellicia*, robe of skin), and *sigel* (brooch, necklace; L. *sigillum*). Certain other words of a similar kind probably belong here although the evidence for their adoption thus early is not in every case conclusive: *cycene* (kitchen; L. *coquīna*), *cuppe* (L. *cuppa*, cup), *disc* (dish; L. *discus*), *cucler* (spoon; L. *coclearium*), *mortere* (L. *mortārium*, a mortar, a vessel of hard material), *līnen* (cognate with or from L. *līnum*, flax), *līne* (rope, line; L. *līnea*), and *gimm* (L. *gemma*, gem). The Teutons adopted Roman words for certain foods, such as *cīese* (L. *cāseus*, cheese), *spelt* (wheat), *pipor* (pepper), *senep* (mustard; L. *sināpi*), *popig* (poppy), *cisten* (chestnut-tree; L. *castanea*), *cires(bēam)* (cherry-tree; L. *cerasus*), while to this period are probably to be assigned *butere* (butter; L. *būtȳrum*),[1] *ynne(lēac)* (L. *ūnio*, onion), *plūme* (plum), *pise* (L. *pisum*, pea), and *minte* (L. *mentha*, mint). Roman contributions to the building arts are evidenced by such words as *cealc* (chalk), *copor* (copper), *pic* (pitch), and *tigele* (tile), while miscellaneous words such as *mūl* (mule), *draca* (dragon), *pāwa* (peacock), the adjectives *sicor* (L. *sēcūrus*, safe) and *calu* (L. *calvus*, bald), *segne* (seine), *pīpe* (pipe, musical instrument), *cirice* (church), *biscop* (bishop), *cāsere* (emperor), and *Sæternesdæg* (Saturday) may be mentioned.[2]

In general, if we are surprised at the number of words acquired from the Romans at so early a date by the Germanic tribes that came to England, we can see nevertheless that the words were such as they would be likely to borrow and such as reflect in a very reasonable way the relations that existed between the two peoples.

59. Latin through Celtic Transmission (Latin Influence of the First Period). The circumstances responsible for the slight influence which Celtic exerted on Old English limited in like manner the Latin influence that sprang from the period of Roman occupation. From what has been said above (see p. 45) about the Roman rule in Britain, the extent to which

---

[1] *Butter* is a difficult word to explain. The unweakened *t* suggests early borrowing. Butter was practically unknown to the Romans; Pliny has to explain its meaning and use. But a well-known allusion in Sidonius Apollinaris testifies to its use among the Burgundians on their hair. The good bishop complains of the rancid odor of Burgundian chiefs with buttered hair.

[2] Other words which probably belong to the period of continental borrowing are *ynce* (ounce, inch), *palentse* (palace), *solor* (upper room), *tæfel* (chessboard), *miscian* (to mix), and *olfend* (camel), but there is some uncertainty about their origin or history.

the country was Romanized, and the employment of Latin by certain elements in the population, one would expect a considerable number of Latin words from this period to have remained in use and to appear in the English language today. But this is not the case. It would be hardly too much to say that not five words outside of a few elements found in place-names can be really proved to owe their presence in English to the Roman occupation of Britain.[1] It is probable that the use of Latin as a spoken language did not long survive the end of Roman rule in the island and that such vestiges as remained for a time were lost in the disorders that accompanied the Germanic invasions. There was thus no opportunity for direct contact between Latin and Old English in England, and such Latin words as could have found their way into English would have had to come in through Celtic transmission. The Celts, indeed, had adopted a considerable number of Latin words—over six hundred have been identified—but the relations between the Celts and the English were such, as we have already seen, that these words were not passed on. Among the few Latin words that the Anglo-Saxons seem likely to have acquired upon settling in England, one of the most likely, in spite of its absence from the Celtic languages, is *ceaster*. This word, which represents the Latin *castra* (camp), is a common designation in Old English for a town or enclosed community. It forms a familiar element in English place-names such as *Chester, Colchester, Dorchester, Manchester, Winchester, Lancaster, Doncaster, Gloucester, Worcester*, and many others. Some of these refer to sites of Roman camps, but it must not be thought that a Roman settlement underlies all the towns whose names contain this common element. The English attached it freely to the designation of any enclosed place intended for habitation, and many of the places so designated were known by quite different names in Roman times. A few other words are thought for one reason or another to belong to this period: *port* (harbor, gate, town) from L. *portus* and *porta; munt* (mountain) from L. *mōns, montem; torr* (tower, rock) possibly from L. *turris*, possibly from Celtic; *wīc* (village) from L. *vīcus*. All of these words are found also as elements in place-names. It is possible that some of the Latin words which the Teutons had acquired on the continent, such as *street* (L. *strāta via*), *wall, wine*, etc., were reinforced by the presence of the same words in Celtic. At best, however, the Latin influence of the First Period remains much the slightest of all the influences which Old English owed to contact with Roman civilization.

---

[1] J. Loth in *Les Mots latins dans les langues brittoniques* (Paris, 1892, p. 29) assigns fifteen words to this period. Some of these, however, are more probably to be considered continental borrowings.

60. *Latin Influence of the Second Period: The Christianizing of Britain.*
The greatest influence of Latin upon Old English was occasioned by the
introduction of Christianity into Britain in 597. The new faith was far from
new in the island, but this date marks the beginning of a systematic attempt
on the part of Rome to convert the inhabitants and make England a
Christian country. According to the well-known story reported by Bede as
a tradition current in his day, the mission of St. Augustine was inspired by
an experience of a man who later became Pope Gregory the Great. Walking
one morning in the marketplace at Rome, he came upon some fair-haired
boys about to be sold as slaves and was told that they were from the island
of Britain and were pagans. "'Alas! what pity,' said he, 'that the author of
darkness is possessed of men of such fair countenances, and that being
remarkable for such a graceful exterior, their minds should be void of
inward grace?' He therefore again asked, what was the name of that
nation and was answered, that they were called Angles. 'Right,' said he,
'for they have an angelic face, and it is fitting that such should be co-heirs
with the angels in heaven. What is the name,' proceeded he, 'of the
province from which they are brought?' It was replied that the natives of
that province were called Deiri. 'Truly are they *de ira*,' said he, 'plucked
from wrath, and called to the mercy of Christ. How is the king of that
province called?' They told him his name was Ælla; and he, alluding to
the name, said 'Alleluia, the praise of God the Creator, must be sung in
those parts.'" The same tradition records that Gregory wished himself to
undertake the mission to Britain, but could not be spared. Some years
later, however, when he had become pope, he had not forgotten his former
intention, and looked about for someone whom he could send at the head
of a missionary band. Augustine, the person of his choice, was a man well
known to him. The two had lived together in the same monastery, and
Gregory knew him to be modest and devout and thought him well suited
to the task assigned him. With a little company of about forty monks
Augustine set out for what seemed then like the end of the earth.

It is not easy to appreciate the difficulty of the task which lay before this
small band. Their problem was not so much to substitute one ritual for
another as to change the philosophy of a nation. The religion which the
Anglo-Saxons shared with the other Germanic tribes seems to have had
but a slight hold on the people at the close of the sixth century; but their
habits of mind, their ideals, and the action to which these gave rise were
often in sharp contrast to the teachings of the New Testament. Germanic
philosophy exalted physical courage, independence even to haughtiness,
loyalty to one's family or leader that left no wrong unavenged. Christianity

preached meekness and humility, patience under suffering, and said that
if a man struck you on one cheek you should turn the other. Clearly it was
no small task which Augustine and his forty monks faced in trying to alter
the age-old mental habits of such a people. They might even have expected
difficulty in obtaining a respectful hearing. But they seem to have been men
of exemplary lives, appealing personality, and devotion to purpose, and
owed their ultimate success as much to what they were as to what they
said. Fortunately, upon their arrival in England one circumstance was in
their favor. There was in the kingdom of Kent, in which they landed, a
small number of Christians. But the number, though small, included no
less a person than the queen. Æthelberht, the king, had sought his wife
among the powerful nation of the Franks, and the princess Bertha had
been given to him only on condition that she be allowed to continue
undisturbed in her Christian faith. Æthelberht set up a small chapel near
his palace in Kent-wara-byrig (Canterbury), and there the priest who
accompanied Bertha to England conducted regular services for her and the
numerous dependents whom she brought with her. The circumstances
under which Æthelberht received Augustine and his companions are
related in the extract from Bede given in § 47 above. Æthelberht was
himself baptized within three months, and his example was followed by
numbers of his subjects. By the time Augustine died seven years later, the
kingdom of Kent had become wholly Christian.

The conversion of the rest of England was a gradual process. In 635
Aidan, a monk from the Scottish monastery of Iona, undertook independently the conversion of Northumbria. He was a man of great sympathy and
tact. With a small band of followers he journeyed from town to town, and
wherever he preached he drew crowds to hear him. Within twenty years he
had made all Northumbria Christian. There were periods of reversion to
paganism, and some clashes between the Celtic and the Roman leaders
over doctrine and authority, but England was slowly won over to the faith.
It is significant that the Christian missionaries were allowed considerable
freedom in their labors. There is not a single instance recorded in which
any of them suffered martyrdom in the cause which they espoused.
Possibly the fact that the important nation of the Franks was known to
have accepted the new religion was a significant factor in rendering the
English more receptive. At all events, within a hundred years of the landing
of Augustine in Kent all England was permanently Christian.

61. *Effects of Christianity on English Civilization.* The introduction of
Christianity meant the building of churches and the establishment of
monasteries. Latin, the language of the services and of ecclesiastical

learning, was once more heard in England. Schools were established in most of the monasteries and larger churches. Some of these became famous through their great teachers and from them trained men went out to set up other schools at other centers. The beginning of this movement was in 669, when a Greek bishop, Theodore of Tarsus, was made archbishop of Canterbury. He was accompanied by Hadrian, an African by birth, a man described by Bede as "of the greatest skill in both the Greek and Latin tongues." They devoted considerable time and energy to teaching. "And because," says Bede, "they were abundantly learned in sacred and profane literature, they gathered a crowd of disciples . . . and together with the books of Holy Writ, they also taught the arts of poetry, astronomy, and ecclesiastical arithmetic; a testimony of which is that there are still living at this day some of their scholars, who are as well versed in the Greek and Latin tongues as in their own, in which they were born." A decade or two later Aldhelm carried on a similar work at Malmesbury. He was a remarkable classical scholar. He had an exceptional knowledge of Latin literature, and he wrote Latin verse with ease. In the north the school at York became in time almost as famous as that of Canterbury. The two monasteries of Wearmouth and Jarrow were founded by Benedict Biscop, who had been with Theodore and Hadrian at Canterbury, and who on five trips to Rome brought back a rich and valuable collection of books. His most famous pupil was the Venerable Bede, a monk at Jarrow. Bede assimilated all the learning of his time. He wrote on grammar and prosody, science and chronology, and composed numerous commentaries on the books of the Old and New Testament. His most famous work is the *Ecclesiastical History of the English People* (731), from which we have already had occasion to quote more than once and from which we derive a large part of our knowledge of the early history of England. Bede's spiritual grandchild was Alcuin, of York, whose fame as a scholar was so great that in 782 Charlemagne called him to be the head of his Palace School. In the eighth century England held the intellectual leadership of Europe, and it owed this leadership to the church. In like manner vernacular literature and the arts received a new impetus. Workers in stone and glass were brought from the continent for the improvement of church building. Rich embroidery, the illumination of manuscripts, and church music occupied others. Moreover the monasteries cultivated their land by improved methods of agriculture and made numerous contributions to domestic economy. In short, the church as the carrier of Roman civilization influenced the course of English life in many directions, and, as is to be expected, numerous traces of this influence are to be seen in the vocabulary of Old English.

62. *The Earlier Influence of Christianity on the Vocabulary.* From the introduction of Christianity in 597 to the close of the Old English period is a stretch of over five hundred years. During all this time Latin words must have been making their way gradually into the English language. It is likely that the first wave of religious feeling which resulted from the missionary zeal of the seventh century, and which is reflected in intense activity in church building and the establishing of monasteries during this century, was responsible also for the rapid importation of Latin words into the vocabulary. The many new conceptions which followed in the train of the new religion would naturally demand expression and would at times find the resources of the language inadequate. But it would be a mistake to think that the enrichment of the vocabulary which now took place occurred overnight. Some words came in almost immediately, others only at the end of this period. In fact it is fairly easy to divide the Latin borrowings of the Second Period into two groups, more or less equal in size but quite different in character. The one group represents words whose phonetic form shows that they were borrowed early and whose early adoption is attested also by the fact that they had found their way into literature by the time of Alfred. The other contains words of a more learned character first recorded in the tenth and eleventh centuries and owing their introduction clearly to the religious revival that accompanied the Benedictine Reform. It will be well to consider them separately.

It is obvious that the most typical as well as the most numerous class of words introduced by the new religion would have to do with that religion and the details of its external organization. Words are generally taken over by one language from another in answer to a definite need. They are adopted because they express ideas that are new or because they are so intimately associated with an object or a concept that acceptance of the thing involves acceptance also of the word. A few words relating to Christianity such as *church* and *bishop* were, as we have seen, borrowed earlier. The Anglo-Saxons had doubtless plundered churches and come in contact with bishops before they came to England. But the great majority of words in Old English having to do with the church and its services, its physical fabric and its ministers, when not of native origin were borrowed at this time. Since most of these words have survived in only slightly altered form in Modern English, the examples may be given in their modern form. The list includes *abbot, alms, altar, angel, anthem, Arian, ark, candle, canon, chalice, cleric, cowl, deacon, disciple, epistle, hymn, litany, manna, martyr, mass, minster, noon, nun, offer, organ, pall, palm, pope, priest, provost, psalm, psalter, relic, rule, shrift, shrine, shrive, stole, sub-*

deacon, synod, temple, and *tunic.* Some of these were reintroduced later. But the church also exercised a profound influence on the domestic life of the people. This is seen in the adoption of many words, such as the names of articles of clothing and household use—*cap, sock, silk, purple, chest, mat, sack;* [1] words denoting foods, such as *beet, caul* (cabbage), *lentil* (O.E. *lent*), *millet* (O.E. *mil*), *pear, radish, doe, oyster* (O.E. *ostre*), *lobster, mussel,* to which we may add the noun *cook;* [2] names of trees, plants, and herbs (often cultivated for their medicinal properties), such as *box, pine,* [3] *aloes, balsam, fennel, hyssop, lily, mallow, marshmallow, myrrh, rue, savory* (O.E. *sæperige*), and the general word *plant.* A certain number of words having to do with education and learning reflect another aspect of the church's influence. Such are *school, master, Latin* (possibly an earlier borrowing), *grammatic(al), verse, meter, gloss, notary* (a scribe). Finally we may mention a number of words too miscellaneous to admit of profitable classification, like *anchor, coulter, fan* (for winnowing), *fever, place* (cf. *marketplace*), *spelter* (asphalt), *sponge, elephant, phoenix, mancus* (a coin), and some more or less learned or literary words, such as *calend, circle, legion, giant, consul,* and *talent.* The words cited in these examples are mostly nouns, but Old English borrowed also a number of verbs and adjectives such as *āspendan* (to spend; L. *expendere*), *bemūtian* (to exchange; L. *mūtāre*), *dihtan* (to compose; L. *dictāre*), *pīnian* (to torture; L. *poena*), *pinsian* (to weigh; L. *pēnsāre*), *pyngan* (to prick; L. *pungere*), *sealtian* (to dance; L. *saltāre*), *temprian* (to temper; L. *temperāre*), *trifolian* (to grind; L. *trībulāre*), *tyrnan* (to turn; L. *tornāre*), and *crisp* (L. *crispus,* 'curly'). But enough has been said to indicate the extent and variety of the borrowings from Latin in the early days of Christianity in England and to show how quickly the language reflected the broadened horizon which the English people owed to the church.

63. *The Benedictine Reform.* The flourishing state of the church which resulted in these significant additions to the English language unfortunately did not continue uninterrupted. One cause of the decline is to be attributed to the Danes, who at the end of the eighth century began their ravages upon the country. Lindisfarne was burnt in 793 and Jarrow, Bede's monastery, was plundered the following year. In the ninth century throughout Northumbria and Mercia churches and monasteries lay everywhere in

[1] Other words of this sort, which have not survived in Modern English, are *cemes* (shirt), *swiftlere* (slipper), *sūtere* (shoemaker), *byden* (tub, bushel), *bytt* (leather bottle), *cēac* (jug), *læfel* (cup), *orc* (pitcher), and *stræl* (blanket, rug).

[2] Cf. also O.E. *cīepe* (onion, L. *cēpa*), *næp* (turnip, L. *nāpus*), *sigle* (rye, V.L. *sigale*).

[3] Also *sæppe* (spruce-fir), *mōrbēam* (mulberry tree).

ruins. By the tenth century the decline had affected the moral fiber of the church. It would seem as though once success had been attained and a reasonable degree of security, the clergy relaxed their efforts. Wealthy men had given land freely to religious foundations in the hope of laying up spiritual reserves for themselves against the life in the next world. Among the clergy poverty gave way to ease, and ease by a natural transition passed into luxury. Probably a less worthy type was drawn by these new conditions into the religious profession. We hear much complaint about immoderate feasting and drinking and vanity in dress. In the religious houses discipline became lax, services were neglected, monasteries were occupied by groups of secular priests, many of them married, immorality was flagrant. The work of education was neglected and learning decayed. By the time of Alfred things had reached such a pass that he looked upon the past as a golden age which had gone, "when the Kings who ruled obeyed God and His evangelists," and when "the religious orders were earnest about doctrine, and learning, and all the services they owed to God"; and he lamented that the decay of learning was so great at the beginning of his reign "that there were very few on this side of the Humber who could understand their rituals in English, or translate a letter from Latin into English, and I believe not many beyond the Humber. So few were there that I cannot remember a single one south of the Thames when I came to the kingship." Two generations later Ælfric, abbot of Eynsham, echoed the same sentiment when he said, "Until Dunstan and Athelwold revived learning in the monastic life no English priest could either write a letter in Latin, or understand one." It is hardly likely, therefore, that many Latin words were added to the English language during these years when religion and learning were both at such a low ebb.

But abuses when bad enough have a way of bringing about their own reformation. What is needed generally is an individual with the zeal to lead the way and the ability to set an example that inspires imitation. King Alfred had made a start. Besides restoring churches and founding monasteries, he strove for twenty years to spread education in his kingdom and foster learning. His efforts bore little fruit. But in the latter half of the tenth century three great religious leaders, imbued with the spirit of reform, arose in the church: Dunstan, archbishop of Canterbury (d. 988), Athelwold, bishop of Winchester (d. 984), and Oswald, bishop of Worcester and archbishop of York (d. 992). With the sympathetic support of King Edgar these men effected a genuine revival of monasticism in England. The true conception of the monastic life was inseparable from the observance of the Benedictine Rule. Almost everywhere in England this had ceased to be adhered to. As the first step in the reform the secular clergy were turned out of the monasteries and their places filled by monks pledged to the threefold vow of chastity, obedience, and poverty. In their work of restoration the reformers received powerful support from the example of continental monasteries, notably those at Fleury and Ghent. These had recently undergone a similar reformation under the inspiring leadership of Cluny, where in 910 a community had been established on even stricter lines than those originally laid down by St. Benedict. Dunstan had spent some time at the Abbey of Blandinium at Ghent; Oswald had studied the system at Fleury; and Athelwold, although wanting to go himself, had sent a representative to Fleury for the same purpose. On the pattern of these continental houses a number of important monasteries were recreated in England, and Athelwold prepared a version of the Benedictine Rule, known as the *Concordia Regularis*, to bring about a general uniformity in their organization and observances. The effort toward reform extended to other divisions of the church, indeed to a general reformation of morals, and brought about something like a religious revival in the island. One of the objects of special concern in this work of rehabilitation was the improvement of education—the establishment of schools and the encouragement of learning among the monks and the clergy. The results were distinctly gratifying. By the close of the century the monasteries were once more centers of literary activity. Works in English for the popularizing of knowledge were prepared by men who thus continued the example of King Alfred, and manuscripts both in Latin and the vernacular were copied and preserved. It is significant that the four great codices in which the bulk of Old English poetry is preserved date from this period. We doubtless owe their existence to the reform movement.

64. *Benedictine Reform's Influence on English.* The influence of Latin upon the English language rose and fell with the fortunes of the church and the state of learning so intimately connected with it. As a result of the renewed literary activity just described, a new series of Latin importations took place. These differed somewhat from the earlier Christian borrowings in being words of a less popular kind and expressing more often ideas of a scientific and learned character. They are especially frequent in the works of Ælfric and reflect not only the theological and pedagogical nature of his writings but also his classical tastes and attainments. His literary activity and his vocabulary are equally representative of the movement. As in the earlier Christian borrowings a considerable number of words have to do with religious matters: *alb, Antichrist, antiphoner, apostle, canticle, cantor, cell, chrism, cloister, collect, creed, dalmatic, demon, dirge, font, idol,* *nocturn, prime, prophet, sabbath, synagogue, troper.* But we miss the group of words relating to everyday life characteristic of the earlier period. Literary and learned words predominate. Of the former kind are *accent, brief* (the verb), *decline* (as a term of grammar), *history, paper, pumice, quatern* (a quire or gathering of leaves in a book), *term(inus), title.* A great number of plant names are recorded in this period. Many of them are familiar only to readers of old herbals. Some of the better known include *celandine, centaury, coriander, cucumber, ginger, hellebore, lovage, periwinkle, petersili* (parsley), *verbena.*[1] A few names of trees might be added, such as *cedar, cypress, fig, laurel,* and *magdāla* (almond).[2] Medical terms, like *cancer, circulādl* (shingles), *paralysis, scrofula, plaster,* and words relating to the animal kingdom, like *aspide* (viper), *camel, lamprey, scorpion, tiger,* belong apparently to the same category of learned and literary borrowings. It would be possible to extend these lists considerably by including words which were taken over in their foreign form and not assimilated. Such words as *epactas, corporale, confessores, columba* (dove), *columne, cathedra, catacumbas, apostata, apocalipsin, acolitus, absolutionem, invitatorium, unguentum, cristalla, cometa, bissexte, bibliothece, basilica, adamans,* and *prologus* show at once by their form their foreign character. Although many of them were later reintroduced into the language, they do not constitute an integral part of the vocabulary at this time. In general the later borrowings of the Christian period come through books. An occasional word assigned to this later period may have been in use earlier, but there is nothing in the form to indicate it, and in the absence of any instance of its use in the literature before Alfred it is safer to put such borrowings in the latter part of the Old English period.

65. *The Application of Native Words to New Concepts.* The words which Old English borrowed in this period are only a partial indication of the extent to which the introduction of Christianity affected the lives and thoughts of the English people. The English did not always adopt a foreign word to express a new concept. Often an old word was applied to a new thing and by a slight adaptation made to express a new meaning. The Anglo-Saxons, for example, did not borrow the Latin word *deus,* since their own word *God* was a satisfactory equivalent. Likewise *heaven* and *hell* express conceptions not unknown to Anglo-Saxon paganism and are conse-

---

[1] A number of interesting words of this class have not survived in modern usage, such as *aprotane* (wormwood), *armelu* (wild rue), *caric* (dry fig), *elehtre* (lupin), *mārūfie* (horehound), *nepte* (catnip), *pollegie* (pennyroyal), *hymele* (hop-plant).

[2] Most of these words were apparently bookish at this time and had to be reintroduced later from French.

quently English words. *Patriarch* was rendered literally by *hēahfæder* (high father), *prophet* by *wītega* (wise one), *martyr* often by the native word *prōwere* (one who suffers pain), and saint by *hālga* (holy one). Specific members of the church organization such as *pope*, *bishop*, and *priest*, or *monk* and *abbot* represented individuals for which the English had no equivalent and therefore borrowed the Latin terms; however they did not borrow a general word for clergy but used a native expression, *ðæt gāstlice folc* (the spiritual folk). The word *Easter* is a Germanic word taken over from a pagan festival, likewise in the spring, in honor of Eostre, the goddess of dawn. Instead of borrowing the Latin word *praedicāre* (to preach) the English expressed the idea with words of their own, such as *lǣran* (to teach) or *bodian* (to bring a message); *to pray* (L. *precāre*) was rendered by *biddan* (to ask) and other words of similar meaning, *prayer* by a word from the same root, *gebed*. For *baptize* (L. *baptizāre*) the English adapted a native word *fullian* (to consecrate) while its derivative *fulluht* renders the noun *baptism*. The latter word enters into numerous compounds, such as *fulluht-bæþ* (font), *fulwere* (baptist), *fulluht-fæder* (baptizer), *fulluht-hād* (baptismal vow), *fulluht-nama* (Christian name), *fulluht-stōw* (baptistry), *fulluht-tīd* (baptism time), and others. Even so individual a feature of the Christian faith as the sacrament of the Lord's Supper was expressed by the Germanic word *hūsl* (modern *housel*), while *lāc*, the general word for sacrifice to the gods, was also sometimes applied to the Sacrifice of the Mass. The term *Scriptures* found its exact equivalent in the English word *gewritu*, and *ēvangelium* was rendered by *godspell*, originally meaning good tidings. *Trinity* (L. *trinitas*) was translated *prines* (three-ness), the idea of God the Creator was expressed by *scieppend* (one who shapes or forms), *fruma* (creator, founder), or *metod* (measurer). Native words like *fæder* (father), *dryhten* (prince), *wealdend* (ruler), *þēoden* (prince), *weard* (ward, protector), *hlāford* (lord) are frequent synonyms. Most of them are also applied to *Christ*, originally a Greek word and the most usual name for the Second Person of the Trinity, but *Hǣlend* (Savior) is also commonly employed. The Third Person (Spiritus Sanctus) was translated *Hālig Gāst* (Holy Ghost). Latin *diabolus* was borrowed as *dēofol* (devil) but we find *fēond* (fiend) as a common synonym. Examples might be multiplied. Cross is *rōd* (rood), *trēow* (tree), *gealga* (gallows), etc.; resurrection is *ǣrist*, from *ārīsan* (to arise); *peccatum* is *synn* (sin), while other words like *mān*, *firen*, *leahtor*, *wōh*, and *scyld*, meaning 'vice', 'crime', 'fault', and the like, are commonly substituted. The Judgment Day is *Doomsday*. Many of these words are translations of their Latin equivalents and their vitality is attested by the fact that in a great many cases they have continued in use down to the present day. It is important to recognize that the significance of a foreign influence is not to be measured simply by the foreign words introduced but is revealed also by the extent to which it stimulates the language to independent creative effort and causes it to make full use of its native resources.

66. The Extent of the Influence.   To be sure, the extent of a foreign influence is most readily seen in the number of words borrowed. As a result of the Christianizing of Britain some 450 Latin words appear in English writings before the close of the Old English period. This number does not include derivatives or proper names, which in the case of biblical names are very numerous. But about one hundred of these were purely learned or retained so much of their foreign character as hardly to be considered part of the English vocabulary. Of the 350 words that have a right to be so considered some did not make their way into general use until later—were, in fact, reintroduced later. On the other hand, a large number of them were fully accepted and thoroughly incorporated into the language. The real test of a foreign influence is the degree to which the words that it brought in were assimilated. This is not merely a question of the power to survive; it is a question of how completely the words were digested and became indistinguishable from the native word-stock, so that they could enter into compounds and be made into other parts of speech, just like native words. When, for example, the Latin noun *planta* comes into English as the noun *plant* and later is made into a verb by the addition of the infinitive ending *–ian* (*plantian*) and other inflectional elements, we may feel sure that the word has been assimilated. This happened in a number of cases as in *gemartyrian* (to martyr), *sealmian* (to play on the harp), *culpian* (to humiliate oneself), *fersian* (to versify), *glēsan* (to gloss), and *crispian* (to curl).[1] Assimilation is likewise indicated by the use of native formative suffixes such as *–dōm*, *–hād*, *–ung* to make a concrete noun into an abstract (*martyrdōm, martyrhād, martyrung*). The use of a foreign word in making compounds is evidence of the same thing. The word *church* enters into more than forty compounds and derivatives (*church-bell, church-book, church-door*, etc.). The Latin influence of the Second Period was not only extensive but thorough and marks the real beginning of the English habit of freely incorporating foreign elements into its vocabulary.

67. The Scandinavian Influence: The Viking Age.   Near the end of the Old English period English underwent a third foreign influence, the result

---

[1] On this general subject see Donald W. Lee, *Functional Change in Early English* (Springfield, Mass., 1948).

of contact with another important language, the Scandinavian. In the course of history it is not unusual to witness the spectacle of a nation or people, through causes too remote or complex for analysis, suddenly emerging from obscurity, playing for a time a conspicuous, often brilliant, part, and then, through causes equally difficult to define, subsiding once more into a relatively minor sphere of activity. Such a phenomenon is presented by the Germanic inhabitants of the Scandinavian peninsula and Denmark, one-time neighbors of the Anglo-Saxons and closely related to them in language and blood. For some centuries the Scandinavians had remained quietly in their northern home. But in the eighth century a change, possibly economic, possibly political, occurred in this area and provoked among them a spirit of unrest and adventurous enterprise. They began a series of attacks upon all the lands adjacent to the North Sea and the Baltic. Their activities began in plunder and ended in conquest. The Swedes established a kingdom in Russia; Norwegians colonized parts of the British Isles, the Faroes, and Iceland, and from there pushed on to Greenland and the coast of Labrador; the Danes founded the dukedom of Normandy and finally conquered England. The pinnacle of their achievement was reached in the beginning of the eleventh century when Cnut, king of Denmark, obtained the throne of England, conquered Norway, and from his English capital ruled the greater part of the Scandinavian world. The daring sea-rovers to whom these unusual achievements were due are commonly known as Vikings,[1] and the period of their activity, extending from the middle of the eighth century to the beginning of the eleventh, is popularly known as the Viking Age. It was to their attacks upon, settlements in, and ultimate conquest of England that the Scandinavian influence upon Old English was due.

68. The Scandinavian Invasions of England. In the Scandinavian attacks upon England three well-marked stages can be distinguished. The first is the period of early raids, beginning according to the Anglo-Saxon Chronicle in 787 and continuing with some intermissions until about 850. The raids of this period were simply plundering attacks upon towns and monasteries near the coast. Sacred vessels of gold and silver, jeweled shrines, costly robes, valuables of all kinds, and slaves were carried off. Noteworthy instances are the sacking of Lindisfarne and Jarrow in 793 and 794. But with the plundering of these two famous monasteries the attacks apparently

---

[1] The term *viking* is usually thought to be derived from Old Norse *vík*, a bay, as indicating 'one who came out from, or frequented, inlets of the sea'. It may, however, come from O.E. *wíc*, a camp, "the formation of temporary encampments being a prominent feature of viking raids." (*OED*.)

ceased for forty years, until renewed in 834 along the southern coast and in East Anglia. These early raids were apparently the work of small isolated bands.

The second stage is the work of large armies and is marked by widespread plundering in all parts of the country and by extensive settlements. This new development was inaugurated by the arrival in 850 of a Danish fleet of 350 ships. Their pirate crews wintered in the isle of Thanet and the following spring captured Canterbury and London and ravaged the surrounding country. Although finally defeated by a West Saxon army, they soon renewed their attacks. In 866 a large Danish army plundered East Anglia and in 867 captured York. In 869 the East Anglian king, Edmund, met a cruel death in resisting the invaders. The incident made a deep impression on all England, and the memory of his martyrdom was vividly preserved in English tradition for nearly two centuries. The eastern part of England was now largely in the hands of the Danes, and they began turning their attention to Wessex. The attack upon Wessex began shortly before the accession of King Alfred (871–899). Even the greatness of this greatest of English kings threatened to prove insufficient to withstand the repeated thrusts of the Northmen. After seven years of resistance, in which temporary victories were invariably succeeded by fresh defeats, Alfred was forced to take refuge with a small band of personal followers in the marshes of Somerset. But in this darkest hour for the fortunes of the English, Alfred's courage and persistence triumphed. With a fresh levy of men from Somerset, Wiltshire, and Hampshire, he suddenly attacked the Danish army under Guthrum at Ethandun (now Edington, in Wiltshire). The result was an overwhelming victory for the English and a capitulation by the Danes (878).

The Treaty of Wedmore (near Glastonbury), which was signed by Alfred and Guthrum the same year, marks the culmination of the second stage in the Danish invasions. Wessex was saved. The Danes withdrew from Alfred's territory. But they were not compelled to leave England. The treaty merely defined the line, running roughly from Chester to London, to the east of which the foreigners were henceforth to remain. This territory was to be subject to Danish law and is hence known as the Danelaw. In addition the Danes agreed to accept Christianity, and Guthrum was baptized. This last provision was important. It might secure the better observance of the treaty, and, what was more important, it would help to pave the way for the ultimate fusion of the two groups.

The third stage of the Scandinavian incursions covers the period of political adjustment and assimilation from 878 to 1042. The Treaty of

Wedmore did not put an end to Alfred's troubles. Guthrum was inclined to break faith and there were fresh invasions from outside. But the situation slowly began to clear. Under Alfred's son Edward the Elder (900–925) and grandson Athelstan (925–939) the English began a series of counter-attacks that put the Danes on the defensive. One of the brilliant victories of the English in this period was Athelstan's triumph in 937 in the battle of Brunanburh, in Northumbria, over a combined force of Danes and Scots, a victory celebrated in one of the finest of Old English poems. By the middle of the century a large part of eastern England, though still strongly Danish in blood and custom, was once more under English rule.

Toward the end of the century, however, when England seemed at last on the point of solving its Danish problem, a new and formidable succession of invasions began. In 991 a fleet of ninety-three ships under Olaf Tryggvason and his associates suddenly entered the Thames. They were met by Byrhtnoth, the valiant earl of the East Saxons, in a battle celebrated in another famous Old English war poem, *The Battle of Maldon*. Here the English, heroic in defeat, lost their leader, and soon the invaders were being bribed by large sums to refrain from plunder. The invasions now began to assume an official character. In 994 Olaf, who shortly became king of Norway, was joined by Svein, king of Denmark, in a new attack on London. The sums necessary to buy off the enemy became greater and greater, rising in 1012 to the amazing figure of £48,000. In each case the truce thus bought was temporary, and Danish forces were soon again marching over England, murdering and pillaging. Finally Svein determined to make himself king of the country. In 1014, supported by his son Cnut, he crowned a series of victories in different parts of England by driving Æthelred, the English king, into exile and seizing the throne. Upon his sudden death the same year his son succeeded him. Three years of fighting established Cnut's claims to the throne, and for the next twenty five years England was ruled by Danish kings.

69. The Settlement of the Danes in England. The events here rapidly summarized had as an important consequence the settlement of large numbers of Scandinavians in England. However temporary may have been the stay of many of the attacking parties, especially those which in the beginning came simply to plunder, many individuals remained behind when their ships returned home. Often they became permanent settlers in the island. Some indication of their number may be had from the fact that more than 1,400 places in England bear Scandinavian names. Most of these are naturally in the north and east of England, the district of the Danelaw, for it was here that the majority of the invaders settled. Most of the new inhabitants were Danes, although there were considerable Norwegian settlements in the northwest, especially in what is now Cumberland and Westmoreland, and in a few of the northern counties. The presence of a large Scandinavian element in the population is indicated not merely by place-names but by peculiarities of manorial organization, local government, legal procedure, and the like. Thus we have to do not merely with large bands of marauders, marching and countermarching across England, carrying hardship and devastation into all parts of the country for upward of two centuries, but with an extensive peaceable settlement by farmers who intermarried with the English, adopted many of their customs, and entered into the everyday life of the community. In the districts where such settlements took place conditions were favorable for an extensive Scandinavian influence on the English language.

70. *The Amalgamation of the Two Peoples.* The amalgamation of the two peoples was greatly facilitated by the close kinship that existed between them. The problem of the English was not the assimilation of an alien people representing an alien culture and speaking a wholly foreign tongue. The policy of the English kings in the period when they were reestablishing their control over the Danelaw was to accept as an established fact the mixed population of the district and to devise a *modus vivendi* for its component elements. In this effort they were aided by the natural adaptability of the Scandinavian. Generations of contact with foreign communities, into which their many enterprises had brought them, had made the Scandinavians a cosmopolitan people. The impression derived from a study of early English institutions is that in spite of certain native customs which the Danes continued to observe, they adapted themselves largely to the ways of English life. That many of them early accepted Christianity is attested by the large number of Scandinavian names found not only among monks and abbots, priests and bishops, but also among those who gave land to monasteries and endowed churches. It would be a great mistake to think of the relation between Anglo-Saxon and Dane, especially in the tenth century, as uniformly hostile. One must distinguish, as we have said, between the predatory bands that continued to traverse the country and the large numbers that were settled peacefully on the land. Alongside the ruins of English towns—Symeon of Durham reports that the city of Carlisle remained uninhabited for two hundred years after its destruction by the Danes—there existed important communities established by the newcomers. They seem to have grouped themselves at first in concentrated centers, parceling out large tracts of land from which the owners had fled, and preferring this form of settlement to too scattered a distribution in a strange land. Among such centers the Five Boroughs—Lincoln, Stamford, Leicester, Derby, and Nottingham—became important *foci* of Scandinavian influence. It was but a question of time until these large centers and the multitude of smaller communities where the Northmen gradually settled were absorbed into the general mass of the English population.

71. *The Relation of the Two Languages.* The relation between the two languages in the district settled by the Danes is a matter of inference rather than exact knowledge. Doubtless the situation was similar to that observable in numerous parts of the world today where people speaking different languages are found living side by side in the same region. While in some places the Scandinavians gave up their language early[1] there were certainly communities in which Danish or Norse remained for some time the usual language. Up until the time of the Norman Conquest the Scandinavian language in England was constantly being renewed by the steady stream of trade and conquest. In some parts of Scotland, Norse was still spoken as late as the seventeenth century. In other districts in which the prevailing speech was English there were doubtless many of the newcomers who continued to speak their own language at least as late as 1100 and a considerable number who were to a greater or lesser degree bilingual. The last-named circumstance is rendered more likely by the frequent intermarriage between the two peoples and by the similarity between the two tongues. The Anglian dialect resembled the language of the Northmen in a number of particulars in which West Saxon showed divergence. The two may even have been mutually intelligible to a limited extent. Contemporary statements on the subject are conflicting, and it is difficult to arrive at a conviction. But wherever the truth lies in this debatable question, there can be no doubt that the basis existed for an extensive interaction of the two languages upon each other, and this conclusion is amply borne out by the large number of Scandinavian elements subsequently found in English.

72. *The Tests of Borrowed Words.* The similarity between Old English and the language of the Scandinavian invaders makes it at times very difficult to decide whether a given word in Modern English is a native or a borrowed word. Many of the commoner words of the two languages were identical, and if we had no Old English literature from the period before the Danish invasions, we should be unable to say that many words were not

---

[1] On this question see E. Ekwall, "How Long Did the Scandinavian Language Survive in England?" *Jespersen Miscellany*, pp. 17–30, and R. I. Page, "How Long Did the Scandinavian Language Survive in England? The Epigraphical Evidence," in *England Before the Conquest: Studies in Primary Sources Presented to Dorothy Whitelock*, ed. P. Clemoes and K. Hughes (Cambridge, 1971), pp. 165–81.

of Scandinavian origin. In certain cases, however, we have very reliable criteria by which we can recognize a borrowed word. These tests are not such as the layman can generally apply, although occasionally they are sufficiently simple. The most reliable depend upon differences in the development of certain sounds in the North Germanic and West Germanic areas. One of the simplest to recognize is the development of the sound *sk*. In Old English this was early palatalized to *sh* (written *sc*), except possibly in the combination *scr*, whereas in the Scandinavian countries it retained its hard *sk* sound. Consequently, while native words like *ship*, *shall*, *fish* have *sh* in Modern English, words borrowed from the Scandinavians are generally still pronounced with *sk*: *sky*, *skin*, *skill*, *scrape*, *scrub*, *bask*, *whisk*. The O.E. *scyrte* has become *shirt*, while the corresponding O.N. form *skyrta* gives us *skirt*. In the same way the retention of the hard pronunciation of *k* and *g* in such words as *kid*, *dike*[1] (cf. *ditch*), *get*, *give*, *gild*, and *egg* is an indication of Scandinavian origin. Occasionally, though not very often, the vowel of a word gives clear proof of borrowing. For example, the Germanic diphthong *ai* became *ā* in Old English (and has become *ō* in Modern English), but became *ei* or *ē* in Old Scandinavian. Thus *aye*, *nay* (beside *no* from the native word), *hale* (cf. the English form *(w)hole*), *reindeer*, *swain* are borrowed words, and many more examples can be found in Middle English and in the modern dialects. Thus there existed in Middle English the forms *geit*, *gait*, which are from Scandinavian, beside *gāt*, *gōt* from the O.E. word. The native word has survived in Modern English *goat*. In the same way the Scandinavian word for *loathsome* existed in Middle English as *leiþ*, *laiþ* beside *lāþ*, *lōþ*. Such tests as these, based on sound-developments in the two languages, are the most reliable means of distinguishing Scandinavian from native words. But occasionally meaning gives a fairly reliable test. Thus our word *bloom* (flower) could come equally well from O.E. *blōma* or Scandinavian *blōm*. But the O.E. word meant an 'ingot of iron', whereas the Scandinavian word meant 'flower, bloom'. It happens that the Old English word has survived as a term in metallurgy, but it is the Old Norse word that has come down in ordinary use. Again, if the initial *g* in *gift* did not betray the Scandinavian origin of this word, we should be justified in suspecting it from the fact that the cognate O.E. word *gift* meant the 'price of a wife', and hence in the plural 'marriage', while the O.N. word had the more general sense of 'gift, present'. The word *plow* in Old English meant a

---

[1] The *k* in this word could be accounted for on the basis of the oblique cases, but it is more probably due to Scandinavian influence. It is possible that the retention of the hard *k* and *g* is due to Anglian rather than Scandinavian tendencies.

measure of land, in Scandinavian the agricultural implement, which in Old English was called a *sulh*. When neither the form of a word nor its meaning proves its Scandinavian origin we can never be sure that we are dealing with a borrowed word. The fact that an original has not been preserved in Old English is no proof that such an original did not exist. Nevertheless when a word appears in Middle English which cannot be traced to an Old English source but for which an entirely satisfactory original exists in Old Norse, and when that word occurs chiefly in texts written in districts where Danish influence was strong, or when it has survived in dialectal use in these districts today, the probability that we have here a borrowed word is fairly strong. In every case final judgment must rest upon a careful consideration of all the factors involved.

73. *Scandinavian Place-names.* Among the most notable evidences of the extensive Scandinavian settlement in England is the large number of places that bear Scandinavian names. When we find more than six hundred places like *Grimsby, Whitby, Derby, Rugby,* and *Thoresby,* with names ending in *–by,* nearly all of them in the district occupied by the Danes, we have a striking evidence of the number of Danes who settled in England. For these names all contain the Danish word *by,* meaning 'farm' or 'town', a word which is also seen in our word *by-law* (town law). Some three hundred names like *Althorp, Bishopsthorpe, Gawthorpe, Linthorpe* contain the Scandinavian word *thorp* (village). An almost equal number contain the word *thwaite* (an isolated piece of land)—*Applethwaite, Braithwaite, Cowperthwaite, Langthwaite, Satterthwaite.* About a hundred places bear names ending in *toft* (a piece of ground, a messuage)—*Brimtoft, Eastoft, Langtoft, Lowestoft, Nortoft.* Numerous other Scandinavian elements enter into English place-names, which need not be particularized here. It is apparent that these elements entered intimately in the speech of the people of the Danelaw. It has been remarked above that more than 1,400 Scandinavian place-names have been counted in England, and the number will undoubtedly be increased when a more careful survey of the material has been made. These names are not uniformly distributed over the Danelaw. The largest number are found in Yorkshire and Lincolnshire. In some districts in these counties as many as 75 percent of the place-names are of Scandinavian origin. Cumberland and Westmoreland contribute a large number, reflecting the extensive Norse settlements in the northwest, while Norfolk, with a fairly large representation, shows that the Danes were numerous in at least this part of East Anglia. It may be remarked that a similar high percentage of Scandinavian personal names have been found in the medieval records of these districts. Names ending in *–son,* like

Stevenson or *Johnson*, conform to a characteristic Scandinavian custom, the equivalent Old English patronymic being –*ing*, as in *Browning*.

74. The Earliest Borrowing. The extent of this influence on English place-nomenclature would lead us to expect a large infiltration of other words into the vocabulary. But we should not expect this infiltration to show itself at once. The early relations of the invaders with the English were too hostile to lead to much natural intercourse, and we must allow time for such words as the Anglo-Saxons learned from their enemies to find their way into literature. The number of Scandinavian words that appear in Old English is consequently small, amounting to only about two score. The largest single group of these is such as would be associated with a sea-roving and predatory people. Words like *barda* (beaked ship), *cnearr* (small warship), *scegþ* (vessel), *liþ* (fleet), *scegþmann* (pirate), *dreng* (warrior), *hā* (oarlock) and *hā-sǣta* (rower in a warship), *bātswegen* (boatman), *hofding* (chief, ringleader), *orrest* (battle), *rān* (robbery, rapine), and *fylcian* (to collect or marshal a force) show in what respects the invaders chiefly impressed the English. A little later we find a number of words relating to the law or characteristic of the social and administrative system of the Danelaw. The word *law* itself is of Scandinavian origin, as is the word *outlaw*. The word *māl* (action at law), *hold* (freeholder), *wapentake* (an administrative district), *hūsting* (assembly), and *riding* (originally *thriding*, one of the above divisons of Yorkshire) owe their use to the Danes. In addition to these, a number of genuine Old English words seem to be translations of Scandinavian terms: *bōtlēas* (what cannot be compensated), *hāmsōcn* (attacking an enemy in his house), *lahcēap* (payment for reentry into lost legal rights), *landcēap* (tax paid when land was bought) are examples of such translations.[1] English legal terminology underwent a complete reshaping after the Norman Conquest, and most of these words have been replaced now by terms from the French. But their temporary existence in the language is an evidence of the extent to which Scandinavian customs entered into the life of the districts in which the Danes were numerous.

75. Scandinavian Loan-words and Their Character. It was after the Danes had begun to settle down peaceably in the island and enter into the ordinary relations of life with the English that Scandinavian words commenced to enter in numbers into the language. If we examine the bulk of these words with a view to dividing them into classes and thus discovering in what domains of thought or experience the Danes contributed especially

[1] Cf. E. Björkman, *Scandinavian Loan-words in Middle English* (Halle, 1900–1902), p. 12.

to English culture and therefore to the English language, we shall not arrive at any significant result. The Danish invasions were not like the introduction of Christianity, bringing the English into contact with a different civilization and introducing them to many things, physical as well as spiritual, that they had not known before. The civilization of the invaders was very much like that of the English themselves, if anything somewhat inferior to it. Consequently the Scandinavian elements that entered the English language are such as would make their way into it through the give and take of everyday life. Their character can best be conveyed by a few examples, arranged simply in alphabetical order. Among nouns that came in are *axle-tree, band, bank, birth, boon, booth, brink, bull, calf* (of leg), *crook, dirt, down* (feathers), *dregs, egg, fellow, freckle, gait, gap, girth, guess, hap, keel, kid, leg, link, loan, mire, race, reef* (of sail), *reindeer, rift, root, scab, scales, score, scrap, seat, sister, skill, skin, skirt, sky, slaughter, snare, stack, steak, swain, thrift, tidings, trust, want, window.* The list has been made somewhat long in order to better illustrate the varied and yet simple character of the borrowings. Among adjectives we find *awkward, flat, ill, loose, low, meek, muggy, odd, rotten, rugged, scant, seemly, sly, tattered, tight,* and *weak.* There are also a surprising number of common verbs among the borrowings, like *to bait, bask, batten, call, cast, clip, cow, crave, crawl, die, droop, egg* (*on*), *flit, gape, gasp, get, give, glitter, kindle, lift, lug, nag, raise, rake, ransack, rid, rive, scare, scout* (an idea), *scowl, screech, snub, sprint, take, thrive, thrust.* Lists such as these suggest better than any explanation the familiar, everyday character of the words which the Scandinavian invasions and subsequent settlement brought into English.

76. *The Relation of Borrowed and Native Words.* It will be seen from the words in the above lists that in many cases the new words could have supplied no real need in the English vocabulary. They made their way into English simply as the result of the mixture of the two peoples. The Scandinavian and the English words were being used side by side, and the survival of one or the other must often have been a matter of chance. Under such circumstances a number of things might happen. (1) Where words in the two languages coincided more or less in form and meaning, the modern word stands at the same time for both its English and its Scandinavian ancestors. Examples of such words are *burn, cole, drag, fast, gang, murk*(*y*), *scrape, thick.* (2) Where there were differences of form, the English word often survived. Beside such English words as *bench, goat, heathen, yarn, few, grey, loath, leap, flay,* corresponding Scandinavian forms are found quite often in Middle English literature and in some cases still exist in dialectal use. We find *screde, skelle, skere* with the hard pronunciation of the initial consonant group beside the standard English *shred, shell, sheer; wae* beside *woe,* the surviving form except in *welaway; trigg* the Old Norse equivalent of O.E. *trēowe* (true). Again where the same idea was expressed by different words in the two languages it was often, as we should expect, the English word that lived on. We must remember that the area in which the two languages existed for a time side by side was confined to the northern and eastern half of England. Examples are the Scandinavian words *attlen* beside English *think* (in the sense of *purpose, intend*), *bolnen* beside *swell, tinen* (O.N. *tȳna*) beside *lose, site* (O.N. **sȳt*) beside *sorrow, roke* (fog) beside *mist, reike* beside *path.* (3) In other cases the Scandinavian word replaced the native word, often after the two had long remained in use concurrently. Our word *awe* from Scandinavian, and its cognate *eye* (*aye*) from Old English are both found in the *Ormulum* (c. 1200). In the earlier part of the Middle English period the English word is commoner, but by 1300 the Scandinavian form begins to appear with increasing frequency, and finally replaces the Old English word. The two forms must have been current in the everyday speech of the northeast for several centuries, until finally the pronunciation *awe* prevailed. The Old English form is not found after the fourteenth century. The same thing happened with the two words for egg, *ey* (English) and *egg* (Scandinavian). Caxton complains at the close of the fifteenth century (see the passage quoted in § 151) that it was hard even then to know which to use. In the words *sister* (O.N. *syster,* O.E. *sweostor*), *boon* (O.N. *bōn,* O.E. *bēn*), *loan* (O.N. *lān,* O.E. *lǣn*), *weak* (O.N. *veikr,* O.E. *wāc*) the Scandinavian form lived. Often a good Old English word was lost, since it expressed the same idea as the foreign word. Thus the verb *take* replaced the O.E. *niman;*[1] *cast* superseded the O.E. *weorpan,* while it has itself been largely displaced now by *throw; cut* took the place of O.E. *snīðan* and *ceorfan.* Old English had several words for *anger* (O.N. *angr*), including *torn, grama,* and *irre,* but the Old Norse word prevailed. In the same way the Scandinavian word *bark* replaced O.E. *rind, wing* replaced O.E. *feþra, sky* took the place of *ūprodor* and *wolcen* (the latter now being preserved only in the poetical word *welkin*), and *window* (= wind-eye) drove out the equally appropriate English word *ēagþȳrel* (eye-thirl, i.e., eye-hole; cf. *nostril* = nose thirl, nose hole). (4) Occasionally both the English and the Scandinavian words were retained with a difference of meaning or use, as in the following pairs

---

[1] For a detailed study, see Alarik Rynell, *The Rivalry of Scandinavian and Native Synonyms in Middle English, especially* taken *and* nimen . . . (Lund, 1948; *Lund Studies in English,* vol. 13).

(the English word is given first): *no—nay, whole—hale, rear—raise, from—fro, craft—skill, hide—skin, sick—ill.* (5) In certain cases a native word which was apparently not in common use was reinforced, if not reintroduced, from the Scandinavian. In this way we must account for such words as *till, dale, rim, blend, run,* and the Scotch *bairn.* (6) Finally, the English word might be modified, taking on some of the character of the corresponding Scandinavian word. *Give* and *get* with their hard *g* are examples, as are *scatter* beside *shatter,* and *Thursday* instead of the O.E. *Thunresdæg.* Some confusion must have existed in the Danish area between the Scandinavian and the English form of many words, a confusion that is clearly betrayed in the survival of such hybrid forms as *shriek* and *screech.* All this merely goes to show that in the Scandinavian influence on the English language we have to do with the intimate mingling of two tongues. The results are just what we should expect when two rather similar languages are spoken for upwards of two centuries in the same area.

77. *Form Words.* If further evidence were needed of the intimate relation that existed between the two languages, it would be found in the fact that the Scandinavian words that made their way into English were not confined to nouns and adjectives and verbs, but extended to pronouns, prepositions, adverbs, and even a part of the verb *to be.* Such parts of speech are not often transferred from one language to another. The pronouns *they, their,* and *them* are Scandinavian. Old English used *hīe, hiera, him* (see § 45). Possibly the Scandinavian words were felt to be less subject to confusion with forms of the singular. Moreover, though these are the most important, they are not the only Scandinavian pronouns to be found in English. A late Old English inscription contains the Old Norse form *hanum* for *him.* *Both* and *same,* though not primarily pronouns, have pronominal uses and are of Scandinavian origin. The preposition *till* was at one time widely used in the sense of *to,* besides having its present meaning; and *fro,* likewise in common use formerly as the equivalent of *from,* survives in the phrase *to and fro.* Both words are from the Scandinavian. From the same source comes the modern form of the conjunction *though,* the Old Norse equivalent of O.E. *þēah.* The Scandinavian use of *at* as a sign of the infinitive is to be seen in the English *ado* (*at-do*) and was more widely used in this construction in Middle English. The adverbs *aloft, athwart, aye* (ever), and *seemly,* and the earlier *heþen* (hence) and *hweþen* (whence), are all derived from the Scandinavian. Finally the present plural *are* of the verb *to be* is a most significant adoption. While *we aron* was the Old English form in the north, the West Saxon plural was *syndon* (cf. German *sind*) and the form *are* in Modern English undoubtedly owes its extension to the influence of the Danes. When we remember that in the expression *they are* both the pronoun and the verb are Scandinavian we realize once more how intimately the language of the invaders has entered into English.

   78. *Scandinavian Influence outside the Standard Speech.* We should miss the full significance of the Scandinavian influence if we failed to recognize the extent to which it is found outside the standard speech. Our older literature and the modern dialects are full of words which are not now in ordinary use. The ballads offer many examples. When the *Geste of Robin Hood* begins "*Lythe* and listin, gentilmen" it has for its first word an Old Norse synonym for *listen*. When a little later on the Sheriff of Nottingham says to Little John, "Say me nowe, *wight* yonge man, What is nowe thy name?" he uses the O.N. *vigt* (strong, courageous). In the ballad of *Captain Car* the line "*Busk* and *bowne*, my merry men all" contains two words from the same source meaning *prepare*. The word *gar*, meaning *to cause* or *make one do something*, is of frequent occurrence. Thus, in *Chevy Chace* we are told of Douglas' men that "Many a doughetë the(y) *garde* to dy"—i.e., they made many a doughty man die. In *Robin Hood and Guy of Gisborne* the Virgin Mary is addressed: "Ah, deere Lady! sayd Robin Hoode, Thou art both mother and *may!*" in which *may* is a Scandinavian form for *maid*. Bessie Bell and Mary Gray, in the ballad of that name, "*bigget* a bower on yon burn-brae," employing in the process another word of Norse origin, *biggen* (to build), a word also used by Burns in *To a Mouse:* "Thy wee bit housie, too, in ruin! . . . And naething now to big a new ane." In Burns and Scott we find the comparative *worse* in the form *waur:* "A' the warld kens that they maun either marry or do waur" (*Old Mortality*), also an old word (O.N. *verre*) more commonly found in the form used by Chaucer in the *Book of the Duchess:* "Allas! how myghte I fare werre?" Examples could be multiplied, but it is sufficiently evident that there is much Scandinavian material in the dialects besides what has found its way into the standard speech.

   79. *Effect on Grammar and Syntax.* That the Scandinavian influence not only affected the vocabulary but extended to matters of grammar and syntax as well is less capable of exact demonstration but is hardly to be doubted. Inflections are seldom transferred from one language to another. A certain number of inflectional elements peculiar to the Northumbrian dialect have been attributed to Scandinavian influence,[1] among others the –*s* of the third person singular, present indicative, of verbs and the parti-

---

[1] W. Keller, "Skandinavischer Einfluss in der englischen Flexion," *Probleme der englischen Sprache und Kultur: Festschrift Johannes Hoops* (Heidelberg, 1925), pp. 80–87.

cipial ending *–and* (*bindand*), corresponding to *–end* and *–ind* in the
Midlands and South, and now replaced by *–ing*. The words *scant, want,
athwart* preserve in the final *t* the neuter adjective ending of Old Norse.
But this is of no great significance. It is much more important to recognize
that in many words the English and Scandinavian languages differed
chiefly in their inflectional elements. The body of the word was so nearly
the same in the two languages that only the endings would put obstacles
in the way of mutual understanding. In the mixed population which existed
in the Danelaw these endings must have led to much confusion, tending
gradually to become obscured and finally lost. It seems but natural that
the tendency toward the loss of inflections, which was characteristic of the
English language in the north even in Old English times, was strengthened
and accelerated by the conditions that prevailed in the Danelaw, and that
some credit must be given the Danes for a development which, spreading
to other parts and being carried much further, resulted after the Norman
Conquest in so happily simplifying English grammar. Likewise, the way
words are put together in phrases and clauses—what we call syntax—is
something in which languages less often influence each other than in
matters of vocabulary. The probability of such influence naturally varies
with the degree of intimacy that exists between the speakers of two
languages. In those parts of Pennsylvania—the "Pennsylvania Dutch"
districts—where German and English have mingled in a jargon peculiar to
itself, German turns of expression are frequently found in the English
spoken there. It is quite likely that the English spoken in the districts where
there were large numbers of Danes acquired certain Danish habits of
expression. A modern Dane like Jespersen [1] notes that the omission of the
relative pronoun in relative clauses (rare in Old English) and the retention
or omission of the conjunction *that* are in conformity with Danish usage;
that the rules for the use of *shall* and *will* in Middle English are much the
same as in Scandinavian; and that some apparently illogical uses of these
auxiliaries in Shakespeare (e.g., "besides it *should* appear" in the *Merchant
of Venice*, III, ii, 289) do not seem strange to a Dane, who would employ
the same verb. Logeman [2] notes the tendency, common to both languages,
to put a strong stress at times on the preposition, and notes the occurrence
of locutions such as "he has some one to work for," which are not shared

---

[1] *Growth and Structure of the English Language*, 4th ed., pp. 82–83. Jespersen's views
have been objected to by E. Einenkel, "Die dänischen Elemente in der Syntax der
englischen Sprache," *Anglia*, 29 (1906), 120–28. They also are unsupported by the earliest
Danish and Norwegian usage as recorded in runic inscriptions. See Max S. Kirch,
"Scandinavian Influence on English Syntax," *PMLA*, 74 (1959), 503–10.
[2] *Archiv für das Studium der neueren Sprachen*, 116 (1906), 281–86.

by the other Germanic languages. It is possible, of course, that similarities such as these are merely coincidences, that the Scandinavian languages and English happened to develop in these respects along similar lines. But there is nothing improbable in the assumption that certain Scandinavian turns of phrase and certain particular usages should have found their way into the idiom of people in no small part Danish in descent and living in intimate contact with the speakers of a Scandinavian tongue.

80. *Period and Extent of the Influence.* It is hardly possible to estimate the extent of the Scandinavian influence by the number of borrowed words that exist in Standard English. That number, if we restrict the list to those for which the evidence is fully convincing, is about nine hundred. These, as the examples given above show, are almost always words designating common everyday things and fundamental concepts. To this group we should probably be justified in adding an equal number in which a Scandinavian origin is probable or in which the influence of Scandinavian forms has entered. Furthermore there are, according to Wright, the editor of the *English Dialect Dictionary*, thousands of Scandinavian words which are still a part of the everyday speech of people in the north and east of England and in a sense are just as much a part of the living language as those that are used in other parts of the country and have made their way into literature. He notes that "if we exclude all *sc–* words of various origins which are common to the standard language and the dialects, it is a remarkable fact that the *English Dialect Dictionary* contains 1,154 simple words beginning with *sc–* (*sk–*)."[1] Locally, at least, the Scandinavian influence was tremendous. The period during which this large Danish element was making its way into the English vocabulary was doubtless the tenth and eleventh centuries. This was the period during which the merging of the two peoples was taking place. The occurrence of many of the borrowed words in written records is generally somewhat later. A considerable number first make their appearance in the *Ormulum* at the beginning of the thirteenth century. But we must attribute this fact to the scarcity of literary texts of an earlier date, particularly from the region of the Danelaw. Because of its extent and the intimate way in which the borrowed elements were incorporated, the Scandinavian influence is one of the most interesting of the foreign influences that have contributed to the English language.

BIBLIOGRAPHY

On the relation of the various peoples in Anglo-Saxon England some interesting observations, especially inferences drawn from place-names, will be found in

---

[1] Joseph and Elizabeth M. Wright, *An Elementary Middle English Grammar*, p. 82.

R. E. Zachrisson's *Romans, Kelts, and Saxons in Ancient Britain* (Uppsala, 1927). For the history of the period, see F. M. Stenton, *Anglo-Saxon England* (3rd ed., Oxford, 1971). A readable account of the introduction of Christianity will be found in W. Hunt's *The English Church from Its Foundation to the Norman Conquest* (London, 1899), or, in more detail, in A. J. Mason, *The Mission of St. Augustine to England according to the Original Documents* (Cambridge, 1897). Among modern histories of the English church, see especially Margaret Deanesly, *The Pre-Conquest Church in England* (2nd ed., London, 1963), and H. Mayr-Harting, *The Coming of Christianity to Anglo-Saxon England* (London, 1972). These may be supplemented for the period of the Benedictine Reform by J. A. Robinson's *The Times of St. Dunstan* (Oxford, 1923) and David Knowles, *The Monastic Order in England* (2nd ed., Cambridge, 1963). The fullest discussion of the Latin element in Old English is Alois Pogatscher, *Zur Lautlehre der griechischen, lateinischen und romanischen Lehnworte im Altenglischen* (Strassburg, 1888). A. Keiser's *The Influence of Christianity on the Vocabulary of Old English Poetry* (Urbana, 1919), Otto Funke's *Die gelehrten lateinischen Lehn- und Fremdwörter in der altenglischen Literatur von der Mitte des X. Jahrhunderts bis um das Jahr 1066* (Halle, 1914), and Helmut Gneuss's *Lehnbildungen und Lehnbedeutungen im Altenglischen* (Berlin, 1955) are also valuable. A general discussion of the Latin and Greek element in English will be found in Roland G. Kent, *Language and Philology* (Boston, 1923), in the series *Our Debt to Greece and Rome*.

The most extensive consideration of the Celtic loan-words in Old English is Max Förster, *Keltisches Wortgut im Englischen* (Halle, 1921), which may be supplemented by the important reviews of Ekwall (*Anglia Beiblatt*, XXXIII, 74–82) and Pokorny (*Zeit. für Celtische Phil.*, XIV, 298). Förster adds to his findings in "Englisch-Keltisches," *Englische Studien*, 56 (1922), 204–39, and Wolfgang Keller discusses "Keltisches im englischen Verbum" in *Anglica: Untersuchungen zur englischen Philologie, Alois Brandl zum 70. Geburtstage überreicht* (Leipzig, 1925; *Palaestra*, 147–48), I, 55–66. Two excellent, comprehensive accounts of early Scandinavian activities are T. D. Kendrick, *A History of the Vikings* (New York, 1930), and Gwyn Jones, *A History of the Vikings* (Oxford, 1968). Sven A. Anderson, *Viking Enterprise* (New York, 1936; *Columbia University Studies in Hist., Econ., and Public Law*, No. 424) is readable and has a valuable bibliography. A shorter sketch will be found in A. Mawer's *The Vikings* (Cambridge, 1913). C. Plummer's *Life and Times of Alfred the Great* (Oxford, 1902) and L. M. Larson's *Canute the Great, 995 (circa)–1035, and the Rise of Danish Imperialism during the Viking Age* (New York, 1912) are useful for background. F. M. Stenton's Raleigh Lectures, "The Danes in England," *Proc. of the British Academy*, vol. 13 (1927), are fresh and illuminating. These and much else of value by Stenton are reprinted in *Preparatory to Anglo-Saxon England*, ed. Doris Stenton (Oxford, 1970). Gillian F. Jensen, "The Vikings in England: A Review," *Anglo-Saxon England*, 4 (1975), 181–206, is a valuable discussion of recent scholarship. The standard discussion of the Scandinavian element in English is E. Björkman's *Scandinavian Loan-words in Middle English* (Halle, 1900–1902), which may be supplemented by his "Zur dialektischen Provenienz der nordischen Lehnwörter im Englischen," *Språkvetenskapliga sällskapets i Upsala forhandlingar 1897–1900* (1901), pp. 1–28, and *Nordische Personnamen in England in alt- und frühmittelenglischer Zeit* (Halle, 1910). Earlier studies include A. Wall's "A Contribution towards the Study of the Scandinavian Element in the English Dialects," *Anglia*, 20 (1898), 45–135, and G. T. Flom's *Scandinavian Influence on Southern Lowland Scotch* (New York, 1900). The Scandinavian influence on local nomenclature is most extensively treated in H. Lindkvist's *Middle-English Place-Names of Scandinavian Origin*, part I (Uppsala, 1912). A later summary of the question will be found in Allen Mawer's "The Scandinavian Settlements in England as Reflected in English Place-names," *Acta Philologica Scandinavica*, 7 (1932), 1–30. An extensive list of place-names is discussed by Assar Janzén, "Scandinavian Place-Names in England," a series of articles in *Names*, vols. 5–11 (1957–1963). The claims for Scandinavian influence on English grammar and syntax are set forth in the articles mentioned in footnotes to § 79. Much of this material is embodied in an excellent overall treatment by John Geipel, *The Viking Legacy: The Scandinavian Influence on the English and Gaelic Languages* (Newton Abbot, 1971).

[5]

The Norman Conquest and the Subjection
of English, 1066–1200

81. *The Norman Conquest*. Toward the close of the Old English period
an event occurred which had a greater effect on the English language than
any other in the course of its history. This event was the Norman Conquest
in 1066. What the language would have been like if William the Conqueror
had not succeeded in making good his claim to the English throne can only
be a matter of conjecture. It would probably have pursued much the same
course as the other Germanic languages, retaining perhaps more of its
inflections and preserving a preponderantly Germanic vocabulary, adding
to its word-stock by the characteristic methods of word-formation already
explained, and incorporating words from other languages much less freely.
In particular it would have lacked the greater part of that enormous
number of French words which today make English seem, on the side of
vocabulary, almost as much a Romance as a Germanic language. The
Norman Conquest changed the whole course of the English language. An
event of such far-reaching consequences must be considered in some
detail.

82. *The Origin of Normandy*. On the northern coast of France directly
across from England is a district extending some seventy-five miles back
from the Channel and known as Normandy. It derives its name from the
bands of Northmen who settled there in the ninth and tenth centuries, at
the same time as similar bands were settling in the north and east of
England. The Seine offered a convenient channel for penetration into the
country, and the settlements of Danes in this region furnish a close parallel
to those around the Humber. A generation after Alfred reached an agreement with the Northmen in England, a somewhat similar understanding
was reached between Rollo, the leader of the Danes in Normandy, and

Charles the Simple, king of France. In 912 the right of the Northmen to occupy this part of France was recognized; Rollo acknowledged the French king as his overlord and became the first duke of the Normans. In the following century and a half a succession of masterful dukes raised the dukedom to a position of great influence, overshadowing at times the power of the king of France.

The adaptability of the Scandinavian, always a marked characteristic of this people, nowhere showed itself more quickly. Readily adopting the ideas and customs of those among whom he came to live, the Norman had soon absorbed the most important elements of French civilization. Moreover he injected fresh vigor into what he borrowed. He profited from his contact with French military forces and, adding French tactics to his own impetuous courage, soon had one of the best armies, if we may use the term, in Europe. He took important features of Frankish law, including the idea of the jury, and with a genius for organization which shows up as clearly in the Norman kingdom of Sicily as in Normandy and later in England, made it one of the outstanding legal systems of the world. He accepted Christianity and began the construction of those great Norman cathedrals that are still marvels to the modern architect. But most important of all, for us, he soon gave up his own language and learned French. So rapidly did the old Scandinavian tongue disappear in the Norman capital that the second duke was forced to send his son to Bayeux that he might learn something of the speech of his forefathers. In the eleventh century, at the time of the Norman Conquest, the civilization of Normandy was essentially French, and the Normans were among the most advanced and progressive of the peoples of Europe.

For some years before the Norman Conquest the relations between England and Normandy had been fairly close. In 1002 Æthelred the Unready had married a Norman wife, and, when driven into exile by the Danes, took refuge with his brother-in-law, the duke of Normandy. His son Edward, who had thus been brought up in France, was almost more French than English. At all events, when in 1042 the Danish line died out and Edward, known as the Confessor, was restored to the throne from which his father had been driven, he brought with him a number of his Norman friends, enriched them, and gave them important places in the government. A strong French atmosphere pervaded the English court during the twenty-four years of his reign.

83. *The Year 1066.* When in January 1066, after a reign of twenty-four years, Edward the Confessor died childless, England was again faced with the choice of a successor. And there was not much doubt as to where the choice would fall. At his succession Edward had found England divided into a few large districts, each under the control of a powerful earl. The most influential of these nobles was Godwin, earl of the West Saxon earldom. He was a shrewd, capable man and was soon Edward's principal adviser. Except for one brief interval, he was the virtual ruler of England until the time of his death. His eldest son Harold succeeded to his title and influence, and during the last twelve years of Edward's reign exercised a firm and capable influence over national affairs. The day after Edward's death Harold was elected king.

His election did not long go unchallenged. William, the duke of Normandy at this time, was a second cousin to the late king. While this relationship did not give him any right of inheritance to the English throne, he had nevertheless been living in expectation of becoming Edward's successor. Edward seems to have encouraged him in this hope. While William had been on a brief visit in England, Edward had assured him that he should succeed him. Even Harold had been led, though unwillingly, to acknowledge his claim. Having on one occasion fallen into William's hands, it seems he had been forced to swear, as the price of his freedom, not to become a candidate or oppose William's election. But the English had had enough of French favorites, and when the time came Harold did not consider himself bound by his former pledge.

Only by force could William hope to obtain the crown to which he believed himself entitled. Perhaps the difficulty involved in an armed invasion of England would have discouraged a less determined claimant. But William was an exceptionally able man. From infancy he had surmounted difficulties. Handicapped by the taint of illegitimacy, the son of his father by a tanner's daughter of Falaise, he had succeeded to the dukedom of Normandy at the age of six. He was the object of repeated attempts upon his life, and only the devoted care of his regents enabled him to reach maturity. In early manhood he had had to face a number of crucial contests with rebellious barons, powerful neighbors, and even his overlord, the French king. But he had emerged triumphantly from them all, greatly strengthened in position and admirably schooled for the final test of his fortune. William the Great, as the chroniclers called him, was not the man to relinquish a kingdom without a struggle.

Having determined upon his course of action, he lost no time in beginning preparations. He secured the cooperation of his vassals by the promise of liberal rewards, once England was his to dispose of. He came to terms with his rivals and enemies on the continent. He appealed to the Pope for the sanction of his enterprise and received the blessing of the

Church. As a result of these inducements, the ambitious, the adventurous, and the greedy flocked to his banner from all over France and even other parts of Europe. In September he landed at Pevensey, on the south coast of England, with a formidable force.

His landing was unopposed. Harold was occupied in the north of England meeting an invasion by the king of Norway, another claimant to the throne, who had been joined by a brother of Harold's, Tostig, returning from exile. Hardly had Harold triumphed in battle over the invaders when word reached him of William's landing. The news was scarcely unexpected, but the English were not fully prepared for it. It was difficult to keep a medieval army together over a protracted period. William's departure had been delayed, and with the coming of the harvest season many of those whom Harold had assembled a few months before, in anticipation of an attack, had been sent home. Harold was forced to meet the invader with such forces as he had. He called upon his brothers-in-law in the earldoms of Mercia and Northumbria to join him and repel the foreigner by a united effort. But they hung back. Nevertheless, hurrying south with his army, Harold finally reached a point between the Norman host and London. He drew up his forces on a broad hill at Senlac, not far from Hastings, and awaited William's attack. The battle began about nine o'clock in the morning. So advantageous was Harold's position and so well did the English defend themselves that in the afternoon they still held their ground. For William the situation was becoming desperate, and he resorted to a desperate stratagem. His only hope lay in getting the English out of their advantageous position on the hill. Since he could not drive them off, he determined to try to lure them off and ordered a feigned retreat. The English fell into the trap. Thinking the Normans were really fleeing, a part of the English army started in pursuit, intending to cut them down in their flight. But the Normans made a stand and the battle was renewed on more even terms. Then happened one of those accidents more easily possible in medieval than in modern warfare. Harold, always in the thick of the fight, was pierced in the eye by a Norman arrow. His death was instantaneous. Two of his brothers had already fallen. Deprived of their leaders, the English became disorganized. The confusion spread. The Normans were quick to profit by the situation, and the English were soon in full retreat. When night fell they were fleeing in all directions, seeking safety under the cover of darkness, and William was left in possession of the field.

While William had won the battle of Hastings and eliminated his rival, he had not yet attained the English crown. It was only after he had burnt and pillaged the southeast of England that the citizens of London decided that further resistance would be useless. Accordingly they capitulated, and on Christmas day, 1066, William was crowned king of England.

84. *The Norman Settlement.* William's victory at Hastings and his subsequent coronation in London involved more than a mere substitution of one monarch for another. It was not as though he had been chosen originally as the successor of Edward. In that case there would doubtless have been more French favorites at court, as in the time of the Confessor, and Normans in certain important offices. But the English nobility would have remained intact, and the English government would have continued with its tradition unbroken. But William's possession of the throne had been a matter of conquest and was attended by all the consequences of the conquest of one people by another.

One of the most important of these consequences was the introduction of a new nobility.[1] Many of the English higher class had been killed on the field at Hastings. Those who escaped were treated as traitors, and the places of both alike were filled by William's Norman followers. This process was repeated several times during the next four years while the Conquest was being completed. For William's coronation did not win immediate recognition throughout England. He was in fact acknowledged only in the southeast. Upon his return from a visit to Normandy the following year he was faced with serious rebellions in the southwest, the west, and the north. It was necessary for him to enter upon a series of campaigns and to demonstrate, often with ruthless severity, his mastery of the country. As a result of these campaigns the Old English nobility was practically wiped out. While many lesser landholders kept small estates, the St. Albans Chronicler was but slightly exaggerating when he said that scarcely a single noble of English extraction remained in the kingdom.[2] In 1072 only one of the twelve earls in England was an Englishman, and he was executed four years later.[3] What was true in the time of the Conqueror was true also in the reigns of his sons, and later. For several generations after the Conquest the important positions and the great estates were almost always held by Normans or men of foreign blood. As an English poet, Robert of Brunne (1338), sums up the situation,

> To Frankis & Normanz, for þar grete laboure,
> To Flemmynges & Pikardes, þat were with him in stoure,

---

[1] On the fate of the Old English aristocracy see F. M. Stenton, "English Families and the Norman Conquest," *Trans. Royal Hist. Soc.*, 4th ser., 26 (1944), 1–12.

[2] Roger of Wendover, ed. H. O. Coxe, II, 23 (Eng. Hist. Soc.).

[3] P. V. D. Shelly, *English and French in England, 1066–1100* (Philadelphia, 1921), p. 32.

He gaf londes bityme, of whilk þer successoure
Hold ʒit þe seysyne, with fulle grete honoure.[1]

In like manner Norman prelates were gradually introduced into all important positions in the church. The two archbishops were Normans. Wulfstan of Worcester was the only Old English bishop who retained his office till the end of the Conqueror's reign, and even his exceptional personality did not prevent him from being scorned by Lanfranc as a simple and untutored man, ignorant of the French language, and unable to assist in the king's councils.[2] The English abbots were replaced more slowly, but as fast as vacancies occurred through death or deprivation they were filled generally by foreigners. In 1075 thirteen of the twenty-one abbots who signed the decrees of the Council of London were English; twelve years later their number had been reduced to three. Foreign monks and priests followed the example of their superiors and sought the greater opportunities for advancement which England now offered. A number of new foundations were established and entirely peopled by monks brought over from Norman houses.

It is less easy to speak with certainty of the Normans in the lower walks of life who came into England with William's army. Many of them doubtless remained in the island, and their number was increased by constant accretions throughout the rest of the eleventh century and the whole of the next. The numerous castles which the Conqueror built were apparently garrisoned by foreign troops.[3] In the chroniclers of the period we find instances extending all through the twelfth century of foreign forces being brought to England. Many of these doubtless made but a short stay in the island, but it is safe to say that every Norman baron was surrounded by a swarm of Norman retainers. William of Newburgh speaks of the bishop of Ely, in the reign of Richard I, as surrounding his person with an army of friends and foreign soldiers, as well as arranging marriages between Englishmen of position and his relations, "of whom he brought over from Normandy multitudes for this purpose."[4] Ecclesiastics, it would seem, sometimes entered upon their office accompanied by an armed band of

---

[1] *Chronicle*, ed. Hearne, I, 72:

> To French and Normans, for their great labor,
> To Flemings and Picards, that were with him in battle,
> He gave lands betimes, of which their successors
> Hold yet the seizin, with full great honor.

[2] Roger of Wendover, II, 52.
[3] Orderic Vitalis, Bk. IV, *passim*.
[4] William of Newburgh, Bk. IV, chap. 14, 16.

supporters. Turold, who became abbot of Peterborough in 1070, is described as coming at the head of 160 armed Frenchmen to take possession of his monastery;[1] and Thurston, appointed abbot of Glastonbury in 1082, imposed certain innovations in the service upon the monks of the abbey by calling for his Norman archers, who entered the chapter house fully armed and killed three of the monks, besides wounding eighteen.[2] Likewise merchants and craftsmen from the continent seem to have settled in England in considerable numbers.[3] There was a French town beside the English one at Norwich and at Nottingham,[4] and French Street in Southampton, which retains its name to this day, was in the Middle Ages one of the two principal streets of the town.[5] It is quite impossible to say how many Normans and French people settled in England in the century and a half following the Conquest,[6] but since the governing class in both church and state was almost exclusively made up from among them, their influence was out of all proportion to their number.

85. *The Use of French by the Upper Class.* Whatever the actual number of Normans settled in England, it is clear that the members of the new ruling class were sufficiently predominant to continue to use their own language. This was natural enough at first, since they knew no English; but they continued to do so for a long time to come, picking up some knowledge of English gradually, but making no effort to do so as a matter of policy. For two hundred years after the Norman Conquest, French remained the language of ordinary intercourse among the upper classes in England. At first those who spoke French were those of Norman origin, but soon through intermarriage and association with the ruling class numerous people of English extraction must have found it to their advantage to learn the new language, and before long the distinction between those who spoke French and those who spoke English was not ethnic but largely social. The language of the masses remained English, and it is

---

[1] Freeman, *Norman Conquest*, IV, 457, 459.

[2] Freeman, IV, 390–93. Both incidents are related in the Peterborough Chronicle.

[3] A contemporary biographer of Thomas Becket tells us that many natives of Rouen and Caen settled in London, preferring to dwell in this city because it was better fitted for commerce and better supplied with the things in which they were accustomed to trade. *Materials for the History of Thomas Becket*, IV, 81. (Rolls Series.)

[4] W. Cunningham, *Alien Immigrants to England*, pp. 35–36.

[5] P. Studer, *Oak Book of Southampton*, I, xii ff.

[6] F. York Powell in Traill's *Social England*, I, 346, says: "One may sum up the change in England by saying that some 20,000 foreigners replaced some 20,000 Englishmen; and that these newcomers got the throne, the earldoms, the bishoprics, the abbacies, and far the greater portion of the big estates, mediate and immediate, and many of the burgess holdings in the chief towns." We do not know what the estimate is based upon, but unless it refers, as it seems to do, to the years immediately following the Conquest, it does not seem to be too high.

reasonable to assume that a French soldier settled on a manor with a few hundred English peasants would soon learn the language of the people among whom his lot was cast. The situation was well described, about the year 1300, by the writer of a chronicle which goes by the name of Robert of Gloucester:

þus com lo engelond in to normandies hond.
& þe normans ne couþe speke þo bote hor owe speche
& speke french as hii dude atom, & hor children dude also teche;
So þat heiemen of þis lond þat of hor blod come
Holdeþ alle þulke spreche þat hii of hom nome.
Vor bote a man conne frenss me telþ of him lute.
Ac lowe men holdeþ to engliss & to hor owe speche ȝute.
Ich wene þer ne beþ in al þe world contreyes none
þat ne holdeþ to hor owe speche bote engelond one.
Ac wel me wot uor to conne boþe wel it is,
Vor þe more þat a mon can, þe more wurþe he is.[1]   (7537–47)

An instructive parallel to the bilingual character of England in this period is furnished by the example of Belgium today. Here we find Flemish and French (Walloon) in use side by side. (Flemish is only another name for the Dutch spoken in Belgium, which is practically identical with that of southern Holland.) Although the use of the two languages here is somewhat a matter of geography—Flemish prevailing in the north and French in the part of the country lying toward France—it is also to some extent dependent upon the social and cultural position of the individual. French is often spoken by the upper classes, even in Flemish districts, while in such a city as Brussels it is possible to notice a fairly clear division between the working classes, who speak Flemish, and the higher economic and social groups, who attend French schools, read French newspapers, and go to French theaters. In the interest of accuracy, it may be noted parenthetically that fluency in French is becoming less common in the north, especially among the younger generation.

---

[1] Thus came, lo! England into Normandy's hand.
And the Normans didn't know how to speak then but their own speech
And spoke French as they did at home, and their children did also teach;
So that high men of this land that of their blood come
Hold all that same speech that they took from them.
For but a man know French men count of him little.
But low men hold to English and to their own speech yet.
I think there are in all the world no countries
That don't hold to their own speech but England alone.
But men well know it is well for to know both,
For the more that a man knows, the more worth he is.

86. *Circumstances Promoting the Continued Use of French.*   The most important factor in the continued use of French by the English upper class until the beginning of the thirteenth century was the close connection that existed through all these years between England and the continent. From the time of the Conquest the kings of England were likewise dukes of Normandy. To the end of his life William the Conqueror seems to have felt more closely attached to his dukedom than to the country he governed by right of conquest. Not only was he buried there, but in dividing his possessions at his death he gave Normandy to his eldest son. and England to William, his second son. Later the two domains were united again in the hands of Henry I. Upon the accession of Henry II, English possessions in France were still further enlarged. Henry, as count of Anjou, inherited from his father the districts of Anjou and Maine. By his marriage with Eleanor of Aquitaine he came into possession of vast estates in the south, so that when he became king of England he controlled about two-thirds of France, all the western part of the country from the English Channel to the Pyrenees.

Under the circumstances it is not surprising that the attention of the English should often be focused upon affairs in France. Indeed English kings often spent a great part of their time there. The Conqueror and his sons were in France for about half of their respective reigns. Henry I (1100–1135) was there for a total of more than seventeen out of the thirty-five years of his reign, sometimes for periods of three and four years at a time.[1] Although conditions at home kept Stephen (1135–1154) for the most part in England, Henry II (1154–1189) spent nearly two-thirds of his long reign in France. When we remember that, except for Henry I, no English king till Edward IV (1461–1483) sought a wife in England, it is easy to see how continentally minded English royalty was and how natural a thing would seem the continued use of French at the English court.

What was true of the royal family was equally true of the nobility in general. The English nobility was not so much a nobility of England as an Anglo-French aristocracy. Nearly all the great English landowners had possessions likewise on the continent, frequently contracted continental marriages, and spent much time in France, either in pursuance of their own interests or those of the king. When we remember that on many of the occasions when the king and his nobles crossed the Channel they were engaged in military operations and were accompanied by military forces, that the business of ecclesiastics and merchants constantly took them

[1] W. Farrer, "An Outline Itinerary of King Henry the First," *Eng. Hist. Rev.*, 34 (1919), 303–82, 505–79.

abroad, we can readily see how this constant going and coming across the narrow seas made the continued use of French by those concerned not only natural but inevitable.

87. The Attitude toward English.   There is no reason to think that the preference which the governing class in England showed for French was anything more than a natural result of circumstances. The idea that the newcomers were actively hostile to the English language is without foundation.[1] It is true that English was now an uncultivated tongue, the language of a socially inferior class, and that a bishop like Wulfstan might be subjected to Norman disdain in part, at least, because of his ignorance of that social shibboleth.[2] Henry of Huntington's statement that it was considered a disgrace to be called an Englishman may be set down to rhetorical exaggeration. It is unreasonable to expect a conquered people to feel no resentment or the Norman never to be haughty or overbearing. But there is also plenty of evidence of mutual respect and peaceful cooperation, to say nothing of intermarriage, between the Normans and the English from the beginning. The chronicler Orderic Vitalis, himself the son of a Norman father and an English mother, in spite of the fact that he spent his life from the age of ten in Normandy, always refers to himself as an Englishman.

According to the same chronicler[3] William the Conqueror made an effort himself at the age of forty-three to learn English, that he might understand and render justice in the disputes between his subjects, but his energies were too completely absorbed by his many other activities to enable him to make much progress. There is nothing improbable in the statement. Certainly the assertion of a fourteenth-century writer[4] that the Conqueror considered how he might destroy the "Saxon" tongue in order that English and French might speak the same language seems little less than silly in view of the king's efforts to promote the belief that he was the authentic successor of the Old English kings and in the light of his use of English alongside of Latin, to the exclusion of French, in his charters. His youngest son, Henry I, may have known some English, though we must give up the pretty story of his interpreting the English words in a charter to the monks of Colchester.[5] If later kings for a time seem to have been

---

[1] On this subject see the excellent discussion in Shelly, *English and French in England.*

[2] Roger of Wendover, ed. H. O. Coxe, II, 52.

[3] Ordericus Vitalis, ed. Prevost, II, 215.

[4] Robert Holkot, on the authority of John Selden, *Eadmeri Monachi Cantuariensis Historiae Novorum siue sui Saeculi Libri VI* (London, 1623), p. 189.

[5] The story was considered authentic by so critical a student as J. Horace Round ("Henry I as an English Scholar," *Academy*, Sept. 13, 1884, p. 168), but the charter has since been proved by J. Armitage Robinson to be a forgery. Cf. C. W. David, "The Claim of King Henry I to Be Called Learned," *Anniversary Essays in Medieval History by Students of Charles Homer Haskins* (Boston, 1929), pp. 45–56.

ignorant of the language,[1] their lack of acquaintance with it is not to be attributed to any fixed purpose. In the period with which we are at the moment concerned—the period up to 1200—the attitude of the king and the upper classes toward the English language may be characterized as one of simple indifference. They did not cultivate English—which is not the same as saying that they had no acquaintance with it—because their activities in England did not necessitate it and their constant concern with continental affairs made French for them much more useful.

88. *French Literature at the English Court.* How completely French was the English court at this time is clearly shown by the literature produced for royal and noble patronage. In an age which had few of our modern means of entertainment, literature played a much more important part in the lives of the leisured class. And it is interesting to find a considerable body of French literature being produced in England from the beginning of the twelfth century, addressed to English patrons and directed toward meeting their special tastes and interests. We do not know much about the literary conditions at the court of the Conqueror himself, although his recognition of learning is to be seen in many of his appointments to high ecclesiastical positions. His daughter Adela was a patron of poets, and his son Henry I, whether or not he deserved the title Beauclerc which contemporaries gave him,[2] was at least married successively to two queens who were generous in their support of poets. His court was the center of much literary activity.[3] Matilda, his first wife, was especially partial to foreign poets.[4] For Adelaide of Louvain, his second wife, David related the achievements of her husband, the king, in French verse. The work is lost, but we know of it from the statement of a contemporary poet, Geoffrey Gaimar, who boasted that he knew more tales than David ever knew or than Adelaide had in books. Likewise for Adelaide, Philippe de Thaun wrote his *Bestiary*, a poem describing rather fancifully the nature of various animals and adding to each description a moral still more fanciful. Gaimar wrote his *History of the English*, likewise in French verse, for Lady Custance "li Gentil," who also paid him a mark of silver for a copy

---

[1] We do not know whether William Rufus and Stephen knew English. Henry II understood it although he apparently did not speak it (see § 91). Richard I was thoroughly French; his whole stay in England amounted to only a few months. He probably knew no English. Concerning John's knowledge of English we have no evidence. As Freeman remarks (*Norman Conquest*, II, 128), the royal family at this time is frequently the least English in England and is not to be used as a norm for judging the diffusion of the two languages.

[2] The question is decided in the negative by David, "The Claim of King Henry I."

[3] For a fuller treatment of the subject, see an excellent study by K. J. Holzknecht, *Literary Patronage in the Middle Ages* (Philadelphia, 1923), chap. 12.

[4] William of Malmesbury, *Gesta Regum Anglorum*, II, 494. (Rolls Series.)

of David's poem, which she kept in her chamber. At the same time Samson de Nanteuil devoted 11,000 lines of verse to the *Proverbs of Solomon* for Lady Adelaide de Condé, wife of a Lincolnshire baron. In the reign of Henry II Wace wrote his celebrated *Roman de Brut* and presented it to the queen, Eleanor of Aquitaine. It is a legendary history of Britain, in which the exploits of King Arthur occupy a prominent place, and was certain to interest a royal family anxious to know something about the history of the country over which it had come to rule. Later Wace undertook in his *Roman de Rou* to write a similar account of the dukes of Normandy. Works of devotion and edification, saints' lives, allegories, chronicles, and romances of Horn, Havelok, Tristan, and other heroes poured forth in the course of the twelfth century. It is indicative of the firm roots which French culture had taken on English soil that so important a body of literature in the French language could be written in or for England, much of it under the direct patronage of the court.

89. *Fusion of the Two Peoples.*   As we look back over any considerable stretch of history we are likely to experience in the perspective a fore-shortening that makes a period of 150 years seem relatively small, and we fail to realize that changes that seem sudden are in reality quite natural in the course of a lifetime or a succession of generations. In the years follow-ing the Norman Conquest the sting of defeat and the hardships incident to so great a political and social disturbance were gradually forgotten. People accepted the new order as something accomplished; they accepted it as a fact and adjusted themselves to it. The experience of our own time shows how quickly national antagonisms and the bitterness of war can be allayed, and what a decade or two in the twentieth century can accomplish in this respect must be allowed to have been possible also in the eleventh. The fusion of Normans and English was rapid, but not more rapid than national interest and the intercourse of everyday life would normally bring about. The distinction between French and English which appears among the Domesday jurors[1] or a document of 1100 addressed by Henry I "to all his faithful people, both French and English, in Hertfordshire" does not long survive. When a distinction is made it soon comes to be between the English, meaning all the people of England, and the French, meaning the inhabitants of France. This early fusion of French and English in England is quite clear from a variety of evidences. It is evident in the marriage of Normans to English women, as when Robert d'Oily further enriched himself by marrying Eadgyth, the daughter of a great English landowner,

---

[1] Round, *Feudal England*, pp. 120–21.

or when the parents of Orderic Vitalis, already mentioned, were united.[1] It is evident from the way in which the English gave their support to their rulers and Norman prelates, as when William II and Henry I drove off foreign invaders with armies made up almost wholly of English troops or when Anselm and Becket found their staunchest supporters among the English.[2] It is evident in many other ways. Between 1072 and 1079 Wulfstan brought about some sort of spiritual federation between the monks of Worcester and six other English monasteries—Evesham, Chertsey, Bath, Pershore, Winchecombe, and Gloucester—in which we find "the heads of these great monasteries, some Norman, some English, . . . binding themselves together without respect of birth or birthplace, in the closest spiritual fellowship."[3] Norman nobles identified themselves with their new country by founding monasteries on their estates, and chose burial for themselves and their families in their adopted land rather than in Normandy.[4] In the towns the associations incident to trade are spoken of by Orderic Vitalis as another factor in bringing about a union between the two peoples.[5] Everywhere there are signs of convergence. The fusion seems to have gone forward rapidly in the reign of Henry I, and by the end of the twelfth century an English jurist was able to write: "Now that the English and Normans have been dwelling together, marrying and giving in marriage, the two nations have become so mixed that it is scarcely possible to-day, speaking of free men, to tell who is English, who of Norman race."[6] Only the events of the next century, the loss of Normandy, and the growing antagonism toward France, were necessary to complete the union, psychological as well as physical, of all the inhabitants of England.

90. The Diffusion of French and English.   The difficult question of the extent to which English and French were used in England after the Norman Conquest is not to be lightly answered. The evidence on which we can base a conclusion is scattered, must be carefully appraised, and is not always easy to harmonize. From time to time writers of the period tell us that such a one spoke both French and English or that he was ignorant of one or the other language. At times incidents in the chroniclers enable us to draw a pretty safe inference. Books and treatises, such as the *Ancrene Riwle* and

---

[1] Matthew Paris speaks of the Conqueror as promoting marriages between Norman and English. Cf. *Gesta Abbatum*, I, 44. (Rolls Series.)

[2] Hardy, *Catalogue of Materials*, II, xxiv.

[3] Freeman, *Norman Conquest*, IV, 382–87.

[4] Shelly, *English and French in England*, p. 42.

[5] Freeman, IV, chap. VII.

[6] Dialogus de Scaccario (1177). Stubbs, *Select Charters* (4th ed., 1881), p. 168. The *Dialogus de Scaccario* is edited and translated by Charles Johnson (London, 1950).

the various thirteenth-century works on husbandry, when we know the individuals for whom they were written, or the social class, at least, to which they belong, shed some light on the problem. From the thirteenth century on, something can be gleaned from the proceedings of the courts, where the language in which a man testifies is occasionally noted. The appearance of manuals from about 1250 for the teaching of French is significant. In the fourteenth century poets and writers often preface their works with an explanation of the language employed and incidentally indulge from time to time in valuable observations of a more general linguistic nature. In the fifteenth century the evidence becomes fairly abundant—letters public and private, the acts and records of towns, gilds, and the central government, and a variety of incidental allusion. From all of this accumulated testimony the situation can be easily enough stated in general terms, as, indeed, has already been done (§ 85): French was the language of the court and the upper classes, English the speech of the mass of the people. Can we, however, define the position of the two languages more specifically? The question to be asked is really twofold: (1) When and how generally did the upper class learn English? (2) How far down in the social scale was a knowledge of French at all general?

91. *Knowledge of English among the Upper Class.* We have already remarked that the use of French was not confined to persons of foreign extraction, but that all those who were brought into association with the governing class soon acquired a command of it. It was a mark of social distinction. On the other hand the fact that English was the language of the greater part of the population made it altogether likely that many of the upper class would acquire some familiarity with it. Such appears to have been the case, at least by the twelfth century. The evidence comes mostly from the reign of Henry II.[1] The most striking instance is that reported (c. 1175) by William of Canterbury in his life of Becket. On one occasion Helewisia de Morville, wife of a man of Norman descent and mother of one of Becket's murderers, invoked the aid of her husband in an emergency by crying out, "Huge de Morevile, ware, ware, ware, Lithulf heth his swerd adrage!"[2] Clearly her husband, whatever language he spoke, under-

---

[1] Some of William the Conqueror's English writs were addressed to Normans. But this hardly implies that they understood English any more than the king himself did. It is doubtful whether the recipients in many cases could have read the writ themselves in any language.
[2] *Materials for the History of Thomas Becket*, I, 128. (Rolls Series.)

stood English. Henry II himself seems to have understood English, though he did not speak it. According to a story twice told by Giraldus Cambrensis[1] he was once addressed by a Welshman in English. Understanding the remark, "the king, in French, desired Philip de Mercros, who held the reins of his horse, to ask the rustic if he had dreamt this." When the knight explained the king's question in English, the peasant replied in the same language he had used before, addressing himself to the king, not the interpreter. That the king's knowledge of English did not extend to an ability to speak the language is in harmony with the testimony of Walter Map, who credits him with "having a knowledge of all the languages which are spoken from the Bay of Biscay to the Jordan, but making use only of Latin and French."[2] His wife, however, Eleanor of Aquitaine, always required an interpreter when people spoke English.[3] The three young women of aristocratic family for whom the *Ancrene Riwle*, or *Rule for Anchoresses*, was probably written about 1200 were advised to do their reading in either French or English, and the original language of the *Rule* itself was almost certainly English.

That English survived for a considerable time in some monasteries is evident from the fact that at Peterborough the Anglo-Saxon Chronicle was continued until 1154. Among churchmen the ability to speak English was apparently fairly common. Gilbert Foliot, bishop of London, a man of Norman descent, was, according to Walter Map,[4] very fluent in Latin, French, and English. Hugh of Nonant, bishop of Coventry, a native of Normandy, must have known English, since he criticizes a fellow-bishop for his ignorance of it,[5] while Giraldus Cambrensis, bishop-elect of St. Davids, had such a knowledge of English that he could read and comment upon the language of Alfred and compare the dialects of northern and southern England.[6] At the same date Abbot Samson, head of the great abbey of Bury St. Edmunds, is thus described by Jocelyn de Brakelond: "He was an eloquent man, speaking both French and Latin, but rather careful of the good sense of that which he had to say than of the style of his words. He could read books written in English very well, and was wont

---

[1] *Itinerary through Wales*, Bk. I, chap. 6; *Conquest of Ireland*, Bk. I, chap. 40.

[2] *De Nugis Curialium*, V, vi (trans. Tupper and Ogle).

[3] Richard of Devizes, in *Chronicles of the Reigns of Stephen, Henry II, and Richard I*, III, 431. (Rolls Series.)

[4] *De Nugis*, I, xii. However, his fluency in three languages may have been mentioned because it was unusual.

[5] Cf. Freeman, *Norman Conquest*, V, 831.

[6] *Descr. of Wales*, Bk. I, chap. 6.

to preach to the people in English, but in the dialect of Norfolk where he was born and bred."

From these instances we must not make the mistake of thinking such a knowledge of English universal among men of this station. Others could be cited in which bishops and abbots were unable to preach in anything but Latin or French.[1] St. Hugh, bishop of Lincoln in the time of Henry II, did not understand English but required an interpreter.[2] One of the most notorious cases of a man who did not know English and who was not only an important ecclesiastic but one of the chief men of the kingdom is that of William Longchamp, bishop of Ely and chancellor of England in the reign of Richard I. The incident is alluded to in a number of chroniclers, of his seeking to escape from England in 1191, disguised as a woman and carrying under his arm some cloth as if for sale. When approached at Dover by a possible purchaser, who asked how much he would let her have an ell for, he was unable to reply because he was utterly unacquainted with the English language.[3] It is true that both of these men were foreigners, one a Burgundian, the other a Norman, and the fact of their not knowing English is set down by contemporaries as something worth noting. Among men of lower rank, whose position brought them into contact with both the upper and the lower class, stewards and bailiffs, for example, or men like the knight of Glamorgan, whom we have seen acting as Henry's interpreter, the ability to speak English as well as French must have been quite general. And among children whose parents spoke different languages a knowledge of English is to be assumed even from the days of the Conqueror if we may consider the case of Orderic Vitalis as representative. His father was Norman and his mother (presumably) English. He was taught Latin by an English priest and at the age of ten was sent to St. Evroult in Normandy. There he says "like Joseph in Egypt, I heard a language which I did not know."

The conclusion that seems to be justified by the somewhat scanty facts which we have to go on in this period is that a knowledge of English was not uncommon at the end of the twelfth century among those who habitually used French; that among churchmen and men of education it was even to be expected; and that among those whose activities brought them into

---

[1] E.g., Jofrid, abbot of Croyland, if we can trust the fourteenth-century continuation of Pseudo-Ingulph. The abbot of Durham who visited St. Godric (died 1170) needed an interpreter since Godric spoke English. Cf. *Libellus de Vita et Miracula S. Godrici*, p. 352. (*Surtees Soc.*, xx.)

[2] *Magna Vita*, ed. Dimick, pp. 157, 268. (Rolls Series.)

[3] One of the fullest accounts is in Roger of Hoveden, III, 141–47. (Rolls Series.)

contact with both upper and lower classes the ability to speak both languages was quite general.[1]

92. *Knowledge of French among the Middle Class.*   If by the end of the twelfth century a knowledge of English was not unusual among members of the highest class, it seems equally clear that a knowledge of French was often found somewhat farther down in the social scale. Among the knightly class French seems to have been cultivated even when the mother tongue was English. In the reign of Henry II a knight in England got a man from Normandy to teach his son French.[2] That an ability to speak French was expected among this class may be inferred from an incident in one of the chroniclers describing a long-drawn-out suit (1191) between the abbey of Croyland and the prior of Spalding. Four supposed knights were called to testify that they had made a view of the abbot. They were neither knights nor holders of a knight's fee, and the abbot testified that they had never come to make a view of him. The chronicler adds that "the third one of them did not so much as know how to speak French."[3] Next to the knights the inhabitants of towns probably contained the largest number of those among the middle class who knew French. In many towns, especially in important trading centers, men with Norman names were the most prominent burgesses and probably constituted a majority of the merchant class.[4] As Mary Bateson remarks, "Burgesses were writing French and clerks who did not keep Latin accounts kept French."[5] The likelihood that stewards and bailiffs on manors spoke both languages has already been mentioned. In fact a knowledge of French may sometimes have extended to the free tenants. At any rate Jocelyn de Brakelond relates that the Abbot Samson conferred a manor upon a man bound to the soil "because

---

[1] The statement of Scheibner, *Ueber die Herrschaft*, p. 17, that by about 1200 at the latest English had become the mother tongue of those of Norman descent seems to me clearly to go beyond the evidence. In the same way Freeman, who is usually quite reasonable in his view of the matter, seems to imply a little too much when he says (*Short History of the Norman Conquest*, p. 143), "Before long the Normans in England learned to speak English, and they seem to have done so commonly by the end of the twelfth century, though of course they could speak French as well." Mary Bateson (*Medieval England*, p. 175) represents the other extreme when she says that "few of the barons who were not court officials knew any language besides Norman French."

[2] *Materials for the History of Thomas Becket*, I, 347; Freeman, V, 891.

[3] Continuation of Pseudo-Ingulph, trans. H. T. Riley, p. 286. The continuation in which this incident occurs is not to be confused with the fourteenth-century forgery but is a genuine work of considerable value. (Gross.)

[4] At Southampton at the time of the Domesday survey the number of those who settled in the borough "after King William came into England" was sixty-five French born and thirty-one English born. The figures represent men and many of them doubtless had families. Cf. J. S. Davies, *A History of Southampton* (Southampton, 1883), pp. 26–28.

[5] *Medieval England*, p. 244.

he was a good farmer and didn't know how to speak French." It has some-times been urged that since preaching to the people was often done in French, such a fact argues for an understanding of the language. But we are more than once told in connection with such notices that the people, although they did not understand what was said, were profoundly moved.[1] It would be a mistake to consider that a knowledge of French was anything but exceptional among the common people as a whole. The observation of a writer at the end of the thirteenth century,

> Lewede men cune Ffrensch non,
> Among an hondryd vnneþis on[2]

was probably true at all times in the Middle Ages.[3]

Thus in the period preceding the loss of Normandy in 1204 there were. some who spoke only French and many more who spoke only English. There was likewise a considerable number who were genuinely bilingual as well as many who had some understanding of both languages while speaking only one. That the latter class—those who were completely or to some extent bilingual—should have been fairly numerous need cause no surprise. Among people accustomed to learn more through the ear than through the eye, learning a second language presents no great problem. The ability to speak one or more languages besides one's native tongue is largely a matter of opportunity, as can be seen in a number of European countries today. In this connection we may again recall the situation of Belgium, where the majority of the people can get along in either Flemish or French, regardless of which of the two languages they habitually use.

---

[1] As, for example, by Giraldus Cambrensis, *Itinerary through Wales*, Bk. I, chap. 22. A similar instance, equally specific though less trustworthy, is in the continuation of Pseudo-Ingulph attributed to Peter of Blois (trans. Riley, p. 238).

[2] *The Romance of Richard the Lion-hearted*, ed. Brunner, lines 23–24:

> Common men know no French.
> Among a hundred scarcely one.

[3] Vising, in his *Anglo-Norman Language and Literature*, pp. 15–18, and in his other contributions mentioned in the bibliography to this chapter, cites a number of passages from poets who explain why they are writing in French as evidence for "the complete dominance of the Anglo-Norman language during the second half of the twelfth and most of the thirteenth century in nearly all conditions of life, and of its penetration even into the lower strata of society." But the point in every case is that their work is "trans-laté hors de latin en franceys a l'aprise de lay gent" and is intended for those "ke de clergie ne ount apris," that is, who know no Latin. Even in the one instance in which the poet included in his appeal "Li grant e li mendre," his words need apply only to those less than "the great" who can understand his work in French, "Q'en franceis le poent entendre."

BIBLIOGRAPHY

Charles H. Haskins' *The Normans in European History* (Boston, 1915) furnishes an excellent background to the events discussed in this chapter. Norman influence in England before the Conquest is discussed by J. H. Round, "Normans under Edward the Confessor," in his *Feudal England* (London, 1895), pp. 317–31. E. A. Freeman's *History of the Norman Conquest* (6 vols., 1867–1879) is still standard, though often and sharply criticized. The same author published convenient small volumes on the period in *A Short History of the Norman Conquest of England* (Oxford, 1880) and *William the Conqueror* (London, 1888). The chapter in John Beddoe's *The Races of Britain* (Bristol, 1885) on the Norman immigration is largely based on the evidence of personal names, and while the results are interesting, the evidence is untrustworthy because of the fashion of employing French names and the uncertainties of nomenclature during the period under discussion. For the general history of the period Austin L. Poole's *From Domesday Book to Magna Carta 1087–1216* (2nd ed., Oxford, 1955) is excellent. Henry G. Richardson and George O. Sayles' *The Governance of Mediaeval England from the Conquest to Magna Carta* (Edinburgh, 1963) is contentious but valuable. On the relations between France and England, see T. F. Tout, *France and England: Their Relations in the Middle Ages and Now* (Manchester, 1922), especially chap. 3. The first attempt of much value to determine the position of the French and English languages in England, except for Freeman's discussion, was Oscar Scheibner, *Ueber die Herrschaft der französischen Sprache in England vom XI. bis zum XIV. Jahrhundert* (Annaberg, 1880). Bertrand Clover's *The Mastery of the French Language in England from the XIth to the XIVth Century* borrows heavily from Scheibner and adds nothing of value. Behrens' discussion in Paul's *Grundriss der Germanischen Philologie* is rather brief. The fullest attempt to collect the documentary evidence is Johan Vising's *Franska Språket i England* (3 parts, Göteborg, 1900–1902). The author's views are epitomized in *Le Français en Angleterre: mémoire sur les études de l'anglo-normand* (Macon, 1901) and *Anglo-Norman Language and Literature* (London, 1923). Chapter 9 (Le français à l'étranger) of F. Brunot's *Histoire de la langue française*, vol. 1 (Paris, 1905) presents clearly the international character of French in the Middle Ages.

$\begin{bmatrix} 6 \end{bmatrix}$

The Re-establishment of English, 1200–1500

93. *Changing Conditions after 1200.* How long the linguistic situation just described would have continued if the conditions under which it arose had remained undisturbed is impossible to say. As long as England held her continental territory and the nobility of England were united to the continent by ties of property and kindred, a real reason existed for the continued use of French among the governing class in the island. If the English had permanently retained control over the two-thirds of France that they once held, French might have remained permanently in use in England. But shortly after 1200 conditions changed. England lost an important part of her possessions abroad. The nobility gradually relinquished their continental estates. A feeling of rivalry developed between the two countries, accompanied by an antiforeign movement in England and culminating in the Hundred Years' War. During the century and a half following the Norman Conquest, French had been not only natural but more or less necessary to the English upper class; in the thirteenth and fourteenth centuries its maintenance became increasingly artificial. For a time certain new factors helped it to hold its ground, socially and officially. Meanwhile, however, social and economic changes affecting the English-speaking part of the population were taking place, and in the end numbers told. In the fourteenth century English won its way back into universal use, and in the fifteenth century French all but disappeared. We must now examine in detail the steps by which this situation came about.

94. *The Loss of Normandy.* The first link in the chain binding England to the continent was broken in 1204 when King John lost Normandy. John, seeing the beautiful Isabel of Angoulême, fell violently in love with her and, no doubt having certain political advantages in mind, married her in great haste (1200), notwithstanding the fact that she was at the time formally betrothed to Hugh of Lusignan, the head of a powerful and ambitious family. To make matters worse, John, anticipating hostility from the Lusignans, took the initiative and wantonly attacked them. They appealed for redress to their common overlord, the king of France. Philip saw in the situation an opportunity to embarrass his most irrritating vassal. He summoned John (1202) to appear before his court at Paris, answer the charges against him, and submit to the judgment of his peers. John maintained that as king of England he was not subject to the jurisdiction of the French court; Philip replied that as duke of Normandy he was. John demanded a safe conduct, which Philip offered to grant only on conditions which John could not accept. Consequently, on the day of the trial the English king did not appear, and the court declared his territory confiscated according to feudal law. Philip proceeded at once to carry out the decision of the court and invaded Normandy. A succession of victories soon put the greater part of the duchy in his control. One after another of John's supporters deserted him. His unpopularity was increased by the news of the death of the young prince Arthur, John's nephew and captive, who was married to Philip's daughter and who, it was firmly believed, had been murdered. In 1204 Rouen surrendered and Normandy was lost to the English crown.

So far as it affected the English language, as in other respects as well, the loss of Normandy was wholly advantageous. King and nobles were now forced to look upon England as their first concern. Although England still retained large continental possessions, they were in the south of France and had never been so intimately connected by ties of language, blood, and property interests as had Normandy. It gradually became apparent that the island kingdom had its own political and economic ends and that these were not the same as those of France. England was on the way to becoming not merely a geographical term but once more a nation.

95. *Separation of the French and English Nobility.* One of the important consequences of the event just described was that it brought to a head the question whether many of the nobility owed their allegiance to England or to France. After the Norman Conquest a large number of men held lands in both countries. A kind of interlocking aristocracy existed, so that it might be difficult for some of the English nobility to say whether they belonged more to England or to the continent. Some steps toward a separation of their interests had been taken from time to time. The example of the Conqueror, who left Normandy to his son Robert and England to William Rufus, was occasionally followed by his companions. The Norman and English estates of William Fitz Osbern were divided in this way at his death in 1071, and of Roger de Montgomery in 1094, though the latter were afterwards reunited.[1] On several occasions Henry I confiscated the English estates of unruly Norman barons. But in 1204 the process of separation was greatly accelerated, for by a decree of 1204–1205 the king of France announced that he had confiscated the lands of several great barons, including the earls of Warenne, Arundel, Leicester, and Clare, and of all those knights who had their abode in England.[2] For the most part the families that had estates on both sides of the Channel were compelled to give up one or the other. Sometimes they divided into branches and made separate terms; in other cases great nobles preferred their larger holdings in England and gave up their Norman lands.[3] John's efforts at retaliation came to the same effect. It is true that the separation was by no means complete. In one way or another some nobles succeeded in retaining their position in both countries. But double allegiance was generally felt to be awkward,[4] and the voluntary division of estates went on. The action of Simon de Montfort in 1229 must have had many parallels. "My brother Amaury," he says, "released to me our brother's whole inheritance in England, provided that I could secure it; in return I released to him what I had in France."[5] The course of the separation may be said to culminate in an incident of 1244, which may best be told in the words of a contemporary chronicler:

> In the course of those days, the king of France having convoked, at Paris, all the people across the water who had possessions in England thus addressed them: "As it is impossible that any man living in my kingdom, and having possessions in England, can competently serve two masters, he must either inseparably attach himself to me or to the king of England." Wherefore those who had possessions and revenues in England were to relinquish them and keep those which they had in France, and *vice versa*. Which, when it came to the knowledge of the king of England, he ordered that all people of the French nation, and especially Normans, who had possessions in England, should be disseized of them. Whence it appeared to the king of France that the king of England had broken the treaties concluded between them, because he had not, as the king of France

---

[1] For other instances see F. M. Powicke, *The Loss of Normandy* (Manchester, 1913), p. 482.

[2] Powicke, pp. 403, 415.

[3] Stubbs, *Constitutional History of England*, I, 557; J. R. Strayer, *The Administration of Normandy under Saint Louis* (Cambridge, Mass., 1932), p. 7.

[4] Confiscations continued, as in 1217 and 1224. Cf. Kate Norgate, *The Minority of Henry III* (London, 1912), pp. 77, 220–21.

[5] Charles Bémont, *Simon de Montfort* (Oxford, 1930), p. 4.

had done, given the option to those who were to lose their lands in one or other of the two kingdoms, so that they might themselves choose which kingdom they would remain in. But as he was much weakened in body since his return from Poitou, he did not wish to renew the war, and preferred to keep silence; he even sought to repress the impetuous complaints of the Normans, as well as the furious and greedy desire that they manifested to rise against the king of England.[1]

The action of Louis was no doubt a consequence of the assistance Henry III attempted to give to the Count de la Marche and other rebellious French nobles in 1243, and although Matthew Paris is our only authority for it, there is no reason to doubt its authenticity. We may perhaps doubt whether these decrees were any more rigidly enforced than previous orders of a similar sort had been, but the cumulative effect of the various causes described was to make the problem of double allegiance henceforth negligible. We may be sure that after 1250 there was no reason for the nobility of England to consider itself anything but English. The most valid reason for its use of French was gone.

96. French Reinforcements. At the very time when the Norman nobility was losing its continental connections and had been led to identify itself wholly with England, the country suffered from a fresh invasion of foreigners, this time mostly from the south of France. The invasion began in the reign of King John, whose wife, mentioned above, was from the neighborhood of Poitou. A Poitevin clerk, Peter des Roches, was made bishop of Winchester, and rose to be chancellor and later justiciar of England. He is only the most important among a considerable number of foreign adventurers who attracted John's attention and won his favor. But what began as a mere infiltration in the time of John became a flood in that of his son. Henry III, in spite of his devotion to English saints, was wholly French in his tastes and connections. Not only was he French on his mother's side, but was related through his wife to the French king, St. Louis. How intimate were the relations between the royal families of France and England at this time may be seen from the fact that Henry III, his half-brother Richard of Cornwall, Louis IX, and Louis' brother Charles

---

[1] Matthew Paris, *Chronica Majora*, trans. J. A. Giles, I, 482. Although Matthew Paris puts this action of Louis IX and Henry III under the year 1244, it is possible that it belongs to the previous year. As early as July 1243, Henry ordered inquiry to be made to determine what magnates of England had stood with the king of France in the last war (*Cal. Close Rolls, 1242–47*, p. 69), and on January 24, 1244, he granted to his son Edward "a moiety of all the lands which the king has ordered to be taken into his hands and which belonged to men of the fealty of the king of France, and those holding of him." (*Cal. Pat. Rolls, 1232–47*, p. 418.)

of Anjou were married to the four daughters of the count of Provence. As a result of Henry's French connections three great inundations of foreigners poured into England during his reign. The first occurred in the year 1233, during the rule of Peter des Roches, a vivid picture of which is given by a contemporary: "The seventeenth year of King Henry's reign he held his court at Christmas at Worcester, where, by the advice of Peter bishop of Winchester, as was said, he dismissed all the native officers of his court from their offices, and appointed foreigners from Poitou in their places. . . . All his former counsellors, bishops and earls, barons and other nobles, he dismissed abruptly, and put confidence in no one except the aforesaid bishop of Winchester and his son Peter de Rivaulx; after which he ejected all the castellans throughout all England, and placed the castles under the charge of the said Peter. . . . The king also invited men from Poitou and Britanny, who were poor and covetous after wealth, and about two thousand knights and soldiers came to him equipped with horses and arms, whom he engaged in his service, placing them in charge of the castles in the various parts of the kingdom; these men used their utmost endeavors to oppress the natural English subjects and nobles, calling them traitors, and accusing them of treachery to the king; and he, simple man that he was, believed their lies, and gave them the charge of all the counties and baronies."[1] The king, the same chronicler adds, "invited such legions of people from Poitou that they entirely filled England, and wherever the king went he was surrounded by crowds of these foreigners; and nothing was done in England except what the bishop of Winchester and his host of foreigners determined on."[2]

In 1236 Henry's marriage to Eleanor of Provence brought a second stream of aliens to England. The new queen inherited among other blessings eight maternal uncles and a generous number of more distant relatives. Many of them came to England and were richly provided for. Matthew Paris writes, under the following year, "Our English king . . . has fattened all the kindred and relatives of his wife with lands, possessions, and money, and has contracted such a marriage that he cannot be more enriched, but rather impoverished."[3] One of the queen's uncles, Peter of Savoy, was given the earldom of Richmond; another, Boniface, was made archbishop of Canterbury. Peter was further empowered by letters-patent to enlist in Henry's service as many foreigners as he saw fit.[4] The Provençals

---

[1] Roger of Wendover, trans. J. A. Giles, II, 565–66.
[2] *Ibid.*, II, 567–68.
[3] *Chronica Majora*, trans. Giles, I, 122.
[4] O. H. Richardson, *The National Movement in the Reign of Henry III* (New York, 1897), p. 75.

who thus came to England as a consequence of Henry's marriage were followed ten years later, upon the death of his mother, by a third alien influx, this one, like the first, from Poitou. Upon the death of King John, Henry's mother had married her first love and borne him five sons. Henry now enriched his Poitevin half-brothers and their followers, and married their daughters to English nobles. To one he gave the castle of Hertford and a rich wife. Another he made bishop of Winchester, "notwithstanding his youth, his ignorance of learning, and his utter incapacity for such a high station."[1] Of a third the same chronicler says that when he left England "the king filled his saddle bags with such a weight of money that he was obliged to increase the number of his horses."[2] Meanwhile marriages with the strangers were promoted by both the king and the queen,[3] Henry's own brother, Richard, earl of Cornwall, for example, being married to the queen's sister. Everywhere ecclesiastical dignities were given to strangers, sometimes to reward favorites, sometimes to please the Pope. The great bishop Grosseteste, who lived at this time, made an estimate of all the revenues of foreigners in England and found that the income of foreign ecclesiastics alone was three times that of the king. In short, in the course of Henry III's long reign (1216–1272), the country was eaten up by strangers. Even London, says Matthew Paris, whom we have so often quoted, "was full to overflowing, not only of Poitevins, Romans, and Provençals, but also of Spaniards, who did great injury to the English."[4]

[1] Matthew Paris, II, 433.

[2] *Ibid.*, II, 247. For the extent to which these foreigners were enriched, see Harold S. Snellgrove, *The Lusignans in England, 1247–1258* (Albuquerque, 1950; *Univ. of New Mexico Pub. in History*, No. 2).

[3] Nothing can equal the impression that would be gained of this period by reading a hundred pages of Matthew Paris. Perhaps a few quotations will help to complete the picture: "My dear earl, I will no longer conceal from you the secret desire of my heart, which is, to raise and enrich you, and to advance your interests, by marrying your eldest legitimate son to the daughter of Guy, count of Angoulême, my uterine brother." (III, 15.) "At the instigation of the queen, Baldwin de Rivers married a foreign lady, a Savoyard, and a relation of the queen's. The county of Devon belonged to this Baldwin, and thus the noble possessions and heritages of the English daily devolved to foreigners." (III, 219.) "At the beginning of the month of May [1247], ... two ladies of Provence were, by the forethought and arrangement of Peter of Savoy, married to two noble youths, namely, Edmund earl of Lincoln, and Richard de Bourg, whom the king had for some years brought up in his palace. At this marriage the sounds of great discontent and anger were wafted through the kingdom, because, as they said, these females, although unknown, were united to the nobles against their wills." (II, 230.) "In the same year, on the 13th of August, by the wish of the king, Johanna, the daughter of Warin de Muntchesnil, was married to William de Valence, the king's uterine brother; for, the eldest son and heir of the said Warin being dead, a very rich inheritance awaited this daughter Johanna, who was the only daughter left." (II, 230–31.)

[4] III, 151.

97. *The Reaction against Foreigners and the Growth of National Feeling.*
The excesses of Henry III in his reckless bestowal of favor upon foreigners
were not so completely unfavorable to the English language as might be
supposed. A reaction was bound to follow. Even the milder tendencies of
John toward the favoring of aliens led the patriotic chancellor, Hubert de
Burgh, during the minority of John's son, to adopt a vigorous policy of
"England for the English." When Henry came of age and under the rule
of Peter des Roches the first great inpouring of Poitevins occurred, the
antagonism aroused was immediate. At a council held at Winchester in
1234 a number of the bishops told the king: "Lord king, . . . the counsel
which you now receive and act upon, namely, that of Peter bishop of
Winchester, and Peter de Rivaulx, is not wise or safe, but . . . cruel and
dangerous to yourselves and to the whole kingdom. In the first place, they
hate the English people . . . ; they estrange your affections from your
people, and those of your people from you . . . ; they hold your castles and
the strength of your dominions in their own hands, as though you could
not place confidence in your own people; . . . they have your treasury, and
all the chief trusts and escheats under their own control; . . . [and] by the
same counsel all the natural subjects of your kingdom have been dismissed
from your court."[1] Upon the threat of excommunication the king yielded
and dismissed the foreigners from office. But they were soon back, and
popular feeling grew steadily more bitter. As Matthew Paris wrote, "At
this time (1251), the king day by day lost the affections of his natural
subjects." The following year the great reforming bishop, Grosseteste,
expressed the feeling of native churchmen when he said: "The church is
being worn out by constant oppressions; the pious purposes of its early
benefactors are being brought to naught by the confiscation of its ample
patrimony to the uses of aliens, while the native English suffer. These
aliens are not merely foreigners; they are the worst enemies of England.
They strive to tear the fleece and do not even know the faces of the sheep;
they do not understand the English tongue, neglect the cure of souls, and
impoverish the kingdom."[2] Opposition to the foreigner became the principal ground for such national feeling as existed and drove the barons and
the middle class together in a common cause. It is significant that the
leader of this coalition, Simon de Montfort, was Norman-born, though he
claimed his inheritance in England by right of his grandmother. The
practical outcome of the opposition was the Provisions of Oxford (1258)
and their aftermath, the Barons' War (1258–1265). Twice during these

---

[1] Roger of Wendover, II, 583–85.
[2] Quoted by Richardson, *National Movement* (New York, 1897), pp. 32–33.

years the foreigners were driven from England, and when peace was finally restored and a little later Edward I (1272–1307) came to the throne we enter upon a period in which England becomes conscious of its unity, when the governmental officials are for the most part English, and when the king, in a summons to parliament (1295), can attempt to stir up the feelings of his subjects against the king of France by claiming that it was "his detestable purpose, which God forbid, to wipe out the English tongue."

The effect of the foreign incursions in the thirteenth century was undoubtedly to delay somewhat the natural spread of the use of English by the upper classes which had begun. But it was also to arouse such widespread hostility to foreigners as greatly to stimulate the consciousness of the difference between those who for a generation or several generations had so participated in English affairs as to consider themselves Englishmen, and to cause them to unite against the newcomers who had flocked to England to bask in the sun of Henry's favor. One of the reproaches frequently leveled at the latter is that they did not know English. It would be natural if some knowledge of English should come to be regarded as a proper mark of an Englishman.

98. *French Cultural Ascendancy in Europe.* The stimulus given to the use of French in England by foreign additions to the upper class coincides by accident with another circumstance tending in the same direction. This was the wide popularity which the French language enjoyed all over civilized Europe in the thirteenth century. At this time France was commonly regarded as representing chivalrous society in its most polished form, and the French language was an object of cultivation at most of the other courts of Europe, just as it was in the eighteenth century. Adenct lc Roi tells us in one of his romances that all the great lords in Germany had French teachers for their children.[1] Brunetto Latini, the master of Dante, in explaining why he wrote his great encyclopedia, *Li Tresor* (c. 1265), in French, says: "And if anyone should ask why this book is written in Romance, according to the language of the French, seeing that I am Italian, I should say that it is for two reasons: one, because I am now in France, and the other because that speech is the most delectable and the most

---

[1] Avoit une coustume ens el tiois pays
Que tout li grant seignor, li conte et li marchis
Avoient entour aus gent françoise tousdis
Pour aprendre françois lor filles et lor fis;
Li rois et la roïne et Berte o le cler vis
Sorent près d'aussi bien le françois de Paris
Com se il fussent né au bourc à Saint Denis.
(*Berte aus Grans Piés*, 148 ff.)

common to all people." At about the same time another Italian, Martino da Canale, translated "the ancient history of the Venetians from Latin into French" "because the French language is current throughout the world and is the most delightful to read and to hear." Similar testimony comes from Norway and Spain, even Jerusalem and the East.[1] The prestige of French civilization, a heritage to some extent from the glorious tradition of Charlemagne, carried abroad by the greatest of medieval literatures, by the fame of the University of Paris, and perhaps to some extent by the enterprise of the Normans themselves, would have constituted in itself a strong reason for the continued use of French among polite circles in England.

99. *English and French in the Thirteenth Century.* The thirteenth century must be viewed as a period of shifting emphasis upon the two languages spoken in England. The upper classes continued for the most part to speak French, as they had done in the previous century, but the reasons for doing so were not the same. Instead of being a mother tongue inherited from Norman ancestors, French became, as the century wore on, a cultivated tongue supported by social custom and by business and administrative convention. Meanwhile English made steady advances. A number of considerations make it clear that by the middle of the century, when the separation of the English nobles from their interests in France had been about completed, English was becoming a matter of general use among the upper classes. It is at this time, as we shall see, that the adoption of French words into the English language assumes large proportions. The transference of words occurs when those who know French and have been accustomed to use it try to express themselves in English. It is at this time also that the literature intended for polite circles begins to be made over from French into English (see § 110). There is evidence that by the close of the century some children of the nobility spoke English as their mother tongue and had to be taught French through the medium of manuals equipped with English glosses.

There is no need to heap up evidence of the continued use of French by the upper class in this century. Even at the close of the century it was used

---

[1] Cf. Nyrop, *Grammaire historique de la langue française*, I, 30; Brunot, *Histoire de la langue française*, I, 358–99. Writers still speak of the wide popularity of French at a much later date. Christine de Pisan at the beginning of the fifteenth century calls it "la plus commune par l'universel monde" (*Le Livre des Trois Vertus*, quoted in R. Thomassy, *Essai sur les écrits politiques de Christine de Pisan* (Paris, 1838), pp. lxxxi–lxxxii) and cf. the anonymous author of *La Manière de langage* (1396), ed. P. Meyer, *Rev. Critique*, 10 (1870), 373–408.

in parliament,[1] in the law courts, in public negotiations generally.[2] Treatises on husbandry which have come down to us from this time are all in French. All of them[3] seem intended for the owners of estates, except possibly *Seneschaucie*, which is on the duties of the seneschal. French was read by the educated, including those who could not read Latin.[4] That the ability was on the decline is suggested by the action of a chronicler at the end of the century who, after citing a petition to parliament "written in the French language in conformity with the usual custom," translates it into Latin in order that it "may be more easily understood by those of posterity who may not be so well versed in the above language."[5]

That the knowledge of French, even of those who attempted to use it in this period, was sometimes imperfect is quite clear. One author of a French poem says he hardly knows how to write the language because he was never in Paris or at the abbey of St. Denis.[6] The most interesting evidence, however, is to be found in the bills or petitions presented to the justices in eyre at the close of the thirteenth and the beginning of the fourteenth centuries by those seeking redress at the law. Custom required these bills to be in French. They are obviously not written by lawyers or by the complainants themselves, but by professional scribes or possibly the parish priest. As the editor of a volume of such petitions[7] says, "The text of the bills makes it

---

[1] In the reign of Edward I the archbishop of Canterbury presented to the king and the leaders of the army a Latin letter from the Pope and explained its contents in French. (Matthew of Westminster, trans. C. D. Young, II, 546.) The petitions to parliament at this time are mostly in French, and sometimes the statutes themselves, though these were commonly drawn up in Latin. (*Statutes of the Realm*, I, xl, and R. L. Atkinson, "Interim Report on Ancient Petitions," typed transcript bound in the copy of *Lists and Indexes*, no. 1, in the Literary Search Room of the Public Record Office.)

[2] As when Edward I was called in (1291) to settle the dispute concerning the Scottish succession. (Rymer, *Foedera*, II, 553.)

[3] Four are edited by E. Lamond, *Walter of Henley's Husbandry* (London, 1890). One was supposedly written by Bishop Grosseteste in 1240–1241 for the countess of Lincoln. Walter of Henley's treatise exists in an English version which is attributed in the manuscripts to Grosseteste. If we could trust the attribution, it would constitute evidence that some of the landowners at this time preferred to read English. But the translation belongs probably to a later date.

[4] A French poem on the calendar is addressed to "simpli gent lettre," i.e., those who could read, while Grosseteste's *Château d'Amour* was "por ceus ki ne sevent mie ne lettrure ne clergie," i.e., those who could neither read at all nor understand Latin, but could understand French when it was read to them.

[5] Continuation of Pseudo-Ingulph, *Ingulph's Chronicle*, trans. H. T. Riley, p. 330.

[6] Je ne sai guers romanz faire ...
   Car jeo ne fu unques a Parye
   Ne al abbaye de saint Denys.
(*Antikrist*, latter part of the thirteenth century, cited by Vising, *Franska Språket i England*, III, 9.)

[7] W. C. Bolland, *Select Bills in Eyre, A.D. 1292–1333* (London, 1914), pp. xix–xx, xxx–xxxi. (Selden Soc.)

plain that the draftsmen were struggling with the forms of a language that was far from being a living tongue with them," and he offers good reason for believing "that they neither spoke French nor were accustomed to hear it spoken in their own neighborhood." Furthermore, declension and conjugation are often incorrect or peculiar, and the writers make the most obvious mistakes in gender, such as using *la* before a man's name and *le* before a woman's ("*le* avant dit Aliz"). Yet, singularly enough, the handwriting of some of the worst is excellent and seems clearly to point to an educated man.

The spread of English among the upper classes was making steady progress. References to a knowledge of the language on the part of members of this class are now seldom found, especially in the latter part of the century, probably because it had become general. We do not know whether Henry III understood English, though he probably did. His brother, Richard, earl of Cornwall, who was elected emperor of Germany in 1257, certainly did, for Matthew Paris tells us that he was chosen partly "on account of his speaking the English language, which is similar in sound to the German."[1] Henry's son, Edward I, notwithstanding his Provençal mother, spoke English readily, perhaps even habitually.[2] While the references to the language are not numerous, they are suggestive. Here a bishop preaches in it;[3] there a judge quotes it,[4] monks joke in it;[5] friars use it to explain to the people of Worcester a legal victory.[6] A royal proclamation is issued in it.[7]

The clearest indication of the extent to which the English language had risen in the social scale by the middle of the thirteenth century is furnished

---

[1] *Chronica Majora*, trans. Riley, III, 209.
[2] Cf. an incident in Walter of Hemingburgh, I, 337 (Eng. Hist. Soc.); Freeman, V, 533.
[3] Grosseteste (cf. Stevenson, *Robert Grosseteste*, p. 32).
[4] W. C. Bolland, *The Year Books* (Cambridge, 1921), p. 76.
[5] Giraldus Cambrensis, *Opera*, IV, 209. (Rolls Series.)
[6] Annals of Worcester, *Annales Monastici*, IV, 504. (Rolls Series.)
[7] The agreement reached by the barons and the king in 1258 and known as the Provisions of Oxford was made public by a proclamation which bound every one in England to the acceptance of it. The proclamation, issued by the king October 18, 1258, was in French and English and was directed "To alle hise holde ilaerde and ileawede" (to all his faithful subjects, learned and lay) in every county. It is the first proclamation to be issued in English since the Norman Conquest, and, although the only one for a good while, is very likely the result of Simon de Montfort's desire to reach the people of the middle class, the lesser barons, and the inhabitants of the towns.

For the text of the proclamation, as entered on the Patent Roll, see A. J. Ellis, "On the Only English Proclamation of Henry III," *Trans. Philol. Soc.* (1868), pp. 1–135. The actual copy sent to the sheriff of Oxford was later found and published by W. W. Skeat, "The Oxford MS. of the Only English Proclamation of Henry III," *ibid.* (1880–1881), Appendix VI. A facsimile of this copy is given in Octavus Ogle, *Royal Letters Addressed to Oxford* (Oxford, 1892).

by a little treatise written by Walter of Bibbesworth to teach children French—how to speak and how to reply, "Which every gentleman ought to know." French is treated as a foreign language, and the child is taken on a very practical course through life, learning the names of the parts of the body, the articles of its clothing, food, household utensils and operations, meals, and the like, together with terms of falconry and the chase and other polite accomplishments. The important words are provided with an interlinear English gloss. The person for whom the little manual was prepared was Dionysia, the daughter of William de Munchensy. The latter was among the leaders of the barons in the battle of Lewes and was related, through his sister's marriage, to the half-brother of King Henry III. Dionysia herself was later married to one of the sons of the earl of Oxford. She thus belonged to the upper circle of the nobility, and it is therefore highly significant that the language she knew, and through which she acquired French, was English. Since the treatise was certainly written in the thirteenth century (not later than 1250) and the number of manuscripts that have come down to us shows that it had a much wider circulation than in just the family for which it was originally written, we may feel quite sure that the mother tongue of the children of the nobility in the year 1300 was, in many cases, English.[1]

Finally, it is interesting to note the appearance at this time of an attitude that becomes more noticeable later, the attitude that the proper language for Englishmen to know and use is English. In the *Cursor Mundi*, an encyclopedic poem on biblical subjects, written shortly before or shortly after the year 1300, we may detect a mild but nonetheless clear protest against the use of French and a patriotic espousal of English:

> Þis ilk bok es translate
> Into Inglis tong to rede
> For the love of Inglis lede,[2]
> Inglis lede of Ingland,
> For the commun at[3] understand.
> Frankis rimes here I redd
> Comunlik in ilka sted;[4]
> Mast[5] es it wroght for Frankis man,
> Quat[6] is for him na Frankis can?

---

[1] The treatise has been most recently edited by Annie Owen, *Le Traité de Walter de Bibbesworth sur la langue française* (Paris, 1929). On the date see Baugh, "The Date of Walter of Bibbesworth's Traité," *Festschrift für Walther Fischer* (Heidelberg, 1959), pp. 21–33.

[2] people   [3] to   [4] place   [5] most   [6] what

> In Ingland the nacion,
> Es Inglis man þar in commun;
> Þe speche þat man wit mast may spede;
> Mast þarwit to speke war nede.
> Selden was for ani chance
> Praised Inglis tong in France;
> Give we ilkan[1] þare langage,
> Me think we do þam non outrage.
> To laud[2] and Inglis man I spell
> Þat understandes þat I tell . . .
> (*Cursor Mundi*, Prologue, ll. 232–50)

The Provisions of Oxford, mentioned above, were in Latin, French, and English. Latin was naturally the language of record. It is certain that the document was sent in English to the sheriffs of every county to be publicized. Whether it was also sent in French is not known but seems likely. At all events, four years before (1244), the *Annals of Burton* record a letter from the dean of Lincoln asking the bishop of Lichfield to proclaim a directive from the Pope excommunicating those who broke the provisions of Magna Carta, the pronouncement to be *in lingua Anglicana et Gallicana*.[3] In 1295 a document was read before the county court at Chelmsford, Essex, and explained *in gallico et anglico*,[4] but this may represent no more than the survival of a custom of making important announcements in both languages. We may sum up the situation by saying that in the latter part of the thirteenth century English was widely known among all classes of people, though not necessarily by everyone.

100. *Attempts to Arrest the Decline of French.* At the close of the thirteenth century and especially in the course of the next we see clear indications that the French language was losing its hold on England in the measures adopted to keep it in use. The tendency to speak English was becoming constantly stronger even in those two most conservative institutions, the church and the universities. Already in the last decades of the thirteenth century the great Benedictine monasteries of Canterbury and Westminster adopted regulations forbidding the novices to use English in school or cloister and requiring all conversation to be in French.[5] Similar regulations were found necessary at the universities. A fourteenth-century

---

[1] each one   [2] ignorant, lay
[3] *Annales Monastici*, I, 322. (Rolls Series.)
[4] W. A. Morris, *The Early English County Court* (Berkeley, 1926), p. 173.
[5] *Customary of the Benedictine Monasteries of Saint Augustine, Canterbury, and Saint Peter, Westminster*, ed. E. H. Thompson, Henry Bradshaw Soc., XXIII, 210; XXVIII, 164.

statute of Oxford required the students to construe and translate in both English and French "lest the French language be entirely disused."[1] Supplementary ordinances drawn up for Exeter College by Bishop Stapleton in 1322 and 1325, and the foundation statutes of Oriel (1326) and Queen's (1340), required that the conversation of the students be in Latin or in French. As early as 1284 at Merton, Archbishop Peckham found that Latin was not spoken, as the rules required. Some time later conditions at this fine old college were clearly in a bad way; the Fellows talked English at table and wore "dishonest shoes."[2] Among the Cambridge colleges Peterhouse had a similar rule. Students were expected to talk Latin except that they might use French "for a just or reasonable cause . . . but very rarely English."[3] The primary purpose of these regulations was of course to insure an easy command of the Latin language, but it is evident that without them the language that would have been spoken, if not Latin, would have been English. According to Froissart, a further effort to keep the French language from going out of use was made by parliament in 1332, which decreed "that all lords, barons, knights, and honest men of good towns should exercise care and diligence to teach their children the French language in order that they might be more able and better equipped in their wars."[4] Such efforts as these indicate how artificial was the use of French in England by the fourteenth century.

If further evidence were needed it would be found in the appearance of numerous manuals for learning French. As early as 1250 we find a short Latin treatise on the French verb. Walter of Bibbesworth's *Traité* of about the same date has already been mentioned. In succeeding years there are several adaptations of it, fuller in treatment and with more attention to pronunciation. They form an unbroken series from that time down to our own textbooks of the present day, and in them all French is treated frankly as a foreign language.[5]

101. Provincial Character of French in England. One factor against the continued use of French in England was the circumstance that Anglo-French was not "good" French. In the Middle Ages there were four principal dialects of French spoken in France: Norman, Picard (in the

---

[1] *Munimenta Academica*, II, 438. (Rolls Series.)
[2] C. E. Mallet, *A History of the University of Oxford* (3 vols., London, 1924–1927), I, 118.
[3] *Documents Relating to the University and Colleges of Cambridge* (1852), II, 31.
[4] *Œuvres de Froissart*, ed. Kervyn de Lettenhove, II, 419.
[5] A full account of these books is given in K. Lambley, *The Teaching and Cultivation of the French Language in England* (Manchester, 1920), and G. T. Clapton and W. Stewart, *Les Études françaises dans l'enseignement en Grande-Bretagne* (Paris, 1929).

northeast), Burgundian (in the east), and the Central French of Paris (the Ile-de-France). At the date of the Norman Conquest and for some time after, each enjoyed a certain local prestige,[1] but with the rapid rise of the Capetian power in the thirteenth century the linguistic supremacy of Paris followed upon its political ascendancy. The French introduced into England was possibly a mixture of various northern dialectal features, but with Norman predominating, and under the influence of English linguistic tendencies, it gradually developed into something quite different from any of the continental dialects. The difference was noticed quite early,[2] and before long the French of England drew a smile from continental speakers. It was the subject of humorous treatment in literature,[3] and English writers became apologetic. One poet says, "A false French of England I know, for I have not been elsewhere to acquire it; but you who have learned it elsewhere, amend it where there is need."[4] The more ambitious sent their children to France to have the "barbarity" taken off their speech.[5] But the situation did not mend. Everybody is familiar with the gentle fun that Chaucer makes of the Prioress:

> And Frensh she spak ful faire and fetisly,
> After the scole of Stratford atte Bowe,
> For Frensh of Paris was to hir unknowe.

One might well feel some hesitancy about speaking a language of which one had to be slightly ashamed.

102. *The Hundred Years' War.* In the course of the centuries following the Norman Conquest the connection of England with the continent, as we have seen, had been broken. It was succeeded by a conflict of interests and a growing feeling of antagonism that culminated in a long period of open hostility with France (1337–1453). The causes of this struggle are too complex to be entered into here, but the active interference of France in

[1] Roger Bacon notes the four dialects and says: "A fitting and intelligible expression in the dialect of the Picards is out of place among the Burgundians, nay, among their nearer Gallic neighbors." *The Opus Majus of Roger Bacon*, trans. R. B. Burke (Philadelphia, 1928), I, 75.

[2] Walter Map says that " if one is faulty in his use of this tongue, we say that he speaketh French of Marlborough." *De Nugis Curialium*, V, vi (trans. Tupper and Ogle).

[3] H. Albert, *Mittelalterlicher Englisch-französischer Jargon* (Halle, 1922).

[4] A life of Edward the Confessor in Anglo-French verse of the latter part of the thirteenth century; cf. A. T. Baker in the *Mod. Lang. Rev.*, 3 (1907–1908), 374–75. William of Wadington makes a similar excuse: "No one ought to blame me for the French or the verse, for I was born in England and nourished and brought up there." So too does Gower. (Vising, *Franska Språket i England*, III, 9.)

[5] Gervase of Tilbury, *Otia Imperialia* (1212), chap. 20, ed. G. G. Leibnitz, *Scriptores Rerum Brunsvicensium* (Hanover, 1707), I, 945.

England's efforts to control Scotland led Edward III finally to put forth a claim to the French throne and to invade France. The great victories of the English at Crécy (1346) and Poitiers (1356) fanned English patriotism to a white heat, though this auspicious beginning of the struggle was followed by a depressing period of reverses and though the contest was interrupted by long periods of truce. In the reign of Henry V England again enjoyed a brief period of success, notably in the victory against great odds at Agincourt (1415). But the success did not continue after the young king's death, and the exploits of Joan of Arc (1429) marked the beginning of the end. Although this protracted war again turned people's attention to the continent, and the various expeditions might have tended to keep the French language in use, it seems to have had no such effect, but rather the opposite. Probably the intervals between the periods of actual fighting were too long and the hindrances to trade and other intercourse too discouraging. The feeling that remained uppermost in the minds of most people was one of animosity, coupled with a sense of the inevitability of renewed hostilities. During all this time it was impossible to forget that French was the language of an enemy country, and the Hundred Years' War is probably to be reckoned as one of the causes contributing to the disuse of French.

103. *The Rise of the Middle Class.* A feature of some importance in helping English to recover its former prestige is the improvement in the condition of the mass of the people and the rise of a substantial middle class. As we have seen, the importance of a language is largely determined by the importance of the people who speak it. During the latter part of the Middle English period the condition of the laboring classes was rapidly improving. Among the rural population villeinage was dying out. Fixed money payments were gradually substituted for the days' work due the lord of the manor, and the status of the villein more nearly resembled that of the free tenants. The latter class was itself increasing; there was more incentive to individual effort and more opportunity for a man to reap the rewards of enterprise. The process by which these changes were being brought about was greatly accelerated by an event that occurred in the year 1349.

In the summer of 1348 there appeared in the southwest of England the first cases of a disease that in its contagiousness and fatality exceeded anything previously known. It spread rapidly over the rest of the country, reaching its height in 1349 but continuing in the north into the early months of 1350. The illness, once contracted, ran a very rapid course. In two or three days the victim either died or showed signs of recovery.

Generally he died. Immunity was slight and in the absence of any system of quarantine the disease spread unimpeded through a community. The mortality was unbelievably high, though it has often been exaggerated. We can no more believe the statement that scarcely one-tenth of the people were left alive than we can the assertion of the same chronicler that all those born after the pestilence had two "cheek-teeth in their head less than they had afore." Careful modern studies based on the data contained in episcopal registers show that 40 percent of the parish clergy died of the plague, and while this is apparently higher than for the population at large, the death rate during the plague approximated 30 percent. It is quite sufficient to justify the name "The Black Death."

The effects of so great a calamity were naturally serious, and in one direction at least are fully demonstrable. As in most epidemics, the rich suffered less than the poor. The poor man could not shut himself up in his castle or betake himself off to a secluded manor. The mortality was accordingly greatest among the lower orders, and the result was a serious shortage of labor. This is evident in the immediate rise in wages, a rise which the Statute of Laborers was insufficient to control or prevent. Nor was this result merely temporary if we may judge from the thirteen reenactments of the statute in the course of the next hundred years. Villeins frequently made their escape, and many cotters left the land in search of the high wages commanded by independent workers. Those who were left behind felt more acutely the burden of their condition, and a general spirit of discontent arose, which culminated in the Peasants' Revolt of 1381. By and large, the effect of the Black Death was to increase the economic importance of the laboring class and with it the importance of the English language which they spoke.[1]

We may also note at this time the rise of another important group—the craftsmen and the merchant class. By 1250 there had grown up in England about two hundred towns with populations of from 1,000 to 5,000; some, like London or York, were larger. These towns became free, self-governing communities, electing their own officers, assessing taxes in their own way,

[1] As a result of the plague English must also have made its way more rapidly in the monasteries, as we know it did in the schools, and probably elsewhere. Forty-seven monks and the abbot died at St. Albans in 1349. Their places were filled by men who often knew no other language than English. We may judge of the situation from the words of the chronicler Knighton: "But, within a short time, a very great multitude of men whose wives had died of the pestilence flocked to Holy Orders, of whom many were illiterate and almost sheer lay folk, except in so far as they could read, though not understand."

collecting them and paying them to the king in a lump sum, trying their own cases, and regulating their commercial affairs as they saw fit. The townsfolk were engaged for the most part in trade or in the manufacturing crafts and banded together into commercial fraternities or gilds for their mutual protection and advantage. In such an environment there arose in each town an independent, sometimes a wealthy and powerful class, standing halfway between the rural peasant and the hereditary aristocracy.

Such changes in the social and economic life benefited particularly the English-speaking part of the population, and enable us better to understand the final triumph of English in the century in which these changes largely occur.

104. *General Adoption of English in the Fourteenth Century*. At the beginning of the fourteenth century English was once more known by everyone. The most conclusive evidence of this is the direct testimony of contemporaries. So much of the polite literature of England until a generation or two before had been in French that writers seemed to feel called upon to justify their use of English. Accordingly they frequently begin with a prologue explaining their intention in the work which follows and incidentally make interesting observations on the linguistic situation. From a number of such statements we may select three quotations. The first is from a collection of metrical homilies written in the north of England about the year 1300:

> Forthi wil I of my povert
> Schau sum thing that Ik haf in hert,
> On Ingelis tong that alle may
> Understand quat I wil say;
> For laued men havis mar mister
> Godes word for to her
> Than klerkes that thair mirour lokes,
> And sees hou thai sal lif on bokes.
> And bathe klerk and laued man
> Englis understand kan,
> That was born in Ingeland,
> And lang haves ben thar in wonand,
> Bot al men can noht, I-wis,
> Understand Latin and Frankis.
> Forthi me think almous it isse

> To wirke sum god thing on Inglisse,
> That mai ken lered and laued bathe.[1]

Here we are told that both learned and unlearned understand English. A still more circumstantial statement, serving to confirm the above testimony, is found in William of Nassyngton's *Speculum Vitae* or *Mirror of Life* (c. 1325):

> In English tonge I schal ʒow telle,
> ʒif ʒe wyth me so longe wil dwelle.
> No Latyn wil I speke no waste,
> But English, þat men vse mast,[2]
> Þat can eche man vnderstande,
> Þat is born in Ingelande;
> For þat langage is most chewyd,[3]
> Os wel among lered[4] os lewyd.[5]
> Latyn, as I trowe, can nane
> But þo, þat haueth it in scole tane,[6]
> And somme can Frensche and no Latyn,
> Þat vsed han[7] cowrt and dwellen þerein,
> And somme can of Latyn a party,
> Þat can of Frensche but febly;
> And somme vnderstonde wel Englysch,
> Þat can noþer Latyn nor Frankys.

---

[1] North English Homily Cycle, ed. John Small, *English Metrical Homilies from Manuscripts of the Fourteenth Century* (Edinburgh, 1862), pp. 3–4:

> Therefore will I of my poverty
> Show something that I have in heart
> In English tongue that all may
> Understand what I will say;
> For laymen have more need
> God's word for to hear
> Than clerks that look in their *Mirror*
> And see in books how they shall live.
> And both clerk and layman
> Can understand English,
> Who were born in England
> And long have been dwelling therein,
> But all men certainly cannot
> Understand Latin and French.
> Therefore methinks it is alms (an act of charity)
> To work some good thing in English
> That both learned and lay may know.

The allusion to clerks that have their *Mirror* is probably a reference to the *Miroir*, or *Les Evangiles des Domees*, an Anglo-French poem by Robert of Gretham.

[2] most   [3] showed, in evidence   [4] learned   [5] unlearned, lay
[6] taken, learned   [7] have

Boþe lered and lewed, olde and ȝonge,
Alle vnderstonden english tonge.[1]   (ll, 61–78)

Here the writer acknowledges that some people who have lived at court know French, but he is quite specific in his statement that old and young, learned and unlearned, all understand the English tongue. Our third quotation, although the briefest, is perhaps the most interesting of all. It is from the opening lines of a romance called *Arthur and Merlin*, written not later than the year 1325 and probably in the opening years of the century:

Riȝt is, þat Inglische[2] Inglische[3] vnderstond,
Þat was born in Inglond;
Freynsche vse þis gentilman,
Ac euerich[4] Inglische can.[5]
Mani noble ich haue yseiȝe[6]
Þat no Freynsche couþe[7] seye.[8]

The special feature of this passage is not the author's statement that everybody knows English, which we have come to expect, but his additional assertion that at a time when gentlemen still "used" French he had seen many a noble who could not speak that language.

Although, as these quotations show, English was now understood by everyone, it does not follow that French was unknown or had entirely gone out of use. It still had some currency at the court although English had largely taken its place; we may be sure that the court that Chaucer knew talked English even if its members commonly wrote and often read French. A dozen books owned by Richard II in 1385, most of them romances, seem from their titles to have been all French, though he spoke English fluently and Gower wrote the *Confessio Amantis* for him in English. Robert of Brunne, who wrote his *Chronicle* in 1338, implies that French is chiefly the language of two groups, the educated classes and the French.[9] That in England French was the accomplishment mainly of the educated in the fourteenth century is implied by the words of Avarice in *Piers Plowman* (B-text, V, 239): "I lerned nevere rede on boke, And I can no Frenche in feith but of the ferthest ende of Norfolke." Among the learned we must include the legal profession and the church. French was the language of lawyers and of the law courts down to 1362. We may likewise believe that ecclesiastics could still commonly speak French. We are told that Hugh of

---

[1] *Englische Studien*, 7 (1884), 469.
[2] English people   [3] English language   [4] everybody   [5] knows   [6] seen
[7] could   [8] *Arthour and Merlin*, ed. E. Kölbing (Leipzig, 1890).
[9] Frankis spech is cald Romance,
So sais clerkes & men of France. (Prol. to part II.)

Eversdone, the cellarer, who was elected abbot of St. Albans in 1308, knew English and French very well, though he was not so competent in Latin;[1] and an amusing story of the bishop of Durham who was consecrated in 1318 attests his knowledge of French while revealing an even greater ignorance of the language of the service.[2] We have already seen that French was kept up as the language of conversation in the monasteries of St. Augustine at Canterbury and St. Peter at Westminster. It was so also at St. Mary's Abbey, York, as appears from the *Ordinal* drawn up in 1390, and was probably the case generally. Chaucer's prioress spoke French, though she told her tale to the Canterbury pilgrims in English, and the instructions from the abbot of St. Albans to the nuns of Sopwell in 1338 are in French.[3] But clerks of the younger generation in Langland's time seem to have been losing their command of the language.[4] Outside the professions, French seems to have been generally known to government officials and the more substantial burgesses in the towns. It was the language of parliament and local administration. The business of town councils and the gilds seems to have been ordinarily transacted in French, though there are scattered instances of the intrusion of English. French was very common at this time in letters and dispatches and local records, and was probably often written by people who did not habitually speak it. An anonymous chronicle of about 1381 is written in French, but, as the editor remarks, it is the French of a man who is obviously thinking in English;[5] and the poet Gower, who wrote easily in Latin, French, and English, protests that he knows little French.[6] In spite of Trevisa's statement (see § 106) about the efforts of " uplondish " men to learn French in order to liken themselves to gentlemen,[7] French can have had but little

---

[1] Walsingham, *Gesta Abbatum*, II, 113–14. (Rolls Series.)

[2] Although he had been carefully coached for his consecration, he stumbled at the word *metropoliticae*, and finally, when he could not pronounce it, ejaculated, *Seit pur dite* (let it be considered as said). Later, after making a vain effort to achieve the word *aenigmate*, he remarked to those present, *Par Seint Lowys, il ne fu pas curteis, qui ceste parole ici escrit*. (Robert de Graystanes, *Historia . . . Ecclesiae Dunelmensis*. Chap. 48, in *Historiae Dunelmensis Scriptores Tres*, Surtees Soc., IX, 118.)

[3] *Monast. Ang.*, III, 365–66.

[4]   Gramer, the grounde of al, bigyleth now children;
          For is none of this newe clerkes, who so nymeth hede,
          That can versifye faire ne formalich enditen;
          Ne nou3t on amonge an hundreth that an auctour can construe,
          Ne rede a lettre in any langage but in Latyn or in Englissh.
                              (*Piers Plowman*, B-text, XV, 365–69)

[5] *The Anonimalle Chronicle, 1333 to 1381, from a MS. written at St. Mary's Abbey, York*, ed. V. H. Galbraith (Manchester, 1927), p. xvii.

[6] *Mirour de l'Omme*, ed. Macaulay, I, 21775.

[7] It must be remembered that the term "uplondish" does not only refer to the rural population but doubtless includes everyone outside of London, just as the word "country" on London pillar-boxes does today.

currency among the middle classes outside of the towns.[1] It is interesting to note that the chief disadvantage that Trevisa sees in the fact that children no longer learn French is that "it will be harm for them if they shall pass the sea and travel in strange lands," though his scholarly instincts led him to add "and in many other places."

It is clear that the people who could speak French in the fourteenth century were bilingual. Edward III knew English,[2] and Richard II addressed the people in it at the time of Wat Tyler's rebellion. Outside the royal family it would seem that even among the governing class English was the language best understood. When Edward III called a parliament in 1337 to advise him about prosecuting his claim to the throne of France, it was addressed by a lawyer who, according to Froissart, was very competent in Latin, French, and English. And he spoke in English, although, as we have seen, French was still the usual language of parliament, "to the end that he might be better understood by all, for one always knows better what one wishes to say and propose in the language to which he is introduced in his infancy than in any other."[3] Ten years before, a similar incident occurred when the privileges which Edward II confirmed to the city of London were read before the mayor, aldermen, and citizens assembled in the Guildhall and were explained to them in English by Andrew Horn, the city chamberlain.[4] In 1362 the chancellor opened parliament for the first time with a speech in English.[5] English likewise appears at this time in the acts of towns and gilds. In 1388 parliament required all gilds to submit a report on their foundation, statutes, property, etc. The returns are mostly in Latin, but forty-nine of them are in English, outnumbering those in French.[6] The Custumal of Winchester, which exists in an Anglo-Norman text of about 1275, was translated into English at the end of the fourteenth century.[7] Finally, in the last year of the century, in

[1] It is a mistake to argue, as has been several times done, from the *Contes Moralisés* of Nichole Bozon that French was widely known among the English middle class. Though this Minorite of the later fourteenth century seems to have the middle class chiefly in mind, these brief items are not sermons, but anecdotes and memoranda for sermons, and do not furnish any evidence that the author or those for whose help he made the collection actually preached in French. They are like the similar collections in Latin.

[2] O. F. Emerson, "English or French in the Time of Edward III," *Romanic Rev.*, 7 (1916), 127–43.

[3] *Œuvres de Froissart*, ed. Kervyn de Lettenhove, II, 326.

[4] *Chronicles of the Reigns of Edward I and Edward II*, I, 325. (Rolls Series.) Andrew Horn was a member of the Fishmongers' Company and the author of *Le Miroir des Justices*. He could doubtless have explained the privileges in French.

[5] English was again used in 1363, 1365, and 1381. *Rotuli Parliamentorum*, II, 268, 275, 283; III, 98.

[6] Printed in Toulmin Smith, *English Gilds*. (Early English Text Soc., O.S. 40.)

[7] J. S. Furley, *The Ancient Usages of the City of Winchester* (Oxford, 1927), p. 3.

the proceedings at the deposition of Richard II, the articles of accusation were read to the assembled parliament in Latin and English, as was the document by which Richard renounced the throne. The order deposing him was read to him in English, and Henry IV's speeches claiming the throne and later accepting it were delivered in English.[1] Thus the proceedings would seem to have been conspicuous for the absence of French. There can be no doubt in the light of instances such as these that in the fourteenth century English is again the mother tongue of all England.

105. *English in the Law Courts.* In 1362 an important step was taken toward restoring English to its rightful place as the language of the country. For a long time, probably from a date soon after the Conquest, French had been the language of all legal proceedings. But in the fourteenth century such a practice was clearly without justification, and in 1356 the mayor and aldermen of London ordered that proceedings in the sheriffs' court of London and Middlesex be in English.[2] Six years later, in the parliament held in October 1362, the *Statute of Pleading* was enacted, to go into effect toward the end of the following January:

> Because it is often shewed to the king by the prelates, dukes, earls, barons, and all the commonalty, of the great mischiefs which have happened to divers of the realm, because the laws, customs, and statutes of this realm be not commonly known in the same realm; for that they be pleaded, shewed, and judged in the French tongue, which is much unknown in the said realm; so that the people which do implead, or be impleaded, in the king's court, and in the courts of others, have no knowledge nor understanding of that which is said for them or against them by their serjeants and other pleaders; and that reasonably the said laws and customs shall be most quickly learned and known, and better understood in the tongue used in the said realm, and by so much every man of the said realm may the better govern himself without offending of the law, and the better keep, save, and defend his heritage and possessions; and in divers regions and countries, where the king, the nobles, and others of the said realm have been, good governance and full right is done to every person, because that their laws and customs be learned and used in the tongue of the country: the king, desiring the good governance and tranquillity of his people, and to put out and eschew the harms

---

[1] *Annales Ricardi II et Henrici IV*, pp. 281–86 (Rolls Series); *Rotuli Parliamentorum*, III, 423; J. H. Wylie, *History of England under Henry the Fourth*, I, 4–18.

[2] R. R. Sharpe, *Calendar of Letter-Books . . . of the City of London*, Letter-Book G (London, 1905), p. 73. There are sporadic instances of the use of English in other courts even earlier. Thus in the action against the Templars in 1310 "frater Radulphus de Malton, ordinis Templi . . . deposuit in Anglico." Wilkins, *Concilia* (1737), II, 357; cf. also p. 391.

and mischiefs which do or may happen in this behalf by the occasions aforesaid, hath ordained and established by the assent aforesaid, that all pleas which shall be pleaded in his courts whatsoever, before any of his justices whatsoever, or in his other places, or before any of his other ministers whatsoever, or in the courts and places of any other lords whatsoever within the realm, shall be pleaded, shewed, defended, answered, debated, and judged in the English tongue, and that they be entered and enrolled in Latin.[1]

All this might have been said in one sentence: Hereafter all lawsuits shall be conducted in English. But it is interesting to note that the reason frankly stated for the action is that "French is much unknown in the said realm." Custom dies hard, and there is some reason to think that the statute was not fully observed at once. It constitutes, however, the official recognition of English.

106. *English in the Schools.*   From a time shortly after the Conquest, French had replaced English as the language of the schools. In the twelfth century there are patriotic complaints that Bede and others formerly taught the people in English, but their lore is lost; other people now teach our folk.[2] A statement of Ranulph Higden in the fourteenth century shows that in his day the use of French in the schools was quite general. At the end of the first book of his *Polychronicon* (c. 1327), a universal history widely circulated, he attributes the corruption of the English language which he observes in part to this cause:

> This apayrynge of þe burþe tunge is bycause of tweie þinges; oon is for children in scole aȝenst þe vsage and manere of alle oþere naciouns beeþ compelled for to leue hire owne langage, and for to construe hir lessouns and here þynges in Frensche, and so þey haueþ seþ þe Normans come first in to Engelond. Also gentil men children beeþ i-tauȝt to speke Frensche from þe tyme þat þey beeþ i-rokked in here cradel, and kunneþ speke and playe wiþ a childes broche; and vplondisshe men wil likne hym self to gentil men, and fondeþ wiþ greet besynesse for to speke Frensce, for to be [more] i-tolde of.[3]

However, after the Black Death, two Oxford schoolmasters were responsible for a great innovation in English education. When the

---

[1] *Statutes of the Realm*, I, 375–76. The original is in French. The petition on which it was based is in *Rotuli Parliamentorum*, II, 273.

[2] *Anglia*, 3 (1880), 424.

[3] *Polychronicon*, II, 159 (Rolls Series), from the version of Trevisa made 1385–1387.

translator of Higden's book, John Trevisa, came to the above passage he added a short but extremely interesting observation of his own:

> Þis manere was moche i-vsed to fore þe firste moreyn and is siþþe sumdel i-chaunged; for Iohn Cornwaile, a maister of grammer, chaunged þe lore in gramer scole and construccioun of Frensche in to Englische; and Richard Pencriche lerned þat manere techynge of hym and oþere men of Pencrich; so þat now, þe ȝere of oure Lorde a þowsand þre hundred and foure score and fyue, and of þe secounde kyng Richard after þe conquest nyne, in alle þe gramere scoles of Engelond, children leueþ Frensche and construeþ and lerneþ an Englische, and haueþ þerby auauntage in oon side and disauauntage in anoþer side; here auauntage is, þat þey lerneþ her gramer in lasse tyme þan children were i-woned to doo; disauauntage is þat now children of gramer scole conneþ na more Frensche þan can hir lift heele, and þat is harme for hem and þey schulle passe þe see and trauaille in straunge landes and in many oþer places. Also gentil men haueþ now moche i-left for to teche here children Frensche.

By a fortunate circumstance we know that there was a John Cornwall licensed to teach Latin grammar in Oxford at this time; his name appears in the accounts of Merton in 1347, as does that of Pencrich a few years later.[1] The innovation was probably due to a scarcity of competent teachers. At any rate, after 1349 English began to be used in the schools and by 1385 the practice had become general.

107. *Increasing Ignorance of French in the Fifteenth Century.* The statement already quoted (p. 145) from a writer of the beginning of the fourteenth century to the effect that he had seen many nobles who could not speak French indicates a condition that became more pronounced as time went on. By the fifteenth century the ability to speak French fluently seems to have been looked upon as an accomplishment.[2] Even the ability to write it was becoming less general among people of position. In 1400 George Dunbar, earl of March, in writing to the king in English, says: "And, noble Prince, marvel ye not that I write my letters in English, for that is more clear to my understanding than Latin or French."[3] Another very interesting case is offered by a letter from Richard Kingston, dean of Windsor, addressed to the king in 1403. Out of deference to custom, the dean begins bravely enough in French, but toward the close, when he

---

[1] W. H. Stevenson, "The Introduction of English as the Vehicle of Instruction in English Schools," *Furnivall Miscellany* (Oxford, 1901), pp. 421–29.

[2] Cf. the case of Richard Beauchamp, earl of Warwick, mentioned by Kingsford, *Eng. Hist. Lit.*, p. 195.

[3] *Royal and Historical Letters during the Reign of Henry IV*, I, 23–25. (Rolls Series.

becomes particularly earnest, he passes instinctively from French to English in the middle of a sentence.[1]

An incident that occurred in 1404 seems at first sight to offer an extreme case. The king of France had refused to recognize Henry IV when he seized the English throne, and his kinsman, the count of Flanders, supported him in his refusal. Outrages were soon committed by the French on English subjects, to which the English retaliated, and finally an attempt was made to settle the matter by negotiation. The English representatives included Sir Thomas Swynford[2] and one Nicholas de Ryssheton, who signs himself "Professor of Both Laws," i.e., civil and ecclesiastical. Now there would be nothing remarkable about these negotiations were it not for the fact that several times the English ambassadors complain about the use of French by their French correspondents and ask them to write only in Latin. On two occasions they speak of the French language as being as unknown to them as Hebrew.[3] This statement, if taken at its face value, as has generally been done, is astonishing, to say the least. But it is quite unbelievable. De Ryssheton, as a lawyer, must have known French well.[4] We need not pause over the reasons for the statement.[5] The statement was not true; but the English delegates would not have alleged such a reason for carrying on negotiations in Latin if it had not had a certain plausibility. Ignorance of French must have been quite common among the governing class in England from the beginning of the fifteenth century. Before the middle of the century it was necessary to have a "Secretary in the French

---

[1] *Ibid.*, pp. 155–59. The letter ends in a strange mixture:

"Jeo prie a la Benoit Trinite que vous ottroie bone vie ove tresentier sauntee a treslonge durre, and sende ȝowe sone to ows in helþ and prosperitee; for, in god fey, I hope to Al Mighty God that, ȝef ȝe come ȝoure owne persone, ȝe schulle have the victorie of alle ȝoure enemyes.

"And for salvation of ȝoure Schire and Marches al aboute, treste ȝe nought to no Leutenaunt.

"Escript a Hereford, en tresgraunte haste, a trois de la clocke apres noone, le tierce jour de Septembre."

[2] He was the son of Katherine de Swynford and a fairly prominent person. Indeed he was believed to have been the murderer of Richard II. At any rate he was a strong supporter of Henry IV and was one of Richard's guardians.

[3] The letters are printed in *Royal and Historical Letters during the Reign of Henry IV.*

[4] On one occasion the English king sends him instructions in French.

[5] The explanation is probably to be found in a passage in Froissart (ed. Kervyn de Lettenhove, XV, 114–15) from which it appears that ten years before, the English had had to proceed very warily in negotiating a treaty of peace; they had had trouble before through the use of French. But there was also some feeling against the desire of France to have French recognized as the language of diplomacy. A somewhat similar instance of friction occurred in 1413–1414 when a compromise was finally reached by drawing up an agreement between the two countries in both Latin and French in parallel columns. Cf. J. H. Wylie, *The Reign of Henry the Fifth*, I, 156.

language" among the government officials.[1] At the end of the century Caxton could write: "For the mooste quantyte of the people vnderstonde not latyn ne frensshe here in this noble royame of englond."

108. *French as a Language of Culture and Fashion.*   When French went out of use as a spoken language in England not only was its sphere more restricted but the reasons for its cultivation changed. In the first decade of the fifteenth century, John Barton wrote a *Donet François*, a treatise intended for adults who wished to learn French. It is interesting to note the three reasons which he gives for Englishmen's learning the language. He says nothing about their needing it to communicate among themselves, but says, first, it will enable them to communicate with their neighbors of the realm of France. In the second place, the laws are largely in French. And finally, he says, gentlemen and women willingly write to each other in French. The first of these reasons would be equally valid today. The other two are a heritage of the past, which in time disappeared. Later Caxton in his *Dialogues in French and English* has the merchant chiefly in mind: "Who this booke shall wylle [wish to] lerne may well enterprise or take on honde marchandises fro one land to anothir." But French had been for so long the mark of the privileged class that such cultivation of it as persisted in this century and in after times was prompted largely by the feeling that it was the language of culture and fashion. This feeling was strengthened in the eighteenth century and it is present in the minds of many people today.

109. *The Use of English in Writing.*   The last step which the English language had to make in its gradual ascent was its employment in writing. For here it had to meet the competition of Latin as well as French. The use of Latin for written communication and record was due partly to a habit formed at a time when most people who could write at all could write Latin, partly to its international character, and partly to the feeling that it was a language that had become fixed while the modern languages seemed to be variable, unregulated, and in a constant state of change. Modern languages began to encroach upon this field of Latin at a time when French was still the language of the educated and the socially prominent. French accordingly is the first language in England to dispute the monopoly of Latin in written matter, and only in the fifteenth century does English succeed in displacing both.[2] In private and semiofficial correspondence

---

[1] *Cal. Pat. Rolls, 1436–41*, pp. 41, 471, 555, and later entries in the Close and Patent Rolls.

[2] The widespread use of French in writing, especially in official documents and letters, is chronicled by Helen Suggett, "The Use of French in England in the Later Middle Ages," *Trans. Royal Hist. Soc.*, 4th ser., 28 (1946), 61–83.

French is at its height at about 1350; the earliest English letters appear in the latter part of the century, but there are few before 1400. English letters first occur among the Paston letters and in the Stonor correspondence between 1420 and 1430. After 1450 English letters are everywhere the rule.[1] It is rather similar with wills. The earliest known English will subsequent to the Conquest dates from 1383, and English wills are rare before 1400. But in 1397 the earl of Kent made his will in English, and in 1438 the countess of Stafford in doing likewise said, "I . . . ordeyne and make my testament in English tonge, for my most profit, redyng, and understandyng in yis wise." The wills of Henry IV, Henry V, and Henry VI are all in English.[2]

The fifteenth century also saw the adoption of English for the records of towns and gilds and in a number of branches of the central government. About 1430 a number of towns are seen translating their ordinances and their books of customs into English, and English becomes general in their transactions after 1450. It is so likewise with the gilds. English was used along with French in the ordinances of the London pepperers as early as 1345. At York the ordinances of the crafts begin to be in English from about 1400 on. An interesting resolution of the London brewers, dating about 1422, shows them adopting English by a formal action:

> Whereas our mother tongue, to wit, the English tongue, hath in modern days begun to be honorably enlarged and adorned; for that our most excellent lord king Henry the Fifth hath, in his letters missive, and divers affairs touching his own person, more willingly chosen to declare the secrets of his will [in it]; and for the better understanding of his people, hath, with a diligent mind, procured the common idiom (setting aside others) to be commended by the exercise of writing; and there are many of our craft of brewers who have the knowledge of writing and reading in the said English idiom, but in others, to wit, the Latin and French, before these times used, they do not in any wise understand; for which causes, with many others, it being considered how that the greater part of the lords and trusty commons have begun to make their matters to be noted down in our mother tongue, so we also in our craft, following in some manner their steps, have decreed in future to commit to memory the needful things which concern us.[3]

---

[1] See F. J. Tanquerey, *Recueil de lettres anglo-françaises, 1265–1399* (Paris, 1916), and C. L. Kingsford, *Prejudice and Promise in XVth Century England* (Oxford, 1925), pp. 22–47.

[2] The wills mentioned are all in J. Nichols, *A Collection of All the Wills . . . of the Kings . . .* (London, 1780).

[3] William Herbert, *The History of the Twelve Great Livery Companies of London* (2 vols., London, 1834–1836), I, 106.

The records of parliament tell a similar story. The petitions of the commons, on which statutes were based if they met with approval, are usually in French down to 1423 and seem to have been enrolled in French even when originally presented in English. After 1423 they are often in English.[1] The statutes themselves are generally in Latin down to about 1300, in French until the reign of Henry VII. In 1485 they begin to appear in English alongside of French, and in 1489 French entirely disappears.

The reign of Henry V (1413–1422) seems to have marked the turning point in the use of English in writing.[2] The example of the king in using English in his letters and certain efforts of his to promote the use of English in writing, which we would gladly know more about, are specifically referred to as a precedent in the resolution of the London brewers quoted above. Apparently his brilliant victories over the French at Agincourt and elsewhere gave Englishmen a pride in things English. The end of his reign and the beginning of the next mark the period at which English begins to be generally adopted in writing. If we want a round number, the year 1425 represents very well the approximate date.

110. *Middle English Literature.* The literature written in England during the Middle English period reflects fairly accurately the changing fortunes of English. During the time that French was the language best understood by the upper classes, the books they read or listened to were in French. All of continental French literature was available for their enjoyment, and we have seen above how this source was supplemented by an important body of French poetry written in England (§ 88). The rewards of patronage were seldom to be expected by those who wrote in English; with them we must look for other incentives to writing. Such incentives were most often found among members of the religious body, interested in promoting right living and in the care of souls. Accordingly, the literature in English that has come down to us from this period (1150–1250) is almost exclusively religious or admonitory. The *Ancrene Riwle*, the *Ormulum* (c. 1200), a series of paraphrases and interpretations of Gospel passages, and a group of saints' lives and short homiletic pieces showing the survival of an Old English literary tradition in the southwest are the principal works

---

[1] Cf. H. L. Gray, *The Influence of the Commons on Early Legislation* (Cambridge, 1932), p. 231.

[2] New evidence is constantly coming to light reinforcing this opinion. For example, R. B. Dobson, working with the incredibly rich collection of records preserved by the Dean and Chapter of Durham, observes, "It was precisely in the second decade of the fifteenth century that the monastic and prior's registers reveal the complete and remarkably abrupt extinction of French as a language of written as well as verbal communication." See *Durham Priory, 1400–1450* (Cambridge, 1973), p. 73.

of this class. The two outstanding exceptions are Layamon's *Brut* (c. 1205), a translation of Wace (cf. § 88), and the astonishing debate between *The Owl and the Nightingale* (c. 1195), a long poem in which two birds exchange recriminations in the liveliest fashion. There was certainly a body of popular literature that circulated orally among the people, just as at a later date the English and Scottish popular ballads did, but such literature has left slight traces in this early period. The hundred years from 1150 to 1250 have been justly called the Period of Religious Record. It is not that religious works were not written in French too for the upper classes; it is rather the absence in English of works appealing to courtly tastes that marks the English language at this time as the language of the middle and lower classes.

The separation of the English nobility from France by about 1250 and the spread of English among the upper class is manifest in the next hundred years of English literature. Types of polite literature which had hitherto sufficed in French now appear in English. Of these types the most popular was the romance. Only one English romance exists from an earlier date than 1250, but from this time translations and adaptations from the French begin to be made, and in the course of the fourteenth century their number becomes really large. The religious literature characteristic of the previous period continues; but we now have other types as well. The period from 1250 to 1350 is a Period of Religious and Secular Literature in English and indicates clearly the wider diffusion of the English language.

The general adoption of English by all classes, which had taken place by the latter half of the fourteenth century, gave rise to a body of literature which represents the high point in English literary achievement in the Middle Ages. The period from 1350 to 1400 has been called the Period of Great Individual Writers. The chief name is that of Geoffrey Chaucer (1340–1400), the greatest English poet before Shakespeare. Not to mention his delightful minor poems, he is the author of a long narrative poem telling the story of the unhappy love of *Troilus and Criseyde* and, most famous of his works, the *Canterbury Tales*, which, besides giving us in the general prologue a matchless portrait gallery of contemporary types, constitutes in the variety of the tales a veritable anthology of medieval literature. To this period belong William Langland, the reputed author of a long social allegory, *Piers Plowman* (1362–1387); John Wycliffe (d. 1384), putative translator of the Bible and author of a large and influential body of controversial prose; and the unknown poet who wrote not only the finest of the Middle English romances, *Sir Gawain and the Green Knight*, but three allegorical and religious poems of great beauty. Any one of these men would have made the later fourteenth century an outstanding period in Middle English literature. Together they constitute a striking proof of the secure position the English language had attained.

The fifteenth century is sometimes known as the Imitative Period since so much of the poetry then written was written in emulation of Chaucer. It is also spoken of as a Transition Period, since it covers a large part of the interval between the age of Chaucer and the age of Shakespeare. The period has been unjustly neglected. Writers like Lydgate, Hoccleve, Skelton, and Hawes are not negligible, though admittedly overshadowed by some of their great predecessors, and at the end of the century we have the prose of Malory and Caxton. In the north the Scottish Chaucerians, particularly Henryson, Dunbar, Gawin Douglas, and Lindsay, produced significant work. These men carry on the tradition of English as a literary medium into the Renaissance. Thus, except in the fifteenth century, when little further extension of English was possible, Middle English literature follows and throws interesting light on the fortunes of the English language.

BIBLIOGRAPHY

F. M. Powicke's *The Loss of Normandy, 1189–1204* (Manchester, 1913) offers a good point of departure for the study of conditions affecting the position of English in the latter part of our period. The same author's *The Thirteenth Century* (2nd ed., Oxford, 1962) may also be consulted. The influx of foreigners in the thirteenth century is treated in François Mugnier, *Les Savoyards en Angleterre au XIIIe siècle* (Chambéry, 1890). The reaction against them is well represented by Oliver H. Richardson, *The National Movement in the Reign of Henry III and Its Culmination in the Barons' War* (New York, 1897), which may be supplemented by Charles Bémont's masterly study of *Simon de Montfort* (Oxford, 1930). O. F. Emerson's "English or French in the Time of Edward III," *Romanic Rev.*, 7 (1916), 127–43, offers evidence chiefly drawn from Froissart. On the whole, the best discussion of the Black Death is the little book by G. G. Coulton, *The Black Death* (London, 1929). For estimates of the mortality, see Josiah C. Russell, *British Medieval Population* (Albuquerque, 1948). The later cultivation of French in England is treated in Kathleen Lambley, *The Teaching and Cultivation of the French Language in England during Tudor and Stuart Times, with an Introductory Chapter on the Preceding Period* (Manchester, 1920), and G. T. Clapton and William Stewart, *Les Études françaises dans l'enseignement en Grande-Bretagne* (Paris, 1929). Walter of Bibbesworth's treatise is edited by Annie Owen, *Le Traité de Walter de Bibbesworth sur la langue française* (Paris, 1929), and discussed at length by John Koch, "Der Anglonormannische Traktat des Walter von Bibbesworth in seiner Bedeutung für die Anglistic," *Anglia*, 58 (1934), 30–77. W. H. Stevenson does much to make John Cornwall a real person in "The Introduction of English as the Vehicle of Instruction in English Schools," *Furnivall Miscellany* (Oxford, 1901), pp. 421–29. On individual points the works cited in the footnotes to the chapter should be consulted. Since the original publication of this book the following articles bearing on the relation of French and English may be noted: M. Dominica Legge, "Anglo-Norman and the Historian," *History*, N.S., 26 (1941), 163–75; George E. Woodbine, "The Language of English Law," *Speculum*, 18 (1943), 395–436, parts of which must be used with caution; R. M. Wilson, "English and French in England 1100–1300," *History*, N.S., 28 (1943), 37–60; and two articles by Rolf Berndt which are largely a recapitulation of familiar evidence, "The Linguistic Situation in England from the Norman Conquest to the Loss of Normandy (1066–1204)," *Philologica Pragensia*, 8 (1965), 145–63, and "The Period of the Final Decline of French in Medieval England (Fourteenth and Early Fifteenth Centuries)," *Zeitschrift für Anglistik und Amerikanistik*, 20 (1972), 341–69.

[7]

Middle English

111. *Middle English a Period of Great Change.* The Middle English period (1150–1500) was marked by momentous changes in the English language, changes more extensive and fundamental than those that have taken place at any time before or since. Some of them were the result of the Norman Conquest and the conditions which followed in the wake of that event. Others were a continuation of tendencies that had begun to manifest themselves in Old English. These would have gone on even without the Conquest, but they took place more rapidly because the Norman invasion removed from English those conservative influences that are always felt when a language is extensively used in books and is spoken by an influential educated class. The changes of this period affected English in both its grammar and its vocabulary. They were so extensive in each department that it is difficult to say which group is the more significant. Those in the grammar reduced English from a highly inflected language to an extremely analytic one.[1] Those in the vocabulary involved the loss of a large part of the Old English word-stock and the addition of thousands of words from French and Latin. At the beginning of the period English is a language which must be learned like a foreign tongue; at the end it is Modern English.

112. *Decay of Inflectional Endings.* The changes in English grammar may be described as a general reduction of inflections. Endings of the noun and adjective marking distinctions of number and case and often of gender were so altered in pronunciation as to lose their distinctive form and hence

---

[1] That the change was complete by 1500 has been shown with convincing statistics by Charles C. Fries, "On the Development of the Structural Use of Word-Order in Modern English," *Language*, 16 (1940), 199–208.

their usefulness. To some extent the same thing is true of the verb. This leveling of inflectional endings was due partly to phonetic changes, partly to the operation of analogy. The phonetic changes were simple but far-reaching. The earliest seems to have been the change of final $-m$ to $-n$ wherever it occurred, i.e., in the dative plural of nouns and adjectives and in the dative singular (masculine and neuter) of adjectives when inflected according to the strong declension (see § 43). Thus *mūðum* (to the mouths) > *mūðun*, *gōdum* > *gōdun*. This $-n$, along with the $-n$ of the other inflectional endings, was then dropped (**mūðu*, **gōdu*). At the same time,[1] the vowels *a*, *o*, *u*, *e* in inflectional endings were obscured to a sound, the so-called "indeterminate vowel," which came to be written *e* (less often *i*, *y*, *u*, depending on place and date). As a result, a number of originally distinct endings such as $-a$, $-u$, $-e$, $-an$, $-um$ were reduced generally to a uniform $-e$, and such grammatical distinctions as they formerly expressed were no longer conveyed. Traces of these changes have been found in Old English manuscripts as early as the tenth century.[2] By the end of the twelfth century they seem to have been generally carried out. The leveling is somewhat obscured in the written language by the tendency of scribes to preserve the traditional spelling, and in some places the final *n* was retained even in the spoken language, especially as a sign of the plural (cf. § 113). The effect of these changes on the inflection of the noun and the adjective, and the further simplification that was brought about by the operation of analogy, may be readily shown.

113. The Noun. A glance at the few examples of common noun declensions in Old English given in § 41 will show how seriously the inflectional endings were disturbed. For example, in the first declension the forms *mūð*, *mūðes*, *mūðe*, *mūð* in the singular, and *mūðas*, *mūða*, *mūðum*, *mūðas* in the plural were reduced to three: *mūð*, *mūðes*, and *mūðe*. In such words the $-e$ which was organic in the dative singular and the genitive and dative plural (i.e., stood for an ending in the Old English paradigm) was extended by analogy to the nominative and accusative singular, so that forms like *stōne*, *mūðe* appear, and the only distinctive termination is the $-s$ of the possessive singular and of the nominative and accusative plural. Since these two cases of the plural were those most frequently used, the $-s$ came to be thought of as the sign of the plural and was extended to all

---

[1] The chronology of these changes has been worked out by Samuel Moore in two articles: "Loss of Final *n* in Inflectional Syllables of Middle English," *Language*, 3 (1927), 232–59; "Earliest Morphological Changes in Middle English," *Language*, 4 (1928), 238–66.

[2] Kemp Malone, "When Did Middle English Begin?" *Curme Volume of Linguistic Studies* (Philadelphia, 1930), pp. 110–17.

plural forms. We get thus an inflection of the noun identical with that which we have today.[1] Other declensions suffered even more, so that in many words (*giefu*, *sunu*, etc.) the distinctions of case and even of number were completely obliterated.

In early Middle English only two methods of indicating the plural remained fairly distinctive: the *–s* or *–es* from the strong declension and the *–en* (as in *oxen*) from the weak (see § 41). And for a time, at least in southern England, it would have been difficult to predict that the *–s* would become the almost universal sign of the plural that it has become. Until the thirteenth century in the south the *–en* plural enjoyed great favor, being often added to nouns which had not belonged to the weak declension in Old English. But in the rest of England the *–s* plural (and genitive singular) of the old first declension (masculine) was apparently felt to be so distinctive that it spread rapidly. Its extension took place most quickly in the north. Even in Old English many nouns originally of other declensions had gone over to this declension in the Northumbrian dialect. By 1200 *–s* was the standard plural ending in the north and north Midland areas; other forms were exceptional. Fifty years later it had conquered the rest of the Midlands, and in the course of the fourteenth century it had definitely been accepted all over England as the normal sign of the plural in English nouns. Its spread may have been helped by the early extension of *–s* throughout the plural in Anglo-Norman, but in general it may be considered as an example of the survival of the fittest in language.

114. *The Adjective.* In the adjective the leveling of forms had even greater consequences. Partly as a result of the sound-changes already described, partly through the extensive working of analogy, the form of the nominative singular was early extended to all cases of the singular, and that of the nominative plural to all cases of the plural, both in the strong and the weak declensions. The result was that in the weak declension there was no longer any distinction between the singular and the plural: both ended in *–e* (*blinda* > *blinde* and *blindan* > *blinde*). This was also true of those adjectives under the strong declension whose singular ended in *–e*. By about 1250 the strong declension had distinctive forms for the singular and plural only in certain monosyllabic adjectives which ended in a consonant in Old English (sing. *glad*, plur. *glade*). Under the circumstances the only ending which remained to the adjective was often without distinctive grammatical meaning and its use was not governed by any strong sense of adjectival inflection. When in the fourteenth century final *e* largely

---

[1] For the use of the apostrophe in the possessive, see § 180.

ceased to be pronounced, it became a mere feature of spelling. Except for
a few archaic survivals, such as Chaucer's *oure aller cok*, the adjective had
become an uninflected word by the close of the Middle English period.[1]

115. *The Pronoun.*   The decay of inflections which brought about such
a simplification of the noun and the adjective as has just been described
made it necessary to depend less upon formal indications of gender, case,
and (in adjectives) number, and to rely more upon juxtaposition, word
order, and the use of prepositions to make clear the relation of words in a
sentence. This is apparent from the corresponding decay of pronominal
inflections, where the simplification of forms was due in only a slight
measure to the weakening of final syllables that played so large a part in
the reduction of endings in the noun and the adjective. The loss was
greatest in the demonstratives. Of the numerous forms of *sē, sēo, þæt* (cf.
§ 44) we have only *the* and *that* surviving through Middle English and
continuing in use today. A plural *tho* (those) survived to Elizabethan times.
All the other forms indicative of different gender, number, and case disappeared in most dialects early in the Middle English period. The same
may be said of the demonstrative *þēs, þēos, þis*[2] (this). Everywhere but in
the south the neuter form *þis* came to be used early in Middle English for
all genders and cases of the singular, while the forms of the nominative
plural were similarly extended to all cases of the plural, appearing in
Modern English as *those* and *these*.

In the personal pronoun the losses were not so great. Here there was
greater need for separate forms for the different genders and cases, and
accordingly most of the distinctions that existed in Old English were
retained (see the paradigm given in § 45). However the forms of the dative
and accusative cases were early combined, generally under that of the
dative (*him, her,* [*t*]*hem*). In the neuter the form of the accusative (*h*)*it*
became the general objective case, partly because it was like the nominative,
and partly because the dative *him* would have been subject to confusion
with the corresponding case of the masculine. One other general simplification is to be noted: the loss of the dual number. Language can get along

---

[1] Today we have what may be considered an inflected adjective in such combinations
as *men students, women patrons.*

[2] In Old English it had the following inflection:

	SINGULAR			PLURAL
	Masc.	*Fem.*	*Neut.*	*All Genders*
N.	þēs	þēos	þis	þās
G.	þisses	þisse	þisses	þissa
D.	þissum	þisse	þissum	þissum
A.	þisne	þās	þis	þās
I.	þȳs		þȳs	

without such nice distinctions as are expressed by separate pronouns for two persons and more than two. Accordingly the forms *wit, ʒit,* and their oblique cases did not survive beyond the thirteenth century.

It will be observed that the pronoun *she* had the form *hēo* in Old English. The modern form could have developed from the Old English *hēo,* but it is believed by some that it is due in part at least to the influence of the demonstrative *sēo.* A similar influence of the demonstrative is perhaps to be seen in the forms of the third person plural, *they, their, them,* but here the modern developments were undoubtedly due mainly to Scandinavian influence (cf. § 77). The normal development of the Old English pronouns would have been *hi* (*he*), *here, hem,* and these are very common. In the districts, however, where Scandinavian influence was strong, the nominative *hi* began early to be replaced by the Scandinavian form *þei* (O.N. *þeir*), and somewhat later a similar replacement occurred in the other cases, *their* and *them.* The new forms were adopted more slowly farther south, and the usual inflection in Chaucer is *thei, here, hem.* But by the end of the Middle English period the forms *they, their, them* may be regarded as the normal English plurals.

116. The Verb. Apart from some leveling of inflections and the weakening of endings in accordance with the general tendency,[1] the principal changes in the verb during the Middle English period were the serious losses suffered by the strong conjugation (see §§ 117–18). This conjugation, although including some of the most important verbs in the language, was relatively small[2] as compared with the large and steadily growing body of weak verbs. While an occasional verb developed a strong past tense or past participle by analogy with similar strong verbs, new verbs formed from nouns and adjectives or borrowed from other languages were regularly conjugated as weak. Thus the minority position of the strong conjugation was becoming constantly more appreciable. After the Norman Conquest the loss of native words further depleted the ranks of the strong verbs. Those that survived were exposed to the influence of the majority, and many have changed over in the course of time to the weak inflection.

117. Losses among the Strong Verbs. Nearly a third of the strong verbs

---

[1] For example, the *–an* of the Old English infinitive became *–en* and later *–e:* O.E. *drīfan* > M.E. *drīven* > *drīve.*

[2] The facts stated in this section are based upon collections for 333 strong (and reduplicating) verbs in Old English. This number includes a few verbs for which only isolated forms occur and one (**stecan*) which is not recorded at all, although its existence is to be inferred from its surviving forms in Middle English.

in Old English seem to have died out early in the Middle English period. In any case about ninety of them have left no traces in written records after 1150. Some of them may have been current for a time in the spoken language, but except where an occasional verb survives in a modern dialect they are not recorded. Some were rare in Old English and others were in competition with weak verbs of similar derivation and meaning which superseded them. In addition to verbs that are not found at all after the Old English period there are about a dozen more that appear only in Layamon (c. 1205) or in certain twelfth-century texts based directly on the homilies of Ælfric and other Old English works. In other words, more than a hundred of the Old English strong verbs were lost at the beginning of the Middle English period.

But this was not all. The loss has continued in subsequent periods. Some thirty more became obsolete in the course of Middle English, and an equal number, which were still in use in the sixteenth and seventeenth centuries, finally died out except in the dialects, often after they had passed over to the weak conjugation or had developed weak forms alongside the strong. Today more than half of the Old English strong verbs have disappeared completely from the standard language.

118. *Strong Verbs Which Became Weak.* The principle of analogy—the tendency of language to follow certain patterns and adapt a less common form to a more familiar one—is well exemplified in the further history of the strong verbs. The weak conjugation offered a fairly consistent pattern for the past tense and the past participle, whereas there was much variety in the different classes of the strong verb. We say *sing—sang—sung*, but *drive—drove—driven, fall—fell—fallen*, etc. At a time when English was the language chiefly of the lower classes and largely removed from the restraining influences of education and a literary standard, it was natural that many speakers should wrongly apply the pattern of weak verbs to some which should have been strong. The tendency was not unknown even in Old English. Thus *rædan* (to advise) and *sceððan* (to injure) had already become weak in Old English, while other verbs show occasional weak forms.[1] In the thirteenth century the trend becomes clear in the written literature. Such verbs as *bow, brew, burn, climb, flee, flow, help, mourn, row, step, walk, weep* were then undergoing change. By the fourteenth century the movement was at its height. No less than thirty-two verbs in

---

[1] E.g., *dwīnan* (to disappear), *rēocan* (to smoke). Ten strong verbs had developed weak forms by the twelfth century. Doubtless most of these weak forms were of occasional occurrence in Old English though they have not been recorded.

addition to those already mentioned now show weak forms. After this there are fewer changes. The impulse seems to have been checked, possibly by the steady rise of English in the social scale and later by the stabilizing effect of printing. At all events the fifteenth century shows only about a dozen new weak formations and in the whole modern period there are only about as many more.

In none of the many verbs which have thus become weak was the change from the strong conjugation a sudden one. Strong forms continued to be used while the weak ones were growing up, and in many cases they continued in use long after the weak inflection had become well established. Thus *oke* as the past tense of *ache* was still written throughout the fifteenth century although the weak form *ached* had been current for a hundred years. In the same way we find *stope* beside *stepped, rewe* beside *rowed, clew* beside *clawed.* In a good many cases the strong forms remained in the language well into modern times. *Climb,* which was conjugated as a weak verb as early as the thirteenth century, still has an alternative past tense *clomb* not only in Chaucer and Spenser but in Dryden, and the strong past tense *crope* was more common than *crept* down to Shakespeare's day. *Low* for *laughed, shove* for *shaved, yold* for *yielded,* etc., were still used in the sixteenth century although these verbs were already passing over to the weak conjugation two centuries before. While the weak forms commonly won out, this was not always the case. Many strong verbs also had weak forms (*blowed* for *blew, knowed* for *knew, teared* for *tore*) which did not survive in the standard speech, while in other cases both forms have continued in use (*cleft—clove, crowed—crew, heaved—hove, sheared— shore, shrived—shrove*).

119. Survival of Strong Participles. For some reason the past participle of strong verbs seems to have been more tenacious than the past tense. In a number of verbs weak participles are later in appearing and the strong form often continued in use after the verb had definitely become weak. In the verb *beat* the participle *beaten* has remained the standard form, while in a number of other verbs the strong participle (*cloven, graven, hewn, laden, molten, mown, (mis)shapen, shaven, sodden, swollen*) are still used, especially as adjectives.

120. Surviving Strong Verbs. When we subtract the verbs that have been lost completely and the eighty-one that have become weak, there remain just sixty-eight of the Old English strong verbs in the language today. To this number may be added thirteen verbs which are conjugated in both ways or have kept one strong form. These figures indicate how extensive has been the loss of strong verbs in the language. Beside this loss the number of new strong formations has been negligible.[1] Since the irregularity of such verbs constitutes a difficulty in language, the loss in this case must be considered a gain.

The surviving strong verbs have seldom come down to the present day in the form which would represent the normal development of their principal parts in Old English. In all periods of the language they have been subjected to various forms of leveling and analogical influence from one class to another. For example, the verb *to slay* had in Old English the forms *slēan—slōg—slōgon—slægen*. These would normally have become *slea* (pronounced *slee*)—*slough*—*slain*, and the present tense *slea* actually existed down to the seventeenth century. The modern *slay* is reformed from the past participle. The past tense *slew* is due to the analogy of preterites like *blew, grew*. In Old English the past tense commonly had a different form in the singular and the plural,[2] and in two large classes of verbs the vowel of the plural was also like that of the past participle (e.g., *bindan— band—bundon—bunden*). Consequently, although normally the singular form survived in Modern English, in many cases the vowel of the plural or of the past participle has taken its place. Thus *cling, sting, spin*, etc., should have had a past tense *clang, stang, span* (like *sing*), but these forms have been replaced by *clung, stung, spun* from the plural and the past participle. The past tense of *slide* should have been *slode*, but the plural and the past participle had *i* and we now say *slide—slid—slid*. Sometimes a verb has changed from one class to another. *Break* belonged originally to the fifth class of strong verbs, and had it remained there, would have had a past participle *breken*. But in Old English it was confused with verbs of the fourth class, which had *o* in the past participle, whence our form *broken*. This form has now spread to the past tense. We should be saying *brack* or *brake*, and the latter is still used in the Bible, but except in biblical language the current form is now *broke*. *Speak* has had a similar development. Almost every strong verb in the language has an interesting

---

[1] There are fifteen such verbs. *Strive* (from French) has been inflected on the pattern of *drive*, as have *thrive* and *rive* (both from Old Norse). *Dive* has in recent years developed a past tense *dove*. Since the eighteenth century *stave* has had a strong form *stove*. So, too, has *reeve*, a nautical term. *Wear—wore—worn*, a weak verb in Old English, has been reformed on the analogy of verbs like *bear* and *swear*. *Spat* has been the past tense of *spit* since the sixteenth century, and the strong forms of *stick* date from the same time. An analogous formation *dug* appears as a past participle at this date and since the eighteenth century has been used as the past tense. *Fling, ring*, and *string* are conjugated like *cling, sting*, and *swing*. *Hide* and occasionally *chide* have strong past participles like *ride—ridden*. *Tug* and *drug* (like *dug*) are sometimes heard for *tagged* and *dragged*, but are not in standard use. A few verbs like *show* have developed past participles on the analogy of *know*.

[2] The second person singular had the vowel of the plural.

form-history, but our present purpose will be sufficiently served by these few examples of the sort of fluctuation and change that was going on all through the Middle English period and has not yet ended.

121. *Loss of Grammatical Gender*. One of the consequences of the decay of inflections described above was the elimination of that troublesome feature of language, grammatical gender. As explained in § 42, the gender of Old English nouns was not often determined by meaning. Sometimes it was in direct contradiction with the meaning. Thus *woman* (O.E. *wīf-mann*) was masculine, because the second element in the compound was masculine; *wife* and *child*, like German *Weib* and *Kind*, were neuter. Moreover the gender of nouns in Old English was not so generally indicated by the declension as it is in a language like Latin. Instead it was revealed chiefly by the concord of the strong adjective and the demonstratives. These by their distinctive endings generally showed, at least in the singular, whether a noun was masculine, feminine, or neuter. When the inflections of these gender-distinguishing words were reduced to a single ending for the adjective, and the fixed forms of *the*, *this*, *that*, *these*, and *those* for the demonstratives, the support for grammatical gender was removed. The weakening of inflections and the confusion and loss of the old gender proceeded in a remarkably parallel course. In the north, where inflections weakened earliest, grammatical gender disappeared first. In the south it lingered longer because there the decay of inflections was slower.

Our present method of determining gender was no sudden invention of Middle English times. The recognition of sex which lies at the root of natural gender is shown in Old English by the noticeable tendency to use the personal pronouns in accordance with natural gender, even when such use involves a clear conflict with the grammatical gender of the antecedent. For example, the pronoun *it* in *Etað þisne hlāf* (masculine), *hit is mīn līchama* (Ælfric's Homilies) is exactly in accordance with modern usage when we say, *Eat this bread, it is my body*. Such a use of the personal pronouns is clearly indicative of the feeling for natural gender even while grammatical gender was in full force. With the disappearance of grammatical gender the idea of sex became the only factor in determining the gender of English nouns.

122. *Grammatical Changes and the Norman Conquest*. It is a general observation that languages borrow words but do not borrow their grammar from other languages. The changes which affected the grammatical structure of English after the Norman Conquest were not the result of contact with the French language. Certain idioms and syntactical usages that appear in Middle English are clearly the result of such contact.[1] But the decay of inflections and the confusion of forms that constitute the really significant development in Middle English grammar are the result of the Norman Conquest only in so far as that event brought about conditions favorable to such changes. By making English the language mainly of uneducated people, the Norman Conquest made it easier for grammatical changes to go forward unchecked. Beyond this it is not to be considered a factor in such changes.

123. *French Influence on the Vocabulary.* While the loss of inflections and the consequent simplification of English grammar were thus only indirectly due to the use of French in England, French influence is much more direct and observable upon the vocabulary. Where two languages exist side by side for a long time and the relations between the people speaking them are as intimate as they were in England, a considerable transference of words from one language to the other is inevitable. As is generally the case, the interchange was to some extent mutual. A good many English words found their way into the French spoken in England. We are naturally less interested in them, since they concern rather the history of the Anglo-Norman language. Their number was not so large as that of the French words introduced into English. English, representing an inferior culture, had more to learn from French, and there were other factors involved. The number of French words that poured into English was unbelievably great. There is nothing comparable to it in the previous or subsequent history of the language.

Although this influx of French words was brought about by the victory of the Conqueror and by the political and social consequences of that victory, it was neither sudden nor immediately apparent. Rather it began slowly and continued with varying tempo for a long time. Indeed it can hardly be said to have ever stopped. The large number of French words borrowed during the Middle Ages has made it easy for us to go on borrowing, and the close cultural relations between France and England in all subsequent periods have furnished a constant opportunity for the transfer of words. But there was a time in the centuries following the Conquest

---

[1] F. H. Sykes, *French Elements in Middle English* (Oxford, 1899) makes an attempt to support this view. The most extensive treatment of the subject is A. A. Prins, *French Influence in English Phrasing* (Leiden, 1952), supplemented by articles in *English Studies*, vols. 40–41. A striking array of instances in which English reflects the use of prepositions and adverbs in French, Latin, and Danish is given in H. T. Price, *Foreign Influences on Middle English* (Ann Arbor, 1947; *Univ. of Michigan Contributions in Modern Philology*, no. 10). The standard work on Middle English syntax is Tauno F. Mustanoja, *A Middle English Syntax*, part 1 (Helsinki, 1960). Part 2 is in preparation.

when this movement had its start and a stream of French words poured into English with a momentum that continued until toward the end of the Middle English period.

In this movement two stages can be observed, an earlier and a later, with the year 1250 as the approximate dividing line. The borrowings of the first stage differ from those of the second in being much less numerous, in being more likely to show peculiarities of Anglo-Norman phonology, and, especially, in the circumstances that brought about their introduction. When we study the French words appearing in English before 1250, roughly 900 in number, we find that many of them were such as the lower classes would become familiar with through contact with a French-speaking nobility (*baron, noble, dame, servant, messenger, feast, minstrel, juggler, largess*). Others, such as *story, rime, lay, douzepers* (the twelve peers of the Charlemagne romances), obviously owed their introduction into English to literary channels. The largest single group among the words that came in early was associated with the church, where the necessity for the prompt transference of doctrine and belief from the clergy to the people is sufficient to account for the frequent transfer of words. In the period after 1250 the conditions under which French words had been making their way into English were supplemented by a new and powerful factor: those who had been accustomed to speak French were turning increasingly to the use of English. Whether to supply deficiencies in the English vocabulary or in their own imperfect command of that vocabulary, or perhaps merely yielding to a natural impulse to use a word long familiar to them and to those they addressed, the upper classes carried over into English an astonishing number of common French words. In changing from French to English they transferred much of their governmental and administrative vocabulary, their ecclesiastical, legal, and military terms, their familiar words of fashion, food, and social life, the vocabulary of art, learning, and medicine. In general we may say that in the earlier Middle English period the French words introduced into English were such as men speaking one language often learn from those speaking another; in the century and a half following 1250, when all classes were speaking or learning to speak English, they were also such words as people who had been accustomed to speak French would carry over with them into the language of their adoption. Only in this way can we understand the nature and extent of the French importations in this period.

124. *Governmental and Administrative Words.* We should expect that English would owe many of its words dealing with government and administration to the language of those who for more than two hundred years made public affairs their chief concern. The words *government, govern, administer* might appropriately introduce a list of such words. It would include such fundamental terms as *crown, state, empire, realm, reign, royal, prerogative, authority, sovereign, majesty, scepter, tyrant, usurp, oppress, court, council, parliament, assembly, statute, treaty, alliance, record, repeal, adjourn, tax, subsidy, revenue, tally, exchequer.* Intimately associated with the idea of government are also words like *subject, allegiance, rebel, traitor, treason, exile, public, liberty.* The word *office* and the titles of many offices are likewise French: *chancellor, treasurer, chamberlain, marshal, governor, councilor, minister, viscount, warden, castellan, mayor, constable, coroner,* and even the humble *crier.* Except for the words *king* and *queen, lord, lady,* and *earl,* most designations of rank are French: *noble, nobility, peer, prince, princess, duke, duchess, count, countess, marquis, baron, squire, page,* as well as such words as *courtier, retinue,* and titles of respect like *sir, madam, mistress.* The list might well be extended to include words relating to the economic organization of society—*manor, demesne, bailiff, vassal, homage, peasant, bondman, slave, servant,* and *caitiff*—since they often have a political or administrative aspect.

125. Ecclesiastical Words. The church was scarcely second to the government as an object of Norman interest and ambition. The higher clergy, occupying positions of wealth and power, were, as we have seen, practically all Normans. Ecclesiastical preferment opened the way to a career that often led to the highest political offices at court. In monasteries and religious houses French was for a long time the usual language. Accordingly we find in English such French words as *religion, theology, sermon, homily, sacrament, baptism, communion, confession, penance, prayer, orison, lesson, passion, psalmody;* such indications of rank or class as *clergy, clerk, prelate, cardinal, legate, dean, chaplain, parson, pastor, vicar, sexton, abbess, novice, friar, hermit;* the names of objects associated with the service or with the religious life, such as *crucifix, crosier, miter, surplice, censer, incense, lectern, image, chancel, chantry, chapter, abbey, convent, priory, hermitage, cloister, sanctuary;* words expressing such fundamental religious or theological concepts as *creator, savior, trinity, virgin, saint, miracle, mystery, faith, heresy, schism, reverence, devotion, sacrilege, simony, temptation, damnation, penitence, contrition, remission, absolution, redemption, salvation, immortality,* and the more general virtues of *piety, sanctity, charity, mercy, pity, obedience,* as well as the word *virtue* itself. We should include also a number of adjectives, like *solemn, divine, reverend, devout,* and verbs, such as *preach, pray, chant, repent, confess, adore, sacrifice, convert, anoint, ordain.*

126. *Law.* French was so long the language of the law courts in England that the greater part of the English legal vocabulary comes from the language of the conquerors. The fact that we speak of *justice* and *equity* instead of *gerihte, judgment* rather than *dom* (doom), *crime* in place of *synn, gylt, undæd*, etc., shows how completely we have adopted the terminology of French law. Even where the Old English word survives it has lost its technical sense. In the same way we say *bar, assize, eyre, plea, suit, plaintiff, defendant, judge, advocate, attorney, bill, petition, complaint, inquest, summons, hue and cry, indictment, jury, juror, panel, felon, evidence, proof, bail, ransom, mainpernor, judgment, verdict, sentence, decree, award, fine, forfeit, punishment, prison, gaol, pillory.* We have likewise a rich array of verbs associated with legal processes: *sue, plead, implead, accuse, indict, arraign, depose, blame, arrest, seize, pledge, warrant, assail, assign, judge, condemn, convict, award, amerce, distrain, imprison, banish, acquit, pardon.* The names of many crimes and misdemeanors are French: *felony, trespass, assault, arson, larceny, fraud, libel, slander, perjury, adultery,* and many others. Suits involving property brought into use such words as *property, estate, tenement, chattels, appurtenances, encumbrance, bounds, seisin, tenant, dower, legacy, patrimony, heritage, heir, executor, entail.* Common adjectives like *just, innocent, culpable* have obvious legal import though they are also of wider application.

127. *Army and Navy.* The large part which war played in English affairs in the Middle Ages, the fact that the control of the army and navy was in the hands of those who spoke French, and the circumstance that much of English fighting was done in France all resulted in the introduction into English of a number of French military terms. The art of war has undergone such changes since the days of Hastings and Lewes and Agincourt that many words once common are now obsolete or only in historical use. Their places have been taken by later borrowings, often likewise from French, many of them being words acquired by the French in the course of their wars in Italy during the sixteenth century. Nevertheless we still use medieval French words when we speak of the *army* and the *navy*, of *peace, enemy, arms, battle, combat, skirmish, siege, defense, ambush, stratagem, retreat, soldier, garrison, guard, spy,* and we have kept the names of officers such as *captain, lieutenant, sergeant.* We recognize as once having had greater significance words like *dart, lance, banner, mail, buckler, hauberk, archer, chieftain, portcullis, barbican,* and *moat.* Sometimes we have retained a word while forgetting its original military significance. The word "*Havoc!*" was originally an order giving an army the signal to commence plundering and seizing spoil. Verbs like *to arm, array, harness, brandish,* *vanquish, besiege, defend,* among many, suffice to remind us of this important French element in our vocabulary.

128. *Fashion, Meals, and Social Life.* That the upper classes should have set the standard in fashion and dress is so obvious an assumption that the number of French words belonging to this class occasions no surprise. The words *fashion* and *dress* are themselves French, as are *apparel, habit, gown, robe, garment, attire, cape, cloak, coat, frock, collar, veil, train, chemise, petticoat.* So too are *lace, embroidery, pleat, gusset, buckle, button, tassel, plume,* and the names of such articles as *kerchief, mitten, garter, galoshes,* and *boots.* Verbs like *embellish* and *adorn* often occur in contexts which suggest the word *luxury,* and this in turn carries with it *satin, taffeta, fur, sable, beaver, ermine.* The colors *blue, brown, vermilion, scarlet, saffron, russet,* and *tawny* are French borrowings of this period. *Jewel, ornament, brooch, chaplet, ivory,* and *enamel* point to the luxuries of the wealthy, and it is significant that the names of all the more familiar precious stones are French: *turquoise, amethyst, topaz, garnet, ruby, emerald, sapphire, pearl, diamond,* not to mention *crystal, coral,* and *beryl.*

The French-speaking classes, it would seem, must also be credited with a considerable adornment of the English table. Not only are the words *dinner* and *supper* French, but also the words *feast, repast, collation,* and *mess* (now military). So, too, are *appetite, taste, victuals, viand,* and *sustenance.* One could have found on the medieval menu, had there been one, among the fish, *mackerel, sole, perch, bream, sturgeon, salmon, sardine, oyster, porpoise;* among meats, *venison, beef, veal, mutton, pork, bacon, sausage, tripe,* with a choice of *loin, chine, haunch,* or *brawn,* and with *gravy* included; among fowl, *poultry, pullet, pigeon,* and various game birds mentioned below. One could have *pottage, gruel, toast, biscuit, cream, sugar, olives, salad, lettuce, endive,* and for dessert *almonds,* and many *fruits,* including *raisin, fig, date, grape, orange, lemon, pomegranate, cherry,*[1] *peach,* or a *confection, pasty, tart, jelly, treacle.* Among seasoning and condiments we find *spice, clove, thyme, herb, mustard, vinegar, marjoram, cinnamon, nutmeg.* The verbs *roast, boil, parboil, stew, fry, broach, blanch, grate,* and *mince* describe various culinary processes, and *goblet, saucer, cruet, plate, platter* suggest French refinements in the serving of meals. It is melancholy to think what the English dinner table would have been like had there been no Norman Conquest.

A variety of new words suggest the innovations made by the French in domestic economy and social life. *Arras, curtain, couch, chair, cushion,*

---

[1] Like *fig, cherry* is a reintroduction; cf. pp. 79 and 88.

screen, lamp, lantern, sconce, chandelier, blanket, quilt, coverlet, counter-pane, towel, and *basin* indicate articles of comfort or convenience, while *dais, parlor, wardrobe, closet, pantry, scullery,* and *garner* (storehouse) imply improvements in domestic arrangements. *Recreation, solace, jollity, leisure, dance, carol, revel, minstrel, juggler, fool, ribald, lute, tabor, melody, music, chess, checkers, dalliance,* and *conversation* reveal various aspects of entertainment in a baronial hall, while numerous words associated with hunting and riding are a reflection of the principal outdoor pastime of the noble class: *ambler, courser, hackney, palfrey, rouncy, stallion* for various types of horse, together with *rein, curb, crupper, rowel, curry, trot, stable, harness; mastiff, terrier, spaniel, leash, kennel, scent, retrieve; falcon, merlin, tercelet, mallard, partridge, pheasant, quail, plover, heron, squirrel; forest, park, covert, warren.* One might extend the list to include other activities, with terms like *joust, tournament, pavilion,* but those given are sufficient to show how much the English vocabulary owes to French in matters of domestic and social life.

129. *Art, Learning, Medicine.* The cultural and intellectual interests of the ruling class are reflected in words pertaining to the arts, architecture, literature, learning, and science, especially medicine. Such words as *art, painting, sculpture, music, beauty, color, figure, image, tone* are typical of the first class, while architecture and building have given us *cathedral, palace, mansion, chamber, ceiling, joist, cellar, garret, chimney, lintel, latch, lattice, wicket, tower, pinnacle, turret, porch, bay, choir, cloister, baptistry, column, pillar, base,* and many similar words. Literature is represented by the word itself and by *poet, rime, prose, romance, lay, story, chronicle, tragedy, prologue, preface, title, volume, chapter, quire, parchment, vellum, paper,* and *pen,* and learning by *treatise, compilation, study, logic, geometry, grammar, noun, clause, gender,* together with verbs like *copy, expound,* and *compile.* Among the sciences, medicine has brought in the largest number of early French words still in common use, among them the word *medicine* itself, *chirurgy, physician, surgeon, apothecary, malady, debility, distemper, pain, ague, palsy, pleurisy, gout, jaundice, leper, paralytic, plague, pestilence, contagion, anatomy, stomach, pulse, remedy, ointment, balm, pellet, alum, arsenic, niter, sulphur, alkali, poison.* It is clear that the arts and sciences, being largely cultivated or patronized by the higher classes, owe an important part of their vocabulary to French.

130. *Breadth of the French Influence.* Such classes of words as have been illustrated in the foregoing paragraphs indicate important departments in which the French language altered the English vocabulary in the Middle Ages. But they do not sufficiently indicate how very general was the adoption of French words in every province of life and thought. One has only to glance over a miscellaneous list of words—nouns, adjectives, verbs—to realize how universal was the French contribution. In the noun we may consider the range of ideas in the following list, made up of words which were already in English by 1300: *action, adventure, affection, age, air, bucket, bushel, calendar, carpenter, cheer, city, coast, comfort, cost, country, courage, courtesy, coward, crocodile, cruelty, damage, debt, deceit, dozen, ease, envy, error, face, faggot, fame, fault, flower, folly, force, gibbet, glutton, grain, grief, gum, harlot, honor, hour, jest, joy, labor, leopard, malice, manner, marriage, mason, metal, mischief, mountain, noise, number, ocean, odor, opinion, order, pair, people, peril, person, pewter, piece, point, poverty, powder, power, quality, quart, rage, rancor, reason, river, scandal, seal, season, sign, sound, sphere, spirit, square, strife, stubble, substance, sum, tailor, task, tavern, tempest, unity, use, vision, waste.* The same universality is shown in the adjective. Here the additions were of special importance since Old English was not very well provided with adjective distinctions. From nearly a thousand French adjectives in Middle English we may consider the following selection, all the words in this list being in use in Chaucer's time: *able, abundant, active, actual, amiable, amorous, barren, blank, brief, calm, certain, chaste, chief, clear, common, contrary, courageous, courteous, covetous, coy, cruel, curious, debonair, double, eager, easy, faint, feeble, fierce, final, firm, foreign, frail, frank, gay, gentle, gracious, hardy, hasty, honest, horrible, innocent, jolly, large, liberal, luxurious, malicious, mean, moist, natural, nice, obedient, original, perfect, pertinent, plain, pliant, poor, precious, principal, probable, proper, pure, quaint, real, rude, safe, sage, savage, scarce, second, secret, simple, single, sober, solid, special, stable, stout, strange, sturdy, subtle, sudden, supple, sure, tender, treacherous, universal, usual.* A list of the verbs borrowed at the same time shows equal diversity. Examples are: *advance, advise, aim, allow, apply, approach, arrange, arrive, betray, butt, carry, chafe, change, chase, close, comfort, commence, complain, conceal, consider, continue, count, cover, covet, cry, cull, deceive, declare, defeat, defer, defy, delay, desire, destroy, embrace, enclose, endure, enjoy, enter, err, excuse, flatter, flourish, force, forge, form, furnish, grant, increase, inform, inquire, join, languish, launch, marry, mount, move, murmur, muse, nourish, obey, oblige, observe, pass, pay, pierce, pinch, please, practise, praise, prefer, proceed, propose, prove, purify, pursue, push, quash, quit, receive, refuse, rejoice, relieve, remember, reply, rinse, rob, satisfy, save, scald, serve, spoil, strangle, strive, stun, succeed, summon, suppose, surprise, tax, tempt, trace, travel, tremble, trip, wait, waive, waste, wince.* Finally, the influence of French may be seen in numerous phrases and turns of expression, such as *to take leave, to draw near, to hold one's peace, to come to a head, to do justice,* or *make believe, hand to hand, on the point of, according to, subject to, at large, by heart, in vain, without fail.* In these and other phrases, even when the words are English the pattern is French.[1]

These four lists have been presented for the general impression which they create and as the basis for an inference which they clearly justify. This is, that so far as the vocabulary is concerned, what we have in the influence of the Norman Conquest is a merging of the resources of two languages, a merger in which thousands of words in common use in each language became partners in a reorganized concern. English retains a controlling interest, but French as a large minority stockholder supplements and rounds out the major organization in almost every department.

131. *Anglo-Norman and Central French.* It will be observed that the French words introduced into English as a result of the Norman Conquest often present an appearance quite different from that which they have in Modern French. This is due first of all to subsequent developments which have taken place in the two languages. Thus the O.F. *feste* passed into Middle English as *feste,* whence it has become *feast* in Modern English, while in French the *s* disappeared before other consonants at the end of the twelfth century and we have in Modern French the form *fête.* The same difference appears in *forest—forêt, hostel—hôtel, beast—bête,* and many other words. The difference is not always fully revealed by the spelling but is apparent in the pronunciation. Thus the English words *judge* and *chant* preserve the early French pronunciation of *j* and *ch,* which was softened in French in the thirteenth century to [ʒ] and [ʃ] as in the Modern French *juge* and *chant.* Therefore we may recognize *charge, change, chamber, chase, chair, chimney, just, jewel, journey, majesty, gentle,* and many other words as early borrowings, while such words as *chamois, chaperon, chiffon, chevron, jabot, rouge,* and the like, show by their pronunciation that they have come into the language at a later date. The word *chivalry* is an early word and should be pronounced [tʃ] but it has been influenced by such words as *chevalier* and by Modern French. A similar case is that of words like *police* and *ravine,* where we pronounce the *i* in the French manner. If these words had been borrowed early, we should pronounce them as we do *nice* and *vine.*

A second cause of difference between English words and their French counterparts is the fact that the Anglo-Norman or Anglo-French dialect spoken in England differed from the language of Paris (Central French) in

---

[1] See the references on p. 167.

numerous respects. A few examples will make this clear. In Anglo-Norman[1] initial *ca–* was often retained, whereas it became *cha–, chie–* in Central French.[2] For example, our word *caitiff* represents the A.N. *caitif*, whereas the Central French form was *chaitif*. In the same way are explained words like *carry, carriage, case* (box), *cauldron, carrion*, etc., since the corresponding words in the dialect of Paris were pronounced with *ch* (*charrier, chaudron*, etc.). In some cases English has taken over the same word in both its Norman and its Central French form. Thus A.N. *catel* corresponds to Central French *chatel:* one gives us our word *cattle*, the other *chattel(s)*. The English verb *catch* represents the Anglo-Norman *cachier*, while the Central French *chacier* (Modern French *chasser*) appears in the English *chase*. Or we may take another peculiarity of Anglo-Norman which appears in English. It is a well-known fact that Central French showed an early avoidance of the *w–* sound, both separately and in combination with other consonants, and whether found in Latin or in words borrowed from the Germanic languages. But the dialects of northern and especially northeastern France, possibly because of their proximity to Flemish and Dutch, showed less hostility to this sound and it accordingly is found in Anglo-Norman. And so we have English *wicket* representing the old Norman French *wiket*, which became in the Paris dialect *guichet*, the form which it has in Modern French. In the same way *waste* (A.N. *waster*) was in Central French *guaster* or *gaster* (Mod. F. *gâter*). Other examples are *wasp* (F. *guêpe*), *warrant* (F. *garantir*), *reward* (F. *régarder*), *wardrobe, wait, warden* (cf. *guardian*, from Central French), *wage, warren, wince*. In the combination *qu–* Central French likewise dropped the labial element while it was retained for a time in Anglo-Norman. For this reason we say *quit, quarter, quality, question, require*, etc., all with the sound of [kw], where French has a simple [k] (*quitter, quartier, qualité*, etc.).

The consonants were not alone in showing special developments in England. The vowels also at times developed differently, and these differences are likewise reflected in the words borrowed by English. One or two illustrations will have to suffice. In Old French the diphthong *ui* was originally accented on the first element (*úi*). This accentuation was retained

[1] There is still considerable difference of opinion as to whether this dialect was in any real sense a unified speech. It shows great diversity of forms and this diversity may reflect the variety of the French people who settled in England. Many others besides Normans took part in William's invasion, and among those who came later every part of France was represented. In this mixture, however, it is certain that Normans predominated, and the Anglo-Norman dialect agrees in its most characteristic features with the dialects of northern France and especially with that of Normandy. Some features of the Norman dialect were characteristic also of its neighbor, Picard, and such features would be reinforced in England by the speech of those who came from the Picard area.

[2] This distinction as it appears in Middle English has been studied by S. H. Bush, "Old Northern French Loan-words in Middle English," *PQ*, 1 (1922), 161–72.

in Anglo-Norman and the *i* disappeared, leaving a simple *u* [y]. In Middle English this [y] became [u] or [iu], written *u, ui, ew*, etc. Hence the English word *fruit*. In Central French, on the other hand, the accentuation of this diphthong was shifted in the twelfth century from *úi* to *uí*, and as a consequence we have in Modern French the form *fruit* with a quite different pronunciation. Again, the diphthong *ei* was retained in Anglo-Norman, but early in the twelfth century it had become *oi* in Central French. Thus we have in English *leal, real* (A.N. *leial, reial*) as compared with French *loyal, royal* (which we have also subsequently adopted). The Latin endings *–ārius, –ōrius* appear in Anglo-Norman as *–arie*,[1] *–orie*, but in Central French they developed into *–aire, –oire*. Hence we have English *salary, victory*, but in French *salaire, victoire*. Of course, in many respects the French spoken in England was identical in its forms with that of Paris, but the cases in which it differed are sufficient to establish the conclusion that until well into the fourteenth century English borrowed its French words pretty generally in the form which they had in the spoken French of England.

While this statement is in accordance with inherent probability and is supported by abundant evidence so far as that evidence enables us to recognize dialectal differences, it must be qualified in one way. We have already seen (§ 101) that by the thirteenth century the preeminence of the Paris dialect was making itself felt outside the capital and it is probable that the French of England was gradually modified in the direction of conformity with that dialect. In spite of Chaucer's jest about the French of Stratford-at-Bow and the undoubted fact that the French of England was ridiculed by those who spoke the dialect of the Ile-de-France, we know that English children were at times sent abroad to correct their accent and that there was much travel to the continent. All this could not have been without some effect in making the forms of Central French more familiar in England. There was moreover the constant influence of French literature. It is reasonable to suppose, therefore, that as time went on and the use of French in England became more artificial, a larger share of the English borrowing was from Central French. This was more particularly the case in the fifteenth century when the less popular character of many of the words borrowed suggests that they came more often through literary than through colloquial channels.[2]

132. Popular and Literary Borrowings. There can be little doubt that a large proportion of the words borrowed from French were thoroughly

---

[1] Also as *–er*, as in *carpenter, danger*.
[2] There is a discussion of the Central French element in English in Skeat, *Principles of English Etymology*, Second Series (Oxford, 1891), chap. 8.

popular in character, that is, words current in the everyday French spoken in England. At the same time the importance of literature is not to be underestimated as a means of transfer. So much of Middle English literature was based directly on French originals that it would have been rather exceptional if English writers had consistently resisted the temptation to carry French words over into their adaptations. Layamon resisted, but most others did not, and when in the thirteenth and fourteenth centuries French words were being taken by the hundreds into the popular speech, the way was made easier for the entrance of literary words as well. Although literature was one of the channels by which French words entered English all through the Middle English period, in the fifteenth century it became the principal source. Words like *adolescence, affability, appellation, cohort, combustion, destitution, harangue, immensity, ingenious, pacification, representation, sumptuous* betray their learned or bookish origin, and in the works of Caxton at the end of the century new words like *aggravation, diversify, furtive, prolongation,* and *ravishment* abound. The number of such words entering the language at this time is probably no greater than in the preceding century, but they are more prominent because the adoption of popular words was now greatly curtailed by the practical disappearance of French as a spoken language in England.

133. *The Period of Greatest Influence.* Some time elapsed after the Norman Conquest before its effects were felt to any appreciable degree by the English vocabulary. This fact has long been recognized in a general way, but it is only within this century that the materials have been available which enable us to speak with any assurance as to the exact period when the greatest number of French words came into the language. These materials are the dated quotations in the *Oxford English Dictionary.* In 1905 Otto Jespersen made a statistical study of one thousand words borrowed from French, classifying them according to the dates when they were first recorded in English and grouping them by half centuries.[1] The

---

[1] *Growth and Structure of the English Language* (4th ed., 1928), p. 94. The following table differs somewhat from his. It represents an independent calculation based upon the completed dictionary. Professor Jespersen took the first hundred words under the letters A–H and the first fifty under I and J. The method followed in compiling the present table is described in *Modern Language Notes*, 50 (1935), 90–93.

.... 1050	2	1301–1350	108	1601–1650	61
1051–1100	0	1351–1400	198	1651–1700	37
1101–1150	2	1401–1450	74	1701–1750	33
1151–1200	7	1451–1500	90	1751–1800	26
1201–1250	35	1501–1550	62	1801–1850	46
1251–1300	99	1551–1600	95	1851–1900	25

For statistics based on the letter A only, see F. Mossé, "On the Chronology of French Loan-Words in English," *English Studies*, 25 (1943), 33–40.

result is highly illuminating. For a hundred years after the Conquest there is no increase in the number of French words being adopted. In the last half of the twelfth century the number increases slightly and in the period from 1200 to 1250 somewhat more rapidly. But it does not become really great until after 1250. Then the full tide sets in, rising to a climax at the end of the fourteenth century. By 1400 the movement has spent its force. A sharp drop in the fifteenth century has been followed by a gradual tapering off ever since.

While there is no way of knowing how long a word had been in the language before the earliest recorded instance, it is a striking fact that so far as surviving records show, the introduction of French words into English follows closely the progressive adoption of English by the upper classes (cf. above, § 95). As we have seen, the years from 1250 to 1400 mark the period when English was everywhere replacing French. During these 150 years 40 percent of all the French words in the English language came in.[1]

A further calculation shows that the total number of French words adopted during the Middle English period was slightly over ten thousand. Of these about 75 percent are still in current use.

134. *Assimilation.* ˈ The rapidity with which the new French words were assimilated is evidenced by the promptness with which many of them became the basis of derivatives. English endings were apparently added to them with as much freedom as to English words. For example, the adjective *gentle* is recorded in 1225 and within five years we have it compounded with an English noun to make *gentlewoman* (1230). A little later we find gentle*man* (1275), gentle*ness* (1300), and gent*ly* (1330). These compounds and derivatives all occur within about a century of the time when the original adjective was adopted. In the same way we have *faith* (1250) giving *faithless* and *faithful* (both by 1300), *faithfully* (1362), and *faithfulness* (1388), as well as the obsolete *faithly* (1325). The adverbial ending –*ly* seems to have been added to adjectives almost as soon as they appeared in the language. The adverbs *commonly, courteously, eagerly, feebly, fiercely, justly, peacefully,* and many more occur almost as early as the adjectives from which they are derived, while *faintly* by mere chance has been preserved in writing from a slightly earlier date than *faint.* Hybrid forms (French root with English prefix or suffix) like chast*hed* (chastity), lecher-*ness*, debonair*ship*, poor*ness*, spus*bruche* (spouse-breach, adultery), *be*catch,

---

[1] As indicated in the text, a word may have been in use some time before the date at which it is first recorded in the *Oxford English Dictionary*, but such a circumstance can hardly invalidate the conclusion here stated.

*un*gracious, *over*praising, *for*scald[1] occur quite early (mostly before 1250), while *common* (1297) has been made into *commonweal* (O.E. *wela*) by 1330, *battle* (1297) combined with *ax* (O.E. *æx*) by 1380, and so on. It is clear that the new French words were quickly assimilated, and entered into an easy and natural fusion with the native element in English.

135. Loss of Native Words. Language often seems lavish, if not wasteful, in having many words which appear to duplicate each other. And yet it has been said that there are no exact synonyms in English. There are usually certain peculiarities of meaning or use that distinguish a word from others with which it has much in common. This seems to indicate that a certain sense of economy characterizes people in their use of language and causes them to get rid of a word when its function is fully performed by some other word. After the Norman Conquest, duplications frequently resulted, for many of the French words that came into use bore meanings already expressed by a native word. In such cases one of two things happened: of the two words one was eventually lost, or, where both survived, they were differentiated in meaning. In some cases the French word disappeared, but in a great many cases it was the Old English word that died out. The substitution was not always immediate; often both words continued in use for a longer or shorter time, and the English word occasionally survives in the dialects today. Thus the O.E. *ēam*, which has been replaced in the standard speech by the French word *uncle*, is still in use (*eme*) in Scotland. The O.E. *anda* contested its position with the French *envy* until the time of Chaucer, but eventually lost out and with it went the adjective *andig* (envious) and the verb *andian* (to envy). In this way many common Old English words succumbed. The O.E. *æþele* yielded to F. *noble*, and *æþeling* became *nobleman*. *Dryhten* and *frēa* were displaced by the French *prince*, although the English word *lord*, which survived as a synonym, helped in the elimination. At the same time *lēod* was being ousted by *people*. The O.E. *dēma* (judge), *dēman* (to judge), and *dōm* (judgment) gave way before French influence in matters of law, but we still use *deem* in the sense of to think or hold an opinion, and *dōm* has survived in special senses, as in *the day of doom*, or *to meet one's doom*. O.E. *cȳþere* (witness), *firen* (crime), and *scyldig* (guilty) have likewise disappeared, as have *here* (army), *cempa* (warrior), and *sibb* (peace). O.E. *blæd* lived on beside *flower* from French until the thirteenth century, and *blēo* (color) survives dialectally as *blee*. Other common words that were lost may be illustrated by *ādl* (disease), *ieldu* (age), *lof* (praise), *lyft* (air), *hold* (gracious), *earm* (poor),

---

[1] Behrens, *Beiträge zur Geschichte der französischen Sprache in England* (Heilbronn, 1886), p. 9.

slīþe (cruel), *gecynde* (natural), although it survived as *kind* with this meaning until the sixteenth century, *wuldor* (glory) with its adjective *wuldrig* (glorious), and *wlite* (beauty), *wlitig* (beautiful). In all these cases the place of the English word was taken by the word in parentheses, introduced from French. Many common verbs died out in the same way, such as *andettan* (confess), *beorgan* (preserve, defend), *bieldan* and *elnian* (encourage), *dihtan* (compose), *flītan* (contend; flite [dialect]), *gōdian* (improve), *healsian* (implore), *herian* (praise), *lēanian* (reward), *belīfan* (remain), *miltsian* (pity). Here likewise the words in parentheses are the French verbs that replaced the native word. Not all the Old English words that have disappeared were driven out by French equivalents. Some gave way to other more or less synonymous words in Old English. Many independently fell into disuse. Nevertheless the enormous invasion of French words not only took the place of many English words that had been lost but itself accounts for a great many of the losses from the Old English vocabulary.

136. Differentiation in Meaning. Where both the English and the French words survived they were generally differentiated in meaning. The words *doom* and *judgment*, *to deem* and *to judge* are examples which have already been mentioned. In the fifteenth century *hearty* and *cordial* came to be used for feelings which were supposed to spring from the heart. Etymologically they are alike, coming respectively from the Old English and the Latin words for heart. But we have kept them both because we use them with a slight difference in meaning, *hearty* implying a certain physical vigor and downrightness, as in *a hearty dinner*, *cordial* a more quiet or conventional manifestation, as in *a cordial reception*. In the same way we have kept a number of words for *smell*. The common word in Old English was *stench*. During the Middle English period this was supplemented by the word *smell* (of unknown origin) and the French words *aroma*, *odor*, and *scent*. To these we have since added *stink* (from the verb) and *perfume* and *fragrance*, from French. Most of these have special connotations and *smell* has become the general word. *Stench* now always means an unpleasant smell. An interesting group of words illustrating the principle is *ox*, *sheep*, *swine*, and *calf* beside the French equivalents *beef*, *mutton*, *pork*, and *veal*. The French words primarily denoted the animal, as they still do, but in English they were used from the beginning to distinguish the meat from the living beast.[1] Other cases of differentiation are English *house* beside

---

[1] The well-known passage in Scott's *Ivanhoe* in which this distinction is entertainingly introduced into a conversation between Wamba and Gurth (chap. 1) is open to criticism only because the episode occurs about a century too early. *Beef* is first found in English at about 1300.

mansion from French, *might* beside *power*, and the pairs *ask—demand*, *shun—avoid, seethe—boil, wish—desire*. In most of these cases where duplication occurred, the French word, when it came into English, was a close synonym of the corresponding English word. The discrimination between them has been a matter of gradual growth, but it justifies the retention of both words in the language.

137. ***Curtailment of O.E. Processes of Derivation.*** Since language is a form of human activity, it often displays habits or tendencies which one recognizes as characteristic of the speech of a given people at a given time. These habits may be altered by circumstances. As we have already seen (§§ 49–50), Old English, like other Indo-European languages, enlarged its vocabulary chiefly by a liberal use of prefixes and suffixes and an easy power of combining native elements into self-interpreting compounds. In this way the existing resources of the language were expanded at will and any new needs were met. In the centuries following the Norman Conquest, however, there is a visible decline in the use of these old methods of word-formation.

138. ***Prefixes.*** This is first of all apparent in the matter of prefixes. Many of the Old English prefixes gradually lost their vitality, their ability to enter into new combinations. The Old English prefix *for–* (corresponding to German *ver–*) was often used to intensify the meaning of a verb or to add the idea of something destructive or prejudicial. For a while during the Middle English period it continued to be used occasionally in new formations. Thus at about 1300 we find *forhang* (put to death by hanging), *forcleave* (cut to pieces), and *forshake* (shake off). It was even combined with words borrowed from French: *forcover, forbar, forgab* (deride), *fortravail* (tire). But while these occasional instances show that the prefix was not dead, it seems to have had no real vitality. None of these new formations lived long, and the prefix is now entirely obsolete. The only verbs in which it occurs in Modern English are *forbear, forbid, fordo, forget, forgive, forgo, forsake, forswear,* and the participle *forlorn*. All of them had their origin in Old English. The prefix *to–* (German *zer–*) has disappeared even more completely. While the 1611 Bible tells us that the woman who cast a millstone upon Abimelech's head "all tobrake his skull," and expressions like *tomelt* and *toburst* lived on for a time, there is no trace of the prefix in current use. *With–* (meaning *against*) gave a few new words in Middle English such as *withdraw, withgo, withsake,* etc. *Withdraw* and *withhold* survive, together with the Old English *withstand,* but other equally useful words have been replaced by later borrowings from Latin: *withsay* by *renounce, withspeak* by *contradict, withset* by *resist,* etc. Some prefixes which are still productive today, like *over–* and *under–*, fell into comparative disuse for a time after the Norman Conquest. Most compounds of *over–* which are not of Old English origin have arisen in the modern period. The prefix *on–* (now *un–*), which was used to reverse the action of a verb as in *unbind, undo, unfold, unwind,* and which in Middle English gave us *unfasten, unbuckle, uncover,* and *unwrap,* seems to owe such life as it still enjoys to association with the negative prefix *un.* The productive power which these formative elements once enjoyed has in many cases been transferred to prefixes like *counter–, dis–, re–, trans–,* etc., of Latin origin. It is possible that some of them would have gone out of use had there been no Norman Conquest, but when we see their disuse keeping pace with the increase of the French element in the language and find them in many cases disappearing at the end of the Middle English period, at a time when French borrowings have reached their maximum, it is impossible to doubt that the wealth of easily acquired new words had weakened English habits of word-formation.

139. Suffixes.   A similar decline is observable in the formative power of certain suffixes which were widely used in Old English. The loss here is perhaps less distinctly felt because some important endings have remained in full force. Such are the noun suffix *–ness* and the adjective endings *–ful, –less, –some,* and *–ish.* But others equally important were either lost or greatly diminished in vitality. Thus the abstract suffix *–lock* (O.E. *lāc*) survives only in *wedlock, –red* (O.E. *ræden*) only in *hatred* and *kindred.* The ending *–dom* was used in Old English to form abstract nouns from other nouns (*kingdom, earldom, martyrdom*) and from adjectives (*freedom, wisdom*). In Middle English there are some new formations such as *dukedom* and *thralldom,* but most of the formations from adjectives, like *falsedom* and *richdom,* did not prove permanent, and the suffix is to all intents and purposes now dead. When used today it is for the most part employed in half serious coinages, such as *fandom, stardom, topsy-turvydom.*[1] The endings *–hood* and *–ship* have had a similar history. *Manhood, womanhood, likelihood* are new formations in Middle English, showing that the suffix retained its power for a while. In fact it occasionally reasserts itself in modern times. *Boyhood* and *girlhood* date from the eighteenth century, while *hardihood* is apparently a creation of Milton's which was revived by Macaulay. Many of the Old English abstracts in *–ship* were lost. We have kept *friendship* but not *fiendship,* and of those formed from adjectives in Old English the only one still in use is *worship*

---

[1] See Harold Wentworth, "The Allegedly Dead Suffix *–dom* in Modern English," *PMLA,* 56 (1941), 280–306.

(worthship). Most of the new formations in Middle English had a short life. We have retained *hardship* but not *boldship, busiship, cleanship, kindship,* etc. In all these instances the ending *–ness* was preferred. As in the case of prefixes, we can see here a gradual change in English habits of word-formation resulting from the available supply of French words with which to fill the needs formerly met by the native resources of the language.

140. *Self-explaining Compounds.* One further habit which was somewhat weakened, although by no means broken, was that of combining native words into self-interpreting compounds. The extent to which words like *bookhouse* or *boatswain* entered into Old English has been pointed out above (§ 49). The practice was not abandoned in Middle English, but in many cases where a new word could have been easily formed on the native model, a ready-made French word was borrowed instead. Today self-explaining compounds are still formed by a sure instinct (*picture tube, four-wheel brakes, oil-burner*), but the method is much less universal than it once was because of new habits introduced after the Norman Conquest.

141. *The Language Still English.* It must not be thought that the extensive modification of the English language caused by the Norman Conquest had made of it something else than English. The language had undergone much simplification of its inflections, but its grammar was still English. It had absorbed several thousand French words as a natural consequence of a situation in which large numbers of people were for a time bilingual and then gradually turned from the habitual use of French to the habitual use of English. It had lost a great many native words and abandoned some of its most characteristic habits of word-formation. But great and basic elements of the vocabulary were still English. No matter what class of society he belonged to, the Englishman *ate, drank,* and *slept,* so to speak, in English, *worked* and *played, spoke* and *sang, walked, ran, rode, leaped,* and *swam* in the same language. The *house* he lived in, with its *hall, bower, rooms, windows, doors, floor, steps, gate,* etc., remind us that his language was basically Germanic. His *meat* and *drink, bread, butter, fish, milk, cheese, salt, pepper, wine, ale,* and *beer* were inherited from pre-Conquest days, while he could not refer to his *head, arms, legs, feet, hands, eyes, ears, nose, mouth,* or any common part of his body without using English words for the purpose. While we are under the necessity of paying considerable attention to the large French element that the Norman Conquest brought directly and indirectly into the language, we must see it in proper perspective. The language which the Normans and their successors finally adopted was English, and while it was an English changed in many important particulars from the language of King Alfred, its predominant features were those inherited from the Germanic tribes that settled in England in the fifth century.

142. *Latin Borrowings in Middle English.*   The influence of the Norman Conquest is generally known as the Latin Influence of the Third Period in recognition of the ultimate source of the new French words. But it is right to include also under this designation the large number of words borrowed directly from Latin in Middle English. These differed from the French borrowings in being less popular and in gaining admission generally through the written language. Of course, it must not be forgotten that Latin was a spoken language among ecclesiastics and men of learning, and a certain number of Latin words could well have passed directly into spoken English. Their number, however, is small in comparison with those that we can observe entering by way of literature. In a single work like Trevisa's translation of the *De Proprietatibus Rerum* of Bartholomew Anglicus we meet with several hundred words taken over from the Latin original. Since they are not found before this in English, we can hardly doubt that we have here a typical instance of the way such words first came to be used. The fourteenth and fifteenth centuries were especially prolific in Latin borrowings. An anonymous writer of the first half of the fifteenth century complains that it is not easy to translate from Latin into English, for "there ys many wordes in Latyn that we have no propre Englysh accordynge therto."[1] Wycliffe and his associates are credited with more than a thousand Latin words not previously found in English.[2] Since many of them occur in the so-called Wycliffe translation of the Bible and have been retained in subsequent translations, they have passed into common use. The innovations of other writers were not always so fortunate. Many of them, like the inkhorn terms of the Renaissance, were but passing experiments. Nevertheless the permanent additions from Latin to the English vocabulary in this period are much larger than has generally been realized.

It is unnecessary to attempt a formal classification of these borrowings. Some idea of their range and character may be gained from a selected but miscellaneous list of examples: *abject, adjacent, allegory, conspiracy, contempt, custody, distract, frustrate, genius, gesture, history, homicide, immune, incarnate, include, incredible, incubus, incumbent, index, individual, infancy, inferior, infinite, innate, innumerable, intellect, interrupt, juniper,*

---

[1] *The Myroure of Oure Ladye, EETSES*, 19, p. 7.
[2] Otto Dellit, *Über lateinische Elemente im Mittelenglischen* (Marburg, 1905), p. 38.

lapidary, legal, limbo, lucrative, lunatic, magnify, malefactor, mechanical, minor, missal, moderate, necessary, nervous, notary, ornate, picture, polite, popular, prevent, private, project, promote, prosecute, prosody, pulpit, quiet, rational, reject, remit, reprehend, rosary, script, scripture, scrutiny, secular, solar, solitary, spacious, stupor, subdivide, subjugate, submit, subordinate, subscribe, substitute, summary, superabundance, supplicate, suppress, temperate, temporal, testify, testimony, tincture, tract, tributary, ulcer, zenith, zephyr. Here we have terms relating to law, medicine, theology, science, and literature, words often justified in the beginning by technical or professional use and later acquiring a wider application. Among them may be noticed several with endings like *–able, –ible, –ent, –al, –ous, –ive,* and others, which thus became familiar in English and, reinforced often by French, now form common elements in English derivatives. All the words in the above list are accepted by the *Oxford English Dictionary* as direct borrowings from Latin. But in many cases Latin words were being borrowed by French at the same time and the adoption of a word in English may often have been due to the impact of both languages.

143. *Aureate Terms.* The introduction of unusual words from Latin (and occasionally elsewhere) became a conscious stylistic device in the fifteenth century, extensively used by poets and occasionally by writers of prose. By means of such words as *abusion, dispone, diurne, equipolent, palestral,* and *tenebrous,* poets attempted what has been described as a kind of stylistic gilding, and this feature of their language is accordingly known as "aureate diction."[1] The beginnings of this tendency have been traced back to the fourteenth century. It occurs in moderation in the poetry of Chaucer, becomes a distinct mannerism in the work of Lydgate, and runs riot in the productions of the Scottish Chaucerians—James I, Henryson, Dunbar, and the rest. How far this affectation went may be seen in the opening lines of Dunbar's *Ballad of Our Lady:*

> Hale, sterne superne! Hale, in eterne,
>   In Godis sicht to schyne!
> Lucerne in derne,[2] for to discerne
>   Be glory and grace devyne;
> Hodiern, modern, sempitern,
>   Angelicall regyne!
> Our tern[3] infern for to dispern
>   Helpe, rialest Rosyne![4]

---

[1] The standard treatment of the subject is John C. Mendenhall, *Aureate Terms* (Lancaster, Pa., 1919).

[2] lamp in darkness   [3] woe   [4] rose

The use of such "halff chongyd Latyne," as a contemporary poet describes it,[1] was quite artificial. The poets who affected aureate terms have been described as tearing up words from Latin "which never took root in the language, like children making a mock garden with flowers and branches stuck in the ground, which speedily wither."[2] This is essentially true, but not wholly so. The novelty which was sought after, and which such words had in the beginning, wore off with use; and words which were "aureate" in Chaucer, like *laureate, mediation, oriental, prolixity,* have sometimes become part of the common speech. These innovations are of considerable interest in the history of style; in the history of language they appear as a minor current in the stream of Latin words flowing into English in the course of the Middle Ages.

144. *Synonyms at Three Levels.*   Much nonsense has been written on the relative merits of the Germanic and Romance elements in the English vocabulary.[3] The Latinized diction of many seventeenth- and eighteenth-century writers brought up in the tradition of the classics provoked a reaction in which the "Saxon" element of the language was glorified as the strong, simple, and direct component in contrast with the many abstract and literary words derived from Latin and French. It is easy to select pairs like *deed—exploit, spell—enchantment, take—apprehend, weariness—lassitude,* and on the basis of such examples make generalizations about the superior directness, the homely force and concreteness of the Old English words. But such contrasts ignore the many hundreds of words from French which are equally simple and as capable of conveying a vivid image, idea, or emotion—nouns like *bar, beak, cell, cry, fool, frown, fury, glory, guile, gullet, horror, humor, isle, pity, river, rock, ruin, stain, stuff, touch, wreck,* or adjectives such as *calm, clear, cruel, eager, fierce, gay, mean, rude, safe, tender,* to take examples almost at random. The truth is that many of the most vivid and forceful words in English are French, and even where the French and Latin words are more literary or learned, as indeed they often are, they are no less valuable and important. Language has need for the simple, the polished, and even the recondite word. The richness of English in synonyms is largely due to the happy mingling of Latin, French, and native elements. It has been said that we have a synonym at each level— popular, literary, and learned. While this statement must not be pressed

---

[1] John Metham. Cf. P. H. Nichols, "Lydgate's Influence on the Aureate Terms of the Scottish Chaucerians," *PMLA,* 47 (1932), 516–22.

[2] Thomas Campbell, *Essay on English Poetry* (London, 1848), p. 39.

[3] Even so sensible a scholar as Freeman could write: "This abiding corruption of our language I believe to have been the one result of the Norman Conquest which has been purely evil." (*Norman Conquest,* V, 547.)

too hard, a difference is often apparent, as in *rise—mount—ascend,
ask—question—interrogate, goodness—virtue—probity, fast—firm—secure,
fire—flame—conflagration, fear—terror—trepidation, holy—sacred—consecrated, time—age—epoch.* In each of these sets of three words the first is
English, the second is from French, and the third from Latin. The difference in tone between the English and the French words is often slight; the
Latin word is generally more bookish. However, it is more important to
recognize the distinctive uses of each than to form prejudices in favor of
one group above another.

145. *Words from the Low Countries.* The importance of the Romance
element in English has overshadowed and caused to be neglected another
source of foreign words in the vocabulary, the languages of the Low
Countries—Flemish, Dutch, and Low German. The similarity of these
languages to English makes it difficult often to tell whether a word has been
adopted from one of them or is of native origin. Moreover, the influence
was not the result of some single cause, like the introduction of Christianity
or the Norman Conquest, confined more or less to a given period of time,
but was rather a gradual infiltration due to the constant and close relations
between England and the people of Flanders, Holland, and northern
Germany. This intercourse extends from the days of William the Conqueror, whose wife was Flemish, down to the eighteenth century. All
through the Middle Ages Flemings came to England in considerable
numbers. In the English wars at home and abroad we repeatedly find
Flemish mercenaries fighting with the English forces. Others came for
more peaceful purposes and settled in the country. The woolen industry
was the major industry of England in the Middle Ages. Most of the wool
exported from England went to supply Flemish and Dutch looms. On the
other hand, weavers from the Low Countries, noted for their superior
cloths, were encouraged to come to England and at various times came in
large numbers. They were sufficiently numerous to arouse at intervals the
antagonism of the native population. In the Peasants' Revolt of 1381 we
are told that "many fflemmynges loste here heedes . . . and namely they
that koude nat say Breede and Chese, But Case and Brode."[1] Trade
between these countries and England was responsible for much travel to
and fro. Flemish and German merchants had their hanse at London,
Boston, Lynn, and elsewhere. The English wool staple was at different
times at Dordrecht, Louvain, Bruges, and other towns near the coast. Add
to this the fact that the carrying trade was largely in the hands of the Dutch

---

[1] C. L. Kingsford, *Chronicles of London* (Oxford, 1905), p. 15.

until the Navigation Act of 1651 and we see that there were many favorable conditions for the introduction of Low German words into English. At the end of the Middle Ages we find entering the language such words as *nap* (of cloth), *deck, bowsprit, lighter, dock, freight, rover, mart, groat, guilder.* Later borrowings include *cambric, duck* (cloth), *boom* (of a boat), *beleaguer, furlough, commodore, gin, gherkin, dollar.* Dutch eminence in art is responsible for *easel, etching, landscape,* while Dutch settlers in America seem to have caused the adoption of *cruller, cookie, cranberry, bowery, boodle,* and other words. The latest study of the Low Dutch element in English considers some 2,500 words. Many of these are admittedly doubtful, but one must grant the possibility of more influence from the Low Countries upon English than can be proved by phonological or other direct evidence.[1]

146. *Dialectal Diversity of Middle English.* One of the striking characteristics of Middle English is its great variety in the different parts of England. This variety was not confined to the forms of the spoken language, as it is to a great extent today, but appears equally in the written literature. In the absence of any recognized literary standard before the close of the period, writers naturally wrote in the dialect of that part of the country to which they belonged. And they did so not through any lack of awareness of the diversity that existed. Giraldus Cambrensis in the twelfth century remarked that the language of the southern parts of England, and particularly of Devonshire, was more archaic and seemed less agreeable than that of other parts with which he was familiar;[2] and at a slightly earlier date (c. 1125) William of Malmesbury had complained of the harshness of the speech of Yorkshire, saying that southerners could not understand it.[3] Such observations continue in subsequent centuries.[4] The author of the

---

[1] The fullest discussion of the Flemings in England and English relations with the Low Countries generally is J. F. Bense, *Anglo-Dutch Relations from the Earliest Times to the Death of William the Third* (London, 1925). J. A. Fleming, *Flemish Influence in Britain* (2 vols., Glasgow, 1930), is rather discursive and concerned mostly with Scotland. The Low German influence on English has been treated by Wilhelm Heuser, "Festländische Einflüsse im Mittelenglischen," *Bonner Beiträge zur Anglistik*, 12 (1902), 173–82; J. M. Toll, *Niederländisches Lehngut im Mittelenglischen* (Halle, 1926); J. F. Bense, *A Dictionary of the Low-Dutch Element in the English Vocabulary* (The Hague, 1939); H. Logeman, "Low-Dutch Elements in English," *Neophilologus*, 16 (1930–1931), 31–46, 103–16 (a commentary on Bense); T. de Vries, *Holland's Influence on English Language and Literature* (Chicago, 1916), a work of slighter value; and E. Ekwall, *Shakspere's Vocabulary* (Uppsala, 1903), pp. 92 ff.

[2] *Description of Wales*, Bk. I, chap. 6.

[3] *Gesta Pontificum*, Bk. III. The remark is repeated in Higden, and in Trevisa's translation of Higden.

[4] "Our language is also so dyverse in yt selfe, that the commen maner of spekyng in Englysshe of some contre [i.e., county] can skante be understonded in some other contre of the same londe." *The Myroure of Oure Ladye* (first half of the fifteenth century), *EETSES*, 19, pp. 7–8.

Cursor Mundi, a northern poem of about 1300, notes that he found the story of the Assumption of Our Lady in Southern English and turned it into his own dialect for "northern people who can read no other English."[1] Even Chaucer, by whose time a literary standard was in process of creation, sends off his *Troilus and Criseyde* with the famous "Go, little book," adding,

> And for ther is so gret diversite
> In Englissh, and in writyng of oure tonge,
> So prey I god that non myswrite the,
> Ne the mys-metre for defaute of tonge.

147. *The Middle English Dialects.* The language differed almost from county to county, and noticeable variations are sometimes observable between different parts of the same county. The features characteristic of a given dialect do not all cover the same territory; some extend into adjoining districts or may be characteristic also of another dialect. Consequently it is rather difficult to decide how many dialectal divisions should be recognized and to mark off with any exactness their respective boundaries. In a rough way, however, it is customary to distinguish four principal dialects of Middle English: Northern, East Midland, West Midland, and Southern. Generally speaking, the Northern dialect extends as far south as the Humber river; East Midland and West Midland together cover the area between the Humber and the Thames; and Southern occupies the district south of the Thames, together with Gloucestershire and parts of the counties of Worcester and Hereford, thus taking in the West Saxon and Kentish districts of Old English. Throughout the Middle English period and later, Kentish preserves individual features marking it off as a distinct variety of Southern English.[2]

The peculiarities that distinguish these dialects are of such a character that their adequate enumeration would carry us beyond our present

---

[1] In sotherin englis was it draun,
And turnd it haue I till our aun
Langage o northrin lede
þat can nan oiþer englis rede. (ll. 20,061–64)

[2] A pioneering attempt to define significant dialect features was "Middle English Dialect Characteristics and Dialect Boundaries," by Samuel Moore, Sanford B. Meech, and Harold Whitehall, in *Univ. of Michigan Pubns in Lang. and Lit.*, vol. 13 (1935). It was based primarily on localized documents, which are not sufficiently numerous. The limitations of this study are pointed out in A. McIntosh, "A New Approach to Middle English Dialectology," *English Studies*, 44 (1963), 1–11. See also M. L. Samuels, "Some Applications of Middle English Dialectology," *ibid.*, pp. 81–94. McIntosh and Samuels have prepared a survey of Middle English dialects, including over a hundred maps, which except for a few maps and articles is not yet published.

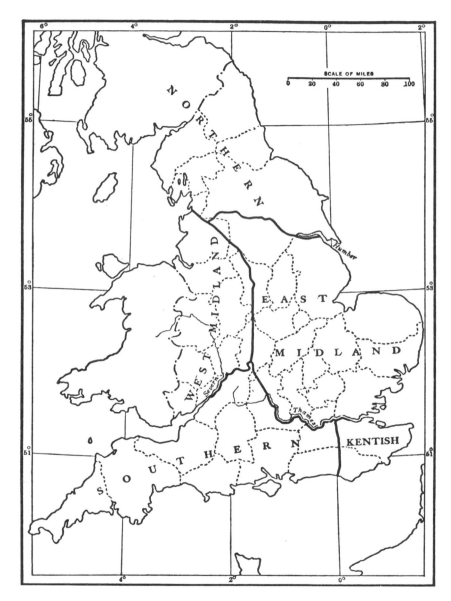

THE DIALECTS OF MIDDLE ENGLISH

purpose. They are partly matters of pronunciation, partly of vocabulary, partly of inflection. A few illustrations will give some idea of the nature and extent of the differences. The feature most easily recognized is the ending of the plural, present indicative, of verbs. In Old English this form always ended in *–th* with some variation of the preceding vowel. In Middle English this ending was preserved as *–eth* in the Southern dialect. In the Midland district, however, it was replaced by *–en*, probably taken over from the corresponding forms of the imperfect and the subjunctive or from preterite-present verbs and the verb *to be*,[1] while in the north it was altered to *–es*, an ending that makes its appearance in Old English times. Thus we have *loves* in the north, *loven* in the Midlands, and *loveth* in the south. Another fairly distinctive form is the present participle before the spread of the ending *–ing*. In the north we have *lovande*, in the Midlands *lovende*, and in the south *lovinde*. In later Middle English the ending *–ing* appears in the Midlands and the south, thus obscuring the dialectal distinction. Dialectal differences are more noticeable between Northern and Southern; the Midland dialect often occupies an intermediate position, tending toward the one or the other in those districts lying nearer to the adjacent dialects. Thus the characteristic forms of the pronoun *they* in the south were *hi, here* (*hire, hure*), *hem*, while in the north forms with *th–* (modern *they, their, them*) early became predominant. In matters of pronunciation the Northern and Southern dialects sometimes presented notable differences. Thus O.E. *ā*, which developed into an *ǭ* south of the Humber, was retained in the north, giving us such characteristic forms as Southern *stone* and *home*, beside *stane* and *hame* in Scotland today. Initial *f* and *s* were often voiced in the south to *v* and *z*. In Southern Middle English we find *vor, vrom, vox, vorzoþe* instead of *for, from, fox, forsoþe* (forsooth). This dialectal difference is preserved in Modern English *fox* and *vixen*, where the former represents the Northern and Midland pronunciation and the latter the Southern. Similarly *ch* in the south often corresponds to a *k* in the north: *bench* beside *benk*, or *church* beside *kirk*. Such variety was fortunately lessened toward the end of the Middle English period by the general adoption of a standard written (and later spoken) English.[2]

148. *The Rise of Standard English.* Out of this variety of local dialects there emerged toward the end of the fourteenth century a written language that in the course of the fifteenth won general recognition and has since become the recognized standard in both speech and writing. The part of

---

[1] W. F. Bryan, "The Midland Present Plural Indicative Ending *–e(n)*," *MP*, 18 (1921), 457–73.

[2] For further illustration see Appendix A.

England that contributed most to the formation of this standard was the East Midland district, and it was the East Midland type of English that became its basis, particularly the dialect of the metropolis, London. Several causes contributed to the attainment of this result.

In the first place, as a Midland dialect the English of this region occupied a middle position between the extreme divergences of the north and south. It was less conservative than the Southern dialect, less radical than the Northern. In its sounds and inflections it represents a kind of compromise, sharing some of the characteristics of both its neighbors. Its intermediate position was recognized in the fourteenth century by Trevisa, the translator of numerous Latin works. In a well-known passage in his version of Higden's *Polychronicon* (c. 1385) he wrote:

> for men of þe est wiþ men of þe west, as it were vnder þe same partie of heuene, acordeþ more in sownynge of speche þan men of þe norþ wiþ men of þe souþ; þerfore it is þat Mercii, þat beeþ men of myddel Engelond, as it were parteners of þe endes, vnderstondeþ bettre þe side langages, Norþerne and Souþerne, þan Norþerne and Souþerne vnderstondeþ eiþer oþer.

In the second place, the East Midland district was the largest and most populous of the major dialect areas. The land was more valuable than the hilly country to the north and west, and in an agricultural age this advantage was reflected in both the number and the prosperity of the inhabitants. As Maitland remarks, "If we leave Lincolnshire, Norfolk and Suffolk out of account we are to all appearances leaving out of account not much less than a quarter of the whole nation. . . . No doubt all inferences drawn from medieval statistics are exceedingly precarious; but, unless a good many figures have conspired to deceive us, Lincolnshire, Norfolk and Suffolk were at the time of the Conquest and for three centuries afterwards vastly richer and more populous than any tract of equal area in the West."[1] Only the southern counties possessed natural advantages at all comparable, and they were much smaller. The prominence of Middlesex, Oxford, Norfolk, and the East Midlands generally in political affairs all through the later Middle Ages is but another evidence of the importance of the district and of the extent to which its influence was likely to be felt.

A third factor, more difficult to evaluate, was the presence of the universities, Oxford and Cambridge, in this region. In the fourteenth century the monasteries were playing a less important rôle in the dissemination of learning than they had once played, while the two universities had

---

[1] *Domesday Book and Beyond*, pp. 20–22.

developed into important intellectual centers. So far as Cambridge is concerned any influence which it had would be exerted in support of the East Midland dialect. That of Oxford is less certain since Oxfordshire is on the border between Midland and Southern and its dialect shows certain characteristic Southern features. Moreover, we can no longer attribute to Wycliffe an important part in the establishment of a written standard.[1] Though he spent much of his life at Oxford, he seems not to have conformed fully to the Oxford dialect. All we can say is that the dialect of Oxford had no apparent influence on the form of London English, which was ultimately adopted as standard. Such support as the East Midland type of English received from the universities must have been largely confined to that furnished by Cambridge.

Much the same uncertainty attaches to the influence of Chaucer. It was once thought that Chaucer's importance was paramount among the influences bringing about the adoption of a written standard. And, indeed, it is unbelievable that the language of the greatest English poet before Shakespeare was not spread by the popularity of his works and, through the use of that language, by subsequent poets who looked upon him as their master and model. But it is nevertheless unlikely that the English used in official records and in letters and papers by men of affairs was greatly influenced by the language of his poetry. Yet it is the language found in such documents rather than the language of Chaucer that is at the basis of Standard English. Chaucer's dialect is not in all respects the same as the language of these documents, presumably identical with the ordinary speech of the city. It is slightly more conservative and shows a greater number of Southern characteristics. Chaucer was a court poet and his usage may reflect the speech of the court and to a certain extent literary tradition. His influence must be thought of as lending support in a general way to the dialect of the region to which he belonged rather than as determining the precise form which Standard English was to take in the century following his death.

149. *The Importance of London English.* By far the most influential factor in the rise of Standard English was the importance of London as the capital of England. Indeed, it is altogether likely that the language of the city would have become the prevailing dialect without the help of any of the factors previously discussed. In doing so it would have been following the course of other national tongues—French as the dialect of Paris, Spanish

---

[1] Wycliffe was credited with the chief part in the establishment of Standard English by Koch, as Chaucer was by Ten Brink. Later Dibelius (*Anglia*, 23–24) argued for the existence of an Oxford standard, recognized for a time beside the language of London. This view has now generally been abandoned.

as that of Castile, etc. London was, and still is, the political and commercial center of England. It was the seat of the court, of the highest judicial tribunals, the focus of the social and intellectual activities of the country. To it were drawn in a constant stream those whose affairs took them beyond the limits of their provincial homes. They brought to it traits of their local speech, there to mingle with the London idiom and to survive or die as the silent forces of amalgamation and standardization determined. They took back with them the forms and usages of the great city by which their own speech had been modified. The influence was reciprocal. London English took as well as gave. It began as a Southern and ended as a Midland dialect. By the fifteenth century there had come to prevail in the East Midlands a fairly uniform dialect and the language of London agrees in all important respects with it. We can hardly doubt that the importance of the eastern counties, pointed out above, is largely responsible for this change. Even such Northern characteristics as are found in the standard speech seem to have entered by way of these counties. The history of Standard English is almost a history of London English.

150. *The Spread of the London Standard.* In the latter part of the fifteenth century the London standard had been accepted, at least in writing, in most parts of the country. Its prestige may possibly be reflected in the fact that Mak the sheep-stealer in the *Towneley Plays* attempts to impose upon the Yorkshire shepherds by masquerading as a person of some importance and affects a "Southern tooth." Considerable diversity still existed in the spoken dialects, as will be apparent from what is said in the next paragraph. But in literary works after 1450 it becomes almost impossible, except in distinctly northern texts, to determine with any precision the region in which a given work was written. And in correspondence and local records there is a widespread tendency to conform in matters of language to the London standard. A factor more difficult to assess is the influence which the Chancery clerks may have had. By the middle of the century they had developed a fairly consistent variety of London English in both spelling and accidence, and as the language of official use it was likely to have some influence in similar situations elsewhere.[1] With the introduction of printing in 1476 a new influence of great importance in the dissemination of London English came into play. From the beginning London has been the center of book publishing in England. Caxton, the first English printer, used the current speech of London in his numerous

---

[1] See John H. Fisher, "Chancery and the Emergence of Standard Written English in the Fifteenth Century," *Speculum*, 52 (1977), 870–99.

translations, and the books that issued from his press and from the presses of his successors gave a currency to London English that assured more than anything else its rapid adoption. In the sixteenth century the use of London English had become a matter of precept as well as practice. The author of *The Arte of English Poesie* (attributed to Puttenham) advises the poet: "ye shall therefore take the usuall speach of the Court, and that of London and the shires lying about London within lx. myles, and not much above."

151. *Complete Uniformity Still Unattained.* It would be a mistake to think that complete uniformity was attained within the space of a few generations. Even in matters of vocabulary dialectal differences have persisted in cultivated speech down to the present day, and they were no less noticeable in the period during which London English was gaining general acceptance. Then, too, there were many French and Latin words, such as the aureate stylists were indulging in, that had not been assimilated. It was not easy for a writer at the end of the fifteenth century to choose his words so that his language would find favor with all people. How difficult it was may be seen from the remarks which Caxton prefixed to his *Eneydos*, a paraphrase of Virgil's *Aeneid* which he translated from French and published in 1490:

> After dyverse werkes made, translated, and achieved, havyng noo werke in hande, I, sittyng in my studye where as laye many dyverse paunflettis and bookys, happened that to my hande came a lytyl booke in frenshe, whiche late was translated oute of latyn by some noble clerke of fraunce, whiche booke is named Eneydos. . . . And whan I had advysed me in this sayd boke, I delybered and concluded to translate it into englysshe, and forthwyth toke a penne & ynke, and wrote a leef or tweyne, whyche I oversawe agayn to corecte it. And whan I sawe the fayr & straunge termes therin I doubted that it sholde not please some gentylmen whiche late blamed me, sayeng that in my translacyons I had over curyous termes whiche coude not be understande of comyn peple, and desired me to use olde and homely termes in my translacyons. And fayn wolde I satysfye every man, and so to doo, toke an olde boke and redde therin; and certaynly the englysshe was so rude and brood that I coude not wele understande it. And also my lorde abbot of westmynster ded do shewe to me late, certayn evydences wryton in olde englysshe, for to reduce it in-to our englysshe now usid. And certaynly it was wreton in suche wyse that it was more lyke to dutche than englysshe; I coude not reduce ne brynge it to be understonden. And certaynly our langage now used varyeth ferre from that whiche was used and spoken whan I was borne. For we englysshe men ben borne under the domynacyon of the mone, whiche is never stedfaste, but ever waverynge, wexynge one season, and waneth & dyscreaseth another

season. And that comyn englysshe that is spoken in one shyre varyeth from a nother. In so moche that in my dayes happened that certayn marchauntes were in a shippe in tamyse, for to have sayled over the see into zelande, and for lacke of wynde, thei taryed atte forlond, and wente to lande for to refreshe them. And one of theym named Sheffelde, a mercer, cam in-to an hows and axed for mete; and specyally he axyd after eggys. And the goode wyf answerde, that she coude speke no frenshe. And the marchaunt was angry, for he also coude speke no frenshe, but wolde have hadde egges, and she understode hym not. And thenne at laste a nother sayd that he wolde have eyren. Then the good wyf sayd that she understod hym wel. Loo, what sholde a man in thyse dayes now wryte, egges or eyren? Certaynly it is harde to playse every man by cause of dyversite & chaunge of langage. For in these dayes every man that is in ony reputacyon in his countre, wyll utter his commynycacyon and maters in suche maners & termes that fewe men shall understonde theym. And som honest and grete clerkes have ben wyth me, and desired me to wryte the moste curyous termes that I coude fynde. And thus bytwene playn, rude, & curyous, I stande abasshed. But in my judgemente the comyn termes that be dayli used ben lyghter to be understonde than the olde and auncyent englysshe. And for as moche as this present booke is not for a rude uplondyssh man to laboure therin, ne rede it, but onely for a clerke & a noble gentylman that feleth and understondeth in faytes of armes, in love, & in noble chyvalrye, therfor in a meane bytwene bothe I have reduced & translated this sayd booke in to our englysshe, not ouer rude ne curyous, but in suche termes as shall be understanden, by goddys grace, accordynge to my copye.

BIBLIOGRAPHY

The changes in Middle English are discussed in the various Middle English grammars listed in the footnote to § 174. On the loss of grammatical gender, see L. Morsbach, *Grammatisches und psychologisches Geschlecht im Englischen* (2nd ed., Berlin, 1926), and Samuel Moore, "Grammatical and Natural Gender in Middle English," *PMLA*, 36 (1921), 79–103, where references to the previous literature will be found. On the later history of strong verbs, see Mary M. Long, *The English Strong Verb from Chaucer to Caxton* (Menasha, 1944). A pioneer in the study of the French element in English and its dependence on the Anglo-Norman dialect was Joseph Payne, whose paper on "The Norman Element in the Spoken and Written English of the 12th, 13th, and 14th Centuries, and in Our Provincial Dialects" was published in the *Trans. of the Philological Soc., 1868–1869*, pp. 352–449. His views largely underlie the treatment of Skeat in his *Principles of English Etymology*, Second Series (Oxford, 1891). Dietrich Behrens dealt in detail with the French borrowings before 1250 in his *Beiträge zur Geschichte der französischen Sprache in England: I, Zur Lautlehre der französischen Lehnwörter im Mittelenglischen* (Heilbronn, 1886). J. Derocquigny's *A Contribution to the Study of the French Element in English* (Lille, 1904) is of slight value except for the remarks on individual words. Other treatments of the subject in various aspects are Robert Mettig, *Die französische Elemente im Alt- und Mittelenglischen (800–1258)* (Marburg, 1910); O. Funke, "Zur Wortgeschichte der französischen Elemente im Englischen," *Englische Studien*, 55 (1921), 1–25; S. H. Bush, "Old Northern French Loan-words in Middle-English," *Philol. Qu.*, 1 (1922), 161–72; Robert Feist, *Studien zur Rezeption des französischen Wortschatzes im Mittelenglischen* (Leipzig, 1934); and Emrik Slettenger, *Contributions to the Study of French Loanwords in Middle English* (Örebro, 1932), the last dealing with phonological developments in Anglo-French and Middle English. The extent of the French penetration in certain sections of the vocabulary can be seen in such studies as Bruno Voltmer, *Die mittelenglische Terminologie der ritterlichen Verwandtschafts- und Standesverhältnisse nach der höfischen Epen und Romanzen des 13. und 14. Jahrhunderts* (Pinneberg, 1911), and Helene Döll, *Mittelenglische Kleidernamen im Spiegel literarischer Denkmäler des 14. Jahrhunderts* (Giessen, 1932). Comprehensive, and treating borrowings down to the nineteenth century, is Fraser Mackenzie, *Les Relations de l'Angleterre et de la France d'après le vocabulaire*, vol. 2 (Paris, 1939). There are also special treatments of the Romance element in individual writers, such as Hans Remus, *Die kirchlichen und speziellwissenschaftlichen romanischen Lehnworte Chaucers* (Halle, 1906); Joseph Mersand, *Chaucer's Romance Vocabulary* (2nd ed., New York, 1939); Georg Reismüller, *Romanische Lehnwörter (erstbelege) bei Lydgate* (Leipzig, 1911); and Hans Faltenbacher, *Die romanischen, speziell französischen und lateinischen (bezw. latinisierten) Lehnwörter bei Caxton* (Munich, 1907). Much additional material is becoming available with the publication of the new *Middle English Dictionary*, ed. Hans Kurath, Sherman M. Kuhn, and John Reidy (Ann Arbor, 1952–, in progress).

For the study of Anglo-Norman the appendix to A. Stimming's *Der Anglonormannische Boeve de Haumtone* (Halle, 1899) is invaluable. For the earlier period J. Vising's *Étude sur le dialecte anglo-normand du XIIᵉ siècle* (Uppsala, 1882) is important, and Emil Busch, *Laut- und Formenlehre der Anglonormannischen Sprache des XIV. Jahrhunderts*, is helpful for the later. L. E. Menger's *The Anglo-Norman Dialect* (New York, 1904) attempts to survey the phonology and morphology down to the early fourteenth century. M. K. Pope's *From Latin to Modern French with Especial Consideration of Anglo-Norman* (2nd ed., Manchester, 1952) contains a chapter on the special developments in England. Skeat's two lists in the *Trans. of the Philological Soc.*, 1880–1881 and 1888–1890, offer a convenient collection of French words used in England.

The loss of native words is treated in a series of monographs, such as Emil Hemken, *Das Aussterben alter Substantiva im Verlaufe der englischen Sprachgeschichte* (Kiel, 1906). Similar treatments are those of Oberdörffer on the adjective (Kiel, 1908), Offe on the verb (Kiel, 1908), Rotzoll on diminutives (Heidelberg, 1909), and the more general dissertations of Fr. Teichert, *Über das Aussterben alter Wörter im Verlaufe der englischen Sprachgeschichte* (Kiel, 1912), and Kurt Jaeschke, *Beiträge zur Frage des Wortschwundes im Englischen* (Breslau, 1931). The curtailment of prefix and suffix derivatives can be seen in such studies as T. P. Harrison, *The Separable Prefixes in Anglo-Saxon* (Baltimore, 1892), and the studies of individual prefixes in Old English such as *uz* by Lehmann (Hamburg, 1905), *bi* by Lenze (Kiel, 1909), *for(e)* by Siemerling (Kiel, 1909), *on(d)* by Lüngen (Kiel, 1911), *wið(er)* by Hohenstein (Kiel, 1912), and *ofer* by Röhling (Heidelberg, 1914). Full titles of all these works can be found in Kennedy's *Bibliography*. Among other studies mention may be made of F. Martin, *Die produktiven Abstraktsuffixe des Mittelenglischen* (Strassburg, 1906); O. Höge, *Die*

Deminutivbildungen im Mittelenglischen (Heidelberg, 1906); and K. H. Schmidt, *Präfixwandlungen in Me. und Ne. bei Verben, Substantiven und Adjektiven* (Strassburg, 1909).

The Latin borrowings in Middle English and the affectation of aureate terms are treated in the works of Dellit and Mendenhall mentioned in the footnotes to § 142 and § 143. The important references for the influence of the Low Countries are given in the footnote to § 145.

There are individual studies of particular dialect features and dialect areas, including the works of Wyld, Ekwall, Serjeantson, and others. A more extensive monograph is Gillis Kristensson, *A Survey of Middle English Dialects 1290–1350: The Six Northern Counties and Lincolnshire* (Lund, 1967; *Lund Stud. in English*, vol. 35), with a useful bibliography covering the whole of England.

On the rise of Standard English the fundamental work is L. Morsbach, *Ueber den Ursprung der neuenglischen Schriftsprache* (Heilbronn, 1888), which may be supplemented by H. M. Flasdieck, *Forschungen zur Frühzeit der neuenglischen Schriftsprache* (2 parts, Halle, 1922). Contributing elements are discussed by R. E. Zachrisson, "Notes on the Essex Dialect and the Origin of Vulgar London Speech," *Englische Studien*, 59 (1925), 346–60; Agnes Peitz, *Der Einfluss des nördlichen Dialektes in Mittelenglischen auf die entstehende Hochsprache* (Bonn, 1933); and H. C. Wyld, "South-Eastern and South-East Midland Dialects in Middle English," *Essays and Studies*, 6 (1920), 112–45. The characteristics of the London dialect are treated by B. A. Mackenzie, *The Early London Dialect* (Oxford, 1928), to which may be added two articles by P. H. Reaney, "On Certain Phonological Features of the Dialect of London in the Twelfth Century," *Englische Studien*, 59 (1925), 321–45, and "The Dialect of London in the Thirteenth Century," *ibid.*, 61 (1926), 9–23. A later period is treated in Hans Friederici, *Der Lautstand Londons um 1400* (Jena, 1937; *Forsch. zur engl. Phil.*, no. 6). Important collections of localized documents will be found in L. Morsbach, *Mittelenglische Originalurkunden von der Chaucer-Zeit bis zur Mitte des XV. Jahrhunderts* (Heidelberg, 1923); H. M. Flasdieck, *Mittelenglische Originalurkunden (1405–1430)* (Heidelberg, 1926); and, most important, R. W. Chambers and Marjorie Daunt, *A Book of London English, 1384–1425* (2nd ed., enlarged, Oxford, 1967).

[8]

The Renaissance, 1500–1650

152. *Changing Conditions in the Modern Period.* In the development of
languages particular events often have recognizable and at times far-
reaching effects. The Norman Conquest and the Black Death are typical
instances that we have already seen. But there are also more general conditions which come into being and are no less influential. In the Modern
English period, the beginning of which is conveniently placed at 1500,
certain of these new conditions come into play, conditions which previously
either had not existed at all or were present in only a limited way, and they
cause English to develop along somewhat different lines from those that *changes*
had characterized its history in the Middle Ages. The new factors were the
printing press, the rapid spread of popular education, the increased
communication and means of communication, and the growth of what may
be called social consciousness.

The invention of the process of printing from movable type, which
occurred in Germany about the middle of the fifteenth century, was destined
to exercise a far-reaching influence on all the vernacular languages of
Europe. Introduced into England about 1476 by William Caxton, who had
learned the art on the continent, printing made such rapid progress that a
scant century later it was observed that manuscript books were seldom to
be seen and almost never used. Some idea of the rapidity with which the
new process swept forward may be had from the fact that in Europe the
number of books printed before the year 1500 reaches the surprising figure
of 35,000. The majority of these, it is true, were in Latin, whereas it is in
the modern languages that the effect of the printing press was chiefly to be
felt. But in England over 20,000 titles in English had appeared by 1640,

ranging all the way from mere pamphlets to massive folios. The result was to bring books, which had formerly been the expensive luxury of the few, within the reach of all. More important, however, was the fact, so obvious today, that it was possible to reproduce a book in a thousand copies or a hundred thousand, every one exactly like the other. A powerful force thus existed for promoting a standard, uniform language, and the means were now available for spreading that language throughout the territory in which it was understood.

Such a widespread influence would not have been possible were it not for the fact that education was making rapid progress among the people and literacy was becoming much more common. In the later Middle Ages a surprising number of people of the middle class could read and write, as the Paston Letters abundantly show. In Shakespeare's London, though we have no accurate means of measurement, it is probable that not less than a third and probably as many as half of the people could at least read. In the seventeenth and eighteenth centuries there arose a prosperous tradesman class with the means to obtain an education and the leisure to enjoy it, attested, for example, by the great increase in the number of schools, the tremendous journalistic output of a man like Defoe, and the rapid rise of the novel. Nowadays, when practically everyone goes to school, we witness the phenomenon of newspapers with circulations of several hundred thousand copies daily, even up to two million, and magazines which in an exceptional case reach a total of 80 million copies per month. As a result of popular education the printing press has been able to exert its influence upon language as upon thought.

A third factor of great importance to language in modern times is the way in which the different parts of the world have been brought together through commerce, transportation, and the rapid means of communication which we have developed. The exchange of commodities and the exchange of ideas are both stimulating to language. We shall see later how the expansion of the British Empire and the extension of trade enlarged the English vocabulary by words drawn from every part of the world, besides spreading the language over vast areas whose existence was undreamed of in the Middle Ages. But while diversification has been one of the results of transportation, unification has also resulted from ease of travel and communication. The steamship and the railroad, the automobile, and the airplane have brought people into contact with one another and joined communities hitherto isolated, while the post office and the telegraph, the telephone, the radio, the movies, and television have been influential in the intermingling of language and the lessening of the more easily altered local idiosyncrasies.[1]

Finally there is the important factor which we have called <u>social consciousness</u>. It is no new thing, but something which in the modern world has been given freer play. It is everyone's natural tendency to identify himself with a certain social or economic group, if possible with a slightly higher group. As long as the lines between social classes were fairly tightly drawn, a man was likely to speak the language of his class without much thought as to the consequences, but under the democratic conditions that prevail today, where a man can lift himself into a different economic or intellectual or social level, he is likely to make an effort to adopt the standards of grammar and pronunciation of the people with whom he has become identified, just as he tries to conform to their fashions and tastes in his dress or his amusements. He is as careful of his speech as of his manners. Awareness that there are standards of language is a part of his social consciousness.

153. *Effect upon Grammar and Vocabulary.* The forces here mentioned may be described as both radical and conservative—radical in matters of vocabulary, conservative in matters of grammar. By a radical force is meant anything that promotes change in language; by conservative, what tends to preserve the existing status. Now it is obvious that the printing press, the reading habit, and all forms of communication are favorable to the spread of ideas and stimulating to the growth of the vocabulary, while these same agencies, together with social consciousness as we have described it, work actively toward the promotion and maintenance of a standard, especially in grammar and usage. They operate both singly and in combination. Education, for example, exerts its influence not only through formal instruction in language—grammar, spelling, pronunciation, etc.— but by making possible something more important, the unconscious absorption of a more or less standard English through books, magazines, and newspapers. We shall accordingly be prepared to find that in modern times changes in grammar have been relatively slight and changes in vocabulary extensive. This is just the reverse of what was true in the Middle English period. Then the changes in grammar were revolutionary, but,

---

[1] On the efforts of the British Broadcasting Company to standardize the pronunciation of announcers, see A. Lloyd James, *The Broadcast Word* (London, 1935). In America we have W. Cabell Greet, *World Words, Recommended Pronunciations* (New York, 1948, by arrangement with CBS), and J. F. Bender, *NBC Handbook of Pronunciation* (3rd ed., New York, 1964).

apart from the special effects of the Norman Conquest, those in vocabulary were not so great.

154. *The Problems of the Vernaculars.* In the Middle Ages the development of English took place under conditions which, because of the Norman Conquest, were largely peculiar to England. None of the other modern languages of Europe had had to endure the consequences of a foreign conquest that temporarily imposed an outside tongue upon the dominant social class and left the native speech chiefly in the hands of the uncultivated. But by the close of the Middle English period English had passed through this experience, and, though bearing deep and abiding marks of what it had gone through, had made a remarkable recovery. From this time on the course of its history runs in many ways parallel with that of the other important European languages. In the sixteenth century the modern languages faced three great problems: (1) recognition in the fields where Latin had for centuries been supreme, (2) the establishment of a more uniform orthography, and (3) the enrichment of the vocabulary so that it would be adequate to meet the demands that would be made upon it in its wider use. Each of these problems received extensive consideration in the England of the Renaissance, but it is interesting to note that they were likewise being discussed in much the same way in France and Italy, and to some extent in Germany and Spain. Italy had the additional task of deciding upon the basis of her literary dialect, a matter which in France and England had been largely taken care of by the ascendancy of Paris and London.

155. *The Struggle for Recognition.* Although English, along with the other vernaculars, had attained an established position as the language of popular literature, there was still a strong tradition that sanctioned the use of Latin in all the fields of knowledge. This tradition was strengthened by the "revival of learning," in which the records of Greek civilization became once more available in the original. Latin and Greek were not only the key to the world's knowledge, but the languages in which much highly esteemed poetry, oratory, and philosophy were to be read. And Latin, at least, had the advantage of universal currency, so that the educated all over Europe could freely communicate with each other, both in speech and writing, in a common idiom. Beside the classical languages, which seemingly had attained perfection, the vulgar tongues seemed immature, unpolished, and limited in resource. It was felt that they could not express the abstract ideas and the range of thought embodied in the ancient languages. Scholars alone had access to this treasure; they could cultivate the things of the spirit and enrich their lives. It would seem at times as though they felt their superiority to the less highly educated and were jealous of a prerogative which belonged to them alone. The defenders of the classical tradition were at no loss for arguments in support of their position. It was feared that the study of the classical languages, and even learning itself, would suffer if the use of the vernaculars were carried too far. And there were many who felt that it would be dangerous if matters like the disputes of theology and discussions in medicine fell into the hands of the indiscreet.

Against this tradition the modern languages now had their champions. In Italy as early as 1434 Alberti, himself a humanist whose reputation was secured by numerous works in Latin, defends his use of the vernacular also, saying: "I confess that the ancient Latin language is very copious and highly adorned; but I do not see why our Tuscan of today should be held in so little esteem that whatever is written in it, however excellent, should be displeasing to us. . . . And if it is true, as they say, that this ancient language is full of authority among all people, only because many of the learned have written in it, it will certainly be the same with ours if scholars will only refine and polish it with zeal and care."[1] His position had strong supporters in Speroni and Cardinal Bembo. In France Du Bellay wrote his vigorous *Deffence et Illustration de la Langue Françoyse* (1549) "in order to show that our language did not have at its birth such enemies in the gods and the stars that it cannot arrive one day at the same state of excellence and of perfection as others, inasmuch as all sciences can be faithfully and copiously treated in it." Du Bellay's point of view was expressed many times by other members of the Pléiade. And in England likewise there were many defenders of English against those who wished to discriminate against it, among them influential names like Elyot and Ascham, Wilson, Puttenham, and Mulcaster. Of those champions none was more enthusiastic than Richard Mulcaster, Head Master of the Merchant Taylors' School: "But why not all in English, a tung of it self both depe in conceit, and frank in deliverie? I do not think that anie language, be it whatsoever, is better able to utter all arguments, either with more pith, or greater planesse, then our English tung is, if the English utterer be as skilfull in the matter, which he is to utter: as the foren utterer is." He expresses his opinion many times, but perhaps nowhere more eloquently than in the words: "For is it not in dede a mervellous bondage, to becom servants to one tung for learning sake, the most of our time, with losse of most time, whereas we maie have

---

[1] *Proemio* to Book III of his *Della Famiglia* (*Opera Volgari di Leon Batt. Alberti* (5 vols., Florence, 1843–1849), II, 221–22). Cf. G. Mancini, *Vita di Leon Battista Alberti* (2nd ed., rev., Florence, 1911), p. 198.

the verie same treasur in our own tung, with the gain of most time? our own bearing the joyfull title of our libertie and fredom, the Latin tung remembring us of our thraldom and bondage? I love Rome, but London better, I favor Italie, but England more, I honor the Latin, but I worship the English."

Influential as utterances such as these were, their importance lies in the fact that they voiced a widespread feeling. The real force behind the use of English was a popular demand, the demand of all sorts of men in practical life to share in the fruits of the Renaissance. The Revival of Learning had revealed how rich was the store of knowledge and experience preserved from the civilizations of Greece and Rome. The ancients not only had lived but had thought about life and drawn practical conclusions from experience. Much was to be learned from their discussion of conduct and ethics, their ideas of government and the state, their political precepts, their theories of education, their knowledge of military science, and the like. The Renaissance would have had but a limited effect if these ideas had remained the property solely of academic men. If the diplomat, the courtier, and the man of affairs were to profit by them, they had to be expressed in the language that everybody read.

The demand was soon met. Translations (and, it might be added, original works generated by the same intellectual ferment) literally poured from the press in the course of the sixteenth century. The historians were great favorites, probably because their works, as so often described on the title-pages, were "very delectable and profitable to read." Thucydides and Xenophon had been Englished before Shakespeare started to school, and Herodotus appeared before the dramatist had begun his career. Caesar was translated by Arthur Golding in 1565, Livy and Sallust and Tacitus before the close of the century, and one of the great translations of the age, Plutarch's *Lives of the Noble Grecians and Romans*, in the version of Sir Thomas North, was published in 1579. Works dealing with politics and morals were equally popular. *The Doctrinal of Princes, made by the noble oratour Isocrates* was translated from the Greek as early as 1534 by Sir Thomas Elyot, who had already given Englishmen a taste of Plato in *The Knowledge Which Maketh a Wise Man*. Aristotle, Cicero, Seneca, Epictetus, and Marcus Aurelius appeared in whole or in part, while the poets and dramatists included Virgil, Ovid (1567), Horace (1566–1567), Terence, Theocritus, and most of the lesser names. Various partial translations of Homer were printed before Chapman's version began to appear in 1598. The translators did not stop with the great works of antiquity, but drew also upon medieval and contemporary sources. Saint Augustine, Boethius,

Peter Martyr, Erasmus, Calvin, and Martin Luther were among those rendered into English. It would seem that while scholars were debating the merits of Latin and English the issue was being decided by the translators.

Other factors, however, contributed to the victory. One was the overzeal of the humanists themselves. Not content with the vigorous and independent Latin that was written in the Middle Ages, they attempted to reform Latin prose on the style and vocabulary of Cicero. Ciceronianism substituted slavish imitation for what had been a natural and spontaneous form of expression. Not only was the vocabulary of Cicero inadequate for the conveyance of modern ideas, but there was no hope of being able to surpass one's model. As Ascham confessed in his *Toxophilus*, "as for ye Latin or greke tonge, every thyng is so excellently done in them, that none can do better." Another factor was the Protestant Reformation, itself a phase of the Renaissance. From the time that Wycliffe refused to carry on his quarrel with the church in the language of the schools and took his cause directly to the people in their own tongue, one of the strongholds of Latin was lost. The amount of theological writing in English is almost unbelievable, for as one Elizabethan remarked, "The dissension in divinity is fierce beyond God's forbid." Finally, we must not overlook the fact that the context between Latin and English had a commercial side. The market for English books was naturally greater than for Latin, and we cannot blame the Elizabethan printer if he sometimes thought, as one said to Thomas Drant in 1567, "Though, sir, your book be wise and full of learning, yet peradventure it will not be so saleable."

Although it is plain to us nowadays that from the beginning the recognition of English was assured, the victory was not lightly won. The use of English for purposes of scholarship was frankly experimental. Sir Thomas Elyot in his *Doctrinal of Princes* (1534) says: "This little book . . . I have translated out of greke . . . to the intent onely that I wolde assaie, if our English tongue mought receive the quicke and proper sentences pronounced by the greekes." The statement is slightly apologetic. Certainly those who used English where they might have been expected to write in Latin often seem to anticipate possible criticism and they attempt to justify their action. Ascham prefaces his *Toxophilus* with the statement: "And althoughe to have written this boke either in latin or Greke . . . had bene more easier and fit for mi trade in study, yet neverthelesse, I supposinge it no point of honestie, that mi commodite should stop and hinder ani parte either of the pleasure or profite of manie, have written this Englishe matter in the Englische tongue, for Englische men." In his *Castle of Health* (1534) Elyot is somewhat bolder in his attitude: "If physicians be angry, that I have written physicke in englische, let them remember that the grekes wrate in greke, the Romains in latine, Avicenna, and the other in Arabike, whiche were their own proper and maternall tongues. And if thei had bene as muche attached with envie and covetise, as some nowe seeme to be, they wolde have devised some particuler language, with a strange cipher or forme of letters, wherin they wold have written their scyence, whiche language or letters no manne should have knowen that had not professed and practised physicke." All these attempts at self-justification had as their strongest motive the desire to reach the whole people in the language they understood best. This is stated with engaging frankness by Mulcaster: "I do write in my naturall English toungue, bycause though I make the learned my judges, which understand Latin, yet I meane good to the unlearned, which understand but English, and he that understands Latin very well, can understand English farre better, if he will confesse the trueth, though he thinks he have the habite and can Latin it exceeding well." Statements such as these, which could be multiplied many times from the literature of the period, show that the recognition of English was achieved in spite of a rather persistent opposition.

As we approach the end of the century and see that English has slowly won recognition as a language of serious thought, we detect a note of patriotic feeling in the attitude of many men. They seem to have grown tired of being told that English was crude and barbarous. This is apparent in the outburst of George Pettie in his book on *Civile Conversation* (1586): "There are some others yet who wyll set lyght by my labours, because I write in Englysh: and . . . the woorst is, they thinke that impossible to be doone in our Tongue: for they count it barren, they count it barbarous, they count it unworthy to be accounted of." "But," he adds, "how hardly soever you deale with your tongue, how barbarous soever you count it, how litle soever you esteeme it, I durst my selfe undertake (if I were furnished with Learnying otherwyse) to wryte in it as copiouslye for varietie, as compendiously for brevitie, as choycely for woordes, as pithily for sentences, as pleasauntly for figures, and every way as eloquently, as any writer should do in any vulgar tongue whatsoever." Mulcaster goes so far as to say: "I take this present period of our English tung to be the verie height therof, bycause I find it so excellentlie well fined, both for the bodie of the tung it self, and for the customarie writing thereof, as either foren workmanship can give it glosse, or as homewrought hanling can give it grace. When the age of our peple, which now use the tung so well, is dead and departed there will another succede, and with the peple the tung will alter and change. Which change in the full harvest thereof maie prove comparable to this, but sure for this which we now use, it semeth even now to be at the best for substance, and the bravest for circumstance, and whatsoever shall becom of the English state, the English tung cannot prove fairer, then it is at this daie, if it maie please our learned sort to esteme so of it, and to bestow their travell upon such a subject, so capable of ornament, so proper to themselves, and the more to be honored, bycause it is their own." In 1595 Richard Carew wrote a discourse on *The Excellency of the English Tongue,* and about 1583 Sir Philip Sidney could say, "But for the uttering sweetly and properly the conceit of the minde, which is the end of speech, that [English] hath it equally with any other tongue in the world."

156. The Problem of Orthography. Spelling is for most people a pedestrian subject, but for the English, as for the French and the Italians, in the sixteenth century the question of orthography or "right writing," as Mulcaster preferred to call it, was a matter of real importance and the subject of much discussion. The trouble was not merely that English spelling was bad, for it is still bad today, but that there was no generally accepted system that everyone could conform to. In short, it was neither phonetic nor fixed. Speaking generally, the spelling of the modern languages in the Middle Ages had attempted with fair success to represent the pronunciation of words, and this is true of English in spite of the fact that Norman scribes introduced considerable confusion when they tried to write a language which they imperfectly knew and carried over habits which they had formed in writing French. The confusion was increased when certain spellings gradually became conventional while the pronunciation slowly changed (see, for example, § 177). In some cases a further discrepancy between sound and symbol arose when letters were inserted in words where they were not pronounced (like the *b* in *debt* or *doubt*) because the corresponding word in Latin was so spelled (*debitum, dubitare*), or in other cases (for example, the *gh* in *delight, tight*) by analogy with words similarly pronounced (*light, night*) where the *gh* had formerly represented an actual sound. The variability of English spelling was an important part of the instability which people felt characterized the English language in the sixteenth century, especially as compared with a language like Latin. To many it seemed that English spelling was chaotic.

In reality it was not so bad as that. There were limits to its variety and inconsistency. It varied more from writer to writer, according to education and temperament, than within the practice of the individual. Then as now, some men were more inclined than others to adopt a given way of doing a thing and to stick to it. Consistency in a matter like spelling often went with a scholarly temperament. Sir John Cheke, for example, has a system of spelling which he adheres to fairly closely. He doubles long vowels (*taak, haat, maad, mijn, thijn*, etc., for *take, hate, made, mine, thine*), discards final *–e* (*giv, belev*), always uses *i* for *y* (*mighti, dai*), and so forth. It is not our system or that of most of his contemporaries, but it is a system and he observed it.[1] Some men observed a system for a particular reason. Thus Richard Stanyhurst, attempting a translation of Virgil (1582) in quantitative verse after the model of Latin poetry, employs a special spelling to help bring out what he believes to be the length of English syllables. He is consistent about spellings like *thee* (for *the*), *too* (for *to*), *mee, neere, coonning, woorde, yeet*, but he writes *featlye, neatlie, aptly* within three lines. He is strictly speaking consistent only so far as it serves his purpose to be. On the other hand, it is clear from the letters of such a man as John Chamberlain, which begin toward the end of the century, that the average man of education in Shakespeare's day did not spell by mere whim or caprice, but had formed fairly constant spelling habits.[2] Such habits were to some extent personal with each individual and differed in some particulars from those of the next man, but each writer will show a fair degree of consistency within his own practice. It was somewhat different with the hastier writing of the more popular playwrights and pamphleteers. It is not always clear how much of their spelling is to be credited to them and how much to the printer. Most printers probably took advantage of the variability of English spelling to "justify" a line, with as little scruple about optional letters as about extra spaces. In any case a certain difference is to be noticed between the spelling of pamphlets like those of Greene, which we can hardly believe were proofread, and a book like North's *Plutarch* or Holinshed's *Chronicles*. In one of Greene's coney-catching pamphlets, *A Notable Discovery of Coosnage* (1591), we find *coñey* spelled *cony, conny, conye, conie, connie, coni, cuny, cunny, cunnie*, while in other words there are such variations as *coosnage, coosenage, cosenage, cosnage, been, beene, bin, fellow, felow, felowe, fallow, fallowe, neibor, neighbor, go, goe, their, theyr*, etc. But in spite of all the variety that Elizabethan spelling presents, there was by 1550 a nucleus of common practice, and many of the features of English spelling today were clearly becoming established.

That the problem of bringing about greater agreement in the writing of English was recognized in the sixteenth century is apparent from the attempts made to draw up rules and to devise new systems. The earliest of

---

[1] There were some spellings about which he had apparently not made up his mind. He writes *borrowing* in three ways within a single paragraph.

[2] See Appendix B.

these, *An A. B. C. for Children* (before 1558), is almost negligible. It consists of only a few pages, and part of the space is devoted to "precepts of good lyvynge," but the author manages to formulate certain general rules such as the use of the final *e* to indicate vowel length (*made, ride, hope*). Certain more ambitious treatises attacked the problem in what their authors conceived to be its most fundamental aspect. This was the very imperfect way in which the spelling of words represented their sound. These writers were prepared to discard the current spelling entirely and respell the language phonetically with the use of additional symbols where needed. Thus in 1568 Thomas Smith published a *Dialogue concerning the Correct and Emended Writing of the English Language.* He increased the alphabet to thirty-four letters and marked the long vowels. Smith's reform did not win much favor. His work, moreover, was in Latin, and this would further limit its chance of popular influence. The next year another attempt at phonetic writing was made in a work by John Hart called *An Orthographie*, elaborated in the following year in *A Method or Comfortable Beginning for All Unlearned, Whereby They May Bee Taught to Read English* (1570).[1] Hart makes use of special characters for *ch, sh, th*, etc., but his system seems to have won no more favor than Smith's. A more considerable attempt at phonetic reform was made in 1580 by William Bullokar in his *Booke at Large, for the Amendment of Orthographie for English Speech.* He confesses that he has profited by the mistakes of Smith and Hart, whose works were "not received in use (the chiefe cause whereof, I thinke, was their differing so farre from the old)." So he says, "My chiefe regard (from the beginning) was to follow the figures of the old letters and the use of them . . . as much as possible." He accordingly invents few special characters, but makes liberal use of accents, apostrophes, and numerous hooks above and below the letters, both vowels and consonants. If his innovations in this way had been more moderate, English spelling might have come to the use of accents such as were being adopted for French at this time, but one glance at a specimen page printed according to his system shows why it could not possibly win acceptance.[2] Attempts such as the foregoing continued well into the seventeenth century. Many of them represented mere exercises in ingenuity, as when Charles Butler, in *The English Grammar, or The Institution of Letters, Syllables, and Woords in the English Tung* (1634), substitutes an inverted apostrophe for final *e*'s

---

[1] On Hart see Bror Danielsson, *John Hart's Works on English Orthography and Pronunciation* (2 vols., Stockholm, 1955–1964), a model of scholarly editing.

[2] Bullokar's *Booke at Large* has been reprinted in facsimile with an introduction by Diane Bornstein (Delmar, New York, 1977).

1 6　If any half voẃel, ̈ɔ foloẃ: r,
　　our ſpeȼh ſerúȩ̈th ẃel, ̃ɔ ſpel them togeȼher.

1 7　And this ſtrŷk (,) iȥ erȼepȼion generaľ,
　　̃ɔ ſpel ẃoȥdȥ trulȳ, ̈hen thæ̃ȥ rulȥ fail aľ.

1 8　Ƞot ẃel, thér iȥ neuer tru ſillabľ,
　　ẃithout voẃel, diᵽhthong, oȥ half voẃel.

1 9　And thoŵh half voẃelȥ bé ſpelḑ beſt alóñ,
　　ȳet the nert conſonant it depenḑȩth on.

2 0　By eȥ, oȥ ȥ, the pluraľ ̈ɔ ges,
　　̈ǿȥ ſimplȥ genitíuȥ, enḑ éȥ, oȥ ȥ.

¶ The 12. Chapter,

ſheweth the vſe of this amendment, by matter in
proſe with the ſame ortography, conteíning
arguments for the premiſſes.

An exer-
ȼŷȥ for
erampľ.

Ŵér-in iȥ ŵeẃeḑ an ererȼŷȥ of the amenḑeḑ oȥtogra-
ᵽhy befóȥ ŵeẃeḑ, and the vȼ of the pȥikȥ, ſtrŷkȥ, and
nótȥ, for deuȳding of ſillabľȥ accoȥding ̃ɔ the rulȥ
befóȥ ŵeẃeḑ. Ŵær-in iȥ ̃ɔ bé noteḑ, that no art, ererȼŷȥ, mirtur, ſȼienȼ, oȥ occupaȼion, ̈hat-ſocuer, iȥ included in óñ thing ónly: but haȼh in it ſeueraľ diſtincȼionȥ, elementȥ, prinȼiplȥ, oȥ deuiȥionȥ, by the ̈hich the ſám comȩth ̃ɔ hiȥ perfet vȼ.
And bicauȥ the ſingľ deuiȥionȥ for engliŵ ſpeȼh, ár at this day ſo unperfetly picˇtureḑ, by the elementȥ (̈hich ẃe caľ letterȥ) prouȳdeḑ for

Of pro-
fit̃ the
græteſt
iȥ ̃ɔ bé
ȼhóȥñ.
Ignoranȼ cauȥ-
ȥȩȼh many ̃ɔ faľ
& offenḑ.

the ſám, (aȥ may apper plainly in this fóȥmer træti̇c) I haui ſet furth
this ẃoȥk for the amendment of the ſám: ̈hich I hóp ̈il bé tákñ
in gǿd part accoȥding ̃ɔ my mæning: for that, that it haľ ſaui chargeȥ in the elder ſoȥt, & ſaui græt tŷm in the pȳth, ̃ɔ the græt comoditȳ of aľ eſtátȥ, unto ̈ǿm it iȥ neceſſarȳ, that thér bé a knowledg of
their dutȳ, unto God ȼhefly, and then their dutȳ óñ ̃ɔ an oȼher: in
knowing of ̈,ich dutȳ, conſiſtȩth the hapi eſtát of manȥ lȳf: for ignoranȼ cauȥȩȼh many ̃ɔ go out-of the way, and that of aľ eſtátȥ, in
̈ǿm ignoȥanȼ doȼh reſt: thær-by God iȥ grætly diſ-plæȥeḑ, the
comon qietnes of meñ hinḑereḑ: græt comion welȼhȥ deuȳdeḑ, ma-
giſtrátȥ

WILLIAM BULLOKAR'S *BOOKE AT LARGE* (1580)

(see § 156)

and ʒ for *th* (*boʒ*, *wiʒout*, ʒird). Efforts at such a radical reform as these enthusiasts proposed were largely wasted.

This was clearly perceived by Richard Mulcaster, the teacher of Spenser, whose *Elementarie* (1582), "which entreateth chefelie of the right writing of our English tung," is the most extensive and the most important treatise on English spelling in the sixteenth century. Mulcaster's great virtue is his moderation. He saw the futility of trying to make English spelling phonetic in any scientific sense. He was therefore willing to compromise between the ideal and the practical. He did not believe that the faults of English spelling were so desperate that they could be removed only by desperate remedies. The way to correct an existing difficulty was not to substitute a new and greater one. This seemed to him to be the effect of all those proposals that took into consideration only the sound of words. Even at its best, he did not think that spelling could ever perfectly represent sound. The differences between one sound and another were often too subtle. "Letters," he says, "can expresse sounds withall their joynts & properties no fuller then the pencill can the form & lineaments of the face." It was inevitable, he thought, that the same letter must sometimes be used for different sounds, but this was no worse than to use the same word, as we often do, in very different senses. Another difficulty that he saw was that pronunciation constantly changes. These were his theoretical reasons for refusing to go along with the phonetic reformers. His practical reason was that their systems were too cumbersome ever to be accepted. "But sure I take the thing to be to combersom and inconvenient, . . . where no likeliehood of anie profit at all doth appear in sight." Every attempt to force people against established custom "hath alwaie mist, with losse of labor where it offered service."

The basis of his reform, therefore, was custom or usage. This he defines not as the practice of the ignorant, but that "wherein the skilfull and best learned do agre." "The use & custom of our cuntrie hath allredie chosen a kinde of penning wherein she hath set down hir relligion, hir lawes, hir privat and publik dealings." This cannot now be completely changed, although it can be pruned "so that the substance maie remain, and the change take place in such points onelie as maie please without noveltie and profit without forcing." "I will therefor do my best," he says, "to confirm our custom in his own right, which will be easilie obtained where men be acquainted with the matter allredie and wold be verie glad to se wherein the right of their writing standeth." In making usage his point of departure he does not ignore sound; he merely insists that it shall not be given an undue share of attention. We must use common sense and try to remove defects in the existing system, not substitute a new one. He thinks ease and convenience in writing should be considered, for popular approval is the final authority. Only a general goodness, not perfection in each detail, can be expected. No set of rules can cover all points; some things must be left to observation and daily practice.

The details of his system we cannot enter into here. We must be content with a statement of his general aims. He would first of all get rid of superfluous letters. There is no use in writing *putt, grubb, ledd* for *put, grub, led,* "and a thowsand such ignorant superfluities." On the other hand, we must not omit necessary letters such as the *t* in *fetch* or *scratch*. He allows double consonants only where they belong to separate syllables (*wit–ting*), and almost never at the end of a word except in the case of *ll* (*tall, generall*). Words ending in *–ss* he writes *–sse* (*glasse, confesse*). Otherwise final *–e* is used regularly to indicate a preceding long vowel, distinguishing *made* from *mad, stripe* from *strip,* and at the end of words ending in the sound of *v* or *z* (*deceive, love, wise*). An *e* is added to words that end in a lightly pronounced *i: daie, maie, trewlie, safetie;* but when the *i* is sounded "loud and sharp" it is spelled *y: deny, cry, defy.* Analogy, or as he calls it, "proportion," plays a justly important part in his system. Since we write *hear,* we should therefore write *fear* and *dear.* This principle, he admits, is subject to exceptions which must be made in deference to "prerogative," that is, the right of language to continue a common custom, as in employing an analogous spelling for *where, here, there.* In such a case he becomes frankly the apologist, justifying the common practice. He is really more interested in having everyone adopt the same spelling for a given word than he is in phonetic consistency. It is not so much a question of whether one should write *where* as that he should adopt a single spelling and use it regularly instead of writing *where, wher, whear, wheare, were, whair,* etc. To this end he prints in the latter part of his book a *General Table* giving the recommended spelling for some 7,000 of the commonest words. Mulcaster's spelling is not always the one which ultimately came to be adopted. In spite of his effort for the most part to follow current usage, he seems sometimes to have gone counter to the tendency of his own and later times. He advocates spelling *guise, guide, guest,* and the like without the *u* and writes *băble, dăble,* indicating the length of the vowel by a short mark over it. But his book had the great merit—or demerit—of standardizing a large number of current spellings, justifying them, and advocating the consistent use of them.

It is impossible to say how influential Mulcaster's work was. The effect of his precepts seems to be evident in certain later writers. Ben Jonson quotes from him, often without acknowledgment. That English spelling developed along the lines laid down by him is certain, but this may have been due largely to the fact that it was already developing along these lines and would have done so even without the help of his book.

During the first half of the next century the tendency toward uniformity increased steadily. The fixation of English spelling is associated in most people's minds with the name of Dr. Johnson, and a statement in the preface of his dictionary might lend color to this idea. In reality, however, our spelling in its modern form had been practically established by about 1650. In *The New World of English Words* published in 1658 by Milton's nephew, Edward Phillips, the compiler says: "As for orthography, it will not be requisite to say any more of it then may conduce to the readers direction in the finding out of words," and he adds two or three remarks about Latin *prae–* being rendered in English by *pre–*, and the like. Otherwise he seemed to think that the subject did not call for any discussion. And in reality it did not. The only changes we should make in the sentence just quoted are in the spelling *then* (for *than*) and the addition of an apostrophe in *readers*. A closer scrutiny of the preface as a whole[1] would reveal a few other differences such as an occasional *e* where we have dropped it (*kinde*), *ll* and *sse* at the end of words (*gratefull, harshnesse*), *–ick* for *–ic* (*logick*), and a contracted form of the past participle (*authoriz'd, chanc't*). Even these differences are not very noticeable. Spelling was one of the problems which the English language began consciously to face in the sixteenth century. During the period from 1500 to 1650 it was fairly settled.[2]

157. The Problem of Enrichment. In 1531 Sir Thomas Elyot, statesman as well as scholar, published what has been described as the first book on education printed in English. He called it *The Governour* since it had to do with the training of those who in the future would be occupied at court. The dedication to Henry the Eighth is couched in the following terms:

> I late consideringe (moste excellent prince and myne onely redoughted soveraigne lorde) my duetie that I owe to my naturall contray with my faythe also of aliegeaunce and othe . . . I am (as God juge me) violently stered to *devulgate* or sette fourth some part of my studie, trustynge therby tacquite me of my dueties to God, your hyghnesse, and this my contray. Wherfore takinge comfort and boldenesse, partly of your graces moste benevolent inclination towarde the universall weale of your subjectes, partly inflamed with zele, I have now enterprised to *describe* in our vulgare tunge the

---

[1] See the extract printed in Appendix B.
[2] For a comprehensive account of the English orthoepists see E. J. Dobson, *English Pronunciation 1500–1700* (2 vols., 2nd ed., Oxford, 1968), vol. 1.

fourme of a juste publike weale: ... Whiche *attemptate* is nat of presumption to teache any persone, I my selfe havinge moste nede of teachinge: but onely to the intent that men which wil be studious about the weale publike may fynde the thinge therto expedient compendiously writen. And for as moch as this present boke treateth of the *education* of them that hereafter may be demed worthy to be governours of the publike weale under your hyghnesse ... I *dedicate* it unto your hyghnesse as the fyrste frutes of my studye, verely trustynge that your moste excellent wysedome wyll therein *esteme* my loyall harte and diligent endevour ... Protestinge unto your excellent majestie that where I commende herin any one vertue or *dispraise* any one vice I meane the generall description of thone and thother without any other particuler meanynge to the reproche of any one persone. To the whiche protestation I am nowe dryven throughe the malignite of this present tyme all disposed to malicious detraction ...

In this passage we have an early example of the attempt to improve the English language. The words printed in italics were all new in Elyot's day; two of them (*education, dedicate*) are first found in the English language as he uses them in this dedication. Two others (*esteem* and *devulgate*) are found in the sense here employed only one year earlier. Several others could be instanced which, although recorded slightly earlier, were not yet in general use.[1] In so short a passage these new words are fairly numerous, but not more numerous than in the rest of his book, and, what is more important, they are not the innovations of a pedant or an extremist. Other writers who could be cited were less restrained in their enthusiasm for words drawn from Latin, Greek, and French. Nor are these new words in Elyot the result of chance. They are part of a conscious effort to enrich the English vocabulary.

We have already indicated that enlarging the vocabulary was one of the three major problems confronting the modern languages in the eyes of men in the sixteenth century. And it is not difficult to see why this was so. The Renaissance was a period of increased activity in almost every field.

---

[1] *Benevolent, enterprise, studious, endeavor, protest, reproach, malignity.* The statements in the text are based upon the dated citations in the *OED.* An earlier occurrence of any word is always possible. For example, in a translation by Skelton (c. 1485) of the *History of the World* by Diodorus Siculus, over 800 Latin innovations occur, many earlier than the first instance recorded in the *OED.* But the work exists in a unique Ms. and has never been published. While its influence on the English language was probably negligible, it shows that the attitude of the sixteenth-century innovators was not without precedent. See F. M. Salter, *John Skelton's Contribution to the English Language* (Ottawa, 1945; *Trans. Royal Soc. of Canada*). The purpose of this and the following paragraphs, of course, is to record the efforts of Elyot and others to enrich the English language by the conscious importation of words which they believed were needed.

It would have been strange if the spirit of inquiry and experiment that led to the discovery of America, the reform of the church, the Copernican theory, and the revolution of thought in many fields should have left only language untouched. The rediscovery of Latin and Greek literature led to new activity in the modern languages and directed attention to them as the medium of literary expression. The result was a healthy desire for improvement. The intellectual aspect of the Revival of Learning had a similar effect. The scholarly monopoly of Latin throughout the Middle Ages had left the vernaculars undeveloped along certain lines. Now that this monopoly was being broken, the deficiencies of English were at the same time revealed. English was undoubtedly inadequate, as compared with the classical languages, to express the thought which those languages embodied and which in England was now becoming part of a rapidly expanding civilization. The translations that appeared in such numbers convinced men of the truth of this fact. The very act of translation brings home to the translator the limitations of his medium and tempts him to borrow from other languages the terms whose lack he feels in his own. For men to whom Latin was almost a second mother tongue the temptation to transfer and naturalize in English important Latin radicals was particularly great. This was so, too, with French and Italian. In this way many foreign words were introduced into English. One may say that the same impulse that led men to furnish the English mind with the great works of classical and other literatures led them to enrich the English language with words drawn from the same source. New words were particularly needed in various technical fields, where English was notably weak. The author of a *Discourse of Warre* justifies his introduction of numerous military terms by an argument that was unanswerable: "I knowe no other names than are given by strangers, because there are fewe or none at all in our language."

It is not always easy, however, to draw the line between a word that is needed because no equivalent term exists, and one which merely expresses more fully an idea that could be conveyed in some fashion with existing words. We can appreciate the feeling of a scholar for whom a familiar Latin word had a wealth of associations and a rich connotation; we must admit the reasonableness of his desire to carry such a word over into his English writing. The transfer is all the more excusable when one is convinced that English would be better for having it and that it is a patriotic duty to employ one's knowledge in so worthy a cause as that of improving the national speech. This motive actuated many men who were both earnest and sincere in their desire to relieve English of the charge of inadequacy and inelegance. Thus Elyot apologizes for introducing the word *maturity:*

"Wherfore I am constrained to usurpe a latine worde . . . , which worde,
though it be strange and darke [obscure], yet . . . ones brought in custome,
shall be facile to understande as other wordes late commen out of Italy and
Fraunce. . . . Therefore that worde *maturitie* is translated to the actis of
man, . . . reservyng the wordes *ripe* and *redy* to frute and other thinges
seperate from affaires, as we have nowe in usage. *And this do I nowe
remember for the necessary augmentation of our langage.*" In another place
he says, "I intended to augment our Englyshe tongue, wherby men shulde
as well expresse more abundantly the thynge that they conceyved in theyr
hartis, . . . havyng wordes apte for the pourpose: as also interprete out of
greke, latyn or any other tonge into Englysshe as sufficiently as out of any
one of the said tongues into an other." In any case, whether "of pure
necessitie in new matters, or of mere braverie to garnish it self withall"—to
quote a phrase of Mulcaster's—English acquired in the sixteenth and early
seventeenth centuries thousands of new and strange words.

The greater number of these new words were borrowed from Latin. But
they were not exclusively drawn from that source. Some were taken from
Greek, a great many from French, and not a few from Italian and Spanish.
Even the older periods of English and occasionally the local dialects were
drawn upon to embellish the language, in this case chiefly the language of
poetry. We shall see more particularly in a moment the character of the
additions made at this time, but before doing so we must consider the
conflicting views that different people held concerning their desirability.

158. The Opposition to Inkhorn Terms. The wholesale borrowing of
words from other languages did not meet with universal favor. The
strangeness of the new words was an objection to some people. As Edward
Phillips said in his *New World of Words*, "some people if they spy but a
hard word are as much amazed as if they had met with a Hobgoblin."
Even Elyot's prestige did not save him from criticism on this score. In a
book published two years after *The Governour* he alludes to "divers men . . .
[who] doo shewe them selfes offended (as they say) with my strange
termes," and he attempts to justify his practice. Other men were purists by
nature and took their stand on general principles. Such a man was Sir John
Cheke. His attitude is interesting because he was himself a fine classical
scholar and might have been expected to show sympathy for classical
borrowings. In a letter to Sir Thomas Hoby, prefaced to Hoby's translation
of *The Courtier* (1561), he wrote:

> I am of this opinion that our own tung shold be written cleane
> and pure, unmixt and unmangeled with borowing of other tunges,
> wherin if we take not heed by tijm, ever borowing and never payeng,

she shall be fain to keep her house as bankrupt. For then doth our tung naturallie and praisablie utter her meaning, when she bouroweth no counterfeitness of other tunges to attire her self withall, but useth plainlie her own, with such shift, as nature, craft, experiens and folowing of other excellent doth lead her unto, and if she want at ani tijm (as being unperfight she must) yet let her borow with suche bashfulnes, that it mai appeer, that if either the mould of our own tung could serve us to fascion a woord of our own, or if the old denisoned wordes could content and ease this neede, we wold not boldly venture of unknowen wordes.

Ascham's admiration for Cheke led him to a similar attitude. Some considered the use of learned words mere pedantry and tried to drive them out by ridicule, calling them "inkhorn" terms. Sir Thomas Chaloner, who translated Erasmus' *Praise of Folly* in 1549, is an example:

Such men therfore, that in deede are archdoltes, and woulde be taken yet for sages and philosophers, maie I not aptelie calle theim foolelosophers? For as in this behalfe I have thought good to borowe a littell of the Rethoriciens of these daies, who plainely thynke theim selfes demygods, if lyke horsleches thei can shew two tongues, I meane to mingle their writings with words sought out of strange langages, as if it were alonely thyng for theim to poudre theyr bokes with ynkehorne termes, although perchaunce as unaptly applied as a gold rynge in a sowes nose. That and if they want suche farre fetched vocables, than serche they out of some rotten Pamphlet foure or fyve disused woords of antiquitee, therewith to darken the sence unto the reader, to the ende that who so understandeth theim maie repute hym selfe for more cunnyng and litterate: and who so dooeth not, shall so muche the rather yet esteeme it to be some high mattier, because it passeth his learnyng.

The strongest objection to the new words, however, was on the score of their obscurity. The great exponent of this view was Thomas Wilson, whose *Arte of Rhetorique* (1553) was several times reprinted in the course of the century and was used by Shakespeare. In a classic passage on "Plainnesse, what it is" he makes a savage attack on inkhorn terms and illustrates the fault by a burlesque letter overloaded with them:

Among all other lessons this should first be learned, that wee never affect any straunge ynkehorne termes, but to speake as is commonly received: neither seeking to be over fine, nor yet living over-carelesse, using our speeche as most men doe, and ordering our wittes as the fewest have done. Some seeke so far for outlandish English, that they forget altogether their mothers language. And I dare sweare this, if some of their mothers were alive, thei were not able to tell what they say: and yet these fine English clerkes will say, they speake in their mother tongue, if a man should charge them for counterfeiting the Kings English. Some farre journeyed gentlemen at their returne home, like as they love to goe in forraine apparell, so thei wil pouder their talke with oversea language. He that commeth lately out of Fraunce will talke French English and never blush at the matter. An other chops in with English Italienated, and applieth the Italian phrase to our English speaking, the which is, as if an Oratour that professeth to utter his mind in plaine Latine, would needes speake Poetrie, and farre fetched colours of straunge antiquitie. . . . The unlearned or foolish phantasticall, that smelles but of learning (such fellowes as have seen learned men in their daies) wil so Latin their tongues, that the simple can not but wonder at their talke, and thinke surely they speake by some revelation. I know them that thinke *Rhetorique* to stande wholie upon darke wordes, and hee that can catche an ynke horne terme by the taile, him they coumpt to be a fine Englisheman, and a good *Rhetorician*. And the rather to set out this foly, I will adde suche a letter as William Sommer himselfe, could not make a better for that purpose. Some will thinke and sweare it too, that there was never any such thing written: well, I will not force any man to beleeve it, but I will say thus much, and abide by it too, the like have been made heretofore, and praised above the Moone.

A letter devised by a Lincolneshire man, for a voyde benefice, to a gentleman that then waited upon the Lorde Chauncellour, for the time being.

Pondering, *expending*,[1] and *revoluting* with my selfe, your *ingent*[2] *affabilitie*, and *ingenious capacity* for *mundaine* affaires: I cannot but *celebrate*, & *extol* your *magnifical dexteritie* above all other. For how could you have *adepted*[3] such *illustrate* prerogative, and *dominicall* *superioritie*, if the fecunditie of your *ingenie*[4] had not been so *fertile* and wonderfull pregnant. Now therefore being *accersited*[5] to such *splendente* renoume and dignitie *splendidious:* I doubt not but you will *adjuvate*[6] such poore *adnichilate*[7] orphanes, as whilome ware *condisciples*[8] with you, and of *antique* familiaritie in Lincolneshire. Among whom I being a *scholasticall panion*,[9] *obtestate*[10] your *sublimitie*, to *extoll* mine infirmitie. There is a Sacerdotall dignitie in my *native* Countrey, *contiguate* to me, where I now *contemplate:* which your worshipfull benignitie could sone *impetrate*[11] for mee, if it would like you to extend your sedules, and *collaude*[12] me in them to the right honourable lord Chaunceller, or rather *Archgrammacian* of

---

[1] weighing mentally (L. *expendere*)   [2] huge (L. *ingens*)
[3] attained (L. *adeptus*)   [4] mind, intellect (L. *ingenium*)
[5] brought (L. *accersitus*)   [6] aid (L. *adjuvare*)
[7] reduced to nothing (L. *ad nihil*)   [8] fellow-students   [9] companion
[10] call upon (L. *obtestari*, to call upon as a witness)   [11] procure (L. *impetrare*)
[12] recommend

Englande. You know my literature, you knowe the *pastorall* promotion. I *obtestate* your *clemencie*, to *invigilate*[1] thus much for me, according to my *confidence*, and as you knowe my condigne meritcs for such a *compendious* living. But now I *relinquish* to *fatigate* your intelligence, with any more *frivolous verbositie*, and therfore he that rules the climates, be evermore your beautreux, your fortresse, and your bulwarke. *Amen.*

Dated at my *Dome*,[2] or rather Mansion place in Lincolnshire, the *penulte* of the moneth Sextile. *Anno Millimo, quillimo, trillimo.*

Per me Johannes Octo.

What wiseman reading this Letter, will not take him for a very Caulf that made it in good earnest, and thought by his ynke pot termes to get a good Parsonage?

In the letter included in the above passage the italicized words were new in Wilson's day and therefore somewhat strange and obscure—dark, as he says—to the ordinary reader. Of the forty-five, thirty are not found before the sixteenth century, and the remaining fifteen are of such infrequent occurrence as to be considered by him inkhorn terms. It is interesting to note in passing that many of them are in common use today.

159. *The Defense of Borrowing.* The attitude revealed in these utterances was apparently not the prevailing one. There were many more who in precept or practice approved of judicious importations. As Dryden wrote somewhat later, "I trade both with the living and the dead, for the enrichment of our native tongue. We have enough in England to supply our necessity, but if we will have things of magnificence and splendour, we must get them by commerce."[3] The innovators had precedent on their side. Not only had English borrowed much in the past, but, as they frequently pointed out, all other languages, including Latin and Greek, had enriched themselves in this way.[4] The strangeness of the new words, they argued, would soon wear off. As Mulcaster observed, we must first become acquainted with any new thing "and make the thing familiar if it seme to be strange. For all strange things seme great novelties, and hard of entertainment at their first arrivall, till theie be acquainted: but after acquaintance theie be verie familiar, and easie to entreat.... Familiaritie and

---

[1] be watchful   [2] house (L. *domus*)

[3] Dedication to his translation of the *Aeneid* (1697).

[4] In France the same argument was being employed: "To wish to take away from a learned man who desires to enrich his language the freedom sometimes to adopt uncommon words would be to restrain our language, not yet rich enough, under a more rigorous law than that which the Greeks and Romans gave themselves." (Du Bellay, *Deffence et Illustration*, chap. 6.)

acquaintance will cause facilitie, both in matter and in words." The charge
of obscurity was also met. Elyot maintained that throughout *The Governour*
"there was no terme new made by me of a latine or frenche worde, but it is
there declared so playnly by one mene or other to a diligent reder that no
sentence is therby made derke or harde to be understande." Not all men
could say as much, but in theory this was their aim. The position of the
defender was in general summed up by George Pettie, the translator of
Guazzo's *Civile Conversation:*

> For the barbarousnesse[1] of our tongue, I must lykewyse say that
> it is much the worse for them [the objectors], and some such curious
> fellowes as they are: who if one chaunce to derive any woord from
> the Latine, which is insolent to their eares (as perchaunce they wyll
> take that phrase to be) they foorthwith make a jest at it, and terme
> it an Inkehorne terme. And though for my part I use those woords
> as litle as any, yet I know no reason why I should not use them, and
> I finde it a fault in my selfe that I do not use them: for it is in deed
> the ready way to inrich our tongue, and make it copious, and it is the
> way which all tongues have taken to inrich them selves. . . . Where-
> fore I marveile how our English tongue hath crackt it credite,[2] that it
> may not borrow of the Latine as well as other tongues: and if it have
> broken, it is but of late, for it is not unknowen to all men how many
> woordes we have fetcht from thence within these fewe yeeres, which
> if they should be all counted inkepot termes, I know not how we
> should speake any thing without blacking our mouthes with inke:
> for what woord can be more plaine then this word *plaine*, and yet
> what can come more neere to the Latine? What more manifest then
> *manifest?* and yet in a maner Latine: What more commune then *rare*,
> or lesse rare then *commune*, and yet both of them comming of the
> Latine? But you wyll say, long use hath made these woords curraunt:
> and why may not use doo as much for these woords which we shall
> now derive? Why should not we doo as much for the posteritie as
> we have received of the antiquitie?[3]

A little later some sanction for the borrowings was derived from authority.
Bullokar says (1616) "it is familiar among best writers to usurpe strange
words."

160. Compromise. The opposition to inkhorn terms was at its height
in the middle of the sixteenth century. At the end of Elizabeth's reign it had
largely spent its force. By this time borrowing had gone so far that the

[1] Corruption by foreign elements.
[2] An allusion to Cheke's statement quoted on p. 216.
[3] Edited by Sir Edward Sullivan (2 vols., London, 1925), Pettie's Preface.

attack was rather directed at the abuse of the procedure than at the procedure itself. The use of unfamiliar words could easily be overdone. It was the enthusiast and the pedant who brought down the criticism of reasonable men upon the practice and caused them to condemn it in more sweeping terms than they knew at heart were justified or were consistent with their own usage. Puttenham, for example, although issuing a warning against inkhorn terms, admits having to use some of them himself, and seeks to justify them in particular instances. He defends the words *scientific*, *major domo*, *politien* (politician), *conduct* (verb), and others. The word *significative*, he says, "doth so well serve the turne, as it could not now be spared: and many more like usurped Latine and French words: as, *Methode, methodicall, placation, function, assubtiling, refining, compendious, prolixe, figurative, inveigle*, a term borrowed of our common lawyers, *impression*, also a new terme, but well expressing the matter, and more than our English word. . . . Also ye finde these wordes, *penetrate, penetrable, indignitie*, which I cannot see how we may spare them, whatsoever fault wee finde with Ink-horne termes: for our speach wanteth wordes to such sence so well to be used." Even Wilson, after exercising his wit in the lively bit of burlesque quoted above, proceeds at once to qualify his disapproval: "Now whereas wordes be received, as well Greke as Latine, to set furthe our meanyng in thenglishe tongue, either for lacke of store, or els because wee would enriche the language: it is well doen to use them, and no man therin can be charged for any affectation when all other are agreed to folowe the same waie," and he cites some that meet with his approval. Each man who used a new word doubtless felt the justification of it and, in a matter about which only time could bring agreement, ran the risk of having his innovations disliked by others. As Ben Jonson remarked in his *Discoveries*, "A man coins not a new word without some peril and less fruit; for if it happen to be received, the praise is but moderate; if refused, the scorn is assured." Some of the words which Puttenham defends have not stood the test of time, and some of those he objects to, such as *audacious, egregious, compatible*, have won a permanent place in the language. One who used any considerable number of new words was in a way on the defensive. Chapman in presenting his translation of Homer says: "For my varietie of new wordes, I have none Inckepot I am sure you know, but such as I give pasport with such authoritie, so significant and not ill sounding, that if my countrey language were an usurer, or a man of this age speaking it, hee would thanke mee for enriching him." Obscurity is always a valid object of criticism, and if the word "inkhorn" could be hurled at an opponent, it was sure to strike him in a vulnerable spot. It was thus that Nash attacked Harvey,[1] who, it must be confessed, lent himself to such an attack. He replied in kind[2] and was able to convict Nash of *interfuseth, finicallitie, sillogistrie, disputative, hermaphrodite, declamatorie, censoriall moralizers, unlineall usurpers of judgement, infringement to destitute the inditement,* and a dozen similar expressions. Not the least interesting feature about the whole question of learned borrowings is the way it aroused popular interest. It even got into the playhouses. In the stage quarrel known as the "War of the Theatres" Ben Jonson delivered a purge to Marston in the *Poetaster* (1601), relieving him of *retrograde, reciprocal, incubus, lubrical, defunct, magnificate, spurious, inflate, turgidous, ventosity, strenuous, obstupefact,* and a number of similar words. The attitude of most men seems to have been one of compromise. No Elizabethan could avoid wholly the use of the new words. Men differed chiefly in the extent to which they allied themselves with the movement or resisted the tendency. As is so often the case, the safest course was a middle one, to borrow, but "without too manifest insolence and too wanton affectation."

161. Permanent Additions. From the exaggeration of a man like Wilson one might get the impression that much of the effort to introduce new words into the language was pedantic and ill-advised. Some of the words Wilson ridicules seem forced and in individual cases were certainly unnecessary. But it would be a mistake to conclude that all or even a large part of the additions were of this sort. Indeed the surprising thing about the movement here described is the number of words that we owe to this period and that seem now to be indispensable. Many of them are in such common use today that it is hard for us to realize that to the Elizabethan they were so strange and difficult as to be a subject of controversy. When Elyot wished to describe a democracy he said, "This maner of governaunce was called in Greke *democratia*, in Latine *popularis potentia*, in Englisshe the rule of the comminaltie." If he were not to have to refer to "the rule of the commonalty" by this roundabout phrase, he could hardly do better than to try to naturalize the Greek word. Again he felt the need of a single word for "all maner of lerning, which of some is called the world of science, of other the circle of doctrine, which is in one word of Greke, *encyclopedia*." Though purists might object, the word *encyclopedia* filled a need in English and it has lived on. The words that were introduced at this time were often basic words—nouns, adjectives, verbs. Among nouns we may note as random examples *allurement, allusion, anachronism, atmosphere, autograph, capsule, denunciation, dexterity, disability, disrespect, emanation, excres-*

[1] In *Strange Newes, or Four Letters Confuted* (1592).
[2] *Pierce's Supererogation* (1593).

cence, excursion, expectation, halo, inclemency, jurisprudence. Among adjectives we find *abject* (in our sense of "down in spirit"), *agile, appropriate, conspicuous, dexterous, expensive, external, habitual, hereditary, impersonal, insane, jocular, malignant.* Few of these could we dispense with. But it is among the verbs, perhaps, that we find our most important acquisitions, words like *adapt, alienate, assassinate, benefit* (first used by Cheke, who thought "our language should be writ pure"!), *consolidate, disregard* (introduced by Milton), *emancipate, eradicate, erupt, excavate, exert, exhilarate, exist, extinguish, harass, meditate* (which Sidney apparently introduced). It is hard to exaggerate the importance of a movement which enriched the language with words such as these.

Most of the words in this list are Latin. But some of them were earlier acquired by Latin from Greek. Examples are *anachronism, atmosphere, autograph.* Others might be added, such as *antipathy, antithesis, caustic, chaos, chronology, climax, crisis, critic, dogma, emphasis, enthusiasm, epitome, parasite, parenthesis, pathetic, pneumonia, scheme, skeleton, system, tactics.* Indeed most of the Greek words in English until lately have come to us either through Latin or French. But in the Renaissance the renewed study of Greek led to the introduction of some Greek words at first hand. Such, for example, are *acme, anonymous, catastrophe, criterion, ephemeral, heterodox, idiosyncrasy, lexicon, misanthrope, ostracize, polemic, tantalize, thermometer,* and *tonic.*

162. Adaptation. Some words, in entering the language, retained their original form; others underwent change. Words like *climax, appendix, epitome, exterior, delirium,* and *axis* still have their Latin form. The adaptation of others to English was effected by the simple process of cutting off the Latin ending. *Conjectural* (L. *conjectural–is*), *consult* (L. *consult–are*), *exclusion* (L. *exclusion–em*), and *exotic* (L. *exotic–us*) show how easily in many cases this could be done. But more often a further change was necessary to bring the word into accord with the usual English forms. Thus the Latin ending *–us* in adjectives was changed to *–ous* (*conspicu–us > conspicuous*) or was replaced by *–al* as in *external* (L. *externus*). Latin nouns ending in *–tas* were changed in English to *–ty* (*celerity < celeritas*) because English had so many words of this kind borrowed from French where the Latin *–tatem* regularly became *–té.* For the same reason nouns ending in *–antia, –entia* appear in English with the ending *–ance, –ence* or *–ancy, –ency,* while adjectives ending in *–bilis* take the usual English (or French) ending *–ble.* Examples are *consonance, concurrence, constancy, frequency, considerable, susceptible.* Many English verbs borrowed from Latin at this time end in *–ate* (*create, consolidate,* *eradicate*). These verbs were formed on the basis of the Latin past participle (e.g., *exterminatus*, whereas the French *exterminer* represents the Latin infinitive *exterminare*). The English practice arose from the fact that the Latin past participle was often equivalent to an adjective and it was a common thing in English to make verbs out of adjectives (*busy, dry, darken*).

163. *Reintroductions and New Meanings.* Sometimes the same word has been borrowed more than once in the course of time. The Latin words *episcopus* and *discus* appear in Old English as *bishop* and *dish* and were again borrowed later to make our words *episcopal* and *disc* (also *dais, desk,* and *discus*). In the same way *chaos* and *malignity* were apparently reintroduced in the sixteenth century. The word *intelligence* is used once in Gower and occasionally in the fifteenth century, but in *The Governour* Elyot remarks that "*intelligence* is nowe used for an elegant worde where there is mutuall treaties or appoyntementes, eyther by letters or message." A word when introduced a second time often carries a different meaning, and in estimating the importance of the Latin and other loan-words of the Renaissance it is just as essential to consider new meanings as new words. Indeed, the fact that a word had been borrowed once before and used in a different sense is of less significance than its reintroduction in a sense that has continued or been productive of new ones. Thus the word *fastidious* is found once in 1440 with the significance 'proud, scornful', but this is of less importance than the fact that both More and Elyot use it a century later in its more usual Latin sense of 'distasteful, disgusting'. From this it was possible for the modern meaning to develop, aided no doubt by the frequent use of the word in Latin with the force of 'easily disgusted, hard to please, over nice'. Chaucer uses the words *artificial, declination, hemisphere* in astronomical senses, but their present use is due to the sixteenth century; and the word *abject*, although found earlier in the sense of 'cast off, rejected', was reintroduced in its present meaning in the Renaissance.

164. *Rejected Words.* There are some things about language that we cannot explain. One of them is why certain words survive while others, apparently just as good, do not. Among the many new words that were introduced into English at this time there were a goodly number that we have not permanently retained. Some are found used a few times and then forgotten. Others enjoyed a rather longer life without becoming in any sense popular. A few were in sufficiently common use for a while to seem assured of a permanent place, but later, for some reason, lost favor and dropped out of use. *Uncounsellable*, for example, was very common in the seventeenth century, but after that practically disappeared. Some of the new words were apparently too learned and smelled too much of the lamp. *Anacephalize*, a Greek word meaning 'to sum up', was of this sort and the more unnecessary since we had already adopted the Latin *recapitulate*. *Deruncinate* (to weed) was another, although it was no worse than *eradicate* for which we had the English expression *to root out*. Elyot's *adminiculation* (aid), *illecebrous* (delicate, alluring), and *obfuscate* (hidden) are of the same sort. Some words might logically have survived but did not. *Expede* (to accomplish, expedite) would have been parallel to *impede*. *Cohibit* (to restrain) is like *inhibit* and *prohibit*. *Demit* (to send away) was common in the sixteenth and seventeenth centuries and would have been as natural as *commit* or *transmit*, but *dismiss* gradually replaced it. It is in fact not uncommon to find words discarded in favor of somewhat similar formations. Examples are *exsiccate* (to dry) alongside of *desiccate*, *emacerate* (emaciate), *discongruity* (incongruity), *appendance* (appendage). In some cases we have preferred a word in a shorter form: *cautionate* (caution), *consolate* (console), *attemptate* (attempt), *denunciate* (denounce). Often there seems to be no explanation but chance or caprice to account for a word's failure to survive. *Eximious* (excellent, distinguished) is frequently found in seventeenth-century literature and was used by Browning, but is now unknown or at least very rare. Similarly, *mansuetude* (mildness) has a history that extends from Chaucer to Browning but it is no longer used. We have given up *disaccustom*, *disacquaint*, *disadorn*, etc., but we say *disabuse*, *disaffect*, *disagree*. Shakespeare used *disquantity* as a verb meaning 'to lessen in quantity' or 'diminish'. Sometimes we have kept one part of speech and discarded another. We say *exorbitant* but not *exorbitate* (to stray from the ordinary course), *approbation* but not *approbate*, *consternation* but not *consternate*. The most convincing reason for the failure of a new word to take hold is that it was not needed. *Aspectable* (visible), *assate* (to roast) and the noun *assation*, *exolete* (faded), *suppeditate* (furnish, supply), and many other rejected words were unnecessary, and there was certainly no need for *temulent* when we had *drunk*, *intoxicated*, and a score of other expressions of various degrees of respectability to express the idea. We must look upon the borrowings of this period as often experimental. New words were being freely introduced at the judgment or caprice of the individual. They were being tried out, sometimes in various forms. In Shakespeare's day no one could have told whether we should say *effectual*, *effectuous*, *effectful*, *effectuating*, or *effective*. Two of these five options have survived. It was necessary for time to do the sifting.

165. *Reinforcement through French.* It is not always possible to say whether a word borrowed at this time was taken over directly from Latin or indirectly through French, for the same wholesale enrichment was going on in French simultaneously and the same words were being introduced in both languages. Often the two streams of influence must have merged. But that English borrowed many words from Latin firsthand is indicated in a number of ways. The word *fact* represents the Latin *factum* and not the French *fait*, which was taken into English earlier as *feat*. Many verbs like *confiscate, congratulate,* and *exonerate* are formed from the Latin participle (*confiscat–us,* etc.) and not from the French *confisquer, congratuler, exonerer,* which are derived from the infinitives *confiscare,* etc. Caxton has the form *confisk,* which is from French, but the word did not survive in this shape. The form *prejudicate* is from Latin while *prejudge* represents the French *prejuger*. In the same way *instruct* and *subtract* show their Latin ancestry (*instructus, subtractus*) since the French *instruire* and *subtraire* would have become in English *instroy* (like *destroy*) and *subtray* (which is found in the fifteenth century). Our word *conjugation* is probably a direct importation from Latin (*conjugation–em*) since the more usual form in French was *conjugaison.* Sometimes the occurrence of a word in English earlier than in French (e.g., *obtuse*) points to the direct adoption from Latin, as do words like *confidence, confident,* which are expressed in French by the forms *confiance, confiant,* but which in English are used in senses that the French forms do not have.

There still remain, however, a good many words which might equally well have come into English from Latin or French. Verbs like *consist* and *explore* could come either from the Latin *consistere* and *explorare* or the French *consister* and *explorer. Conformation, conflagration,* and many other similar nouns may represent either Latin *conformation–em, conflagration–em,* or French *conformation, conflagration.* It is so with words like *fidelity, ingenuity, proclivity,* where the Latin *fidelitat–em* developed into French *fidélité,* but English possessed so many words of this kind from French that it could easily have formed others on the same pattern. So adjectives like *affable, audible, jovial* may represent the Latin *affabilis* or the French *affable,* etc., and others like *consequent, modest, sublime* can have come equally well from the Latin or the French forms. It is really not important which language was the direct source of the English words since in either case they are ultimately of Latin origin. In many cases French may have offered a precedent for introducing the Latin words into English and may have assisted in their general adoption.

166. *Words from the Romance Languages.* Sixteenth-century purists objected to three classes of strange words, which they characterized as *inkhorn terms, oversea language,* and *Chaucerisms.* For the foreign borrowings in this period were by no means confined to learned words taken from Latin and Greek. The English vocabulary at this time shows words adopted from more than fifty languages,[1] the most important of which (besides Latin and Greek) were French, Italian, and Spanish. English travel in France and consumption of French books are reflected in such words as *alloy, ambuscade, baluster, bigot, bizarre, bombast, chocolate, comrade, detail, duel, entrance, equip, equipage, essay, explore, genteel, mustache, naturalize, probability, progress, retrenchment, shock, surpass, talisman, ticket, tomato, vogue,* and *volunteer.* But the English also traveled frequently in Italy, observed Italian architecture, and brought back not only Italian manners and styles of dress but Italian words. Protests against the Italianate Englishman are frequent in Elizabethan literature, and the objection is not only that the Englishmen came back corrupted in morals and affecting outlandish fashions, but that they "powdered their talk with oversea language."[2] Nevertheless, Italian words, like Italian fashions, were frequently adopted in England. Words like *algebra, argosy, balcony, cameo, capricio* (the common form of *caprice* until after the Restoration), *cupola, design, granite, grotto, piazza, portico, stanza, stucco, trill, violin, volcano* began to be heard on the lips of Englishmen or to be found in English books. Many other Italian words were introduced through French or adapted to French forms, words like *battalion, bankrupt, bastion, brigade, brusque, carat, cavalcade, charlatan, frigate, gala, gazette, grotesque, infantry, parakeet,* and *rebuff.* Many of these preserved for a time their Italian form. From Spanish and Portuguese, English adopted *alligator* (*el lagarto,* the lizard), *anchovy, apricot, armada, armadillo, banana, barricade* (often *barricado,* as in Shakespeare), *bastiment, bastinado, bilbo, bravado, brocade* (often employed in the form *brocado*), *cannibal, canoe, cedilla, cocoa, corral, desperado, embargo, hammock, hurricane, maize, mosquito, mulatto, negro, peccadillo, potato, renegado* (the original form of *renegade*), *rusk, sarsaparilla, sombrero, tobacco,* and *yam.* Many of these words reflect the Spanish enterprise on the sea and colonization of the American continent. Like Italian words, Spanish words sometimes entered English through French or took a French form. *Grenade, palisade, escalade,* and *cavalier* are examples, although commonly found in the sixteenth and seventeenth centuries in the form *grenado, palisado, escalado,* and *cavaliero,* even when the correct Spanish form would have been *granada, palisada,*

---

[1] See Murray's preface to vol. 7 of the *OED.*

[2] Carew, in *The Excellency of the English Tongue,* says: "Soe have our Italyan travilers brought us acquainted with their sweet relished phrases which (soe their condicions crept not in withall) weere the better tollerable." (*Eliz. Critical Essays,* II, 290.)

escalada, and *caballero.* Sometimes the influence of all these languages combined to give us our English word, as in the case of *galleon, gallery, pistol, cochineal.*[1] Thus the cosmopolitan tendency, the spirit of exploration and adventure, and the interest in the New World which was being opened up show themselves in an interesting way in the growth of our vocabulary, and contributed along with the more intellectual forms of activity to the enrichment of the English language.

167. The Method of Introducing the New Words. The Latin words which form so important an element in the English vocabulary have generally entered the language through the medium of writing. Unlike the Scandinavian influence and to a large extent the French influence after the Norman Conquest, the various Latin influences, except the earliest, have been the work of churchmen and scholars. If the words themselves have not always been learned words, they have needed the help of learned men to become known. This was particularly true in the Renaissance. Even the words borrowed from the Romance languages in this period often came in through books, and the revivals and new formations from native material were due to the efforts of individual writers and their associates. It is impossible, of course, to say who was responsible for the introduction of each particular word, but in certain cases we can see an individual man at work—like Sir Thomas Elyot—conscious of his innovations and sometimes pausing to remark upon them. Another writer who introduced a large number of new words was Elyot's older contemporary, Sir Thomas More. To More we owe the words *absurdity, acceptance, anticipate, combustible, compatible* (in our sense), *comprehensible, concomitance, congratulatory, contradictory, damnability, denunciation, detector, dissipate, endurable, eruditely, exact, exaggerate, exasperate, explain, extenuate, fact, frivolous, impenitent, implacable, incorporeal, indifference, insinuate, inveigh, inviolable, irrefragable, monopoly, monosyllable, necessitate, obstruction, paradox, pretext,* and others. Elyot, besides using some of these, gives us *accommodate, adumbrate, adumbration, analogy, animate, applicate* (as an alternative to the older *apply*), *beneficence, encyclopedia, excerp, excogitate, excogitation, excrement, exhaust, exordium, experience* (verb), *exterminate,*

---

[1] galleon = F. *galion,* Sp. *galeon,* Ital. *galeone.*
gallery = F. *galerie,* Sp., Port., and Ital. *galeria.*
pistol = F. *pistole,* Sp. and Ital. *pistola.*
cochineal = F. *cochenille,* Sp. *cochinilla,* Ital. *cocciniglia.*
  That the Italian and Spanish words borrowed by English at this time reflect the general commerce of ideas is clear from the fact that the same words were generally being adopted by French. Cf. B. H. Wind, *Les Mots italiens introduits en français au XVIᵉ siècle* (Deventer, 1928), and Richard Ruppert, *Die spanischen Lehn- und Fremdwörter in der französischen Schriftsprache* (Munich, 1915).

frugality, implacability, infrequent, inimitable, irritate, modesty, placability, etc.[1] The lists have been made long, at the risk of being wearisome, in order that they might be the more impressive. So far as we now know, these words had not been used in English previously. In addition both writers employ many words which are recorded from only a few years before. And so they either introduced or helped to establish many new words in the language. What More and Elyot were doing was being done by numerous others, and it is necessary to recognize the importance of individuals as "makers of English" in the sixteenth and early seventeenth century.

168. *Enrichment from Native Sources.* By far the greater part of the additions to the English vocabulary in the period of the Renaissance was drawn from sources outside of English. The popular favor shown to all kinds of foreign words seems to have implied a disparagement of English resources that was resented in some quarters. Gabriel Harvey remarked that "in Inglande . . . nothinge is reputid so contemptible, and so baselye and vilelye accountid of, as whatsoever is taken for Inglishe, whether it be handsum fasshions in apparrell, or seemely and honorable in behaviour, or choise wordes and phrases in speache, or anye notable thinge else . . . that savorith of our owne cuntrye and is not ether merely or mixtely out-landishe."[2] But, as we have seen, there were purists like Cheke, and there were also others who believed that English could very well develop new words from old roots or revive expressions that had gone out of use. Cheke was so strongly opposed to the borrowing of Latin and Greek words that he sought wherever possible for English equivalents. Thus, in his transla-tion of the Gospel of St. Matthew, where the Authorized Version reads *lunatic* he wrote *mooned,* and in the same way he said *toller* for *publican, hundreder* for *centurion, foresayer* for *prophet, byword* for *parable, freshman* for *proselyte, crossed* for *crucified, gainrising* for *resurrection.* The poets, of course, were rather more given to the revival of old words, especially words that were familiar to them in Chaucer. For this reason their revivals and new formations that suggested an older period of English were sometimes referred to as "Chaucerisms." Among poets who consciously made use of old words to enlarge the poetical vocabulary the most important was

---

[1] A number of the words here listed antedate the earliest quotation in the *Oxford English Dictionary*. The More list is based (with additions) upon J. Delcourt, *Essai sur la langue de Sir Thomas More d'après ses œuvres anglaises* (Paris, 1914). Both lists, but especially Elyot's, could be largely extended by words which have not survived, such as *adminiculation* (aid), *allect* (allure), *allective, circumscription* (description or account) *comprobate* (sanction), *concinnity* (harmony, congruity), *condisciple* (schoolfellow), etc. It may be noted that More was equally given to new formations from native material (see § 168).

[2] *Eliz. Crit. Essays,* I, 124.

Spenser, although there were also others, such as Thomas Drant, the translator of Horace, whose influence on Spenser has not been fully appreciated, and to a lesser degree Milton.

These poetical innovations were of several kinds. Some were old words revived, like *astound, blameful, displeasance, enroot, doom, forby* (hard by, past), *empight* (fixed, implanted), *natheless, nathemore, mickle, whilere* (a while before). Others were new, such as *askew, filch, flout, freak*. The origin of these is often uncertain; they may have been of dialectal provenience. Some were definitely coinages, such as Spenser's *bellibone* (a fair maid, possibly from *belle et bonne*), *blatant, braggadocio, chirrup, cosset* (lamb), *delve* (pit, den), *dit* (song), *scruze* (apparently a telescope word combining *screw* and *squeeze*), *squall* (to cry), and *wrizzled* (wrinkled, shriveled). Finally, many were simply adaptations and derivatives of old words, such as *baneful, briny, changeful, drear* (from *dreary*), *hapless, oaten, sunshiny*, or *wolfish*. Some of the innovations had a look much more rustic and strange than these, and, as in the case of inkhorn terms and oversea words, opinion varied as to their desirability. Sidney criticized Spenser for the "framing of his stile to an old rustick language," and Ben Jonson went so far as to say that "Spenser in affecting the ancients writ no language." But the poet also had his defenders. His friend "E.K." wrote, ". . . in my opinion it is one special prayse of many whych are dew to this poete, that he hath laboured to restore as to their rightfull heritage such good and naturall English words as have ben long time out of use and almost cleane disherited." The defenders, moreover, could have pointed to the fact that the same method of enriching the language was being urged in France. The words which English acquired in this way are not nearly so numerous as those obtained from outside, but when all is said the fact remains that to Spenser and others who shared his views we owe a great many useful words. *Belt, bevy, craggy, dapper, forthright, glen, glee, glance, surly, blandishment, birthright, changeling, elfin, endear, disrobe, don, enshrine, drizzling, fleecy, grovel, gaudy, gloomy, merriment, rancorous, shady, verdant, wakeful, wary*, and *witless* by no means exhaust the list. Many of these have passed from the language of poetry into common use, and, what is equally important, a vital principle of English word-formation was being kept alive.

169. *Methods of Interpreting the New Words.* The difficulty for the reader presented by these new words of many different origins was met in various ways. In many cases the context or the reader's knowledge of Latin was expected to make the meaning clear. But the interpretation was not left entirely to chance. Explanations were sometimes added parenthetically. When Elyot uses the word *circumspection* he adds, "whiche signifieth as

moche as beholdynge on every parte." In using the word *magnanimity* he
says, "But nowe I remembre me, this worde *magnanimitie* beinge yet
straunge, as late borowed out of the latyne, shall nat content all men";
he therefore explains what it means. Again, he says, "*Industrie* hath nat
ben so longe tyme used in the englisshe tonge. . . . It is a qualitie procedyng
of witte and experience, by the whiche a man perceyveth quickly, inventeth
fresshly, and consayleth spedily." This is not our way of using the word,
but he also uses it in the sense of diligence in performance. A simpler way,
where an equivalent word or expression existed, was to combine the new
and the old in a self-interpreting pair. Thus he says "*animate* or give
courage," "*devulgate* or set forth," "*explicating* or unfolding," "*difficile*
or hard," "*education* or bringing up of children," "*adminiculation* or aid,"
"*ostent* or show," "*excerped* or gathered out of," "*obfuscate* or hid," and
"*celerity*, commonly called speediness." Where no help like this was given,
however, many a word must have remained troublesome to the ordinary
reader. Another means was therefore provided for his "adminiculation."

170. Dictionaries of Hard Words.   As early as 1582 Mulcaster had
written: "It were a thing verie praiseworthie in my opinion, and no lesse
profitable than praise worthie, if som one well learned and as laborious a
man, wold gather all the words which we use in our English tung, whether
naturall or incorporate, out of all professions, as well learned as not, into
one dictionarie, and besides the right writing, which is incident to the
alphabete, wold open unto us therein both their naturall force and their
proper use." This statement shows another of the many ways in which
Richard Mulcaster was in advance of his time. It was not until nearly 150
years later, when Nathaniel Bailey published his *Universal Etymological
English Dictionary* (1721), that anyone attempted to list all the words in the
language. The earliest dictionaries were those explaining the words in Latin
or some other foreign language, and the earliest English dictionaries were
dictionaries of hard words. The first of these was a little book of 120 pages
by Robert Cawdrey, called *The Table Alphabeticall of Hard Words* (1604),
explaining some 3,000 terms.[1] It was followed in 1616 by John Bullokar's
English Expositor and in 1623 by the *English Dictionarie* of Henry
Cockeram, both of which passed through numerous editions. Blount's
Glossographia (1656), Edward Philipps' *New World of Words* (1658), and
other later compilations continued to treat only the more difficult words
until the time of Bailey, mentioned above, whose book held the field until
the appearance of Dr. Johnson's. An interesting feature of Cockeram's

---

[1] Cawdrey's little book has been reprinted in facsimile, with an introduction by
Robert A. Peters (Gainesville, 1966).

work and the later editions of Bullokar was a section "serving for the translation of ordinary English words into the more scholastick, or those derived from other languages." By means of this supplement a person might write in ordinary English and then, by making a few judicious substitutions, convey a fine impression of learning. The development of dictionaries was a consequence of the extensive additions that had been made to the language and in turn helped to facilitate their adoption into general use.

171. *Nature and Extent of the Movement.* In order to appreciate the importance of the Renaissance in enriching the English vocabulary it is worthwhile to form some idea of the number of new words added at this time. A calculation based upon the data available in the *Oxford Dictionary* gives a figure somewhat above 12,000. This number is certain to be reduced somewhat when all of the materials assembled for the *Middle English Dictionary* are published; but it is likely to remain close to 10,000, since the calculation has been made conservatively, taking no account of minor variations of the same word, or of words which, while appearing before 1500, were reintroduced in the sixteenth century or first gained currency at that time. Many of the new words, of course, enjoyed but a short life. Some even were used only once or twice and forgotten. But about half of the total number have become a permanent part of the language. A very large majority were from Latin, and this accession from Latin is sometimes known as the Latin Influence of the Fourth Period. Not all of the additions filled gaps in the existing vocabulary, but they gave the language a wealth of synonyms. In the course of time these have often become differentiated, enabling us to express slight shades of meaning that would otherwise have been unattainable. Most of the new words entered English by way of the written language. They are a striking evidence of the new force exerted by the printing press. They also furnish a remarkable instance of the ease with which the printed word can pass into everyday speech. For while many of the new words were of a distinctly learned character in the beginning, they did not remain so very long, a fact which not only can be inferred from their widespread popular use today but can be illustrated from the plays of Shakespeare or almost any of his contemporaries.

172. *The Movement Illustrated in Shakespeare.* It is a well-known fact that, except for a man like the Elizabethan translator, Philemon Holland, Shakespeare had the largest vocabulary of any English writer. This is due not only to his daring and resourceful use of words, but in part to his ready acceptance of new words of every kind. It is true that he could make sport of the inkhorn terms of a pedant like Holofernes, who quotes Latin, affects words like *intimation, insinuation, explication, replication,* and who has a high scorn for anyone like the slow-witted Dull who, as another character remarks, "hath not eat paper." Shakespeare had not read Wilson in vain. But he was also not greatly impressed by Wilson's extreme views. Among Shakespearian words are found *agile, allurement, antipathy, catastrophe, consonancy, critical, demonstrate, dire, discountenance, emphasis, emulate, expostulation, extract, hereditary, horrid, impertinency, meditate, modest, pathetical, prodigious, vast,* the Romance words *ambuscado, armada, barricade, bastinado, cavalier, mutiny, palisado, pell-mell, renegado*—all new to English in the latter half of the sixteenth century. Some of the words Shakespeare uses must have been very new indeed, since the earliest instance in which we find them at all is only a year or two before he uses them (e.g., *exist, initiate, jovial*), and in a number of cases his is the earliest occurrence of the word in English (*accommodation, apostrophe, assassination, dexterously, dislocate, frugal, indistinguishable, misanthrope, obscene, pedant, premeditated, reliance, submerged,* etc.). He would no doubt have been classed among the liberals in his attitude toward foreign borrowing. Shakespeare's use of the new words illustrates an important point in connection with them. This is the fact that they were often used, upon their first introduction, in a sense different from ours, closer to their etymological meaning in Latin. Thus, *to communicate* nowadays means to exchange information, but in Shakespeare's day it generally preserved its original meaning 'to share or make common to many'. This is its force when Adriana says in the *Comedy of Errors:*

> Thou art an elm, my husband, I a vine,
> Whose weakness married to thy stronger state
> Makes me with thy strength to *communicate,*

i.e., she shares his strength with him. When Lorenzo in the *Merchant of Venice* says "let's in and there *expect* their coming," he is using *expect* in its original sense of 'to await'. In the sixteenth century, when the verb *to atone* was first used, it did not have its modern meaning 'to make amends' but simply 'to set at one, reconcile', as when Desdemona says, "I would do much to atone them." *Enlargement* meant freedom from confinement ("take this key, give *enlargement* to the swain") and *humorous* might mean 'damp' (as in "the *humorous* night" of *Romeo and Juliet*) or 'capricious', 'moody', 'peevish', that is, showing the effect of the various bodily humors which, according to medieval belief, determined one's disposition. The word did not acquire its present meaning until the time of Addison. It would be easy to multiply examples from almost any page of

Shakespeare. The few that have been given will suffice to show that the new words often remained close to their etymological meaning, like recent immigrants who still show traces of their foreign ways.

173. *Shakespeare's Pronunciation.* Shakespeare's pronunciation, though not ours, was much more like ours than has always been realized. He pronounced [e] for [i] in some words just as Pope could still say *tay* for *tea*.[1] The falling together of *er, ir, ur* (e.g., *herd, birth, hurt*) was under way but not yet completed. As explained in § 175, M.E. $\bar{e}$ was sometimes open, sometimes close [ɛː eː] and the two sounds were still distinct in Shakespeare's day, [eː] and [iː] respectively. Consequently *sea* [seː] does not normally rime with *see* [siː], *heap* with *keep*, *speak* with *seek*, etc. Toward the close of the fifteenth century an attempt was made to distinguish between them by the spelling. The closer sound was often spelled with *ee* or *ie* (*deep, field*) while the more open sound was as often written *ea* (*sea, clean*). But the practice was not consistently carried out. Although the two sounds are now identical, this variation in spelling is a reminder of the difference in pronunciation that long existed. We should also probably notice considerable difference in the pronunciation of words containing a M.E. $\bar{o}$. This regularly developed into [uː], as in *room, food, roof, root*, and it retains this sound in many words today. In some words the vowel was shortened in the fifteenth century and was unrounded to the sound in *blood, flood*. In still other words, however, it retained its length until about 1700, but was then shortened without being unrounded, giving us the sound in *good, stood, book, foot*. It is apparent that in Shakespeare's day there was much fluctuation in the pronunciation of words containing this Middle English vowel, both in the different parts of the country and in the usage of different individuals. Consequently we find in the poetry of the period a word like *flood* riming not only with *blood* but with *mood* and *good*. In fact, as late as Dryden we find in the same rime *flood—mood—good*, the three developments of the sound at the present day. It is only in recent times that the pronunciation of these words has been standardized, and even today there is some vacillation between a long and short vowel in some of them, e.g., in *broom, room*, and *roof*. In addition to such differences in the quality of vowels there were some differences of accent. Shakespeare said *persev'er, demon'strate*, and generally *aspect', de'testable*, while he has *charact'er, com'mendable, envy', se'cure, welcome'*, etc., in contrast to the accentuation that is customary in these words today. On the whole, however, we should probably have little more difficulty in understanding Shakespeare's pronun-

---

[1] Cf. p. 17.

ciation than we experience in listening to a broad Irish brogue. The situation would be very different with the language of Chaucer. And the reason is that in the course of the fifteenth and sixteenth centuries the vowels of Middle English, especially the long vowels, underwent a wholesale but quite regular shifting, about which something must be said.

174. *The Importance of Sound-changes.* The subject of sound-changes is just as important in the history of language as the changes in grammar and vocabulary. But it lends itself less readily to generalization and brief presentation. Any treatment of even the vowels, if it would have value, must proceed by one's examining each of the vowel sounds individually, determining its character at a given time, tracing its source in the preceding period, and following its subsequent development both independently and under the influence of neighboring sounds and varying conditions of accent, often noting significant differences in its development in different dialects, and, sometimes, in individual words, its modification through the analogical influence of other words. It is obviously impossible to enter upon such a study here. Some sounds in English have been less subject to change than others and would offer little difficulty. For example, the short *e* under certain conditions has remained unchanged since Old English times: O.E. *bĕdd* is still *bed* today. On the other hand, to take a fairly simple case, the *ā* in O.E. *stān* (stone) became about 1100 a sound like that in *law* [stɔːn] in central and southern England. In the great vowel shift that began to take place in all long vowels in the fifteenth century this sound underwent a further change so that in Shakespeare's pronunciation it has become a close *ǭ* similar to its pronunciation at the present day (*stone*). Today the *o* is followed by a slight *u* glide [stoᵘn] or [stoun] which some authorities believe arose in the nineteenth century, while others trace it back as far as the seventeenth. On the other hand, the development here described did not take place in the north of England. There the O.E. *ā* instead of being rounded to an *ǭ*, developed into a sound that rimes with *lane* (*stane*), and this is its pronunciation in Scotland today. For the detailed treatment of English sounds the student must be referred to the various historical grammars and works which make it their special concern.[1] Here we must confine ourselves to a few broad observations.

---

[1] The study of sounds and sound-changes is known as *phonology*. Most of the grammars of Old and Middle English deal fully with this aspect of the language. Standard treatments of Old English have been mentioned in the footnote of § 40. The principle Middle English grammars are those of Morsbach (1896), Wright (2nd ed., 1928), and Jordan (1925; 3rd ed. 1968, trans. and rev. Eugene J. Crook, 1974). An exhaustive treatment of Middle English phonology is contained in K. Luick, *Historische Grammatik der englischen Sprache* (1914–1940), the final fasciculi edited by Fr. Wild and H. Koziol;

175. From Old to Middle English. In considering the changes in pronunciation which English words underwent in passing from Old to Middle English we may say that qualitatively they were slight, at least in comparison with those that occurred later. Changes in the consonants were rather insignificant, as they have always been in English. Some voiced consonants became voiceless, and vice versa, and consonants were occasionally lost. Thus *w* before a following *o* was lost when it followed another consonant: *sō* (O.E. *swā*), *hō* (who, O.E. *hwā*). *Sc* became *sh* (O.E. *scip* > M.E. *ship* or *schip*), or had already done so in Old English. But we do not expect much change in the consonantal framework of words. Nor was there much alteration in the quality of vowels in accented syllables. Most of the short vowels, unless lengthened, passed over into Middle English unaltered. But short *æ* became *a*, and *y* [y] was unrounded to *i* in most districts, either early or eventually (O.E. *cræft* > M.E. *craft; brycg* > *brigge*). The other short vowels, *ă, ĕ, ĭ, ŏ, ŭ*, remained (O.E. *catte* > *cat, bedd* > *bed, scip* > *schip, folc* > *folk, full* > *ful*). Among the long vowels the most important change was that of *ā* to *ọ̄*, mentioned in the preceding paragraph (O.E. *bān* > *bọ̄n*, bone; *bāt* > *bọ̄t*, boat). The long *ȳ* developed in the same way as short *ў* (O.E. *brȳd* > *brīde*, bride; *fȳr* > *fīr*, fire). The long *æ*, so characteristic a feature of Old English spelling, represented two sounds. In some words it stood for an *ā* in West Germanic. This sound appears as a close *ẹ̄* outside the West Saxon area and remains *ē* in Middle English (Non-W.S. *dēd* > *dẹ̄d*, deed; *slēpan* > *slẹ̄pen*, sleep). In many

---

reprinted with a new index (2 vols., Oxford, 1964). Vol. 2 of Max Kaluza's *Historische Grammatik der englischen Sprache* (2nd ed., 1907) covers the same period, and a briefer treatment is offered by Kluge in Paul's *Grundriss der germanischen Philologie* (vol. I, 2nd ed., 1901). B. A. Mackenzie's *The Early London Dialect* (1928) is important for the sources of the standard speech. In the study of English pronunciation in the modern period Ellis was a pioneer, but his work *On Early English Pronunciation* (5 vols., 1869–1889) must now be considered an unsafe guide, to be used with extreme caution. The best introduction to modern views of the later English sound-changes is to be found in W. Horn, *Historische neuenglische Grammatik* (1908); Otto Jespersen, *A Modern English Grammar* (vol. I, 1909); R. E. Zachrisson, *Pronunciation of English Vowels 1400–1700* (1913); Joseph and E. M. Wright, *An Elementary Historical New English Grammar* (1924); E. Ekwall, *Historische neuenglische Laut- und Formenlehre* (3rd ed., 1956); and the works of Wyld mentioned below. The more important surveys covering the whole or most of the sound-history of English are Henry Sweet, *History of English Sounds* (1888), the same author's *New English Grammar*, Part I (1892), both now somewhat antiquated, and the following works of H. C. Wyld: *Historical Study of the Mother Tongue* (1906), *A History of Modern Colloquial English* (rev. ed., 1921), *A Short History of English* (3rd ed., 1927). The same author's *Studies in English Rhymes from Surrey to Pope* (1924) presents some of the more important changes in popular form. A comprehensive and indispensable treatment based on a fresh study of the sixteenth- and seventeenth-century orthoepists is E. J. Dobson, *English Pronunciation 1500–1700* (2 vols., 2nd ed., Oxford, 1968).

words O.E. *ǣ* was a sound resulting from the *i*-umlaut of *ā*.[1] This was a more open vowel and appears as *ę̄* in Middle English (O.E. *clǣne* > *clę̄ne*, clean; *dǣlan* > *dę̄len*, deal). These two sounds have now become identical (cf. *deed* and *clean*). The other long vowels of Old English preserved their original quality in Middle English (*mēd* > *mēde*, meed; *fīf* > *fīf*, five; *bōc* > *bōk*, book; *hūs* > *hūs*, house, often written *hous* through the influence of Anglo-Norman scribes). The Old English diphthongs were all simplified, and all diphthongs in Middle English are new formations resulting chiefly from the combination of a simple vowel with a following consonant (*ʒ*, *w*) which vocalized.

If the quality of Old English vowels did not change much in passing into Middle English, their quantity or length was subject to considerable alteration. For example, Old English long vowels were shortened late in the Old English period or early in Middle English when followed by a double consonant or by most combinations of consonants (*grětter*, comparative of *grēt* < O.E. *grēat;* *ăsken* < O.E. *āxian*, ask). Conversely, short vowels in open syllables were lengthened in Middle English (O.E. *băcan* > M.E. *bāken*, bake; *ĕtan* > *ę̄ten*, eat). Such changes in length are little noticeable in the spelling, but they are of great importance since they determine the course which these vowels pursued in their subsequent development.

176. *From Middle English to Modern.* When we come to the vowel changes in Modern English we see the importance of the factors that determined the length of vowels in Middle English. All Middle English long vowels underwent extensive alteration in passing into Modern English, but the short vowels, in accented syllables, remained comparatively stable. If we compare Chaucer's pronunciation of the short vowels with ours, we note only two changes of importance, those of *a* and *u*. By Shakespeare's day (i.e., at the close of the sixteenth century) Chaucer's *a* had become an [æ] in pronunciation (*cat, thank, flax*). In some cases this M.E. *a* represented an O.E. *æ* (*at, apple, back*) and the new pronunciation was therefore a return to approximately the form which the word had in Old English. It is the usual pronunciation in America and a considerable part of southern England today. The change which the *u* underwent was what is known as unrounding. In Chaucer's pronunciation this vowel was like the *u* in *full*. By the sixteenth century it seems to have become in most words the sound which we have in *but* (e.g., *cut, sun; love*, with the Anglo-Norman spelling of *o* for *u*). So far as the short vowels are concerned it is clear that a person today would have little difficulty in understanding the English of any period of the language.

[1] See p. 76.

177. *The Great Vowel Shift.* The situation is very different when we consider the long vowels. In Chaucer's pronunciation these had still their so-called "continental" value—i.e., *a* was pronounced like the *a* in *father* and not as in *name*, *e* was pronounced either like the *e* in *there* or the *a* in *mate*, but not like the *ee* in *meet*, and so with the other vowels. But in the fifteenth century a great change is seen to be under way. All the long vowels gradually came to be pronounced with a greater elevation of the tongue and closing of the mouth, so that those that could be raised (*a, ę, ẹ, ǫ, ọ*) were raised, and those that could not without becoming consonantal (*i, u*) became diphthongs. The change may be visualized in the following diagram:

Such a diagram must be taken as only a very rough indication of what happened, especially in the breaking of *i* and *u* into the diphthongs *ai* and *au*. Nor must the changes indicated by the arrows be thought of as taking place successively, but rather as all part of a general movement with slight differences in the speed with which the results were accomplished (or the date at which evidence for them can be found). The effects of the shift can be seen in the following comparison of Chaucer's and Shakespeare's pronunciation:

M.E.	Chaucer		Shakespeare	
ī	[fiːf]	*five*	[faɪv][1]	
ẹ̄	[meːdə]	*meed*	[miːd]	
ę̄	[klɛːnə]	*clean*	[kleːn]	(*now* [kliːn])
ā	[naːmə]	*name*	[neːm]	
ǭ	[gɔːtə]	*goat*	[goːt]	
ọ̄	[roːtə]	*root*	[ruːt]	
ū	[duːn]	*down*	[daʊn][1]	

From this it is apparent that most of the long vowels had acquired at least by the sixteenth century (and probably earlier) approximately their present pronunciation. The most important development that has taken place since is the further raising of M.E. *ę̄* to *ī*. Whereas in Shakespeare *clean* was

---

[1] The pronunciations [aɪ] and [aʊ] may not have been fully attained in Shakespeare's day, but they were apparently well on the way. Cf. Wyld, *History of Modern Colloquial English*, pp. 223 ff., 230 ff.

pronounced like our *lane*, it now rimes with *lean*.[1] The change occurred at the end of the seventeenth century and had become general by the middle of the eighteenth.[2] Such other changes as have occurred are slight and must be sought by the interested reader in the books devoted especially to the history of English sounds.[3]

It will be noticed that the Great Vowel Shift is responsible for the unorthodox use of the vowel symbols in English spelling. The spelling of English had become fixed in a general way before the shift and therefore did not change when the quality of the long vowels changed. Consequently our vowel symbols no longer correspond to the sounds which they once represented in English and still represent in the other modern languages.[4]

178. *Weakening of Unaccented Vowels*. A little observation and reflection will show the student that in unaccented syllables, too, the spelling does not accurately represent the pronunciation today. This is because in all periods of the language the vowels of unstressed syllables have had a tendency to weaken and then often to disappear. This is true of all parts of a word. For example, we do not distinguish in ordinary or rapid speech between the vowels at the beginning of *ago, upon, opinion*. The sound in all three words is [ə]; in other cases it is commonly [ə] or [ɪ]. Consider the unstressed middle or final syllable in the words *introduce, elegant* [ə, ɪ], *drama, color, kingdom, breakfast* (brɛkfəst *or* brɛkf'st), *Monday* [i]. The weakening is especially noticeable in words from French where an accented vowel came to be unaccented in English (cf. French *mouton, raisin, bonté* with English *mutton, raisin, bounty*). One must not be misled by the spelling. The original spelling was generally retained and in recent times has occasionally influenced the pronunciation so that the quality of the vowel has been restored to something like its earlier character. *Window* now has a fairly well-defined diphthong in the final syllable [ou] or [oᵘ] but the

---

[1] A pronunciation approximating that of today was apparently in use among some speakers but was considered substandard.

[2] There are three exceptions: *break, great, steak*. The pronunciation [i] was apparently considered vulgar at first, later alternated with [e], and finally became the accepted form in most words. See Wyld, *Short History of English*, p. 173.

[3] For descriptions of the vowel shift within the theory of generative phonology, see Noam Chomsky and Morris Halle, *The Sound Pattern of English* (New York, 1968), chap. 6, and Patricia M. Wolfe, *Linguistic Change and the Great Vowel Shift in English* (Berkeley and Los Angeles, 1972).

[4] A comprehensive history of English spelling has yet to be written. The fullest survey is by D. G. Scragg, *A History of English Spelling* (New York, 1974). For a brief treatment the reader may consult W. W. Skeat, *Principles of English Etymology*, First Series (2nd ed., Oxford, 1892), chap. 16. A clear statement of modern usage is given in W. A. Craigie, *English Spelling: Its Rules and Reasons* (New York, 1927).

weakened vowel is evident in the vulgar pronunciation *winder*. Misguided purists often try to pronounce the final syllable of *Monday*, etc., with the full quality of the diphthong in *day*. But even when the vowel has been restored in standard speech the weakened form is generally apparent in informal speech and in the dialects.

179. *Grammatical Features.* English grammar in the sixteenth and early seventeenth century is marked more by the survival of certain forms and usages that have since disappeared than by any fundamental developments. The great changes which reduced the inflections of Old English to their modern proportions had already taken place. In the few parts of speech which retain some of their original inflections, the reader of Shakespeare or the Authorized Version is conscious of minor differences of form, and in the framing of sentences he may note differences of syntax and idiom which, while they attract attention, are not sufficient to interfere seriously with understanding. The more important of these differences we may pass briefly in review.

180. *The Noun.* The only inflections retained in the noun were, as we have seen above, those marking the plural and the possessive singular. In the former the *s*–plural had become so generalized that except for a few nouns like *sheep* and *swine* with unchanged plurals, and a few others like *mice* and *feet* with mutated vowels, we are scarcely conscious of any other forms. In the sixteenth century, however, there are certain survivals of the old weak plural in *–n* (see § 113). Most of these had given way before the usual *s*–forms: *fon* (foes), *kneen* (knees), *fleen* (fleas). But beside the more modern forms Shakespeare occasionally has *eyen* (eyes), *shoon* (shoes), and *kine*, while the plural *hosen* is occasionally found in other writers. Today, except for the poetical *kine* and mixed plurals like *children* and *brethren*, the only plural of this type in general use is *oxen*.

An interesting peculiarity of this period, and indeed later, is the *his*–genitive. In Middle English the *–es* of the genitive, being unaccented, was frequently written and pronounced *–is*, *–ys*. The ending was thus often identical with the pronoun *his*, which commonly lost its *h* when unstressed. Thus there was no difference in pronunciation between *stonis* and *ston is* (his), and as early as the thirteenth century the ending was sometimes written separately as though the possessive case were a contraction of a noun and the pronoun *his*.[1] This notion was long prevalent and Shakespeare writes '*Gainst the count his galleys I did some service* and *In characters as red as Mars his heart*. Until well into the eighteenth century people were

---

[1] Wyld, *History of Modern Colloquial English*, p. 315, calls attention to instances in *Genesis and Exodus* (c. 1250).

troubled by the illogical consequences of this usage;[1] Dr. Johnson points out that one can hardly believe that the possessive ending is a contraction of *his* in such expressions as *a woman's beauty* or *a virgin's delicacy*. He, himself, seems to have been aware that its true source was the Old English genitive, but the error has left its trace in the apostrophe which we still retain as a graphic convenience to mark the possessive.

One other construction affecting the noun becomes established during this period, the group possessive: *the Duke of Gloucester's niece, the King of England's nose, somebody else's hat*. The construction is perhaps illogical, since even a king may be considered to have some rights in his nose, and the earlier construction was *the Duke's niece of Gloucester*, etc. But the expressions *Duke of Gloucester, King of England*, and the like, occurred so commonly as a unit that in the fifteenth century we begin to get the sign of the possessive added to the group. Instances are not common before the sixteenth century, and the construction may be thought of properly as belonging to the modern period. Nowadays we may say *the writer of the book's ambition* or *the chief actor in the play's illness*.[2]

181. The Adjective.   Since the adjective had already lost all its endings, so that it no longer expressed distinctions of gender, number, and case, the chief interest of this part of speech in the modern period is in the forms of the comparative and superlative degrees. In the sixteenth century these were not always precisely those now in use. For example, comparatives such as *lenger, strenger* remind us that forms like our *elder* were once more common in the language. The two methods commonly used to form the comparative and superlative, with the endings *–er* and *–est* and with the adverbs *more* and *most*, had been customary since Old English times. But there was more variation in their use. Shakespearian comparisons like *honester, violentest* are now replaced by the analytical forms. A double comparative or superlative is also fairly frequent in the work of Shakespeare and his contemporaries: *more larger, most boldest*, or Mark Antony's *This was the most unkindest cut of all*. The chief development affecting the adjective in modern times has been the gradual settling down of usage so that monosyllables take *–er* and *–est* while most adjectives of two or more syllables (especially those with suffixes like those in frug*al*, learn*ed*, care*ful*, poet*ic*, act*ive*, fam*ous*) take *more* and *most*.

---

[1] For example, Robert Baker in his *Remarks on the English Language* (2nd ed., 1779) enters into a long polemic against Dr. Johnson and others on the subject. Logic was sometimes conciliated by expressions like *my sister her watch*.

[2] See Eilert Ekwall, *Studies on the Genitive of Groups in English* (Lund, 1943; *K. Humanistika Vetenskapssamfundets i Lund, Årsberättelse*, 1942–1943).

182. *The Pronoun.*   The sixteenth century saw the establishment of the personal pronoun in the form which it has had ever since. In attaining this result three changes were involved: the disuse of *thou, thy, thee;* the substitution of *you* for *ye* as a nominative case; and the introduction of *its* as the possessive of *it*.

(1) In the earliest period of English the distinction between *thou* and *ye* was simply one of number; *thou* was the singular and *ye* the plural form for the second person pronoun. In time, however, a quite different distinction grew up. In the thirteenth century the singular forms (*thou, thy, thee*) were used among familiars and in addressing children or persons of inferior rank, while the plural forms (*ye, your, you*) began to be used as a mark of respect in addressing a superior.[1] In England the practice seems to have been suggested by French usage in court circles, but it finds a parallel in many other modern languages. In any case, the usage spread as a general concession to courtesy until *ye, your,* and *you* became the usual pronoun of direct address irrespective of rank or intimacy. By the sixteenth century the singular forms had all but disappeared from polite speech and are in ordinary use today only among the Quakers.[2]

(2) Originally a clear distinction was made between the nominative *ye* and the objective *you*. But since both forms are so frequently unstressed, they were often pronounced alike [jə]. A tendency to confuse the nominative and the accusative forms can be observed fairly early, and in the fourteenth century *you* began to be used as a nominative. By a similar substitution *ye* appears in the following century for the objective case, and from this time on the two forms seem to have been used pretty indiscriminately until *ye* finally disappeared. It is true that in the early part of the sixteenth century some men (Lord Berners, for example) were careful to distinguish the two forms, and in the Authorized Version of the Bible (1611) they are often nicely differentiated: *No doubt but ye are the people, and wisdom shall die with you* (Job). On the other hand Ascham and Sir Thomas Elyot appear to make no distinction in the nominative, while Shakespeare says *A southwest wind blow on ye And blister you all over!* In *The Two Gentlemen of Verona* occurs the line *Stand, sirs, and throw us that*

---

[1] Cf. A. G. Kennedy, *The Pronoun of Address in English Literature of the Thirteenth Century* (Stanford University, 1915); R. O. Stidston, *The Use of Ye in the Function of Thou in Middle English Literature from MS. Auchinleck to MS. Vernon: A Study of Grammar and Social Intercourse in Fourteenth-Century England* (Stanford University, 1917); and Thomas Finkenstaedt, *You und Thou: Studien zur Anrede im Englischen* (Berlin, 1963).

[2] On the Quaker position, see William Penn's *No Cross, No Crown* (1669), in *A Collection of the Writings of William Penn*, vol. 1 (London, 1726).

you have about ye, where the two pronouns represent the exact reverse of their historical use. Although in the latter instance, *ye* may owe something to its unemphatic position, as in similar cases it does in Milton, it is evident that there was very little feeling any more for the different functions of the two words, and in the course of the seventeenth century *you* becomes the regular form for both cases.

(3) In some ways the most interesting development in the pronoun at this time was the formation of a new possessive neuter, *its.* As we have seen above, the neuter pronoun in Old English was declined *hit, his, him, hit,* which by the merging of the dative and accusative under *hit* in Middle English became *hit, his, hit.* In unstressed positions *hit* weakened to *it,* and at the beginning of the modern period *it* was the usual form for the subject and object. *His,* however, remained the proper form of the possessive. Although it was thus identical with the possessive case of *he,* its occurrence where we should now use *its* is very common in written English down to the middle of the seventeenth century. Thus Portia's words *How far that little candle throws his beams* are quite natural, as is the Biblical *if the salt have lost his savor, wherewith shall it be salted?*

If grammatical gender had survived in English the continued use of *his* when referring to neuter nouns would probably never have seemed strange. But when, with the substitution of natural gender, meaning came to be the determining factor in the gender of nouns, and all lifeless objects were thought of as neuter, the situation was somewhat different. The personal pronouns of the third person singular, *he, she, it,* had a distinctive form for each gender in the nominative and objective cases, and a need seems to have been felt for some distinctive form in the possessive case as well. Various substitutes were tried, clearly indicating a desire, conscious or unconscious, to avoid the use of *his* in the neuter. Thus, we find frequently in the Bible expressions like *Two cubits and a half was the length of it* and *nine cubits was the length thereof.* Not infrequently the simple form *it* was used as a possessive, as when Horatio, describing the ghost in *Hamlet,* says *It lifted up it head,* or when the Fool in *Lear* says:

> The hedge-sparrow fed the cuckoo so long,
> That it had it head bit off by it young.

The same use of the pronoun *it* is seen in the combination *it own: We enjoin thee . . . that there thou leave it, Without more mercy, to it own protection (Winter's Tale).* Similarly *the* was used in place of the pronoun: *growing of the own accord* (Holland's *Pliny,* 1601). Both of these makeshifts are as old as the fourteenth century.

It was perhaps inevitable that the possessive of nouns (*stone's, horse's*) should eventually suggest the analogical form *it's* for the possessive of *it*. (The word was spelled with an apostrophe down to about 1800.) The first recorded instance of this form is in *The Second Book of Madrigals* published by Nicholas Yonge in 1597,[1] but, like most novelties of this kind in language, it had probably been in colloquial use for a time before it appeared in print. Nevertheless, it is not likely to have been common even at the end of the sixteenth century, considering the large amount of fairly colloquial English that has come down to us from this period with no trace of such a form. At the beginning of the seventeenth century it was clearly felt as a neologism not yet admitted to good use. There is no instance of it in the Bible (1611) or in any of the plays of Shakespeare printed during his lifetime. In the First Folio of 1623 there are only ten instances, and seven of these were in plays written near the end of the dramatist's career. Milton, although living till 1674, seems to have admitted it but grudgingly to his writings; there are only three occurrences of the word in all his poetry and not many in his prose. Yet so useful a word could hardly fail to win a place for itself among the rank and file of men. Toward the close of the seventeenth century its acceptance seems to have gained momentum rapidly, so that to a man like Dryden (1631–1700) the older use of *his* as a neuter seemed an archaism worthy of comment.[2]

Finally, mention should be made of one other noteworthy development of the pronoun in the sixteenth century. This is the use of *who* as a relative. Refinements in the use of subordinate clauses are a mark of maturity in style. As the loose association of clauses (parataxis) gives way to more precise indications of logical relationship and subordination (hypotaxis) there is need for a greater variety of words effecting the union. Old English had no relative pronoun proper. It made use of the definite article (*sē, sēo, þæt*), which, however it was felt in Old English times, strikes us as having more demonstrative force than relative. Sometimes the indeclinable particle *þe* was added (*sē þe*, which that) and sometimes *þe* was used alone. At the end of the Old English period the particle *þe* had become the most usual relative pronoun, but it did not long retain its popularity. Early in the Middle English period its place was taken by *þæt* (that) and this was the almost universal relative pronoun, used for all genders, throughout the Middle English period. In the fifteenth century *which* begins to alternate fairly frequently with *that*. At first it referred mostly to neuter antecedents, although occasionally it was used for persons, a use that survives in *Our*

---

[1] See C. L. Quinton in *LTLS*, April 29, 1944, p. 211.
[2] *Dramatic Poetry of the Last Age.*

Father, which art in heaven. But the tendency to employ *that* as a universal relative has never been lost in the language, and was so marked in the eighteenth century as to provoke Steele to address to the *Spectator* (No. 78) his well-known "Humble Petition of *Who and Which*" in protest. It was not until the sixteenth century that the pronoun *who*[1] as a relative came into use. Occasional instances of such a use occur earlier, but they are quite exceptional. There is no example of the nominative case in Chaucer. Chaucer, however, does use the oblique cases *whose* and *whom* (infrequently) as relative pronouns, and it is clear that the use of *who* as a pure relative began with these forms.[2] Two earlier uses of *who* are the sources of the new construction: *who* as an indefinite pronoun (*Who hath ears to hear, let him hear; Who steals my purse steals trash*) and as an interrogative in indirect questions. The latter appears to have been the more important. The sequence *Whom do you want?* (direct question), *They asked whom you wanted* (indirect question), *I know the man whom you wanted* (relative) is not a difficult one to assume. In any case, our present-day widespread use of *who* as a relative pronoun is primarily a contribution of the sixteenth century to the language.

183. The Verb. Even the casual reader of Elizabethan English is aware of certain differences of usage in the verb which distinguish this part of speech from its form in later times. These differences are sometimes so slight as to give only a mildly unfamiliar tinge to the construction. When Lennox asks in *Macbeth, Goes the King hence today?* we have merely an instance of the more common interrogative form without an auxiliary, where we should say *Does the king go?* or *Is the king leaving today?* Where we should say *has been* Shakespeare often says *is: Is execution done on Cawdor?* and *'Tis unnatural, Even like the deed that's done;* or *Arthur, whom* [who] *they say is killed tonight.* A very noticeable difference is the scarcity of progressive forms. Polonius asks, *What do you read, my Lord?*—i.e., *What are you reading?* The large increase in the use of the progressive is one of the important developments of later times (see §§ 209–10). Likewise the compound participle, *having spoken thus, having decided to make the attempt,* etc., is conspicuous by its infrequency. There are only three

---

[1] *Hwā* was in Old English an interrogative pronoun.

[2] This was first pointed out by O. F. Emerson (*Hist. of the English Lang.*, p. 338). The most valuable collection of data for tracing the beginnings of the relative *who* is in J. Steinki, *Die Entwicklung der englischen Relativpronomina in spätmittelenglischer und frühneuenglischer Zeit* (Breslau, 1932), chap. 3. See also L. R. Wilson, "Chaucer's Relative Constructions," *Studies in Philology*, 1 (1906), 1–58, and G. O. Curme, "A History of English Relative Constructions," *JEGP*, 11 (1912), 10–29, 180–204, 355–80. Other references may be found in Steinki.

instances in Shakespeare and less than threescore in the Bible. The construction arose in the sixteenth century.[1] On the other hand, impersonal uses of the verb were much more common than they are today. *It yearns me not, it dislikes me, so please him come* are Shakespearian expressions which in more recent English have been replaced by personal constructions. In addition to such features of Elizabethan verbal usage, there are certain differences in inflection which are more noticeable, particularly the ending of the third person singular of the present indicative, an occasional *–s* in the third person plural, and many forms of the past tense and past participle, especially of strong verbs.

The regular ending of the third person singular in the whole south and southeastern part of England—that is, the district most influential in the formation of the standard speech—was *–eth* all through the Middle English period. It is universal in Chaucer: *telleth, giveth, saith, doth,* etc. In the fifteenth century, forms with *–s* occasionally appear. These are difficult to account for, since it is not easy to see how the Northern dialect, where they were normal, could have exerted so important an influence upon the language of London and the south. But in the course of the sixteenth century their number increases, especially in writings which seem to reflect the colloquial usage. By the end of this century forms like *tells, gives, says* predominate, though in some words, such as *doth* and *hath*, the older usage may have been the commoner. One was free to use either. In the famous plea for mercy in the *Merchant of Venice* Portia says:

> The quality of mercy is not strain'd,
> It dropp*eth* as a gentle rain from heaven
> Upon the place beneath: it is twice bless'd;
> It bless*eth* him that giv*es* and him that tak*es:* . . .

It is worth noting, however, that in the trial scene as a whole, forms in *–s* outnumber those in *–eth* two to one. Certainly, during the first half of the next century *–s* had become universal in the spoken language. This is beyond doubt, even though *–eth* continued to be quite commonly written. A writer toward the middle of the century observes that "howsoever wee use to Write thus, *leadeth* it, *maketh* it, *noteth* it, *raketh* it, per-*fumeth* it, &c. Yet in our ordinary speech (which is best to bee understood) wee say, *leads* it, *makes* it, *notes* it, *rakes* it, per-*fumes* it."[2] It is altogether probable that during Shakespeare's lifetime *–s* became the usual ending for this part of the verb in the spoken language.

[1] Jespersen, *Modern English Grammar*, IV, 94.
[2] Richard Hodges, *A Special Help to Orthographie* (London, 1643), p. 26.

Another feature of the English verb in the sixteenth century, more noticeable at the close than at the opening, is the occurrence of this –s as an ending also of the third person plural. Normally at this time the plural had no ending in the language of literature and the court, a circumstance resulting from the disappearance of the East Midland –en, –e, the characteristic endings of the plural in Chaucer. But alongside this predominant plural without ending, we find occasionally expressions like *troubled minds that wakes* in Shakespeare's *Lucrece*, or *Whose own hard dealings teaches them suspect the deeds of others* in the *Merchant of Venice*. These are not solecisms or misprints, as the reader might suppose. They represent forms in actual, if infrequent, use. Their occurrence is also often attributed to the influence of the Northern dialect, but this explanation has been quite justly questioned,[1] and it is suggested that they are due to analogy with the singular. While we are in some danger here of explaining *ignotum per ignotius*, we must admit that no better way of accounting for this peculiarity has been offered. And when we remember that a certain number of Southern plurals in –eth continued apparently in colloquial use, the alternation of –s with this –eth would be quite like the alternation of these endings in the singular. Only they were much less common. Plural forms in –s are occasionally found as late as the eighteenth century.

We have already seen (§ 117) that during the Middle English period extensive inroads were made in the ranks of the Old English strong verbs. Many of these verbs were lost and many became weak. Moreover, those that remained were subject to considerable fluctuation and alteration in the past tense and past participle. Since all of these tendencies were still operative in the beginning of the modern period, we may expect to find them reflected in the language of Shakespeare and his contemporaries. Among verbs which developed weak forms in this period were *bide, crow, crowd, flay, mow, dread, sprout,* and *wade,* and we accordingly find corresponding strong forms which have since disappeared, still in common use. Strong forms also alternate with weak in verbs which had begun to change earlier. Some of these are mentioned in § 118. Others were *waxen,* more frequent in the Bible than *waxed, sew* beside *sowed, gnew* beside *gnawed, holp* beside *helped.* A number of weak forms like *blowed, growed, shined, shrinked, swinged* were in fairly common use, although these verbs ultimately remained strong. In certain common verbs the form of the past tense differed from that of today. Such preterites as *brake* and *spake, drave* and *clave, tare, bare,* and *sware* are familiar to us from the Bible. *Bote* as

---

[1] Wyld, *History of Modern Colloquial English*, p. 340.

the past tense of *bite* (like *write—wrote*) was still in occasional use. The participle *baken* is more frequent in the Bible than *baked*. *Brent* and *brast* were common forms for *burnt* and *burst*, while *wesh* and *washen* were prevalent as the past tense and past participle of *wash* until the close of the sixteenth century. Since in all these cases the forms current today were also in use, it is apparent that in Shakespeare's day there was much more latitude in the inflection of the verb than is permitted today.

184. *Usage and Idiom.* Language is not merely a matter of words and inflections. We should neglect a very essential element if we failed to take account of the many conventional features—matters of idiom and usage—that often defy explanation or logical classification but are nevertheless characteristic of the language at a given time and, like other conventions, subject to change. Such a matter as the omission of the article where we customarily use it is an illustration in point. Shakespeare says *creeping like snail, with as big heart as thou, in number of our friends, within this mile and half, thy beauty's form in table of my heart,* where modern idiom requires an article in all these cases. On the other hand, where we say *at length, at last,* Shakespeare says *at the length, at the last.* Again, usage permitted a different placing of the negative—before the verb—as in such expressions as *I not doubt, it not appears to me, she not denies it.* For a long time English permitted the use of a double negative. We have now discarded it through a false application of mathematical logic to language; but in Elizabethan times it was felt merely as a stronger negative, as indeed it is today in the instinct of the uneducated. So Shakespeare could say *Thou hast spoken no word all this while—nor understood none neither; I know not, nor I greatly care not; Nor this is not my nose neither; First he denied you had in him no right; My father hath no child but I, nor none is like to have; Nor never none shall mistress be of it, save I alone.* It is a pity we have lost so useful an intensive.

Perhaps nothing illustrates so richly the idiomatic changes in a language from one age to another as the uses of prepositions. When Shakespeare says *I'll rent the fairest house in it after threepence a bay,* we should say *at;* in *Our fears in Banquo stick deep,* we should say *about.* The single preposition *of* shows how many changes in common idioms have come about since 1600: *One that I brought up of* (from) *a puppy; he came of* (on) *an errand to me; 'Tis pity of* (about) *him; your name.... I know not, nor by what wonder you do hit of* (upon) *mine; And not be seen to wink of* (during) *all the day; it was well done of* (by) *you; I wonder of* (at) *their being here together; I am provided of* (with) *a torch-bearer; I have no mind of* (for) *feasting forth tonight; I were better to be married of* (by) *him than of another;*

That did but show thee of (as) *a fool.* Many more examples could be added. While matters of idiom and usage generally claim less attention from students of the language than do sounds and inflections or additions to the vocabulary, no picture of Elizabethan English would be adequate which did not give them a fair measure of recognition.

185. *General Characteristics of the Period.* As we survey the period of the sixteenth and early seventeenth centuries—the period of early Modern English—we recognize certain general characteristics, some of which are exemplified in the foregoing discussion, while others concern the larger spirit of the age in linguistic matters. These may be stated in the form of a brief summary as a conclusion to the present chapter.

First, a conscious interest in the English language and an attention to its problems are now widely manifested. The fifteenth century had witnessed sporadic attempts by individual writers to embellish their style with "aureate terms." These attempts show in a way a desire to improve the language, at least along certain limited lines. But in the sixteenth century we meet with a considerable body of literature—books and pamphlets, prefaces and incidental observations—defending the language against those who were disposed to compare it unfavorably to Latin or other modern tongues, patriotically recognizing its position as the national speech, and urging its fitness for learned and literary use. At the same time it is considered worthy of cultivation, and to be looked after in the education of the young. Whereas a century or two before, the upper classes seemed more interested in having their children acquire a correct French accent, and sometimes sent them abroad for the purpose, we now find Elyot urging that noblemen's sons should be brought up by those who "speke none englisshe but that which is cleane, polite, perfectly and articulately pronounced, omittinge no lettre or sillable," and observing that he knew some children of noble birth who had "attained corrupte and foule pronuntiation"[1] through the lack of such precautions. Numerous books attempt to describe the proper pronunciation of English, sometimes for foreigners but often presumably for those whose native dialect did not conform to the standard of London and the court. Along with this regard for English as an object of pride and cultivation went the desire to improve it in various ways—particularly to enlarge its vocabulary and to regulate its spelling. All of these efforts point clearly to a new attitude toward English, an attitude which makes it an object of conscious and in many ways fruitful consideration.

---

[1] *The Governour*, chap. 5.

In the second place, we attain in this period to something in the nature of a standard, something moreover that is recognizably "modern." The effect of the Great Vowel Shift was to bring the pronunciation within measurable distance of that which prevails today. The influence of the printing press and the efforts of spelling reformers had resulted in a form of written English that offers little difficulty to the modern reader. And the many new words added by the methods already discussed had given us a vocabulary that has on the whole survived. Moreover, in the writings of Spenser and Shakespeare, and their contemporaries generally, we are aware of the existence of a standard literary language free from the variations of local dialect. Although Sir Walter Raleigh might speak with a broad Devonshire pronunciation,[1] and for all we know Spenser and Shakespeare may have carried with them through life traces in their speech of their Lancashire and Warwickshire ancestry, yet when they wrote they wrote a common English without dialectal idiosyncrasies. This, as Puttenham (1589) reminds us, was to be the speech of London and the court. It is not without significance that he adds, "herein we are already ruled by th' English Dictionaries and other bookes written by learned men, and therefore it needeth none other direction in that behalfe." However subject to the variability characteristic of a language not yet completely settled, written English in the latter part of the sixteenth century is fully entitled to be called a standard speech.

Thirdly, English in the Renaissance, at least as we see it in books, was much more plastic than now. Men felt freer to mould it to their wills. Words had not always distributed themselves into rigid grammatical categories. Adjectives appear as adverbs or nouns or verbs, nouns appear as verbs—in fact, any part of speech as almost any other part. When Shakespeare wrote *stranger'd with an oath* he was fitting the language to his thought, rather than forcing his thought into the mold of conventional grammar. This was in keeping with the spirit of his age. It was in language, as in many other respects, an age with the characteristics of youth—vigor, a willingness to venture, and a disposition to attempt the untried. The spirit that animated Hawkins and Drake and Raleigh was not foreign to the language of their time.

Finally, we note that in spite of all the progress that had been made toward a uniform standard, there were a good many features of the

---

[1] "Old Sir Thomas Malette, one of the judges of the King's Bench, knew Sir Walter Ralegh, and sayd that, notwithstanding his great travells, conversation, learning, etc., yet he spake broade Devonshire to his dyeing day." John Aubrey, *Brief Lives*, ed. Andrew Clark (2 vols., Oxford, 1898), I, 354.

language that were still unsettled. There still existed a considerable variety of use—alternative forms in the grammar, experiments with new words, variations in pronunciation and spelling. A certain latitude was clearly permitted among speakers of education and social position, and the relation between the literary language and good colloquial English was so close that this latitude appears also in the written language. Where one might say *have wrote* or *have written* with equal propriety,[1] as well as *housen* or *houses*, *shoon* or *shoes*, one must often have been in doubt over which to use. One heard *service* also pronounced *sarvice*, and the same variation occurred in a number of other words (*certain—sartin, concern— consarn, divert—divart, clerk—clark, smert—smart*, etc.). These and many other matters were still unsettled at the close of the period. Their settlement, as we shall see, was one of the chief concerns of the next age.

BIBLIOGRAPHY

Good brief discussions of the language in this period will be found in Henry Bradley's article, "Shakespeare's English," in *Shakespeare's England* (2 vols., Oxford, 1916), II, 539–74, and J. W. H. Atkins' chapter, "The Language from Chaucer to Shakespeare," in the *Cambridge Hist. of English Lit.*, III, 499–530. A fuller and more recent account is by Charles Barber, *Early Modern English* (London, 1976). J. L. Moore, *Tudor-Stuart Views on the Growth, Status, and Destiny of the English Language* (Halle, 1910), gathers together the most important contemporary pronouncements. Convenient facsimile reprints of many of the sources cited in this chapter and the next have been published by the Scolar Press in its series *English Linguistics, 1500–1800* (365 vols., Menston, England, 1967–1972). An admirable introduction to the problem of recognition which the vernacular languages faced in France and Italy, necessary as a background to the problem in England, is Pierre Villey, *Les Sources italiennes de la "Deffense et Illustration de la Langue Françoise" de Joachim du Bellay* (Paris, 1908). The situation in France is treated fully by F. Brunot, *Histoire de la langue française*, 2 (Paris, 1922), 1–91. Du Bellay's *Deffence* may now be read in an English translation by Gladys M. Turquet (New York, 1940). Other treatments of the struggle of the vernacular for recognition in Italy are V. Vivaldi, *Storia delle controversie linguistiche in Italia da Dante ai nostri giorni* (Catanzaro, 1925); T. Labande-Jeanroy, *La Question de la langue en Italie* (Strassburg, 1925); and Robert A. Hall, Jr., *The Italian Questione della Lingua, An Interpretative Essay* (Chapel Hill, 1942; *Univ. of No. Carolina Stud. in Romance Lang. and Lit.*, no. 4). J. A. Symonds' chapter, "The Purists," in his *Renaissance in Italy*, vol. 2, is a fairly good account of the linguistic situation in the sixteenth century. The parallel conditions in Spain are treated by M. Romera-Navarro, "La defensa de la lengua española en el siglo XVI," *Bulletin Hispanique*, 31 (1929), 204–55. Mulcaster's *Elementaire* is edited by E. T. Campagnac (Oxford, 1925), and his views are discussed by Richard F. Jones, "Richard Mulcaster's View of the

---

[1] Gray's *Elegy* (1751) was originally published with the title *An Elegy Wrote in a Country Churchyard*.

English Language," *Washington Univ. Studies*, Humanistic Ser., 13 (1926), 267–303. For a comprehensive treatment, see the same author's more recent *The Triumph of the English Language: A Survey of Opinions Concerning the Vernacular from the Introduction of Printing to the Restoration* (Stanford, 1953). Elizabethan translations are well treated in F. O. Mathiessen, *Translation, An Elizabethan Art* (Cambridge, Mass., 1931), and H. B. Lathrop, *Translations from the Classics into English from Caxton to Chapman, 1477–1620* (Madison, 1933). As an example of the new words introduced by individual writers the student may consult an excellent monograph by Joseph Delcourt, *Essai sur la langue de Sir Thomas More d'après ses œuvres anglaises* (Paris, 1914), especially chap. 5 and Appendix III. The purist reaction is studied by Wilhelm Prein, *Puristische Strömungen im 16. Jahrhundert* (Eickel i. W., 1909). An excellent account of the early dictionaries interpreting hard words is given by Sir James A. H. Murray in his *Evolution of English Lexicography* (Oxford, 1900). For a more extended treatment, see D. T. Starnes and Gertrude E. Noyes, *The English Dictionary from Cawdrey to Johnson, 1604–1755* (Chapel Hill, 1946). Mario Praz treats fully the Italian borrowings in "The Italian Element in English," *Essays and Studies*, 15 (1929), 20–66. Since the same words were often being borrowed by French at this time and their introduction into English was thus strengthened, the special student will find of value such works as B. H. Wind, *Les Mots italiens introduits en français au XVIe siècle* (Deventer, 1928), and Richard Ruppert, *Die spanischen Lehn- und Fremdwörter in der französischen Schriftsprache* (Munich, 1915). George Gordon's *Shakespeare's English* (Oxford, 1928) is an excellent essay on Shakespeare's innovations, coinages, and general daring in matters of vocabulary. Eilert Ekwall discusses *Shakspere's Vocabulary: Its Etymological Elements*, vol. 1 (Uppsala, 1903). For his pronunciation special mention may be made of Wilhelm Viëtor's *Shakespeare's Pronunciation* (Marburg, 1906); Helge Kökeritz, *Shakespeare's Pronunciation* (New Haven, 1953); and R. E. Zachrisson's *Pronunciation of English Vowels 1400–1700* (Göteborg, 1913), along with the works of Wyld and others mentioned in the footnote to § 174. More general is E. J. Dobson, "Early Modern Standard English," *Trans. Philol. Soc.* (1955), 25–54. Changes in the pronoun and the verb are treated in J. Steinki, *Die Entwicklung der englischen Relativpronomina in spätmittelenglischer und frühneuenglischer Zeit* (Breslau, 1932), and H. T. Price, *A History of Ablaut in the Strong Verbs from Caxton to the End of the Elizabethan Period* (Bonn, 1910). Interesting statistics on the incidence of –s and –th in the third person singular of verbs are given by Rudolph C. Bambas, "Verb Forms in –s and –th in Early Modern English Prose," *JEGP*, 46 (1947), 183–87. Two exceptionally full treatments of topics in Renaissance syntax are F. T. Visser, *A Syntax of the English Language of St. Thomas More* (3 vols., Louvain, 1946–1956), and Mats Rydén, *Relative Constructions in Early Sixteenth Century English, with Special Reference to Sir Thomas Elyot* (Uppsala, 1966).

$\begin{bmatrix} 9 \end{bmatrix}$

The Appeal to Authority,
1650–1800

186. *The Temper of the Eighteenth Century.* The first half of the eighteenth century is commonly designated in histories of literature as the Augustan Age in England. During the half-century preceding, the principal characteristics of this period may be seen taking form, and in the fifty years following it they are still clearly visible, however mixed with new tendencies foreign to it. It is not unreasonable, therefore, to attempt to include this century and a half in one view, and if we survey it from a sufficient distance to obscure minor features (that would reveal its actual complexity), we may simplify without falsifying the picture and thus recognize certain dominant characteristics that emerge, reach their height, and decline, in the manner indicated, and that affect the course of the English language no less than that of the literature.

One of the first of these characteristics to be mentioned is a strong sense of order and the value of regulation. Adventurous individualism and the spirit of independence characteristic of the previous era give way to a desire for system and regularity. This involves conformity to a standard that the consensus recognizes as good. It sets up correctness as an ideal and attempts to formulate rules or principles by which correctness may be defined and achieved. The most important consideration in the foundation of this standard is reason. The spirit of scientific rationalism in philosophy was reflected in many other domains of thought. A great satisfaction was felt in things that could be logically explained and justified. Where it was possible, reason was often supported by the force of authoritative example, particularly classical example. Not only in literature but in language Latin was looked upon as a model, and classical precedent was often generalized into precept. It is easy to see how a standard having its basis in regularity, justified by reason, and supported by authority might be regarded as approaching perfection, and how an age which set much store by elegance and refinement might come to believe in this standard as an indispensable criterion of "taste." The eighteenth century, like many other periods in history, was quietly conscious of its own superiority, and not being trammeled by any strong historical sense, any belief in the validity of other ideals than its own, or any great interest in the factors by which the ideals of former ages might be justified, it could easily come to believe in the essential rightness of its judgment and think that its own ideals could be erected into something like a permanent standard. We may well believe that permanence and stability would seem like no inconsiderable virtues to a generation that remembered the disorders and changes of the Revolution and Restoration.

187. *Its Reflection in the Attitude toward the Language.* The intellectual tendencies here noted are seen quite clearly in the eighteenth-century efforts to standardize, refine, and fix the English language. In the period under consideration discussion of the language takes a new turn. Previously interest had been shown chiefly in such questions as whether English was worthy of being used for writings in which Latin had long been traditional, whether the large additions being made to the vocabulary were justified, and whether a more adequate system of spelling could be introduced. Now for the first time attention was turned to the grammar, and it was discovered that English had no grammar. At any rate its grammar was largely uncodified, unsystematized. The ancient languages had been reduced to rule; one knew what was right and what was wrong. But in English everything was uncertain. One learned to speak and write as one learned to walk, and in many matters of grammatical usage there was much variation even among men of education. This was clearly distasteful to an age that desired above all else an orderly universe. The spontaneous creativeness of a Shakespeare, verbing it with nouns and adjectives, so to speak, sublimely indifferent to rules, untroubled by any considerations in language save those springing from a sure instinct, had given place to hesitation and uncertainty, so that a man like Dryden confessed that at times he had to translate an idea into Latin in order to decide on the correct way to express it in English.

In its effort to set up a standard of correctness in language the rationalistic spirit of the eighteenth century showed itself in the attempt to settle disputed points logically, that is, by simply reasoning about them, often arriving at entirely false conclusions. The respect for authoritative example, especially for classical example, takes the form of appeals to the analogy of Latin, while a different manifestation of the respect for authority is at the bottom of the belief in the power of individuals to legislate in matters of language, and accounts for the repeated demand for an English Academy. Finally it is an idea often expressed that English has been and is being daily corrupted, that it needs correction and refinement, and that when the necessary reforms have been effected it should be fixed permanently and protected from change. In other words, it was the desire of the eighteenth century to give the English language a polished, rational, and permanent form. How mistaken were some of its methods will be shown later. The various features of its program will constitute the major topics for discussion in the remainder of this chapter.

188. *Ascertainment.* Eighteenth-century attempts to deal with the English language and to direct its course fall, we may repeat, under three main heads: (1) to reduce the language to rule and set up a standard of correct usage; (2) to refine it—that is, to remove supposed defects and introduce certain improvements; and (3) to fix it permanently in the desired form.

As pointed out in the preceding section, one of the chief defects of English which people became acutely conscious of in the latter part of the seventeenth century was the absence of a standard, the fact that the language had not been reduced to rule so that a man could express himself at least with the assurance that he was doing so correctly. Dryden sums up this attitude in the words: "we have yet no prosodia, not so much as a tolerable dictionary, or a grammar, so that our language is in a manner barbarous."[1] That is, the language did not possess the character of an orderly and well-regulated society. One must write it according to one's individual judgment and therefore without the confidence which one might feel if there were rules on which to lean and a vocabulary sanctioned by some recognized authority. It was a conviction of long standing with him. In his dedication of *Troilus and Cressida* to the earl of Sunderland (1679) he says: "how barbarously we yet write and speak, your lordship knows, and I am sufficiently sensible in my own English. For I am often put to a stand, in considering whether what I write be the idiom of the tongue, or false grammar." And he adds: "I am desirous, if it were possible, that we might all write with the same certainty of words, and purity of phrase, to which the Italians first arrived, and after them the French; at least that we might advance so far, as our tongue is capable of such a standard." The idea was expressed many times in the earlier part of the eighteenth century, perhaps nowhere more accurately than in the words, "we write by guess,

---

[1] *Discourse concerning Satire* (1693).

more than any stated rule, and form every man his diction, either according to his humour and caprice, or in pursuance of a blind and servile imitation." [1]

In the eighteenth century the need for standardization and regulation was summed up in the word *ascertainment*. The force of this word then was somewhat different from that which it has today. To *ascertain* was not so much to learn by inquiry as to settle a matter, to render it certain and free from doubt. Dr. Johnson defined *ascertainment* as "a settled rule; an established standard"; and it was in this sense that Swift used the verb in his *Proposal for Correcting, Improving, and Ascertaining the English Tongue.* [2] When reduced to its simplest form the need was for a dictionary which should record the proper use of words, and a grammar which should settle authoritatively the correct usages in matters of construction. How it was proposed to attain these ends we shall see shortly.

189. The Problem of "Refining" the Language. Uncertainty was not the only fault which the eighteenth century found with English. The lack of a standard to which all might conform was believed to have resulted in many corruptions which were growing up unchecked. It is the subject of frequent lament that for some time the language had been steadily going down. Such observations are generally accompanied by a regretful backward glance at the good old days. Various periods in the past were supposed to represent the highest perfection of English. It was Dryden's opinion that "from Chaucer the purity of the English tongue began," but he was not so completely convinced as some others that its course had been always downward. For Swift the golden age was that of the great Elizabethans. "The period," he says, "wherein the English tongue received most improvement, I take to commence with the beginning of Queen Elizabeth's reign, and to conclude with the great rebellion in forty-two. From the civil war to this present time, I am apt to doubt whether the corruptions in our language have not at least equalled the refinements of it; and these corruptions very few of the best authors in our age have wholly escaped. During the usurpation, such an infusion of enthusiastic jargon prevailed in every writing, as was not shaken off in many years after. To this succeeded the licentiousness which entered with the restoration, and from infecting our religion and morals fell to corrupt our language." [3]

---

[1] Thomas Stackhouse, *Reflections on the Nature and Property of Language in General, on the Advantages, Defects, and Manner of Improving the English Tongue in Particular* (1731), p. 187.

[2] Cf. § 193, below.

[3] *Proposal for Correcting, Improving, and Ascertaining the English Tongue.*

With this opinion Dr. Johnson agreed. In his *Dictionary* he says, "I have studiously endeavoured to collect examples and authorities from the writers before the restoration, whose works I regard as the wells of English undefiled, as the pure sources of genuine diction." It is curious to find writers later in the century, such as Priestley, Sheridan, and the American Webster, looking back upon the Restoration and the period of Swift himself as the classical age of the language. It is apparent that much of this talk springs merely from a sentimental regard for the past and is to be taken no more seriously than the perennial belief that our daughters are not what their mothers were. Certainly the corruptions which Swift cites seem to us rather trivial. But the significance of such utterances lies in the fact that they reveal an attitude of mind and lead to many attempts in the course of the century to "purify" the language and rid it of supposed imperfections.

There have always been, and doubtless always will be, men who feel a strong antipathy toward certain words or expressions or particular constructions, especially those with the taint of novelty about them. Usually such men do not make their objections felt beyond the circle of their friends. But occasionally an individual whose name carries weight and who is possessed with a crusading spirit offers his views to the public. However much the condemned usages may represent mere personal prejudice, they are often regarded by others as veritable faults in the language and continue to be condemned in words that echo those of the original critic until the objections attain a currency and assume a magnitude out of all proportion to their significance. Such seems to have been the case with the strictures of Dean Swift on the English of his day.

In matters of language Swift was a conservative. The things which troubled the gloomy dean in his reflections on the current speech were chiefly innovations which he says had been growing up in the last twenty years. One of these was the tendency to clip and shorten words which should have retained their full polysyllabic dignity. He would have objected to *taxi, phone, bus, ad*, and the like, as he did to *rep, mob, penult*, and others. The practice seems to have been a temporary fad, although not unknown to any period of the language. It continued, however, to be condemned for fifty years. Thus George Campbell in his *Philosophy of Rhetoric* (1776) says: "I shall just mention another set of barbarisms, which also comes under this class, and arises from the abbreviation of polysyllables, by lopping off all the syllables except the first, or the first and second. Instances of this are *hyp* for *hypochondriac, rep* for *reputation, ult* for *ultimate, penult* for *penultimate, incog* for *incognito, hyper* for *hypercritic, extra* for *extraordinary*. Happily all these affected terms have been denied

the public suffrage. I scarcely know any such that have established themselves, except *mob* for *mobile*. And this it hath effected at last, notwithstanding the unrelenting zeal with which it was persecuted by Dr. Swift,
wherever he met with it. But as the word in question hath gotten use, the
supreme arbitress of language, on its side, there would be as much ob-
stinacy in rejecting it at present, as there was perhaps folly at first in
ushering it upon the public stage."[1] Campbell's admission of the word *mob*
is interesting, since in theory he accepted the test of usage, but he could not
quite free himself from prejudice against this word.

A second innovation which Swift opposed was the tendency to contract
verbs like *drudg'd, disturb'd, rebuk'd, fledg'd* "and a thousand others everywhere to be met with in prose as well as verse, where, by leaving out a
vowel to save a syllable, we form a jarring sound, and so difficult to utter,
that I have often wondered how it could ever obtain." His ostensible
reason for rejecting this change, which time has fully justified, is that "our
language was already overstocked with monosyllables." We accordingly
hear a good bit in the course of the century about the large number of
monosyllabic words in English, an objection which seems to have no more
to support it than the fact that a person of Swift's authority thought
monosyllables "the disgrace of our language."

A third innovation which aroused Swift's ire has to do with certain
words then enjoying a considerable vogue among wits and people of
fashion. They had even invaded the pulpit. Young preachers, fresh from
the universities, he says, "use all the modern terms of art, *sham, banter,
mob, bubble, bully, cutting, shuffling*, and *palming*, all which, and many
more of the like stamp, as I have heard them often in the pulpit, so I have
read them in some of those sermons that have made most noise of late."
Swift was by no means alone in his criticism of new words. Each censor of
the language has his own list of objectionable expressions (cf. § 205). But
this type of critic may be illustrated here by its most famous representative.

All of these faults which Swift found in the language he attacked in a
letter to the *Tatler* (No. 230) in 1710, and he called attention to them again
two years later in his *Proposal for Correcting, Improving, and Ascertaining
the English Tongue*. In the former paper, in order to set out more clearly
the abuses he objected to, he published a letter supposedly "received some
time ago from a most accomplished person in this way of writing":

Sir,
    I *cou'dn't* get the things you sent for all *about Town.*—I *thôt* to *ha'*
come down myself, and then *I'd ha' brout'um;* but I *han't don't*, and

[1] I. 428–29.

I believe *I can't do't*, that's *pozz.*—*Tom* begins to *g'imself* airs because *he's* going with the *plenipo's.*—'Tis said, the French King will *bamboozl' us agen*, which *causes many speculations.* The *Jacks*, and others of that *kidney*, are very *uppish*, and *alert upon't*, as you may see by their *phizz's.*—*Will Hazzard* has got the *hipps*, having lost *to the tune of* five hundr'd pound, *thô* he understands play very well, *nobody better.* He has promis't me upon *rep*, to leave off play; but you know 'tis a weakness *he's* too apt to *give into, thô* he has as much wit as any man, *nobody more.* He has lain *incog* ever since.—The *mobb's* very quiet with us now.—I believe you *thôt* I *banter'd* you in my last like a *country put.*—I *sha'n't* leave Town this month, &c.

"This letter," he says, "is in every point an admirable pattern of the present polite way of writing." The remedy which he proposes is for the editor (Steele) to use his position to rid the language of these blemishes, "First, by argument and fair means; but if these fail, I think you are to make use of your authority as Censor, and by an annual *index expurgatorius* expunge all words and phrases that are offensive to good sense, and condemn those barbarous mutilations of vowels and syllables." Later, in his *Proposal*, he was to go much further.

190. The Desire to "Fix" the Language.   One of the most ambitious hopes of the eighteenth century was to stabilize the language, to establish it in a form which would be permanent. Swift talked about "fixing" the language, and the word was echoed for fifty years by lesser men who shared his desire and, like him, believed in the possibility of realizing it. The fear of change was an old one. Bacon at the end of his life had written to his friend, Sir Toby Matthew (1623): "It is true, my labours are now most set to have those works, which I had formerly published, . . . well translated into Latin. . . . For these modern languages will, at one time or other, play the bankrupts with books."[1]

A succession of writers voiced the fear that in a few generations their works would not be understood. Shortly after the Restoration the poet Waller wrote (*Of English Verse*):

> But who can hope his lines should long
> Last, in a daily changing tongue?
> While they are new, Envy prevails;
> And as that dies, our language fails. . . .
>
> Poets that Lasting Marble seek,
> Must carve in Latin or in Greek;
> We write in Sand. . . .

[1] *Works*, ed. Basil Montagu (Philadelphia, 1841), III, 151.

A little later Swift wrote: "How then shall any man, who hath a genius for history equal to the best of the ancients, be able to undertake such a work with spirit and cheerfulness, when he considers that he will be read with pleasure but a very few years, and in an age or two shall hardly be understood without an interpreter?" And he added, "The fame of our writers is usually confined to these two islands, and it is hard it should be limited in *time* as much as *place* by the perpetual variations of our speech."[1] Pope echoed the sentiment when he wrote in his *Essay on Criticism*, "And such as Chaucer is, shall Dryden be." Even after the middle of the century, when the hope of fixing the language was less frequently expressed, Thomas Sheridan addressed a plea to the earl of Chesterfield to exert his influence toward stabilizing the language: "Suffer not our Shakespear, and our Milton, to become two or three centuries hence what Chaucer is at present, the study only of a few poring antiquarians, and in an age or two more the victims of bookworms."[2]

It is curious that a number of men notable in various intellectual spheres in the late seventeenth and early eighteenth centuries should have been blind to the testimony of history and believed that by taking thought it would be possible to suspend the processes of growth and decay that characterize a living language. It is the more remarkable in that the truth had been recognized by some from a considerably earlier date. The anonymous author of the pamphlet *Vindex Anglicus: or, The Perfections of the English Language Defended and Asserted* (1644)[3] noted that changes in language are inevitable. Even earlier (1630) that delightful letter writer, James Howell, had observed: "that as all other sublunary things are subject to corruptions and decay, . . . so the learnedest and more eloquent languages are not free from this common fatality, but are liable to those alterations and revolutions, to those fits of inconstancy, and other destructive contingencies which are unavoidably incident to all earthly things."[4] Nevertheless, laboring under the mistaken notion that the classical languages, particularly Greek, had continued unchanged for many centuries, some men held that English might be rendered equally stable. That great scholar Bentley explained the changes that English had undergone in the last two centuries as due chiefly to the large number of Latin words incorporated into the language, and he thought that it would not change so much in the future, adding: "Nay, it were no difficult contrivance, if the

[1] *Proposal.*
[2] *British Education* (1756), p. xvii.
[3] *Harleian Miscellany*, 5 (1808–1811), 428–34.
[4] *Epistolae Ho-Elianae*, Bk. II, Sec. VII, Letter LX.

Public had any regard to it, to make the English Tongue unmutable; unless here after some Foreign Nation shall invade and overrun us."[1] Bentley's influence is apparent in Swift's opinion that "if it [English] were once refined to a certain standard, perhaps there might be ways found out to fix it for ever, or at least till we are invaded and made a conquest by some other state." In the same place Swift says: "But what I have most at heart, is, that some method should be thought on for ascertaining and fixing our language for ever, after such alterations are made in it as shall be thought requisite. For I am of opinion, it is better a language should not be wholly perfect, than that it should be perpetually changing." And again he adds, "I see no absolute necessity why any language should be perpetually changing; for we find many examples to the contrary."[2] It would be possible to show the continuance of this idea through much of the rest of the century, but it is sufficient to recognize it as one of the major concerns of the period with respect to the language.

191. *The Example of Italy and France.* It was perhaps inevitable that those who gave thought to the threefold problem which seemed to confront English—of standardizing, refining, and fixing it—should consider what had been done in this direction by other countries. Italy and France were the countries to which the English had long turned for inspiration and example, and in both of these lands the destiny of the language had been confided to an academy. In Italy, prolific in academies, the most famous was the Accademia della Crusca, founded as early as 1582. Its avowed object was the purification of the Italian language, and to this end, it published in 1612 a dictionary, the famous *Vocabolario degli Accademici della Crusca*. The dictionary provoked controversy, one of the most effective kinds of publicity, and, though subsequently modified in important ways, it went through several editions. In the third (1691) it had reached the proportions of three folio volumes, and the fourth edition (1729–1738) filled six. Here then was an impressive example of the results attained in at least one country from an effort to improve its language. Perhaps an even more effective precedent was furnished by France. In 1635 Cardinal Richelieu offered a royal charter to a small group of men who for several years had been meeting once a week to talk about books and to exchange views on literature. The original group was composed of only six or eight; the maximum membership was set at forty. The society was to be known as the French Academy (l'Académie française) and in the statutes which

---

[1] *Dissertation upon the Epistles of Phalaris* (1699), p. 406.
[2] *Proposal.*

were drawn up defining its purpose it was declared: "The principal function of the Academy shall be to labor with all possible care and diligence to give definite rules to our language, and to render it pure, eloquent, and capable of treating the arts and sciences." It was to cleanse the language of impurities, whether in the mouths of the people or among men of affairs, whether introduced by ignorant courtiers or preachers or writers. It would be well "to establish a certain usage of words" and accordingly it should undertake to compile a dictionary, a grammar, a rhetoric, and a treatise on the art of poetry. The most important of these projects was the dictionary. Work on it proceeded slowly, but in 1694 it appeared. Thus while England continued to lament the lack of an adequate dictionary, Italy and France had both apparently achieved this object through the agency of academies.

192. *An English Academy.* There can be little doubt that the vital incentive to the establishment of an academy in England came from the example of France and Italy. The suggestion of an English Academy occurs early in the seventeenth century. Indeed learned societies had been known in England from 1572, when a Society of Antiquaries founded by Archbishop Parker began holding its meetings at the house of Sir Robert Cotton and occupied itself with the study of antiquity and history. It might in time have turned its attention to the improvement of the language, but it languished after the accession of James. A proposal that promised even more was made about the year of Shakespeare's death by Edmund Bolton, an enthusiastic antiquary. It was for a society to be composed of men famous in politics, law, science, literature, history, and the like. Those proposed for membership, beside the originator, included such well-known names as George Chapman, Sir Edward Coke, Sir Robert Cotton, Sir Kenelm Digby, Michael Drayton, Ben Jonson, Inigo Jones, John Selden, Sir Henry Spelman, and Sir Henry Wotton,[1] all men with scholarly tastes and interests. But the project died with James I.

In time, however, the example of the French Academy began to attract attention in England. In 1650 James Howell spoke approvingly of its intentions to reform French spelling, and in 1657 its history appeared in English, translated from the French of Pellisson. With the Restoration, discussion of an English Academy became much more frequent. In the very year that Charles II was restored to the throne, a volume was published with the title *New Atlantis . . . Continued by R. H. Esquire* (1660) in which, as a feature of his ideal commonwealth, the author pictured an

---

[1] B. S. Monroe, "An English Academy," *MP*, 8 (1910), 107–16.

academy "to purifie our Native Language from Barbarism or Solecism, to the height of Eloquence, by regulating the termes and phrases thereof into constant use of the most significant words, proverbs, and phrases, and justly appropriating them either to the Lofty, mean, or Comic stile."[1]

Shortly thereafter the idea of an academy received support from several influential persons, notably from Dryden and John Evelyn. In the dedication of the *Rival Ladies* (1664) Dryden says, "I am Sorry, that (Speaking so noble a Language as we do) we have not a more certain Measure of it, as they have in France, where they have an Academy erected for the purpose, and Indow'd with large Privileges by the present King." A few months later the Royal Society took a step which might have led it to serve the purpose of an academy. This society, founded in 1662, was mainly scientific in its interests, but in December 1664 it adopted a resolution to the effect that as "there were persons of the Society whose genius was very proper and inclined to improve the English tongue, Particularly for philosophic purposes, it was voted that there should be a committee for improving the English language; and that they meet at Sir Peter Wyche's lodgings in Gray's-Inn once or twice a month, and give an account of their proceedings, when called upon." The committee was a large one; among its twenty-two members were Dryden, Evelyn, Sprat, and Waller. Evelyn, on one occasion, unable to attend the meeting of the committee, wrote out at length what he conceived to be the things which they might attempt. He proposed the compilation of a grammar and some reform of the spelling, particularly the leaving out of superfluous letters. This might be followed by a "Lexicon or collection of all the pure English words by themselves; then those which are derivative from others, with their prime, certaine, and natural signification; then, the symbolical: so as no innovation might be us'd or favour'd, at least, 'till there should arise some necessity of providing a new edition, & of amplifying the old upon mature advice." He further suggested collections of technical words, "exotic" words, dialect expressions, and archaic words which might be revived. Finally, translations might be made of some of the best of Greek and Latin literature, and even out of modern languages, as models of elegance in style. He added the opinion in conclusion that "there must be a stock of reputation gain'd by some public writings and compositions of ye Members of this Assembly, and so others may not think it dishonor to come under the test, or accept them for judges and approbators." Evelyn's statement is important not so

[1] Edmund Freeman, "A Proposal for an English Academy in 1660," *MLR*, 19 (1924), 291–300. The author of this article plausibly suggests Robert Hooke as the R. H. Esquire.

much for the authority that attaches to his words as for the fact that his notions are quite specific and set out at length. Whether because the program which he outlined appeared too ambitious or for some other reason, nothing was done about it. The committee seems to have held only three or four meetings. The Royal Society was not really interested in linguistic matters.

It is quite likely, as Professor Emerson thought,[1] that the moving spirit in this gesture of the Royal Society was John Dryden. Though he was certainly not a pioneer in suggesting the creation of an English Academy, he was the most distinguished and consistent advocate of it in public. Later he seems to have joined forces with the earl of Roscommon. Horace Walpole, in his life of the earl, says: "we are told that his Lordship in conjunction with Dryden projected a society for refining and fixing the standard of our language. It never wanted this care more than at that period; nor could two men have been found more proper to execute most parts of that plan than Dryden, the greatest master of the powers of language, and Roscommon, whose judgment was sufficient to correct the exuberances of his associate."[2] Thus the movement for an academy did not lack the support of well-known and influential names.

But at the end of the century the idea was clearly in the air. In 1697, Defoe in his *Essay upon Projects* devoted one article to the subject of academies. In it he advocated an academy for England. He says: "I would therefore have this society wholly composed of gentlemen, whereof twelve to be of the nobility, if possible, and twelve private gentlemen, and a class of twelve to be left open for mere merit, let it be found in who or what sort it would, which should lie as the crown of their study, who have done something eminent to deserve it." He had high hopes of the benefits to be derived from such a body: "The voice of this society should be sufficient authority for the usage of words, and sufficient also to expose the innovations of other men's fancies; they should preside with a sort of judicature over the learning of the age, and have liberty to correct and censure the exorbitance of writers, especially of translators. The reputation of this society would be enough to make them the allowed judges of style and language; and no author would have the impudence to coin without their authority. Custom, which is now our best authority for words, would always have its original here, and not be allowed without it. There should

---

[1] O. F. Emerson, *John Dryden and a British Academy* (London, 1921; *Proc. of the British Academy*).

[2] *Catalogue of the Royal and Noble Authors of England* (2nd ed., 1959). The statement is echoed by Dr. Johnson in his *Lives of the Poets*.

be no more occasion to search for derivations and constructions, and it would be as criminal then to coin words as money."

193. *Swift's Proposal, 1712*.   By the beginning of the eighteenth century the ground had been prepared and the time was apparently ripe for an authoritative plan for an academy. With the example of Richelieu and the French Academy doubtless in his mind, Swift addressed a letter in 1712 to the earl of Oxford, Lord Treasurer of England. It was published under the title *A Proposal for Correcting, Improving, and Ascertaining the English Tongue*. After the usual formalities he says: "My Lord, I do here in the name of all the learned and polite persons of the nation complain to your Lordship as *first minister*, that our language is extremely imperfect; that its daily improvements are by no means in proportion to its daily corruptions; that the pretenders to polish and refine it have chiefly multiplied abuses and absurdities; and, that in many instances it offends against every part of grammar." He then launches an attack against the innovations which he had objected to in his paper in the *Tatler* two years before, observing, "I have never known this great town without one or more *dunces* of figure, who had credit enough to give rise to some new word, and propagate it in most conversations, though it had neither humour nor significancy."

The remedy which he proposes is an academy, though he does not call it by that name. "In order to reform our language, I conceive, my lord, that a free judicious choice should be made of such persons, as are generally allowed to be best qualified for such a work, without any regard to quality, party, or profession. These, to a certain number at least, should assemble at some appointed time and place, and fix on rules, by which they design to proceed. What methods they will take, is not for me to prescribe." The work of this group, as he conceives it, is described in the following terms: "The persons who are to undertake this work will have the example of the French before them to imitate, where these have proceeded right, and to avoid their mistakes. Besides the grammar-part, wherein we are allowed to be very defective, they will observe many gross improprieties, which however authorized by practice, and grown familiar, ought to be discarded. They will find many words that deserve to be utterly thrown out of our language, many more to be corrected, and perhaps not a few long since antiquated, which ought to be restored on account of their energy and sound." And then he adds the remark which we have quoted in a previous paragraph, that what he has most at heart is that they will find some way to fix the language permanently. In setting up this ideal of permanency he allows for growth but not decay: "But when I say, that I would have our language, after it is duly correct, always to last, I do not mean that it should never be enlarged. Provided that no word, which a society shall give a sanction to, be afterwards antiquated and exploded, they may have liberty to receive whatever new ones they shall find occasion for." He ends with a renewed appeal to the earl to take some action, indulging in the characteristically blunt reflection that "if genius and learning be not encouraged under your Lordship's administration, you are the most inexcusable person alive."

194. The Effect of Swift's Proposal. The publication of Swift's *Proposal* marks the culmination of the movement for an English Academy. It had in its favor the fact that the public mind had apparently become accustomed to the idea through the advocacy of it by Dryden and others for more than half a century. It came from one whose judgment carried more weight than that of anyone else at the beginning of the eighteenth century who might have brought it forward. It was supported by important contemporary opinion. Only a few months before, Addison, in a paper in the *Spectator* (No. 135) which echoes most of Swift's strictures on the language, observed that there were ambiguous constructions in English "which will never be decided till we have something like an Academy, that by the best Authorities and Rules drawn from the Analogy of Languages shall settle all Controversies between Grammar and Idiom."

Apparently the only dissenting voice was that of John Oldmixon, who, in the same year that Swift's *Proposal* appeared, published *Reflections on Dr. Swift's Letter to the Earl of Oxford, about the English Tongue.* It was a violent Whig attack inspired by purely political motives. He says, "I do here in the Name of all the Whigs, protest against all and everything done or to be done in it, by him or in his Name." Much in the thirty-five pages is a personal attack on Swift, in which he quotes passages from the *Tale of a Tub* as examples of vulgar English, to show that Swift was no fit person to suggest standards for the language. And he ridicules the idea that anything can be done to prevent languages from changing. "I should rejoice with him, if a way could be found out to *fix our Language for ever*, that like the *Spanish* cloak, it might always be in Fashion." But such a thing is impossible.

Oldmixon's attack was not directed against the idea of an academy. He approves of the design, "which must be own'd to be very good in itself." Yet nothing came of Swift's *Proposal.* The explanation of its failure in the Dublin edition is probably correct; at least it represented contemporary opinion. "It is well known," it says, "that if the Queen had lived a year or two longer, this proposal would, in all probability, have taken effect.

For the Lord Treasurer had already nominated several persons without distinction of quality or party, who were to compose a society for the purposes mentioned by the author; and resolved to use his credit with her Majesty, that a fund should be applied to support the expence of a large room, where the society should meet, and for other incidents. But this scheme fell to the ground, partly by the dissensions among the great men at court; but chiefly by the lamented death of that glorious princess."

This was the nearest England ever came to having an academy for the regulation of the language. Though Swift's attempt to bring about the formation of such a body is frequently referred to with approval by the advocates of the idea throughout the century, no serious effort was made to accomplish the purpose again. Apparently it was felt that where Swift had failed it would be useless for others to try. Meanwhile opposition to an academy was slowly taking shape. The importance of the *Proposal* lies in the fact that it directed attention authoritatively to the problems of language which then seemed in need of solution.

195. *Objection to an Academy.* Though the idea of establishing an academy died hard, if indeed it has ever completely died, the eighteenth century showed a growing skepticism toward it and an increasing attitude of dissent. The early enthusiasm for the example of France had given place, in the minds of some, to doubts about the value of the results obtained by the French Academy. As an anonymous writer in 1724 observes, "many say, that they have been so far from making their language better, that they have spoiled it."[1] Certainly they had not prevented it from changing. The claim that a language could be fixed in permanent form was the rock on which the hope for an academy seems first to have split. Oldmixon, in his attack on Swift's *Proposal* referred to above, vigorously opposes the notion. "The Doctor," he says, "may as well set up a Society to find out the *Grand Elixir*, the *Perpetual Motion*, the *Longitude*, and other such Discoveries, as to fix our Language beyond their own Times ... This would be doing what was never done before, what neither *Roman* nor *Greek*, which lasted the longest of any in its Purity, could pretend to." A much more authoritative utterance was that of Dr. Johnson in the Preface to his *Dictionary* (1755): "Those who have been persuaded to think well of my design, require that it should fix our language, and put a stop to those alterations which time and chance have hitherto been suffered to make in it without opposition. With this consequence I will confess that I flattered myself for a while; but now begin to fear that I have indulged expectation which neither reason

[1] Cf. H. M. Flasdieck, *Der Gedanke einer englischen Sprachakademie* (Jena, 1928), p. 95.

nor experience can justify. When we see men grow old and die at a certain time one after another, from century to century, we laugh at the elixir that promises to prolong life to a thousand years; and with equal justice may the lexicographer be derided, who being able to produce no example of a nation that has preserved their words and phrases from mutability, shall imagine that his dictionary can embalm his language, and secure it from corruption and decay, that it is in his power to change sublunary nature, or clear the world at once from folly, vanity, and affectation.

"With this hope, however, academies have been instituted, to guard the avenues of their languages, to retain fugitives, and repulse intruders; but their vigilance and activity have hitherto been vain; sounds are too volatile and subtile for legal restraints; to enchain syllables, and to lash the wind, are equally the undertakings of pride, unwilling to measure its desires by its strength. The French language has visibly changed under the inspection of the academy . . . and no Italian will maintain, that the diction of any modern writer is not perceptibly different from that of Boccace, Machiavel, or Caro."

Other grounds for objecting to an academy were not wanting. When in the same preface Johnson said, "If an academy should be established . . . which I, who can never wish to see dependance multiplied, hope the spirit of English liberty will hinder or destroy," he was voicing a prevailing English attitude. Englishmen have always been moved by a spirit of personal liberty in the use of their language. A policy of noninterference appeals to them much more than one of arbitrary regulation. As Johnson late in life again remarked of Swift's *Proposal*, "The certainty and stability which, contrary to all experience, he thinks attainable, he proposes to secure by instituting an academy; the decrees of which every man would have been willing, and many would have been proud to disobey."

Johnson's views apparently had a decided influence. After the publication of his *Dictionary*, advocacy of an academy becomes less frequent. Instead we find his views reflected in the opinions expressed by other men. Sheridan in his *British Education*, published a year later, says: "The only scheme hitherto proposed for correcting, improving, and ascertaining our language, has been the institution of a society for that purpose. But this is liable to innumerable objections; nor would it be a difficult point to prove, that such a method could never effectually answer the end." He then repeats Johnson's objections. At least some men realized that language has a way of taking care of itself, and that features which appear objectionable to one age are either accepted by the next or have been eliminated by time. Joseph Priestley, who, as we shall see, was remarkably liberal in his views upon language, anticipating the attitude of later times, inserts a passage in his *Grammar* (1761) which may be taken as indicating the direction which opinion on the subject of an academy was taking in the latter half of the eighteenth century: "As to a public Academy, invested with authority to ascertain the use of words, which is a project that some persons are very sanguine in their expectations from, I think it not only unsuitable to the genius of a free nation, but in itself ill calculated to reform and fix a language. We need make no doubt but that the best forms of speech will, in time, establish themselves by their own superior excellence: and, in all controversies, it is better to wait the decisions of time, which are slow and sure, than to take those of synods, which are often hasty and injudicious."[1]

196. Substitutes for an Academy. Since the expectation of those who put their hopes in an academy must have been considerably lessened by the failure of Swift's *Proposal*, the only means left to them was to work directly upon the public. What could not be imposed by authoritative edict might still win adoption through reason and persuasion. Individuals sought to bring about the reforms which they believed necessary and to set up a standard which might gain general acceptance. In 1724 there appeared an anonymous treatise on *The Many Advantages of a Good Language to Any Nation: with an Examination of the Present State of Our Own*. This repeats the old complaints that English has too many monosyllables, uses too many contractions, and has no adequate grammar or dictionary. But what is of more importance is that it seeks to stir up popular interest in matters of language, calls upon the public to take part in the discussion, and proposes the publication of a series of weekly or monthly pamphlets on grammar and other linguistic topics. In 1729 one Thomas Cooke published "Proposals for Perfecting the English Language."[2] The reforms which he suggests extend to the changing of all strong verbs to weak, the formation of all plurals of nouns by means of –s or –es, the comparison of adjectives only with *more* and *most*, etc. Cooke was both an idealist and an optimist, but he did not put his faith in academies. The change in attitude, the belief that a standard was to be brought about not by force but by general consent, is revealed in the words of Sheridan: "The result of the researches of rational enquirers, must be rules founded upon rational principles; and a general agreement amongst the most judicious, must occasion those rules

---

[1] That the idea of an academy was not dead is shown by Allen W. Read, "Suggestions for an Academy in England in the Latter Half of the Eighteenth Century," *MP*, 36 (1938), 145–56.

[2] As an appendix to his *Tales, Epistles, Odes*, etc.

to be as generally known, and established, and give them the force of laws. Nor would these laws meet with opposition, or be obeyed with reluctance, inasmuch as they would not be established by the hand of power, but by common suffrage, in which every one has a right to give his vote: nor would they fail, in time, of obtaining general authority, and permanence, from the sanction of custom, founded on good sense."[1]

The two greatest needs, still felt and most frequently lamented, were for a dictionary and a grammar. Without these there could be no certainty in diction and no standard of correct construction. The one was supplied in 1755 by Johnson's *Dictionary*, the other in the course of the next half-century by the early grammarians.

197. Johnson's Dictionary. The publication in 1755 of *A Dictionary of the English Language*, by Samuel Johnson, A.M., in two folio volumes, was hailed as a great achievement. And it was justly so regarded, when we consider that it was the work of one man laboring almost without assistance for the short space of seven years. True, it had its defects. Judged by modern standards it was painfully inadequate. Its etymologies are often ludicrous. It is marred in places by prejudice and caprice. Its definitions, generally sound and often discriminating, are at times truly Johnsonian.[2] It includes a host of words with a very questionable right to be regarded as belonging to the language.[3] But it had positive virtues. It exhibited the English vocabulary much more fully than had ever been done before. It offered a spelling, fixed, even if sometimes badly, that could be accepted as standard. It supplied thousands of quotations illustrating the use of words, so that, as Johnson remarked in his preface, where his own explanation is inadequate "the sense may easily be collected entire from the examples."

It is the first purpose of a dictionary to record usage. But even today, when the scientific study of language makes us much less disposed to pass

---

[1] T. Sheridan, *British Education*, pp. 370–71.

[2] *Network:* Any thing reticulated or decussated, at equal distances, with interstices between the intersections. *Cough:* A convulsion of the lungs, vellicated by some sharp serosity.

[3] Webster was severe in his judgment of the work on this score: "From a careful examination of this work and its effect upon the language, I am inclined to believe that Johnson's authority has multiplied instead of reducing the number of corruptions in the English Language. Let any man of correct taste cast his eye on such words as *denominable, opiniatry, ariolation, assation, ataraxy, clancular, comminuible, conclusible, detention, deuteroscopy, digladiation, dignotion, cubiculary, discubitory, exolution, exenterate, incompossible, incompossibility, indigitate,* etc., and let him say whether a dictionary which gives *thousands* of such terms, as *authorized English words,* is a safe standard of writing." Cf. Stanley Rypins, "Johnson's Dictionary Reviewed by His Contemporaries," *PQ,* 4 (1925), 281–86. *Denominable, detention, exolution, exenterate* were not in the original edition.

judgment upon, and particularly to condemn, its phenomena, many people look upon the editor of a dictionary as a superior kind of person with the right to legislate in such matters as the pronunciation and use of words. This attitude was well-nigh universal in Johnson's day and was not repugnant to the lexicographer himself. In many ways he makes it clear that he accepts the responsibility as part of his task. "Every language," he says in the preface, "has its anomalies, which, though inconvenient, and in themselves once unnecessary, must be tolerated among the imperfections of human things, and which require only to be registred, that they may not be increased, and ascertained, that they may not be confounded: but every language has likewise its improprieties and absurdities, which it is the duty of the lexicographer to correct or proscribe." In a paper which he published in the *Rambler* (No. 208) while he was still engaged on the *Dictionary* he wrote: "I have laboured to refine our language to grammatical purity, and to clear it from colloquial barbarisms, licentious idioms, and irregular combinations." He condemns the word *lesser* as a barbarous corruption, though he admits that "it has all the authority which a mode originally erroneous can derive from custom." Under *nowise* he says, "this is commonly spoken and written by ignorant barbarians, *noways*." But *noways* was once much used and, as a later contemporary observed, "These ignorant barbarians . . . are only Pope, and Swift, and Addison, and Locke, and several others of our most celebrated writers."[1] In addressing the *Plan* of his work to the earl of Chesterfield, Johnson said: "And though, perhaps, to correct the language of nations by books of grammar, and amend their manners by discourses of morality, may be tasks equally difficult; yet, as it is unavoidable to wish, it is natural likewise to hope, that your Lordship's patronage may not be wholly lost."

That Johnson's *Dictionary* should suggest comparison with similar works in France and Italy, prepared by academies, is altogether natural. Garrick wrote an epigram on his friend's achievement in which occur the lines

> And Johnson, well arm'd like a hero of yore,
> Has beat forty French, and will beat forty more.

A notice which appeared on the continent observes that Johnson may boast of being in a way an academy for his island.[2] Johnson himself envisaged his work as performing the same function as the dictionary of an academy. Speaking of pronunciation, he says, "one great end of this undertaking is

---

[1] Campbell, *Philosophy of Rhetoric*, I, 371.
[2] *Journal Britannique*, 17 (1755), 219.

to fix the English language"; and in the same place he explains, "The chief intent of it is to preserve the purity, and ascertain the meaning of our English idiom." Summing up his plan he says, "This . . . is my idea of an English Dictionary; a dictionary by which the pronunciation of our language may be fixed, and its attainment facilitated; by which its purity may be preserved, its use ascertained, and its duration lengthened."[1] These statements sound like the program of an academy. Chesterfield felt that it would accomplish the same purpose. In the paper published in the *World* (No. 100), by which he is supposed to have angled for the dedication of the work, he said: "I had long lamented, that we had no lawful standard of our language set up, for those to repair to, who might choose to speak and write it grammatically and correctly." Johnson's *Dictionary*, he believed, would supply one. "The time for discrimination seems to be now come. Toleration, adoption, and naturalization, have run their lengths. Good order and authority are now necessary. But where shall we find them, and at the same time the obedience due to them? We must have recourse to the old Roman expedient in times of confusion, and choose a Dictator. Upon this principle, I give my vote for Mr. Johnson to fill that great and arduous post." In 1756 Sheridan wrote, "if our language should ever be fixed, he must be considered by all posterity as the founder, and his dictionary as the corner stone."[2] Boswell was apparently expressing the opinion of his age when he spoke of Johnson as "the man who had conferred stability on the language of his country."

198. *The Eighteenth-century Grammarians and Rhetoricians.* What Dr. Johnson had done for the vocabulary was attempted for the syntax by the grammarians of the eighteenth century. Treatises on English grammar had begun to appear in the sixteenth century,[3] and in the seventeenth were compiled by even such men as Ben Jonson and Milton. These early works, however, were generally written for the purpose of teaching foreigners the language or providing a basis for the study of Latin grammar. Occasional writers like John Wallis (*Grammatica Linguae Anglicanae*, 1653) recognized that the plan of Latin grammar was not well suited to exhibiting the structure of English, but not until the eighteenth century, generally speaking, was English grammar viewed as a subject deserving of study in itself. Even then freedom from the notions derived from Latin was something to be claimed as a novelty and not always observed. William Loughton, School-

---

[1] *The Plan of an English Dictionary.*
[2] T. Sheridan, *British Education*, I, 376.
[3] See Emma Vorlat, *The Development of English Grammatical Theory 1586–1737, with Special Reference to the Theory of Parts of Speech* (Leuven, 1975).

master at Kensington, whose *Practical Grammar of the English Tongue* (1734) went through five editions, inveighs against those who "have attempted to force our Language (contrary to its Nature) to the Method and Rules of the Latin Grammar" and goes so far as to discard the terms *noun, adjective, verb*, etc., substituting *names, qualities, affirmations*. But most of the compilers of English grammars came equipped for their task only with a knowledge of the classical languages and tried to keep as many of the traditional concepts as could be fitted to a more analytic language.

The decade beginning in 1760 witnessed a striking outburst of interest in English grammar. In 1761 Joseph Priestley published *The Rudiments of English Grammar*. In it he showed the independence, tolerance, and good sense that characterized his work in other fields, and we shall have more to say of it below. It was followed about a month later by Robert Lowth's *Short Introduction to English Grammar* (1762). Lowth was a clergyman who ultimately rose to be bishop of London. He was much more conservative in his stand, a typical representative of the normative and prescriptive school of grammarians. His grammar was more in accordance with the tendencies of the time and soon swept the field. At least twenty-two editions appeared during the eighteenth century, and its influence was spread by numerous imitators, including the well-known Lindley Murray. *The British Grammar* by James Buchanan appeared in the same year.[1] A somewhat more elementary manual, by John Ash, was published in 1763 with the title *Grammatical Institutes*. It was designed as an "easy introduction to Dr. Lowth's English Grammar." These were the most popular grammars in the eighteenth century. In 1784 Noah Webster published the second part of *A Grammatical Institute of the English Language*, which enjoyed much prestige in America and not a little circulation in England. Most of these books were the work of men with no special qualifications for the thing they attempted to do. There were, to be sure, writings on linguistic matters which were not in the mold of the practical, prescriptive grammars. A philosophical concern for linguistic universals, especially lively in France at the time, found expression in England in works such as John Wilkins' *Essay towards a Real Character and a Philosophical Understanding* (1668) and James Harris' *Hermes* (1751). After more than a century of relative neglect these and other "universal grammars" have recently been revived because of similarities that have been found between them and certain

---

[1] Cf. Arthur G. Kennedy, "Authorship of *The British Grammar*," *MLN*, 41 (1926), 388–91, and Bert Emsley, "James Buchanan and the Eighteenth Century Regulation of English Usage," *PMLA*, 48 (1933), 1154–66.

aspects of contemporary linguistics.[1] The effect of these philosophical writings upon the development of specific structures in the English language is difficult to assess, but it seems to have been negligible. More important for the history of the English language are the works of more practical and often less gifted grammarians who turned philosophical concerns into linguistic prescriptions. They exerted a considerable influence, especially through the use of their books in the schools, and it will be necessary to consider their aims, the questions they attempted to settle, their method of approach, and the results which they achieved.[2]

With them belongs another group which may be called the rhetoricians. Though they did not compile grammars, they often discussed the same questions of usage. Of these one of the most important was Thomas Sheridan, father of the dramatist. His most important work was a lengthy treatise called *British Education* (1756), in which he attempted to show "that a revival of the art of speaking, and the study of our language, might contribute, in a great measure," to the cure of "the evils of immorality, ignorance and false taste." The second part of his work discussed the absolute necessity for such study "in order to refine, ascertain, and fix the English language." He held "that the study of eloquence was the necessary cause of the improvement, and establishment of the Roman language: and the same cause would infallibly produce the same effect with us. Were the study of oratory once made a necessary branch of education, all our youth of parts, and genius, would of course be employed in considering the value of words both as to sound and sense." His interest in language thus grew out of his interest in elocution, but his opinions throw an interesting light on the eighteenth-century attitude toward language. More influential was George Campbell, a learned Scottish divine, whose *Philosophy of Rhetoric* appeared in two volumes in 1776. Campbell professed greater respect for the evidence of usage and is responsible for the definition of "good use" that is still accepted today. His book is the ancestor of numerous later works, such as those of Blair (1783) and Whateley (1828) and a succession of nineteenth-century treatises.

Questions of grammar and usage had become a matter of popular

---

[1] See Noam Chomsky, *Cartesian Linguistics* (New York, 1966), an influential but professedly polemical account, which must be used with caution. Cf. Robin Lakoff, rev. of facsimile ed. of *Grammaire générale et raisonée, ou La Grammaire du Port-Royal*, *Language*, 45 (1969), 343–64, and Hans Aarsleff, "The History of Linguistics and Professor Chomsky," *Language*, 46 (1970), 570–85.

[2] Here, too, discriminations must be made among grammars such as Lowth's, which by the light of the times was by no means contemptible, and inferior imitations such as Murray's. See R. S. Sugg, Jr., "The Mood of Eighteenth-Century English Grammar," *PQ*, 43 (1964), 239–52.

interest. In 1770 one Robert Baker published *Reflections on the English Language*, "in the Manner of those of Vaugelas on the French; being a detection of many improper expressions used in conversation, and of many others to be found in authors." As qualifications for his task he mentions the fact that he knows no Greek and very little Latin, and he adds, "It will undoubtedly be thought strange, when I declare that I have never yet seen the folio edition of Mr. Johnson's dictionary: but, knowing nobody that has it, I have never been able to borrow it; and I have myself no books; at least, not many more than what a church-going old woman may be supposed to have of devotional ones upon her mantlepiece: for, having always had a narrow income, it has not been in my power to make a collection without straightening myself. Nor did I ever see even the Abridgment of this Dictionary till a few days ago, when, observing it inserted in the catalogue of a Circulating Library, where I subscribe, I sent for it." Nevertheless Baker's book went through two editions. By men such as these was the English language "ascertained."

199. The Aims of the Grammarians. Just as the goals of linguistic scholarship vary from author to author in the present century, so one must recognize a variety of concerns in the eighteenth century. In a comprehensive and balanced history of linguistic thought, which has yet to be written, it would be necessary to consider the full range of writings, from the most specific rules of the handbooks to the speculations of the universal grammars.[1] For a history of the English language it is appropriate to single out those efforts which most directly affected structures of English, especially as they were taught in the classroom. There was undeniably a coherent prescriptive tradition, within which eighteenth-century grammarians aimed to do three things: (1) to codify the principles of the language and reduce it to rule; (2) to settle disputed points and decide cases of divided usage; and (3) to point out common errors or what were supposed to be errors, and thus correct and improve the language. All three of these aims were pursued concurrently.

(1) One of the things which the advocates of an academy had hoped it would do was to systematize the facts of English grammar and draw up rules by which all questions could be viewed and decided. In his *Dictionary* Johnson had declared, "When I took the first survey of my undertaking, I found our speech copious without order, and energetick without rules:

---

[1] See, for example, Hans Aarsleff, "The Eighteenth Century, Including Leibniz," in *Current Trends in Linguistics*, 13, *Historiography of Linguistics*, ed. Thomas A. Sebeok *et al.* (The Hague, 1975), pp. 383–479, and James Knowlson, *Universal Language Schemes in England and France, 1600–1800* (Toronto, 1975).

wherever I turned my view, there was perplexity to be disentangled, and confusion to be regulated." It was necessary to demonstrate that English was not incapable of orderly treatment, was not so "irregular and capricious" in its nature that it could not be reduced to rule and used with accuracy.[1] As Lowth said in the preface to his grammar, "It doth not then proceed from any peculiar irregularity or difficulty of our Language, that the general practice both of speaking and writing it is chargeable with inaccuracy. It is not the Language, but the Practice that is in fault. The Truth is, Grammar is very much neglected among us: and it is not the difficulty of the Language, but on the contrary the simplicity and facility of it, that occasions this neglect. Were the Language less easy and simple, we should find ourselves under a necessity of studying it with more care and attention. But as it is, we take it for granted, that we have a competent knowledge and skill, and are able to acquit ourselves properly, in our own native tongue: a faculty, solely acquired by use, conducted by habit, and tried by the ear, carries us on without reflexion; we meet with no rubs or difficulties in our way, or we do not perceive them; we find ourselves able to go on without rules, and we do not so much as suspect, that we stand in need of them." This need had obviously to be met. The grammarians of the eighteenth century would, without exception, have agreed with Campbell, whose *Philosophy of Rhetoric* has been mentioned above: "The man who, in a country like ours, should compile a succinct, perspicuous, and faithful digest of the laws, though no lawgiver, would be universally acknowledged to be a public benefactor." And he adds that the grammarian is a similar benefactor in a different sphere.

(2) But the grammarian set himself up as a lawgiver as well. He was not content to record fact; he pronounced judgment. It seems to have been accepted as self-evident that of two alternate forms of expression one must be wrong. As nature abhors a vacuum, so the eighteenth-century grammarians hated uncertainty. A choice must be made; and once a question had been decided, all instances of contrary usage were unequivocally condemned. Of all the grammarians of this period only Priestley seems to have doubted the propriety of *ex cathedra* utterances and to have been truly humble before the facts of usage.

(3) "The principal design of a Grammar of any Language," says Lowth, "is to teach us to express ourselves with propriety in that Language; and to enable us to judge of every phrase and form of construction, whether it

---

[1] John Ash, in the preface to his *Grammatical Institutes*, says: ". . . it has been supposed, even by Men of Learning, that the English Tongue is too vague, and untractable to be reduced to any certain Standard, or Rules of Construction."

be right or not. The plain way of doing this is, to lay down rules, and to illustrate them by examples. But, beside shewing what is right, the matter may be further explained by pointing out what is wrong." The last-named procedure is a prominent feature of his and other contemporary grammars. Indeed, one may question whether it is not too prominent. One grows weary in following the endless bickering over trivialities. However the grammarians might justify the treatment of errors pedagogically, one cannot escape the feeling that many of them took delight in detecting supposed flaws in the grammar of "our most esteemed writers" and exhibiting them with mild self-satisfaction. One wishes there had been more Priestleys, or men who shared his opinion: "I . . . think a man cannot give a more certain mark of the narrowness of his mind . . . then to shew, either by his vanity with respect to himself, or the acrimony of his censure with respect to others, that this business is of much moment with him. We have infinitely greater things before us; and if these gain their due share of our attention, this subject, of grammatical criticism, will be almost nothing. The noise that is made about it, is one of the greatest marks of the frivolism of many readers, and writers too, of the present age." [1]

200. *The Beginnings of Prescriptive Grammar.* To prescribe and to proscribe seem to have been coordinate aims of the grammarians. Many of the conventions now accepted and held up as preferable in our handbooks were first stated in this period. The distinction between *lie* and *lay* was apparently first specifically made in the second half of the eighteenth century. The expressions *had rather, had better* were condemned by Johnson, Lowth, and Campbell. Lowth says: "It has been very rightly observed, that the Verb *had*, in the common phrase, *I had rather*, is not properly used, either as an Active or as an Auxiliary Verb; that, being in the Past time, it cannot in this case be properly expressive of time Present; and that it is by no means reducible to any Grammatical construction. In truth, it seems to have arisen from a mere mistake, in resolving the familiar and ambiguous abbreviation, *I'd rather*, into *I had rather*, instead of *I would rather;* which latter is the regular, analogous, and proper expression." This attitude is still found in some current books. Various opinions were expressed on the propriety of using *whose* as the possessive of *which*, and in spite of historical justification, opposition to this use is still found among purists. The preference for *different from* (rather than *different than* or *to*), the condemnation of *between you and I, it is me*, and *who is it for* (although on the last two points opinion was for a time divided) are among

---

[1] *Rudiments of English Grammar*, Preface.

the attitudes which, generally speaking, have been subsequently approved in the standard speech. Such is the case also with the differentiation of *between* and *among*, the use of the comparative rather than the superlative where only two things are involved (*the larger*, not *largest*, of two), the feeling that incomparables such as *perfect, chief, round*, should not be compared (*more perfect*, etc.), the defense of *from hence* and the condemnation of *this here* and *that there* (although Webster defended these as ancient usage). Webster also defended *you was* as a singular, and the expression was certainly common in literature. But Lowth and Priestley and others were against it and subsequent usage has settled upon *were*.

It would be possible to point out many other matters of usage which were disputed by the grammarians. The nature of the questions considered, however, is sufficiently clear from those cited above. One or two more of special interest may be mentioned. The proper case after *than* and *as* was a question that troubled the eighteenth century greatly (*he is taller than I*, or *me*), but Lowth expressed the view that has since been accepted, that the pronoun is determined by the construction to be supplied or understood (*he is older than she; he likes you better than me*). Another puzzling question concerned the case before the gerund (*I don't like him doing that* or *his doing that*). *His* in this construction was vigorously opposed by Harris, Lowth, and others; but Webster held that this was "the genuine English idiom" and the only permissible form. His opinion has come to be the one widely held. Finally we may note that the eighteenth century is responsible for the condemnation of the double negative. Lowth stated the rule that we are now bound by: "Two Negatives in English destroy one another, or are equivalent to an Affirmative." Thus a useful idiom was banished from polite speech.

One important series of prescriptions that now form part of all our grammars—that governing the use of *shall* and *will*—had its origin in this period. Previous to 1622 no English grammar recognized any distinction between these words. In 1653 Wallis, in his *Grammatica Linguae Anglicanae* stated for the benefit of foreigners that simple futurity is expressed by *shall* in the first person, by *will* in the second and third. It was not until the second half of the eighteenth century, however, that the usage in questions and subordinate clauses was explicitly defined. In 1755 Johnson, in his *Dictionary*, stated the rule for questions and in 1765 William Ward, in his *Grammar of the English Language*, drew up for the first time the full set of prescriptions which underlies, with individual variations, the rules found in modern books. His pronouncements were not followed generally by other grammarians until Lindley Murray gave them greater currency in

1795. Since about 1825 they have often been repeated in English grammars.[1] Here, as elsewhere, the grammarians seem to have been making absolute what was apparently a common but not universal tendency in the written language, evident in the letter-writers of the seventeenth and early eighteenth centuries.[2] That the distinction was not observed in colloquial speech may be inferred from the language of plays, and today it is commonly ignored except by speakers who conform consciously to the rules or inherit a tradition which has been influenced by rules.

201. *Methods of Approach.* The considerations by which these questions were settled were three in number: reason, etymology, and the example of Latin and Greek.

Dryden had asserted that "the foundation of the rules is reason." But reason covered a multitude of sins. Johnson argued from it when he condemned *the grammar is now printing*,[3] because the active participle was "vulgarly used in a passive sense." By similar logic Lowth objected to *I am mistaken*, since it should properly mean *I am misunderstood* and not *I am wrong*. But reason was commonly taken to mean consistency or, as it was called, analogy. Analogy appeals to an instinct very common at all times in matters of language, the instinct for regularity. Even Priestley was influenced by it. "The chief thing to be attended to in the improvement of a language," he says, "is the *analogy* of it. The more consistent are its principles, the more it is of a piece with itself, the more commodious it will be for use." Consequently, where one expression could be paralleled by another in the language it was commonly preferred for that reason. Campbell erects this into one of his general "canons." He says: "If by the former canon the adverbs *backwards* and *forwards* are preferable to *backward* and *forward;* by this canon, from the principle of analogy, *afterwards* and *homewards* should be preferred to *afterward* and *homeward*. Of the two adverbs *thereabout* and *thereabouts*, compounded of the particle *there* and the preposition, the former alone is analogical, there being no such word in the language as *abouts*. The same holds of *hereabout* and *whereabout*. In the verbs *to dare* and *to need*, many say, in the third person present singular, *dare* and *need*, as 'he *need* not go' ; 'he *dare* not do it.' Others

---

[1] See Charles C. Fries, "The Periphrastic Future with *shall* and *will* in Modern English," *PMLA*, 40 (1925), 963–1024.

[2] For evidence drawn from letters of a preference for *shall* in the first person in simple future statements, see J. R. Hulbert, "On the Origin of the Grammarians' Rules for the Use of *shall* and *will*," *PMLA*, 62 (1947), 1178–82. For evidence that the grammarians' rules for direct statements, indirect statements, and questions had a basis in usage, see J. Taglicht, "The Genesis of the Conventional Rules of *Shall* and *Will*," *English Studies*, 51 (1970), 193–213.

[3] On this construction see § 210.

say, *dares* and *needs*. As the first usage is exceedingly irregular, hardly any thing less than uniform practice could authorize it."[1] It was also reasoned, however, that where two expressions often used interchangeably could be differentiated, it was better to make a distinction. Accordingly Campbell argued: "In the preposition *toward* and *towards*, and the adverbs *forward* and *forwards*, *backward* and *backwards*, the two forms are used indiscriminately. But as the first form in all these is also an adjective, it is better to confine the particles to the second. Custom, too, seems at present to lean this way."[2] The same consideration led Priestley to say, "As the paucity of inflections is the greatest defect in our language, we ought to take advantage of every variety that the practice of good authors will warrant; and therefore, if possible, make a participle different from the preterite of a verb; as, a book is *written*, not *wrote;* the ships are *taken*, not *took*." With this opinion Dr. Johnson was in sympathy.

A second consideration was etymology. On this account Johnson and Lowth preferred *averse from* to *averse to*. Campbell again states this principle most fully. He says, "When etymology plainly points to a signification different from that which the word commonly bears, propriety and simplicity both require its dismission. I use the word *plainly*, because, when the etymology is from an ancient or foreign language, or from obsolete roots in our own language, or when it is obscure or doubtful, no regard should be had to it. The case is different, when the roots either are, or strongly appear to be, English, are in present use, and clearly suggest another meaning. Of this kind is the word *beholden*, for obliged or indebted. It should regularly be the passive participle of the verb to *behold*, which would convey a sense totally different. Not that I consider the term as equivocal, for in the last acceptation it hath long since been disused, having been supplanted by *beheld*. But the formation of the word is so analogical, as to make it have at least the appearance of impropriety, when used in a sense that seems naturally so foreign to it."[3] By the same reasoning he maintains, "The verb *to unloose*, should analogically signify *to tie*, in like manner as *to untie* signifies *to loose*. To what purpose is it then, to retain a term, without any necessity, in a signification the reverse of that which its etymology manifestly suggests?"[4]

Fortunately the third consideration, occasionally made the basis on which questions of grammar were decided, the example of the classical

[1] *Philosophy of Rhetoric*, I, 378–79.
[2] *Ibid.*, I, 374–75.
[3] *Ibid.*, I, 397–98.
[4] *Ibid.*, I, 398.

languages, and especially of Latin, was not so commonly cited. It is true that Johnson is quoted as saying, "It is, seriously, my opinion, that every language must be servilely formed after the model of some one of the ancient, if we wish to give durability to our works."[1] Such an attitude derived in part from concerns with universal grammar, which Harris defines as "that grammar, which without regarding the several idioms of particular languages, only respects those principles, that are essential to them all."[2] Harris was more interested in the philosophical problems involving language than in any practical applications that discussions of those problems might have.[3] There were other grammarians with more normative goals who found it natural to turn descriptive comparisons into prescriptive rules, especially since most of the ideas of universal grammar were derived from the literary traditions of Latin and Greek. In the course of the eighteenth century a fairly definite feeling grew up that there were more disadvantages than advantages in trying to fit English into the pattern of Latin grammar, and though its example was called upon by one even so late as Noah Webster and is occasionally appealed to even today, this approach to grammatical questions was fortunately not often consciously employed. The interest in universal grammar for its own sake waned during the following century, and it was not until the mid-twentieth century that the works of Wilkins, Harris, and other philosophically oriented grammarians in England and France were revived as precursors of transformational approaches to linguistic analysis.

202. *The Doctrine of Usage.* In the latter half of the eighteenth century we find the beginnings of the modern doctrine that the most important criterion of language is usage. Sporadic recognition of this principle is encountered in the previous century, doubtless inspired by the dictum of Horace that "use is the sole arbiter and norm of speech." Thus John Hughes, who quotes the remark of Horace, says in his essay *Of Style* (1698) that "general acceptation . . . is the only standard of speech." In the fifty years following, Dennis, Johnson, and Chesterfield spoke to the same effect. In the *Plan* of his dictionary Johnson said, "It is not in our power to have recourse to any established laws of speech; but we must remark how the writers of former ages have used the same word. . . . I shall therefore, since the rules of stile, like those of law, arise from precedents often repeated, collect the testimonies on both sides, and endeavour to discover and promulgate the decrees of custom, who has so long possessed, whether by

---

[1] Leonard, *Doctrine of Correctness*, p. 50.
[2] *Hermes* (1751), p. x.
[3] *Ibid.*, pp. 293–96.

right or by usurpation, the sovereignty of words." But he constantly strayed from his intention. Chesterfield spoke in similar terms: "Every language has its peculiarities; they are established by usage, and whether right or wrong, they must be complied with. I could instance very many absurd ones in different languages; but so authorized by the *jus et norma loquendi* [Horace again], that they must be submitted to."

The person who more wholeheartedly than anyone else advocated the doctrine, however, was Joseph Priestley. His voluminous writings on chemistry, natural philosophy, theology, and politics have overshadowed his contributions to the study of language. In this field, however, as in all others, he was independent and original, and in his *Rudiments of English Grammar* (1761) he repeatedly insisted upon the importance of usage. "Our grammarians," he says, "appear to me to have acted precipitately in this business" of writing a grammar of the language. "This will never be effected by the arbitrary rules of any man, or body of men whatever." "It must be allowed, that the custom of speaking is the original and only just standard of any language. We see, in all grammars, that this is sufficient to establish a rule, even contrary to the strongest analogies of the language with itself. Must not this custom, therefore, be allowed to have some weight, in favour of those forms of speech, to which our best writers and speakers seem evidently prone . . . ?" He states his own practice accordingly: "The best and the most numerous authorities have been carefully followed. Where they have been contradictory, recourse hath been had to analogy, as the last resource. If this should decide for neither of two contrary practices, the thing must remain undecided, till all-governing custom shall declare in favour of the one or the other." In his lectures on the *Theory of Language*, written the following year, he again affirmed his creed: "In *modern* and *living* languages, it is absurd to pretend to set up the compositions of any person or persons whatsoever as the standard of writing, or their conversation as the invariable rule of speaking. With respect to custom, laws, and every thing that is changeable, the body of a people, who, in this respect, cannot but be free, will certainly assert their liberty, in making what innovations they judge to be expedient and useful. The general prevailing custom, whatever it happen to be, can be the only standard for the time that it prevails."[1]

Of almost equal importance in representing this point of view, and perhaps more influential in giving it currency, was George Campbell, whose *Philosophy of Rhetoric* (1776) in two substantial volumes has already

---

[1] *Theological and Miscellaneous Works* (25 vols., n.p., n.d.), XXIII, 198.

been referred to. Proceeding from Priestley's position, which he refers to with approval, he states his own views in very similar terms: "Language is purely a species of fashion. . . . It is not the business of grammar, as some critics seem preposterously to imagine, to give law to the fashions which regulate our speech. On the contrary, from its conformity to these, and from that alone, it derives all its authority and value. For, what is the grammar of any language? It is no other than a collection of general observations methodically digested, and comprising all the modes previously and independently established, by which the significations, derivations, and combinations of words in that language, are ascertained. It is of no consequence here to what causes originally these modes or fashions owe their existence, to imitation, to reflection, to affectation, or to caprice; they no sooner obtain and become general, than they are laws of the language, and the grammarian's only business is to note, collect, and methodise them."[1] This sounds peculiarly modern. What is even more important, however, is the fact that Campbell did not stop here, but went on to inquire what constituted this body of usage which he recognized as so authoritative. And he defined it as *present*, *national*, and *reputable* use, a definition so reasonable and sound that it has been accepted ever since. It is so well known that it needs no explanation other than the remark that by reputable use Campbell meant "whatever modes of speech are authorized as good by the writings of a great number, if not the majority of celebrated authors."

The difference between Priestley and Campbell is that whereas Campbell expounded the doctrine of usage with admirable clarity and then violated it, Priestley was almost everywhere faithful to his principles. Campbell is frankly inconsistent. In one place he holds "that to the tribunal of use, as to the supreme authority, and consequently, in every grammatical controversy, the last resort, we are entitled to appeal from the laws and the decisions of grammarians; and that this order of subordination ought never, on any account, to be reversed." In another passage, however, he says that everything favored by good use is "not on that account worthy to be retained" and he sets up canons by which features of the language sanctioned by good use may be pronounced objectionable and discarded. Thus Priestley stands alone in his unwavering loyalty to usage. After the perpetual dogmatizing of other eighteenth-century grammarians, it is refreshing to find on almost every page of his grammar statements like "This may be said to be ungrammatical; or, at least, a very harsh ellipsis; but custom authorizes it, and many more departures from strict grammar,

[1] I, 340–41.

particularly in conversation." "The word *lesser*, though condemned by Dr. Johnson, and other English grammarians, is often used by good writers." "It is very common to see the superlative used for the comparative degree, when only two persons or things are spoken of. . . . This is a very pardonable oversight." "The word *whose* begins likewise to be restricted to persons, but it is not done so generally but that good writers, and even in prose, use it when speaking of things." "A language can never be properly fixed, till all the varieties with which it is used, have been held forth to public view, and the general preference of certain forms have been declared, by the general practice afterwards. Whenever I have mentioned any variety in the grammatical forms that are used to express the same thing, I have seldom scrupled to say which of them I prefer; but this is to be understood as nothing more than a conjecture, which time must confirm or refute."

One must come down almost to our own day to find an attitude so tolerant and so liberal. And the doctrine of usage is so fundamental to all sound discussion of linguistic matters that it is important to recognize the man in whom it first found real expression.

203. Results. If we attempt to view the work of the eighteenth-century grammarians in retrospect and estimate the results that they achieved, we shall find them not inconsiderable. It must be remembered that consciously or unconsciously these men were attempting to "ascertain" the language and to give definiteness and order to a body of hitherto uncodified practice. As a consequence it could no longer be said that English was a language without rules. It might almost be said that we had too many rules. Some of them have since been set aside. Others are of doubtful validity, although they still find a place in our handbooks and are imposed upon those who consider conformity to supposed authority a sufficient criterion of correctness. But though we may recognize that the grounds on which decisions were reached were often faulty, and the decisions themselves were often arbitrary, we must admit that a considerable number of disputed points, rightly or wrongly, were settled and have since become established. Some of the more significant of these have already been mentioned. Thus, with the codification of usage and the settlement of many matters which were in dispute, much of the uncertainty that troubled Dryden and Swift was removed. For this and other reasons English escaped the artificial restraints and the repressive influence of an academy.

204. Weakness of the Early Grammarians. While acknowledging the results attained by the eighteenth-century grammarians and reformers, it is necessary to emphasize the serious limitations in nearly all of them. Their

greatest weakness was, of course, their failure, except in one or two conspicuous cases, to recognize the importance of usage as the sole arbiter in
linguistic matters. They did not realize, or refused to acknowledge, that
changes in language often appear to be capricious and unreasonable—in
other words, are the result of forces too complex to be fully analyzed or
predicted. Accordingly they approached most questions in the belief that
they could be solved by logic and that the solutions could be imposed upon
the world by authoritative decree. Hence the constant attempt to legislate
one construction into use and another out of use. In this attempt little or
no recognition was shown for the legitimacy of divided usage. Thus, as
Noah Webster pointed out, every time they refused to base their statements
on the facts of current use they were also refusing to preserve an agreement
between books and practice and were contributing "very much to create
and perpetuate differences between the written and spoken language." At
the root of all their mistakes was their ignorance of the processes of
linguistic change. The historical study of English was still in its infancy,[1]
and though the materials were rapidly becoming available on which
sounder opinions could be formed, most men in the eighteenth century did
not realize their importance.

205. *Attempts to Reform the Vocabulary.* Similar weaknesses characterized the attempts to reform the vocabulary at this time. Every man felt
competent to "purify" the language by proscribing words and expressions
because they were too old or too new, or were slang or cant or harsh
sounding, or for no other reason than that he disliked them. Swift's
aversions have already been referred to. "I have done my best," he said,
"for some Years past to stop the Progress of *Mobb* and *Banter*, but have
been plainly borne down by Numbers, and betrayed by those who promised
to assist me." George Harris objected to expressions such as *chaulking out
a way, handling a subject, driving a bargain,* and *bolstering up an argument.*
In a volume of *Sketches* by "Launcelot Temple" the author attacks
encroach, inculcate, purport, betwixt, methinks, and *subject-matter.* Of the

---

[1] The study of Old English had its beginnings in the Reformation in an effort on the
part of the reformers to prove the continuity and independence of the English church
and its doctrines. This motive was accompanied by the desire to discredit the doctrine
of the divine right of kings and to find the source of English law and administrative
practice. The first specimen of the language to be printed, Ælfric's Easter homily,
appeared about 1566–1567 in a volume called *A Testimonie of Antiquity.* In 1659 William
Somner published a *Dictionarium Saxonico-Latino-Anglicum,* the first Old English
dictionary. In 1689 the first Old English grammar was published, the work of George
Hickes. In 1755 the first permanent chair of Anglo-Saxon was established at Oxford by
Richard Rawlinson. See Eleanor N. Adams, *Old English Scholarship in England from
1566–1800* (New Haven, 1917), and Ewald Flügel, "The History of English Philology,"
Flügel Memorial Volume (Stanford University, 1916), pp. 9–35.

last he says: "in the Name of every thing that's disgusting and detestable, what is it? Is it one or two ugly words? What's the Meaning of it? Confound me if I ever could guess! Yet one dares hardly ever peep into a Preface, for fear of being stared in the Face with this nasty *Subject Matter*." Campbell, referring to the strictures in this volume, says: "I think there is at present a greater risk of going too far in refining, than of not going far enough. The ears of some critics are immoderately delicate." Yet he himself has his own list of words to be banned, some of which "though favoured by custom, being quite unnecessary, deserve to be exploded. Such, amongst others, are the following: the *workmanship* of God, for the work of God; a *man of war*, for a *ship of war;* and a *merchantman*, for a trading vessel. The absurdity in the last two instances is commonly augmented by the words connected in the sequel, in which, by the application of the pronouns *she* and *her*, we are made to understand that the man spoken of is a female. I think this gibberish ought to be left entirely to mariners; amongst whom, I suppose, it hath originated." He objected to other words because "they have a pleonastic appearance. Such are the following, *unto, until, selfsame, foursquare, devoid, despoil, disannul, muchwhat, oftentimes, nowadays, downfall, furthermore, wherewithal;* for *to, till, same, square, void, spoil, annul, much, often, now, fall, further, wherewith.* The use of such terms many writers have been led into, partly from the dislike of monosyllables, partly from the love of variety. . . . However, with regard to the words specified, it would not be right to preclude entirely the use of them in poetry, where the shackles of metre render variety more necessary, but they ought to be used very sparingly, if at all, in prose." Individual objection to particular expressions is not confined to the eighteenth century, but it is here a part of the prevailing attitude toward language. Most of the words criticized are still in use, and these misguided efforts to ban them show the futility of trying to interfere with the natural course of linguistic history.

206. *Objection to Foreign Borrowings.* The concern which the eighteenth century expressed for the purity of the language included what seems like an undue apprehension that English was being ruined by the intrusion of foreign words, especially French. Defoe observed that "an Englishman has his mouth full of borrow'd phrases . . . he is always borrowing other men's language."[1] And in his *Review* (October 10, 1708) he complained: "I cannot but think that the using and introducing foreign terms of art or foreign words into speech while our language labours under no penury or scarcity

---

[1] *Complete English Gentleman*, p. 220.

of words is an intolerable grievance." Shortly before, Dryden had expressed a similar feeling: "I cannot approve of their way of refining, who corrupt our English idiom by mixing it too much with French: that is a sophistication of language, not an improvement of it; a turning English into French, rather than a refining of English by French. We meet daily with those fops who value themselves on their travelling, and pretend they cannot express their meaning in English, because they would put off on us some French phrase of the last edition; without considering that, for aught they know, we have a better of our own. But these are not the men who are to refine us; their talent is to prescribe fashions, not words."[1] The feeling was very common. In 1711 Addison wrote in the *Spectator* (No. 165): "I have often wished, that as in our constitution there are several persons whose business is to watch over our laws, our liberties, and commerce, certain men might be set apart as superintendents of our language, to hinder any words of a foreign coin, from passing among us; and in particular to prohibit any French phrases from becoming current in this kingdom, when those of our own stamp are altogether as valuable." Even quite late in the century Campbell could say, "Nay, our language is in greater danger of being overwhelmed by an inundation of foreign words, than of any other species of destruction."

It is not difficult to see how French was in a strong position to influence English at this time. The language was then at the height of its prestige. It was used at almost every court in Europe. The knowledge of the language among the upper classes in England was quite general, equaled only by the ignorance of English on the part of the French. Sheridan, speaking of the widespread use of Latin in the Middle Ages, says that it was written by all the learned of Europe "with as much fluency and facility as the polite now speak or write French." Travel in France was considered a necessary part of one's education, and the cultural relations between the two countries were very close. And yet the danger does not seem to have been acute. The number of French words admitted to the language in the period from 1650 to 1800 was not unusually large.[2] The *Oxford English Dictionary* records a fair number that did not win permanent acceptance, but among those that have been retained are such useful words as *ballet, boulevard, brunette, canteen, cartoon, champagne, chenille, cohesion, coiffure, connoisseur, coquette, coterie, dentist, negligee, patrol, pique, publicity, routine, soubrette, syndicate*. Most of these are words which we could ill afford to lose. Time has again done the sifting and clearly done it well.

[1] *Dramatic Poetry of the Last Age.*
[2] See table in footnote, § 133.

207. *The Expansion of the British Empire.*   When we take our eyes from the internal problems which the language was facing and Englishmen were attempting to solve, we observe that in this period the foundations were being laid for that wide extension of English in the world which has resulted in its use throughout more than a quarter of the earth's surface. Although we occasionally come across references in those who wrote about the language suggesting that the reforms they hoped for and the changes they were suggesting would be advantageous to the language in its use abroad, it is doubtful whether the future greatness of the English language was suspected any more than the growth of the empire itself. For the British Empire was not the result of a consciously planned and aggressively executed program, but the product of circumstances and often of chance.

England entered the race for colonial territory late. It was the end of the fifteenth century that witnessed the voyages which opened up the East and the West to European exploitation. And when Columbus discovered America in 1492 and Vasco da Gama reached India in 1498 by way of the Cape of Good Hope, their achievements were due to Spanish and Portuguese enterprise. It was only when the wealth of America and India began pouring into Spanish and Portuguese coffers that the envy and ambition of other countries were aroused. In the sixteenth century Spain was the greatest of the European powers, but she was ruined by her own wealth and by the effects of the Inquisition. Thereafter England's real rival for a colonial empire was France.

The English settlements at Jamestown and Plymouth were the beginning of a process of colonization in North America that soon gave to England the Atlantic seaboard. The French settlements began in Montreal, Quebec, and on the St. Lawrence, and then pressed vigorously to the west and south, toward the Great Lakes and the Gulf of Mexico. Wolfe's victory (1759) over Montcalm paved the way for the ultimate control of most of this continent by the English. Although the American Revolution deprived the mother country of one of her most promising colonies, it did not prevent the language of this region from remaining English. Meanwhile England was getting a foothold in India. At the end of the sixteenth century the revolt of the Netherlands and the rapid rise of Holland as a maritime power soon brought the Dutch into active competition with the Portuguese in the trade with India. Inspired by the Dutch example, the English entered the contest and in 1600 the East India Company was founded to promote this trade, establishing settlements at Madras, Bombay, and Calcutta. In the reign of Louis XIV the French formed similar settlements not far from Calcutta and Madras. By the middle of the eighteenth century the two great rivals in India, as in America, were England and France. Largely through the accomplishments of a young Englishman named Clive, a clerk in the East India Company with a genius for military matters, the struggle that ensued ended in a series of triumphs for the English, and thus an area almost equal to that of European Russia became part of the British Empire.

The beginnings of the English occupation of Australia also occurred in the eighteenth century. In 1768 the Royal Society persuaded the king to sponsor an expedition into those parts of the Pacific to observe the transit of Venus across the sun. Their ship was under the command of an enterprising seaman, Captain Cook, and after the astronomical observations had been completed he undertook to explore the lands which were vaguely known to be in the neighborhood. He sailed around the islands of New Zealand and then continued twelve hundred miles westward until he reached Australia. In both places he planted the British flag. A few years later the English discovered a use to which this territory could be put. The American Revolution had deprived them of a convenient place to which to deport criminals. The prisons were overcrowded and in 1787 it was decided to send several shiploads of convicts to Australia. Soon after, the discovery that sheep raising could be profitably carried on in the country led to considerable immigration, which later became a stampede when gold was discovered in the island in 1851.

The opening up of Africa was largely the work of the nineteenth century, although it had its start likewise at the close of the eighteenth century. Early in the Napoleonic Wars Holland had come under the control of France and in 1795 England seized the Dutch settlement at Cape Town. From this small beginning sprang the control of England over a large part of South Africa. This is not the place to pursue the complicated story of how the attitude of the Boers and the native tribes forced the English to push farther and farther north, how the missionary efforts and the explorations of Livingstone played their part and had their culmination in the work of the great financier and empire builder, Cecil Rhodes. Nor can we pause over the financial embarrassments of Egypt and the necessity for English control over the Suez Canal which led to the British protectorate over the region of the Nile. We can note only the result, the control by England of so large a part of southern and eastern Africa as to make possible the building of a railroad from Cape Town to Cairo. Our interest is merely in sketching in the background for the extension of the English language and the effect which this extension had upon it.

208. Some Effects of Expansion on the Language. Apart from the greatly enlarged sphere of activity which the English language thus acquired and the increased opportunity for local variation that has naturally resulted, the most obvious effects of English expansion are to be seen in the vocabulary. New territories mean new experiences, new activities, new products, all of which are in time reflected in the language. Trade routes have always been important avenues for the transmission of ideas and words. In America contact with the Indians resulted in a number of characteristic words such as *caribou, hickory, hominy, moccasin, moose, opossum, papoose, raccoon, skunk, squaw, terrapin, toboggan, tomahawk, totem, wampum*, and *wigwam*. From other parts of America, especially where the Spanish and the Portuguese were settled, we have derived many more words, chiefly through Spanish. Thus we have in English Mexican words such as *chili, chocolate, coyote, tomato;* from Cuba and the West Indies come *barbecue, cannibal, canoe, hammock, hurricane, maize, potato, tobacco;* from Peru we get through the same channel *alpaca, condor, jerky, llama, pampas, puma, quinine;* from Brazil and other South American regions *buccaneer, cayenne, jaguar, petunia, poncho, tapioca*. English contact with the East has been equally productive of new words. From India come *bandana, bangle, bengal, Brahman, bungalow, calico, cashmere, cheroot, china, chintz, coolie, cot, curry, dinghy, juggernaut, jungle, jute, loot, mandarin, nirvana, pariah, polo, punch* (drink), *pundit, rajah, rupee, sepoy, thug, toddy, tom-tom*, and *verandah*. From a little farther east come *gingham, indigo, mango*, and *seersucker*, the last an East Indian corruption of a Persian expression meaning 'milk and sugar' and transferred to a striped linen material. From Africa, either directly from the natives or from Dutch and Portuguese traders, we obtain *banana, Boer, boorish, chimpanzee, gorilla, guinea, gumbo, Hottentot, palavar, voodoo*, and *zebra*. Australia has not contributed so much to the general language. *Boomerang* and *kangaroo* are interesting examples of native words that have passed into universal use. Other words are sometimes found in the English of Australians—*wombat*, a kind of burrowing animal, *paramatta*, a light dress fabric, and *cooey*, a signal cry used by the aborigines and adopted by the colonists; one is said to be 'within cooey' of Sydney when he is within an easy journey of the city. Thus, one of the reasons for the cosmopolitan character of the English vocabulary today is seen to be the multitude of contacts the English language has had with other tongues in widely scattered parts of the world.

209. *Development of Progressive Verb Forms.* Before concluding this survey of the factors affecting the language in the eighteenth century we must notice in particular one characteristic development in English grammar. In a work such as this it is impossible to follow in detail the history of each part of speech. All that can be done is to indicate the more important grammatical changes that have taken place since Old English times and to note such new developments as are of most significance in the language of today. Of these, one of great importance concerns the verb. It is a commonplace that English is distinctly more varied and flexible in some of its verbal expressions than the other better-known modern languages. Thus, where French says *je chante* or German *ich singe*, English may say *I sing, I do sing*, or *I am singing*. The *do-* forms are often called emphatic forms, and this they sometimes are; but their most important uses are in negative and interrogative sentences (*I don't sing, do you sing*). The forms with *to be* and the present participle are generally called progressive forms since their most common use is to indicate an action as being in progress at the time implied by the auxiliary.[1] The wide extension of the use of progressive forms is one of the most important developments of the English verb in the modern period.

In Old English such expressions as *he wæs lærende* (he was teaching) are occasionally found, but usually in translations from Latin.[2] In early Middle English, progressive forms are distinctly rare, and although their number increases in the course of the Middle English period,[3] we must credit their development mainly to the period since the sixteenth century. The chief factor in their growth is the use of the participle as a noun governed by the preposition *on* (*he burst out on laughing*).[4] This weakened to *he burst out a-laughing* and finally to *he burst out laughing*. In the same way *he was on laughing* became *he was a-laughing* and *he was laughing*. Today such forms are freely used in all tenses (*is laughing, was laughing, will be laughing*, etc.).

210. *The Progressive Passive.* The extension of such forms to the passive (*the house is being built*) was an even later development. It belongs to the very end of the eighteenth century. Old English had no progressive passive. Such an expression as *the man is loved, feared, hated* is progressive only in so far as the verbs *loving, fearing, hating* imply a continuous state. But no such force attaches to *the man is killed*, which does not mean *the man is being killed* but indicates a completed act. The construction *the man is on laughing* was capable also of a passive significance under certain

---

[1] For an attempt to distinguish other uses of the progressive form, see J. Van der Laan, *An Inquiry on a Psychological Basis into the Use of the Progressive Form in Late Modern English* (Gorinchem, Holland, 1922).

[2] A thorough study of the contexts in which this pattern occurs in Old English, including contexts not influenced by Latin, is by Gerhard Nickel, *Die Expanded Form im Altenglischen* (Neumünster, 1966).

[3] A valuable list of early occurrences is given in W. Van der Gaff, "Some Notes on the History of the Progressive Form," *Neophilologus*, 15 (1930), 201–15.

[4] In Middle English, forms without the preposition are usually accompanied by an adverb like *always, all day*, etc. (cf. Chaucer's *syngynge he was, or floytynge, al the day*).

circumstances. Thus *the house is on building* can only suggest that the house is in process of construction. This use is found from the fourteenth century on, and in its weakened form the construction is not unknown today. Colloquially, at least, we say *there is nothing doing at the mill this week. The dinner is cooking* and *the tea is steeping* are familiar expressions. In some parts of America one may hear *there's a new barn a-building down the road.* When the preposition was completely lost (*on building* > *a-building* > *building*) the form became *the house is building.* Since such an expression may at times be either active or passive, it had obvious limitations. Thus *the wagon is making* is a passive, but *the wagon is making a noise* is active. And whenever the subject of the sentence is animate or capable of performing the action, the verb is almost certain to be in the active voice (*the man is building a house*). With some verbs the construction was impossible in a passive sense. Thus the idea *he is always being called* could not be expressed by *he is always calling.*

In the last years of the eighteenth century we find the first traces of our modern expression *the house is being built.* The combination of *being* with a past participle to form a participial phrase had been in use for some time. Shakespeare says: *which, being kept close, might move more grief to hide* (*Hamlet*). This is thought to have suggested the new verb phrase. The earliest instance of the construction which has been noted is from the year 1769.[1] In 1795 Robert Southey wrote: *a fellow, whose uppermost upper grinder is being torn out by a mutton-fisted barber.* It seems first to have been recognized in an English grammar in 1802.[2] As yet it is generally used only in the present and simple past tense (*is* or *was being built*). We can hardly say *the house has been being built for two years*, and we avoid saying *it will be being built next spring.*

The history of the new progressive passive shows that English is a living and growing thing, that its grammar is not fixed, that it will continue to change in the future as it has changed in the past, even if more slowly. If the need is felt for a new and better way of expressing an idea, we may rest assured that a way will be found. But it is interesting to note that even so useful a construction was at first resisted by many as an unwarranted innovation. Although supported by occasional instances in Coleridge,

[1] *OED*, s.v. *be.*
[2] The history of this construction was first traced by Fitzedward Hall in his book *Modern English* (New York, 1873). Much valuable material is assembled by Alfred Akerlund in *On the History of the Definite Tenses in English* (Cambridge, 1911). More recent treatments are Jespersen, *Modern English Grammar*, vol. 4 (1931), and Fernand Mossé, *Histoire de la forme périphrastique* être + participe présent *en germanique* (2 parts, Paris, 1938).

Lamb, Landor, Shelley, Cardinal Newman, and others, it was consciously avoided by some (Macaulay, for example) and vigorously attacked by others. In 1837 a writer in the *North American Review* condemned it as "an outrage upon English idiom, to be detested, abhorred, execrated, and given over to six thousand penny-paper editors." And even so enlightened a student of language as Marsh, in 1859, noted that it "has widely spread, and threatens to establish itself as another solecism." "The phrase 'the house *is being built*' for 'the house *is building*'," he says, "is an awkward neologism, which neither convenience, intelligibility, nor syntactical congruity demands, and the use of which ought therefore to be discountenanced, as an attempt at the artificial improvement of the language in a point which needed no amendment."[1] Artificial it certainly was not. Nothing seems to have been more gradual and unpremeditated in its beginnings. But, as late as 1870 Richard Grant White devoted thirty pages of his *Words and Their Uses* to an attack upon what still seemed to him a neologism. Although the origin of the construction can be traced back to the latter part of the eighteenth century, its establishment in the language and ultimate acceptance required the better part of the century just past.

BIBLIOGRAPHY

The appeal to authority and its reflection in the efforts to set up an academy are discussed in detail by H. M. Flasdieck, *Der Gedanke einer englischen Sprachakademie* (Jena, 1928), where references to the previous literature will be found. D. M. Robertson, *A History of the French Academy* (London, 1910), treats the model which Swift and others had most in mind. The fullest study of Johnson's dictionary is James H. Sledd and Gwin J. Kolb, *Dr. Johnson's Dictionary: Essays in the Biography of a Book* (Chicago, 1955). Sterling A. Leonard's *The Doctrine of Correctness in English Usage, 1700–1800* (Madison, 1929) surveys the points most often in dispute among the eighteenth-century grammarians. The most comprehensive study of early grammars of English is Ian Michael, *English Grammatical Categories and the Tradition to 1800* (Cambridge, 1970). A full list of the works of the grammarians will be found in Kennedy's *Bibliography*, supplemented by R. C. Alston, *A Bibliography of the English Language . . . to the Year 1800* (Leeds, 1965–). Important also are A. F. Bryan's "Notes on the Founders of Prescriptive English Grammar," *Manly Anniversary Studies* (Chicago, 1923), pp. 383–93, and "A Late Eighteenth-Century Purist" (George Campbell), *Studies in Philology*, 23 (1926), 358–70. A useful collection of excerpts from sixteenth- to eighteenth-century writings is Susie I. Tucker, *English Examined: Two Centuries of Comment on the Mother-Tongue* (Cambridge, 1961). The same author's *Protean Shape: A Study in Eighteenth-Century Vocabulary and Usage* (London, 1967) discusses a large number of words which have undergone semantic change since the eighteenth century. The borrowings from French in

---

[1] George P. Marsh, *Lectures on the English Language* (4th ed., New York, 1872), p. 649.

this period are treated by Anton Ksoll, *Die französischen Lehn- und Fremdwörter in der englischen Sprache der Restaurationszeit* (Breslau, 1933), and Paul Leidig, *Französische Lehnwörter und Lehnbedeutungen im Englischen des 18. Jahrhunderts: Ein Spiegelbild französischer Kultureinwirkung* (Bochum-Langendreer, 1941; *Beiträge zur engl. Philologie*, no. 37). An excellent account of the colonial expansion of England is C. F. Lavell and C. E. Payne, *Imperial England* (New York, 1919). For a fuller treatment of the development of progressive verb forms the student may consult the works referred to in §§ 209–10.

[10]

The Nineteenth Century and After

211. *Influences Affecting the Language.* The events of the nineteenth and twentieth centuries affecting the English-speaking countries have been of great political and social importance, but in their effect on the language they have not been of a revolutionary character. The success of the British on the sea in the course of the Napoleonic Wars, culminating in Nelson's famous victory at Trafalgar in 1805, left England in a position of undisputed naval supremacy and gave her control over most of the world's commerce. The war against Russia in the Crimea (1854–1856) and the contests with native princes in India had the effect of again turning English attention to the East. The great reform measures—the reorganization of parliament, the revision of the penal code and the poor laws, the restrictions placed on child labor, and the other industrial reforms—were important factors in establishing English society on a more democratic basis. They lessened the distance between the upper and the lower classes and greatly increased the opportunities for the mass of the population to share in the economic and cultural advantages that became available in the course of the century. The establishment of the first cheap newspaper (1816) and of cheap postage (1840), and the improved means of travel and communication brought about by the railroad, the steamboat, and the telegraph had the effect of uniting more closely the different parts of England and of spreading the influence of the standard speech. During the first half of the twentieth century the world wars and the troubled periods following them affected the life of almost everyone and left their mark on the language. At the same time, the growth in importance of some of England's larger colonies, their eventual independence, and the rapid development of the United States, have given increased significance to the forms of English

295

spoken in these territories and have led their populations to the belief that
their use of the language is as entitled to be considered a standard as that
of the mother country.

Some of these events and changes are reflected in the English vocabulary.
But more influential in this respect are the great developments in science
and the rapid progress that has been made in every field of intellectual
activity in the last hundred years. Periods of great enterprise and activity
seem generally to be accompanied by a corresponding increase in new
words. This is the more true when all classes of the people participate in
such activity, both in work and play, and share in its benefits. Accordingly,
the great developments in industry, the increased public interest in sports
and amusements, and the many improvements in the mode of living, in
which even the humblest worker has shared, have all contributed to the
vocabulary. The last two centuries offer an excellent opportunity to observe
the relation between a civilization and the language which is an expression
of it.

212. *The Growth of Science.*   The most striking thing about our present-
day civilization is probably the part which science has played in bringing
it to pass. We have only to think of the progress which has been made in
medicine and the sciences auxiliary to it, such as bacteriology, biochemistry,
and the like, to realize the difference that marks off our own day from that
of only a few generations ago in the diagnosis, treatment, prevention, and
cure of disease. Or we may pause to reflect upon the relatively short period
that separates the Wright brothers, making history's first powered and
controlled airplane flight, from the landings of astronauts on the moon and
unmanned spacecraft on Mars. In every field of science, pure and applied,
there has been need in the last hundred years for thousands of new terms.
The great majority of these are technical words known only to the specialist,
but a certain number of them in time become familiar to the layman and
pass into general use.

In the field of medicine this is particularly apparent. We speak familiarly
of *anemia, appendicitis, arteriosclerosis,* difficult as the word is, of *bronchitis,
diphtheria,* and numerous other diseases and ailments. We use with some
sense of their meaning words like *homeopathic, osteopathy, bacteriology,
immunology, orthodontia.* We maintain *clinics,* administer an *antitoxin* or
an *anesthetic,* and *vaccinate* for smallpox. We have learned the names of
drugs like *aspirin, iodine, insulin, morphine,* and we acquire without effort
the names of antibiotics, such as *penicillin, streptomycin,* and a whole
family of *sulfa* compounds. We speak of *adenoids, endocrine glands,* and
hormones, and know the uses of the *stethoscope* and the *bronchoscope.* We

refer to the combustion of food in the body as *metabolism*, distinguish between *proteins* and *carbohydrates*, know that a dog can digest bones because he has certain *enzymes* or digestive fluids in his stomach, and say that a person who has the idiosyncrasy of being made ill by certain foods has an *allergy*. *Cholesterol* is now a part of everyone's vocabulary. All of these words have come into use during the nineteenth, and in some cases, the twentieth century.

In almost every other field of science the same story could be told. In the field of electricity words like *dynamo, commutator, alternating current, arc light* have been in the language since about 1870. Physics has made us familiar with terms like *calorie, electron, ionization, ultraviolet rays*, the *quantum theory*, and *relativity*, though we don't always have an exact idea of what they mean. More recently *atomic energy, radioactive, hydrogen bomb, chain reaction, fallout, strontium 90*, and *yellowcake* have come into common use. Chemistry has contributed so many common words that it is difficult to make a selection—*alkali, benzine, creosote, cyanide, formaldehyde, nitroglycerine, radium*, to say nothing of such terms as *biochemical, petrochemical*, and the like. The psychologist has taught us to speak of *apperception, egocentric, extravert* and *introvert, behaviorism, inhibition, inferiority complex*, and *psychoanalysis*. Originally scientific words and expressions such as *ozone, natural selection, stratosphere, DNA* (for *deoxyribonucleic acid*) became familiar through the popularity of certain books or scientific reports in magazines and newspapers. Among the most publicized events of the 1960's and 1970's were the achievements of science and engineering in the exploration of space. In addition to *astronaut* and *cosmonaut*, the public regularly hears and reads dozens of new words from space science, especially compounds like *launch pad, countdown, blast off, moon shot, command module, lunar orbiter, spacecraft, space walk, space shuttle, moon buggy, docking cone, splashdown*. Consciously or unconsciously, we have become scientifically minded in the last few generations, and our vocabularies reflect this extension of our consciousness and interest.

213. *Automobile, Film, Broadcasting.* Scientific discoveries and inventions do not always influence the language in proportion to their importance. It is doubtful whether the radio and motion pictures are more important than the telephone, but they have brought more new words into general use. Such additions to the vocabulary depend more upon the degree to which the discovery or invention enters into the life of the community. This can be seen admirably exemplified in the many new words or new uses of old words that have resulted from the popularity of the automobile and the numerous activities associated with it. Many an old word is now used in a special sense. Thus we *park* a car, and the verb to *park* scarcely suggests to the average man anything except leaving his car along the side of a street or road or in a *parking space*. But the word is an old one, used as a military term (*to park cannon*) and later in reference to carriages. The word *automobile* and the more common word in England, *motor car*, are new, but such words as *sedan* (*saloon* in England), *coach*, and *coupe* are terms adapted from earlier types of vehicles. The American *truck* is the English *lorry* to which we may attach a *trailer*. We have learned new words or new meanings in *carburetor*, *spark plug*, *choke*, *clutch*, *gear shift*, *piston rings*, *throttle*, *differential*, *universal*, *steering wheel*, *shock absorber*, *radiator*, *hood* (English *bonnet*), *windshield* (in England *wind screen*), *bumper*, *chassis*, *hubcap*, *power steering*, and *automatic transmission*. We go into *high* and *low*, have a *blowout* or a *flat*, use *radial tires*, carry a *spare*, drive a *convertible* or *station-wagon* (English *estate car*), and put the car in a *garage*. We may *tune up* the engine or *stall* it, it may *knock* or *backfire*, or we may *skid*, *cut in*, *sideswipe* another car, and be fined for *speeding* or passing a *traffic signal*. *Service stations* and *motels* are everywhere along the *interstate highway*, and it is a well-known fact that one buys *gas* in America and *petrol* in England. Many more examples could be added to terms familiar to every motorist, to illustrate further what is already sufficiently clear, the way in which a new thing which becomes genuinely popular makes demands upon and extends the resources of the language.

The same principle might be illustrated by the movies, radio, and television. The words *cinema* and *moving picture* date from 1899, whereas the alternative *motion picture* is somewhat later. *Screen, reel, newsreel, film, scenario, projector, close-up, fade-out, feature picture, animated cartoon* are now common, and new techniques have produced new words like *Cinerama* and *Sensurround*. Although the popularity of *three-D* (or *3-D*) as a cinematic effect was short-lived, the word is still used, and *Technicolor* as a process for color film has become so common that the word is now seldom heard. The word *radio* in the sense of a receiving station dates from about 1925, and we get the first hint of *television* as early as 1904. Since many of the terms from radio broadcasting were applicable in the later development of television, it is not surprising to find a common vocabulary of broadcasting that includes *broadcast* itself, *aerial*, *antenna*, *lead-in*, *loudspeaker*, *stand by*, and the more recent *solid-state*. Words like *announcer*, *reception*, *microphone*, and *transmitter* have acquired special meanings sometimes commoner than their more general senses. The abbreviations *FM* (for *frequency modulation*) and *AM* (for *amplitude modulation*) serve regularly in radio broadcasting for the identification of stations, as do *UHF* (*ultrahigh frequency*) and *VHF* (*very high frequency*) in television, which in addition has need for the terms *cable TV, teleprompter, telethon*, and *videotape*. The related development of increasingly refined equipment for the recording of sound since Thomas Edison's invention of the *phonograph* in 1877 has made the general consumer aware of *stereo* and *stereophonic, quad* and *quadraphonic, tweeter, woofer, tape deck, four-channel*, and *reel-to-reel*.

214. *The World Wars.* As another example of how great developments or events leave their mark upon language we may observe some of the words that came into English between 1914 and 1918 as a direct consequence of World War I. Some of these were military terms representing new methods of warfare, such as *air raid, antiaircraft gun, tank*, and *blimp*. *Gas mask* and *liaison officer* were new combinations with a military significance. *Camouflage* was borrowed from French, where it had formerly been a term of the scene-painter's craft, but it caught the popular fancy and was soon used half facetiously for various forms of disguise or misrepresentation. Old words were in some cases adapted to new uses. *Sector* was used in the sense of a specific portion of the fighting line; *barrage*, originally an artificial barrier like a dam in a river, designated a protective screen of heavy artillery or machine-gun fire; *dud*, a general word for any counterfeit thing, was specifically applied to a shell that did not explode; and *ace* acquired the meaning of a crack airman, especially one who had brought down five of the enemy's machines. In a number of cases a word which had had only limited circulation in the language now came into general use. Thus *hand grenade* goes back to 1661, but attained new currency during the war. Other expressions already in the language but popularized by the war were *dugout, machine gun, periscope, no man's land*, and even the popular designation of an American soldier, *doughboy*, which was in colloquial use in the United States as early as 1867. *Blighty* was a popular bit of British army slang, derived from India and signifying England or home, and was often applied to a wound that sent a man back to England. Other expressions such as *slacker, trench foot, cootie, war bride*, and the like were either struck off in the heat of the moment or acquired a poignant significance from the circumstances under which they were used.

It would seem that World War II was less productive of memorable words, as it was of memorable songs. Nevertheless it made its contribution to the language in the form of certain new words, new meanings, or an increased currency for expressions which had been used before. In connection with the *air raid*, so prominent a feature of the war, we have the words *alert* (air-raid warning), *blackout, blitz* (German *Blitzkrieg*, literally 'lightning war'), *blockbuster, dive-bombing, evacuate,* air-raid *shelter.* The words *beachhead, parachutist, paratroop, landing strip, crash landing, road-block, jeep, fox hole* (as a shelter for one or two men), *bulldozer* (an American word used in a new sense), *decontamination, task force* (a military or naval unit assigned to the carrying out of a particular opera-tion), *resistance movement,* and *radar* are not in the *Oxford Dictionary* or its 1933 Supplement. *To spearhead* an attack, *to mop up,* and *to appease* were new verbs or old verbs with a new military or political significance. *Flack* (antiaircraft fire) was taken over from German, where it is an abbreviation of *Fliegerabwehrkanone,* 'antiaircraft gun'. *Commando,* a word which goes back to the Boer War, acquired a new and specialized meaning. Some words which were either new or enjoyed great currency during the war—*priority, tooling up, bottleneck, ceiling* (upper limit), *backlog, stockpile*—have become a part of the vocabulary of civilian life, while *lend-lease* has passed into history. The aftermath of the war gave us such expressions as *iron curtain, cold war, fellow traveler, front organization, police state,* all with a very special connotation.

215. *Language as a Mirror of Progress.* Words, being but symbols by which a man expresses his ideas, are an accurate measure of the range of his thought at any given time. They obviously designate the things he knows, and just as obviously the vocabulary of a language must keep pace with the advance of his knowledge. The date when a new word enters the language is in general the date when the object, experience, observation, or whatever it is that calls it forth has entered his consciousness. Thus with a work like the *Oxford Dictionary,* which furnishes us with dated quota-tions showing when the different meanings of every word have arisen and when new words first appear in the language, we could almost write the history of civilization merely from linguistic evidence. When in the early part of the nineteenth century we find growing up a word like *horsepower* or *lithograph,* we may depend upon it that some form of mechanical power which needs to be measured in familiar terms or a new process of engraving has been devised. The appearance in the language of words like *railway, locomotive, turntable* about 1835 tells us that steam railways were then coming in. In 1839 the words *photograph* and *photography* first appear, and a beginning is made toward a considerable vocabulary of special words or senses of words such as *camera, film, enlargement, emulsion, focus, shutter, light meter. Concrete* in the sense of a mixture of crushed stone and cement dates from 1834, but *reinforced concrete* is an expression called forth only in the twentieth century. The word *cable* occurs but a few years before the laying of the first Atlantic cable in 1857–1858. *Refrigerator* is first found in

English in an American quotation of 1841. The words *emancipation* and *abolitionist* have for every American specific meanings connected with the efforts to abolish slavery, efforts which culminated in the Civil War. In the last quarter of the nineteenth century an interesting story of progress is told by new words or new meanings such as *typewriter, telephone, apartment house, twist drill, drop-forging, blueprint, oilfield, motorcycle, feminist, fundamentalist, marathon* (introduced in 1896 as a result of the revival of the Olympic games at Athens in that year), *battery* and *bunt*, the last two indicating the growing popularity of professional baseball in America.

The twentieth century permits us to see the process of vocabulary growth going on under our eyes, sometimes, it would seem, at an accelerated rate. At the turn of the century we get the word *questionnaire* and in 1906 *suffragette. Dictaphone, raincoat*, and *Thermos* became a part of the recorded vocabulary in 1907 and *free verse* in 1908. This is the period when many of the terms of aviation that have since become so familiar first came in—*airplane, aircraft, airman, monoplane, biplane, hydroplane, dirigible. Nose-dive* belongs to the period of the war. About 1910 we began talking about the *futurist* and the *postimpressionist* in art, and the *Freudian* in psychology. *Intelligentsia* as a designation for the class to which superior culture is attributed, and *bolshevik* for a holder of revolutionary political views were originally applied at the time of the First World War to groups in Russia. At this time *profiteer* and in America *prohibition* arose with specialized meanings. Meanwhile *foot fault, fairway, fox trot, auction bridge*, and *contract* were indicative of popular interest in certain games and pastimes. The 1933 supplement to the *Oxford Dictionary* records *Cellophane* (1921) and *rayon* (1924), but not *nylon, deep-freeze, air-conditioned*, or *transistor;* and it is not until the first volume of the new supplement in 1972 that the *OED* includes *credit card, ecosystem, existentialism* (1941, though in German a century earlier), *freeze-dried, convenience foods, bionics, electronic computer, automation, cybernetics, bikini, discotheque.* Only yesterday witnessed the birth of *supersonic transport* (or *SST*), *biodegradable, polyunsaturate, pulsar, cryosphere, op art, multiversity, stagflation*, and *biofeedback.* Tomorrow will witness others as the exigencies of the hour call them into being.

216. *Sources of the New Words: Borrowings.* Most of the new words coming into the language since 1800 have been derived from the same sources or created by the same methods as those that have long been familiar, but it will be convenient to examine them here as an illustration of the processes by which a language extends its vocabulary. It should be remembered that the principles are not new, that what has been going on in the last century and a half could be paralleled from almost any period of the language.

As is to be expected in the light of the English disposition to borrow words from other languages in the past, many of the new words have been taken over ready-made from the people from whom the idea or the thing designated has been obtained. Thus from the French come *apéritif, bengaline, charmeuse, chauffeur, chiffon, consommé, garage, marquisette;* from Italian come *confetti* and *vendetta;* and from Spanish, by way of the United States, *bonanza.* German has given us *rucksack, zeppelin,* and *zither.* From Russia come the words *caracul* and *vodka,* like the articles themselves. *Goulash* is a Magyar word, *robot* is from Czech, while the East is represented by *afghan, loot, thug* from India, *pajamas* (British *pyjamas*) from Persia, and *chop suey* from China. The cosmopolitan character of the English vocabulary, already pointed out, is thus being maintained, and we shall see in the next chapter that America has added many other foreign words, particularly from Spanish and the languages of the American Indian.

217. Self-explaining Compounds.   A second source of new words is represented in the practice of making self-explaining compounds, one of the oldest methods of word-formation in the language. In earlier editions of this book such words as *fingerprint* (in its technical sense), *fire extinguisher, hitchhike, jet propulsion,* the colloquial *know-how, lipstick, steamroller, steam shovel,* and *streamline* were mentioned as being rather new. They have now passed into such common use that they no longer carry any sense of novelty. This will probably happen, indeed has already happened, to some of the more recent formations that can be noted, such as *think tank, skydiving, jet lag, body language, life-style, put-on, flashcube, house sitter, spin-off, pantsuit* (or *pants suit*), *software, mobile home,* and *hatchback.* Many of these betray their newness by being written with a hyphen or as separate words, or by preserving a rather strong accent on each element. They give unmistakable testimony to the fact that the power to combine existing words into new ones expressing a single concept, a power that was so prominent a feature of Old English, still remains with us.

218. Compounds Formed from Greek and Latin Elements.   The same method may be employed in forming words from elements derived from Latin and Greek. The large classical element already in the English vocabulary makes such formations seem quite congenial to the language, and this method has long been a favorite source of scientific terms. Thus *eugenics* is formed from two Greek roots, εὐ– meaning *well,* and γεν–

meaning *to be born*. The word therefore means *well-born* and is applied to the efforts to bring about well-born offspring by the selection of healthy parents. The same root enters into *genetics*, the experimental study of heredity and allied topics. In the words *stethoscope, bronchoscope, fluoroscope*, and the like we have *–scope*, which appears in *telescope*. It is a Greek word σκοπός meaning a *watcher*. Just as τῆλε in Greek means *far* and enters into such words as *telephone, telescope, television*, etc., so we have *stethoscope* with the first element from Greek στῆθος (breast or chest), *bronchoscope* from Greek βρόγχος (windpipe), and *fluoroscope* with the same first element as in *fluorine* (from Latin *fluere*, to flow). *Panchromatic* comes from the Greek words παν– (all) and χρωματικός (relating to color), and is thus used in photography to describe a plate or film that is sensitive to all colors. An *automobile* is something that moves of itself (Greek αὐτός 'self' + Latin *mobilis* 'movable'). *Orthodontia* is from Greek ὀρθός 'straight' and ὀδούς (ὀδόντ–) 'tooth', and thus describes the branch of dentistry that endeavors to straighten irregular teeth. A few minutes spent in looking up recent scientific words in any dictionary will supply abundant illustrations of this common method of English word-formation.

219. *Prefixes and Suffixes*. Another method of enlarging the vocabulary is by appending familiar prefixes and suffixes to existing words on the pattern of similar words in the language. Several of the Latin prefixes seem to lend themselves readily to new combinations. Thus in the period under discussion we have formed *transoceanic, transcontinental, trans-Siberian, transliterate, transformer*, and several more or less technical terms such as *transfinite, transmarine, transpontine*, etc. We speak of *postimpressionists* in art, *postprandial* oratory, the *postclassical* period, and *postgraduate* study. In the same way we use *pre–* in such words as *prenatal, preschool* age, *prehistoric, pre-Raphaelite*, and we may *preheat* or *precool* in certain technical processes. In film parlance we may have a *preview* or a *prerelease*, and we may make *prenuptial* arrangements. During the wars we often read that one side or the other had launched a *counterattack*, and we organized a *counterintelligence* service. In biological laboratories a *counterstain* is used to render more visible the effect of another stain on a tissue or specimen. In his *Man and Superman* Bernard Shaw coined the word *superman* to translate the German *Übermensch* of Nietzschian philosophy. We *subirrigate* and build a *subcellar*, and foreign movies sometimes come to us with *subtitles*. We can *decode* a message, *defrost* a refrigerator, *deflate* the currency, and we may *debunk* a statement, *debug* a machine, and *decaffeinate* coffee. It is so also with suffixes. Recent popular creations on old patterns are *stardom, filmdom, fandom, gangster, pollster, profiteer,* *racketeer.* Familiar endings like *–some, –ful, –less* can be freely added in accordance with long-standing habits in the language.

220. Coinages.   A considerable number of new words must be attributed to deliberate invention or coinage. There has probably never been a time when the creative impulse has not spent itself occasionally in inventing new words, but their chances of general adoption are nowadays often increased by a campaign of advertising as deliberate as the effort which created them. They are mostly the product of ingenuity and imitation, the two being blended in variable proportions. Thus the trademark *Kodak*, which seems to be pure invention, was popularly used for years to refer to cameras of any brand, and *Victrola* and *Frigidaire* enjoyed something of the same currency as synonyms for *phonograph* and *refrigerator. Kleenex* and *Xerox* are trade terms that are often treated as common nouns, and *Zipper*, a word coined by the B. F. Goodrich Company and registered in 1925 as the name for a boot fitted with a slide fastener, has become the universal name for the fastener itself. Words formed by combining the initial or first few letters of two or more words are known as acronyms. *Radar* (*ra*dio *de*tecting *a*nd *ra*nging) is an example, as are *scuba* (*s*elf-contained *u*nder-water *b*reathing *a*pparatus) and OPEC (Organization of Petroleum Exporting Countries).[1] In deliberate coinages there is often an analogy with some other word or words in the language. This is felt, consciously or unconsciously, to be desirable. It permits the meaning more easily to be guessed at, reveals a mild degree of ingenuity on the part of the inventor, and focuses the attention on the distinctive syllable or syllables. *Linotype* is merely the running together of "line o' type," since it casts an entire line in one piece of metal, but the word resembles *stereotype*, and as analogous forms with it we now have *Monotype* and *stenotype. Dictaphone* combines elements found in the words *dictate* and *telephone*, just as *travelogue* is a cross between *travel* and *dialogue. Bureaucrat* and *plutocrat* are obviously formed on the model of *aristocrat, autocrat*, etc., as *electrocute* is modeled after *execute*. Sometimes a Latin formative element is used and the new word has a rather specious classical air, as in *novocaine* from Latin *novus* (new) grafted upon the English word *cocaine.*

Words such as *electrocute* or *travelogue* are often called *portmanteau* words, or better, *blends.*[2] In them two words are, as it were, telescoped into

---

[1] More than 100,000 other examples have been collected in *Acronyms and Initialisms Dictionary*, ed. Ellen T. Crowley and Robert C. Thomas (4th ed., Detroit, 1973), and its periodic supplements.

[2] See Louise Pound, *Blends: Their Relation to English Word Formation* (Heidelberg, 1914).

one. This was a favorite pastime of the author of *Alice in Wonderland*, and to him we owe the word *chortle*, a blending of *snort* and *chuckle*, and *snark* (snake + shark). Often such coinages are formed with a playful or humorous intent. The *Oxford Dictionary* records *brunch* in the year 1900. Although it was originally used facetiously in speaking of those who get up too late for breakfast and therefore combine breakfast and lunch, it is now as likely to be used for the name of a social occasion. *Paradoxology*, *alcoholiday*, *revusical*, *yellocution*, *guestimate*, *condomania*, *ecopolypse*, and the like, often reveal flashes of wit. They carry a momentary appeal, like the coinages of *Time* magazine (*cinemactress*, *cinemaddict*, *cinemagnate*, *socialite*), but few of them are likely to find a permanent place in the language since, like epigrams, they lose their luster when passed about at second hand.

221. Common Words from Proper Names. Another source from which many English words have been derived in the past is the names of persons and places. Every one is aware that *morocco* is derived from the corresponding proper name and that *sandwich* owes its use to the fact that the earl of Sandwich on one occasion put slices of meat between pieces of bread. Like other processes of English word derivation this can be well illustrated in the nineteenth century and later. Thus we get the word for *tabasco* sauce from the name of the Tabasco River in Mexico. *Camembert* comes from the village in France from which cheese of this type was originally exported. A *limousine* is so called from the name of a province in France, and during the 1920's the American city Charleston gave its name to a dance. The word *colt* for a certain kind of firearm is merely the name of the inventor. *Wistaria*, the vine whose most common variety is now known as *wisteria*, is named after Caspar Wistar, an American anatomist of the mid-1800's. The type of one-horse, closed carriage known as a *brougham* owes its name to Lord Brougham of about the same date. In 1880 Captain Boycott, the agent of an Irish landowner, refused to accept rents at the figure set by the tenants. His life was threatened, his servants were forced to leave, and his figure was burnt in effigy. Hence from Ireland came the use of the verb *to boycott*, meaning to coerce a person by refusing to have, and preventing others from having, dealings with him. Similarly, from evidence recently published it seems clear that *lynch law* owes its origin to Captain William Lynch of Virginia, about 1776. In the early nineteenth century we find the verb *to lynch*, and it is now a familiar word. *Mackintosh* is derived from the name of a Glasgow chemist, and *raglan* comes from Lord Raglan, the British commander in the Crimean War. *Shrapnel* is from the name of the British general who invented the type of missile, while in the period of World War II we called a person who collaborated with the enemy a *quisling*, after the Norwegian Vidkun Quisling yielded to the German occupation and became the head of a puppet state. More than five hundred common words in English have been traced to proper names, and they must be considered as illustrating one of the sources from which new words are still being derived.

222. Old Words with New Meanings.   The resources of the vocabulary are sometimes extended from within by employment of an old word in a new sense. We have already seen many examples of this in some of the paragraphs preceding, especially many of the words now applied to the automobile. But the process can be illustrated on almost every hand, for it is one of the commonest phenomena in language. *Skyline* formerly meant the horizon, but it is now commoner in such an expression as the New York *skyline*. *Broadcast* originally had reference to seed, but its application to radio seems entirely appropriate. A *record* may be many other things than a phonograph disc, and *radiator* was used for anything which radiated heat or light before it was applied specifically to steam heat or the automobile. *Cabaret* is an old word meaning a booth or shed, and later a small drinking place. Today it signifies only a certain type of restaurant. We *sign off* or *stand by* in radio, *take off* in an airplane, *kick off* in football, *carry on* in war, *call up* on the telephone, and in each of these cases we convey a specific, often technical meaning, quite different from the sense which these expressions previously had.

A certain amount of experimenting with words is constantly going on, and at times the new use of a word may meet with opposition. Many people object to the use of *intrigue* in the sense of 'to interest greatly or arouse curiosity', and the American businessman's employment of *contact* as a verb has met with resistance in certain quarters. (It is well to remember that Swift objected to *behave* without the reflexive pronoun.) Time will decide the fate of these words, but whether or not the new uses establish themselves in the language, they must be considered as exemplifying a well-recognized phenomenon in the behavior of words.

223. The Influence of Journalism.   In the introduction and popularizing of new words journalism has been a factor of steadily increasing importance. The newspaper and the more popular type of magazine not only play a large part in spreading new locutions among the people but are themselves fertile producers of new words. The reporter necessarily writes under pressure and has not long to search for the right word. In the heat of the moment he is as likely as not to strike off a new expression or wrench the language to fit his idea (*pacifist, socialize*). In his effort to be interesting and

racy he adopts an informal and colloquial style, and many of the colloquialisms current in popular speech find their way into writing first in the
magazine and the newspaper. In this way we have come to *back* a horse or
a candidate, to *boost* our community, *comb* the woods for a criminal, *hop*
the Atlantic, *oust* a politician, and *spike* a rumor, and we speak of a *probe*,
a *cleanup*, a business *deal*, a *go-between*, a political *slate*. *Egghead* sprang
from a telephone conversation between Stewart Alsop, the columnist, and
his brother during Adlai Stevenson's campaign in 1952. Most of these
expressions are still limited to the newspaper and colloquial speech and are
properly classed as journalistic. The sportswriter is often hard pressed to
avoid monotony in his description of similar contests day after day, and in
his desire to be picturesque he seldom feels any scruple about introducing
the latest slang in his particular field of interest. Many an expression
originating in the sports page has found its way into general use. We owe
crestfallen, fight shy, and *show the white feather* to cockfighting, *neck and
neck* and *out of the running* to the race track, and *sidestep, down and out,
straight from the shoulder*, and many other expressions to boxing. In
America we owe *caught napping* and *off base* to baseball. If some of these
locutions are older than the newspaper, there can be no question but that
today much similar slang is given currency through this medium. The terms
Radical Chic, Jet Set, Beautiful People, Bamboo Curtain, Yippie mix the
tone of the spoken language and the capital letters of the printed page. One
of our popular news weeklies makes the use of verbal novelties a feature of
its style, routinely identifying people through capitalized epithets (*Swedish
Film Maker, Candy Tycoon, Pundit*) and strings of hyphenated words
(*show-biz-struck*). So too we find puns, rhymes, coinages (*nobelity* for
winners of a Nobel prize, *jeerworthy*), and many other examples of the
search for novelty. We must recognize that in the nineteenth century a new
force affecting language arose, and that among the many ways in which it
affects the language not the least important are its tendency constantly to
renew the vocabulary and its ability to bring about the adoption of new
words.

224. Changes of Meaning. It is necessary to say something about the
way in which words gradually change their meaning. That words do
undergo such change is a fact readily perceived, and it can be illustrated
from any period of the language. That we should choose to illustrate it by
more or less recent examples is a matter merely of convenience. Differences
of meaning are more readily perceived when they affect current use. It
should be clearly recognized, however, that the tendencies here discussed
are universal in their application and are not confined to the nineteenth

century or to the English language. They will be found at work in every
language and at all times. The branch of linguistic study which concerns
itself with the meanings of words and the way meanings develop is known
as *semasiology* or *semantics*.

It has been observed that in their sense development, words often pursue
certain well-marked tendencies. Among the more common of these are
extension of meaning, *narrowing* of meaning, *degeneration*, and *regeneration*. By *extension of meaning* is meant the widening of a word's signification
until it covers much more than the idea originally conveyed. The tendency
is sometimes called *generalization*. The word *lovely*, for example, means
primarily worthy to be loved, and *great* means large in size, the opposite of
small. But today the schoolgirl's *lovely* and the average man's *great* have no
such meaning. A box of candy or a chair may be *lovely*, and anything from
a ball game to the weather may be *great*. When a college student says that
he found a certain book *great*, it is more than likely that his statement has
nothing to do with the value of the book judged as a work of art but simply
means that he thoroughly enjoyed it. In everyday use these words have
come to express only enthusiastic approval of a rather vague sort. The
word *proposition* primarily means a statement set forth for purposes of
discussion, or in mathematics, for demonstration. It was so used by
Lincoln in his Gettysburg Address: "... a new nation dedicated to the
proposition that all men are created equal." But in America during the last
century it began to be used more loosely. Owen Wister says in *The Virginian*,
"Proposition in the West does, in fact, mean whatever you at the moment
please." Today if a man wants to buy a house and offers the owner a certain
price for it, we say that he made him a *proposition*. "That's a different
proposition" expresses an idea which in more formal English becomes
"That's a different matter" (an equally general word). The word is often
accompanied by an adjective: *a tough proposition; he was the coolest
proposition I ever met*. All of these uses are distinctly colloquial and are not
accepted in England, but they illustrate the principle of generalization. A
more acceptable illustration is the word *dean*. It has, of course, its proper
meanings, such as the head of the chapter in a cathedral church or the head
of the faculty in a college. But it has come to be used as a designation for
the senior or foremost person of any group or class, so that we may speak
of the *dean* of American critics, or indeed, of sportswriters.

The opposite tendency is for a word gradually to acquire a more
restricted sense, or to be chiefly used in one special connection. A classic
example of this practice is the word *doctor*. There were doctors (i.e., learned
men) in theology, law, and many other fields beside medicine, but nowadays

when we send for *the* doctor we mean a member of only one profession. In some of the preceding paragraphs, especially that in which were presented examples of old words in new meanings, will be found a number of similar instances. The verb to *park* as applied to automobiles and the war word *tank* are cases in point. The use of a word in a restricted sense does not preclude its use also in other meanings. There was a time in the 1890's when the word *wheel* suggested to most people a bicycle, but it could still be used of the wheel of a cart or a carriage. Often the restricted sense of a word belongs to a special or class vocabulary. An *enlargement* means to a photographer a large print made from a small negative, and in educational circles a *senior* is a member of the graduating class. Consequently it sometimes happens that the same word will acquire different restricted meanings for different people. The word *gas* is an inclusive term for the chemist, but it calls up a more restricted idea for the housewife and a still different one for the American owner of an automobile. Narrowing of meaning may be confined to one locality under the influence of local conditions. *Nickel* in America means a coin, and for a number of years the word *prohibition* in this country generally suggested the prohibition of intoxicants. In the same way the terms *democrat* and *republican* seldom have their broader significance to an American, but rather imply adherence to one or the other of the two chief political parties in the United States.

Degeneration of meaning may take several forms. It may take the form of the gradual extension to so many senses that any particular meaning which a word may have had is completely lost. This is one form of generalization already illustrated in the words *lovely* and *great*.[1] *Awful* and *terrible* have undergone a similar deterioration. In other cases a word has retained a very specific meaning but a less favorable one than it originally had. Phillips in his *New World of Words* (1658) defines *garble* as "to purifie, to sort out the bad from the good, an expression borrowed from Grocers, who are said to garble their Spices, i.e. to purifie them from the dross and dirt."

---

[1] Chesterfield has an interesting comment on this development in the word *vast* in his time: "Not contented with enriching our language by words absolutely new, my fair countrywomen have gone still farther, and improved it by the application and extension of old ones to various and very different significations. They take a word and change it, like a guinea into shillings for pocket-money, to be employed in the several occasional purposes of the day. For instance, the adjective *vast*, and its adverb *vastly*, mean anything, and are the fashionable words of the most fashionable people. A fine woman, under this head I comprehend all fine gentlemen too, not knowing in truth where to place them properly, is *vastly* obliged, or *vastly* offended, *vastly* glad, or *vastly* sorry. Large objects are *vastly* great, small ones are *vastly* little; and I had lately the pleasure to hear a fine woman pronounce, by a happy metonymy, a very small gold snuff-box that was produced in company to be *vastly* pretty, because it was *vastly* little." (*The World*, No. 101, December 5, 1754.)

The word was still used in this sense down through the eighteenth century and even beyond. But in the time of Johnson it occasionally carried the implication of selecting in an unfair or dishonest way, and as used today it always signifies the intentional or unintentional mutilation of a statement so that a different meaning is conveyed from that intended. *Smug* was originally a good word, meaning neat or trim; its present suggestion of objectionable self-satisfaction seems to have grown up during the nineteenth century. The same thing is true of *vulgar* in the meaning bordering on obscene, and of *pious* in its contemptuous sense. *Amateur* and *dilettante* now imply inexpertness or superficiality, although the former word still conveys a favorable idea when applied to athletics. In England one speaks only of *insects*, since the word *bug* has degenerated to the specialized meaning 'bedbug'. A very interesting form of degeneration often occurs in words associated with things which it is not considered polite to talk about. In 1790 the satirist Peter Pindar wrote:

> I've heard that breeches, petticoats and smock,
> Give to thy modest mind a grievous shock
> And that thy brain (so lucky its device)
> Christ'neth them *inexpressibles* so nice.[1]

Thus the common word for a woman's undergarment down to the eighteenth century was *smock*. It was then replaced by the more delicate word *shift*. In the nineteenth century the same motive led to the substitution of the word *chemise*, and in the twentieth this has been replaced by *combinations*, *step-ins*, and other euphemisms. Until the recent movement for women's rights, *bra* occurred but seldom in polite mixed company, as did *panties* and *slip* (the last of which referred to an outer garment in the eighteenth century and an undergarment as early as the mid-nineteenth). Changing attitudes toward this part of the vocabulary may halt the process of degeneration and give a longer life to those terms currently in use.

If words sometimes go downhill, they also undergo the opposite process, known as *regeneration*. Words like *budge, coax, nonplus, shabby, squabble, stingy, tiff, touchy, wobbly*, which were recorded with proper disparagement by Dr. Johnson, have since passed into the standard speech. In the eighteenth century *snob* and *sham* were slang, but in the nineteenth they attained respectability, the former word partly through the influence of Thackeray. The word *sturdy* originally meant harsh, rough, or intractable. We now use it in a wholly complimentary sense. Even the word *smock*, which was mentioned above as losing caste in the eighteenth century, has

---

[1] *Roland for Oliver.*

now been rehabilitated as applied to an outer garment. We use it for a certain type of woman's dress and we speak of an artist's smock. The changes of meaning which words undergo are but another evidence of the constant state of flux which characterizes the living language.

225. Slang. All the types of semantic change discussed in the preceding paragraph could be illustrated from that part of the vocabulary which at any given time is considered slang. It is necessary to say "at any given time" not only because slang is fleeting and the life of a slang expression likely to be short, but because what is slang today may have been in good use yesterday and may be accepted in the standard speech of tomorrow. Slang has been aptly described as "a peculiar kind of vagabond language, always hanging on the outskirts of legitimate speech, but continually straying or forcing its way into the most respectable company."[1] Yet it is a part of language and cannot be ignored or dismissed with a contemptuous sneer. One of the developments which must certainly be credited to the nineteenth century is the growth of a more objective and scientific attitude toward this feature of language. The word *slang* does not occur in Johnson's *Dictionary*. It first occurs a few years later and in its early use always has a derogatory force. Webster in 1828 defines it as "low, vulgar, unmeaning language." But the definition in the *Oxford Dictionary*, expressing the attitude of 1911, is very different: "Language of a highly colloquial type, below the level of standard educated speech, and consisting either of new words, or of current words employed in some special sense." Here the words "low" and "vulgar" have disappeared, and this element in language is treated frankly as a scientific fact.

One reason why slang cannot be ignored even by the strictest purist is that it has not infrequently furnished expressions which the purist uses without suspecting their origin. Even the student of language is constantly surprised when he comes across words which he uses naturally and with entire propriety but finds questioned or condemned by writers of a generation or a few generations before. The expression *what on earth* seems to us an idiomatic intensive and certainly would not be objected to in the speech of anyone today. But De Quincey condemned it as slang and expressed horror at hearing it used by a government official. The word *row* in the sense of a disturbance or commotion was slang in the eighteenth century and described by Todd (1818) as "a very low expression," but today we find it in the works of reputable writers as a word that fittingly suggests the qualities of a vulgar brawl. *Boom, slump, crank*, and *fad*, in becoming

---

[1] Greenough and Kittredge, *Words and Their Ways in English Speech* (New York, 1901), p. 55.

respectable, have acquired an exact and sometimes technical meaning. Even the harmless word *joke* was once slang.

In surveying contemporary English, not only do we have to consider the slang which has lifted itself into the level of educated speech but we must recognize the part played by slang in its own character. For there is hardly a person who does not make use of it upon occasion. Slang results from an instinctive desire for freshness and novelty of expression. Naturally the less a person is inclined to submit to the restraints imposed by a formal standard, the more ready he is to accept indiscriminately the newest slang locution. *To criticize* seems to the man in the street tame and colorless, if not stilted, so he substitutes *to bad-mouth*. For the same reason a woman who fails to keep an engagement with a man *stands him up*. Since novelty is a quality which soon wears off, slang has to be constantly renewed. *Vamoose, skedaddle, twenty-three skiddoo, beat it, scram, buzz off* have all had their periods of popularity in the twentieth century as expressions of roughly the same idea, usually in imperative form. It can hardly be denied that some slang expressions, while they are current, express an idea that it would be difficult to convey by other means. *Hassle, boob tube, vibes, clout, pizzazz, rip-off, laid-back, antsy, knee-jerk, trendy* undoubtedly owe their popularity to some merit which is recognized by a sure instinct among the people. It is sometimes difficult to define the precise quality which makes an expression slang. It is often not in the word itself, but in the sense in which it is used. *Put down* is proper enough if we speak of soldiers who put down a rebellion, but it is slang when we speak of a remark which *put someone down* or refer to the remark as a *put-down*. So far as colloquial use is concerned it is impossible to shut our eyes to the prominent part which slang plays in the language.

It is dangerous to generalize about the relative prominence of slang in this and former times. But it would seem as though the role which it plays today is greater than it has been at certain times in the past, say in the Elizabethan age or the eighteenth century, to judge by the conversation of plays and popular fiction. The cultivation of slang has become a feature of certain types of popular writing. We think of men like George Ade, who wrote *Fables in Slang*, or Ring Lardner or O. Henry. They are not only the creators of locutions which have become part of the slang of the day, but they have popularized this outer fringe of the colloquial and given it greater currency. It would certainly be an incomplete picture of the language of today which failed to include slang as a present feature and a source from which English will doubtless continue to be fed in the future.

226. *Cultural Levels and Functional Varieties*.[1]   The discussion of slang has clearly indicated that there is more than one type of speech. Within the limits of any linguistic unity there are as many languages as there are groups of people thrown together by propinquity and common interests. Beyond the limits of the general language there are local and class dialects, technical and occupational vocabularies, slang, and other forms of speech less reputable. Even within the region of the common language from which these are diverging forms it is possible to distinguish at least three broad types.

Occupying a sort of middle ground is the *spoken standard*. It is the language heard in the conversation of educated people. It is marked by conformity to the rules of grammar and to certain considerations of taste which are not easily defined but are present in the minds of those who are conscious of their speech. Whatever its dialectal coloring or qualities varying with the particular circumstances involved, it is free from features that are regarded as substandard in the region. To one side of this spoken standard lies the domain of the *written standard*. This is the language of books and it ranges from the somewhat elevated style of poetry to that of simple but cultivated prose. It may differ both in vocabulary and idiom from the spoken standard, although the two frequently overlap. When we say *tip* and write *gratuity* we are making a conscious choice between these two functional varieties. In the other direction we pass from one cultural level to another, from the spoken standard to the region of *vulgar* or *illiterate speech*. This is the language of those who are ignorant of or indifferent to the ideals of correctness by which the educated are governed. It is especially sympathetic to all sorts of neologisms and generally is rich in slang.

While the three types—the literary standard, the spoken standard, and vulgar speech—are easily recognized, it is not possible to draw a sharp line of demarcation between them. To a certain extent they run into one another. The spoken standard itself covers a wide range of usage. In speech suitable to formal occasions the spoken standard approaches the written standard, whereas in easy and colloquial conversation it may tend in the direction of its more unconventional neighbor. Some interchange between one type and the next is constantly going on. The written and the spoken standards have been drawing appreciably closer, possibly because reading is such a widespread accomplishment today, possibly because we have

---

[1] For the distinction, see John S. Kenyon, "Cultural Levels and Functional Varieties of English," *College English*, 10 (1948), 1–6. For a criticism of the distinction, see William Labov, *The Study of Nonstandard English* (Champaign, Ill., 1970), pp. 22–28.

come to feel that the simplest and best prose is that which most resembles the easy and natural tone of cultivated speech. In the same way words and locutions current among the masses sometimes find their way into the lower reaches of the spoken standard. This is particularly true of slang. One may reason that when slang is acceptable to those who in general conform to the spoken standard it should no longer be called slang. But such a conclusion is hardly justified. It is better to hold that there are different levels in slang, and that some use of slang is tolerated in the lighter conversation of most educated speakers.

It is necessary to recognize that from a linguistic point of view each of the varieties—whether of cultural level or degree of formality—has its own right to exist. If we judge them simply on their capacity to express ideas clearly and effectively, we must admit that one kind of English is seldom superior to another. *I seen it* and *I knowed it* may not conform to the standard of correctness demanded of cultivated speech, but these expressions convey their meaning just as clearly as the standard forms and historically are no worse than dozens of others now in accepted use. Likewise much could be said, historically and logically, for *it's me* and the double negative. It is rather in their social implications that the varieties of English differ. The difference between the spoken standard and vulgar speech is in their association with broadly different classes. As Bernard Shaw once remarked, "People know very well that certain sorts of speech cut off a person for ever from getting more than three or four pounds a week all their life long—sorts of speech which make them entirely impossible in certain professions." The recognition of this fact does not prevent speakers who represent different levels of usage from mixing in the daily contacts of life and communicating with each other without restraint. The fact that one happens to conform to the accepted standard need not make him less ready to recognize the admirable qualities in those whose speech does not. He may also possibly find the speech of one who employs language of the literary variety in his conversation, who talks like a book, an obstacle to free intercourse, because he associates such language with stiff and pedantic qualities of mind or a lack of social ease. In this case what he objects to has clearly nothing to do with the question of correctness. It is a question merely of appropriateness to the occasion. As in numerous other linguistic matters, we have come in recent times to look upon the different types of speech more tolerantly, to recognize them as one of the phenomena of language. We do not expect (or wish) men to talk like Matthew Arnold, and we do not include in a sweeping condemnation all those who fail to conform to the spoken standard of the educated. In recent years a sometimes strident discussion among linguists and sociologists has dealt with the relations between the standard dialects of the middle classes and the nonstandard dialects of lower socioeconomic groups. The black English vernacular of the United States presents especially vexed questions for the educational system and society as a whole (see § 250.8). The issues are finally economic, political, and psychological in a debate that seems far from arriving at a satisfactory resolution.

227. *The Standard Speech.* The spoken standard or, as it is sometimes called, the *received standard*, is something which varies in different parts of the English-speaking world. In England it is a type of English perhaps best exemplified in the speech of those educated in the great public schools, but spoken also with a fair degree of uniformity by cultivated people in all parts of the country. It is a class rather than a regional dialect. This is not the same as the spoken standard of the United States or Canada or Australia. Each of these is entitled to recognition. The spread of English to many parts of the world has changed our conception of what constitutes Standard English. The speech of England can no longer be considered the norm by which all others must be judged. The growth of countries like the United States and Canada and the political independence of countries that were once British colonies force us to admit that the educated speech of these vast areas is just as "standard" as that of London or Oxford. It is perhaps inevitable that people will feel a preference for the pronunciation and forms of expression which they are accustomed to, but to criticize the Englishman for omitting many of his *r*'s or the American for pronouncing them betrays an equally unscientific provincialism irrespective of which side of the Atlantic indulges in the criticism. The hope is sometimes expressed that we might have a world standard to which all parts of the English-speaking world would try to conform. So far as the spoken language is concerned it is too much to expect that the marked differences of pronunciation that distinguish the speech of, let us say, England, Australia, India, and the United States will ever be reduced to one uniform mode. We must recognize that in the last two hundred years English has become a cosmopolitan tongue and must cultivate a cosmopolitan attitude toward its various standard forms.[1]

228. *English Dialects.* In addition to the educated standard in each major division of the English-speaking world there are local forms of the language known as regional dialects. In the newer countries where English

---

[1] On the varieties of English today, see Eric Partridge and John W. Clark, *British and American English since 1900* (London, 1951), and G. L. Brook, *Varieties of English* (London, 1973).

has spread in modern times these are not so numerous or so pronounced in their individuality as they are in the British Isles. The English introduced into the colonies was a mixture of dialects in which the peculiarities of each were fused in a common speech. Except perhaps in the United States, there has scarcely been time for new regional differences to grow up, and although one region is sometimes separated from another by the breadth of a continent, the improvements in transportation and communication have tended to keep down differences which might otherwise have arisen. But in Great Britain such differences are very great. They go back to the earliest period of the language and reflect conditions which prevailed at a time when travel was difficult and communication was limited between districts relatively close together. Even among the educated the speech of northern England differs considerably from that of the south. In words such as *butter, cut, gull,* and *some* the southern vowel [ʌ] occurs in the north as [ʊ], and in *chaff, grass,* and *path* the southern retracted vowel [ɑː] occurs as short [a] in northern dialects. In the great Midland district one distinguishes an eastern variety and a western, as well as a central type lying between. But such a classification of the English dialects is sufficient only for purposes of a broad grouping. Every county has its own peculiarities, and sometimes as many as three dialectal regions may be distinguished within the boundaries of a single shire. This wide diversity of dialects is well illustrated by the materials published since 1962 in the *Survey of English Dialects.* In the six northern counties at least seventeen different vowels or diphthongs occur in the word *house,* including the [uː] of Old English *hūs.*[1]

The dialect of southern Scotland has claims to special consideration on historical and literary grounds. In origin it is a variety of Northern English, but down to the sixteenth century it occupied a position both in speech and in writing on a plane with English. In the time of Shakespeare, however, it began to be strongly influenced by Southern English. This influence has been traced in part to the Reformation, which brought in the Bible and other religious works from the south, in part to the renaissance of English literature. The most important factor, however, was probably the growing importance of England and the greatness of London as the center of the English-speaking world. When in 1603 James VI of Scotland became the king of England as James I, and when by the Act of Union in 1707 Scotland

[1] Orton and Dieth, eds., *Survey of English Dialects,* 1, part 2, 459. See also two studies deriving from the *Survey:* Eduard Kolb, *Phonological Atlas of the Northern Region* (Bern, 1966), and Harold Orton and Nathalia Wright, *A Word Geography of England* (London, 1974).

was formally united to England, English was plainly felt to be standard, and Scots became definitely a dialect. During the eighteenth century it managed to maintain itself as a literary language through the work of Ramsay, Ferguson, and Robert Burns. Since then it has gradually lost ground. English is taught in the schools, and cultivation of English has, rightly or wrongly, been taken as the first test of culture. The ambitious have avoided the native dialect as a mark of lowly birth, and those who have a patriotic or sentimental regard for this fine old speech have long been apprehensive of its ultimate extinction.[1] Prompted in part by this concern, three linguistic projects are presently recording Scottish speech. The publication of two major dictionaries began in 1931 and is still in progress. *A Dictionary of the Older Scottish Tongue* records the language before 1700, *The Scottish National Dictionary* after that year.[2] In addition, the Linguistic Survey of Scotland, which has been collecting information since 1949 on both Scots and Gaelic, has begun publishing its *Atlas*.[3]

The characteristics of this dialect are known to most people through the poetry of Robert Burns:

> O ye wha are sae guid yoursel,
>   Sae pious and sae holy,
> Ye've nought to do but mark and tell
>   Your Neebour's fauts and folly!
> Whase life is like a weel-gaun mill, [well-going]
>   Supply'd wi' store o' water,
> The heapet happer's ebbing still, [heaped hopper]
>   And still the clap plays clatter.

Here we see some of the characteristic differences of pronunciation, *wha*, *whase*, *sae*, *weel*, *neebour*, *guid*, etc. These could easily be extended from others of his songs and poems, which all the world knows, and the list would include not only words differently pronounced but many an old word no longer in use south of the Tweed. Familiar examples are *ain* (own), *auld* (old), *lang* (long), *bairn* (child), *bonnie* (beautiful), *braw*

---

[1] See an interesting address by the philologist most responsible for Scottish lexicography in this century, Sir William Craigie, "The Present State of the Scottish Tongue," in *The Scottish Tongue* (London, 1924), pp. 1–46. The survival of the dialect now appears unlikely. Cf. David Murison, "The Scots Tongue—the Folk-Speech," *Folklore*, 75 (1964), 37–47.

[2] A description of the goals and methods of the two dictionaries is given in A. J. Aitken, "Completing the Record of Scots," *Scottish Studies*, 8 (1964), 129–40.

[3] See Angus McIntosh, *An Introduction to a Survey of Scottish Dialects* (Edinburgh, 1952), and J. Y. Mather and H. H. Speitel, eds., *The Linguistic Atlas of Scotland*, vol. 1 (Hamden, Conn., 1975).

(handsome), *dinna* (do not), *fash* (trouble oneself), *icker* (ear of grain), *maist* (almost), *muckle* (much, great), *syne* (since), *unco* (very).

The dialect of Ireland is equally distinct from the standard English of England although it has had no Burns to give it currency in literature. Except in the Scotch-Irish dialect of Ulster, the English language in Ireland has not preserved so many old words as have survived in Scotland. But the Anglo-Irish of the southern part of the island has an exuberance of vocabulary that recalls the lexical inventiveness of Elizabethan times, the period during which English began to spread rapidly in Ireland.[1] It has also been influenced by the native speech of the Celts, sometimes in vocabulary (*blarney*, *galore*, *smithereens*), sometimes in idiom. Although different varieties of the Irish dialect are distinguished, especially in the north and the south, certain peculiarities of pronunciation are fairly general. In dialect stories we are familiar with such spellings as *tay*, *desaive*, *foine*, *Moikle*, *projuce* (produce), *fisht* (fist), *butther*, *thrue*, and the like. As an instance of *sh* for *s* before a long *u*, P. W. Joyce quotes the remark of one Dan Kiely "That he was now looking out for a wife that would *shoot* him."[2] It is needless to say that many cultivated speakers in Ireland speak in full accord with the received standard of England or use a form of that standard only slightly colored by dialectal peculiarities.

229. *English in the Empire.* In the various parts of the former British Empire, as in the United States, the English language has developed differences which distinguish it from the language of England. In Australasia, Africa, South Asia, and Canada, peculiarities of pronunciation and vocabulary have grown up which mark off national and areal varieties from the dialect of the mother country and from one another. These peculiarities are partly such as arise in communities separated by time and space, and are partly due to the influence of a new environment. In some countries the most striking changes are the result of imperfect learning and systematic adaptations by speakers of other languages. Differences of nature and material civilization, and generally contact with some foreign tongue, are clearly reflected in the vocabulary. Thus in Australia it has been well said, "It is probably not too much to say that there never was an instance in history when so many new words were needed, and that there never will be again, for never did settlers come, nor can they ever come again, upon Flora and Fauna so completely different from anything seen by them before. An oak in America is still a *Quercus*, not as in Australia a *Casuarina*.

---

[1] See J. Braidwood, "Ulster and Elizabethan English," in *Ulster Dialects* (Belfast, 1964), pp. 5–109.

[2] *English as We Speak It in Ireland* (Dublin, 1910), p. 96.

But with the whole tropical region intervening it was to be expected that in the South Temperate Zone many things would be different, and such expectation was amply fulfilled."[1] Australian English uses many words which would not be understood in England or America. Some of these are old words which have acquired new meanings by being applied to new things. Thus the term *robin* is used for various birds not known in Europe. The word *jackass* (shortened from *laughing jackass*) means a bird whose cry is like a donkey's bray. Other words have been borrowed from the aboriginal languages of Australia and from Maori in New Zealand. *Kangaroo* and *boomerang* have become general English, but *wombat* is still chiefly Australian because it is the name of an Australian animal.[2] The Australian calls a rowdy street loafer a *larrikin*. A *swagman* is a man traveling through the *bush* (back country) carrying a *swag* (tramp's bundle). Where an American talks of a *ranch*, the Australian speaks of a *station* and, like us, distinguishes between a *sheep station* and a *cattle station*. A *boundary rider* is one who patrols an estate and keeps the owner informed concerning every part of it. The English of Australia not only is characterized by interesting differences of vocabulary, but varies strikingly in pronunciation from the received standard of England. The accent of the majority of Australians has characteristics often associated with Cockney, especially in the quality of the vowels and diphthongs which occur in the words *say, so, beat, boot, high*, and *how*.[3] Because an Australian's pronunciation of *hay* may register on an American as *high*, or *basin* as *bison*, these systematic differences have been the source of misunderstandings between speakers of General Australian and speakers of other national varieties, though not among speakers of General Australian themselves. Within Australia there are possible difficulties in the different patterns of General Australian, the dialect of the great majority, and Cultivated Australian, a minority accent that approaches the received standard of England.[4] Social varieties such as these, and Broad Australian at the uncultivated extreme of the scale, are the only significant dialectal differences in a country where regional variations are negligible. The distinctive characteristics of General Australian pronunciation and the uniformity of the dialect throughout the continent are attributed to the circumstance that the early settlers were

[1] E. E. Morris, *Austral English: A Dictionary of Australasian Words, Phrases and Usages* (London, 1898), p. xii.

[2] Of course, this has not prevented *kangaroo* from gaining general currency.

[3] For important differences with Cockney, see A. G. Mitchell, *The Pronunciation of English in Australia*, rev. ed. with Arthur Delbridge (Sydney, 1965), pp. 7–8.

[4] See A. G. Mitchell and Arthur Delbridge, *The Speech of Australian Adolescents: A Survey* (Sydney, 1965), pp. 37, 83.

deported prisoners and adventurers often drawn from the lower classes of England (cf. § 207). Although detailed information about the dialects spoken by these settlers is lacking, it is clear that the predominant varieties were lower-class urban dialects of southeastern England. In Australia the constant moving of convicts from place to place brought about the development of a mixed dialect which became homogeneous throughout the settled territory and distinct from any of the British dialects that contributed to the mixture. The English of Australia offers an interesting example of the changes that take place in a language transplanted to a remote and totally different environment.

The same thing is true in a somewhat different way of Africa, the most multilingual continent on earth. The present Republic of South Africa had been occupied successively by the Bushmen, Hottentots, Bantus, Portuguese, and Dutch before the English settlers came. From all these sources, but especially from Dutch and its South African development, Afrikaans, the English language has acquired elements. A few words which occurred earlier in peculiarly South African contexts have passed into the general English vocabulary. In addition to *apartheid* and *veldt* (or *veld*), which retain their original associations, British and American speakers use *commando*, *commandeer*, and *trek* in contexts that no longer reflect their South African history. The great majority of Afrikanerisms (i.e., words and expressions borrowed from Dutch and Afrikaans) would still be generally meaningless in other parts of the English-speaking world, yet quite common in the daily life of South Africans. A recently compiled list of words and phrases which South Africans themselves consider to be characteristic of their variety of English includes *biltong* (strips of dried meat), *braaivleis* (a barbecue), *donga* (ravine), *gogga* (insect), *koeksisters* (a confection), *kopje* (hill), *lekker* (nice), *mealies* (Indian corn), *ou* (fellow, U.S. *guy*), *spruit* (gully), *stoep* (verandah, U.S. *stoop*), and *veldskoen* (hide-shoes).[1] As in Australian English, a number of good English words are used in quite new senses. South African racial policies have given a new meaning to *location* as an area in which black Africans are required to live. *Lands* in South Africa are just those portions of a farm that can be used for cultivation of crops, *camp* refers to the fenced-in portion of a farm, and the *leopard* (Afrikaans *tier*, from *tyger*) is sometimes called a *tiger*.[2] An

---

[1] William Branford, "Aardvark to Zwarthout: Social and Historical Aspects of the South African English Vocabulary," in *Seven Studies in English*, ed. Gildas Roberts (Cape Town and London, 1971), p. 134.

[2] See also Charles Pettman, *Africanderisms: A Glossary of South African Colloquial Words and Phrases and Place and Other Names* (London, 1913), and W. S. Mackie, "Afrikanerisms," in *Standard Encyclopaedia of South Africa*, 1 (Cape Town, 1970), 188.

American would find some familiar usages. A *store* means a shop, large or small, and the South African also speaks of a *storekeeper*. *Cookies* (small cakes) is the same as our word, which we also learned from the Dutch. *Divide* (watershed) is said to be borrowed from American use, and *up-country* is used much as we use it in the eastern states. The use of *with* without an object (*Can I come with?*) can be found dialectally in this country, but we do not say "He threw me over the hedge with a rock" (i.e., "He threw a stone over the hedge and hit me"), a syntactic pattern that occurs in the English speech of Afrikaners and in the spoken language of relatively uneducated English speakers. Occasionally an old word now lost to Standard English in England has been preserved in South Africa, although this does not seem to have happened so often as in America. *Dispense* or *spens*, meaning a pantry or kitchen cupboard, is found in Chaucer (Al vinolent as botel in the spence: *Summoner's Tale*). It was doubtless carried to South Africa from one of the English dialects. The variations of the English vocabulary in different parts of the British Empire are so fascinating that one is tempted to pursue them at too great a length. Enough has probably been said to illustrate the individual character of many expressions in South African use. In pronunciation the English of South Africa has been much influenced by the pronunciation of Afrikaans and to a lesser extent by the speech of many Scottish school-masters.[1] To Afrikaans it apparently owes not only the peculiar modification of certain vowels (e.g., [pen] for *pin;* [kɛb] for *cab*, etc.), but also its higher pitch and the tendency to omit one of two or more consonants at the end of a word (e.g., *tex* for *text*). South African shares with American English the general disposition to pronounce the *r* when it appears in the spelling and to give full value to unaccented syllables (*extraordinary*, rather than the English *extraord'n'ry*).

In other parts of sub-Saharan Africa that were once British colonies and are now independent countries, the English language has a complex relationship to the many African languages. Unlike South Africa, where English and Afrikaans are the European languages of the ruling minorities, Ghana, Nigeria, Sierra Leone, Kenya, Uganda, and other former colonies have a choice of retaining their colonial linguistic inheritance or rejecting it. In Nigeria three main African languages—Hausa, Yoruba, and Igbo—and scores of languages spoken by smaller groups exist alongside English. Although only a tiny minority of the population speaks English, almost

[1] See David Hopwood, *South African English Pronunciation* (Cape Town and Johannesburg, 1928), and L. W. Lanham, *The Pronunciation of South African English* (Cape Town, 1967).

always as a second language, it is the official language of the country. Ethnic jealousies that would arise from the selection of one of the African languages, and the advantages of English for communication both internally and internationally, are sufficient to overcome the reluctance toward using a colonial language. Swahili is the official language in Tanzania, but government business is routinely transacted in English. Some nations have deferred making the choice of an official language and continue to use English simultaneously with one or more of the African languages. Even more complex than the choice of an official language is the question of a standard. Among speakers who learn English as a second language there will inevitably be a wide range of varieties, from pidgin at one extreme to a written standard of international acceptability at the other. Because many speakers know no English and many know only the patois of the marketplace, West African English is remarkable for its varieties. With as yet no identifiable West African standard, graders of examinations often have difficulty drawing the line between an incorrect answer and a local variant. Such practicalities illustrate the larger philosophical problem of correctness and acceptability in varieties of English that diverge markedly from the international Standard English of educated speakers in Great Britain, the United States, Canada, Australia, New Zealand, South Africa, and many speakers in the West African countries. The questions of whether a West African standard will emerge, and if so, whether such a standard is desirable and should be taught, evoke a wide range of answers that reflect a bewildering diversity of opinion concerning language and its use.[1]

A similar situation exists in India except that a clearly identifiable Indian variety has emerged over the years. The problems and prospects of Indian English were summarized by Raja Rao nearly half a century ago: "The telling has not been easy. One has to convey in a language that is not one's own the spirit that is one's own. One has to convey the various shades and omissions of a certain thought-movement that looks maltreated in an alien language. I use the word 'alien,' yet English is not really an alien language to us. It is the language of our intellectual make-up . . . but not of our emotional make-up. We are all instinctively bilingual, many of us writing in our own language and in English. We cannot write like the English. We should not. We cannot write only as Indians. We have grown to look at the

[1] Cf. the contrasting views in M. A. K. Halliday, Angus McIntosh, and Peter Strevens, *The Linguistic Sciences and Language Teaching* (London, 1964), pp. 203–4 *et passim*; C. H. Prator, "The British Heresy in TEFL," in *Language Problems of Developing Nations*, ed. Joshua A. Fishman *et al.* (New York, 1968), pp. 459–76; J. H. Sledd, "Un-American English Reconsidered," *American Speech*, 48 (1973), 46–53; and K. A. Sey, *Ghanaian English: An Exploratory Survey* (London, 1973).

large world as part of us. Our method of expression therefore has to be a dialect which will some day prove to be as distinctive and colorful as the Irish or the American. Time alone will justify it."[1] Peculiarly Indian features of pronunciation, vocabulary, and syntax, which the British regarded with condescension during the days of the Empire, have in recent years received more appropriately neutral descriptions from linguists. Certain pronunciations result from the systematic influence of Indian languages. For speakers of the variety of Hindi which does not permit *sk*, *st*, and *sp* at the beginning of words, English *station* is regularly pronounced with an initial vowel [ɪsteːʃən].[2] In some varieties of Indian English [v] and [w] are not distinguished, and [t], [d], [l], and [r] are pronounced with retroflection. Dozens of words and phrases which strike British and American speakers as strange are the natural expressions of cultural contexts that are absent in Western society. Indian English is characterized by greetings such as *bow my forehead, fall at your feet, blessed my hovel with the good dust of your feet;* abuses and curses such as *you eater of your masters, you of the evil stars, the incestuous sister sleeper;* blessings and flattery such as *thou shalt write from an inkwell of your shoe and my head;* and modes of address such as *cherisher of the poor, king of pearls, police-wala, mother of my daughter.*[3] The future of English in India and the rest of South Asia will be determined by a complex set of social, political, and linguistic forces. The Indian Constitution of 1950 recognized fourteen Indian languages, of which Hindi was to be the first national language. English was to serve as a transitional language with Hindi until 1965, but it has continued to be used as an official language. Whatever the stated policies may be in the future, it is certain that the English language will be spoken and written by a small but influential minority of the Indian population, including leaders in government, education, and the press. It is also certain that the variety of English recognized as standard in India—and in Pakistan—will be a distinctively South Asian variety in its pronunciation, syntax, and vocabulary. It will continue to be affected by the culture and native languages of South Asia, and in turn it will affect those languages and serve as the medium for Western influences on the culture.

Canadian English, as would be expected, has much in common with that of the United States while retaining a few features of British

---

[1] *Kanthapura* (1938; reprinted New York, 1963), p. vii. Cf. Noah Webster on American English, § 246.

[2] Braj B. Kachru, "English in South Asia," in *Current Trends in Linguistics*, 5 (The Hague, 1967), 640.

[3] Further examples are given in Braj B. Kachru, "The *Indianness* in Indian English," *Word*, 21 (1965), 391–410.

pronunciation and spelling. Where alternative forms exist the likelihood for a particular choice to be British or American varies with region, education, and age. British items such as *chips, serviette,* and *copse* tend to occur more frequently in the West, while the more common American choices *French fries, napkin,* and *grove* tend to occur in the East. British spellings such as *colour* and pronunciations such as *schedule* with an initial [ʃ] occur most frequently throughout Canada among more highly educated and older speakers.[1] In addition there are a number of words with meanings that are neither British nor American but peculiarly Canadian. Thus one finds *aboiteau* (dam), *Bluenose* (Nova Scotian), *Creditiste* (member of the Social Credit party), *Digby chicken* (smoke-cured herring), *Innuit* (Eskimo), *mukluk* (Eskimo boot), *reeve* (chairman of a municipal council), *salt-chuck* (ocean), and *skookum* (powerful, brave). The *Dictionary of Canadianisms,* published in Canada's Centennial Year, will allow historical linguists to establish in detail the sources of Canadian English.[2] Many of the earlier settlers in Canada came from the United States, and the influence of the United States has always been very strong. A writer in the *Canadian Journal* in 1857 complained of the new words adopted from us, "imported by travellers, daily circulated by American newspapers, and eagerly incorporated into the language of our Provincial press." Needless to say, he considered the influence wholly bad, and his words are still echoed by Canadians who deplore the wide circulation of American books and magazines in Canada and in recent years the further influence of movies and television. Nevertheless a linguistically informed opinion would have to concede that in language as in other activities "it is difficult to differentiate what belongs to Canada from what belongs to the United States, let alone either from what might be called General North American."[3]

230. *Spelling Reform.* In the latter part of the nineteenth century renewed interest was manifested in the problem of English spelling and the question of reform was vigorously agitated. For nearly four hundred years the English have struggled with their spelling. It was one of the chief problems which seemed to confront the language in the time of Shakespeare (see pp. 207–213), and it continued to be an issue throughout the seventeenth and to some extent in the eighteenth century. The publication

---

[1] See H. J. Warkentyne, "Contemporary Canadian English: A Report of the Survey of Canadian English," *American Speech*, 46 (1971; pub. 1975), 193–99.

[2] Walter S. Avis *et al., Dictionary of Canadianisms on Historical Principles* (Toronto, 1967).

[3] Raven I. McDavid, Jr., "Canadian English," *American Speech*, 46 (1971), 287.

in 1837 of a system of shorthand by Isaac Pitman led to his proposal of several plans of phonetic spelling for general use. In these schemes Pitman was assisted by Alexander J. Ellis, a much greater scholar. They were promoted during the 1840's by the publication of a periodical called the *Phonotypic Journal*, later changed to the *Phonetic Journal*. The Bible and numerous classic works were printed in the new spelling, and the movement aroused considerable public interest. By 1870 the English Philological Society had taken up the question, and the *Transactions* contain numerous discussions of it. Prominent members who took part in the debate included Ellis, Morris, Payne, Sweet, Furnivall, Skeat, and Murray. The discussion spread into the columns of the *Academy* and the *Athenaeum*. America became interested in the question, and in 1883 the American Philological Association recommended the adoption of a long list of new spellings approved jointly by it and the English society. Spelling Reform Associations were formed in both countries. In America men like March, Lounsbury, Grandgent, William Dean Howells, and Brander Matthews lent their support to the movement. In 1898 the National Education Association formally adopted for use in its publications twelve simplified spellings— *tho, altho, thoro, thorofare, thru, thruout, program, catalog, prolog, decalog, demagog,* and *pedagog*. Some of these have come into general use, but on the whole the public remained indifferent. In 1906 there was organized in the United States a Simplified Spelling Board, supported by a contribution from Andrew Carnegie. Their first practical step was to publish a list of 300 words for which different spellings were in use (judgement—judgment, mediaeval—medieval, etc.) and to recommend the simpler form. This was a very moderate proposal and met with some favor. Theodore Roosevelt endorsed it. But it also met with opposition, and subsequent lists which went further were not well received. Newspapers, magazines, and book publishers continued to use the traditional orthography, and though the Simplified Spelling Board continued to issue from time to time its publication, *Spelling*, until 1931, its accomplishment was slight and it eventually went out of existence.

The efforts that have been described produced only slender results, but they did succeed in stimulating public interest for a time and gained the support of various people whose names carried weight. This interest, however, was far from universal. Advocates of reform had to contend with the apathy of the public and face at the same time a certain amount of active opposition. Innate conservatism was responsible for some of it, and there are always those who feel that the etymological value of the old spelling is an asset not to be lightly relinquished.[1] An influential opinion was expressed by Henry Bradley in his paper "On the Relation of Spoken and Written Language" (1919). He held that it was a mistake to think that the sole function of writing was to represent sounds. For many people nowadays the written word is as important as the spoken word, and as we read, many words convey their meaning directly without the intermediate process of pronunciation, even mental pronunciation. To change the symbol which long practice enables us instantaneously to translate into an idea would be a handicap to many people, even though a temporary one. Besides, there are the numerous words which are distinguished in writing, though pronounced alike. For these and other reasons he was opposed to any radical change in English spelling. The history of spelling reform makes it clear that in opposing radical change he was expressing the attitude of the majority of people. It is probably safe to say that if our spelling is ever to be reformed, it must be reformed gradually and with as little disruption to the existing system as is consistent with the attainment of a reasonable end.

231. *The International Aspect.* Between the two World Wars the problem of spelling reform was approached from a different point of view. One of the most important benefits which would result from simplified spelling is that it would facilitate the learning of the language by foreigners. British and American speakers might continue to get along well enough with the old makeshift since from childhood we learn the pronunciation of words by ear. But it is different with the foreign student who generally acquires the language to a much greater extent through the eye and gets very little help from the spelling in learning to speak it properly. About 1930 a distinguished Swedish philologist, the late R. E. Zachrisson, Professor of English in the University of Uppsala, made a proposal that has much to recommend it. Believing that the many advantages that would result from having a generally accepted international language (cf. § 7) are universally admitted and that no artificial language will ever suffice for such a purpose, he declared himself in favor of English. "Among national languages," he says, "English has the strongest claim. It is spoken regularly by several hundreds of millions in four continents, and it is the official governing language of many more. It is taught as a compulsory subject in

---

[1] The case against spelling reform is stated by Sir William Craigie, *Problems of Spelling Reform* (Oxford, 1944; *S.P.E. Tract No. 63*). More recently it has been argued that predictable morphophonemic alternations (e.g., *divine* ~ *divinity*) make conventional orthography "a near optimal system for the lexical representation of English words." See Noam Chomsky and Morris Halle, *The Sound Pattern of English* (New York, 1968), p. 49.

most of the higher schools in Europe and in numerous schools in Asia. For simplicity of grammar and a cosmopolitan vocabulary it has no rival among living languages."[1] But the great hindrance to its adoption is the present spelling. Since any radical attempt at reform along strict phonetic lines involves practical difficulties and would undoubtedly meet with opposition, he suggested a compromise. Employing the present Roman alphabet without change and adopting a uniform method of indicating the principal vowels and diphthongs, it has been possible to devise a spelling that does not conflict too violently with old habits. An important feature of the method is the retention of some forty of the commonest words, mostly prepositions and pronouns, in their traditional spelling. These are designated "word signs." By this slight sacrifice of consistency a great practical advantage is gained. Nearly a third of all the words on a printed page remain unchanged, and another third are practically unchanged. How readily a passage printed in such a spelling can be read may be seen from a short specimen:

Lincoln'z Gettysburg Speech[2]

Forskor and sevn yeerz agoe our faadherz braut forth on this kontinent a nue naeshon, konseevd in liberti, and dedikaeted to the propozishon that aul men ar kreaeted eequel.

Now we are engaejd in a graet sivil wor, testing whedher that naeshon, or eni naeshon soe konseevd and so dedikaeted, kan long enduer. We are met on a graet batl-feeld of that wor. We hav kum to dedikaet a porshon of that feeld as a fienl resting-plaes for those who heer gaev their lievz that that naeshon miet liv. It is aultogedher fiting and proper that we shood do this.

But in a larjer sens, we kannot dedikaet—we kannot konsekraet— we kannot halo—this ground. The braev men, living and ded, who strugld heer, hav konsekraeted it far abuv our puur pour to ad or dotrakt. Tho wurld wil litl noot nor long remember what we sae heer, but it kan never forget what they did heer. It is for us, the living, raadher, to be dedikaeted heer to the unfinisht wurk which they who faut heer hav dhus far soe noebli advaanst. It is raadher for us to be heer dedikaeted to the graet taask remaening befor us—that from these onerd ded we taek inkreest devoeshon to that kauz for which they gaev the laast ful mezher of devoeshon; that we heer hieli rezolv that these ded shal not hav died in vaen; that this naeshon, under God, shal hav a nue burth of freedom; and that guvernment of the peepl, by the peepl, for the peepl, shal not perish from the urth.

---

[1] *Anglic, An International Language* (2nd ed., Uppsala, 1932), p. 16.
[2] Accented vowels are indicated by bold-face type when the stress falls on some other syllable than the first.

The name which Professor Zachrisson gave to this respelled English was *Anglic*. There is an advantage in the name. English-speaking people who might be unwilling to accept the new spelling for ordinary use might yet agree to it for special purposes, and foreign nations, unwilling to confer greater prestige upon a rival tongue, might more willingly consent to use a form of that tongue devised especially for international use. During the 1930's *Anglic* received influential support. It was endorsed by linguists and men in public life. A fund of $20,000 was given to aid in diffusing knowledge of it and promote its acceptance. To the present writers, it appeals greatly in principle. It seems to indicate at least the kind of solution that must be found for the problem of an international language.[1] Unfortunately, World War II put an end to its promotion, and the death of Professor Zachrisson in 1937 left it without a leader.

Among attempts to fill the void two deserve mention, both influenced by Zachrisson's proposals. Both avoided one of the most serious obstacles to the acceptance of his plan, which was the expense of using boldface type to indicate primary stress on vowels which did not occur in the first syllable of a word. Newspaper publishers were not equipped to meet this requirement, and other publishers would not have been willing to incur the additional cost. The first of the two proposals was that put forward in 1940 by the British Simplified Spelling Society under the title *New Spelling*.[2] It employed what the Society referred to as a "systematic" method of recording the pronunciation, using the ordinary Roman alphabet. As a result, about 90 percent of the words on a given page are altered, sometimes drastically. Moreover, the British system was apparently designed more for the native speaker who already knew the pronunciation than for the foreign learner who would use English as an international language. Nevertheless it came close to receiving government approval.[3] The shortcomings of the *New Spelling* were pointed out at length by Axel Wijk, who,

---

[1] An alternative suggestion for making English simple for international use is known as Basic English (cf. C. K. Ogden, *Basic English: A General Introduction with Rules and Grammar*, London, 1930). This is a selection of 850 words with which it is claimed any idea may be expressed. The use of so restricted a vocabulary, however, involves considerable juggling to express many ideas, and there are other drawbacks to the scheme. For a very sensible statement of its weaknesses see Janet R. Aiken, "'Basic' and World English," *American Speech*, 8, no. 4, 17–21. There have been many other opponents, as well as staunch advocates.

[2] W. Ripman and W. Archer, *New Spelling*, rev. Harold Orton *et al.* (5th ed., London, 1940).

[3] Through the efforts of the Society, a spelling reform bill providing a program to implement the system came before Parliament and was narrowly defeated in 1949. A similar bill was passed by Parliament in 1953 but was withdrawn in the face of opposition from the Ministry of Education.

like Zachrisson, is a Swedish scholar with a particular interest in English as an international language. His own proposal, which he calls *Regularized Inglish*, likewise uses the ordinary Roman alphabet but is willing to forego rigid phonetic representation for the sake of readability.[1] In this he succeeds. Although Wijk's system received highly favorable reviews, partly because it would require fewer changes than *Anglic* or *New Spelling*, it has had even less success than its predecessors in capturing the public imagination to the extent necessary for general acceptance. The English-speaking world does not appear as yet to be stirred to the necessity for spelling reform, and since it is the nature of language to change over time, no system can hope for immortality.

232. Purist Efforts.   The conservative in matters of language, as in politics, is a hardy perennial. We have seen many examples of the type in the course of this history. He flourished especially during the eighteenth century, but his descendants are fairly numerous in the nineteenth and scarcely less common today. He generally looks upon change with suspicion and is inclined to view all changes in language as corruptions. In retrospect he seems often a melancholy figure, fighting a losing fight, many times living to see the usages against which he fought so valiantly become universally accepted. De Quincy argued at length against the use of *implicit* in such expressions as *implicit faith* or *confidence*, wishing to restrict the word to a sense the opposite of *explicit*. The American philologist Marsh spoke against "the vulgarism of the phrase *in our midst*" and objected to a certain adjectival use of the participle. "There is at present," he says, "an inclination in England to increase the number of active, in America, of passive participles, employed with the syntax of the adjective. Thus, in England it is common to hear: 'such a thing is *very damaging*', and the phrase has been recently introduced into this country. Trench says: 'Words which had become unintelligible or *misleading*', and 'the phrase could not have been other than more or less *misleading*'; 'these are the most serious and most *recurring*'. Now, though *pleasing, gratifying, encouraging*, and many other words have long been established as adjectives, yet the cases cited from Trench strike us as unpleasant novelties."[2] Dean Alford, the author of *The Queen's English*[3] (1864), a curious composite of platitude and prejudice with occasional flashes of unexpected liberality, a book which was reprinted many times, finds much to object to, especially in the

---

[1] Axel Wijk, *Regularized English* (Stockholm, 1959).
[2] *Lectures*, I, 657.
[3] *The Queen's English* called forth a reply by G. W. Moon under the title *The Dean's English*.

English of journalism. "No man ever *shows* any feeling, but always *evinces* it. . . . Again, we never *begin* anything in the newspapers now, but always *commence*. . . . Another horrible word, which is fast getting into our language through the provincial press, is to *eventuate*. . . . *Avocation* is another monster patronised by these writers. . . . *Desirability* is a terrible word. . . . *Reliable* is hardly legitimate . . ." and so with many others. The battle over *reliable* was still being waged at the end of the nineteenth century, as over *lengthy* and *standpoint*. Often the American was accused of introducing these supposed outrages against good English, and just as often accused unjustly.[1] It is unnecessary to multiply examples which could be useful only to the future historian of human error. If we might venture a moral, it would be to point out the danger and the futility of trying to prevent the natural developments of language.

233. The Society for Pure English.   An effort which gave promise of being saved from some of the pitfalls that beset the reformers of language took the form of a *Society for Pure English* (*S.P.E.*). If it were to escape the common fate of such efforts, it would have been because of the moderateness of its aims and the fuller knowledge of the ways of language which some of its members possessed. The society was founded in 1913, but the war delayed its plans and it was not until after the Armistice that it began its activities. The original committee was composed of Henry Bradley, the distinguished philologist, Robert Bridges, the poet, Sir Walter Raleigh, Oxford Professor of English Literature, and Logan Pearsall Smith, a well-known literary man. The moving spirit was the poet laureate. In their proposals they stated their aim to be "to agree upon a modest and practical scheme for informing popular taste on sound principles, for guiding educational authorities, and for introducing into practice certain slight modifications and advantageous changes." They specifically disavowed any intention "of foolish interference with living developments." Their hope of directing the development of the vocabulary seems, in the light of history, perhaps overoptimistic, but their recognition of the popular voice inspired confidence. "Now, believing that language is or should be democratic both in character and origin, and that its best wordmakers are the uneducated classes, we would prefer vivid popular terms to the artificial creations of scientists." This at least is sound doctrine. One must likewise applaud the recognition given to local dialects, from which the standard speech has so often been enriched in the past. But most praiseworthy of all was the intention to achieve its ends not by authorita-

---

[1] See Fitzedward Hall, *Recent Exemplifications of False Philology* (New York, 1872).

tive pronouncement but by the dissemination of fact and enlightened opinion. For this purpose it proposed to issue from time to time short *Tracts* on various linguistic topics and promote the discussion of pertinent questions. In this respect the *S.P.E.* recalls the proposal of the anonymous writer of 1724 (cf. § 196). The difference lies in the fact that this society had already issued more than three score of its *Tracts* before becoming inactive.

Almost from the beginning some skepticism was expressed. Dissent appeared as early as 1926. "The 'Society for Pure English,' recently formed by the Poet Laureate, is getting a great deal of support at this moment, and is the literary equivalent of political Fascism. But at no period have the cultured classes been able to force the habit of tidiness on the nation as a whole. . . . The imaginative genius of the uneducated and half-educated masses will not be denied expression."[1] Nevertheless the movement appealed to many on both sides of the Atlantic. In 1922 a group of Americans proposed that some plan of cooperation between England and America should be devised, and a committee was appointed in England to consider the question.[2] A few years later, at a meeting of the Royal Society of Literature held in London, a number of English and American writers and scholars agreed to form an "International Council for English" to consider the problems of the common language of the English-speaking countries.[3] Such movements indicate that even if the idea of a formal academy was no longer entertained, not all hope had been given up of exercising some control over the development of the language.

234. The Oxford English Dictionary. In the more enlightened attitude of the Society for Pure English, as distinguished from most purist efforts in the past, it is impossible not to see the influence of a great work which came into being in the latter half of the nineteenth century. About 1850 the inadequacy of the existing dictionaries of the English language began to be acutely felt. Those of Johnson and Richardson, even in their later revisions, were sadly incomplete and far below the standards of modern scholarship. In 1857 at a meeting of the Philological Society in London a committee was appointed to collect words not in the dictionaries, with a view to

[1] Robert Graves, *Impenetrability, or The Proper Habit of English* (London, 1926), pp. 30–31. Cf. Basil de Selincourt: "The best and most English instinct is still that of resistance to change, and above all to any plan or method of change, any committee or academy or association to school and enlighten us." (*Pomona, or The Future of English*, London, n.d., p. 69.)

[2] The American invitation and the British answer are printed in *The Literary Review* of the New York *Evening Post*, December 16, 1922.

[3] See J. H. G. Grattan, "On Anglo-American Cultivation of Standard English," *Review of English Studies*, 3 (1927), 430–41, and Kemp Malone, "The International Council for English," *American Speech*, 3 (1928), 261–75. Nothing came of the proposal.

THE EDITORS OF THE NEW (OXFORD) ENGLISH DICTIONARY

Herbert Coleridge   Frederick James Furnivall
Sir James A. H. Murray   Henry Bradley
Sir William A. Craigie   C. T. Onions

(see § 234)

publishing a supplement to them. The committee consisted of Herbert Coleridge, Dean Trench, whose little books *English Past and Present* and *The Study of Words* had shown his interest in word history, and F. J. Furnivall, that great student and inspirer of students of early English literature. Furnivall seems to have suggested the undertaking. The most important outcome of the committee's activity was a paper read to the Society by Dean Trench, "On Some Deficiencies in our English Dictionaries." In it he laid down the historical principles on which a dictionary should be compiled. As a result of this paper the society decided that a supplement would not be satisfactory, and in January 1858 it passed resolutions calling for a new dictionary. A formal "Proposal for the Publication of a New English Dictionary by the Philological Society" was issued the following year. The two principal aims of the new project were to record every word which could be found in English from about the year 1000 and to exhibit the history of each—its forms, its various spellings, and all its uses and meanings, past and present. The last-named feature was especially to be shown by a full selection of quotations from the whole range of English writings. This would of course necessitate the systematic reading of thousands of texts. A call for volunteers was issued and met with a most gratifying response. Hundreds of readers not only from England but all over the world began to send in material. This was the nucleus out of which the future dictionary grew. The number of contributors increased, and before the last part of the dictionary was published some six million slips containing quotations had been gathered. An important by-product of the dictionary enterprise was the founding of a society for the publication of unedited texts, chiefly from the Middle Ages. It was early apparent that the words from this great mass of literature could be obtained only with great difficulty as long as much of it remained in manuscript. In order to provide the machinery for the printing of this material by subscription, Furnivall founded in 1864 the Early English Text Society. Through this society more than four hundred volumes, chiefly of Middle English texts, have been published.

The first editor appointed to deal with the mass of material being assembled was Herbert Coleridge, already mentioned. Upon his sudden death in 1861 at the age of thirty-one, he was succeeded by Furnivall, then in his thirty-sixth year. For a time work went forward with reasonable speed, but then it gradually slowed down, partly because of Furnivall's increasing absorption in other interests. Meanwhile James A. H. Murray, a British (Scottish) schoolmaster with philological tastes, had been approached by certain publishers to edit a dictionary to rival those of

2/4 Hogs that had been fed on acorns and goobers. **1888**
Century Mag. XXXVI. 770/2 Peanuts, known in the vernacular as 'goobers'.

Good (gud), *a.*, *adv.*, and *sb.* Forms: 1 gód,
good, 2–6 god, 4–6 gode, 3–4 guod(e, 4 godd(e,
goed, (gowde), 4–5 goud(e, 4–6 good(d)e, 4–8
Sc. guid(e, 4–9 *Sc.* and *north.* gud(e, (4 gwde, 5
guyd, 6 *north.* gewd), 4– good. [Com. Teut.:
OE. *gód* = OFris., OS. *gôd* (MDu. *goet*, inflected
goed-, Du. *goed*), OHG. *guot*, *kuot*, *guat*, *kuat*,
etc. (MHG. *guot*, G. *gut*), ON. *gôð-r* (Sw., Da.
god), Goth. *gôþ-s*, gen. *gôdis*:—OTeut. *gôðo-*. The
root *gôð-* is perh. an ablaut-variant of *gað-* to
bring together, to unite (see GATHER *v.*), so that
the original sense of 'good' would be that of
'fitting', 'suitable'; cf. OSl. *goditi* to be pleasing,
godĭnŭ pleasing, *godŭ* time, fitting time, Russ.
годный fit, suitable.

The adj., as in the other Teut. langs., has no regular comparative or superlative, the place of these being supplied by
BETTER, BEST; the form *goodest* occurs in jocular or playful
language. The corresponding adv. is WELL.]

A. *adj.*

The most general adj. of commendation, implying
the existence in a high, or at least satisfactory,
degree of characteristic qualities which are either
admirable in themselves or useful for some purpose.

As stronger expressions of commendation than 'good' may
be used, the latter sometimes has by comparison a modified
sense = 'fair', 'passable', 'fairly large', etc.

In OE. (as in OS. and OHG.) the opposite of 'good' was
regularly expressed by *yfel* EVIL, but in ME. this was supplemented by ILL and BAD, the latter of which is now the
more general term.

I. In the widest sense, without other specialization than such as is implied by the nature of the
object which the adj. is used to describe.

1. Of things: Having in adequate degree those
properties which a thing of the kind ought to have.

a. of material things or substances of any kind.

In early use often employed where a word of more definite
meaning would now be substituted; e.g. as an epithet of
gold or silver, = 'fine, pure'; *good stones* = 'precious stones'.

Beowulf (Z.) 1562 Eald sweord eotenisc..þæt wæpna cyst
..god ond ʒeatolic ʒiganta ʒe-weorc. *c* 1000 *Ags. Gosp.*
Matt. vii. 17 Ælc god treow byrð gode wæstmas. *c* 1205
LAY. 26070 Ardur..up ahof his gode brond. *c* 1250 *Gen. &*
Ex. 1191 A ðhusant plates of siluer god Gaf he sarra.
a 1300 *Cursor M.* 21281 Þar es god axultreis tua. *c* 1300
Seyn Julian 162 He let make of wode and col a strong fur
and good. *c* 1400 *Destr. Troy* 1366 No hede toke Of golde
ne of garmenttes, ne of goode stonys. 1484 CAXTON *Fables*
of Poge ii, [She] promysed to him that she shold gyue to
hym a ryght good dyner. 1562 J. HEYWOOD *Prov. & Epigr.*
(1867) 143 It is a good hors, that neuer stumbleth. 1597
SHAKS. *2 Hen. IV*, III. ii. 42 How a good Yoke of Bullocks
at Stamford Fayre? 1599 H. BUTTES *Dyets drie Dinner*
H viij b, Veale..Nourisheth excellently: makes verie good
blood. 1639 DU VERGER tr. *Camus' Admir. Events* 8 We
thinke nothing to good for them. 1698 FRYER *Acc. E. India*
& *P.* 6 A special good Anchor of 2400 weight. 1769 MRS.
RAFFALD *Eng. Housekpr.* (1778) 151 Lay over it a good
cold paste. 1789 BLIGH *Narr. Bounty* (1790) 52 One half of
us slept on shore by a good fire.

b. of food or drink. (Often with mixture of senses
11 a, 12.) (*To keep*) *good*: untainted, fit to eat.

805-31 in *O. E. Texts* 444, xxx ombra godes uuelesces
aloð. 971 [see 12]. *c* 1200 ORMIN 15408 Þin forrme win

Webster and Worcester. After the abandonment of this project Murray was drawn into the Philological Society's enterprise, and in 1879 a formal agreement was entered into with the Oxford University Press whereby this important publishing house was to finance and publish the society's dictionary and Murray was to be its editor. From this time on the work was pushed with new energy and in 1884 the first installment, covering part of the letter A, was issued. By 1900 four and a half volumes had been published, extending as far as the letter H. World War I made serious inroads in the dictionary staff, and progress was for a time retarded. But in 1928 the final section was issued, just seventy years after the Philological Society had passed its now notable resolution looking toward "A New English Dictionary."

Dr. Murray did not live to see the completion of the task which he had undertaken. But his genuine scholarship and sure judgment in laying down the lines along which the work should be carried out were of the greatest importance to its success. In 1887 he secured the services of Henry Bradley, then comparatively unknown, but instantly recognized through the merit of a long review which he wrote of the first installment. In 1888 he became a co-editor. In 1897 William A. Craigie, recently called to Oxford from the University of St. Andrews, joined the staff, and in 1901 became a third editor. Finally, in 1914, Charles T. Onions, who had been working with Dr. Murray since 1895, was appointed the fourth member of the editorial staff. Two of the editors were knighted in recognition of their services to linguistic scholarship, Murray in 1908 and Craigie in 1928. But the list of editors does not tell the story of the large number of skillful and devoted workers who sifted the material and did much preliminary work on it. Nor would the enterprise have been possible at all without the generous support of the Oxford University Press and the voluntary help of thousands who furnished quotations. The name by which the dictionary was originally known, *A New English Dictionary on Historical Principles* (*NED*), has clung to it, although in 1895 the title *The Oxford English Dictionary* (*OED*) was added and has since been widely used as an alternative designation. The completed work fills ten large volumes, occupies 15,487 pages, and treats 240,165 main words. In 1933 a supplementary volume was published, containing additions and corrections accumulated during the forty-four years over which the publication of the original work extended. The first two volumes of a new four-volume Supplement, which will absorb and extend the 1933 Supplement, were published in 1972–76, and the recent micrographic reproduction of the complete work in two volumes has made the dictionary available to many who could not afford it in its original format.

The influence of this great publication—the greatest dictionary of any language in the world—has been far-reaching. Its authority was recognized from the appearance of the first installment. It has provided a wealth of exact data on which many questions relating to the history of the language have been resolved. But it has had a further important effect which was scarcely contemplated by the little committee of the Philological Society to which it owed its inception. It has profoundly influenced the attitude of many people toward language, and toward the English language in particular. By exhibiting the history of words and idioms, their forms and various spellings, their changes of meaning, the way words rise and fall in the levels of usage, and many other phenomena, it has increased our linguistic perspective and taught us to view many questions of language in a more scientific and less dogmatic way. When the historian of English a century or two hence attempts to evaluate the effect of the Oxford Dictionary on the English language he may quite possibly say that it exerted its chief force in making us historically minded about matters of English speech.

235. *Grammatical Tendencies.* The several factors already discussed as giving stability to English grammar (§ 152)—the printing press, popular education, improvements in travel and communication, social consciousness—have been particularly effective in the century just passed. Very few changes in grammatical forms and conventions are to be observed. There has been some schoolmastering of the language. The substitution of *you were* for *you was* in the singular occurs about 1820, and *it is I* is now often considered a social test where propriety is expected. What was left of the subjunctive mood in occasional use has disappeared except in conditions contrary to fact (*if I were you*). Some tendency toward loss of inflection, although we have but little to lose, is noticeable in informal speech. The colloquial *he don't* represents an attempt to eliminate the ending of the third person singular and reduce this verb in the negative to a uniform *do* in the present tense. Likewise the widespread practice of disregarding the objective case form *whom* in the interrogative (*Who do you want?*) illustrates the same impulse. Though many people are shocked by the latter "error," it has a long and honorable history. Shakespeare often commits it, and historically the reduction of case forms in this pronoun is as justifiable as that in the second person (*you* for *ye;* cf. § 182).[1] Occasionally a new grammatical convention may be seen springing up. The *get* passive (*he got hurt*) is largely a nineteenth-century development, called into being because *he is hurt* is too static, *he became hurt* too formal. This construction

---

[1] Cf. J. S. Kenyon, "On *Who* and *Whom*," *American Speech*, 5 (1930), 253–55.

is noted only from 1652[1] and it is unusual before the nineteenth century. One other tendency is sufficiently important to be noticed separately, the extension of verb-adverb combinations discussed in the following paragraph.

236. *Verb-adverb Combinations.* An important characteristic of the modern vocabulary is the large number of expressions like *set out, gather up, put off, bring in,* made up of a common verb, often of one syllable, combined with an adverb.[2] They suggest comparison with verbs having separable prefixes in German, and to a smaller extent with English verbs like *withstand* and *overcome.* The latter were much more common in Old English than they are today, and we have seen (§§ 138–39) that their gradual disuse was one of the consequences of the Norman Conquest. Old English made but slight use of the modern type, and during the Middle English period the large number of new verbs from French seems to have retarded for a time what would probably have been a normal and rapid development. Such combinations as we do find before the modern period are generally expressions in which the meaning is the fairly literal sense of the verb and the adverb in the combination (*climb up, fall down*), often a mere intensification of the idea expressed by the simple verb. One of the most interesting features of such combinations in modern times, however, is the large number of figurative and idiomatic senses in which they have come to be used. Familiar examples are *bring about* (cause or accomplish), *catch on* (comprehend), *give out* (become exhausted), *keep on* (continue), *put up with* (tolerate), *hold up* (rob), *lay off* (cease to employ), *turn over* (surrender), *size up* (estimate), *let up* (cease), *bid up, bid in,* and *knock down* with their meanings at an auction sale. Another is the extensive use, especially in colloquial speech, of these verb-adverb combinations as nouns: *blowout, cave-in, holdup, runaway.*[3]

It will be noticed that many of these expressions are substitutes for single verbs such as *comprehend, continue, surrender,* etc., of more learned or formal character, and the interesting observation has been made that the vocabulary has thus been pursuing a development similar to that which took place in English grammar at an earlier period and which

---

[1] *OED,* s.v. *get,* 34b.

[2] On this subject see A. G. Kennedy, *The Modern English Verb-Adverb Combination* (Stanford University, 1920), and Bruce Fraser, *The Verb-Particle Combination in English* (corrected ed., New York, 1976).

[3] See Edwin R. Hunter, "Verb + adverb = noun," *American Speech,* 22 (1947), 115–19; U. Lindelöf, *English Verb-adverb Groups Converted into Nouns* (Helsingfors, 1937; *Societas Scientiarum Fennica, Commentationes Humanarum Litterarum,* vol. 9, no. 5).

changed the language from a synthetic to an analytic one.[1] It is also apparent that many of the expressions among the examples given are more or less colloquial and betray clearly their popular origin. Many others are slang or considered inelegant. The single adverb *up* enters into such combinations as *bang up, bring up, brace up, cough up, dig up, dish up, drum up, fly up, gum up, hash up, jack up, loosen up, pass up, perk up, scrape up, shut up, spruce up, whack up,* and we have recently seen the frequent use of *crack down.* Every one in America will recognize the familiar meaning that attaches to these expressions in colloquial speech.

Opposition is sometimes expressed toward the extensive growth of these verb-adverb combinations, and not only toward the less reputable ones. Even among those which are universally accepted in both the spoken and written language there are many in which the adverb is, strictly speaking, redundant. Others, to which this objection cannot be made, are thought to discourage the use of more formal or exact verbs by which the same idea could be conveyed. But it is doubtful whether the objection is well founded. Usually the verb-adverb combination conveys a force or a shade of meaning that could not be otherwise expressed, and there can be no question about the fact that the flexibility of the language, to say nothing of its picturesqueness, has been enormously increased. The twenty verbs *back, blow, break, bring, call, come, fall, get, give, go, hold, lay, let, make, put, run, set, take, turn,* and *work* have entered into 155 combinations with over 600 distinct meanings or uses.[2] The historian of language can view this development only as a phenomenon going on actively for over four hundred years, one which shows no tendency to lose its vitality and which has its roots in the most permanent and irresistible source of linguistic phenomena, the people.

237. *A Liberal Creed.* In closing this chapter on the language of our own day it may not be inappropriate to suggest what should be an enlightened modern attitude toward linguistic questions. It has often been necessary in the course of this book to chronicle the efforts of well-meaning but misguided persons who hoped to make over the language in accordance with their individually conceived pattern. And we still find all too often provincialism and prejudice masquerading as scientific truth in discussions of language by men and women who would blush to betray an equal intolerance in the music or furniture or social conventions of other parts of the world than their own. Doubtless the best safeguard against prejudice is knowledge, and some knowledge of the history of English in the past is

[1] Kennedy, p. 42.
[2] Kennedy, p. 35.

necessary to an enlightened judgment in matters affecting present use. Such knowledge warns us to beware of making arbitrary decisions on questions which only time can settle. It teaches us that reason is but a sorry guide in many matters of grammar and idiom, and that the usage of educated speakers and writers is the only standard in language for the educated. It should make us tolerant of colloquial and regional forms, since like the common people, they claim their right to exist by virtue of an ancient lineage. And finally, it should prepare us for further changes since language lives only on the lips and fingers of living people and must change as the needs of people in expressing themselves change. But knowledge of the ways of language in the past is not all that is necessary. Knowledge must be coupled with tolerance, and especially tolerance toward usage that differs from our own. We must avoid thinking that there is some one region where the "best" English is spoken, and particularly that that region is the one in which we ourselves live. We must not think that the English of London or Oxford, or Boston or Philadelphia, is the norm by which all other speech must be judged, and that in whatever respects other speech differs from this norm it is inferior. Good English is the usage—sometimes the divided usage—of cultivated people in that part of the English-speaking world in which one happens to be.

BIBLIOGRAPHY

The best source of information about the growth of the vocabulary in the nineteenth century and since is the *New English Dictionary*, with the subsequently published Supplements. For the ways in which changes in the vocabulary take place, excellent treatments are J. B. Greenough and G. L. Kittredge, *Words and Their Ways in English Speech* (New York, 1901); George H. McKnight, *English Words and Their Background* (New York, 1923); and J. A. Sheard, *The Words We Use* (New York, 1954). A regular department of the quarterly journal *American Speech* is "Among New Words," and annual lists appear in the *Britannica Book of the Year*. For many examples of common words from proper names, see Ernest Weekley, *Words and Names* (London, 1932), and Eric Partridge, *Name into Word* (2nd ed., New York, 1950). A readable account of the growth of scientific English is Theodore H. Savory, *The Language of Science* (2nd ed., London, 1967). Principles of English word-formation are explained and fully illustrated in Herbert Koziol, *Handbuch der englischen Wortbildungslehre* (2nd ed., Heidelberg, 1972); Hans Marchand, *The Categories and Types of Present-Day English Word-Formation* (2nd ed., Munich, 1969); and Valerie Adams, *An Introduction to Modern English Word-Formation* (London, 1973). The general subject of change of meaning is treated in Michel Bréal, *Semantics: Studies in the Science of Meaning* (Eng. trans., New York, 1900), and Stephen Ullmann, *The Principles of Semantics* (2nd ed., Oxford, 1957). Gustav Stern's *Meaning and Change of Meaning, with Special Reference to the English Language* (Göteborg, 1931) is valuable but rather difficult. More accessible are the important work of C. K.

Ogden and I. A. Richards, *The Meaning of Meaning* (10th ed., New York, 1949), and of Stephen Ullmann, *Semantics: An Introduction to the Science of Meaning* (Oxford, 1962). On degeneration and regeneration there are two important monographs: H. Schreuder, *Pejorative Sense Development in English* (Groningen, 1929), and G. A. Van Dongen, *Amelioratives in English* (Rotterdam, 1933). Recent advances in social dialectology are discussed by William Labov, *Sociolinguistic Patterns* (Philadelphia, 1972); his methods have influenced many studies, including in England, Peter Trudgill, *The Social Differentiation of English in Norwich* (Cambridge, 1974). William Matthews, *Cockney Past and Present: A Short History of the Dialect of London* (London, 1938) is a treatment of a perennially interesting subject. For English dialects in general, see G. L. Brook, *English Dialects* (London, 1963), and Martyn F. Wakelin, *English Dialects: An Introduction* (London, 1972), which may be supplemented by Joseph Wright's *English Dialect Grammar* (Oxford, 1905) and his invaluable *English Dialect Dictionary* (6 vols., London, 1898–1905). The Introduction and twelve books of Basic Material in the *Survey of English Dialects*, ed. Harold Orton and Eugen Dieth (Leeds, 1962–), have now been published, and a description of the full projected series appears in Harold Orton, "A Linguistic Atlas of England," *Advancement of Science*, 27 (1970), 80–96. The corresponding survey for Scotland has published the first volume of its *Linguistic Atlas of Scotland: Scots Section*, ed. J. Y. Mather and H. H. Speitel (Hamden, Conn., 1975). Various aspects of the Scottish dialect are treated in *The Scottish Tongue: A Series of Lectures on the Vernacular Language of Lowland Scotland*, by W. A. Craigie *et al.* (London, 1924), and the pronunciation is described in William Grant, *The Pronunciation of English in Scotland* (Cambridge, 1913). The two major Scottish dictionaries are still in progress: William A. Craigie and A. J. Aitken, *A Dictionary of the Older Scottish Tongue* (Chicago, 1931–), and William Grant and David D. Murison, *The Scottish National Dictionary* (Edinburgh, 1931–). One of the few studies of Anglo-Welsh is an essay by David R. Parry, "Anglo-Welsh Dialects in South-East Wales," in a helpful anthology edited by Martyn F. Wakelin, *Patterns in the Folk Speech of the British Isles* (London, 1972), pp. 140–63. Essays on the English of Northern Ireland are collected in *Ulster Dialects: An Introductory Symposium* (Belfast, 1964), which may be used to supplement two older studies, P. W. Joyce, *English as We Speak It in Ireland* (Dublin, 1910), a popular but suggestive work, and Jeremiah S. Hogan, *The English Language in Ireland* (Dublin, 1927). Good introductions to Australasian English are G. W. Turner, *The English Language in Australia and New Zealand* (London, 1966), and W. S. Ramson, ed., *English Transported: Essays on Australasian English* (Canberra, 1970). The only historical dictionary of Australian English is E. E. Morris, *Austral English* (London, 1898). More recent studies are by S. J. Baker, *The Australian Language* (2nd ed., Sydney, 1966), whose scholarly methods have been criticized, and W. S. Ramson, *Australian English: An Historical Study of the Vocabulary, 1788–1898* (Canberra, 1966). Charles Pettman's *Africanderisms* (London, 1913) will eventually be superseded by the forthcoming work described in *Towards a Dictionary of South African English on Historical Principles*, report no. 3 of the Dictionary Committee (Grahamstown, 1971). For South African pronunciation there are descriptions by David Hopwood, *South African English Pronunciation* (Cape Town and Johannesburg, 1928), and L. W. Lanham, *The Pronunciation of South African English: A Phonetic-Phonemic Introduction* (Cape Town, 1967). Useful essays describing the problems and prospects of English in newly independent African states are edited by John Spencer in *The English Language in West Africa* (New York, 1971). A *Dictionary of West African English* is being prepared under the editorship of Peter Young. The only dictionary of Indian English is now dated, Henry Yule and A. C. Burnell, *Hobson-Jobson: A Glossary of Colloquial Anglo-Indian Words and Phrases*, rev. William Crooke (London, 1903). A full survey of English in India, Pakistan, and Ceylon is Braj B. Kachru, "English in South Asia," in *Current Trends in Linguistics*, vol. 5, *Linguistics in South Asia*, ed. Thomas A. Sebeok *et al.* (The Hague, 1967), 627–78. The same series contains an authoritative treatment of Canadian English by Walter S. Avis, "The English Language in Canada," in vol. 10, *Linguistics in North America* (1973), 40–75. Avis is also the editor-in-chief of *A Dictionary of Canadianisms on Historical Principles* (Toronto, 1967). An admirable discussion of the English language in the Caribbean is Frederic G. Cassidy, *Jamaica Talk: Three Hundred Years of the English Language in Jamaica* (2nd ed., London, 1971). The history of spelling reform is given in R. E. Zachrisson, "Four Hundred Years of English Spelling Reform," *Studia Neophilologica*, 4 (1931–1932), 1–19, largely incorporated in his *Anglic: An International Language* (2nd ed., Uppsala, 1932), and Axel Wijk, *Regularized English: An Investigation into the English Spelling Reform Problem with a New, Detailed Plan for a Possible Solution* (Stockholm, 1959). For the earlier part of the period covered in this chapter, Hans Aarsleff, *The Study of Language in England, 1780–1860* (Princeton, 1967) is of interest, and for Sir James Murray's labors on the *OED*, a recent, moving account is by his granddaughter, K. M. Elisabeth Murray, *Caught in the Web of Words* (New Haven, 1977).

[11]

The English Language in America

238. *The Settlement of America.* The English language was brought to America by colonists from England who settled along the Atlantic seaboard in the seventeenth century. It was therefore the language spoken in England at that time, the language spoken by Shakespeare and Milton and Bunyan. In the peopling of this country three great periods of European immigration are to be distinguished. The first extends from the settlement of Jamestown in 1607 to the end of colonial times. This may be put conveniently at 1787, when Congress finally approved the Federal Constitution, or better, 1790, when the last of the colonies ratified it and the first census was taken. At this date the population numbered approximately four million people, 95 percent of whom were living east of the Appalachian Mountains, and 90 percent were from various parts of the British Isles. The second period covers the expansion of the original thirteen colonies west of the Appalachians, at first into the South and into the Old Northwest Territory, ending finally at the Pacific. This era may be said to close with the Civil War, about 1860, and was marked by the arrival of fresh immigrants from two great sources, Ireland and Germany. The failure of the potato crop in Ireland in 1845 precipitated a wholesale exodus to America, a million and a half emigrants coming in the decade or so that followed. At about the same time the failure of the revolution in Germany (1848) resulted in the migration of an equal number of Germans. Many of the latter settled in certain central cities such as Cincinnati, Milwaukee, and St. Louis, or became farmers in the Middle West. The third period, the period since the Civil War, is marked by an important change in the source from which our immigrants have been derived. In the two preceding periods, and indeed up to about 1890, the British Isles and the countries of northern Europe furnished from 75 to 90 percent of all who came to this country. Even in the last quarter of the nineteenth century more than a million Scandinavians, about one-fifth of the total population of Norway and Sweden, settled here, mainly in the upper Mississippi valley. But since about 1890 great numbers from southern Europe and the Slavic countries have poured in. Just before World War I, Italians alone were admitted to the number of more than 300,000 a year, and of our annual immigration of more than a million, representatives of the east and south European countries constituted close to 75 percent.

Outside the patterns of European immigration was the forced immigration of Africans through the slave trade that began in the seventeenth century and continued until the mid-nineteenth. There are presently some 25 million blacks in the United States, mostly settled in the South and in the larger cities of the North. Finally, one should note the influx during the mid-twentieth century of Mexican, Puerto Rican, and other Hispanic immigrants. Extreme economic imbalances among the countries of the Western Hemisphere have caused a sharp increase in migration, both legal and illegal, to the United States during the past decade.

For the student of language the most important period of immigration to America is the first. It was the early colonists who brought us our speech and established its form. Those who came later were largely assimilated in a generation or two, and though their influence may have been felt, it is difficult to define and seems not to have been great.[1] It is to these early settlers that we must devote our chief attention if we would understand the history of the English language in America.

239. *The Thirteen Colonies.* The colonial settlement, the settlement of the thirteen colonies along the Atlantic seaboard, covered a long narrow strip of land extending from Maine to Georgia. This area is familiarly divided into three sections—New England, the Middle Atlantic states, and the South Atlantic states. The earliest New England settlements were made around Massachusetts Bay. Between 1620 and 1640 some two hundred vessels came from England to New England bringing upward of 15,000 immigrants. By the latter year this number had grown to about 25,000 inhabitants. The majority of the settlers came first to Massachusetts, but in a very few years groups in search of cheaper land or greater freedom began to push up and down the coast and establish new communities. In

---

[1] On this question see two papers by E. C. Hills, "The English of America and the French of France," *American Speech*, 4 (1928–1929), 43–47; "Linguistic Substrata of American English," *ibid.*, 431–33. The foreign born in this country in the 1970 census amounted to about 5 percent.

this way Connecticut got its start as early as 1634, and the coasts of Maine and Rhode Island were early occupied. New Hampshire was settled more slowly because of the greater hostility of the Indians. New England was not then misnamed: practically all of the early colonists came from England. East Anglia was the stronghold of English Puritanism, and, as we shall see, there is fair evidence that about two-thirds of the early settlers around Massachusetts Bay came from the eastern counties.

The settlement of the Middle Atlantic states was somewhat different. Dutch occupation of New York began in 1614, but the smallness of Holland did not permit of a large migration, and the number of Dutch in New York was never great. At the time of the seizure of the colony by the English in 1664 the population numbered only about 10,000 and a part of it was English. After the Revolution a considerable movement into the colony took place from New England, chiefly from Connecticut. New York City even then, though small and relatively unimportant, had a rather cosmopolitan population of merchants and traders. New Jersey was almost wholly English. The eastern part was an offshoot of New England, but on the Delaware River there was a colony of Quakers direct from England. At Burlington opposite sides of the town were occupied by a group from Yorkshire and a group from London. Pennsylvania had a mixed population of English Quakers, some Welsh, and many Scotch-Irish and Germans. William Penn's activities date from 1681. Philadelphia was founded the following year, prospered, and grew so rapidly that its founder lived to see it the largest city in the colonies. From about 1720 a great wave of migration set in from Ulster to Pennsylvania, the number of emigrants being estimated at nearly 50,000. Many of these, finding the desirable lands already occupied by the English, moved on down the mountain valleys to the southwest. Their enterprise and pioneering spirit made them the most important element among the vigorous frontiersmen who opened up this part of the South and later other territories farther west into which they pushed. But there were still many of them in Pennsylvania, and Franklin was probably close to the truth in his estimate that in about 1750 one-third of the state was English, one-third Scotch, and one-third German. Germantown, the first outpost of the Germans in Pennsylvania, was founded in 1683 by an agreement with Penn. In the beginning of the eighteenth century Protestants in the districts along the Rhine known as the Palatinate were subject to such persecution that they began coming in large numbers to America. Most of them settled in Pennsylvania, where, likewise finding the desirable lands around Philadelphia already occupied by the English, they went up the Lehigh and Susquehanna valleys and formed communities sufficiently homogeneous to long retain their own language. Even today "Pennsylvania Dutch" is spoken by scattered groups among their descendants. Lancaster was the largest inland town in any of the colonies. Maryland, the southernmost of the middle colonies, and in some ways actually a southern colony, was originally settled by English Catholics under a charter to Lord Baltimore, but they were later outnumbered by new settlers. The Maryland back country was colonized largely by people from Pennsylvania, among whom were many Scotch-Irish and Germans.

The nucleus of the South Atlantic settlements was the tidewater district of Virginia. Beginning with the founding of Jamestown in 1607, the colony attracted a miscellaneous group of adventurers from all parts of England. It is said, however, that the eastern counties were largely represented. There were political refugees, royalists, Commonwealth soldiers, deported prisoners, indentured servants, and many Puritans. The population was pretty mixed both as to social class and geographical source. From Virginia colonists moved south into North Carolina. In South Carolina the English settlers were joined by a large number of French Huguenots. Georgia, which was settled late, was originally colonized by English debtors who, it was hoped, might succeed if given a fresh start in a new country. It was the most sparsely populated of any of the thirteen colonies. The western part of all these South Atlantic colonies was of very different origin from the districts along the coast. Like western Maryland, the interior was largely settled by Scotch-Irish and Germans who moved from western Pennsylvania down the Shenandoah valley and thus into the back country of Virginia, the Carolinas, and even Georgia.

240. *The Middle West*. The country from the Alleghenies to the Mississippi is divided into a northern and a southern half by the Ohio River. South of the Ohio this territory belonged originally to the colonies along the Atlantic, whose boundary in theory extended west to the Mississippi. North of the Ohio was the Old Northwest Territory. The settlement of this whole region illustrates strikingly the spread and inter-mingling of elements in the population of the original thirteen colonies. Kentucky was an offspring of Virginia with many additions from Pennsylvania and North Carolina. Tennessee was an extension of western North Carolina with the same strongly Scotch-Irish coloring that we have seen in this part of the parent colony. Alabama and Mississippi were settled from the districts around them, from Virginia, the Carolinas, Georgia, and Tennessee. Nearly half the population, however, was black. Louisiana, through being so long a French colony, had a population largely French, but even before the Louisiana Purchase there were numerous Scotch and English settlers from the mountainous parts of the southern colonies, and after 1803 this migration greatly increased. Missouri likewise had many French, especially in St. Louis, but as a territory in which slavery was permitted it had numerous settlers from its neighbors to the east, Kentucky and Tennessee, and even Virginia and North Carolina. These soon outnumbered the French in this region.

The Old Northwest Territory began to be opened up shortly after the Revolution by settlers coming from three different directions. One path began in New England and upper New York, earlier colonized from western New England. The movement from this region was greatly stimulated by the opening of the Erie Canal in 1825. A second route brought colonists from Pennsylvania and settlers from other states who came through Pennsylvania. The third crossed the Ohio from Kentucky and West Virginia and accounts for the large number of southerners who migrated into the territory.[1] In 1850 the southerners in Indiana outnumbered those from New England and the Middle States two to one. Michigan and Wisconsin were the only states in this territory with a population predominantly of New England origin. In the latter part of the nineteenth century the Old Northwest Territory and the upper Mississippi valley received large numbers of German and Scandinavian immigrants whose coming has been mentioned above.

241. *The Far West.* The Louisiana Purchase in 1803 opened up the first of the vast territories beyond the Mississippi. From here fur traders, missionaries, and settlers followed the Oregon trail into the Pacific Northwest, and the Santa Fe trail into the sparsely populated Spanish territory in the Southwest. After the Mexican War and the treaty with Great Britain (1846) establishing the forty-ninth parallel as the northern boundary of the United States to the Pacific, when the territory of this country extended to the ocean, it was only a question of time before the Far West would be more fully occupied. Oregon in 1860 had a population of 30,000 pioneers. About half of them had come up from Missouri and farther south, from Kentucky and Tennessee; the other half were largely of New England stock. The discovery of gold in California in 1848 resulted in such a rush

---

[1] "A good illustration of this migration is Daniel Boone, himself of English stock, who was born on the Delaware only a few miles above Philadelphia. The Boone family soon moved to Reading. Thence drifting southwestward with his compatriots, Daniel Boone settled in the North Carolina uplands, along the valley of the Yadkin, then passed beyond into Kentucky, and, after that location began to be civilized, went on as a pioneer to Missouri. His son appears a little later as one of the early settlers of Kansas, his grandson as a pioneer in Colorado." (Madison Grant, *The Conquest of a Continent* [New York, 1933] pp. 122–23.)

to the gold fields that in 1849 the 2,000 Americans that constituted the population in February had become 53,000 by December. When the territory was admitted to the Union as a state in September 1851, its population was at least 150,000, and in not much more than another twelve months it had become a quarter of a million. Every part of America was represented in it.

242. *Uniformity of American English.* In this necessarily rapid survey some emphasis has been laid on the geographical and ethnic groups represented in the settlement of different parts of the country. The reason for this emphasis will appear later (§ 250). But it has been equally the intention to show that except for a few districts, such as the region around Massachusetts Bay and the tidewater section of Virginia, the most prominent characteristic of the occupation of the United States is the constant mingling of settlers from one part with settlers from other parts. Not only were practically all sections of the British Isles represented in the original colonists, with some admixture of the French and the Germans, but as each new section was opened up it attracted colonists from various districts which had become overcrowded or uncongenial to them. Thus colonists from Massachusetts went north into Maine and New Hampshire and south into Rhode Island and Connecticut. Others moved from New England into New York, New Jersey, and colonies as far south as Georgia, as when a body from Dorchester in Massachusetts, known as the Dorchester Society, moved to Georgia in 1752. The Ulster Scots seem to have been of a more roving disposition or a more pioneering spirit than the English, and their movement from Pennsylvania to the South, from there into the Old Northwest Territory, and eventually into the Pacific Northwest seems to indicate that they were generally to be found on each advancing frontier. Except for a few of the larger cities with numerous recent and as yet unassimilated immigrants, and except for certain localities such as Wisconsin and Minnesota where the settlement of large groups of Scandinavians and Germans took place in the nineteenth century, there is probably nowhere a European population of such size and extent with so homogeneous a character.[1]

---

[1] The history of black Americans is strikingly different. The institution of slavery during the seventeenth, eighteenth, and nineteenth centuries, the decades of segregation in the South following the Civil War, and the isolation of blacks in northern cities during the present century have produced a major anomaly in the structure and mobility of American society. This anomaly has had its corresponding linguistic effects, which require separate treatment below (§ 250.8). The uniformity of the language of the majority of Americans, as described in the following paragraphs, makes the contrast with the English of many black Americans more evident than it would appear in a linguistically diverse society.

Linguistically the circumstances under which the American population spread over the country have had one important consequence. It has repeatedly been observed, in the past as well as at the present day, especially by travelers from abroad, that the English spoken in America shows a high degree of uniformity. Those who are familiar with the pronounced dialectal differences that mark the popular speech of different parts of England will know that there is nothing comparable to these differences in the United States. This was the object of remark as early as 1781, when Dr. Witherspoon, the Scottish president of Princeton, observed of the common people in America that "being much more unsettled, and moving frequently from place to place, they are not so liable to local peculiarities either in accent or phraseology."[1] Isaac Candler, an Englishman who traveled in America in 1822–1823, wrote: "The United States having been peopled from different parts of England and Ireland, the peculiarities of the various districts have in a great measure ceased. As far as pronunciation is concerned, the mass of people speak better English, than the mass of people in England. This I know will startle some, but its correctness will become manifest when I state, that in no part, except in those occupied by the descendants of the Dutch and German settlers, is any unintelligible jargon in vogue. We hear nothing so bad in America as the Suffolk whine, the Yorkshire clipping, or the Newcastle guttural. We never hear the letter H aspirated improperly, nor omitted to be aspirated where propriety requires it. The common pronunciation approximates to that of the well educated class of London and its vicinity."[2] We must not be misled by his statement about the goodness of American English. He does not mean that equally good English was not spoken in England. What he says is that in America there was little local variation and in the matter of pronunciation there was a more general conformance to what he conceived to be an educated standard. At about the same time James Fenimore Cooper spoke to much the same effect. "If the people of this country," he said, "were like the people of any other country on earth, we should be speaking at this moment a great variety of nearly unintelligible patois; but, in point of fact, the people of the United States, with the exception of a few of German and French descent, speak, as a body, an incomparably better English than the people of the mother country. There is not, probably, a man (of English descent) born in this country, who would not be perfectly intelligible to all whom he should meet in the streets of London, though a vast number of those he met in the

---

[1] In a paper contributed to the *Pennsylvania Journal*, conveniently reprinted in M. M. Mathews, *The Beginnings of American English* (Chicago, 1931), p. 16.
[2] *A Summary View of America ... by an Englishman* (London, 1824), p. 327.

streets of London would be nearly unintelligible to him. In fine, we speak our language, as a nation, better than any other people speak their language. When one reflects on the immense surface of country that we occupy, the general accuracy, in pronunciation and in the use of words, is quite astonishing. This resemblance in speech can only be ascribed to the great diffusion of intelligence, and to the inexhaustible activity of the population, which, in a manner, destroys space."[1] We may excuse the patriotism that inspired some of these remarks, remembering that Cooper was writing at a time when Americans often felt the need for dwelling on the advantages of their country, but the fact remains that the uniformity of American English seems to have been something generally recognized at the beginning of the nineteenth century. Indeed, in another passage Cooper expresses the opinion that such local differences as did exist and that could be detected "by a practised ear" were diminishing. "It is another peculiarity of our institutions, that the language of the country, instead of becoming more divided into provincial dialects, is becoming, not only more assimilated to itself as a whole, but more assimilated to a standard which sound general principles, and the best authorities among our old writers, would justify. The distinctions in speech between New England and New York, or Pennsylvania, or any other state, were far greater twenty years ago than they are now."[2]

The merging of regional differences through the mixture of the population that has been described has been promoted since by a certain mobility that characterizes the American people. It has been said that it is unusual to find an adult American living in the place in which he was born, and while this is an obvious exaggeration, it is nevertheless true that change of abode is distinctly common. The very extensiveness of the country, moreover, tends to create an attitude of mind that may almost be said to diminish space. We are so accustomed to distance that we disregard it. Witness the willingness of the westerner to make trips of five hundred or a thousand miles upon slight occasions, or to drive across the continent for a vacation. In the past we have had to reckon with the influence of Webster's spelling book (see § 248) and Lindley Murray's grammar, and at all times public education in America has been a standardizing influence. We respect in language the authority of those who are supposed to know;[3] it is part of our faith in specialists, whether in surgeons or "publicity experts."

---

[1] *Notions of the Americans* (2 vols., London, 1828), II, 164–65.

[2] *Ibid.*, II, 165–66.

[3] "If pressed to say definitely what good American English is, I should say, it is the English of those who are believed by the greater number of Americans to know what good English is." R. O. Williams, *Our Dictionaries* (New York, 1890), p. iii.

And we must not forget the American instinct of conformity and the fact that we readily accept standardization in linguistic matters as in houses, automobiles, and other things.[1]

As a result of the homogeneity of the English language in America we have a standard that rests upon general use, albeit a standard for which complete uniformity cannot be claimed.[2] In New England and the South there are particular differences, as of pronunciation, that are easily recognized and that will be pointed out later. They distinguish these sections from the remaining two-thirds of the country. But just because they can be perceived, it is easy to exaggerate them while losing sight of the great majority of features which the speech of all parts of the country shares in common. Such differences as characterize the pronunciation of New England, the South, and the Middle States and the West are not defections from the general standard but variations within it. Even the black English vernacular, the most conspicuous example of a nonstandard dialect, diverges from the uniformity of American English in the most insignificant ways (see § 250.8). The relatively few features which characterize the black English vernacular, some of which are features of standard Southern English, are more important as a social reality than as a linguistic reality.[3] The features are perceived as more pervasive than they actually are, and a few occurrences of patterns such as *He tired* or *She don't be busy* evoke in the listener's mind a full stereotype with its associations, negative or positive, depending on the listener's nonlinguistic sympathies. But regarding the linguistic insignificance of the features themselves, sociolinguists and traditional dialectologists have made the same point. William Labov

---

[1] This is not to deny that currents contrary to standardization have always run through American speech communities. Recent studies in the sociology of language, including especially Joshua Fishman's descriptions of immigrant languages in the United States, remind us of an often neglected point. Fishman writes: "The two processes—de-ethnization and Americanization, on the one hand, and cultural-linguistic self-maintenance, on the other—are equally ubiquitous throughout all of American history. They are neither necessarily opposite sides of the same coin nor conflicting processes. Frequently the same individuals and groups have been simultaneously devoted to both in different domains of behavior. However, as a nation we have paid infinitely more attention to the Americanization process than to the self-maintenance process." *Language Loyalty in the United States* (The Hague, 1966), p. 15.

[2] In his *Dissertations on the English Language* (1789) Noah Webster wrote, "The two points therefore, which I conceive to be the basis of a standard in speaking, are these: *universal undisputed practice*, and the *principle of analogy* [on the doctrine of *analogy* in the eighteenth century, see § 201]. *Universal practice* is generally, perhaps always, a rule of propriety; and in disputed points, where people differ in opinion and practice, *analogy* should always decide the controversey" (p. 28).

[3] This useful distinction is drawn by William Labov, "Some Features of the English of Black Americans," in *Varieties of Present-Day English*, ed. Richard W. Bailey and Jay L. Robinson (New York, 1973), pp. 242–43.

draws upon the deep structures of generative grammar to show that differences between the English of black speakers and that of white speakers "are largely confined to superficial, rather low level processes."[1] And Raven I. McDavid, Jr., who has spent years recording American dialects for the Linguistic Atlas, confirms the conclusions of the less systematic observers quoted above: "To those familiar with the situation in European countries, such as France or Italy or even England, dialect differences in American English are relatively small."[2]

243. *Archaic Features in American English.* A second quality often attributed to American English is archaism, the preservation of old features of the language which have gone out of use in the standard speech of England. Our pronunciation as compared with that of London is somewhat old-fashioned. It has qualities that were characteristic of English speech in the seventeenth and eighteenth centuries. The preservation of the *r* in General American and a flat *a* in *fast, path,* etc. (§ 250.7) were abandoned in southern England at the end of the eighteenth century. In many little ways standard American English is reminiscent of an older period of the language. We pronounce *either* and *neither* with the vowel of *teeth* or *beneath*, while in England these words have changed their pronunciation since the American colonies were established and are now pronounced with an initial diphthong [aɪ]. Our use of *gotten* in place of *got* as the past participle of *get* always impresses the Englishman of today as an old-fashioned feature not to be expected in the speech of a people that prides itself on being up-to-date. It was the usual form in England two centuries ago. We have kept a number of old words or old uses of words no longer usual in England. We still use *mad* in the sense of angry, as Shakespeare and his contemporaries did, and we have kept the general significance of *sick* without restricting it to nausea. We still speak of *rare* meat, whereas the English now say *underdone*. *Platter* is a common word with us, but is seldom used any more in England except in poetry. We have kept the picturesque old word *fall* as the natural word for the season. We learn *autumn*, the word used in England, in the schoolroom, and from books. *Wilt*, which we use so naturally for drooping flowers that we employ it figuratively (a person wilts under a cross-examination), has quite gone out of use in Standard English of the mother country. The American *I guess,*

---

[1] William Labov, *The Study of Nonstandard English* (Champaign, Ill., 1970), p. 40. Labov's analysis shows that the patterns of black English provide systematic aspectual distinctions and thus are not "mistakes" in the usual sense.

[2] "The Dialects of American English," McDavid's chapter in W. Nelson Francis, *The Structure of American English* (New York, 1958), p. 482.

so often ridiculed in England, is as old as Chaucer and was still current in English speech in the seventeenth century. It we were to take the rural speech of New England or that of the Kentucky mountaineer, we should find hundreds of words, meanings, and pronunciations now obsolete in the standard speech of both England and this country. There can be no question about the fact that many an older feature of the language of England can be illustrated from survivals in the United States.

The phenomenon is not unknown in other parts of the world. The English spoken in Ireland illustrates many pronunciations indicated by the rimes in Pope, and modern Icelandic is notably archaic as compared with the languages of the Scandinavian countries of the mainland. Accordingly it has often been maintained that transplanting a language results in a sort of arrested development. The process has been compared to the transplanting of a tree. A certain time is required for the tree to take root, and growth is temporarily retarded. In language this slower development is often regarded as a form of conservatism, and it is assumed as a general principle that the language of a new country is more conservative than the same language when it remains in the old habitat. In this theory there is doubtless an element of truth. It would be difficult to find a student of the Scandinavian languages who did not feel that the preservation of so many of the old inflections in Icelandic, which have been lost in modern Swedish and Danish, speaks strongly in support of it. And it is a well-recognized fact in cultural history that isolated communities tend to preserve old customs and beliefs. To the extent, then, that new countries into which a language is carried are cut off from contact with the old we may find them more tenacious of old habits of speech.

Yet it is open to doubt whether the English language in America can really be considered more conservative than the English of England.[1] It is but a figure of speech when we speak of transplanting a language. Language is only an activity of people, and it is the people who are transplanted to a new country. Language is but the expression of the people who use it, and should reflect the nature and the experiences of the speakers. Now we generally do not think of the pioneer who pulls up roots and tries the experiment of life in a new world as more conservative than the man who stays at home. Moreover, the novel conditions of his new environment and the many new experiences which his language is called upon to express are

---

[1] This doubt has been well expressed by Frank E. Bryant, "On the Conservatism of Language in a New Country," *PMLA*, 22 (1907), 277–90, and supported with additional arguments by George P. Krapp, "Is American English Archaic?" *Southwest Review*, 12 (1927), 292–303.

inducements to change rather than factors tending to conserve his language unaltered. We may well ask ourselves, therefore, whether the archaic features which we have noted in the language of America are evidence of a conservative tendency or are survivals which can be otherwise accounted for—whether, in short, American English is more conservative than the English of England. And here we must ask ourselves what form of American English we are considering and with what we are going to compare it in England—with the received standard which grew up in the southern parts of the island or with the form of the language spoken in the north. If we compare the English spoken in America outside of New England and the South with the received standard of England, it will undoubtedly appear conservative, but it is not noticeably so as compared with the speech of the northern half of England. On the other hand, the language of New England and in some features that of the South have undergone many of the changes in pronunciation which characterize the received standard of England. We must be equally careful in speaking of archaic survivals in the American vocabulary. Illustrations of these are often drawn from the rural speech of New England. But they are no more characteristic of American speech in general than of the received standard of England, and many of them can be matched in the rural dialects of England. In this respect the rural speech of England is just as conservative as that of America. Even the archaisms which are really a part of educated American English can generally be found surviving locally in the mother country. The difference is one of dissemination and social level. It is a question whether an equal number of survivals could not be found, such as *fortnight, porridge, heath, moor, ironmonger*, in educated English that are lost or uncommon on this side of the Atlantic. In general, it seems nearest the truth to say that American English has preserved certain older features of the language which have disappeared from Standard English in England. But it has also introduced innovations equally important, to which we must turn.

244. Early Changes in the Vocabulary. When colonists settle in a new country they find the resources of their language constantly taxed. They have no words for the many new objects on every hand or the constant succession of new experiences which they undergo. Accordingly in a colonial language changes of vocabulary take place almost from the moment the first settlers arrive. When the colonists from England became acquainted with the physical features of this continent they seem to have been impressed particularly by its mountains and forests, so much larger and more impressive than any in England, and the result was a whole series of new words like *bluff, foothill, notch, gap, divide, watershed, clearing,* and *underbrush.* Then there were the many living and growing things which were peculiar to the New World. The names for some of these the colonists learned from the Indian, words like *moose, raccoon, skunk, opossum, chipmunk, porgy, terrapin;* others they formed by a descriptive process long familiar in the language: *mud hen, garter snake, bullfrog, potato bug, groundhog, reed bird.* Tree names such as the *hickory* and *live oak*, and the *locust* are new to colonial English, as are *sweet potato, eggplant, squash, persimmon, pecan.* Contact with the Indians brought into English a number of words having particular reference to the Indian way of life: *wigwam, tomahawk, canoe, toboggan, mackinaw, moccasin, wampum, squaw, papoose.* These are Indian words, but we have also English words formed at the same time and out of the same experience: *war path, paleface, medicine man, pipe of peace, big chief, war paint*, and the verb *to scalp*. Indian words for Indian foods were taken over in the case of *hominy, tapioca, succotash*, and *pone*. The latter is still heard in the South for corn bread, the kind of bread the Indians made. The individual character of our political and administrative system required the introduction of words such as *congressional, presidential, gubernatorial* (in use as early as 1734 but still refused admission to certain editorial offices), *congressman, caucus, mass meeting, selectman, statehouse, land office.* Many other words illustrate things associated with the new mode of life—*back country, backwoodsman, squatter, prairie, log cabin, clapboard, corncrib, popcorn, hoe cake, cold snap, snow plow, bobsled, sleigh.*

As indicated above, the colonists got a number of the words they needed ready-made from the languages of the Indians. They got some, too, from other languages. From the French colonists they learned *portage, chowder, cache, caribou, bureau, bayou, levee*, and others; from the Dutch *cruller, coleslaw, cookie, stoop, boss, scow;* from German *noodle, pretzel, smearcase, sauerkraut.* More interesting, however, are the cases in which the colonist applied an old word to a slightly different thing, as when he gave the name of the English *robin* to a red-breasted thrush, applied the word *turkey* to a distinctive American bird, and transferred the word *corn* to an entirely new cereal. *Indian corn* was known in England only from the accounts of travelers, and naming its various features seems to have taxed the ingenuity of the first Americans. *Maize*, the West Indian name which came into England through the Spanish, was never used by the American settler. Henry Hudson called it *Turkish wheat*, a designation found in French and Italian and among the Pennsylvania Germans. But the colonists used the common English word *corn*, which in England is used of any kind of grain, but especially of wheat. At first they prefixed the distinguishing epithet

"Indian," but this was soon dropped, and consequently *corn* means something quite different in England and in America today. There were other difficulties. *Tassel* and *silk* were natural descriptions of the flower, but the *ear* was more troublesome. The *cob* was known in Virginia as the *husk* or *huss*, and John Smith calls it the *core*. The outer covering, which we generally call the *husk* today, was variously known as the *hose*, the *leaves*, and the *shuck*. The latter word survives in the sociable activity of *corn-shucking*, the equivalent of the New England *husking bee*. In an instance like this we catch a glimpse of the colonist in the very act of shifting and adapting his language to new conditions, and we find him doing the same thing with *rabbit, lumber, freshet*, and other words which have a somewhat different meaning in American and English use. He is perhaps at his best when inventing simple homely words like *apple butter, sidewalk*, and *lightning rod, spelling bee* and *crazy quilt, low-down*, and *know-nothing*, or when striking off a terse metaphor like *log rolling, wire pulling, to have an ax to grind, to be on the fence*. The American early manifested the gift, which he continues to show, of the imaginative, slightly humorous phrase. To it we owe *to bark up the wrong tree, to face the music, fly off the handle, go on the war path, bury the hatchet, come out at the little end of the horn, saw wood*, and many more, with the breath of the country and sometimes of the frontier about them. In this way America began her contributions to the English language, and in this period also we see the beginning of such differentiation as has taken place between the American and the British vocabulary. Both of these matters will be dealt with in their later aspects below.

245. *National Consciousness.* There is evidence that at the time of the American Revolution and especially in the years immediately following it, Americans were beginning to be conscious of their language and to believe that it might be destined to have a future as glorious as that which they confidently expected for the country itself. It was apparent that in the hundred and fifty years since the founding of Jamestown and Plymouth the English language on this continent had developed certain differences which were often the subject of remark. Thomas Jefferson thought that we were more tolerant of innovations in speech than the people of England and that these innovations might eventually justify calling the language of America by a name other than English. The consciousness of an American variety of English with characteristics of its own led to the consideration of a standard which should be recognized on this side of the Atlantic. John Witherspoon, whose papers on the English language in the *Pennsylvania Journal* for 1781 have already been mentioned, believed it probable that

American English would not follow the course of Scottish and become a provincial dialect. "Being entirely separated from Britain," he says, "we shall find some centre or standard of our own, and not be subject to the inhabitants of that island, either in receiving new ways of speaking or rejecting the old." That others were thinking along the same lines and were unwilling that this standard should be left to chance is evident from a communication published in January 1774 in the *Royal American Magazine*. The writer signs himself "An American" and gives evidence of his patriotic fervor by venturing the opinion that although English has been greatly improved in Britain within the last century, "its highest perfection, with every other branch of human knowledge, is perhaps reserved for this Land of light and freedom." He proposes the formation of something like an academy in this country:

> I beg leave to propose a plan for perfecting the English language in America, thro' every future period of its existence; viz. That a society, for this purpose should be formed, consisting of members in each university and seminary, who shall be stiled, *Fellows of the American Society of Language:* That the society, when established, from time to time elect new members, & thereby be made perpetual. And that the society annually publish some observations upon the language and from year to year, correct, enrich and refine it, until perfection stops their progress and ends their labour.
>
> I conceive that such a society might easily be established, and that great advantages would thereby accrue to science, and consequently America would make swifter advances to the summit of learning. It is perhaps impossible for us to form an idea of the perfection, the beauty, the grandeur, & sublimity, to which our language may arrive in the progress of time, passing through the improving tongues of our rising posterity; whose aspiring minds, fired by our example, and ardour for glory, may far surpass all the sons of science who have shone in past ages, & may light up the world with new ideas bright as the sun.[1]

Whether the author of this proposal was John Adams, a future president of the United States, is not certain. His name has sometimes been mentioned in connection with it because a few years later he made a somewhat similar suggestion in a letter to the president of Congress, written from Amsterdam, September 5, 1780. After directing attention to the importance of "eloquence and language" in a republic and citing the example of

---

[1] First republished by Albert Matthews in *Trans. of the Colonial Society of Massachusetts*, XIV, 263–64. It is reprinted in M. M. Mathews, *The Beginnings of American English* (Chicago, 1931), pp. 40–41.

France, Spain, and Italy in forming academies for the improvement of their languages, he continues:

> The honor of forming the first public institution for refining, correcting, improving, and ascertaining the English language, I hope is reserved for congress; they have every motive that can possibly influence a public assembly to undertake it. It will have a happy effect upon the union of the States to have a public standard for all persons in every part of the continent to appeal to, both for the signification and pronunciation of the language. The constitutions of all the States in the Union are so democratical that eloquence will become the instrument for recommending men to their fellow-citizens, and the principal means of advancement through the various ranks and offices of society. . . .
> . . . English is destined to be in the next and succeeding centuries more generally the language of the world than Latin was in the last or French is in the present age. The reason of this is obvious, because the increasing population in America, and their universal connection and correspondence with all nations will, aided by the influence of England in the world, whether great or small, force their language into general use, in spite of all the obstacles that may be thrown in their way, if any such there should be.
> It is not necessary to enlarge further, to show the motives which the people of America have to turn their thoughts early to this subject; they will naturally occur to congress in a much greater detail than I have time to hint at. I would therefore submit to the consideration of congress the expediency and policy of erecting by their authority a society under the name of "the American Academy for refining, improving, and ascertaining the English Language. . . .[1]

There is nothing very original in this suggestion. It follows the proposals which had been made by Swift and others in England (see §§ 192ff.). But it is significant as indicating a growing sense of the importance which Americans were beginning to attach to the form that English was taking and should take in the future in America. That feeling was to find expression in the more extreme views of one of Adams' contemporaries, Noah Webster.

246. *Noah Webster and an American Language.* The Declaration of Independence and the years during which the colonies were fighting to establish their freedom from England produced an important change in American psychology. Accustomed for generations to dependence upon the mother country, the people who settled in America imported most of

[1] Mathews, *The Beginnings of American English*, pp. 42–43.

their books and many of their ideas from Europe. It was a natural and entirely just recognition of the superior civilization of the Old World and the greatness of English literature and learning. But with political independence achieved, many of the colonists began to manifest a distaste for anything that seemed to perpetuate the former dependence. An ardent, sometimes belligerent patriotism sprang up, and among many people it became the order of the day to demand an American civilization as distinctive from that of Europe as were the political and social ideals which were being established in the new world.

No one expressed this attitude more vigorously than Noah Webster (1758–1843). Born on the outskirts of Hartford, Connecticut, he received at Yale such an education as universities in the country then offered, and later undertook the practice of law. But business in the legal profession was slow, and he was forced for a livelihood to turn to teaching. The change determined his entire subsequent career. The available English schoolbooks were unsatisfactory, and the war diminished the supply of such as there were. Webster accordingly set about compiling three elementary books on English, a spelling book, a grammar, and a reader. These he published in 1783, 1784, and 1785 under the high-sounding title *A Grammatical Institute of the English Language*. They were the first books of their kind to be published in this country. The success of the first part was unexpectedly great. It was soon reissued under the title *The American Spelling Book*, and in this form went through edition after edition. It is estimated that in a hundred years, more than 80 million copies of the book were sold. From a profit of less than a cent a copy Webster derived most of his income throughout his life. The influence of the little book was enormous, and will be discussed below. Here it is sufficient to note that it had the effect of turning its author's attention to questions of language and enabled him to devote himself to a number of projects of a linguistic kind. In 1789 he published a volume of *Dissertations on the English Language, with Notes Historical and Critical*. In 1806 he brought out a small *Dictionary*, the prelude to his greatest work. This was *An American Dictionary of the English Language*, published in 1828 in two quarto volumes. In all of these works and in numerous smaller writings he was animated by a persistent purpose: to show that the English language in this country was a distinctly American thing, developing along its own lines, and deserving to be considered from an independent, American point of view. His self-assurance had its faults as well as its virtues. It led him to ignore discoveries from Europe that were establishing the principles of comparative linguistics, and to spend years writing etymologies that were inadequate even for his time.[1] The etymologies could be replaced eventually by a German scholar, C. A. F. Mahn, but the sustaining zeal which carried him to the completion of his work drew on resources of personality more complex and rarer than current knowledge of the discipline.

In the preface to the first part of the *Grammatical Institute* Webster says: "The author wishes to promote the honour and prosperity of the confederated republics of America; and cheerfully throws his mite into the common treasure of patriotic exertions. This country must in some future time, be as distinguished by the superiority of her literary improvements, as she is already by the liberality of her civil and ecclesiastical constitutions. Europe is grown old in folly, corruption and tyranny. . . . For America in her infancy to adopt the present maxims of the old world, would be to stamp the wrinkles of decrepid age upon the bloom of youth and to plant the seeds of decay in a vigorous constitution." Six years later, in his *Dissertations on the English Language*, he went much further. "As an independent nation," he says, "our honor requires us to have a system of our own, in language as well as government. Great Britain, whose children we are, should no longer be *our* standard; for the taste of her writers is already corrupted, and her language on the decline. But if it were not so, she is at too great a distance to be our model, and to instruct us in the principles of our own tongue." But independence of England was not the only factor that colored men's thinking in the new nation. A capital problem in 1789 was that of welding the thirteen colonies into a unified nation, and this is also reflected in Webster's ideas. In urging certain reforms of spelling in the United States he argues that one of the advantages would be that it would make a difference between the English orthography and the American, and "that such an event is an object of vast political consequence." A "national language," he says, "is a band of national union. Every engine should be employed to render the people of this country *national;* to call their attachments home to their own country; and to inspire them with the pride of national character." Culturally they are still too dependent upon England. "However they may boast of Independence, and the freedom of their government, yet their *opinions* are not sufficiently independent; an astonishing respect for the arts and literature of their parent country, and a blind imitation of its manners, are still prevalent among the Americans." It is an idea that he often returns to. In his *Letter*

---

[1] See Allen W. Read, "The Spread of German Linguistic Learning in New England during the Lifetime of Noah Webster," *American Speech*, 41 (1966), 163–81, and Joseph H. Friend, *The Development of American Lexicography, 1798–1864* (The Hague, 1967), pp. 75–79.

to Pickering (1817) he says, "There is nothing which, in my opinion, so debases the genius and character of my countrymen, as the implicit confidence they place in English authors, and their unhesitating submission to their *opinions*, their *derision*, and their *frowns*. But I trust the time will come, when the English will be convinced that the intellectual faculties of their descendants have not degenerated in America; and that we can contend with them in *letters*, with as much success, as upon the *ocean*." This was written after the War of 1812. So far as the language is concerned, he has no doubt of its ultimate differentiation. He is sure that "numerous local causes, such as a new country, new associations of people, new combinations of ideas in arts and science, and some intercourse with tribes wholly unknown in Europe, will introduce new words into the American tongue. These causes will produce, in a course of time, a language in North America, as different from the future language of England, as the Modern Dutch, Danish and Swedish are from the German, or from one another."

The culmination of his efforts to promote the idea of an American language was the publication of his *American Dictionary* in 1828. Residence for a year in England had somewhat tempered his opinion, but it was still fundamentally the same. In the preface to that work he gave final expression to his conviction: "It is not only important, but, in a degree necessary, that the people of this country, should have an *American Dictionary* of the English Language; for, although the body of the language is the same as in England, and it is desirable to perpetuate that sameness, yet some differences must exist. Language is the expression of ideas; and if the people of our country cannot preserve an identity of ideas, they cannot retain an identity of language. Now an identity of ideas depends materially upon a sameness of things or objects with which the people of the two countries are conversant. But in no two portions of the earth, remote from each other, can such identity be found. Even physical objects must be different. But the principal differences between the people of this country and of all others, arise from different forms of government, different laws, institutions and customs ... the institutions in this country which are new and peculiar, give rise to new terms, unknown to the people of England ... No person in this country will be satisfied with the English definitions of the words *congress*, *senate* and *assembly*, *court*, &c. for although these are words used in England, yet they are applied in this country to express ideas which they do not express in that country." It is not possible to dismiss this statement as an advertisement calculated to promote the sale of his book in competition with the English dictionaries of Johnson and others. He had held such a view long before the idea of a dictionary had taken shape in his mind. Webster was a patriot who carried his sentiment from questions of political and social organization over into matters of language. By stressing American usage and American pronunciation, by adopting a number of distinctive spellings, and especially by introducing quotations from American authors alongside of those from English literature, he contrived in large measure to justify the title of his work. If, after a hundred and fifty years, some are inclined to doubt the existence of anything so distinctive as an American language, his efforts, nevertheless, have left a permanent mark on the language of this country.

247. *Webster's Influence on American Spelling.* It is a matter of common observation that American spelling often differs in small ways from that customary in England.[1] We write *honor, color,* and a score of words without the *u* of English *honour, colour,* etc. We sometimes employ one consonant where the English write two: *traveler—traveller, wagon—waggon,* etc. We write *er* instead of *re* in a number of words like *fiber, center, theater.* We prefer an *s* in words like *defense, offense,* and write *ax, plow, tire, story, czar, jail,* and *medieval* for *axe, plough, tyre, storey, tsar, gaol,* and *mediaeval.* The differences often pass unnoticed, partly because a number of English spellings are still current in America, partly because some of the American innovations are now common in England, and in general because certain alternatives are permissible in both countries. Although some of the differences have grown up since Webster's day, the majority of the distinctively American spellings are due to his advocacy of them and the incorporation of them in his dictionary.

Spelling reform was one of the innumerable things that Franklin took an interest in. In 1768 he devised *A Scheme for a New Alphabet and a Reformed Mode of Spelling* and went so far as to have a special font of type cut for the purpose of putting it into effect. Years later he tried to interest Webster in his plan, but without success. According to the latter, "Dr. Franklin never pretended to be a man of erudition—he was self-educated; and he wished to reform the orthography of our language, by introducing new characters. He invited me to Philadelphia to aid in the work; but I differed from him in opinion. I think the introduction of new characters neither practicable, necessary nor expedient."[2] Indeed, Webster

---

[1] For an excellent discussion of English and American spellings see H. L. Mencken, *The American Language* (4th ed., New York, 1936), chap. 8.

[2] *Letter to Pickering* (1817), p. 32. Franklin's letter to Webster on the subject was written June 18, 1786, and indicates that Webster had already devised an alphabet of his own (*Writings of Benjamin Franklin*, ed. A. H. Smyth, IX, 518, 527; for Franklin's *Scheme*, V, 169–78).

was not in the beginning sympathetic to spelling reform. At the time that he brought out the first part of his *Grammatical Institute* (1783) he wrote: "There seems to be an inclination in some writers to alter the spelling of words, by expunging the superfluous letters. This appears to arise from the same pedantic fondness for singularity that prompts new fashions of pronunciation. Thus they write the words *favour, honour,* &c. without *u.* . . . Thus *e* is omitted in *judgment;* which is the most necessary letter in the word. . . . Into these and many other absurdities are people led by a rage for singularity. . . . We may better labour to speak our language with propriety and elegance, as we have it, than to attempt a reformation without advantage or probability of success." But by 1789 Franklin's influence had begun to have its effect. In the *Dissertations on the English Language*, published in that year, Webster admitted: "I once believed that a reformation of our orthography would be unnecessary and impracticable. This opinion was hasty; being the result of a slight examination of the subject. I now believe with Dr. Franklin that such a reformation is practicable and highly necessary." As an appendix to that volume he published *An Essay on the Necessity, Advantages and Practicability of the Mode of Spelling, and of Rendering the Orthography of Words Correspondent to the Pronunciation*. In this he urged the omission of all superfluous or silent letters, such as the *a* in *bread* and the *e* in *give*, the substitution of *ee* for the vowels in *mean, speak, grieve, key*, etc., the use of *k* for *ch* in such words as had a *k*-sound (*character, chorus*), and a few other "inconsiderable alterations." The next year he exemplified his reform in *A Collection of Essays and Fugitive Writings*, from which a few sentences in the preface may be quoted by way of illustration:

> In the essays, ritten within the last yeer, a considerable change of spelling iz introduced by way of experiment. This liberty waz taken by the writers before the age of queen Elizabeth, and to this we are indeted for the preference of modern spelling over that of Gower and Chaucer. The man who admits that the change of *housbonde, mynde, ygone, moneth* into *husband, mind, gone, month*, iz an improovment, must acknowlege also the riting of *helth, breth, rong, tung, munth*, to be an improovment. There iz no alternativ. Every possible reezon that could ever be offered for altering the spelling of wurds, stil exists in full force; and if a gradual reform should not be made in our language, it wil proov that we are less under the influence of reezon than our ancestors.

This is neither consistent nor adequate. The changes here proposed met with so much opposition that he abandoned most of them in favor of a more moderate proposal.

By 1806 when he published his first small dictionary[1] he had come to hold that "it would be useless to attempt any change, even if practicable, in those anomalies which form whole classes of words, and in which, change would rather perplex than ease the learner." The most important modifications which he introduces are that he prints *music, physic, logic,* etc., without a final *k; scepter, theater, meter,* and the like with *er* instead of *re; honor, favor,* etc., without the *u; check, mask, risk,* etc., for *cheque, masque, risque; defense, pretense, recompense,* and similar words with an *s;* and *determin, examin, doctrin, medicin,* etc., without a final *e.* In all except the last of these innovations he has been followed generally in American usage. He was not always consistent. He spelled *traffick, almanack, frolick,* and *havock* with a final *k* where his own rule and modern practice call for its omission. But on the whole the principles here adopted were carried over, with some modifications and additions,[2] into his *American Dictionary* of 1828 and from this they have come into our present use.[3]

It has been thought well to trace in some detail the evolution of Webster's ideas on the subject of spelling, since it is to him that we owe the most characteristic differences between English and American practice today. Some of his innovations have been adopted in England, and it may be said in general that his later views were on the whole moderate and sensible.

248. *Webster's Influence on American Pronunciation.* Though the influence is more difficult to prove, there can be no doubt that to Webster are to be attributed some of the characteristics of American pronunciation, especially its uniformity and the disposition to give fuller value to the unaccented syllables of words. Certainly he was interested in the improvement of American pronunciation and intended that his books should serve that purpose. In the first part of his *Grammatical Institute,* which became the *American Spelling Book,* he says that the system "is designed to

---

[1] *A Compendious Dictionary of the English Language. In which Five Thousand Words are added to the number found in the best English compends. The Orthography is, in some instances, corrected,* etc. By Noah Webster (Hartford, 1806). The work is available in a facsimile edition with an Introduction by Philip B. Gove (New York, 1970).

[2] E.g., he restored the *e* in *determine, examine,* stated the rule for not doubling the consonant in words like *traveler, traveling,* etc.

[3] "Webster inculcated his views on orthography and pronunciation upon all occasions. He wrote, he lectured, he pressed home his doctrines upon persons and assemblies. . . . The present printer [1881] of 'Webster's Dictionary' remembers that when he was a boy of thirteen, working at the case in Burlington, Vermont, a little pale-faced man came into the office and handed him a printed slip, saying, 'My lad, when you use these words, please oblige me by spelling them as here: *theater, center,* etc.' It was Noah Webster traveling about among the printing-offices, and persuading people to spell as he did: a better illustration could not be found of the reformer's sagacity, and his patient method of effecting his purpose." (Horace E. Scudder, *Noah Webster* [Boston, 1882], pp. 213–14.)

introduce uniformity and accuracy of pronunciation into common schools." That it was not without effect can, in one case at least, be shown. In the preface to that work he says, "*Angel, ancient*, the English pronounce *anegel, anecient*, contrary to every good principle." Now James Fenimore Cooper, in his *Notions of the Americans*, tells how as a boy he was sent off to a school in Connecticut, and when he came home for a vacation he was pronouncing the first syllable of *angel* like the article *an*, and *beard* as *berd* or *baird* (another Websterian pronunciation). He was only laughed out of the absurdity by the rest of his family. But he adds: "I think . . . a great deal of the peculiarity of New England pronunciation is to be ascribed to the intelligence of its inhabitants. This may appear a paradox; but it can easily be explained. They all read and write; but the New Englandman, at home, is a man of exceedingly domestic habits. He has a theoretical knowledge of the language, without its practice. . . . It is vain to tell a man who has his book before him, that *cham* spells *chame*, as in *chamber*, or *an*, *ane* as in *angel;* or *dan, dane*, as in *danger*. He replies by asking what sound is produced by *an, dan*, and *cham*. I believe it would be found, on pursuing the inquiry, that a great number of their peculiar sounds are introduced through their spelling books, and yet there are some, certainly, that cannot be thus explained." [1]

In this case the effect was fortunately temporary. But because of the use to which the Webster *Spelling Book* was put in thousands of schools, it is very likely that some of its other effects were more lasting. In the reminiscences of his early life, Joseph T. Buckingham, a newspaper publisher of some prominence in New England, gives an interesting account of the village school at the close of the eighteenth century:

> It was the custom for all such pupils [those who were sufficiently advanced to pronounce distinctly words of more than one syllable] to stand together as one class, and with *one voice* to read a column or two of the tables for spelling. The master gave the signal to begin, and all united to read, letter by letter, pronouncing each syllable by itself, and adding to it the preceding one till the word was complete. Thus a–d *ad*, m–i *mi, admi*, r–a *ra, admira*, t–i–o–n *shun, admiration*. This mode of reading was exceedingly exciting, and, in my humble judgment, exceedingly useful; as it required and taught deliberate and distinct articulation. . . . When the lesson had been thus read, the books were closed, and the words given out for spelling. If one was misspelt, it passed on to the next, and the next pupil in order, and so on till it was spelt correctly. Then the pupil who had spelt correctly went up in the class *above* the one who had misspelt. . . .

[1] Cooper, *Notions of the Americans* (London, 1828), II, 172–74.

> Another of our customs was to choose sides to spell once or twice a
> week. . . . [The losing side] had to sweep the room and build the fires
> the next morning. These customs, prevalent sixty and seventy years
> ago, excited emulation, and emulation produced improvement.[1]

Webster quotes Sheridan with approval to the effect that "A good articulation consists in giving every letter in a syllable its due proportion of sound,
according to the most approved custom of pronouncing it; and in making
such a distinction, between syllables, of which words are composed, that
the ear shall without difficulty acknowledge their number." And he adds
the specific injunction, "Let words be divided as they ought to be pronounced *clus–ter*, *hab–it*, *nos–tril*, *bish–op*, and the smallest child cannot
mistake a just pronunciation." In the light of such precept and evidence of
its practice, and considering the popularity of spelling bees among those
of a former generation, it seems certain that not a little influence on
American pronunciation is to be traced to the old blue-backed spelling
book.

249. *Pronunciation*.   The earliest changes in the English language in
America, distinguishing it from the language of the mother country, were
in the vocabulary. These have already been mentioned. From the time
when the early colonists came, however, divergence in pronunciation began
gradually to develop. This has been due in part to changes that have occurred here, but has resulted still more from the fact that the pronunciation of
England has undergone further change and that a variety of southern
English has come to be recognized as the English received standard. At the
present time American pronunciation shows certain well-marked differences from English use.[2]

Perhaps the most noticeable of these differences is in the vowel sound
in such words as *fast*, *path*, *grass*, *dance*, *can't*, *half*. At the end of the
eighteenth century southern England began to change from what is called
a flat *a* to a broad *a* in these words, that is from a sound like the *a* in *man*
to one like the *a* in *father*. The change affected words in which the vowel
occurred before *f*, *sk*, *sp*, *st*, *ss*, *th*, and *n* followed by certain consonants.
In parts of New England the same change took place, but in most other
parts of the country the old sound was preserved, and *fast*, *path*, etc., are
pronounced with the vowel of *pan*. In some speakers there is a tendency to
employ an intermediate vowel, halfway between the *a* of *pan* and

---

[1] Letter to Henry Barnard, December 10, 1860, printed in Barnard's *American Journal
of Education*, 13 (1863), 129–32.

[2] Eilert Ekwall, *American and British Pronunciation* (Uppsala, 1946; also printed in
Studia Neophilologica, XVIII, 161–90).

com-mon	dol-lar	of-fer	ker-nel
con-duct	fod-der	of-fice	mer-cy*
con-cord	fol-ly	pot-ter	per-fect*
con-grefs	fop-pifh	rob-ber	per-fon
con-queft	hor-rid	fot-tifh	fer-mon
con-ful	juc-ky		fer-pent
con-vert	jol-ly	cler-gy	fer-vant
doc-tor	mot-to	er-rand	ver-min
drofs-y	on-fet	her-mit	

* Not Marty, Parfect, &c.

TABLE V.

Eafy Words of Two Syllables, accented on the Second.

N. B. In general when a vowel, in an unaccented fyllable, ftands alone, or ends a fyllable*, it has its firft found, as in *pro-tect*; yet as we do not dwell upon the vowel, it is fhort and weak. When the vowel, in fuch fyllables, is joined to a confonant, it has its fecond found; as, *ad-drefs*.

A-Bafe	com-pute	de-pute	en-tice
a-bide	com-plete	de-rive	en-tire
a-dore	confine	dif-like	e-vade
a-like	con-jure	dif-place	for-fworn
al-lude	con-fume	dif-robe	fore-feen
a-lone	cre-ate	dif-tafte	im-brue
a-maze	de-cide	di-vine	im-pale
af-pire	de-clare	e-lope	in-cite
a-tone	de-duce	en-dure	in-flame
at-tire	de-fy	en-force	in-trude
be-fore	de-fine	en-gage	in-fure
be-have	de-grade	en-rage	in-vite
be-hold	de-range	en-rol	mif-name
com-ply	de-note	en-fue	mif-place

* But if a vowel unaccented ends the word, it has its fecond found, as in ci-ty.

THE *AMERICAN SPELLING BOOK* OF NOAH WEBSTER
(see § 248)

father, but the "flat *a*" must be regarded as the typical American pronunciation.

Next to the retention of the flat *a*, the most noticeable difference between English and American pronunciation is in the treatment of the *r*. In the received pronunciation of England this sound has disappeared except before vowels. It is not heard when it occurs before another consonant or at the end of a word unless the next word begins with a vowel. In America, eastern New England and most of the South follow the English practice, but in the Middle States and the West the *r* is pronounced in all positions. Thus in the received standard of England *lord* has the same sound as *laud* and *there* is pronounced [ðɛə] with the indeterminate vowel [ə] as a glide at the end. The American *r* is either a retention of older English pronunciation or the result of north of England influence in our speech. It has caused more comment than any other distinction in American pronunciation.

A distinction less apparent to the layman is the pronunciation of the *o* in such words as *not, lot, hot, top*. In England this is still an open *o* pronounced with the lips rounded, but in America except in parts of New England it has commonly lost its rounding and in most words has become a sound identical in quality with the *a* in *father*, only short.

There are other differences of less moment between English and American pronunciation, since they concern individual words or small groups of words. Thus in England *been* has the same sound as *bean*, but in America is like *bin*. *Leisure* often has in America what is popularly called a long vowel but in England usually rimes with *pleasure*. There, too, the last syllable of words like *fertile* and *sterile* rimes with *aisle*. In America we have kept the common eighteenth-century pronunciation with a short vowel or a mere vocalic *l*. The English pronunciation of *either* and *neither* is sometimes heard in America, as is *process* with a close *o*. But we do not suppress the final *t* in *trait* or pronounce an *f* in *lieutenant*. Our pronunciation of *figure* with [jər] would be considered pedantic in England, according to Fowler, who also confirms the pronunciation of *ate* as *et*, while noting that the American pronunciation has been growing in Britain. In this country *figger* and *et* would betray a lack of cultivation.

A more important difference is the greater clearness with which we pronounce unaccented syllables. We do not say *secret'ry* or *necess'ry*. Bernard Shaw said he once recognized an American because he accented the third syllable of *necessary*, and the disposition to keep a secondary stress on one of the unaccented syllables of a long word is one of the consequences of our effort to pronounce all the syllables. Conversely the suppression of syllables in England has been accompanied by a difference at times in the position of the chief stress. The English commonly say *centen'ary* and *labor'atory*, and *adver'tisement* is never *advertise'ment*. There is, of course, more in speech than the quality of the sounds. There is also the matter of pitch and tempo. We speak more slowly and with less variety of tone. There can be no gainsaying the fact that our speech is much more monotonous, is uttered with much less variety in the intonation, than that of England.

The differences between English and American pronunciation are not such as should cause any alarm for the future, any fear that Englishmen and Americans may become unintelligible to each other. As already said, the difference in the pronunciation of the *o* in *lot*, *top*, etc., is one that often escapes the notice of the layman. The pronunciation of the *r* may continue to excite mutual recrimination, but the difference between the broad *a* and the flat *a* affects fewer than a hundred and fifty words in common use.[1] Other differences are sporadic and on the whole negligible.

250. *The American Dialects.*   Certain features of pronunciation characteristic of a part of New England and others associated with many parts of the South are so easily recognized and so well known that for a long time it was customary to distinguish three main dialects in American English—the New England dialect, the Southern dialect, and General American, meaning the dialect of all the rest of the country. Such a division, in a broad way, is not unjustified since each of the dialect types is marked by features which distinguish it clearly from the others. But it is not sufficiently exact. Not all of New England shares in the features—such as the so-called "broad *a*" and the loss of [r] finally and before consonants— which are thought of as most characteristic. Parts of the South were settled from Pennsylvania and are not typically southern in speech. And finally, General American itself shows regional differences which, while not so obvious to the layman, can be recognized by the linguist and charted.

Our ability to distinguish more accurately the various speech areas which exist in this country is due to the fact that we now have a large mass of accurate data gathered by field workers for the *Linguistic Atlas of the United States and Canada* (see p. 390) and a growing number of detailed studies of regional pronunciation and other features. These have contributed greatly to a clearer understanding of some of the speech areas of the country.[2]

---

[1] See J. S. Kenyon, "Flat *a* and Broad *a*," *American Speech*, 5 (1930), 323–26.

[2] The following studies may be mentioned by way of illustration: Hans Kurath and Raven I. McDavid, Jr., *The Pronunciation of English in the Atlantic States* (Ann Arbor, 1961); C. K. Thomas, *An Introduction to the Phonetics of American English* (2nd ed., New York, 1958); the same author's "The Phonology of New England English," *Speech*

In 1949 Professor Hans Kurath published a study of the first importance, *A Word Geography of the Eastern United States.* On the basis of lexical evidence, mainly in the Atlantic Coast states as far south as South Carolina, he distinguished eighteen speech areas, which he grouped into three main groups: Northern, Midland, and Southern. Subsequent studies have extended the areas as far west as the Mississippi and even beyond. The line separating Northern from Midland, confirmed by a number of isoglosses, runs northwest across New Jersey and eastern Pennsylvania and then in a fairly regular westward progression across the northern parts of Pennsylvania, Ohio, Indiana, and Illinois.[1] As the boundary approaches the

---

Monographs, 28 (1961), 223–32; Arthur J. Bronstein, *The Pronunciation of American English* (New York, 1960); Walter S. Avis, "The 'New England Short *o*': A Recessive Phoneme," *Language*, 37 (1961), 544–58; Thomas H. Wetmore, *The Low-Central and Low-Back Vowels in the English of the Eastern United States*, *Pub. of the Amer. Dialect Soc.* (hereafter *PADS*), no. 32 (1959); Lee A. Pederson, *The Pronunciation of English in Metropolitan Chicago*, *PADS*, no. 44 (1965); David DeCamp, "The Pronunciation of English in San Francisco," *Orbis*, 7 (1958), 372–91; 8 (1959), 54–77; Carroll E. Reed, "The Pronunciation of English in the Pacific Northwest," *Language*, 37 (1961), 559–64. The distribution of various dialect features is studied in Hans Kurath, "Mourning and Morning," *Studies for William A. Read* (University, La., 1940), pp. 166–73; E. Bagby Atwood, "*Grease* and *Greasy*—A Study of Geographical Variation," *Texas Stud. in English*, 29 (1950), 249–60, to which may be added the same author's *Survey of Verb Forms in the Eastern United States* (Ann Arbor, 1953) and *The Regional Vocabulary of Texas* (Austin, 1962); Albert H. Marckwardt, "Principal and Subsidiary Dialect Areas in the North-Central States," *PADS*, no. 27 (1957), pp. 3–15; Robert F. Dakin, "South Midland Speech in the Old Northwest," *Jour. of English Ling.*, 5 (1971), 31–48; Roger W. Shuy, *The Northern-Midland Dialect Boundary in Illinois*, *PADS*, no. 38 (1962); Harold B. Allen, "Aspects of the Linguistic Geography of the Upper Midwest," in *Studies . . . in Honor of Charles C. Fries* (Ann Arbor, 1964), pp. 303–14, and "Minor Dialect Areas of the Upper Midwest," *PADS*, no. 30 (1958), pp. 3–16; Gordon R. Wood, "Dialect Contours in the Southern States," *American Speech*, 38 (1963), 243–56, and *Vocabulary Change* (Carbondale, Ill., 1971); Lee Pederson, "Dialect Patterns in Rural Northern Georgia," in *Lexicography and Dialect Geography: Festgabe for Hans Kurath* (Wiesbaden, 1973), pp. 195–207; Arthur M. Z. Norman, "A Southeast Texas Dialect Study," *Orbis*, 5 (1956), 61–79; Katherine E. Wheatley and Oma Stanley, "Three Generations of East Texas Speech," *American Speech*, 34 (1959), 83–94; Fred Tarpley, *From Blinky to Blue-John: A Word Atlas of Northeast Texas* (Wolfe City, Tex., 1970); Elizabeth S. Bright, *A Word Geography of California and Nevada* (Berkeley, 1971); and Carroll E. Reed and David W. Reed, "Problems of English Speech Mixture in California and Nevada," in *Studies . . . in Honor of Raven I. McDavid, Jr.* (University, Ala., 1972), pp. 135–43, the last two items being of particular interest for their evidence of extensive dialect mixture in the West. Mention may also be made of R. I. McDavid's "Postvocalic /-r/ in South Carolina: A Social Analysis," *American Speech*, 23 (1948), 194–203, suggesting that the loss of *r* in the tidewater area is an aristocratic feature, and the same author's "The Position of the Charleston Dialect," *PADS*, no. 23 (1955), pp. 35–49. An excellent account of the more important dialect areas will be found in the chapter contributed by McDavid to W. Nelson Francis, *The Structure of American English* (New York, 1958).

[1] The boundaries (especially the broken lines) on the map are approximations which are crossed by individual features, lexical and phonological. The Norfolk, Virginia, region, for example, is included in the Virginia area, but has largely escaped the Piedmont influence and is more closely related to the adjacent part of North Carolina.

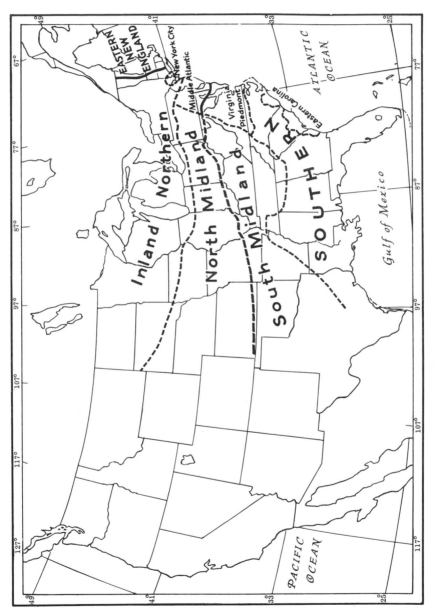

THE DIALECTS OF AMERICAN ENGLISH

Mississippi in northwestern Illinois it turns north and, to the extent that it can be traced as a boundary at all, continues that general course across the upper Midwest. The division between Midland and Southern begins at the Atlantic Ocean at a midpoint on the Delmarva peninsula, describes a northward arc through Maryland, and turns southwest, skirting the eastern edge of the Blue Ridge Mountains in Virginia and North Carolina and turning west just north of Atlanta. To the east lie the Piedmont and the coastal plain. To the west the Midland-Southern boundary continues through northern Georgia and Alabama, then turns north into western Tennessee. West of the Mississippi the boundary becomes predictably more diffuse, but it can still be traced through Arkansas and east Texas. Such a threefold division has the virtue of simplicity, and it is at least one possible classification of the country as far west as the Mississippi. In the region farther west the greater mixture of people from different parts of the country and the corresponding mixture of dialects reduce the utility of any description based on traditional isoglosses. The classification has the weakness of suggesting a greater homogeneity for the Northern type than it actually has, containing as it does the dialect of eastern New England, which must be recognized as a distinct variety of American English, and that, let us say, of most of the state of New York, which on the basis of pronunciation is a part of General American. But such inconsistencies between lexical and phonological criteria are probably inevitable, since words are more easily transferred than regional types of pronunciation.

Within the Northern, Midland, and Southern areas, at least six regional dialects in the eastern half of the country are prominent enough to warrant individual characterization, and two additional dialects of considerable importance extend over several regions:

1. *Eastern New England.* This includes the whole or parts of states that lie to the east of the Connecticut River in Massachusetts and Connecticut and east of the Green Mountains in Vermont. While all features of the dialect are not uniform in their distribution, we may recognize as characteristic the retention of a rounded vowel in words like *hot* and *top*, which the rest of the country has unrounded to a shortened form of the *a* in *father;* the use of the broad *a* in *fast, path, grass*, etc.; and, as we have seen, the loss of the *r* in *car, hard*, etc., except before vowels (*carry, Tory*). Boston is its focal area.[1]

---

[1] A focal area is one which because of its political, commercial, cultural, or other importance (e.g., social) has influenced the speech of surrounding areas. *Tonic* (soft drink), for instance, has spread apparently only to communities served by distributors whose headquarters are in Boston.

2. *New York City.* Although often considered a part of the Eastern New England dialect, the speech of New York City and adjacent counties is on the whole quite different. The occurrence of *r* has increased significantly since the second world war, and its frequency among various groups of speakers has become a reliable indicator of social class.[1] *Cot* and *caught* are phonemically contrasted [kɑt, kɔt] since the *o* in words like *cot* and *top*, before voiceless stops, is almost always unrounded. The pronunciation of *curl* like *coil*, *third* as *thoid* is the characteristic most distinctive of New York City in the popular mind, although it should be added that among cultivated New Yorkers *curl* and *coil* are phonemically distinct [kʌɪl, kɔɪl].

3. *Inland Northern.* Western New England, upstate New York, and the basin of the Great Lakes share features of pronunciation which derive from the original settlement and the spread of the population westward through the water route of the lakes. Like the speech of eastern New England, Inland Northern distinguishes [o] in words like *mourning* and *hoarse* from [ɔ] in *morning* and *horse*. Also like the dialect of eastern New England and in contrast with the prevailing forms of the Pennsylvania settlement area, Northern has [ð] regularly in *with*, [s] in *grease* (verb) and *greasy*, and [ʊ] in *roots*. The recently published volumes of the *Linguistic Atlas of the Upper Midwest* (see § 255) show that traces of the boundary can be extended beyond the Mississippi into Iowa, Nebraska, Minnesota, and the Dakotas, although it is less distinct than the boundary in Illinois, Indiana, and Ohio, just as the boundary in those states is less distinct than that of the original settlements in Pennsylvania. Because the speech of the Inland Northern region differs strikingly from that of eastern New England in its retention of postvocalic [r] and in the occurrence of the vowel [æ] in words like *ask*, it is necessary to separate these two subareas of Northern, with a prominent boundary running in a northerly direction from the mouth of the Connecticut River to the Green Mountains of Vermont.

4. *North Midland.* Like Inland Northern, the North Midland dialect preserves the *r* in all positions and has [æ] in *fast, ask, grass*, etc. Within the North Midland region one of the two major subareas is the Middle Atlantic, which includes the eastern third of Pennsylvania below the Northern-Midland line, the southern half of New Jersey, the northern half of Delaware, and the adjacent parts of Maryland. The speech of this subarea has the unrounded vowel in *forest* as well as in *hot*, the [ɛ] of *egg* in *care, Mary, merry*, and a merging of [o] and [ɔ] before [r] in *four* and *forty*. The other major subarea includes the speech of western Pennsylvania and

---

[1] See William Labov, *The Social Stratification of English in New York City* (Washington, D.C., 1966), pp. 63–89, 207–43, *et passim.*

its derivatives in Ohio, Indiana, and Illinois. Although closely related to the Middle Atlantic dialect, it has some differences of pronunciation such as the merging of the vowels in *cot* and *caught*. The two words are generally homonyms [kɒt], the same vowel occurring with a considerable range of allophones in *lot, John, palm, barn, law, frost, dog, fog,* and *foggy*.

5. *South Midland (Mid Southern).*[1] This area includes all of West Virginia except the counties bordering on Pennsylvania and Maryland,[2] the mountain regions of Virginia and North Carolina, most of Kentucky and Tennessee, with a small portion of the states to the north and the south. At the present stage of investigation it appears that South Midland extends west of the Mississippi through southern Missouri and northern Arkansas into north Texas, where it blends with the Southern dialect. Settled first from Pennsylvania and later from the South, the region shows in its speech the mixed character which is to be expected under the circumstances. Although none of the dialect features of South Midland are unique in themselves and all of them occur in either Midland or Southern, the configuration of features is peculiar to the South Midland. Thus the *r* is sounded as in Midland, but [aɪ] is generally pronounced [aᵋ], or in the southern part of the area [aᵊ, a] as in many parts of the South. Some dialectologists believe that the dialect of this area should be considered a variety of Southern rather than a Midland type (see footnote 1), and the problem, which involves the relative weights to be assigned dialectal features, remains one of continuing investigation in the fieldwork for the regional dialect atlases.

6. *Southern.* The Southern dialect covers a large area, the old plantation country, and it would be unreasonable to expect uniformity in it. Important focal areas are the Virginia Piedmont and the low country near the coast of South Carolina. In many districts it agrees with eastern New England in the loss of *r* finally and before consonants, as in *car* and *hard*, but tends to go even further and omit the *r* before a word beginning with a vowel, as in *far away* [faː əˡwe]. But it does not have the rounded vowel in words like *top* and *hot*, or the broad *a* in *grass* and *dance*. In the latter words it shows a preference for [æə, æɪ]. A distinctive feature of the Southern dialect is the treatment of the diphthong in *out*. Instead of the

[1] Most dialectologists associated with the Linguistic Atlas designate this area South Midland. For evidence supporting Mid Southern, see Wood, *Vocabulary Change*, pp. 28–31, 358. See also C.-J. N. Bailey, "Is There a 'Midland' Dialect of American English?" Paper read at the summer meeting of the Ling. Soc. of Amer., July 27, 1968 (ERIC ED 021 240).

[2] In the southern and eastern part of West Virginia the influence of Virginia speech is strong.

usual [aʊ] the Southern speaker begins this diphthong with [æ] before voiced consonants and finally, while in Virginia and South Carolina this diphthong takes the form [əʊ, ʌʊ] before voiceless consonants. Equally characteristic is the so-called Southern drawl. This is not only a matter of slower enunciation, but involves a dipthongization or double diphthongization of stressed vowels. In its most pronounced form this results in *yes* becoming [jɛɪs] or [jɛjəs], *class* becoming [klæɪs] or [klæjəs], etc. Final consonant groups are likely to suffer from a weakened articulation: *las'*, *kep'*, *fin'*, etc. for *last, kept, find*, especially in nonstandard use. Around New Orleans and Charleston *curl* and *third* are pronounced [kʌɪl] and [θʌɪd], as in New York City, a pattern which may be phonologically related to certain other diphthongizations in the Southern drawl.[1] Many speakers pronounce *Tuesday* and *duty* with a glide [tjus–, dju–] and in much of the South homonomy of mid and high front vowels before nasals is general, no distinction occurring between *pin* and *pen* [pɪn]. There are considerable differences in the speech of the South, enabling a southerner at times to tell from a short conversation the particular state which another southerner comes from. But a northerner can seldom do this.

7. *General American.* This variety and the next one, black English, are controversial and unlike the dialects discussed above in not directly reflecting geographical patterns of migration and settlement. Both varieties can be superimposed on large areas of the map of dialects at the beginning of this section, although many dialectologists would deny the validity of such a description. At the time of the first edition of this history, General American was widely accepted as one of the three main dialects of American English, along with New England and Southern. It was usually said to be characterized by the flat *a* (in *fast, path*, etc.), the unrounded vowel in *hot, top*, etc., the retention of a strong *r* in all positions, and less tendency than British English to introduce a glide after the vowels [e] and [o], *late, note*. The western half of the country and the regions enumerated in the preceding discussions except eastern New England, metropolitan New York, and Southern were often spoken of as constituting General American. Since the 1930's, investigations for the *Linguistic Atlas* (see § 255) have identified dialect areas within the old General American area and have prompted a repudiation of this "prescientific concept."[2] The present authors believe

[1] See James Sledd, "Breaking, Umlaut, and the Southern Drawl," *Language*, 42 (1966), 18–41.
[2] Roger Abrahams and Rudolph C. Troike, eds., *Language and Cultural Diversity in American Education* (Englewood Cliffs, N.J., 1972), p. 130. See also W. R. Van Riper, "General American: An Ambiguity," in *Lexicography and Dialect Geography: Festgabe for Hans Kurath* (Wiesbaden, 1973), pp. 232–42, and J. B. McMillan, "Of Matters

that if the term, which has lost much of its currency, is completely abandoned, something very much like it will have to be invented in the future. Since only one of the published volumes of the *Linguistic Atlas* has described pronunciation west of the Atlantic states,[1] it is difficult to know whether the western areas of the old General American should be subdivided at all.[2] Even when additional volumes of the *Atlas* become available, they will reflect the speech of older inhabitants of the middle decades of this century, a feature of the *Atlas* for which it has often been criticized. The questions asked and the informants interviewed put an emphasis on items of rural vocabulary which are now seldom used by younger speakers. If the trend toward homogeneity within the vast area of General American continues, there will be less utility in the terms "Northern" and "Midland" for identifying speakers from, say, Minnesota (Northern) and southern Iowa (Midland) than in the supplanted term "General American," which would group these speakers together along with the majority of speakers from the West Coast and the states in between.

8. *Black English Vernacular.* One of the most intensively studied varieties of English during the past decade has been the speech of American blacks in the South and in northern cities. This variety, which has been called variously *nonstandard Negro English, black English vernacular,* and simply *black English,* diverges in its very name from a geographical classification of dialects. The actual extent of divergence as well as the degree of homogeneity within the black English vernacular are matters of some debate, which relate directly to theories regarding the origins of the dialect.[3] The view of traditional dialectologists has been that the English of American blacks is essentially that of white speakers from the same socioeconomic

---

Lexicographical," *American Speech* (1970; pub. 1974), 289–92. Frederic G. Cassidy abandoned the term in his 1954 revision of Stuart Robertson, *The Development of Modern English* (New York, 1934), as did C. K. Thomas in his 1958 revision of *An Introduction to the Phonetics of American English* (New York, 1947).

[1] Harold B. Allen, *The Linguistic Atlas of the Upper Midwest,* vol. 3 (Minneapolis, 1976).

[2] In the 1958 edition of his *Introduction,* Thomas proposes four regional dialects in the General American area beyond the Atlantic states. But in an important critique of traditional dialectology in this country, Glenna R. Pickford, "American Linguistic Geography: A Sociological Appraisal," *Word,* 12 (1956), writes of California: "The whirlpool caused by the continual mixing, moving, and intermarriage of peoples of heterogeneous origin renders a sociological analysis by groups of common origin patently impossible" (p. 226), and with reference to a study by David W. Reed, "California vocabulary as Reed describes it appears to be not so much regional as national—the urban speech of most of the rest of the United States" (p. 227).

[3] The one point upon which there is general agreement is that none of the characteristics of black English (or of any other dialect or language in the world) has anything to do with the physical characteristics of the group of speakers. The causes of dialectal differences are cultural, not biological.

class, with a few independent developments, a few relic forms of English origin, and a few superficial features, especially vocabulary, from African languages.[1] This view has been challenged by proponents of the "creole hypothesis," who find deeper structural differences between black English and standard English, and trace those differences ultimately to the linguistic situation on the west coast of Africa during the days of the slave trade. Pidgin English, characterized by syntactic structures and words from West African languages, was the means of communication between English-speaking whites and Africans, and among Africans whose languages were mutually unintelligible. In the New World this pidgin English continued to be spoken by transported slaves and eventually as a creole dialect by their descendants.[2] By this view, the most compelling parallels to American black English are various creolized forms of English in the Caribbean. Both views recognize that the migrations of blacks from the rural South to the cities of the North during this century brought a dialect with distinctly Southern features to the black areas of New York, Philadelphia, Detroit, and other cities, where it has continued to be learned by successive generations. The historical view which one assumes depends partly on the structural descriptions one accepts. Recent studies of the black English vernacular have argued that the syntactic structures which differ from standard English are consistent within their own system and sometimes similar to structures in clear pidgin and creole languages.[3] The best-known example of an English-based creole in the continental United States is the Gullah dialect spoken by blacks along the coast and on the coastal islands of South Carolina and Georgia.[4] The speech of the majority of American blacks is much closer to standard English than is Gullah, but whether the differences that exist are superficial or profound remains a point of controversy, the answer varying in part with the evidence chosen. Those who argue for profound differences have cited a relatively few structures in black English such as the systematic absence of the copula, the use of the auxiliary *be* for expressing durative aspect, the absence of inflection for the

---

[1] See R. I. McDavid, Jr., and V. G. McDavid, "The Relationship of the Speech of American Negroes to the Speech of Whites," *American Speech*, 26 (1951), 3–17.

[2] A creole, like a pidgin, is based on two or more languages, but unlike a pidgin it is learned as a native language, and it contains fuller syntax and vocabulary. See David DeCamp, "Introduction: The Study of Pidgin and Creole Languages," in *Pidginization and Creolization of Languages*, ed. Dell Hymes (Cambridge, 1971), pp. 13–39.

[3] See, for example, the articles by B. L. Bailey, W. A. Stewart, and D. Dalby reprinted in *Black-White Speech Relationships*, ed. Walt Wolfram and Nona H. Clarke (Washington, D.C., 1971).

[4] The standard work on Gullah is Lorenzo D. Turner, *Africanisms in the Gullah Dialect* (1949; reprinted with a new foreword by David DeCamp, Ann Arbor, 1974).

possessive, and the failure of agreement (from the point of view of standard English) of verbs in the present tense third person singular. In considering such arguments, it is easy to overlook the vast ground that all dialects of American English share. Further research will establish more clearly the degree of difference between the black English vernacular and standard English, but it will be surprising if many of the claims of divergence are not found eventually to be overstated, rather like Noah Webster's patriotic assertions on the differences between British English and American English.[1]

Although there may have been influences from African languages on certain structures in black English, the most plausible attempt to account for most major dialectal differences of the United States is that which studies the districts in England from which the earliest settlers came.[2] If this explanation is valid, we must believe that the English spoken by the first colonists—mainly those who came during the seventeenth century—determined the speech of the communities in which they settled, and that later accretions to the population of districts already occupied were made sufficiently gradually to be assimilated to the speech that had become established there. There is nothing in the facts to contradict this assumption. The nucleus of the New England colonies was in the district around Massachusetts Bay, and the earliest settlements in the South were in the tidewater district of Virginia. Fortunately, it is for just these sections that we have the fullest information concerning the English homes of the earliest settlers. In the *Atlas of the Historical Geography of the United States*[3] the evidence has been collected. Of the settlers in New England before 1700, 1,281 have been traced to their source in England, and for Virginia during the same period the English homes have been found for 637. These numbers, to be sure, are not large, but it is believed that the group of

---

[1] In the meantime, the views which individual English teachers assume will have consequences that make the matter more than an academic debate. Cf., for example, the essays in *Teaching Standard English in the Inner City*, ed. Ralph W. Fasold and Roger W. Shuy (Washington, D.C., 1970), and James Sledd, "Doublespeak: Dialectology in the Service of Big Brother," *College English*, 33 (1972), 439–56.

[2] For an excellent statement of this view see Hans Kurath, "The Origin of the Dialectal Differences in Spoken American English," *Modern Philology*, 25 (1928), 385–95. A convenient summary of supporting evidence collected in the years since is Kurath's *Studies in Area Linguistics* (Bloomington, Ind., 1972), especially chap. 5, "The Historical Relation of American English to British English."

[3] Prepared by Charles O. Paullin and John K. Wright (Washington and New York, 1932), pp. 46–47. To this may be added Marcus L. Hansen, *The Atlantic Migration, 1607–1860* (Cambridge, Mass., 1940) and the same author's account of the settlement of New England contributed to the *Handbook of the Linguistic Geography of New England* mentioned on p. 390.

colonists identified in each case is representative of the two settlements. The result shows that the predominant element in New England was from the southeastern and southern counties of England.[1] Sixty-one percent of those traced are accounted for by the larger counties mentioned in the footnote, and since the figures for the smaller counties are not given, we may conservatively say that two-thirds of the New England colonists before 1700 came from the south of England, especially the southeast. For Virginia the percentage is not quite so large, but is still decisive. Forty-two percent were derived from London, Gloucester, and Kent, all in the south. Again figures for the smaller counties are omitted. From the map which these statistics accompany, however, it appears that the south Midlands and the west were more fully represented among the settlers of Virginia than in the New England colonies. In any case, it is certain that more than 50 percent of the Virginia settlers traced came from the southern half of England. The inference is that the English brought to New England and Virginia was that spoken in the southern parts of England, and that the similarity of the New England and Southern dialects in this country to present-day standard English is due to the preponderance of settlers from the south of England in these colonies. The importance of Virginia in the later settlements of the South has already been pointed out, and doubtless accounts for the spread of the early Virginia form of speech in the southern states.

We unfortunately do not have the same sort of information about the early settlers in the middle colonies. But we are not without a basis for inference. We know that the Quakers played the principal part in the settlements along the Delaware, and that this sect had its largest following in the north of England and the north Midlands. We should expect a good many of the settlers in eastern Pennsylvania and the adjacent parts of New Jersey and Delaware to have come from the northern half of England. We know also that large numbers of Scotch-Irish settled in Pennsylvania and were later prominent in the settlement of parts of the South and the West. They were mostly Scots who had been settled for a few generations in northeastern Ireland. They, of course, spoke Northern English. The Germans, who formed a large element in the population of the middle

---

[1] "The number of settlers from London for New England was 193, or 15 percent; for Virginia 179, or 28 percent. The counties (with numbers) sending the most settlers to New England are as follows: Norfolk 125, Suffolk 116, Kent 106, Essex 100, Devon 76, Wiltshire 69; to Virginia, Gloucester 44, Kent 42, Yorkshire 30, and Lancaster 22. Of the emigrants from Gloucester both to New England and Virginia more than half came from Bristol. Of the Norfolk emigrants to New England half came from Hingham and Norwich." (Paullin and Wright, *op. cit.*, p. 46.)

colonies, acquired their English from the English-speaking colonists among whom they settled. It would seem likely that the population of the Middle States was much more northern than that of New England and Virginia, and that the preservation of the *r* and other characteristics of Northern English found in the dialect of these states is to be accounted for in this way. It may not be too much to assert that the prominence of the Scotch-Irish in the constant advance of the western frontier was an influential factor in carrying the form of English spoken in the middle colonies into the newer territories of the West and in making this speech the basis of General American.

In describing the principal dialect areas that can be distinguished in the language of this country we have spoken only of distinctive features of the pronunciation. This does not mean that there are no other local differences. There are also peculiarities of vocabulary or idiom that may represent a survival of some older form of expression or some special development whose origin cannot be traced. They are especially characteristic of the popular speech. When a man calls a certain kind of cheese *smearcase*, we suspect contact at some time with the Pennsylvania Dutch settlements. In the neighborhood of Boston one may call for a *tonic* when he wants only a *soft drink*. In different parts of the country he may get sugar in a *bag*, a *sack*, or a *poke*, and he may either *carry* it or, in the South, *tote* it. The Philadelphian uses the word *square* not only for a small city park but also for what Baedeker describes as "a rectangular mass of buildings bounded by four streets," and what is elsewhere known as a *block*. In most parts of the country one *parks* a car, but until very recently he might *rank* it in Trenton and, for all we know to the contrary, may still *file* it in a certain little town in southern Delaware. Within a small area a number of interesting variants for the same thing can often be found in the half-hidden recesses of popular speech. Thus in different New England communities the *earthworm* exists under the name *angleworm*, *angledog*, *easworm* (with variants *eastworm* and *easterworm*), *fishworm*, *mudworm*, and *rainworm*.[1] There are also odd deviations of idiom from the standard speech. Such are the Middle Western *phone up* and *I want in*, or the expression reported from South Dakota, "I got up at six o'clock this morning although I don't *belong to* get up until seven." It would be easy to multiply local peculiarities of word or phrase in all parts of America, as in other countries. In this country they are not always genuine examples of dialect, since they are not

---

[1] Cf. Rachel S. Harris, "New England Words for the Earthworm," *American Speech*, 8, no. 4 (1933), 12–17, and maps 139 and 140 in Kurath, *Word Geography*, mentioned on p. 369.

peculiar to a particular dialectal region, but may occur in numerous parts of the country, often at a considerable distance from one another.[1] In any case they should not by themselves be made the basis for distinguishing major dialect areas.

In connection with this discussion of American dialects it is necessary to recall what was said above about the general uniformity of the English language in this country. The differences between the English of one section and that of another are not great. The universal spread of education in modern times and the absence of any sharp differentiation of social classes in this country are not favorable to the development or maintenance of dialect. While a southerner or a man from "down East" can usually be recognized by his speech, there are large sections of the country in which it would be impossible to tell within a thousand miles the district from which an individual came. That such differences as exist are more noticeable in the East and are greater from north to south than from east to west is but a natural consequence of the geographical configuration of colonial America.[2]

251. *The Controversy over Americanisms.* From the time that differences in the vocabulary and idiom of Americans began to be noticed, they became the subject of comment and soon of controversy. In the beginning English comment was uniformly adverse, at least as far back as the utterances of Dr. Johnson, and to a large extent it still is today. Often Americans were accused of corrupting the English language by introducing new and unfamiliar words, whereas they were in fact only continuing to employ terms familiar in the seventeenth century which had become obsolete in England. When the injustice of this attitude was perceived, Americans began to defend their use of English and, with a growing sense of their position among nations, to demand parity for their speech with the English of England. Over this difference in point of view a controversy was carried on through most of the nineteenth century and can hardly be said to have died down completely at the present day.

[1] The late Professor Miles L. Hanley, at one time editor of *Dialect Notes*, gave an interesting example of this in the Connecticut term "the minister's face" for the head of a pig after the animal has been butchered and the ears, jowels, eyes, etc., have been removed. The phrase is occasionally found in New Hampshire in parts settled from Connecticut, but also occurs in Virginia.

[2] For discussions of the English language in Hawaii, which touch on some of the same problems found in discussions of black English, see John E. Reinecke, *Language and Dialect in Hawaii: Sociolinguistic History to 1935*, ed. Stanley M. Tsuzaki (Honolulu, 1969); Elizabeth Carr, *Da Kine Talk: From Pidgin to Standard English in Hawaii* (Honolulu, 1972); and the articles by Elizabeth Carr and Stanley Tsuzaki in *Pidginization and Creolization of Languages*, ed. Dell Hymes.

The first person to use the term *Americanism* was John Witherspoon, one of the early presidents of Princeton University. In 1781 he defined it as "an use of phrases or terms, or a construction of sentences, even among persons of rank and education, different from the use of the same terms or phrases, or the construction of similar sentences in Great-Britain." In justification of the word he added, "The word Americanism, which I have coined for the purpose, is exactly similar in its formation and signification to the word Scotticism." Himself a Scot, he naturally did not look upon differences from the English of England as necessarily bad. He said, "It does not follow, from a man's using these, that he is ignorant, or his discourse upon the whole inelegant; nay, it does not follow in every case, that the terms or phrases used are worse in themselves, but merely that they are of American and not of English growth."[1] So independent an attitude is not surprising in one who, if he did not paint his name in characters so bold as John Hancock, was nevertheless one of the signers of the Declaration of Independence. Jefferson, who did not scruple to coin the word *belittle*, was independent without being belligerent. He objected to "raising a hue and cry against every word he [Johnson] has not licensed.... Here where all is new, no innovation is feared which offers good.... And should the language of England continue stationary, we shall probably enlarge our employment of it, until its new character may separate it in name, as well as in power, from the mother tongue." With most, however, the spirit of conformity prevailed. Even so original a thinker as Franklin was ready to accept English usage as his own guide. Acknowledging a criticism of Hume's, he wrote: "I thank you for your friendly admonition relating to some unusual words in the pamphlet. It will be of service to me. The *pejorate* and the *colonize*, since they are not in common use here [in England], I give up as bad; for certainly in writings intended for persuasion and for general information, one cannot be too clear; and every expression in the least obscure is a fault. The *unshakable*, too, tho clear, I give up as rather low. The introducing new words, where we are already possessed of old ones sufficiently expressive, I confess must be generally wrong, as it tends to change the language.... I hope with you, that we shall always in America make the best English of this Island our standard, and I believe it will be so."[2]

[1] In the *Pennsylvania Journal and Weekly Advertiser*, reprinted in M. M. Mathews, *The Beginnings of American English* (Chicago, 1931), p. 17.

[2] *Writings*, ed. A. H. Smyth, IV, 83–84. In the same place Franklin says: "Yet, at the same time, I cannot but wish the usage of our tongue permitted making new words, when we want them, by composition of old ones whose meanings are already well understood...."

The first dictionary of Americanisms was published in 1816 by John Pickering under the title *A Vocabulary, or Collection of Words and Phrases which have been supposed to be Peculiar to the United States of America*. Although the work of an American, it is thoroughly English in its point of view. Both in the introductory essay which accompanies it and in the comment throughout the body of the glossary Pickering shows clearly that he has been inspired by a desire to purify the language of his countrymen by pointing out all departures from English usage and persuading them that only by strict accord with that usage can they hope to write pure English. This attitude aroused the wrath of Noah Webster, who felt that his own position had been attacked. With manifest effort at self-control he replied in a published *Letter to the Honorable John Pickering on the Subject of His Vocabulary* (1817). "With regard to the general principle," he wrote, "that we must use only such words as the English use let me repeat, that the restriction is, in the nature of the thing, impracticable, and the demand that we should observe it, is as improper as it is arrogant. Equally impertinent is it to ridicule us for retaining the use of genuine English words, because they happen to be obsolete in London, or in the higher circles of life." "Let it be further observed," he said, "that the charge against the people of this country, of introducing new words, is, to a great degree, unfounded. Your own researches have proved this fact. I question whether ten words can be found among men of reputable character in the United States, which are not authorized by English usage, either general or local. But whether the number is ten or fifty, is not material. New words will be formed and used, if found necessary or convenient, without a license from Englishmen." The battle was on.

A much more ambitious *Dictionary of Americanisms* was published in 1848 by John R. Bartlett and greatly enlarged in a second edition of 1859. The author was for three years commissioner on the Mexican boundary and had an opportunity to gather many words from prairie and frontier life. Considering the date at which it was compiled, it is a very commendable piece of work. In it the older attitude of Pickering has given place almost entirely to an interest in dialect for its own sake. Bartlett refrains from controversy, and though he has no hope that "the pure old idiomatic English style can ever be restored in this country," he ventures the thought that we may some day have a "style and a literature which will also have their beauties and merits, although fashioned after a somewhat different model."[1]

---

[1] Two other dictionaries of Americanisms may be mentioned. J. S. Farmer's *Americanisms Old and New* (London, 1889) adds little of value except some rather late

Up to the time of our Civil War the prevailing attitude in this country seems to have been one of deference to English usage. In 1866, however, James Russell Lowell published in book form the Second Series of *The Biglow Papers*, and supplied it with a lengthy introduction. Ostensibly an exposition of the dialect in which the *Papers* were written, this essay is in reality one of the most important contributions to the controversy over Americanisms. While it had often been recognized that many of the distinctive features of American English were survivals of the older English of England, no one had been at pains to bring together the enormous mass of evidence on the subject. Lowell filled more than fifty pages with closely packed but eminently readable parallels to American expressions, drawn from his wide reading of the older literature of England. His reputation both in this country and abroad insured a wide public for his views. Since the appearance of this essay, the legitimacy of one large class of Americanisms has not been questioned. Those who have written most on the subject, such as Lounsbury[1] and Brander Matthews, have generally taken Lowell's defense as a point of departure, explicitly or implicitly, and have employed their strength in combating the idea that because an expression is of American origin it has no right to a hearing. They have preached the doctrine of American English for the American as a natural mark of intellectual sincerity. "For our novelists to try to write Americanly, from any motive," said William Dean Howells, "would be a dismal error, but being born Americans, we would have them use 'Americanisms' whenever these serve their turn; and when their characters speak, we should like to hear them speak true American, with all the varying Tennesseean, Philadelphian, Bostonian, and New York accents."[2] What Brander Matthews, in his *Americanisms and Briticisms*, wrote of English criticism of American spelling has a wider significance as indicative of the contemporary attitude in America toward English authority in matters of linguistic usage: "Any American who chances to note the force and the fervor and the frequency

---

quotations. By far the most valuable contribution to the subject is R. H. Thornton's *An American Glossary* (London, 1912) with its 14,000 dated quotations. A supplement, based on additional material which Thornton had collected at the time of his death, is published in *Dialect Notes*, vol. 6 (1931–1939). Gilbert M. Tucker's *American English* (New York, 1921) contains two lists of Americanisms, the alleged and the real. It is a useful contribution. Today we have the modern works mentioned on p. 389.

[1] Lounsbury further stressed the fact that many so-called Americanisms were not Americanisms at all by pointing to parallels in the English dialects. He found such "typically American" expressions as *to ride like blazes, in a jiffy, a tip-top fellow, before you could say Jack Robinson, that's a whopper, gawky* (awkward), *glum* (gloomy), *gumption* (sense), *sappy* (silly) in a glossary for Suffolk, England, published in 1823. Cf. the *International Rev.*, 8 (1880), 479.

[2] *Harper's Magazine*, 32 (1886), 325.

of the objurgations against American spelling in the columns of the *Saturday Review*, for example, and of the *Athenaeum*, may find himself wondering as to the date of the papal bull which declared the infallibility of contemporary British orthography, and as to the place at which it was made an article of faith." Regarding the British side of the question, the English attitude toward Americanisms is still quite frankly hostile. It often seems to be assumed that all Americanisms are vulgarities and colloquialisms, and we need to be reminded of an occasional utterance like that of William Archer: "New words are begotten by new conditions. . . . America has enormously enriched the language."

252. The Purist Attitude. The controversy over Americanisms has at times been more or less connected in this country with the purist attitude,[1] always an element in linguistic discussions in any age. There is nothing, of course, to compel the purist in America to be hostile to an American standard of "purity," but as a matter of fact he was in the beginning almost always identical with one who accepted English usage as a norm and believed that we should conform as completely as possible to it. While theoretically the purist ideal and advocacy of the English standard are two quite distinct things, they are so often united in our guardians of linguistic decorum that it would be difficult to separate them for purposes of discussion. Conversely, in England at any time during the nineteenth century any impurity in the language, meaning anything which the individual purist objected to, was more likely than not to be described as an Americanism. Coleridge objected to "that vile and barbarous word, *talented*," adding, "Most of these pieces of slang come from America." *Talented* did not come from America, though the point is of no consequence. Mr. Mencken tells us that *scientist* was denounced as "an ignoble Americanism" in 1890.[2] It is well known that the word has been disliked by many in England, although it was coined in 1840 by an Englishman.

That the various modifications of the English language in the United States were all "gross corruptions" was a belief vigorously expressed by an anonymous writer of 1800 in *The Monthly Magazine and American Review*. His article "On the Scheme of an American Language" contains an ironical reference to those who "think grammars and dictionaries should be compiled by natives of the country, not of the British or English,

---

[1] *Purist* and *purism* "are for the most part missile words, which we all of us fling at anyone who insults us by finding not good enough for him some manner of speech that is good enough for us . . . ; by *purism* is to be understood a needless and irritating insistence on purity or correctness of speech." (Fowler, *Modern English Usage* [Oxford, 1926], pp. 474–75.)

[2] *The American Language* (1st ed.), p. 38.

but of the American tongue." After thus paying his respects to Webster, he states his conviction that for our standard of language we must look to "the best educated class, whose dialect is purified by intimate intercourse with English books."

Pickering, whose *Vocabulary* of Americanisms has been mentioned above, begins his introductory essay with the statement, "The preservation of the English language in its purity throughout the United States is an object deserving the attention of every American, who is a friend to the literature and science of his country." This seems general enough, but after quoting several pages of extracts from English journals in condemnation of Americanisms, he adds that the language of the United States "has in so many instances departed from the English standard, that our scholars should lose no time in endeavouring to restore it to its purity, and to prevent future corruption." In 1835 an unknown writer in the *Southern Literary Messenger* looked forward (none too hopefully) to the time when "we shall no longer see such a term as *firstly* in a work on metaphysics, nor hear such a double adverb as *illy* on the floor of Congress—no longer hear of an event's *transpiring*, before it has become public, nor of an argument being *predicated* on such and such facts." He stated that our only safeguard against such licenses was the adoption of some common and acknowledged standard. "Such a standard exists in the authorized classics of Great Britain." The famous "Index Expurgatorius" of William Cullen Bryant has often been cited as an example of the purist ideal in journalism. It is a list of words which he excluded from the New York *Evening Post* and which seems to have grown up gradually during the years (1829–1878) when he was the editor of this well-known newspaper. Many of the expressions which he disliked "bear the stamp of vulgarity, pretension, haste, and slang," but the only objection to some of them, such as *dutiable, presidential, lengthy* (defended by Webster fifty years before), seems to have been the fact that they were Americanisms. A purist of a rather extreme type was Richard Grant White. In his books called *Words and Their Uses* (1870) and *Every-Day English* (1880) conformity to the purist ideal and acceptance of the English standard of usage become practically synonymous. In the preface to the former book he specifically disavows any right of Americans "to set up an independent standard." His opinion carried much weight with a certain class of people, a class possessed of a fine, if somewhat old-fashioned, culture. Such people are likely to have the point of view of the purist and to be more or less constantly influenced by English literary tradition.

With the establishment during the last century and the flourishing during the present of a modern tradition in American literature, the authority of English opinion and usage has diminished. Sentiments favoring prescriptivism persist, however, and the purist ideal continues to find expression in the popular press and in lexicographical enterprises.[1] When the Merriam Company published *Webster's Third New International Dictionary* in 1961, an outpouring of reviews ignored the considerable merits of the dictionary to criticize its restraint in legislating on matters of usage. The inclusion of *finalize* and *normalcy* without statements of their acceptability and of *irregardless* (though it was labeled "nonstandard") stirred editorial responses of extraordinary emotion and hostility. When the *New York Times* announced that it would continue to use the *Second International* edition of 1934, Bergen Evans pointed out that the very issue of the *Times* which made the announcement used 153 separate words, phrases, and constructions listed in the *Third International* but not in the *Second* and nineteen others which are condemned in the *Second*. Evans concluded: "Anyone who solemnly announces in the year 1962 that he will be guided in matters of English usage by a dictionary published in 1934 is talking ignorant and pretentious nonsense."[2] It is no more reasonable to look to a past, or a supposed past, in American lexicography for guidance in the current use of the language than to look across the ocean. The purist ideal is a manifestation of the same temperament in America as elsewhere in the world. In this country it has been guided in past years by a considerable respect for English opinion and usage, and in recent times by what seems to be self-confident introspection.[3] In all periods, the purist ideal has made the answers to difficult questions rather easier than they actually are. The judgments which can be asserted for lists of words taken without regard to context, audience, or expository intent imply falsely that linguistic forms have a certain value once and for all, and that the keys to effective writing and speaking can be found in the mastery of a few, clear, permanent proscriptions.

253. *Present Differentiation of Vocabulary.* Except in pronunciation the distance which the English language in America has traveled in its separation from that of England is chiefly measured in its vocabulary. It is

---

[1] One recent example is the "usage panel" of *The American Heritage Dictionary of the English Language* (New York, 1969).

[2] "But What's a Dictionary For?" *Atlantic* (May 1962), p. 62; reprinted in an instructive collection of reviews and essays on the subject, *Dictionaries and* That *Dictionary*, ed. James Sledd and Wilma R. Ebbitt (Chicago, 1962), p. 248.

[3] As, for example, in Dwight Macdonald, "The String Untuned," *The New Yorker* (March 10, 1962), pp. 130–34, 137–40, 143–50, 153–60; reprinted in Sledd and Ebbitt, pp. 166–88.

easy to exaggerate the importance of the differences that can be readily pointed out. The American on going to England or the English traveler on arriving in America is likely to be impressed by them, because each finds the other's expressions amusing when they do not actually puzzle him. As examples of such differences the words connected with the railroad and the automobile are often cited. The English word for *railroad* is *railway*, the *engineer* is a *driver*, the *conductor* a *guard*. The *baggage car* is a *van*, and the *baggage* carried is always *luggage*. Our *freight train, freight yard*, etc., become in England *goods train* and *goods yard*. Some of the more technical terms are likewise different. A *sleeper* in the United States is a sleeping car; in England it is what we call a *tie*. Our *switch* is a *point*, a *grade crossing* a *level crossing*, and so on. In connection with the automobile, the English speak of a *lorry* (truck), *windscreen* (windshield), *bonnet* (hood), *sparking plugs, gear lever* (gearshift), *gearbox* (transmission), *dynamo* (generator), *silencer* (muffler), *boot* (trunk), *petrol* (gasoline or gas). Their *motorway* is our *expressway* and their *dual carriageway* our *divided highway*. Such differences can be found in almost any part of the vocabulary: *ironmongery* (hardware), *lift* (elevator), *post* (mail), *hoarding* (billboard), *nappy* (diaper), *spanner* (wrench), *underground* (subway), *trunk call* (long-distance call), *cotton wool* (absorbent cotton), *barrister* (lawyer), *dustman* (garbage collector). We readily recognize the American character of *ice cream soda, apple pie, popcorn, free lunch, saloon* from their associations, and can understand why some of them would not be understood elsewhere. A writer in the London *Daily Mail* not very long ago complained that an Englishman would find "positively incomprehensible" the American words *commuter, rare* (as applied to underdone meat), *intern, tuxedo, truck farming, realtor, mean* (nasty), *dumb* (stupid), *enlisted man, seafood, living room, dirt road*, and *mortician*. It is always unsafe to say what American words an Englishman will not understand, and there are some words in this list which would be pretty generally "comprehended" in England. Others are not universal in America. At least *realtor* and *mortician* have by no means replaced real-estate agent and undertaker, though they spring from the same impulse that at the beginning of the last century converted the English *apothecary* into a *chemist*. Some of our words have a deceptive familiarity. *Lumber* with us is timber, but in England is discarded furniture and the like. *Laundry* in America is not only the place where clothing and linen are washed but the articles washed as well. A *lobbyist* in England is a parliamentary reporter, not one who attempts to influence legislation, and a *pressman* for us is not a reporter but one who works in the pressroom where a newspaper is printed.

It is of course on the level of more colloquial or popular speech that the greatest differences are noticed. The American seems to have a genius for ephemeral coinages which are naturally quite meaningless to one who is not constantly hearing them. *Bawl out, bonehead, boob, bootlegger, dumb-bell, flivver, go-getter, grafter, hootch, peach of a, pep, punk*, and to *razz* are part of a long list of terms in an American novel which had to be explained by a glossary in the English edition. There is nothing surprising about the geographical limitations of slang. Colloquial language has always shown more local variation than the more formal levels of speech. There were doubtless many colloquialisms current in Shakespeare's London that would not have been understood in contemporary Stratford. These do not constitute the English language either in England or America. It is well to remember that in the written language the difference between the English and the American use of words is often so slight that it is difficult to tell, in the case of a serious book, on which side of the Atlantic it was written.

254. *American Words in General English.* The difference between the English and the American vocabulary today is lessened by the fact that many American words have made their way into English use, and their number appears to be increasing rather than diminishing. Often, one might almost say generally, they have had to make their way against long and bitter opposition. The verbs to *advocate, placate*, and *antagonize* were buried under a literature of protest during most of the nineteenth century. This is not true of most of the early words adopted by the colonists from the Indians for native American things. Other words associated with American things have at times been accepted fairly readily: *telephone, phonograph, typewriter, ticker, prairie* are familiar examples. Some of our political terms, especially those associated with less admirable practices, have also been taken in: *caucus, logrolling, graft, to stump*, among others. It is easy to recognize the American origin of such words as *to lynch, blizzard, jazz, joy-ride, bucket shop*, but in many other cases the American origin of a word has been forgotten or the word has been so completely accepted in England that the dictionaries do not think it important any longer to state the fact. Generally speaking, it may be said that when an American word expresses an idea in a way that appeals to the English as fitting or effective, the word is ultimately adopted in England. Mr. Ernest Weekley, in his *Adjectives—and Other Words*, says: "It is difficult now to imagine how we got on so long without the word *stunt*, how we expressed the characteristics so conveniently summed up in *dope-fiend* or *high-brow*, or any other possible way of describing that mixture of the cheap pathetic and the ludicrous which is now universally labelled *sob-stuff.*" It is difficult to determine how large the debt of English is to the American vocabulary, but in the last hundred and fifty years it has probably exceeded the debt of English to any other source.

255. Scientific Interest in American English.   Apart from the interest in Americanisms, which, as we have seen, goes back to the beginning of the nineteenth century, there has been of late years considerable study of American English as a branch of English philology. It began with the investigation by individual scholars of particular dialects or regional characteristics. Pioneers in the field were George Hempl, Charles H. Grandgent, and O. F. Emerson.[1] Interest in American dialects led to the formation in 1889 of the American Dialect Society, which published a journal called *Dialect Notes*. The society, reorganized, now issues *PADS* (*Publications of the American Dialect Society*). In 1919 H. L. Mencken published a book of nearly five hundred pages which he called *The American Language*. This contained a large amount of entertaining and valuable material presented in a popular way and had the effect of stimulating a wider interest in the subject. It has gone through four editions, and subsequently two supplements were published (1945 and 1948), both larger than the original book.[2] A few years later a magazine called *American Speech* was launched, in which popular and technical discussions appear as evidence of the twofold appeal which American English has for the people of this country. In 1925 George P. Krapp gave us our first comprehensive and scholarly treatment of the language in his two-volume work, *The English Language in America*. This is the work of a philologist, but is not without its attraction for the layman. Subsequently there have been prepared and published at the University of Chicago *A Dictionary of American English on Historical Principles*, edited by Sir William Craigie and James R. Hulbert (4 vols., Chicago, 1938–1944), and *A Dictionary of Americanisms, on Historical Principles*, the work of Mitford M. Mathews (2 vols., Chicago, 1951). An American dictionary comparable with Joseph Wright's *English Dialect Dictionary* has been a goal of the American Dialect Society since its founding. The forthcoming *Dictionary of American Regional English* under the editorship of Frederic G. Cassidy will achieve that goal and provide an invaluable account of American dialects as they were

---

[1] Professor Grandgent was interested in the speech of New England. His most important essays on the New England dialect are reprinted in a volume called *Old and New* (Cambridge, Mass., 1920). Professor Emerson's monograph on the dialect of Ithaca, New York, was the first extensive study of an American dialect.

[2] A convenient abridged edition in one volume, with annotations and new material, is by Raven McDavid, Jr. (New York, 1963).

recorded between 1965 and 1970. The five-year period of fieldwork in more than one thousand communities in all fifty states will provide an almost instantaneous picture in comparison with the time required for most dialect surveys.

Much longer in the making and in many ways the most important of the undertakings designed to record the characteristics of American speech is the *Linguistic Atlas of the United States and Canada*, publication of which began in 1939. Although conceived as a single enterprise, the various regional projects have evolved into a series of independent but closely associated investigations. In this undertaking America has followed the lead of Europe. In the latter part of the nineteenth century there began to grow up an interest in linguistic geography, the study of the geographic distribution of linguistic phenomena. Apart from the value of such study in insuring the preservation of accurate records of dialects and even languages which were in process of dying out, it was seen that it might play an important role in linguistic science. The best way to study the phenomena of linguistic evolution and change is in the living speech of communities whose origin, cultural development, and relation to other communities can still be traced. Accordingly there have been published, or are in course of preparation, linguistic atlases for more than a dozen European speech areas, notably French, German, and Italian.[1] The proposal for an American atlas was made in 1928 at a meeting of the Modern Language Association and, independently, at a session of the Linguistic Society. With the support of the American Council of Learned Societies, work was begun in 1931 under the direction of Professor Hans Kurath of the University of Michigan. The portion of the *Atlas* covering the New England states was published during the first twelve years of the project, the data being presented graphically in a series of 730 maps.[2] Records of the speech of some two hundred communities were made. "In each community at least two informants (subjects) are selected: (1) An elderly representative of the long established families whose speech is felt to be old fashioned. (2) A represen-

---

[1] For an account of the various surveys then being made see J. Schrijnen, *Essai de bibliographie de géographie linguistique générale* (Nimègue, 1933). Later information may be found in the issues of *Orbis: Bulletin internationale de documentation linguistique* (Louvain, 1952–   ). For a survey of earlier work and a general treatment of the province of linguistic geography, see Albert Dauzat, *La Géographie linguistique* (Paris, 1922), and the exhaustive work of Sever Pop, *La Dialectologie: Aperçu historique et méthodes d'enquêtes linguistiques* (2 vols., Louvain, 1950).

[2] *Linguistic Atlas of New England*, ed. Hans Kurath *et al.* (3 vols., in 6 parts, Providence, 1939–1943), with a *Handbook of the Linguistic Geography of New England*, by Kurath *et al.* (Providence, 1939), discussing the dialect areas distinguished, the selection of communities and informants, the settlement of New England, the work sheets, and various procedural matters.

tative of the middle-aged group who has not had too much schooling and has preserved, in the main, the local type of speech." The history of the settlement is traced and generally a fairly full history of the individual informant is obtained before he is approached. The material collected covers pronunciation, grammatical forms, syntactical usages, and vocabulary, and is obtained by means of a carefully prepared questionnaire designed to bring out the most characteristic dialectal features, known or suspected.[1] The answers are recorded in phonetic notation and supplemented by phonograph records and tapes. In the fourth decade after the publication of the *Linguistic Atlas of New England,* the three volumes covering the Upper Midwest (Minnesota, Iowa, Nebraska, South Dakota, and North Dakota) have appeared,[2] and materials for most of the other regions have been collected or are well advanced.[3] Even in their unedited and unpublished form, they have been the source for a number of regional studies (see footnote, pp. 368–69).

Any large project which requires several decades to record features of a language will encounter the problem of changes in the language as well as changes in the methods of studying human institutions. In the half century since the inception of the *Linguistic Atlas,* both kinds of change have occurred at a rapid rate in the United States. While the Atlas fieldworkers were recording rural linguistic items from older, settled speakers, American society was becoming increasingly mobile and urban. At the same time, advances in related social sciences made the traditional methods of

[1] See Alva L. Davis, Raven I. McDavid, Jr., and Virginia G. McDavid, eds., *A Compilation of the Work Sheets of the Linguistic Atlas of the United States and Canada and Associated Projects* (2nd ed., Chicago, 1969).

[2] Harold B. Allen, *The Linguistic Atlas of the Upper Midwest* (3 vols., Minneapolis, 1973–1976).

[3] The materials for practically all the rest of the Atlantic seaboard were collected by Guy S. Lowman, and, after his untimely death, by Raven I. McDavid, Jr. They will be published as the *Linguistic Atlas of the Middle and South Atlantic States.* Fieldwork for the *Linguistic Atlas of the North-Central States* (Wisconsin, Michigan, Illinois, Indiana, Kentucky, Ohio, and southwestern Ontario) was completed in 1958 under the direction of Albert H. Marckwardt. Xerox and microfilm copies of the field records are available from the University of Chicago. A third project between the stage of completed fieldwork and publication is the *Linguistic Atlas of the Pacific Coast,* directed by David Reed and Carroll Reed. Some work has been done in the Rocky Mountain states, and research for the *Linguistic Atlas of the Gulf States,* after beginning later than the others, is now making rapid progress under the direction of Lee Pederson. Meanwhile, Audrey Duckert has revisited the original New England communities in a second round of investigation to record linguistic change. See E. Bagby Atwood, "The Methods of American Dialectology," *Zeitschrift für Mundartforschung,* 30 (1963), 1–30; Wolfgang Viereck, "Britische und amerikanische Sprachatlanten," *Zeitschrift für Dialektologie und Linguistik,* 38 (1971), 167–205; and Lee Pederson, "An Introduction to the LAGS Project," in *A Manual for Dialect Research in the Southern States,* ed. Lee Pederson *et al.* (2nd ed., University, Ala., 1974), pp. 3–31.

selecting and classifying informants, and the goals of the survey, subject to criticism.[1] In recent years linguists have turned more of their attention to the complex patterns of speech in the cities of the United States. William Labov's work has been especially influential in its application of techniques from sociology to the description of urban speech. In studying the social varieties of English, Labov and others have attempted to observe the language in its social setting, outside the artificial context of an interview.[2] The methodological conclusions which these linguists have drawn from their trials, failures, and successes in recording urban English are as important as their descriptions of particular pronunciations or syntactic structures. Labov argues that the lack of verbal ability and logic which some linguists find in nonstandard English is the result of asking the wrong questions in the wrong situations and then analyzing the answers within the investigator's linguistic system rather than the subject's. If the practical implications which have been drawn from recent sociolinguistic studies are often contradictory, the contradictions are hardly surprising at our present stage of understanding.[3] It is unrealistic to expect the discipline of sociolinguistics, which only recently has acquired its name, to provide immediate solutions to problems that are rooted not only in the stratification of the language but finally in the society which the language reflects.

At the same time that linguistic geography and sociolinguistics were contributing so much to our knowledge of the language of this country in its regional and social aspects, the study of American English was making great advances in one other direction, that of its basic structure. In the nineteenth century and the early part of the twentieth the interests of linguistic scholars were mainly historical and comparative. Such studies, of course, still constitute a large and important field of scholarship. But with the increasing interest in this country in the recording and interpretation of the languages of the American Indians, new procedures were found to be necessary to deal with structures totally different from those of the languages most familiar to us, the languages of Europe and western Asia. In the new approach Franz Boas and his pupil Edward Sapir were the pioneers, and their work was supplemented and continued by Leonard

[1] See Glenna Ruth Pickford, "American Linguistic Geography: A Sociological Appraisal," *Word*, 12 (1956), 211–33.

[2] See William Labov, *Sociolinguistic Patterns* (Philadelphia, 1972), chap. 8, and *Language in the Inner City* (Philadelphia, 1972), chaps. 5–7.

[3] Cf. the contrasting conclusions drawn by Labov, "The Logic of Nonstandard English," in *Language in the Inner City*, chap. 5, and those by the influential British sociologist Basil Bernstein, "Elaborated and Restricted Codes: Their Social Origins and Some Consequences," in *The Ethnography of Communication*, ed. J. J. Gumperz and D. Hymes, special pub. of *American Anthropologist*, 66, no. 6, part 2 (1964), 55–69.

Bloomfield. The publication in 1933 of Bloomfield's book *Language*, the most important work on general linguistics in the first half of the present century, marked a turning point in American linguistic scholarship. The methods which had proved their worth in the study of American Indian languages began to be applied to the study of American English (and other modern languages). Starting with the premise that any language is a structured system of arbitrary signals (here conceived of as vocal sounds), structural linguistics sought to determine which elements (including stress, intonation, pauses, etc.) are significant and to describe the pattern in which they are organized. It began with phonemic analysis[1] and proceeded from there to morphology and syntax. It generally ignored semantics, or the study of meaning.[2]

In 1957 Noam Chomsky presented a radically different model of language in a thin, technical book entitled *Syntactic Structures*. Instead of beginning the description with phonology, as the structuralists who followed Bloomfield had done, Chomsky began with syntax and argued that the part of the grammar which describes syntactic structures should have priority as the creative component. By this view, the other two major parts of grammar—semantics and phonology—are "interpretive components," the purpose of which is to act upon and assign meaning and sound to the structures generated by the syntax. In characterizing the syntactic component of grammar as "creative," Chomsky brought attention to certain obvious but easily overlooked facts about English (and every other natural language), and he pointed out inadequacies in existing systems of descriptive grammar. The fact that speakers of English can recognize and produce sentences which they have never before encountered

---

[1] The *phoneme* is a minimum unit of speech sound in any given language or dialect by which a distinction is conveyed. Thus the initial sounds of *pit* and *bit* in English are different phonemes. On the other hand, the initial sounds of *keep* and *coop* (or *Kodak*), though physiologically and acoustically different, are in English (but not, for example, in Arabic) only varieties of the phoneme /k/ since they always occur in different phonetic environments, and in phonemic transcription need not be represented by different symbols. Such varieties of the same phoneme are called *allophones* and are said to be in complementary distribution. It is customary to enclose phonetic symbols within brackets [k], phonemes between diagonal strokes /k/.

[2] H. A. Gleason, *An Introduction to Descriptive Linguistics* (rev. ed., New York, 1961) is a good general treatment of linguistics from a structural point of view. See also G. L. Trager and H. L. Smith, Jr., *An Outline of English Structure* (Norman, Okla., 1951; *Studies in Linguistics, Occasional Papers*, no. 3); C. C. Fries, *The Structure of English* (New York, 1952); and A. A. Hill, *Introduction to Linguistic Structures* (New York, 1958), as well as the numerous publications of B. Bloch, W. N. Francis, R. A. Hall, Z. S. Harris, C. F. Hockett, H. M. Hoenigswald, E. A. Nida, K. L. Pike, M. Swadesh, W. F. Twaddell, and R. S. Wells, to mention only a few. More recently within this general tradition there have been studies in "stratificational grammar" by Sydney M. Lamb and others.

suggests that the grammar which describes English must provide for infinite syntactic novelty. But the grammar itself must be a finite thing if one assumes that a goal of linguistic description is to account for the knowledge—or, in a technical sense of the word, the "competence"—of a native speaker of a language. Chomsky sketched a model of a grammar which was unlike existing grammars in its ability to generate an infinite number of sentences from a finite set of rules. In addition, he formalized the kind of rule necessary to show certain relationships of meaning, as for example between an active sentence and its corresponding passive form. These rules which show relationships are known as *transformational rules*, and the system of description is known as *transformational generative grammar* (often simply *generative grammar* or *transformational grammar*). In its revised form in Chomsky's *Aspects of the Theory of Syntax* (New York, 1965), it has become the most influential system of linguistic description in the second half of the twentieth century, and it has had a significant effect on the related disciplines of psychology and sociology, as well as on the teaching of grammar in the schools.[1] During the past decade a number of linguists have challenged, and others have defended and modified, various parts of the standard theory of transformational grammar.[2] In the 1960's participants in the debate often viewed their discipline as parallel to the natural sciences in its pattern of advancement, and Chomsky's model was seen as a "paradigm change" in the sense described by Thomas S. Kuhn.[3] The lively attacks on Chomsky's model and the counterattacks on competing systems were inspired in part by the belief that further changes in the paradigm were imminent. At present the discipline of linguistics is in an extreme state of fragmentation, and it is uncertain whether a new paradigm will emerge as a synthesis. The differences between the natural sciences and the social sciences may eventually

[1] For the highly abstract phonology of generative grammar, the single major work is by Noam Chomsky and Morris Halle, *The Sound Pattern of English* (New York, 1968).

[2] Among the hundreds of books, articles, and papers on syntactic theory during the past two decades, the advanced student will find important developments in John R. Ross, "Constraints on Variables in Syntax" (Dissertation, M.I.T., 1967); George Lakoff, *Irregularity in Syntax* (New York, 1970); David Perlmutter, *Deep and Surface Structure Constraints in Syntax* (New York, 1971); Ray Jackendoff, *Semantic Interpretation in Generative Grammar* (Cambridge, Mass., 1972); and Noam Chomsky, *Studies on Semantics in Generative Grammar* (The Hague, 1972). More accessible for the beginner is Emmon Bach, *Syntactic Theory* (New York, 1974). A sociolinguistic study which makes strong theoretical claims concerning "variable rules" in transformational grammar is William Labov, "Contraction, Deletion, and Inherent Variability of the English Copula," *Language*, 45 (1969), 715–62 (reprinted in revised form as chap. 3 of Labov's *Language in the Inner City* [Philadelphia, 1972]).

[3] *The Structure of Scientific Revolutions* (2nd ed., Chicago, 1970).

force a reconsideration of the analogies which have been assumed and the goals which have been set in linguistics. Whatever the outcome of the theoretical issues, the specific arguments will continue to draw upon actual syntactic and phonological patterns for evidence. Since the theoretical debates and analytical procedures which have evolved in American linguistics have naturally turned to the language as spoken in this country, the various approaches to grammatical description not only have changed our thinking about language but have contributed to the study of American English.

256. *Is American English Good English?* If the question is asked less often now than in the past, attitudes associated with the question persist. There is nothing at present like the sustained controversy over Americanisms of the nineteenth and early twentieth centuries (see § 251). The steady flood of writings on the English language during recent years includes few that undertake to compare American English unfavorably with British English and even fewer that find it necessary to defend the American variety. And a judgment such as De Selincourt's of half a century ago would be taken as facetious exaggeration on either side of the Atlantic: "Only when we hear English on the lips of Americans do we fear for its integrity."[1] Yet one must recognize that a certain hostility toward American English is still to be encountered, often stated more obliquely than in the past. The English novelist Anthony Burgess asserts with a touch of irony, "There's no doubt at all that the model of spoken English that the whole world is now taking comes from America and not despised and diminished Britain." But he makes clear that he considers the model an inferior one: "American speech seems to me to have difficulty in achieving a mode of converse which shall strike a mean between heavy formality and folkiness—there is a tendency for it to be either brutally and sentimentally colloquial or pentagonally grandiloquent."[2] The Americanism that he cites as especially illustrative of such difficulties in tone is the greeting *Hi*. It is instructive to be aware of linguistic prejudice in others if only to guard against it in ourselves as we observe varieties of English in countries whose traditions are younger and less assured than our own.

The opinion of William Archer, which was markedly liberal at the time and which strikes us now as self-evident, has implications that are broader than the specific question of Americanisms: "We are apt in England to class as an 'Americanism' every unfamiliar or too familiar locution which

---

[1] Basil de Selincourt, *Pomona, or the Future of English* (London, 1928), p. 61. Read in its context, this is not so extreme as it seems.

[2] "Ameringlish Isn't Britglish," *N.Y. Times Mag.*, Sept. 9, 1973, p. 100.

we do not happen to like. . . . But there can be no rational doubt, I think, that the English language has gained, and is gaining, enormously by its expansion over the American continent. The prime function of a language, after all, is to interpret the 'form and pressure' of life—the experience, knowledge, thought, emotion and aspiration of the race which employs it. This being so, the more taproots a language sends down into the soil of life and the more varied the strata of human experience from which it draws its nourishment, whether of vocabulary or idiom, the more perfect will be its potentialities as a medium of expression . . . The English language is no mere historic monument, like Westminster Abbey, to be religiously preserved as a relic of the past, and reverenced as the burial-place of a bygone breed of giants; it is a living organism, ceaselessly busied, like any other organism, in the processes of assimilation and excretion. It has before it, we may fairly hope, a future still greater than its glorious past. And the greatness of that future will greatly depend on the harmonious interplay of spiritual forces throughout the American Republic and the British Empire." [1] With this point of view the American has the most natural sympathy. A flourishing literary tradition that regularly includes Nobel laureates among its numbérs is eloquent testimony that a language gains in extending its taproots, and the history of that tradition serves to remind speakers in both the United States and Britain that similar extensions throughout the world will continue to enrich the language. Along with the good use of English there will be much that is indifferent or frankly bad. In India, Ghana, and the Philippines, in Australia and Jamaica, as in the United States and England, one can find plentiful samples of English that deserve a low estimate. Many earlier attacks on American English were prompted by the slang, colloquialisms, and linguistic novelties of popular fiction and journalism, just as recent criticisms have been directed at jargon in the speech and writings of American government officials, journalists, and social scientists. But the English of a whole country should not be judged by its least graceful examples. Generalizations about the use of English throughout a country or a region are more likely to mislead than to inform, and questions which lead to such generalizations are among the least helpful questions to ask.

Good American English is simply good English, English that differs a little in pronunciation, vocabulary, and occasionally in idiom from good English as spoken in London or South Africa, but differs no more than our physical surroundings, our political and social institutions, and the other

[1] "America and the English Language," *The Living Age*, 219 (1898), 514–19.

circumstances reflected in language differ from those of other English-speaking areas. It rests upon the same basis as that which the standard speech of England rests upon—the usage of reputable speakers and writers throughout the country. No American student of language is so provincial as to hope, or wish, that the American standard may some day be adopted in England. Nor does he share the views of such in England as think that we would do well to take our standard ready-made from them. He will be content with the opinion of Henry Bradley that "the wiser sort among us will not dispute that Americans have acquired the right to frame their own standards of correct English on the usage of their best writers and speakers." And Americans generally will subscribe to the sentiment with which the same scholar continues: "But is it too much to hope that one day this vast community of nations will possess a common 'standard English,' tolerant of minor local varieties . . . ? There are many on both sides of the ocean who cherish this ideal and are eager to do all in their power to bring it nearer to fulfilment."[1]

BIBLIOGRAPHY

An excellent one-volume account of the settlement of America is Curtis P. Nettels, *The Roots of American Civilization: A History of American Colonial Life* (2nd ed., New York, 1963), which may be supplemented by the detailed studies of Charles M. Andrews, *The Colonial Period of American History* (4 vols., New Haven, 1934–1938), and Wesley F. Craven, *The Southern Colonies in the Seventeenth Century, 1607–1689* (Baton Rouge, 1949). For the history of the frontier Ray A. Billington's *Westward Expansion* (3rd ed., New York, 1967) is clear and comprehensive. Standard works on the major immigrant groups are Marcus L. Hansen, *The Atlantic Migration, 1607–1860* (Cambridge, Mass., 1940), and Carl Wittke, *We Who Built America: The Saga of the Immigrant* (rev. ed., Cleveland, 1964). See also George von Skal, *History of German Immigration in the United States* (New York, 1908), and G. T. Flom, *A History of Norwegian Immigration to the United States . . . to 1848* (Iowa City, 1909). On the history of the English language in this country, George P. Krapp's *The English Language in America* (2 vols., New York, 1925) is still indispensable. H. L. Mencken, *The American Language* (4th ed., New York, 1936) contains much valuable material, although overemphasizing colloquial and vulgar speech. For the supplements and an abridged edition, see above, p. 389. Thomas Pyles, *Words and Ways of American English* (New York, 1952) and Albert H. Marckwardt, *American English* (New York, 1958) are readable and informative. M. M. Mathews, *The Beginnings of American English* (Chicago, 1931), reprints in convenient form some of the earlier discussions of English in America, and Jane L. Mesick's *The English Traveller in America, 1785–1835* (New York, 1922) gives references to early comments on American speech. A skillful study based on manuscripts of the eighteenth and nineteenth centuries is Norman E. Eliason, *Tarheel Talk: An Historical Study*

---

[1] *The Literary Review*, December 3, 1921, p. 224.

of the English Language in North Carolina to 1860 (Chapel Hill, 1956). There are biographies of Noah Webster by Horace E. Scudder (Boston, 1882; *American Men of Letters Series*) and Harry R. Warfel (New York, 1936). Emily E. F. Ford, *Notes on the Life of Noah Webster* (2 vols., New York, 1912) contains extensive material from Webster's diaries and correspondence. The fullest account of his work on the dictionary is by Joseph H. Friend, *The Development of American Lexicography, 1798–1864* (The Hague, 1967), which may be supplemented by Kemp Malone, "A Linguistic Patriot," *American Speech*, 1 (1925), 26–31; Edward Wagenknecht, "The Man Behind the Dictionary," *Virginia Qu. Rev.*, 5 (1930), 246–58; and Allen W. Read, "The Spread of German Linguistic Learning in New England during the Lifetime of Noah Webster," *American Speech*, 41 (1966), 163–81. Excellent introductions to American pronunciation are John S. Kenyon, *American Pronunciation* (10th ed., Ann Arbor, 1950), and C. K. Thomas, *An Introduction to the Phonetics of American Pronunciation* (2nd ed., New York, 1958). Studies of the subject based on materials for the *Linguistic Atlas* are Hans Kurath and Raven I. McDavid, Jr., *The Pronunciation of English in the Atlantic States* (Ann Arbor, 1961), and Hans Kurath, *A Phonology and Prosody of Modern English* (Ann Arbor, 1964). Comparison with English pronunciation may be made by means of Daniel Jones's *An Outline of English Phonetics* (9th ed., New York, 1960) and the same author's *Everyman's English Pronouncing Dictionary*, ed. A. C. Gimson (13th ed., London, 1967), along with John S. Kenyon and Thomas A. Knott, *A Pronouncing Dictionary of American English* (Springfield, Mass., 1949). A. C. Gimson, *An Introduction to the Pronunciation of English* (2nd ed., London, 1970) is useful for recent changes in English pronunciation, and J. Windsor Lewis, *A Concise Pronouncing Dictionary of British and American English* (London, 1972) conveniently lists the variants side by side. A number of important articles on American regional dialects are collected in Harold B. Allen and Gary N. Underwood, eds., *Readings in American Dialectology* (New York, 1971), which contains a helpful bibliography, and in Juanita V. Williamson and Virginia M. Burke, eds., *A Various Language: Perspectives on American Dialects* (New York, 1971). An exhaustive bibliography for the Southern dialect is James B. McMillan, *Annotated Bibliography of Southern American English* (Coral Gables, Fla., 1971). In addition to the works mentioned on p. 390, a good introduction to the study of linguistic geography will be found in chap. 19 of L. Bloomfield, *Language*, and for a fuller treatment the student may consult Ernst Gamillscheg, *Die Sprachgeographie und ihre Ergebnisse für die allgemeine Sprachwissenschaft* (Bielefeld, 1928). Many local word lists will be found in *American Speech* and the *Publications of the American Dialect Society*. An attempt to present a regional record of the American vocabulary is Harold Wentworth, *American Dialect Dictionary* (New York, 1944), which will be superseded by publication of the *Dictionary of American Regional English* under the editorship of Frederic G. Cassidy.

On the subject of Americanisms the principal glossaries and dictionaries have been mentioned on p. 382. The American point of view is well represented in T. R. Lounsbury, "The English Language in America," *International Rev.*, 8 (1880), 472–82, 596–608, and Brander Matthews, *Americanisms and Briticisms* (New York, 1892). For an expression of liberal English opinion, see J. Y. T. Greig, *Breaking Priscian's Head* (London, 1928). Studies on sociolinguistics and black English by William Labov are conveniently collected in *Sociolinguistic Patterns* (Philadelphia, 1972) and *Language in the Inner City: Studies in the Black English Vernacular* (Philadelphia, 1972). R. W. Shuy, W. A. Wolfram, R. W. Fasold, and others have presented the results of their sociolinguistic investigations in volumes of the Urban Language Series, published by the Center for Applied Linguistics. A general survey of sociolinguistics in the United States is Walt Wolfram and R. W. Fasold's *The Study of Social Dialects in American English* (Englewood Cliffs, N.J., 1974). Two books by J. L. Dillard, both well known but often objectionable in tone and method, are *Black English* (New York, 1972) and *All-American English* (New York, 1975). Bibliographies of black English and related topics in pidgin and creole languages are Ila W. Brasch and Walter M. Brasch, *A Comprehensive Bibliography of American Black English* (Baton Rouge, 1974), and John E. Reinecke *et al.*, *A Bibliography of Pidgin and Creole Languages* (Honolulu, 1975). For transformational grammar the beginning student can consult Adrian Akmajian and Frank Heny, *An Introduction to the Principles of Transformational Syntax* (Cambridge, Mass., 1975), or Diane Bornstein, *An Introduction to Transformational Grammar* (Cambridge, Mass., 1977), as background for the references cited on p. 394.

APPENDIX A

Specimens of the Middle English Dialects

The discussion of the Middle English dialects in the text (§ 147) is necessarily general. The subject may be further illustrated by the following specimens. It is not to be expected that students without philological training will be able to follow all the details in the accompanying Observations, but these observations may serve to acquaint the reader with the nature of the differences that distinguish one dialect from another. Some of them, such as the endings of the verb or the voicing of initial *f* in Southern and Kentish, are easily enough recognized.

Northern

The Cursor Mundi, c. 1300.

Þis are þe maters redde on raw
Þat i thynk in þis bok to draw,
Schortly rimand on þe dede,
For mani er þai her-of to spede.
Notful me thinc it ware to man   5
To knaw him self how he began,—
How [he] began in werld to brede,
How his oxspring began to sprede,
Bath o þe first and o þe last,
In quatkin curs þis world es past.   10
Efter haly kyrc[es] state
Þis ilk bok it es translate
In to Inglis tong to rede

For þe love of Inglis lede,
Inglis lede of Ingland,   15
For þe commun at understand.
Frankis rimes here I redd,
Comunlik in ilk[a] sted:
Mast es it wroght for frankis man.
Quat is for him na frankis can?   20
Of Ingland þe nacion—
Es Inglis man þar in commun—
Þe speche þat man wit mast may spede,
Mast þar-wit to speke war nede.
Selden was for ani chance   25
Praised Inglis tong in france.
Give we ilkan þare langage,
Me think we do þam non outrage.
To laud and Inglis man i spell
Þat understandes þat i tell. . . .   30

TRANSLATION: These are the matters explained in a row that I think in this book to draw, shortly riming in the doing, for many are they who can profit thereby. Methinks it were useful to man to know himself, how he began,—how he began to breed in the world, how his offspring began to spread, both first and last, through what kind of course this world has passed. After Holy Church's state this same book is translated into the English tongue to read, for the love of English people, English people of England, for the commons to understand. French rimes I commonly hear read in every place: most is it wrought for Frenchmen. What is there for him who knows no French? Concerning England the nation—the Englishman is common therein—the speech that man may speed most with, it were most need to speak therewith. Seldom was by any chance English tongue praised in France. Let us give each their language: methinks we do them no outrage. To layman and Englishman I speak, that understand what I tell.

OBSERVATIONS: The most distinctive feature of the Northern dialect is the retention of O.E. $\bar{a}$ as an a, whereas it became an o in all the other dialects: raw (1), knaw (6), bath (9), haly (11), mast (19, etc.: Northumbrian $m\bar{a}st$), na (20). Northern shares with all non-W.S. districts $\bar{e}$ for W.S. $\bar{æ}$ (= Gmc. $\bar{æ}$): dede (3) riming with spede (O.E. $sp\bar{e}dan$), rede (13) riming with lede (O.E. $l\bar{e}od$), etc. Characteristic of the Northern is the spelling qu– for hw–: quatking (10), quat (20); the retention of a hard consonant in kyrces (11), *ilk* (12), *ilka(n)* (18, 27); *s* for *sh* in *Inglis* (13, 14), *Frankis* (17). The pres. participle ends in *–and: rimand* (3), the 3rd pers. sing. pres. indic. in *–es: understandes* (30). The verb *to be* shows typical Northern forms in *es* (10, 12, etc) for *is*, *er* (4) and *are* (1), and the pret. plur. *ware* (5), with *a* from Scandinavian influence, corresponding to Midland *wẹren*, Southern *wẹren*. With this may be compared *þar* (22: O.N. *þar*) = Southern *þer*. The infinitive *at understand* (16) likewise points to Scandinavian influence and the north. The 3rd pers. plur. pronoun in *th–* is a Northern characteristic at this date, especially in the oblique cases: *þai* (4), *þare* (27), *þam* (28).

East Midland

The Bestiary, c. 1250.

Cethegrande is a fis
ðe moste ðat in water is;
ðat tu wuldes seien get,
gef ðu it soge wan it flet,
ðat it were an eilond   5
ðat sete one ðe se sond.
ðis fis ðat is unride,
ðanne him hungreð he gapeð wide;
ut of his ðrote it smit an onde,
ðe swetteste ðing ðat is on londe;   10
ðer-fore oðre fisses to him dragen;
wan he it felen he aren fagen;
he cumen and hoven in his muð;
of his swike he arn uncuð;
ðis cete ðanne hise chaveles lukeð,   15
ðise fisses alle in sukeð;
ðe smale he wile ðus biswiken,
ðe grete maig he nogt bigripen.
ðis fis wuneð wið ðe se grund,
and liveð ðer evre heil and sund,   20
til it cumeð ðe time
ðat storm stireð al ðe se,
ðanne sumer and winter winnen;
ne mai it wunen ðer-inne,
So drovi is te sees grund,   25
ne mai he wunen ðer ðat stund,

oc stireð up and hoveð stille;
wiles [ðat] weder is so ille,
ðe sipes ðat arn on se fordriven,—
loð hem is ded, and lef to liven,— 30
biloken hem and sen ðis fis;
an eilond he wenen it is,
ðer-of he aren swiðe fagen,
and mid here migt ðar-to he dragen,
sipes on festen, 35
and alle up gangen;
Of ston mid stel in ðe tunder
wel[m] to brennen one ðis wunder,
warmen hem wel and heten and drinken;
ðe fir he feleð and doð hem sinken, 40
for sone he diveð dun to grunde,
he drepeð hem alle wið-uten wunde.

Significacio

Ðis devel is mikel wið wil and magt,
So wicches haven in here craft;
he doð men hungren and haven ðrist, 45
and mani oðer sinful list,
tolleð men to him wið his onde:
wo so him folegeð he findeð sonde;
ðo arn ðe little in leve lage;
ðe mikle ne maig he to him dragen,— 50
ðe mikle, i mene ðe stedefast
in rigte leve mid fles and gast.
wo so listneð develes lore,
on lengðe it sal him rewen sore;
wo so festeð hope on him, 55
he sal him folgen to helle dim.

TRANSLATION: The cetegrande (whale) is a fish, the greatest that is in water; so that thou wouldst say, if thou saw it when it floats, that it was an island that set on the sea-sand. This fish, that is enormous, when hungry gapes wide; out of its throat it casts a breath, the sweetest thing that is on land; therefore other fishes draw to it. When they perceive it they are glad; they come and linger in its mouth—of its deceit they are ignorant. This whale then shuts its jaws, sucks all these fishes in; the small he will thus deceive, the great can he not catch. This fish dwells on the sea-bottom and lives there ever hale and sound till it comes the time that a storm stirs up all the sea, when summer and winter contend. Nor may it dwell therein; so troubled is the bottom of the sea, he can not abide there that hour, but comes to the surface and remains still. Whilst the weather is so ill, the ships (seamen) that are tossed about on the sea—loath to them is death, and to live dear—look about them and see this fish. They think it is an island; thereof they are very glad and draw thereto with all their might, moor fast the ships and all go up (on land) to light a fire on this wonder, from stone with steel in the tinder, to warm themselves well and eat and drink. He feels the fire and doth sink them, for soon he dives down to the ground and kills them all without wound. *Significatio.* This Devil is so great with will and might, as witches have in their craft, that he makes men to hunger and have thirst and many other sinful desires. He draws men to him with his breath. Whoso follows him finds shame: those are the little (who are) low (weak) in faith; the great he can not draw to him,—the great, I mean the steadfast in right belief with flesh and ghost (body and soul). Whoso listeneth to the Devil's lore, at length shall rue it sorely. Whoso finds hope in him shall follow him to Hell dim.

OBSERVATIONS: The East Midland character of this text is not so much indicated by distinctive features as by a combination of phonological characteristics which can be found individually in other dialects. Thus O.E. *ǽ* appears as *a*, as it does also at this date generally: *ðat* (2), *water* (2), *fagen* (12), *craft* (44), etc. As in the north O.E. *ȳ* appears generally as *i: unride* (7), *stireð* (22), *fir* (40), *diveð* (41), *ðrist* (45), *sinfull* (46), *list* (46), and *ĕo* becomes *e: lef* (30), *sen* (31), *devel* (43, 53). But the development of O.E. *ā > ō* in *loð* (30), *wo* (48), *lore, sore* (54) indicates a district south of the Humber. Northern influence is possible in *gast* (52) although the *a* may be due to shortening. The morphology is typically East Midland. The 3rd pers. sing. pres. indic. always ends in *–eð* (except in contractions): *hungreð* (8), *gapeð* (8), *lukeð* (15), etc.; the pres. plur. always ends in *–en: dragen* (11), *felen* (12), *aren* (12), *cumen* (13), etc.; the strong past participle ends in *–en: fordriven* (29), as do all infinitives: *seien* (3), *biswiken* (17), *bigripen* (18), etc.; the 3rd pers. plur. of the pronoun is *he* (12, etc.), *here* (34, 44), *hem* (30, etc.). That the text belongs toward the northern part of the region is indicated by the frequent occurrence of *s* for O.E. *sc: fis, fisses* (1, etc.), *sipes* (29), *sonde* (48), *fles* (52), *sal* (54, 56); by the *–es* of the 2nd pers. sing.: *wuldes* (3); and by the more Northern *aren, arn* (12, 14, etc.) in place of the typical East Midland form *ben* (which occurs in other parts of the poem).

West Midland

St. Katherine, c. 1230.

In þis ilke burh wes wuniende a meiden swiðe ȝung of ȝeres, twa
wone of twenti, feier & freolich o wlite & o westum, ah ȝet, þ is mare
wurð, steðelfest | wiðinnen, of treowe bileave, anes kinges Cost hehte
anlepi dohter icuret clergesse Katerine inempnet. Þis meiden wes
baðe federles & moderles of hire childhade. Ah þah ha ȝung were, ha   5
heold hire aldrene hird wisliche & warliche i þe heritage & i þe herd þ
com of hire burde: nawt for þi þ hire þuhte god in hire heorte to
habben monie under hire & beon icleopet lefdi, þ feole telleð wel to,
ah ba ha wes offearet of scheome & of sunne, ȝef þeo weren todreauet,
oðer misferden, þ hire forðfederes hefden ifostret. For hire seolf ne   10
kepte ha nawt of þe worlde. Þus, lo, for hare sake ane dale ha etheold
of hire ealdrene god & spende al þ oðer in neodfule & in nakede.
Þeos milde, meoke meiden þeos lufsume lefdi mid lastelese lates ne
luvede heo nane lihte plohen ne nane sotte songes. Nalde ha nane
ronnes ne nane luve runes leornin ne lustnen, ah eaver ha hefde on hali   15
writ ehnen oðer heorte, oftest ba togederes.

TRANSLATION: In this same town was dwelling a maiden very young in
years—two lacking of twenty—fair and noble in appearance and form, but
yet, which is more worth, steadfast within, of true belief, only daughter of
a king named Cost, a distinguished scholar named Katherine. This maiden
was both fatherless and motherless from her childhood. But, though she
was young, she kept her parents' servants wisely and discreetly in the
heritage and in the household that came to her by birth: not because it
seemed to her good in her heart to have many under her and be called lady,
that many count important, but she was afraid both of shame and of sin
if they were dispersed or went astray whom her forefathers had brought
up. For herself, she cared naught of the world. Thus, lo, for their sake she
retained one part of her parents' goods and spent all the rest on the needy
and on the naked. This mild, meek maiden, this lovesome lady with fault-
less looks, loved no light playings or foolish songs. She would neither learn
nor listen to any songs or love poems, but ever she had her eyes or heart
on Holy Writ, oftenest both together.

OBSERVATIONS: The more significant West Midland characteristics of the
above passage are: the preservation of O.E. *ȳ* as a rounded vowel, spelled
u: icuret < *cyre* (4), *burde* (7), *sunne* (9), *lustnen* (15); the development of

O.E. *ĕo* as a rounded vowel, spelled *eo, u: ʒung* (1), *freolich* (2), *wurð* (3), etc.; the appearance of O.E. *ă* + nasal as *on, om: wone* (2), *monie* (8); the i-umlaut of O.E. *æl* + cons. as *al: aldrene* (6); the feminine pronoun *ha* (5, etc.), *heo* (14) for *she;* the gen. plur. of the 3rd pers. pronoun *hare* (11); the form *nalde* (14) for *nolde;* the unvoicing of final *d* to *t* in the ending *–et: icuret* (4), *inempnet* (4), *ifostret* (10), etc. The ending *–ende* of the pres. participle (*wuniende*, 1) is common to East and West Midland, but the ending *–eð* of the plur. pres. indic. (*telleð*, 8), characteristic of the south, is found in West Midland where the East would commonly have *–en*.

Southern

The Owl and the Nightingale, c. 1195 (MS. after 1216).

  Al so þu dost on þire side:
  vor wanne snou liþ þicke & wide,
  an alle wiʒtes habbeþ sorʒe,
  þu singest from eve fort amorʒe.
  Ac ich alle blisse mid me bringe: 5
  ech wiʒt is glad for mine þinge,
  & blisseþ hit wanne ich cume,
  & hiʒteþ aʒen mine kume.
  þe blostme ginneþ springe & sprede,
  boþe ine tro & ek on mede.   10
  þe lilie mid hire faire wlite
  wolcumeþ me, þat þu hit w[i]te,
  bit me mid hire faire blo
  þat ich shulle to hire flo.
  þe rose also mid hire rude,   15
  þat cumeþ ut of þe þorne wode,
  bit me þat ich shulle singe
  vor hire luve one skentinge:
  & ich so do þurʒ niʒt & dai,
  þe more ich singe þe more I mai,   20
  an skente hi mid mine songe,
  ac noþeles noʒt over-longe;
  wane ich iso þat men boþ glade,
  ich nelle þat hi bon to sade;
  þan is ido vor wan ich com,   25
  ich fare aʒen & do wisdom.

Wane mon hoȝeþ of his sheve,
an falewi cumeþ on grene leve,
ich fare hom & nime leve:
ne recche ich noȝt of winteres reve.   30
wan ich iso þat cumeþ þat harde,
ich fare hom to min erde
an habbe boþe luve & þonc
þat ich der com & hider swonk.

.   .   .   .

"Abid! abid!" þe ule seide, . . .   35
"þu seist þat þu singist mankunne,
& techest hom þat hi fundieþ honne
up to þe songe þat evre ilest:
ac hit is alre w[u]nder mest,
þat þu darst liȝe so opeliche.   40
Wenest þu hi bringe so liȝtliche
to Godes riche al singin[d]e?
Nai! nai! hi shulle wel avinde
þat hi mid longe wope mote
of hore sunnen bidde bote,   45
ar hi mote ever kume þare."

TRANSLATION: All so thou dost [behave] on thy side: for when snow lies thick and wide, and all wights have sorrow, thou singest from evening until morning. But I bring all happiness with me: each wight is glad for my quality and rejoices when I come and hopes for my coming. The blossoms begin to burst forth and spread, both in tree and eke on meadow. The lily with her fair form welcomes me, as thou dost know, bids me with her fair countenance that I should fly to her. The rose also with her ruddy color, that comes out of the thorn-wood, bids me that I should sing something merry for her love. And I do so through night and day—the more I sing, the more I can—and delight her with my song, but none the less not over long; when I see that men are pleased I would not that they be surfeited. When that for which I came is done I go away and do wisely. When man is intent on his sheaves and russet comes on green leaf, I take leave and go home; I do not care for winter's garb. When I see that the hard (weather) comes I go home to my native country and have both love and thanks that I came here and hither toiled . . .

"Abide! abide!" the owl said, . . . "Thou sayst that thou singest mankind and teachest them that they strive hence up to the song that is everlasting. But it is the greatest of all wonders that thou darest to lie so openly. Weenest thou to bring them so lightly to God's kingdom all singing? Nay, nay! They shall well find that they must ask forgiveness of their sins ere they may ever come there."

OBSERVATIONS: The Southern character of this text is evident from a number of distinctive developments. Noteworthy is the retention of O.E. *ў* as a rounded vowel, characteristic of the west and southwest: *cume* (8), *cumeþ* (16), *mankunne* (36), *sunnen* (45). Likewise characteristic of west and southwest is the development of O.E. *ĕo* as a rounded vowel (*u, ue, o*), here spelled *o: tro* (10), *blo* (13), *flo* (14), *iso* (23), *boþ* (23: O.E. *beoþ*), *bon* (24: O.E. *beon*), *honne* (37). In the southwest O.E. *ĭe* developed into either *ü* or *i*, as contrasted with the *e* of all other dialects: *hi* (24, 41, etc.), *hire* (11, etc.). The 3rd pers. sing. pres. indic. of verbs has the characteristic Southern (and East Midland) ending *–eð* (sometimes contracted): *liþ* (2), *blisseþ* (7), *hiʒteþ* (8), *wolcumeþ* (12), *bit* (13, 17), *cumeþ* (16, 28), *hoʒeþ* (27). The plural always has the Southern ending *–eð*, except *bon* (24), which shows Midland influence: *habbeþ* (3), *ginneþ* (9), *boþ* (23), *fundieþ* (37). Characteristic of the south are the pres. participle in *–inde: singinde* (42); the forms of the plur. personal pronoun: *hi* (24, 37), *hore* (45), *hom* (37); the past participle with the prefix *i–* and loss of final *–n: ido* (25); and the infinitive with the usual Southern absence of final *–n: springe* (9), *sprede* (9), *flo* (14), etc. It is hardly necessary to point out that O.E. *ā* appears as *o: so* (1), *snou* (2), *boþe* (10), *more* (20), etc. The distinctive Southern voicing of *f* at the beginning of syllables is evident in *vor* (18, etc.), *avinde* (43).

Kentish

Dan Michel, *Ayenbite of Inwyt*, 1340.

Þis boc is dan Michelis of Northgate, y-write an englis of his oʒene hand. þet hatte: Ayenbyte of inwyt. And is of þe bochouse of saynt Austines of Canterberi ...

    Nou ich wille þet ye ywyte hou hit is y-went:
    þet þis boc is y-write mid engliss of kent.   5
    þis boc is y-mad vor lewede men,
    Vor vader, and vor moder, and vor oþer ken,
    ham vor to berʒe vram alle manyere zen,
    þet ine hare inwytte ne bleve no voul wen.

'Huo ase god' in his name yzed,　　　　　　　　　　　　10
þet þis boc made god him yeve þet bread,
of angles of hevene and þerto his red,
and ondervonge his zaule huanne þet he is dyad. Amen.
　Ymende þet þis boc is volveld ine þe eve of þe holy apostles Symon
an Iudas, of ane broþer of þe cloystre of saynt austin of Canterberi,　　15
Ine þe yeare of oure lhordes beringe, 1340.
　Vader oure þet art ine hevenes, y-halȝed by þi name, cominde þi
riche, y-worþe þi wil ase ine hevene: and ine erþe. bread oure
echedayes: yef ous to day. and vorlet ous oure yeldinges: ase and
we vorleteþ oure yelderes. and ne ous led naȝt: in-to vondinge. ac vri　　20
ous vram queade. zuo by hit.

TRANSLATION: This book is Dan Michel's of Northgate, written in English
with his own hand. It is called *Ayenbite of Inwit* (Remorse of Conscience)
and belongs to the library of St. Augustine's at Canterbury ... Now I wish
that ye know how it has come about that this book is written with English
of Kent. This book is made for ignorant men,—for father and for mother
and for other kin,—to protect them from all manner of sin, that in their
conscience there may remain no foul blemish. "Who as God" is his name
said [Michael in Hebrew means "Who is like God"], that made this book:
God give him the bread of angels of heaven and thereto his counsel, and
receive his soul when that he is dead. Amen. Mind (note) that this book is
fulfilled on the eve of the holy apostles Simon and Judas, by a brother of
the cloister of Saint Augustine of Canterbury, in the year of our Lord's
bearing, 1340. Our Father that art in heaven, etc.

OBSERVATIONS: Many of the characteristics of Southern English noted in
the preceding specimen are likewise found in Kentish. Thus the Southern
development of O.E. ǽ to e is better preserved in Kentish than in the
southwest: þet (2, 5, 9, etc.). *Vader* (7) is commonly an exception in Kentish
texts. The Southern voicing of *f* and *s* at the beginning of syllables is very
pronounced in Kentish: *vor* (6, 7, 8), *vader* (7, 17), *vram* (8, 21), *voul* (9),
ondervonge (13), *volveld* (14), *vorlet(eþ)* (19, 20), *vondinge* (20), *vri* (20),
zen (8), *yzed* (10), *zaule* (13), *zuo* (21). Kentish shares in the Southern –eð
of the plur. pres. indic.: *vorleteþ* (20); the pres. participle in –*inde: cominde*
(17); the past participle with the *y–* or *i–* prefix and loss of final –*n: y-write*
(1, 5), *y-worþe* (18), etc.; and the loss of –*n* in the infinitive: *to berȝe* (8).
Like the rest of the south, Kentish is marked by the absence of *th–* forms
in the 3rd pers. plur. of the personal pronoun: *ham* (8), *hare* (9). The *a* in

these forms is a Kentish characteristic. The most characteristic feature of
Kentish is the appearance of e for W.S. $\breve{y}$: *ken* (7), *zen* (8), *ymende* (14),
volveld (14), with the complete absence of the Southwestern rounding (cf.
preceding selection). Similar absence of rounding marks the development of
O.E. *ĕo: berȝe* (8), *hevene(s)* (12, 17, 18), *erþe* (18). The typical Kentish
spelling for O.E. *ēa* appears in *dyad* (13). Here also it is hardly necessary to
note the development of O.E. *ā* > *ō: oȝene* (1), *huo* (10), *holy* (14), etc.

London

Geoffrey Chaucer, *Canterbury Tales*, c. 1387.

Whan that Aprille with his shoures sote
The droghte of Marche hath perced to the rote,
And bathed every veyne in swich licour,
Of which vertu engendred is the flour;
Whan Zephirus eek with his swete breeth   5
Inspired hath in every holt and heeth
The tendre croppes, and the yonge sonne
Hath in the Ram his halfe cours y-ronne,
And smale fowles maken melodye,
That slepen al the night with open yë,   10
(So priketh hem nature in hir corages):
Than longen folk to goon on pilgrimages
(And palmers for to seken straunge strondes)
To ferne halwes, couthe in sondry londes;
And specially, from every shires ende   15
Of Engelond, to Caunterbury they wende,
The holy blisful martir for to seke,
That hem hath holpen, whan that they were seke. . . .

   Ther was also a Nonne, a Prioresse,
That of hir smyling was full simple and coy;   20
Hir gretteste ooth was but by sëynt Loy;
And she was cleped madame Eglentyne.
Ful wel she song the service divyne,
Entuned in hir nose ful semely;
And Frensh she spak ful faire and fetisly,   25
After the scole of Stratford atte Bowe,
For Frensh of Paris was to hir unknowe.
At mete wel y-taught was she with-alle;

She leet no morsel from hir lippes falle,
Ne wette hir fingres in hir sauce depe. 30
Wel coude she carie a morsel, and wel kepe,
That no drope ne fille up-on hir brest.
In curteisye was set ful muche hir lest.
Hir over lippe wyped she so clene,
That in hir coppe was no ferthing sene 35
Of grece, whan she dronken hadde hir draughte.
Ful semely after hir mete she raughte,
And sikerly she was of greet disport,
And ful plesaunt, and amiable of port,
And peyned hir to countrefete chere 40
Of court, and been estatlich of manere,
And to ben holden digne of reverence.
But, for to speken of hir conscience,
She was so charitable and so pitous,
She wolde wepe, if that she sawe a mous 45
Caught in a trappe, if it were deed or bledde.
Of smale houndes had she, that she fedde
With rosted flesh, or milk and wastel-breed.
But sore weep she if oon of hem were deed,
Or if men smoot it with a yerde smerte: 50
And al was conscience and tendre herte.
Ful semely hir wimpel pinched was;
Hir nose tretys; hir eyen greye as glas;
Hir mouth ful smal, and ther-to softe and reed;
But sikerly she hadde a fair forheed; 55
It was almost a spanne brood, I trowe;
For, hardily, she was nat undergrowe.
Ful fetis was hir cloke, as I was war.
Of smal coral aboute hir arm she bar
A peire of bedes, gauded al with grene; 60
And ther-on heng a broche of gold ful shene,
On which ther was first write a crowned A,
And after, *Amor vincit omnia.*

OBSERVATIONS: The language of Chaucer may be taken as representing
with enough accuracy the dialect of London at the end of the fourteenth
century. It is prevailingly East Midland with some Southern and Kentish
features. The latter are a little more prominent in Chaucer than in the

nonliterary London documents of the same date. Among the usual East Midland developments may be noted O.E. *ā* as *ō: so* (11), *goon* (12), *holy* (51), etc.; O.E. *ǣ* as *a: that* (1), *spak* (25), *smal* (54), *war* (58), *bar* (59); the unrounding of O.E. *ȳ* to *i: swich* (3), *which* (4), *first* (62), but Kentish *e* is to be noted in *lest* (33: O.E. *lyst*) and possible evidence of the Western and Southwestern rounding in the *u* of *Canterbury* (16) and *much* (33) although the *u* in these words can be otherwise accounted for; O.E. *ĕo* as *e: seke* (18), *cleped* (22), *depe* (30), *brest* (32), *ferthing* (35), *weep* (49), *herte* (51). Since the W.S. diphthong *ĭe* is replaced in all other districts by *e*, Chaucer has *yerde*-(50). His inflectional forms are mostly East Midland. Thus he has the usual East Midland *–eð* in the 3rd pers. sing. pres. indic.: *hath* (2, 6, 8), *priketh* (11), and the plural in *–en* or *–e: maken* (9), *slepen* (10), *longen* (12), *wende* (16), *were* (18). The feminine pronoun in the nominative is *she;* the plural forms are *they* (16, 18), *hir* (11), *hem* (11). In his past participles he shows a mixture of Midland and Southern tendencies. Characteristic of East Midland is the loss of the prefix *y–* and the retention of the final *–n: holpen* (18), *dronken* (36), *holden* (42), but he has the Southern *y–* in *y-ronne* (8), *y-taught* (28), and the loss of *–n* in *unknowe* (27), *write* (62), etc. The infinitive has the usual Midland *–n* in *goon* (12), *seken* (13), *been* (41), *ben* (42), *speken* (43), but the Southern absence of *–n* in *falle* (29), *carie* (31), *kepe* (31), *countrefete* (40), *wepe* (45).

English Spelling

The following specimens are intended to illustrate the discussion in § 156. The first quotation, from the *Ormulum*, is included as the earliest conscious attempt at reform. The others illustrate either avowed efforts at uniform practice, or self-evident striving, within limits, at consistency.

I

Dedication to the *Ormulum, c.* 1200.

Nu, broþerr Wallterr, broþerr min   affterr þe flæshess kinde;
& broþerr min i Crisstenndom   þurrh fulluhht & þurrh trowwþe;
& broþerr min i Godess hus,   ʒét o þe þride wise,
þurrh þatt witt hafenn takenn ba   an reʒhellboc to follʒhenn,
Unnderr kanunnkess had & lif,   swa summ Sannt Awwstin sette;   5
Icc hafe don swa summ þu badd,   & forþedd te þin wille,
Icc hafe wennd inntill Ennglissh   goddspelless hallʒhe láre,
Affterr þatt little witt þatt me   min Drihhtin hafeþþ lenedd.
þu þohhtesst tatt itt mihhte wel   till mikell frame turrnenn,
ʒiff Ennglissh follc, forr lufe off Crist,   itt wollde ʒerne lernenn,   10
& follʒhenn itt, & fillenn itt   wiþþ þohht, wiþþ word, wiþþ dede.
& forrþi ʒerrndesst tu þatt icc   þiss werrc þe shollde wirrkenn;
& icc itt hafe forþedd te,   acc all þurrh Cristess hellpe;
& unnc birrþ baþe þannkenn Crist   þatt itt iss brohht till ende.
Icc hafe sammnedd o þiss boc   þa goddspelless neh alle,   15
þatt sinndenn o þe messeboc   inn all þe ʒer att messe.
& aʒʒ affterr þe goddspell stannt   þatt tatt te goddspell meneþþ,
þatt mann birrþ spellenn to þe follc   off þeʒʒre sawle nede . . .

413

II

Roger Ascham, *Toxophilus*, 1545.

If any man woulde blame me, eyther for takynge such a matter in
hande, or els for writing it in the Englyshe tongue, this answere I may
make hym, that whan the beste of the realme thinke it honest for
them to use, I one of the meanest sorte, ought not to suppose it vile
for me to write: And though to have written it in an other tonge, had   5
bene bothe more profitable for my study, and also more honest for my
name, yet I can thinke my labour wel bestowed, yf with a little
hynderaunce of my profyt and name, maye come any fourtheraunce,
to the pleasure or commoditie, of the gentlemen and yeomen of
Englande, for whose sake I tooke this matter in hande. And as for ye   10
Latin or greke tonge, every thing is so excellently done in them, that
none can do better: In the Englysh tonge contrary, every thinge in a
maner so meanly, bothe for the matter and handelynge, that no man
can do worse. For therein the least learned for the moste part, have
ben alwayes moost redye to wryte. And they whiche had leaste hope   15
in latin, have bene moste boulde in englyshe: when surelye every man
that is moste ready to taulke, is not moost able to wryte. He that wyll
wryte well in any tongue, muste folowe thys councel of Aristotle, to
speake as the common people do, to thinke as wise men do; and so
shoulde every man understande hym, and the judgement of wyse men   20
alowe hym. Many English writers have not done so, but usinge
straunge wordes as latin, french and Italian, do make all thinges
darke and harde . . .

III

Sir John Cheke, *The Gospel according to Saint Matthew, c.* 1550.

On y̆ dai Jesus comming from y̆ hous, sat bi y̆ see sijd, and much
compaini was gay̆erd togiy̆er, in so much y̆ he went into á boot and
set him doun y̆eer. and al y̆ hool companí stood on y̆ bank. And he
spaak unto y̆em much in biwordes and said. On a tijm y̆ souer went
forth to soow, and whil he was in soowíng summ fel bi y̆ wais sijd,   5
and y̆ birds cam and devoured it. and somm fel in stooni places,
wheer it had not much earth, and it cam up bi and bi, becaus it had

no depth in th' earth, and when ẙ sonn was risen it was burnt up,

and bicause it had no root it dried up. . . . Oẙer fel in ẙ good ground,
and ielded fruit, summ an hunderd, sum threescoor, sum thurtí. He   10
ẙᵗ hath ears to heer let him heer.

IV

Richard Stanyhurst, *The First Foure Bookes of Virgil His Æneis*, 1582,
    Dedication.

Hauing therefore (mi good lord) taken vpon mee too execute soom
part of master *Askam* his wyl, who, in his goulden pamphlet, intituled
thee Schoolemayster, dooth wish thee Vniuersitie students too applie
theyre wittes in bewtifying oure English language with heroical
verses: I heeld no *Latinist* so fit, too geeue thee onset on, as *Virgil*,   5
who, for his peerelesse style, and machlesse stuffe, dooth beare thee
prick and price among al thee Roman Poëts. How beyt I haue heere
haulf a guesh, that two sortes of carpers wyl seeme too spurne at this
myne entreprise. Thee one vtterlie ignorant, thee oother meanelye
letterd. Thee ignorant wyl imagin, that thee passage was nothing   10
craggye, in as much as M. *Phaere* hath broken thee ice before mee:
Thee meaner clarcks wyl suppose, my trauail in theese heroical verses
too carrye no great difficultie, in that yt lay in my choise, too make
what word I would short or long, hauing no English writer beefore
mee in this kind of poëtrye with whose squire I should leauel my   15
syllables. Too shape therefor an answer too thee first, I say, they are
altogeather in a wrong box: considering that such woordes, as fit M.
Phaer, may bee very vnapt for mee, which they would confesse, yf
theyre skil were, so much as spare, in theese verses. Further more I
stand so nicelie on my pantofles that way, as yf I could, yeet I would   20
not renne on thee skore with M. *Phaer*, or ennie oother, by borrowing
his termes in so copious and fluent a language, as oure English
tongue is.

V

Richard Mulcaster, *Elementarie*, 1582.

It were a thing verie praiseworthie in my opinion, and no lesse
profitable then praise worthie, if som one well learned and as
laborious a man, wold gather all the words which we vse in our

English tung, whether naturall or incorporate, out of all professions, as well learned as not, into one dictionarie, and besides the right writing, which is incident to the Alphabete, wold open vnto vs therein, both their naturall force, and their proper vse: that by his honest trauell we might be as able to iudge of our own tung, which we haue by rote, as we ar of others, which we learn by rule. The want whereof, is the onelie cause why, that verie manie men, being excellentlie well learned in foren speche, can hardlie discern what theie haue at home, still shooting fair, but oft missing far, hard censors ouer other, ill executors themselues. For easie obtaining is enemie to iudgement, not onlie in words, and naturall speche, but in greater matters, and verie important.

VI

John Chamberlain: Excerpt from a letter to Sir Dudley Carleton, London, October 31, 1618. [S. P. Dom., Jac. I, ciii, 58].

[*Sir Walter Raleigh's conduct on the day of his execution.*]

He made a speach of more than halfe an howre, wherin he cleered himself of having any intelligence with Fraunce, (which had ben objected to him,) more then to save his life and hide himself from the Kinges indignation: then that he never had any yll intent towards his Majestie not so much as in thought, that he had no other pretence nor end in his last viage then the inriching of the King, the realme, himself and his followers: that he never had any undutifull speach concerning his Majestie with the runagate French phisician, nor ever offered to Sir Lewes Stukeley 10000^{li} to go with him into Fraunce, nor told him that the Lord Carew had geven him advise to be gon, and that he and the Lord of Doncaster wold maintain him in Fraunce, of which points he had ben accused by them, and though he protested not only to forgeve them but to pray God to forgeve them, yet he thought fit to geve men warning of such persons. To all this and much more he tooke God so often and so solemnly to witnes, that he was beleved of all that heard him. He spake somwhat of the death of the earle of Essex and how sory he was for him, for though he was of a contrarie faction, yet he fore-saw that those who estemed him then in that respect, wold cast him of as they did afterward. He confessed himself the greatest sinner that he knew, and no marvayle as having ben a souldier, a seaman and a courtier: he excused the

disfiguring of himself by the example of David who fained himself
mad to avoide daunger: and never heard yt imputed to him for a
sinne. In conclusion he spake and behaved himself so, without any
shew of feare or affectation that he moved much commiseration, and   25
all that saw him confesse that his end was *omnibus numeris absolutus*,
and as far as man can discern every way perfect. Yt will not be amisse
to set downe some few passages of divers that I have heard. The
morning that he went to execution there was a cup of excellent sacke
brought him and beeing asked how he liked yt, as the fellow (saide   30
he) that drincking of St. Giles bowle as he went to Tiburn, saide yt
was goode drincke yf a man might tarrie by yt. As he went from
Westminster Hall to the Gatehouse, he espied Sir Hugh Beeston in
the thronge and calling to him prayed he wold see him dye to morow:
Sir Hugh to make sure worke got a letter from Secretarie Lake to the   35
sheriffe to see him placed conveniently, and meeting them as they
came nere to the scaffold delivered his letter but the sheriffe by
mishap had left his spectacles at home and put the letter in his pocket.
In the mean time Sir Hugh beeing thrust by, Sir Walter bad him
farewell and saide I know not what shift you will make, but I am sure   40
to have a place. When the hangman asked him forgivenes he desired
to see the axe, and feeling the edge he saide that yt was a fayre sharpe
medicine to cure him of all his diseases and miseries. When he was
laide downe some found fault that his face was west-ward, and wold
have him turned, wherupon rising he saide yt was no great matter   45
which way a mans head stoode so his heart lay right. He had geven
order to the executioner that after some short meditation when he
strecht forth his handes he shold dispatch him. After once or twise
putting foorth his handes, the fellow out of timerousnes (or what
other cause) forbearing, he was faine to bid him strike, and so at two   50
blowes he tooke of his head, though he stirred not a whit after the
first. The people were much affected at the sight insomuch that one
was heard say that we had not such another head to cut of.

VII

James Howell, *Epistolæ Ho-Elianæ*, 1645.

To the Intelligent *Reader*

Amongst other reasons which make the *English* Language of so
small extent, and put strangers out of conceit to learn it, one is,

That we do not pronounce as we write, which proceeds from divers
superfluous Letters, that occur in many of our words, which adds
to the difficulty of the Language: Therfore the Author hath taken   5
pains to retrench such redundant, unnecessary Letters in this Work
(though the *Printer* hath not bin carefull as he should have bin) as
amongst multitudes of other words may appear in these few, *done,*
some, come; Which though we, to whom the speech is *connaturall,*
pronounce as monosyllables, yet when strangers com to read them,   10
they are apt to make them disillables, as *do–ne, so–me, co–me;*
therfore such an *e* is superfluous.

Moreover, those words that have the *Latin* for their originall, the
Author prefers *that* Orthography, rather then the *French,* wherby
divers Letters are spar'd, as *Physic, Logic, Afric,* not *Physique,*   15
Logique, Afrique; favor, honor, labor, not *favour, honour, labour,* and
very many more, as also he omits the *Dutch k,* in most words; here
you shall read *peeple* not *pe–ople, tresure* not *treasure, toung* not
ton–gue, &c. *Parlement* not *Parliament, busines, witnes, sicknes,* not
businesse, witnesse, sicknesse; star, war, far, not *starre, warre, farre,* 20
and multitudes of such words, wherin the two last Letters may well
be spar'd: Here you shall also read *pity, piety, witty,* not *piti–e,*
pieti–e, witti–e, as strangers at first sight pronounce them, and
abundance of such like words.

The new Academy of wits call'd *l'Academie de beaux esprits,* which   25
the late Cardinall *de Richelieu* founded in *Paris,* is now in hand to
reform the *French* Language in this particular, and to weed it of all
superfluous Letters, which makes the *Toung* differ so much from the
Pen, that they have expos'd themselves to this contumelious Proverb,
The Frenchman doth neither pronounce as he writes, nor speak as he   30
thinks, nor sing as he pricks.

Aristotle hath a topic Axiom, that *Frustra fit per plura, quod fieri*
potest per pauciora, When fewer may serve the turn more is in vain.
And as this rule holds in all things els, so it may be very well observ'd
in Orthography.   35

VIII

Edward Phillips, *The New World of English Words,* 1658, Preface.

Whether this innovation of words deprave, or inrich our English
tongue is a consideration that admits of various censures, according
to the different fancies of men. Certainly as by an invasion of

strangers, many of the old inhabitants must needs be either slain, or
forced to fly the Land; so it happens in the introducing of strange   5
words, the old ones in whose room they come must needs in time be
forgotten, and grow obsolete; sometimes indeed, as Mr. *Cambden*
observes, there is a peculiar significancy in some of the old Saxon
words, as in stead of fertility they had wont to say *Eordswela*, which
is as much as the wealth, or riches of the earth, yet let us not bewail   10
the losse of them for this, for we shall finde divers Latin words, whose
Etymology is as remarkable, and founded upon, as much reason, as
in the word *intricate*, which (coming from *Tricæ* i.e. those small
threads about Chickens legs, that are an encombrance to them in
their going) signifieth entangled; and it is worth the taking notice,   15
that although divers Latin words cannot be explained, but by a
Periphrasis, as *Insinuation* is a winding ones self in by little and little,
yet there are others, both French and Latin, that are match't with
Native words equally significant, equally in use among us, as with
the French *Denie*, we parallel our *gainsay*, with the Latin *resist* our   20
withstand, with *Interiour*, *inward*, and many more of this nature: So
that by this means these forrainers instead of detracting ought from
our tongue, add copiousnesse and vari[e]ty to it, now whether they
add, or take from the ornament of it, it is rather to be referr'd to
sence and fancy, then to be disputed by arguments. That they come   25
for the most part from a language, as civil as the Nation wherein it
was first spoken, I suppose is without controversy, and being of a
soft and even sound, nothing savouring of harshnesse, or barbarisme,
they must needs mollifie the tongue with which they incorporate, and
to which, though of a different nature, they are made fit and adapted   30
by long use; in fine, let a man compare the best English, now written,
with that which was written three, or four ages ago, and if he be not
a doater upon antiquity, he will judge ours much more smooth, and
gratefull to the ear: for my part that which some attribute to *Spencer*
as his greatest praise, namely his frequent use of obsolete expressions,   35
I account the greatest blemish to his Poem, otherwise most excellent,
it being an equal vice to adhere obstinately to old words, as fondly
to affect new ones.

INDEX

Numbers refer to pages